IIFT

Indian Institute of Foreign Trade

by

Gautam Puri

(Alumnus IIM Bangalore)

G K Publications (P) Ltd

CL MEDIA (P) LTD.

Edition : 2019

ISBN   : **978-81-93975-41-1**

Typeset by : *CL Media DTP Unit*

Administrative and Production Offices

Published by : **CL Media (P) Ltd.**

A-45, Mohan Cooperative Industrial Area,
Near Mohan Estate Metro Station,
New Delhi - 110044

Marketed by : **G.K. Publications (P) Ltd.**

A-45, Mohan Cooperative Industrial Area,
Near Mohan Estate Metro Station,
New Delhi - 110044

For product information :

Visit ***www.gkpublications.com*** or email to ***gkp@gkpublications.com***

Preface

Preparing for an entrance exam is like running a marathon - you will have to maintain a steady pace to win the race. This will need clarity of goal, steadfastness, tenacity and self-belief. Understanding the exam you are due to write and developing a strategy accordingly goes a long way in achieving success in an exam. Through this book we aim to equip you with an understanding of one of the most prestigious exams in the Management Entrance Test cadre.

IIFT is not only one of the most coveted but also one of the toughest exams to crack. The reason why most students lose out on scoring in IIFT is because the usual preparation for management entrance test that may get one through most of the aptitude test is not applicable to IIFT. You are likely to find yourself short of time while attempting this exam. You may also find yourselves trapped in the web of IIFT's unique differential marking scheme. This is also one of the few papers to give a G.K. section which possess a challenge for most students.

The key to crack IIFT Exam is to master the art of maximizing your score in the available time. The IIFT Admission Test usually has 4-6 sections with sectional cut-offs. An aspirant needs to balance the sectional attempts while building up an overall score. The pattern of the test has not changed much in the past few years and this has increased the importance of solving past years' specially when questions are grouped Chapter-wise and Topic-wise.

It is against this backdrop that we have come up with Topic-wise & Year-wise solved papers of IIFT containing the questions of the actual papers of 2006 to 2018. The solution to these questions has been prepared by Career Launcher experts who themselves score consistently in IIFT every year. This will not only increase your familiarity with the various question types that appear in the test but will also help you strengthen your fundamentals of each chapter.

Last but not the least, with this book students will get an additional service i.e. 2 online mock tests to help students improve test taking strategy.

Hard work in the right direction will surely fulfill your desires. Have a lot of self-belief; load it with a lot of practice, top it off with a little smart work and you are good to go.

All the best

Contents

English Usage

1. Verbal Logic — 1.1 – 1.14
- Para-Completion — 1.1
- Para-Jumbles — 1.1
- Course of Action — 1.6
- Syllogisms — 1.7
- Critical Reasoning — 1.9
- Logical Consistency — 1.9
- Statement Conclusion — 1.10
- Statement Assumption — 1.10
- *Answers* — 1.10
- *Explanations* — 1.11

2. Vocabulary — 2.1 – 2.25
- Match the Meaning — 2.1
- Synonyms — 2.1
- Antonyms — 2.4
- Spelling — 2.5
- Word/Phrase Replacement — 2.6
- One Word Substitute — 2.8
- Fill in the Blanks — 2.8
- Common Confusables — 2.12
- Odd Word Out — 2.13
- Analogy — 2.13
- Idioms & Phrase — 2.15
- Miscellaneous — 2.15
- *Answers* — 2.17
- *Explanations* — 2.18

3. Grammar — 3.1 – 3.10
- Sentence Selection — 3.1
- IEP — 3.1
- Word Usage — 3.2
- Identify the Erroneous Part — 3.3
- Miscellaneous — 3.6
- *Answers* — 3.7
- *Explanations* — 3.8

4. Reading Comprehension — 4.1 – 4.88
- *Answers* — 4.76
- *Explanations* — 4.77

Quantitative Aptitude

1. Number System — 1.1 – 1.6
- Property — 1.1
- HCF and LCM — 1.2
- Miscellaneous — 1.2
- *Answers* — 1.3
- *Explanations* — 1.4

2. Arithmetic — 2.1 – 2.26
- Percentages and Fraction — 2.1
- Profit, Loss & Discount — 2.2
- Ratio and Proportion — 2.3
- Average — 2.4
- Simple Interest and Compound Interest — 2.5
- Mixture and Solutions — 2.6
- Time, Speed and Distance — 2.7
- Time and Work — 2.10
- Miscellaneous — 2.12
- *Answers* — 2.13
- *Explanations* — 2.14

3. Geometry, Mensuration and Trigonometry — 3.1 – 3.18
- Triangle — 3.1
- Quadrilaterals — 3.1
- Polygons — 3.2
- Circle — 3.3
- Mensuration — 3.4
- Co-ordinate Geometry — 3.6
- Trigonometry — 3.6
- *Answers* — 3.8
- *Explanations* — 3.9

4. Modern Maths   4.1 – 4.15

- Permutation and Combination   4.1
- Probability   4.3
- Set Theory   4.6
  - *Answers*   4.7
  - *Explanations*   4.8

5. Algebra   5.1 – 5.15

- Equations, Polynomials and Inequations   5.1
- Functions   5.2
- Logarithm and Exponents   5.3
- Progressions   5.4
- Matrix and Determinants   5.6
- Miscellaneous   5.6
  - *Answers*   5.6
  - *Explanations*   5.7

Logical Reasoning & Data Interpretation

1. Logical Reasoning   1.1 – 1.49

- Analytical Reasoning   1.1
- Data Sufficiency   1.23
- Input and Output   1.24
- Coding and Decoding   1.27
- General Mental Ability   1.27
  - *Answers*   1.31
  - *Explanations*   1.32

2. Data Interpretation   2.1 – 2.86

- Logic Based DI   2.1
- Calculation Based DI   2.5
  - *Answers*   2.57
  - *Explanations*   2.58

General Knowledge & Current Affairs

1. General Knowledge & Current Affairs   1.1 – 1.34

- Science   1.1
- Polity   1.3
- Geography   1.4
- History   1.6
- Art and Culture   1.8
- Economy   1.9
- Current Affairs   1.13
  - *Answers*   1.33
  - *Explanations*   1.33

Comparative Analysis of IIFT Admission Tests

IIFT Admission Tests over the years

Program Year	2019-21	2018-20	2017-19	2016-18	2015-17	2014-16	2013-15	2012-14
Total no. of questions	114	114	123	124	118	128	128	120
Total marks	100	100	100	100	100	100	100	100
No. of sections	6	6	4	4	4	4	4	6
Negative marking	0.33	0.33	0.33	0.33	0.33	0.33	0.33	0.33

Section-wise Analysis

Section / Subsection	Program Year	2019-21	2018-20	2017-19	2016-18	2015-17	2014-16	2013-15	2012-14
RC	No. of questions	16	16	16	16	17	16	16	15
RC	Marks/Question	1	1	1	1	1	0.75	0.75	0.75
VA	No. of questions	20	20	20	20	20	20	20	23
VA	Marks/Question	0.75	1	0.75	0.75	0.75	0.75	0.75	0.75
GK	No. of questions	18	18	25	28	26	28	28	21
GK	Marks/Question	0.5	0.5	0.5	0.5	0.5	0.5	0.5	0.5
QA	No. of questions	20	20	20	22	20	25	25	24
QA	Marks/Question	1	1	1	1	1	1	1	1
DI	No. of questions	20	18	20	18	15	19	19	16
DI	Marks/Question	1	0.75	1	1	1	1	1	1
LR	No. of questions	20	20	22	20	20	20	20	21
LR	Marks/Question	1	1	0.75	0.75	1	0.75	0.75	1

Sectional Cut-off

2018-20		2017-19		2016-18		2015–17	
LR & DI	5.5–7	LR & DI	6.5–9	LR & DI	7.25	LR	4.34
GK	1.2–1.5	GK	1.5–2.5	GK	2	GK	2.49
VA & RC	7.5–8	VA & RC	6.5–9	VA & RC	6.5	DI & QA	4.67
QA	3.5–4	QA	4–7	QA	6.25	VA & RC	6.5

English Usage

CHAPTER 1

Verbal Logic

Para-Completion

Directions for questions 1 – 2: A partially completed paragraph is below, followed by fillers a,b,c. From options A, B, C and D, identify the right combination and order of fillers a,b or c that will best complete the paragraph.

1. In cultivating team spirit, one should not forget the importance of discipline. (____________) It is the duty of all the members of the team to observe discipline in its proper perspective.

   a. A proper team spirit can seldom be based on discipline.

   b. It is a well known fact that team spirit and discipline can never go hand in hand

   c. Discipline in its right perspective would mean sacrificing self to some extent.

   (a) a and b only   (b) b and c only

   (c) Either a or b only   (d) c only

2. Forests are gifts of nature (________). Yet, with the spread of civilisation, man has not only spurned the forests, but has been ruthlessly destroying them.

   a. It is on historical record that the vast Sahara desert of today once used to be full of thick forests.

   b. A large part of humanity still lives deep inside forests, particularly in the tropical regions of the earth.

   c. Human evolution itself has taken place in the forests.

   (a) Only a and b   (b) Only c and a

   (c) Only c and b   (d) c and a or b

Direction for question 3: Given below are the first and last parts of a sentence, and the remaining sentence is broken into four parts p, q, r and s. From A, B, C and D, choose the arrangement of these parts that forms a complete, meaningful sentence.

3. A number of measures ______ of the Municipal Corporations.

   p. The financial conditions.

   q. For mobilisation of resources

   r. In order to improve

   s. Are being taken by the State Governments

   (a) psqr   (b) qrsp

   (c) rsqp   (d) sqrp

Directions for questions 4 and 5 : The first and last parts of the sentence are marked 1 and 6. The rest of the sentence is spilt into five parts and marked I, ii, iii, iv and v. These five parts are not given in their proper order. From the options given, please choose the most appropriate order to form a coherent, logical and grammatically correct sentence.

4. 1. having started

   i. in less time than it takes

   ii. more than half of your capital

   iii. with just $5.8 million

   iv. you squandered

   v. in seed financing

   6. to soft-boil and egg

   (a) 1, iii, iv, ii, v, i, 6   (b) 1, iii, v, iv, I, ii, 6

   (c) 1, I, v, iii, iv, ii, 6   (d) 1, iii, v, iv, ii, i, 6

5. 1. You could behave badly, say you were sorry,

   i. who now had both to suffer the crime

   ii. in the same position

   iii. and the difficulty of forgiving

   iv. you would get extra fun and be reinstated

   v. as the one who had done nothing

   6. with no goodies in addition at all

   (a) 1, ii, v, iv, iii, i, 6   (b) 1, I, iii, ii, v, iv, 6

   (c) 1, iv, v, ii, i, iii, 6   (d) 1, iv, ii, v, i, iii, 6

Para-Jumbles

Directions for Questions 6 and 7:

Mark the correct option, which puts the parts of the sentence in **_right order:_**

6. I. But she gained courage as she went on.

   II. She was a little nervous about it just at first.

   III. And opened their eyes and mouths so very wide.

   IV. The two creatures got so close to her, one on each side.

   (a) IV, III, II, I   (b) II, IV, III, I

   (c) II, I, IV, III   (d) None of the above

7.
I. It would perhaps be possible for him to be of some use to this brave girl

II. He said to himself, vaguely at first, that

III. Without neglecting anything of what was due to his important mission.

IV. And this idea pleased him.

(a) II, III, I, IV   (b) III, II, I, IV

(c) I, III, II, IV   (d) None of the above

2009-11

Directions for questions 8 – 10: A number of sentences are given below which, when properly sequenced, form a COHERENT PARAGRAPH. Choose the most LOGICAL ORDER of sentences from the choices given to construct a COHERENT PARAGRAPH.

8.
I. The economy's performance in expenditure terms was even poorer, with real GDP contracting by 0.6% after a gain of 0.5% in the October-December quarter.

II. On an output basis – the government's preferred measure because it is less volatile than expenditure – based GDP – the economy contracted by 0.3% in real terms from the previous quarter.

III. Data from Statistics New Zealand, a government agency, published on June 27th show an almost uniformly abysmal economic performance in January – March 2008.

IV. This was the first contraction since late 2005, made worse by the fact that the previous quarter's growth rate was revised down from 1% to 0.8%.

(a) III, IV, II, I   (b) I, II, III, IV

(c) III, II, IV, I   (d) I, III, II, IV

9.
I. Matti Meri, a teacher-trainer at Helsinki University, was a teacher at the time.

II. By the time comprehensives reached the more populous south, teachers were eager to join in what was clearly a roaring success.

III. "Grammar-school teachers were quite afraid of the reforms," he recalls.

IV. "They used to teach only one-third of the students. But the comprehensive schools used almost the same curriculum as the grammar schools had – and we discovered that the two – thirds were mostly able to cope with it."

V. Comprehensive schools were introduced in 1972 in the sparsely populated north, and then over the next four years in the rest o the country.

(a) V, I, III, IV, II   (b) I, II, III, IV, V

(c) V, II, IV, I, III   (d) I, III, II, IV, V

10.
I. "It is a clear illustration of the major role played by diet and culture on your risk of chronic disorders," he says.

II. Little is known about its effects, but changing its levels, possibly through diet or with different gut bacteria, might help to control high blood pressure.

III. Chinese and Japanese people are very similar at a genetic level, but Dr Nicholson found big differences in the type and variety of metabolites in their blood and urine.

IV. "Metabolomics can provide very specific pointers as to what is going wrong and new ways of intervening."

V. For instance, he found an unexpected metabolic marker, called formate, that seems to have a role in regulating blood pressure.

(a) III, II, IV, I, V   (b) III, IV, V, I, II

(c) II, III, IV, I, V   (d) III, I, IV, V, II

2010-12

Directions for questions 11 – 16: A number of sentences are given below which, when properly sequenced, form a COHERENT PARAGRAPH. Choose the most LOGICAL ORDER of sentences from the choices given to construct a COHERENT PARAGRAPH.

11.
I. As a retention strategy, the company has issued many schemes including ESOPs.

II Given the track record and success of our employees, other companies often look to us as a hunting ground for talent.

III. The growth of the Indian economy has led to an increased requirement for talented managerial personnel and we believe that the talented manpower is our key strength.

IV. Further, in order to mitigate the risk we place considerable emphasis on development of leadership skills and on building employee motivation.

(a) I, II, III, IV   (b) II, I, IV, III

(c) II, I, IV   (d) IV, I, III

12.
I. It reverberates throughout the entire Universe. And you are transmitting that frequency with your thoughts!

II. The frequency you transmit reaches beyond cities, beyond countries, beyond the world.

III. You are human transmission tower, and you are more powerful than any television tower created on earth.

IV. Your transmission creates your life and it creates the world.

(a) IV, I, III, II   (b) II, IV, III, I

(c) III, IV, II, I   (d) I, II, III, IV

13.
I. Asian economies will need alternative sources of growth to compensate for the rapid fall in demand from the western markets.

II. But the crisis has exposed the limits of region's dominant economic-growth model.

III. The export-let that propelled many Asian economies so effectively for the past 30 years must be adapted to a different global economic context.

IV. Asia is less exposed to the financial turmoil than the west is, because Asian countries responded to the previous decade's regional crisis by improving their current-account positions, accumulating reserves, and the ensuring that their banking systems operated prudently.

(a) IV, II, I, III   (b) I, II, III, IV

(c) III, I, II, IV   (d) II, III, IV

14.
I. The dangers of conflicting irrational majoritarianism with enlightened consensus are, indeed, great in developing democracy.

II. Real democracy is about mediating the popular will through a network of institutional structure and the law of the land.

III. While law making and governance are meant to articulate the latter, the judiciary is supposed to protect the former any kind of excess that might occur, unwittingly or otherwise, in the conduct of legislative and governmental functions.

IV. The principle of separation of powers is meant to embody a desirable tension between individual rights and social consensus.

(a) I, II, III, IV   (b) II, I, III, IV

(c) IV, III, I, II   (d) II, III, IV

15.
I. First may be necessary for immediate relief.

II. However, to cure the problem from the root the treatment at the elemental level is a must.

III. Therefore synergy of modern medical science and ancient Indian wisdom is in the interest of humanity.

IV. Allopathic treatment is symptomatic while Ayurveda treats at an elemental level.

(a) IV, II, I, III   (b) IV, I, II, III

(c) IV, III, II   (d) II, IV, III

16.
I. He somehow knew he would find what he was looking for. So, with missionary zeal, he started to climb.

II. So instead, for perhaps the first time in his life, he shed the shackles of reason and placed his trust in his intuition.

III. At first he thought about hiring a Sherpa guide to aid him in his climb through the mountains,

but, for some strange reason, his instincts told him this was one journey he would have to make alone.

IV. The next morning, as the first rays of the Indian sun danced along the colourful horizon, Julian set out his trek to the lost land of Savana.

(a) I, II, III, IV   (b) I, III, II, IV

(c) III, IV, I, II   (d) IV, III, II, I

2011-13

Directions for questions 17 to 22: Each question consists of a number of sentences that need to be properly sequenced, to form a meaningful and coherent paragraph/sentences. Choose the most logical order of sentences from the choices given below.

17.
I. of course, it isn't anywhere near as simple as this in real life

II. the diagram is commonly called 'the stack', and the people in the computer industry love to talk about it

III. at the base are components that are assembled into finished hardware products; operating systems, middleware, and software applications sit above the hardware; and it's all topped off by a whole range of services

IV. the stack shows most of the major pieces in a typical computing environment

(a) II, I, III, IV

(b) II, IV, III, I

(c) III, IV, II, I

(d) II, III, I, IV

18.
I. as a skeptical empiricist

II. I do not want to be the turkey

III. since we do not observe

IV. so I do not want to focus

V. solely on specific organs in the brain

VI. brain functions very well

(a) I, II, III, IV, V, VI   (b) II, I, IV, III, V, VI

(c) I, VI, IV, III, V, II   (d) I, II, IV, V, III, VI

19.
I. knowledge, even when it is exact

II. because we tend to forget what we know

III. if we do not pay attention

IV. or forget how to process it properly

V. does not often lead to appropriate actions

VI. even when we are experts

(a) I, V, II, IV, III, VI   (b) I, V, III, IV, II, VI

(c) VI, V, II, I, III, IV   (d) III, VI, I, II, V, IV

20. I. in the classroom

    II. once they are let out on streets

    III. statisticians, it has been shown

    IV. and engage in most trivial inferential errors

    V. tend to leave their brains

    (a) III, V, I, IV, II   (b) II, III, V, I, IV

    (c) I, V, II, III, IV   (d) III, I, V, IV, II

21. I. sure enough failed

    II. I have tested myself and

    III. by carefully setting a wide range

    IV. even while consciously trying to be humble

    V. as we will see the core of my professional activities

    VI. and yet such underestimation happens to be

    (a) I, II, V, III, IV, VI   (b) IV, II, I, III, V, VI

    (c) V, II, I, IV, III, VI   (d) II, I, IV, III, VI, V

22. I. except that people got all excited

    II. so I would not have cared

    III. and talked quite a bit about

    IV. the least about them

    V. pouring verbal sauce around the forecasts

    VI. what these figures were going to mean

    (a) I, II, IV, IV, III, VI   (b) I, III, II, IV, V, VI

    (c) II, IV, I, III, VI, V   (d) V, II, IV, VI, I, III

2012-14

Direction for question 23: In the following question, a sentence has been broken up into parts, and the parts have been scrambled and numbered. Choose the correct order of these parts from the alternatives A, B, C and D.

23. 1. food supply

    2. storage, distribution and handling

    3. pastoral industry and fishing

    4. besides increasing

    5. by preventing wastage in

    6. the productivity from agriculture

    7. can be increased

    (a) 1, 7, 5, 2, 4, 3, 6   (b) 4, 1, 6, 7, 5, 3, 2

    (c) 4, 6, 3 ,1, 7, 5, 2   (d) 6, 3, 5, 7, 4, 1, 2

2013-15

Direction for questions 24 - 25: A number of sentences are given below, which when properly sequenced, form a coherent paragraph. Choose the most logical order of sentences from the choices given to construct a coherent paragraph.

24. I. Have you ever gone through a book that was so good you kept hugging yourself mentally as you read?

    II. Now, notice the examples I have used

    III. Have you ever seen a play or motion picture that was so charming that you felt sheer delight as you watched?

    IV. I have not spoken of books that grip you emotionally, of plays and movies that keep you on the edge of your seat in surprise, or of food that satisfies a ravenous hunger.

    V. Or perhaps you have had a portion of pumpkin pie, light and airy and mildly flavoured, and with a flaky, delicious crust, that was the last word in gustatory enjoyment?

    (a) I, V, III, IV, II   (b) III, V, II, IV, I

    (c) IV, II, I, III, V   (d) I, III, V, II, IV

25. I. All these help hasten download and optimize the farmer's usage of the internet within the available bandwidth.

    II. ITC has learnt invaluable lessons from finding creative local solutions on the ground, to some of these apparently intractable problems.

    III. Solutions include the use of RNS kits in the telephone exchanges, or setting up VSAT to tide over connectivity problems, and using solar power as the back-up source of electricity.

    IV. It has also adopted special imaging techniques.

    V. It has applied the template approach to manage content.

    (a) V, IV, I, II, III   (b) V, IV, III, I, II

    (c) II, IV, I, V, III   (d) II, III, V, IV, I

2014-16

Directions for questions 26 to 27: Arrange the given sentences in the most logical sequence.

26. (i) She was so innovative that she had begun to include the songs composed by Rabindranath Tagore in her repertoire even before the word "Rabindra Sangeet" was coined.

    (ii) Gauhar knew she could gain the goodwill of the Bengali babus by singing as many Bengali songs as she could in her soirees.

    (iii) Instead, she rendered them in her own style, giving them a classical twist.

    (iv) Gauhar was not afraid to defy the norms and in fact she seldom used the tunes that Tagore had set his songs to.

    (a) i, ii, iii, iv   (b) ii, iv, iii, i

    (c) ii, i, iv, iii   (d) iv, ii, i, iii

27. (i) At dusk, I allowed Adele to put away books and work, and to run downstairs.

(ii) Twilight and snowflakes together thickened the air and hid the very shrubs in the lawn.

(iii) The afternoon was wild and snowy and we passed it in the schoolroom.

(iv) Left alone, I walked to the window but nothing was to be seen there.

(a) i, ii, iii, iv   (b) iii, i, iv, ii

(c) i, iii, iv, ii   (d) iv, iii, ii, i

2015-17

Directions for questions 28 and 29: Read the following sets of four sentences and arrange them in the most logical sequence to form a meaningful and coherent paragraph.

28. I. Doubts linger about Facebook's ability to be a business. Financial markets had also cratered since the Microsoft deal.

II. Big, as that is, it's considerably less than the $15 billion valuation that Microsoft and Li Ka-shing accepted in October 2007.

III. Milner's confidence that Facebook will eventually be profitable at a gigantic scale is what emboldened him to invest initially at a price that valued the company at $10 billion.

IV. But Milner's enthusiasm is such that not only did he buy stock from Facebook, he will also be spending as much as $300 million more buying stock from employees and outside investors.

(a) I, II, III, IV   (b) I, IV, II, III

(c) III, II, I, IV   (d) III, IV, II, I

29. I. No light, no sound comes in from the world.

II. My violin misses him more than I do. I tune it, and we enter my soundproof cell.

III. Electrons along copper, horsehair across acrylic create my only impressions of sense.

IV. I have not played Schubert for more than a month.

(a) I, II, III, IV   (b) II, III, I, IV

(c) III, I, IV, II   (d) IV, II, I, III

2016-18

Directions (Q. 30-31): *The first line (SI) of each question is fixed. Arrange the other four lines P, Q, R and S in a logical sequence.*

30. SI : The beginning of the universe had, of course, been discussed for a long time.

P : One argument of such a beginning was the feeling that it was necessary to have a first cause to explain the existence of the universe.

Q : He pointed out that civilization is progressing, and we remember who performed this deed or developed that technique;

R : According to a number of early cosmologies in the Jewish/Christian/Muslim tradition, the universe started at a finite and not very distant time in the past.

S : Another argument was put forward by St. Augustine in his book, *The City of God.*

A. QRSP   B. RPSQ

C. PSQR   D. SQPR

31. SI : I was so eager not to disappoint my parents that I ran errands for anyone.

P : On the way a boy on a bicycle crashed into me and my left shoulder hurt so much that my eyes watered.

Q : Only then did I cry

R : But I still went and bought the maize, took it to my neighbours and then went home

S : One day my neighbours asked me to buy some maize for them from the bazaar

A. SPRQ

B. PQSR

C. QRPS

D. RSQP

2017-19

Directions (Q. 32-33): *In the following questions some parts of the sentence have been jumbled up. Re-arrange these parts which are labelled as (a), (b), (c) and (d) to produce the correct sequence in completing the sentence.*

32. Nelson <u>Mandela modem country in a modern way</u> / (a) <u>and could run a new</u> /(b) <u>shifted the beliefs of the people</u> /(c) <u>so they could heal the racial conflict</u> /(d)

(a) (c), (b), (d), (a)

(b) (c), (d), (b), (a)

(c) (b), (a), (c), (d)

(d) (b), (c), (a), (d)

33. The difference <u>and development on the other affects</u> / (a) <u>in the relationship between death and birth-rates on the one hand</u> /(b) <u>but the age structure of the population</u> /(c) <u>not just the rate of population growth</u> /(d)

(a) (d), (c), (b), (a)

(b) (b), (d), (a), (c)

(c) (b), (a), (d), (c)

(d) (d), (a), (b), (c)

2019-21

Directions (Questions 34-35): The sentences given in each question, when properly sequenced, form a coherent paragraph. Each sentence is labelled with a letter. Choose the most logical order of sentences from among the given choices to construct a coherent paragraph.

34. A. But, clearly, the government still has the final say.

    B. In the past few years, the Reserve Bank of India might have wrested considerable powers from the government when it comes to monetary policy.

    C. The RBI's announcements of certain issues become effective only after the government notifies them.

    D. Isn't it time the government vested the RBI with powers to sanction such changes, leaving their ratification later?

    A. ACBD   B. ACDB

    C. DACB   D. BACD

35. A. All levels of demand, whether individual, aggregate, local, national, or international are subject to change.

    B. At the same time, science and technology add new dimensions to products, their uses and the methods used to market them.

    C. Aggregate demand fluctuates with changes in the level of business activity, GNP and national income.

    D. The demand of individuals tend to vary with changing needs and rising income.

    A. BCAD   B. ADCB

    C. CBDA   D. DCAB

Course of Action

2012-14

Directions for questions 36 – 37: In each question given below, a statement is followed by three courses of action numbered 1, 2 and 3. You have to assume everything in the statement to be true, and then decide which of the three suggested courses of action logically follow(s).

36. Statement: School dropout rate is very high in the rural areas as children support their parents in income earning activities.

Courses of action:

1. Public awareness programme on primary education should be expanded immediately to educate parents.

2. Compensation should be given to those parents whose children are in the school.

3. Law on universal education and ban on child labour should be made rigorous.

(a) Only 1 and 2 follow

(b) Only 2 and 3 follow

(c) Only 1 and 3 follow

(d) All follow

37. Statement: In a recent bulletin the Meteorological Department of India has forecasted severe drought in next cropping season which may cause failure of crops.

Courses of action:

1. The forecast should be widely published in media.

2. The drought relief team should be ready for relief work.

3. The people should be advised to go for drought resistant variety.

(a) Only 1 and 2 follow

(b) Only 2 follows

(c) Only 2 and 3 follow

(d) None of the above

2015-17

Directions for question 38: The statement below is followed by three outcomes numbered I. II and III. An outcome is either a step of administrative decision to be undertaken for improvement, or a follow-up for further action, or natural response by stakeholders, etc. on the basis of the information provided in the statement. Everything mentioned in the statement is to be assumed to be true, on the basis of which the most logically followed course of action has to be decided.

38. **Statement:** The city council of *Brownwood City* has decided to install a plant of mineral water to provide the citizens mineral water bottles at US $ 1 per bottle as against bottles costing US $ 1.5 being sold by local private players.

I. All the local private companies selling bottled water in *Brownwood City* will have to close their operations.

II. The city council of *Brownwood City* will have to provide for the losses from this project in its budget.

III. The normal tap water supply of *Brownwood City* will have no takers and that will have to be discontinued.

(a) None of I, II or III   (b) Only II

(c) Both II and III   (d) All I, II and III

Syllogisms

2009-11

Direction for questions 39 – 40: Answer the questions based on the following information.

In each question below three statements (I, II and III) are given followed by four conclusions numbered 1, 2, 3 and 4. You have to take the given statements to be true even if they seem to be at variance with commonly known facts. Read all the conclusions and then decide which of the given conclusions logically follows from the given statements, disregarding commonly known facts. Choose the correct options (A to D) presented below.

39. Statements:

   I.   Some drivers are technicians

   II.   All technicians are engineers

   III. Some engineers are lecturers

Conclusions:

   1.   Some technicians are lecturers

   2.   Some lecturers are drivers

   3.   All engineers are technicians

   4.   Some engineers are drivers

   (a) Only 3 follows

   (b) Only 4 follows

   (c) Only 3 and 4 follows

   (d) None of the above

40. Statements:

   I.   Some barbers are fashion designers

   II.   No fashion designers are businessmen

   III. Some businessmen are traders

Conclusions:

   1.   No Fashion designers are traders

   2.   Some traders are not fashion designers

   3.   Some fashion designers are traders

   4.   Some barbers are not businessmen

   (a) Either 1, 2 and 4 or 3, 2 and 4 follow

   (b) Either 1 and 4 or 3 and 4 follow

   (c) Either 1 and 2 or 3 and 2 follow

   (d) None of the above

2012-14

Direction for questions 41–42: Each of the questions below starts with a few statements, followed by four conclusions numbered 1, 2, 3 and 4. You have to consider every given statement as true, even if it does not confirm to the accepted facts. Read the conclusions carefully and then decide which of the conclusion(s) logically follow(s) from the given statements, disregarding commonly known facts.

41. Statements:

   a.   Some boys are scholars

   b.   Some teachers are boys

   c.   All scholars are observers

Conclusions:

   1.   Some scholars are boys

   2.   Some scholars are not boys

   3.   Some observers are boys

   4.   Some teachers are scholars

Answer:

   (a) 1, and 3 follow

   (*i*) 1, 3 and 4 follow

   (c) Either 1 or 2 and 3 follow

   (d) None of the above

42. Statements:

   a.   All teachers are professors

   b.   All professors are researchers

   c.   All researchers are consultants

Conclusions:

   1.   Some consultants are teachers

   2.   All professors are consultants

   3.   Some researchers are teachers

   4.   All professors are teachers

Answer:

   (a) Only 1 and 2 follow

   (b) Only 1 and 3 follow

   (c) Either 1 or 4 follow

   (d) None of the above

2013-15

43. Statement 1: All chickens are birds.

   Statement 2: Some chickens are hens.

   Statement 3: Female birds lay eggs.

   If the above statements are facts, then which of the following must also be a fact?

   I.   All birds lay eggs.

   II.   Hens are birds.

   III. Some chickens are not hens.

   (a) II only

   (b) II and III only

   (c) I, II and III

   (d) None of the statements is a known fact

44. Statement 1: Picture can tell a story.

    Statement 2: All storybook have pictures.

    Statement 3: Some storybooks have words.

    If the above statement are facts, then which of the following must also be a fact?

    I.   Pictures can tell a story better than words can.

    II. The stories in storybooks are very simple.

    III. Some storybooks have both words and pictures.

    (a) I only

    (b) II only

    (c) III only

    (d) None of the statements is a known fact.

2015-17

Directions for questions 45 and 46: In each question given below, there are three statements followed by four conclusions numbered I, II, III and IV. You have to take the given statements to be true even if they seem to be at variance with commonly known facts and then decide which of the conclusion(s) logically follows from the given statements.

45. **Statements:**

    a. All tigers are lions.

    b. All lions are horses.

    c. No horses are monkeys.

    Conclusions:

    I.   All tigers are horses.

    II. No tigers are monkeys.

    III. Some lions are tigers.

    IV. Some monkeys are not tigers.

    (a) All follow

    (b) Only I, II and III follow

    (c) Only I, II and IV follow

    (d) Only II, III and IV follow

46. **Statements:**

    a. Same shirts are pants.

    b. All shoes are shirts.

    c. All pants are gloves.

    Conclusions:

    I.   Some shoes are gloves.

    II. Some shirts are gloves.

    III. No pants are shoes.

    IV. All gloves are shirts.

    (a) Only II follows

    (b) Both I and III follow

    (c) Only III follows

    (d) Only I and IV follow

2016-18

47. From the given statements, choose the conclusions which follow logically :

    Statements :

    i.   Some iphones are mobiles

    ii. Some mobiles are ipads

    iii. Some ipads are tablets

    Conclusions :

    I.   Some tablets are iphones

    II. Some mobiles are tablets

    III. Some ipads are iphones

    IV. All iphones are tablets

    (a) Only I & II follow   (b) Only I, II & III follow

    (c) Only II & III follow   (d) None of these

2017-19

48. The diagram below, explains which of the given relationship

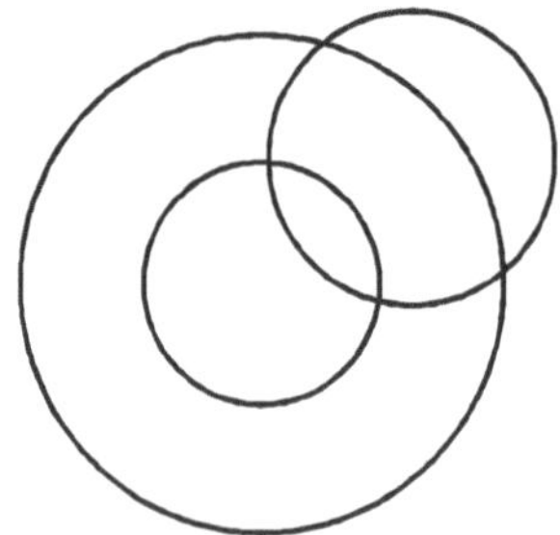

    (a) Judge, Thief, Criminal

    (b) Tea, Coffee, Beverages

    (c) Males, fathers, Doctors

    (d) Cabinet, Minister, Home Minister

49. Choose the conclusion which logically follows from the given statement irrespective of commonly known facts.

    Statement:

    All branches are flowers.

    All flowers are leaves

    Conclusion:

    I.   All branches are leaves

    II. All leaves are branches

    III. All flowers are branches

    IV. Some leaves are branches

    (a) None follows

    (b) Only I and IV follow

    (c) Only II and III

    (d) All follow

2018-20

50. In the following question, two statements are given followed by four conclusions. Taking the given statements to be true, decide which of the given conclusions logically follows from the given statements:

Statements

Some rivers are plateau. No plateau is mountain.

Conclusions

I. Some plateau are rivers.

II. Some mountains are rivers.

III. Some rivers are not mountains.

IV. All mountains are rivers.

(*a*) Only I follows

(*b*) Both II and III follow

(*c*) Both I and III follow

(*d*) Both I and II follow

Critical Reasoning

2008-10

Directions for Questions 51 and 52: Answer the questions based on following information.

In an institute there are five identical rooms having different items in it. Every identical looking room has a name indicating its contents. The details of the contents and the name of each room are as given below.

Contents	Name of Rooms
Two printers	Pashupatti
Two Computers	Chandrachud
Two Bags	Bagbahadur
One printer and one computer	Purnchandra
One bag and one computer	Biswachakra

One day somebody in the institute changed the name plate of every room such that no room contains the name correctly explaining its contents.

51. If supervisor of the institute opened a room named Biswachakra and found that one item was a bag. Which of the following would **definitely be correct**?

(a) the other item will be a bag

(b) the other item will not be bag

(c) the other room named Bagbahadur will contain a bag

(d) the other item is a computer

52. If it is known that room named Purnachandra does not contain either any printer or any computer, the room named Pashupatti does not contain any printer and room named Chandrachud contains one computer and one bag, which of the following will **definitely be true** if only one of the remaining rooms is opened?

(a) It will have at least one computer and printer

(b) It will have two printers

(c) It will have at least one computer

(d) It will have at least one printer

Logical Consistency

2008-10

Directions for Questions 53 to 56: Each question consists of five statements followed by options consists of three statements put together in a specific order. Choose the option which indicates a valid argument, that is, where the third statement is a conclusion drawn from the preceding two statements.

53. a. All universities appoint experienced teachers.

b. Kashi Vidyapeeth appoints experienced teachers.

c. Kashi Vidyapeeth is a university.

d. Some universities employ experienced teachers.

e. Kashi Vidyapeeth only appoints experienced teachers.

(a) abc   (b) cdb

(c) acb   (d) ace

54. a. Migration of people augments housing problem in urban areas.

b. Increase in housing problem in urban areas is determined to economic growth.

c. Migration of people is detrimental to economic growth.

d. Some migration does not cause increase in urban housing problem.

e. Some migration is not detrimental to economic growth.

(a) cba   (b) bde

(c) cde   (d) bac

55. a. Some drivers are drug addicted.

b. All drug addicted drivers should be terminated.

c. Driver Balbeer should be terminated.

d. Driver Balbeer is drug addicted.

e. Some drivers should be terminated.

(a) bae   (b) bde

(c) ade   (d) cdb

56. a. No officer is a teacher

b. Mr. Rangachary is not a teacher.

c. Mr. Rangachary is an officer.

d. Dr. Nandi is not an officer.

e. Dr. Nandi is a teacher.

(a) abe   (c) abc

(c) ade   (d) acb

Statement Conclusion

2016-18

57. Based on the given statement, choose the right conclusion:

    'If the breakfast doesn't have eggs, I will not go for a walk and will not have lunch.'

    (a) If I went for a walk and didn't have lunch, the breakfast didn't have eggs.

    (b) If I went for a walk or I had lunch, the breakfast had eggs.

    (c) If I went for a walk and had lunch, the breakfast had eggs.

    (d) If I didn't go for a walk and had lunch, the breakfast had eggs.

Statement Assumption

2015-17

Direction for question 58: In the question below, a statement is followed by three assumptions numbered I, II and III. An assumption is something supposed or taken for granted. You have to consider the statement and the following assumptions and decide which assumptions are implicit in the statement.

58. It is believed by many economists that to realize a 7 percent GDP growth rate in India, which is very much attainable, the gross fixed capital formation in the country must increase to 30 percent of GDP from the present level of 28 percent.

    I.   The target of 7 percent GDP growth is not feasible.

    II. GDP growth rate is directly related to capital formation rate.

    III. The GDP growth rate in a country is the only indicator of country's economic devlopment.

    (a) Both I and II   (b) Both II and III
    (c) Both III and I   (d) None of A, B or C

ANSWERS

1. (d)	**2.** (c)	**3.** (d)	**4.** (d)	**5.** (d)	**6.** (a)	**7.** (a)	**8.** (c)	**9.** (a)	**10.** (d)
11. (c*)	**12.** (c)	**13.** (a)	**14.** (c)	**15.** (b*)	**16.** (d)	**17.** (b)	**18.** (d)	**19.** (a)	**20.** (a)
21. (d)	**22.** (c)	**23.** (c)	**24.** (d)	**25.** (d)	**26.** (c)	**27.** (b)	**28.** (c)	**29.** (d)	**30.** (b)
31. (a)	**32.** (b)	**33.** (c)	**34.** (d)	**35.** (b)	**36.** (d)	**37.** (c)	**38.** (a)	**39.** (b)	**40.** (d)
41. (a)	**42.** (d)	**43.** (d)	**44.** (c)	**45.** (a)	**46.** (a)	**47.** (d)	**48.** (c)	**49.** (b)	**50.** (c)
51. (a)	**52.** (d)	**53.** (c)	**54.** (d)	**55.** (a)	**56.** (d)	**57.** (b)	**58.** (d)		

EXPLANATIONS

1. Statements A and B can be ruled out because they go against the idea of "importance of discipline" introduced in the first sentence. So the answer would be statement C which carries the same idea forward. Hence, the answer would be option (d).

2. Statement A can be ruled out because it does not fit in the context of the passage. Statement C followed by statement B would be the correct answer since, they agree with the subject of the passage and are in the right chronological order.

3. The correct order would be "A number of measures are being taken by the State Governments for mobilisation of resources in order to improve the financial conditions of the Municipal Corporations".

4. The complete sentence should be – 'Having started with just 5.8 million in seed financing, you squandered more than half of your capital in less time than it takes to soft-boil an egg.' This makes option (d) correct.

5. The complete sentence should be – 'You could behave badly, say you were sorry, you could get extra fun and be reinstated in the same position as the one who had done nothing, who now had both to suffer the crime and the difficulty of forgiving.'. This makes option (d) correct.

6. Statement IV and III form a mandatory pair because 'and' in statement III connects statement IV by explaining how close the creatures got to her and opened their eyes and mouths so wide. Statement II and statement I form a mandatory pair because statement I provides the contrast to statement II.

7. Statement II and III form a mandatory pairs as what is said in the statement III is referred to in statement II. Statement I and IV form a mandatory pair because the idea referred to in statement IV is the one mentioned in statement I.

8. Statement III is the opening statement as it is a general idea. Also, the mandatory pair is statements II and IV are the mandatory pair as 'contracted' in statement II has a link with 'this' in statement IV, The key-words 'even poorer' in statement I take the idea mentioned in statement IV forward.

9. Statement V introduces 'Comprehensive schools' which makes it an obvious opener. "At the time" in statement I refers to 1972 mentioned in statement V, The pronoun 'he' in statement III refers to Matti Meri in statement I, the pronoun 'they' in statement IV refers to 'grammar school teachers' in statement III, which makes statements III and IV a mandatory pair, statement II carries the idea forward.

10. Statement III introduces the idea. The pronoun 'he' in statement I refers to Dr. Nicholson mentioned in statement III. Statement IV is a continuation of what Dr. Nicholson says in statement I. Statement V gives an example of the 'specific pointer' mentioned in statement IV. The pronoun 'its' in statement II refers to 'formate' in statement V. The correct sequence is III, I, IV, V, II. Hence, option (d) is the correct answer.

11. Statement II is an obvious opener as it introduces the topic. Statement I logically follows statement II as it talks about the strategy used by the company to counter the head hunting by other companies. IV carries forward the idea mentioned in statement I. (Statement III could also have been an opener followed by statements II, I and IV necessarily in the same order. Since there was no option starting with statement III option (c) is the best answer among the given options).

In the given paper options (c) and (d) are incomplete.

12. Statement II and I option a mandatory pair because 'frequency' mentioned in statement II is referred to by 'it' in statement I. Only option (c) has the required pair. Hence, option (c) is the correct answer.

13. Statement IV is the oblivious opener as it introduces the subject. Statement II and IV form a mandatory pair. Statement I carries forward the discussion in statement II. Statement III gives the details of the "alternative sources of growth" mentioned in statement I. Hence option (a) is the correct answer.

14. Statement IV and III form a mandatory pair as the words 'latter' and 'former' in III refer to 'individual rights' and 'social consensus' respectively. This mandatory pair only exists in option (c). Hence, option (c) is the correct answer.

15. IV opens the discussion as it introduces the two schools of medicine. I throws more light on the allopathic treatment whereas II highlights the importance of ayurvedic school of medicine thus, I and II would appear in the same sequence. III concludes the discussion.

In the given paper option C and D are incomplete.

16. Option (d) is the correct answer as it presents the information in a chronological manner. Statement IV opens the paragraph because it mentioned the beginning of the track. Statement IV and III form a mandatory pair because statement III follows the event mentioned in statement IV. Hence option (d) is the correct answer.

17. The term 'the stack' is introduced in statement (II) and is discussed in statement (IV). 'Of course' in statement (I) makes it a concluding sentence.

Moreover, 'it' in statement (I) refers to the concept discussed in statement (III). So, statements (II)-(IV) and (III)-(I) are mandatory pairs. Hence, option (b) is the correct answer.

18. (I) reasons out why the speaker does not 'want to be the turkey'. So (I) and (II) are a mandatory pair. 'To focus' in (IV) connects to 'solely on specific organs' in (V). So, (IV) and (V) are also a mandatory pair. There two mandatory pairs make option (d) correct.

19. The subject of the sentence in statement (V) is 'knowledge' in statement (I). So statement (I) and statement (V) form a mandatory pair. Statement (II) and statement (IV) also form a mandatory pair as verb 'tend' in statement (II) has two objects 'to forget' in statement (I) and 'forget' in statement (IV). Statement (III) connects with the context discussed in statement (II) and statement (IV). Hence, option (a) is the correct answer.

20. 'Statisticians, it has been shown, tend to leave their brains in the classroom' is the correct and logical sequence. Statements (V) and (I) form a mandatory pair because statement (I) tells where the statisticians leave their brain (in the classroom). Statements (III), (V) and (I) are in sequence. Hence, option (a) is the correct answer.

21. Statements (II) and (I) form a mandatory pair as the conjuction 'and' in statement (II) connects and completes the thought mentioned in statement (I). Statements (IV) and (III) also form a mandatory pair. Hence, option (d) is the correct answer.

22. 'Cared the least about them' in statements (II) and (IV) is logically consistent. Statements (III) and (VI) are a mandatory pair as statement (VI) indicates what people talked about. Statements (I) and (III) also from a mandatory pair because the idea of getting excited in talking about the figures is connected in these two statements. Hence, option (c) is the correct answer.

23. Statements 4 and 6 form a mandatory pair because 'productivity' in statement 6 refers to 'increasing' in statements 4. Statements 1 and 7 form a mandatory pair because statement 7 refers to the increased food supply mentioned in statement 1. This combination of mandatory pairs does not exist in any other option hence option (c) is the correct answer. The correct order of the sentence is "besides increasing the productivity from agriculture pastoral industry and fishing, food supply can be increased by preventing wastage in storage, distribution and handling."

24. The correct sequence is given in option (d). Clearly, I and III form a mandatory pair with the author addressing the reader by asking similar questions. V follows after I and III as it continues in the same vein posing another question to the reader. II and IV

is another pair. The author elaborates in statement IV on the kind of examples he has used. Thus, option (d) is correct.

25. II introduces the topic; hence it opens the sequence. III follows II as it mentions the solutions talked about in II. V and IV is a mandatory pair. IV suggests another measure that the ITC has taken apart from the one mentioned in V. I concludes the passage by stating the benefits of the measures mentioned before. Option (d) gives the correct sequence.

26. Statement (ii) talks about the way Gauhar thought about gaining the goodwill of the Bengali babus — that is, by singing Bengali songs. Statement (i) follows this up by talking of how she went about her plan – by including 'the songs composed by Rabindranath Tagore'. Statements (iv) and (iii) form a mandatory pairas (iv) says how Gauhar was not afraid to defy norms and hardly used the tunes that Tagore set his songs to and (iii) follows by saying what she did instead – rendered those songs in her own style. Hence, the correct sequence is ii, i, iv, iii and this, option (c) is the correct answer.

27. Statement (iii) talks of the happenings in the afternoon, immediately followed up by the author's description at dusk in statement (i). He talks of Adele running downstairs at dusk. He is left alone, of which he talks in statement (iv). Statements (iv) and (ii) form a mandatory pair as (iv) talks about the author going upto the window but seeing nothing and statement (ii) gives the reason for this – 'twilight and darkness had together thickened the air'. Hence, the correct answer is option (b).

28. III and II form a mandatory pair because III discusses Milner's investment of $10 billion in Facebook and II states that this amount, i.e. $10 billion, is less than what Microsoft and Li Ka-shing accepted in the past. I and IV form a mandatory pair because I states the probability of Financial markets becoming hollow and IV states that despite the doubts (discussed in I), Milner not only spent on buying a stock from Facebook but will also spend more on buying stocks from elsewhere. Since III introduces the idea of Milner having invested in Facebook and its reference is being made in IV, III and II will precede I and IV. Hence, the correct sequence is III, II, I, and IV and option (c) the answer.

29. IV and II form a mandatory pair because the 'him' in II refers to Schubert in IV. II should be followed by I because I, which describes a world devoid of sound or light, follows from II that discusses the process of creation of this world. III should follow I because III discusses the only impressions on sense created after I mentions that the impressions of light and sight do not exist in this world. Hence, the correct answer is option (d).

30. Sentence R correctly elucidates and describes S1. Sentence R describes the process of the origin of the universe which is a continuation of S1. Hence, option (b) is the answer.

31. Sentence S again describes S1. Sentence S describes an errand which correctly follows S1 because S1 mentions the fact that the person 'ran errands for anyone'.

32. Option (b) arranges the sentence correctly as the subject Mandel must be followed by (c) which will lead to (d).

33. Option (c) is the correct choice as the difference mentioned in the beginning is followed the death and birth-rates in (b) which is followed (a).

34. It's an easy question. Only sentence B can open the paragraph. We can't start with 'but'. So, options (a) and (b) are eliminated. Sentence D has a question which has not been answered by the paragraph. So, it can only come at the end. So, option (d) is the correct answer.

35. A is the best opening sentence as it is generic and it covers all the areas mentioned in the other three sentences. So, option (b) is the only possible answer.

36. Courses of action 2 and 3 follow. There are two areas to be addressed: the reluctance of parents to send their children to school and the issue of child labor. The first issue can be addressed by educating the parents about the benefits of education. Since the question mentions that children support their parents in income earning activities therefore giving the parents compensation as in course of action 2 will also be effective. The second issue can be addressed by course of action 3. Thus option (d) is the correct answer.

37. Course of action 1 would cause unnecessary panic and is not valid. Course of action 2 is valid since it is necessary to act on the forecast and be prepared for any eventuality. Course of action 3 is also a necessary preventive measure that needs to be taken.

38. The statement discusses that the plant installed by the city has decided to provide mineral water bottles to its citizens at US $ 0.5 cheaper than that provided by local private players. Assumption I is invalid because it is possible that the citizens only trust the brand of local private players and therefore, prefer mineral water bottles sold by them. Assumption II is invalid because it is possible that the city plant earns profit despite selling the bottles at a cheaper price.

There is no reason why people will stop using normal tap water. It is possible that citizens don't use only mineral water for all purposes, rendering assumption III also invalid. Hence, the answer to this question is option (a).

39. 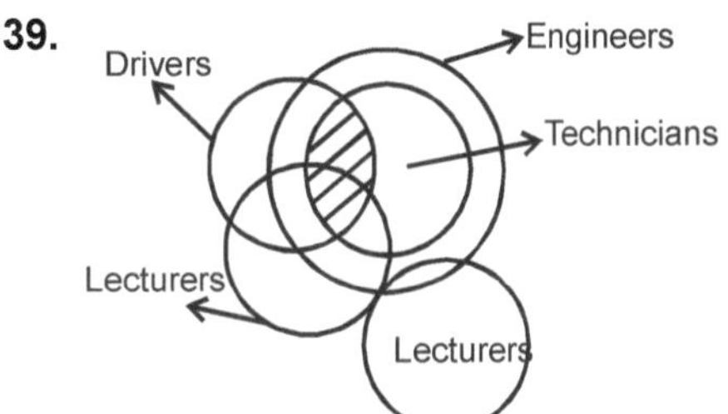

40. 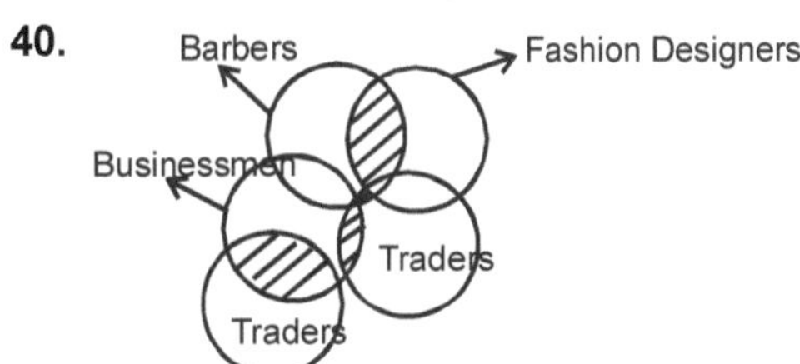

41. 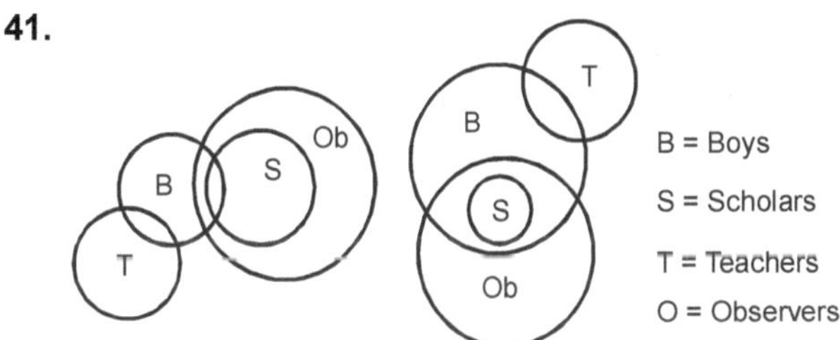

Statements 1 & 3 follow.

42. 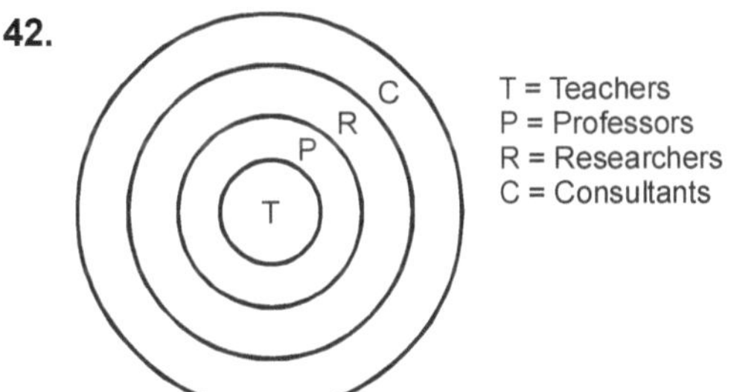

Statements 1, 2 and 3 are correct.

43. 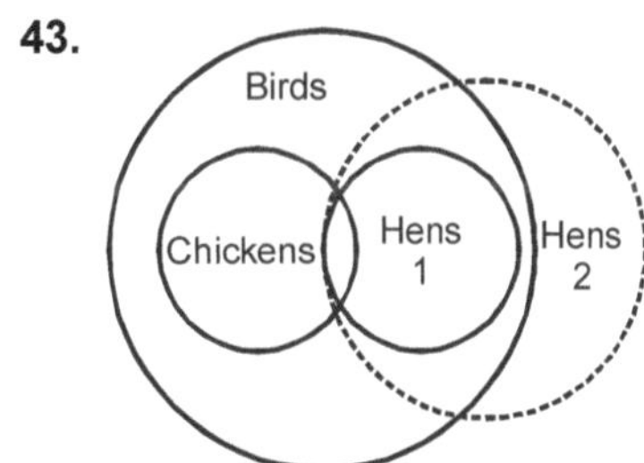

The set 'female birds' will fall under the set 'birds'. This implies that 'female birds' is a subset of 'birds'. So, the possible cases are as follows:

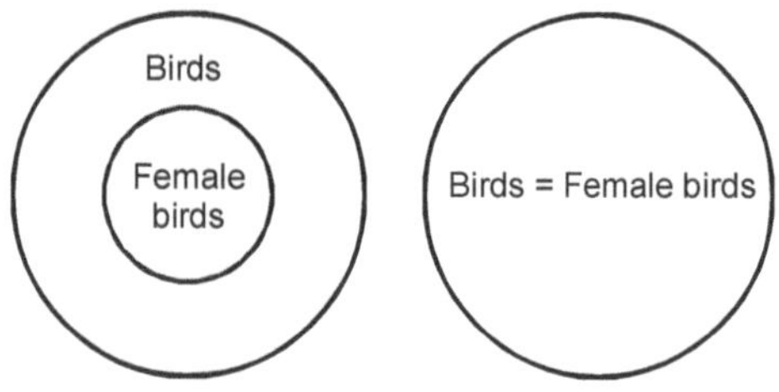

Hence,

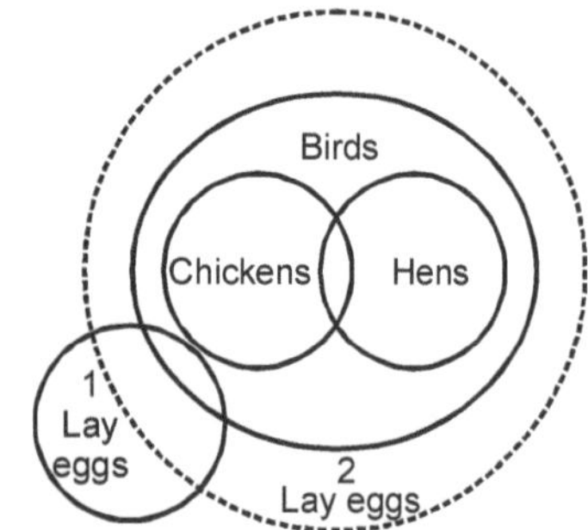

Thus, option (d) is correct.

44.

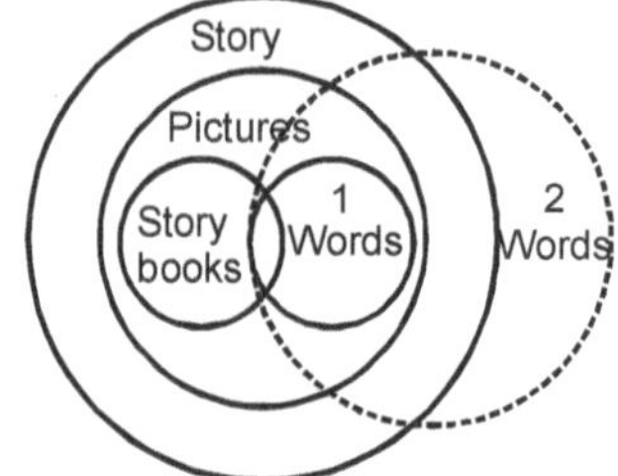

Only statement III follows from the given set of statements. Hence, option (c) is correct.

45.

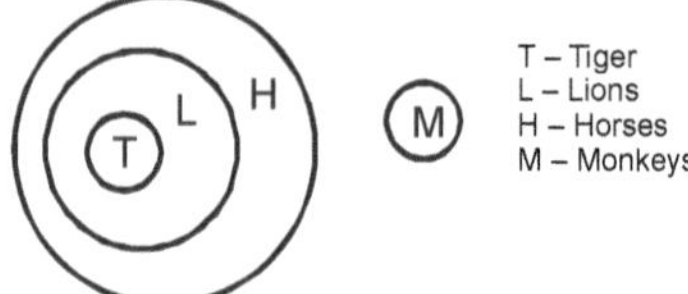

As per the Venn diagram, option (a) is the correct answer.

46.

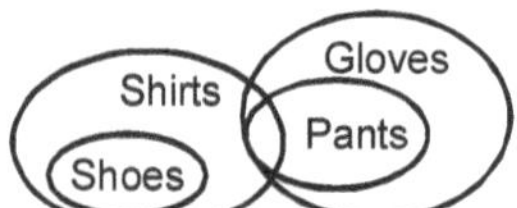

As per the Venn diagram, option (a) is the correct answer.

47.

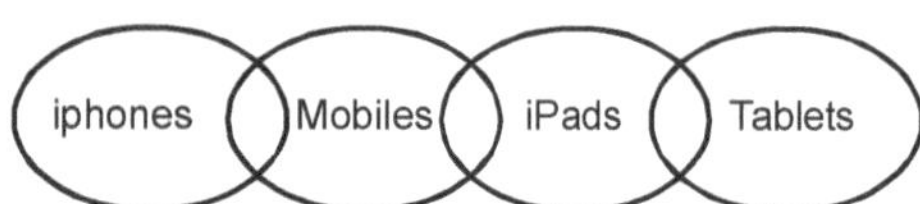

48. As all Fathers are Males, i.e. the set Fathers is a subset of the set Males; and some Doctors may be Males or Fathers, i.e. the set Doctors cuts across the sets Males and Fathers.

49. Option (b) is the right answer as can be confirmed by the following Venn Diagram:

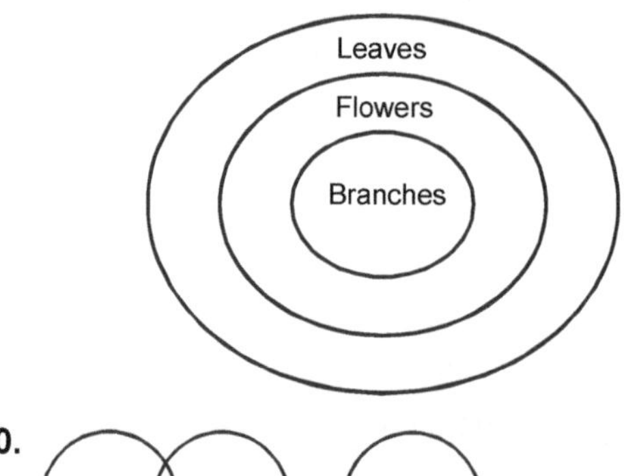

50.

From the diagram Both (i) and (ii) follows

Answer is option (c).

51. Only (A) can be concluded with certainty.

52. Only (D) can be concluded with certainty.

For questions 53 to 56: From the given statement,

53. "acb" is the only order of sentences which gives a valid argument.

54. "bac" is the only order of sentences which gives a valid argument.

55. "bae" is the only order of sentences which gives a valid argument.

56. "acb" is the only order of sentences which gives a valid argument.

57. If the breakfast doesn't have eggs, neither I will go for a walk nor will have lunch.' It means that If I went for a walk or I had lunch, the breakfast had eggs.

58. Assumption I is invalid because the statement suggests that realizing a 7 per cent GDP growth rate in India is very much feasible. Assumption II is valid because according to the statement, increase in GDP will happen if the capital formation increases. Assumption III is invalid because the statement does not state that the GDP growth of a country is the sole indicator of a country's economic development. Since, only assumption II is valid, option (d) is the answer.

Vocabulary

Match the Meaning

2007-09

Directions for Questions 1 and 2: List I gives pronounciation hints; List II gives word meanings and List III gives suggested spellings. Mark all the options whose suggested spellings in List C are correct.

1.

List I	List II	List III
Pronounciation hint	Word Meaning	Suggested Spelling
A. hype-PAL-uh-jee	The interchange in syntactic relationship between two terms	hypallage
B. RAN-tee.pole	characterized by a wild unruly manner or attitude	rantipole
C. in-TAL-yoh	An engraving or incised figured in stone or other hard material	intahlio
D. ICE-uh-goh-jee	A scholarly introduction to a branch of study or research	isagoje

2.

List I	List II	List III
Pronounciation hint	Word Meaning	Suggested Spelling
A. puh-LIFF-uh-jiz-um	the habit of feeding on a variety of plants or animals	polyphajism
B. see-gwuh-TERR-uh	poisoning caused by eating fish or mollusks with flesh toxic to man	siguatera
C. mak-ETT	a preliminary model of something designed	maquet
D. pan-uh-JEER-ik	an oration or writing expressing praise	panegyric

Synonyms

2009-11

Direction for questions 3 – 5: Find the most appropriate word from the given choices which is described by the meaning provided in the question.

3. Meaning: a bowl-shaped drinking vessel

   (a) rumble   (b) fracas

   (c) aquifer   (d) chalice

4. Meaning: definition of a substance, especially a strong acid; erosive; mordant.

   (a) vitriolic   (b) briny

   (c) puerile   (d) prophylactic

5. Meaning: an upward slope or grade (as in a road); rise; raise; climb; upgrade.

   (a) maelstrom   (b) acclivity

   (c) alacrity   (d) slighting

2010-12

Directions for questions 6 – 10: Select the most suitable synonym for the underlined word in the sentence.

6. The book did not get much acclaim because of its <u>pedantic</u> style of writing.

   (a) radical   (b) dogmatic

   (c) esoteric   (d) applicative

7. The policy announcement was made to the much <u>chagrin</u> of the farmers.

   (a) euphoria   (b) placation

   (c) glee   (d) mortification

8. The leader summoned the group and told that the time has come to act and not <u>genuflect</u>.

   (a) grovel   (b) procrastinate

   (c) renounce   (d) incriminate

9. The <u>stentorian</u> honks of the marching fleet could be heard for miles.

   (a) rhythmic   (b) euphonious

   (c) blaring   (d) subdued

10. Noticing the behaviour of the audience in the amphitheater the performer was more <u>bemused</u> than bitter.

    (a) amused   (b) bewildered

    (c) enlightened   (d) enthused

2012-14

Directions for questions 11 – 12: Match the words in column 1 with their appropriate meaning in column 2.

11.

	Column 1		Column 2
a.	Predilection	i.	Vanish
b.	Evanescence	ii.	A gentle, mild breeze
c.	Zephyr	iii.	Inane
d.	Diaphanous	iv.	Completely transparent and translucent
e.	Fatuous	v.	Partiality

(a) a - v; b - iv; c - i; d - ii; e - iii

(b) a - ii; b - i; c - iii; d - v; e - iv

(c) a - v; b - i; c - ii; d - iv; e - iii

(d) a - iii; b - iv; c - i; d - v; e - ii

12.

	Column 1		Column 2
a.	Perspicacity	i.	Doting upon wife
b.	Uxorious	ii.	Insignificant, ineffective person
c.	Nebbish	iii.	Undeveloped, immature
d.	Chicanery	iv.	Keenness of mental perception
e.	Inchoate	v.	to trick, to deceive

(a) a - ii; b - i; c - iv; d - iii; e - v

(b) a - iv; b - i; c - ii; d - v; e - iii

(c) a - iv; b - ii; c - i; d - v; e - iii

(d) a - ii; b - iv; c - i; d -iii; e - v

2013-15

Direction for questions 13 – 14: Choose the option which gives the correct meaning in the same order as the words.

13.

1. Arrogate	i. clinch or seize without right
2. Arraign	ii. embarrassment due to disappointment
3. Chagrin	iii. to enrol for compulsory service
4. Conscript	iv. to swing back and forth
5. Vacillate	v. to bring before court of law

(a) 1-v, 2-i, 3-iv, 4-iii, 5-ii

(b) 1-i, 2-v, 3-ii, 4-iii, 5-iv

(c) 1-ii, 2-v, 3-iii, 4-i, 5-iv

(d) 1-iii, 2-iv, 3-ii, 4-v, 5-i

14.

1. Ephemeral	i. an alcoholic drink taken before a meal
2. Ethereal	ii. fleeting/short lived
3. Aperitif	iii. frankness
4. Candour	iv. illusion
5. Chimera	v. spiritual/not of this world

(a) 1-v, 2-ii, 3-iii, 4-i, 5-iv

(b) 1-ii, 2-iv, 3-i, 4-iii, 5-v

(c) 1-iv, 2-v, 3-i, 4-ii, 5-iii

(d) 1-ii, 2-v, 3-i, 4-iii, 5-iv

2014-16

Directions for questions 15 and 16: Match the word in column 1 with its meaning in column 2.

15.

Column 1	Column 2
i. Anthromorphous	a. Moving upwards
ii. Anachronistic	b. A collection of extracts from the writing of various authors
iii. Anthology	c. Having or resembling human form
iv. Ascension	d. Occurring in the wrong time period

(a) i-b; ii-a; iii-d; iv-c

(b) i-c; ii-b; iii-d; iv-a

(c) i-c; ii-d; iii-b; iv-a

(d) i-b; ii-c; iii-a; iv-d

16.

Column 1	Column 2
i. Cacology	a. Study of human character
ii. Ethology	b. Study of snow and ice
iii. Misology	c. Poor diction or poor choice of words
iv. Cryology	d. Hatred of reasoning

(a) i-d; ii-c; iii-a; iv-b

(b) i-c; ii-a; iii-d; iv-b

(c) i-a; ii-b; iii-c; iv-d

(d) None of the above

2017-19

Directions (Q. 17-20): Use the words in the table below to solve the questions.

i) Equipoise	ii) Assiduous	iii) Emollient	iv) Noxious	v) Nebulous	vi) Dogmatic
vii) Tedious	viii) Obviate	ix) Espouse	x) Enigmatic	xi) Soliloquy	xii) Tranquil
xiii) Militate	xiv) Tenacity	xv) Endemic	xvi) Pursuant	xvii) Encomium	xviii) Obloquy
ixx) Digitise	xx) Tousled				

17. Complete the crossword using the words from the above table. There are more words than required.

Hint:

  1: Across: native to or confined to a certain region;

  1: Down: balance of forces or interests;

  2: inclined to lay down principles as undeniably true;

  3: attempting to avoid confrontation or anger, calming or conciliatory;

  4: a speech or piece of writing that praises someone or something highly

  (a) 1-Across-ix); 1-Down-i); 2-xvi); 3-xi); 4-vi)

  (b) 1-Across-iv); 1-Down-v); 2-xiv); 3-xi); 4-xvii)

  (c) 1-Across-xv); 1-Down-i); 2-vi); 3-iii); 4-xvii)

  (d) 1-Across-xii); 1-Down-xiv); 2-v); 3-ii); 4-xi)

Each question has explained the meaning of two words from the above table. Identify the correct matching words from the table.

18. A. A formal expression of praise
    B. Take up the cause, support
  (a) A-ii; B-xvi   (b) A-xvii; B-ix
  (c) A-ii; B-viii   (d) A-iii; B-vii

19. (a) Devoid of cheer or comfort, dreary
  (b) Stubbornly persevering, doggedness
  (a) A-vii; B-xiv   (b) A-vi; B-xiv
  (c) A-x ; B-iv   (d) None of the above

20. (a) Having a softening or soothing effect
  (b) Verbal abuse, defamation
  (a) A-xii ; B-ii   (b) A-xvii ; B-iv
  (c) A-iii ; B-xviii   (d) A-iii ; B-ix

2018-20

Directions for questions 21-23: Create a word using all the given letters from the jumbled letters and identify its appropriate meaning

21.

E	T	E
I	H	R
M	C	

  (a) Embarrassing Situation
  (b) An official license
  (c) Charming, pleasant
  (d) Completely sealed, isolated

22.

L	I	T
U	C	E
D	A	E

  (a) Denounce
  (b) Sincere
  (c) Enlighten
  (c) Confound

23.

A	I	
	T	O
P	U	N

  (a) Doubtful
  (b) Interesting
  (c) Haughty
  (d) Foremost

2019-21

Directions (Questions 24 and 25): Match the correct answers.

24. 1. Adonis   : A. An idler or loafer
     2. Don Juan   : B. An awkward, rough fellow
     3. Wastrel   : C. A handsome man
     4. Lout   : D. A rake or seducer
  (a) 1 -c, 2-b, 3-d, 4-a
  (b) 1 -b, 2-d, 3-a, 4-c
  (c) 1-b, 2-a, 3-d, 4-c
  (d) 1 -c, 2-d. 3-a, 4-b

25.
1. En Masse   : a. Adjective
2. Fetter   : b. Verb
3. Malinger   : c. Adverb
4. Raspy   : d. Noun

   (a) 1-c, 2-d, 3-b, 4-a
   (b) 1-b, 2-a, 3-d, 4-c
   (c) 1-d, 2-b, 3-c, 4-a
   (d) 1-d, 2-c, 3-a, 4-b

Directions (Questions 26-28): Create a word using all jumbled alphabets as provided in the table below and identify its appropriate meaning.

26.

	O	U
A	L	
I	C	S
Q	U	O

   (a) Verbose   (b) Taciturn
   (c) Rational   (d) Alluring

27.

C	B	A
	R	E
A	M	

   (a) Innocent   (b) Tarried
   (c) Gruesome   (d) Pleasing

28.
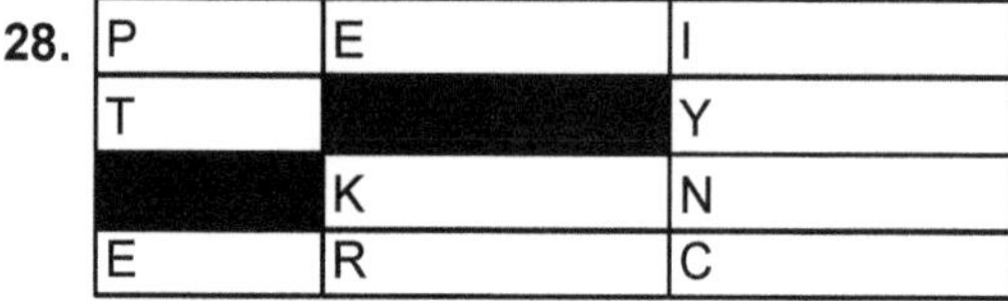

P	E	I
T		Y
	K	N
E	R	C

   (a) Spiteful   (b) Careless
   (c) Ignorant   (d) Fussy

Antonyms

Directions for Questions 29 to 32:

Select the words from the options below that have the *farthest* meaning to the given words:

29. REPUDIATE
   (a) Sanction   (b) Afflict
   (c) Transient   (d) Prowl

30. GRANDILOQUENT
   (a) Immature   (b) Innocent
   (c) Unpleasant   (d) Simple

31. VENERATION
   (a) Congregate   (b) Loquacious
   (c) Consecrate   (d) Burlesque

32. PERSPICACIOUS
   (a) Judicious   (b) Obtuse
   (c) Adroit   (d) Cerebral

Direction for questions 33 – 35: Select the most OPPOSITE of the given word from the given choices.

33. REQUIEM
   (a) Humility   (b) Prerequisite
   (c) Resolution   (d) Reign

34. ASPERSION
   (a) Infamy   (b) Restriction
   (c) Tradition   (d) Obeisance

35. STOLIDITY
   (a) Posterity   (b) Proximity
   (c) Agility   (d) Sobriety

Directions for questions 36 – 40: Select the most suitable antonym for the underlined word in the sentences.

36. The arguments put forth by the speaker were rather <u>specious</u>, but somehow he got away with them.
   (a) fallacious   (b) unfeigned
   (c) obscure   (d) pernicious

37. The trends suggest that most of the new members got themselves deregistered within 7-10 days of their joining due to the <u>exacting</u> instructor.
   (a) insouciant   (b) discourteous
   (c) grievous   (d) fastidious

38. The congregation was awestruck at the sight of the <u>levitating</u> saint.
   (a) gravitating   (b) enchanting
   (c) captivating   (d) vacillating

39. By the time she could realize the gravity of the situation she found herself <u>ensnared</u> in the labyrinth of accusation.
   (a) seized   (b) enmeshed
   (c) intrigued   (d) released

40. The sub-prime crisis has pushed millions of people in the <u>quagmire</u> of financial indebtedness.
   (a) predicament   (b) swamp
   (c) tranquility   (d) impasse

Directions for questions 41 – 42: Identify *antonyms* for the following words.

41. Risible:
   (a) serious   (b) amusing
   (c) ludicrous   (d) ridiculous

42. Tenebrous:
    - (a) dark
    - (b) truthful
    - (c) bright
    - (d) quarrelsome

2013-15

Direction for questions 43 - 44: Pick the correct antonym for the word given

43. PUERILE
    - (a) Adult
    - (b) Servile
    - (c) Peaceful
    - (d) Ambiguous

44. PROSAIC
    - (a) Predisposed
    - (b) Useful
    - (c) Interesting
    - (d) Mundane

2014-16

Directions for questions 45 to 46: Select the most appropriate antonym for the given word.

45. Apocryphal
    - (a) authentic
    - (b) audacious
    - (c) blasphemous
    - (d) none of these

46. Capricious
    - (a) crafty
    - (b) obvious
    - (c) erratic
    - (d) consistent

2016-18

47. Choose the option which is the antonym of the word 'Blasphemous'
    - (a) Ascetic
    - (b) Reverent
    - (c) Inferior
    - (d) Blarney

2017-19

Directions (Q. 48-49): *Match the words in Column A with their **Antonyms** Column B*

Column A	Column B
i) Lament	a. Unique
ii) Irascible	b. Unjustified
iii) Itinerant	c. Benevolent
iv) Apogee	d. Celebrate
v) Baleful	e. Secret
vi) Vexation	f. Extrovert
vii) Warranted	g. Amiable
viii) Epiphany	h. Static
ix) Recluse	i. Happiness
x) Archetypal	j. Nadir

48. (a) iv-j; vii -b; viii -e; x-a
    - (b) i-d; iii -h; viii -e; v-f
    - (c) vi-i; iv -g; iii -b; ix-e
    - (d) x-g; iii -j; ii -h; vii -b

49. (a) vii-b; x-a; ii-h;
    - (b) iv-j; i-d; iii-h; ix-b
    - (c) vi-i; v-c; ix-f; iii-h
    - (d) viii-e; iv-j; vii-b; x-g

Spelling

2008-10

Directions for Questions 50 to 52:

Mark the ***wrongly spelt*** word mentioned among the following options:

50. (a) Contemporaneous
    - (b) Belligerent
    - (c) Epicurean
    - (d) Recalcitrent

51. (a) Opprobrium
    - (b) Iniquitous
    - (c) Vicisitude
    - (d) Pusillanimous

52. (a) Exonerate
    - (b) Unctuous
    - (c) Flatulant
    - (d) Disencumber

2011-13

Directions for questions 53 and 54: Select the pair of wrongly spelt word from the given set of choices.

53. (a) Conscientious: Oleaginous
    - (b) Obstreperous: Supercilious
    - (c) Diletante: Reminiscience
    - (d) Tergiversation: Interstice

54. (a) Irascible: Surreptitious
    - (b) Proclivity: Vicissitude
    - (c) Lassitude: Imperturbable
    - (d) Munificient: Psusillanimous

2012-14

Direction for question 55: In the following question, the options A, B, C and D have a word written in four different ways, of which only one is correct. Identify the correctly spelt word.

55. (a) Septaganarian
    - (b) Septagenarian
    - (c) Septagenurian
    - (d) Septuagenarian

2013-15

Directions for questions 56 - 57: Pick the word with the correct spelling

56. (a) Exorbitant
    - (b) Exhorbitant
    - (c) Exhobitant
    - (d) Exxorhbitant

57. (a) Acqueisence
    - (b) Acquiescence
    - (c) Acaueiscence
    - (d) Acquescience

2014-16

Directions for questions 58 to 59: Select the option with the incorrect spelling.

58. (a) Accidentally
    - (b) Asseverate
    - (c) Assassination
    - (d) Ammelioration

59. (a) Gazzette   (b) Lustre

    (c) Sergeant   (d) Bucolic

2015-17

60. Which of the following words is spelled <u>correctly</u>?

    (a) Decrepit

    (b) Descrepit

    (c) Deceript

    (d) Decript

61. Which of the following options has both words spelled <u>correctly</u>?

    (a) Recieve, Deceive

    (b) Perceive, Believe

    (c) Deceive, Percieve

    (d) Receive, Beleive

62. How many words of four or more letters can be made with the following, with the condition that at least one "E" appears in each word?

E, T, Y, T, E, L, A

    (a) exactly 4   (b) at least 5

    (c) at most 3   (d) None of the above

63. How many words of four or more letters can be made with the following, with the condition that "A" appears in each word?

A, H, N, E, T, E, H

    (a) at most 6

    (b) exactly 5

    (c) at least 8

    (d) exactly 7

2017-19

Directions (Q. 64-65): *Four words are given in each question, out of which one word is correctly spelt. Find the correctly spelt word.*

64. (a) Danseus   (b) Dansueses

    (c) Densuace   (d) Danseuse

65. (a) Narcotic   (b) Permentant

    (c) Pesimist   (d) Acoustic

Word/Phrase Replacement

2009-11

Directions for questions 66 – 69: In each of the following sentences, part or all of the sentence is underlined. The answer-choices offer four ways of phrasing the underlined part. If you think the original sentence is better than the alternatives, choose A, which merely repeats the underlined part; otherwise choose one of the alternatives.

66. <u>Had the President's Administration not lost the vote on the budget reduction package, his first year in office would have been rated an A.</u>

    (a) Had the President's Administration not lost the vote on the budget reduction package, his first year in office would have been rated an A.

    (b) Had the President's Administration not lost the vote on the budget reduction package, it would have been rated an A in the first year.

    (c) If the President's had not lost the vote on the budget reduction package, the Administration's first year in office would have been rated and A.

    (d) Had the President's Administration not lost the vote on its budget reduction package, his first year in office would have been rated an A.

67. This century began with <u>war brewing in Europe, the industrial revolution well-established, and a nascent communication age.</u>

    (a) war brewing in Europe, the industrial revolution well-established, and a nascent communication age.

    (b) war brewing in Europe, the industrial revolution surging, and a nascent communication age.

    (c) war brewing in Europe, the industrial revolution well-established, and the communication age beginning.

    (d) war brewing in Europe, the industrial revolution well-established, and saw the birth of the communication age.

68. The rise in negative attitudes toward foreigners <u>indicate that the country is becoming less tolerant, and therefore that</u> the opportunities are ripe for extremist groups to exploit the illegal immigration problem.

    (a) indicate that the country is becoming less tolerant, and therefore that

    (b) indicates that the country is becoming less tolerant, and therefore

    (c) indicates that the country is becoming less tolerant, and therefore that

    (d) indicates that the country has become less tolerant, and therefore

69. <u>Due to the chemical spill, the commute into the city will be delayed by as much as 2 hours.</u>

    (a) Due to the chemical spill, the commute into the city will be delayed by as much as 2 hours.

    (b) The chemical spill, will be delaying the commute into the city by as much as 2 hours.

    (c) Due to the chemical spill, the commute into the city had been delayed by as much as 2 hours.

    (d) Because of the chemical spill, the commute into the city will be delayed by as much as 2 hours.

2018-20

Directions for questions 70-74: *Passage below is accompanied by a number of questions. For some questions, consider how the passage might be revised to improve the expression of ideas. For other questions, consider how the passage might be edited to correct errors in sentence structure, usage or punctuation.*

After reading the passage, choose the answer to each question that most effectively improves the quality of writing in the passage or that makes the passage confirm to the conventions of standard written English.

The underlined areas in the passage along with the [number] direct you to the question concerned

If you've ever been to an art museum, you know the basic layout: long hallways and large rooms with paintings hung a few feet apart. You know how the paintings are [70] <u>by certain means are marked,</u> and you know that the paintings have been arranged chronologically or thematically.

There's one thing, however, which you've definitely noticed even if you can't quite articulate it. Particularly when looking at old paintings, [71] <u>paintings all have that vividly new look,</u> whether they were painted in 1950 or 1450. Even where the subject matter is older, the colours are vibrant, and you're never forced to wonder exactly what the painting must have looked like in its original state.

[72] <u>The history of painting is nearly as long as the history of mankind.</u> The incredible feat is the work of a highly specialised group: art restorers. Despite this specialisation, the profession has exploded in recent years. Art restoration has been growing steadily since 1930. While the job of an art restorer may seem fairly straightforward [73] <u>when looking,</u> the job is in fact quite complicated. Sometimes, as in the case of Michelangelo's famous sculpture David, the cleaning and restoration of artworks is a simple matter: applying chemicals, washing away grime and scrubbing of the; dirt.

[74] <u>With most paintings, however,</u> the process is a good deal more involved because it is not necessarily just a matter of 'cleaning' the older paintings. One cannot merely take a scrub brush to centuries-old great work, Because of the wide range of restoration techniques, art restoration itself can be controversial business.

70. Identify the best possible change in the underlined area

   (*a*) marked

   (*b*) being marked in a way

   (*c*) by no means of marking

   (*d*) no change

71. Identify the best possible change in the underlined area

   (*a*) No change

   (*b*) you've surely noticed how new all the paintings look,

   (*c*) noticing the new look of all the paintings is something you can do,

   (*d*) the paintings always strike you as very new looking,

72. The writer is considering deleting the underlined sentence. Should the sentence be kept or deleted?

   (*a*) Kept, because it is useful introduction to the topic of this paragraph

   (*b*) Deleted, because it restates a historical detail that is provided in a later paragraph.

   (*c*) Deleted, because it strays from the paragraph's major focus by introducing an irrelevant fact

   (*d*) Kept, because it provides a humorous anecdote regarding the work of art restorers

73. Identify the best possible change in the underlined area

   (*a*) at first glance,   (*b*) beholden,

   (*c*) under your gaze,   (*d*) No Change

74. Identify the best possible change in the underlined area

   (*a*) Anyway,

   (*b*) In this sense,

   (*c*) Alongside cleaning,

   (*d*) No change

2019-21

Directions (Questions 75-76): Choose the appropriate answer for rephrasing the underlined portion of the sentence.

75. Sky-Airlines recently announced aggressive cost-cutting measures <u>ranging from a new airport check-in procedures that encourage passengers to use self-service kiosks and reductions</u> in the size of its fleet.

   (a) such as improvement of airport check-procedures, encouragement of passengers to use self-service kiosks and reducing

   (b) ranging from new airport check-in procedures that encourage passengers to use self-service kiosks and to reductions

   (c) ranging from new airport check-in procedures that encourage passengers to use self-service kiosks to reductions

   (d) ranging from new airport check-in procedures that encourage passengers to use self-service kiosks to reducing

76. Although the square root of a negative number has no real value, it is not necessarily true that <u>equations involving imaginary numbers like these are practically inapplicable</u>.

   (a) equations involving these inapplicable imaginary numbers are practical

   (b) equations involving such imaginary numbers have no practical applications

   (c) there is no practical applications for equations involving such imaginary numbers as these

   (d) equations involving imaginary numbers such as these are inapplicable practically

One Word Substitute

2012-14

Directions for questions 77 and 78: For each of the following sentences, choose the most appropriate "one word" for the given expressions.

77. One who is unrelenting and cannot be moved by entreaties:

   (a) Inexorable   (b) Infallible (c) Impregnable   (d) Inexplicable

78. The art of cutting trees and bushes into ornamental shapes:

   (a) Horticulture   (b) Bonsai

   (c) Pruning   (d) Topiary

2014-16

Directions for questions 79 to 82: Select one word/ phrase which is closest in meaning to the given phrase.

79. Person who knows or can speak many languages

   (a) Polyglot   (b) Potable

   (c) Plebiscite   (d) Paramour

80. Deserving blame for an offence or crime

   (a) Hedonist   (b) Culpable

   (c) Misanthrope   (d) Regicide

81. To have a jaundiced eye

   (a) to be prejudiced

   (b) to have an ailing eye

   (c) to have ill-feeling for someone

   (d) none of the above

82. To lose one's bearings

   (a) to become tired

   (b) to give up

   (c) to become mentally unstable

   (d) to be uncertain of one's position

Fill in the Blanks

2007-09

Directions for Questions 83 to 86: Each question has two sentences. Each sentence contains one blank. From the first three options (A…C) provided below the sentences, pick the one that best fits both the sentences; otherwise, mark option D.

83. i. As indigenous peoples are denied access to their traditional lands, their cultures are dying. The result is that now over half the world's languages are _________, meaning that only elderly people speak those languages.

   ii. The third aim, the big one, is to convince Lockists that their research program is _________, and Gauker's contextualist alternative is the way of the future.

   (a) moribund

   (b) sycophantic

   (c) garrulous

   (d) none of those

84. i. A soft monotonous tone is _________ for the audience.

   ii. It was many months since Whitehead had gone to bed sober. He's started to use vodka as a _________ when the night terrors began.

   (a) maverick

   (b) palladium

   (c) soporific

   (d) none of these

85. i. This seems pretty _________ considering that fair use itself is a grey area rather than a fine line, why superimpose a fine line here?

   ii. He was greeted with half a dozen really _________ comments about his grammar and use of capitals at the beginning of sentences. They completely detailed the thread.

   (a) incriminate   (b) puerile

   (c) adjure   (d) none of these

86. i. The target for reducing the use of penal custody for children by 10% by 2008 is _________ and won't happen unless the youth court magistrates get on board.

   ii. A _________ Prime Minister Jean Chretien, with a keen political eye for embracing these groups, decided to send token and combat-avoiding units to Afghanistan, reinforcing views across Canada that America's pursuits and actions were ignoble from the start.

   (a) placative

   (b) egregious

   (c) congenital

   (d) none of these

2008-10

Directions for Questions 87 to 90:

Select the *right pair of words* to fill in the blanks.

87. The bell, hung on the door by means of a curved ribbon of steel, was _________ to circumvent. It was hopelessly cracked; but of an evening, at the slightest provocation, it clattered behind the customer with _________ virulence.
    (a) impossible, melodious
    (b) effortless, loud
    (c) difficult, impudent
    (d) daunting, harmonious

88. A _________ question caused him to stutter to the point of suffocation. When started by anything perplexing he used to squint _________.
    (a) courteous, palpably
    (b) brusque, horribly
    (c) considerate, genially
    (d) civil, frightfully

89. Vanity and pride are _________ things, though the words are often used _________.A person may be proud without being being vain. Pride relates more to our _________ of ourselves, vanity to what we would have others think of us.
    (a) same, differently, analysis
    (b) analogous, similarly, evaluation
    (c) different, synonymously, opinion
    (d) dissimilar, carelessly, view

90. During the heated discussion, the Leader of the group _________ refuted all the claims brought by his opponents. Later everybody acknowledged that he survived by most _________ luck.
    (a) ingeniously, incredible
    (b) ingeniously, incredulous
    (c) ingenuously, incredible
    (d) ingenuously, incredulous

2009-11

Direction for questions 91 – 94: Select the most appropriate word (s) from the given choice to fill the blanks (s).

91. Justice Minister Bola Ige, confronted with the general incivility of local police, placed a _____ on the cads. Said the Hon. Bola Ige, "I pray that God will make big holes in their pockets."
    (a) malediction   (b) sanction
    (c) proscription   (d) plea

92. I _____ i _____that he will pass his exam and get a good job.
    I will make a _____ ii _____. There will be a new government in less than a year.
    (a) i. prophecy ii. prophesy
    (b) i. prophesy ii. prophecy
    (c) i. prophecy ii. prophecy
    (d) i. prophesy ii. prophesy

93. Imagine an _____ public figure attacked by press and public, who is facing an inquiry into allegations of having obtained money by deception.
    (a) empowered
    (b) endangered
    (c) embattled
    (d) engrossed

94. His listeners enjoyed his _____ wit but his victims often _____ at its satire.
    (a) lugubrious, suffered
    (b) bitter, smarted
    (c) lugubrious, smiled
    (d) trenchant, winced

2010-12

Directions for questions 95 – 98: Select the most appropriate set of words from the given choices to fill in the blanks.

95. The organization takes its cue from the person on the top. I always told our business leaders their personal _____ determined their organization's _____.
    (a) serendipity; faux pas
    (b) predilection; despair
    (c) intensity; success
    (d) oddity; conformity

96. The Himalayas ran from east to west and cut off the cold winds from the north. This allowed agriculture to prosper and _____ wealth, but it also _____ barbarian invaders from the north.
    (a) attracted; dissipated
    (b) created; attracted
    (c) created; restricted
    (d) attracted; evicted

97. Our _____ diversity may also be of some value. Because we have always learned to live with pluralism, it is possible that we may be better prepared to _____ the diversity of global economy.
    (a) stupefying; negotiate
    (b) plural; alleviate
    (c) variegated; annihilate
    (d) dreary; exasperate

98. My inward petition was instantly _____. First, a delightful cold wave descended over my back and under my feet, _____ all discomfort.
    (a) acknowledged; banishing
    (b) repudiated; infuriating
    (c) acceded; exacerbating
    (d) decimated; assuaging

2011-13

Directions for questions 99 to 104: From the given pair of words select the most appropriate pair that fills the gaps and makes the sentence more meaningful.

99. These issues are extremely ______ and any knee jerk reaction will ultimately result in a loss of ______ for all shareholders
    (a) Unassociated, curare
    (b) Ambiguous, plutocracy
    (c) Nuanced, opportunity
    (d) Contexed, serendipity

100. Growth under this government has been ______ high and remarkably ______ even during the worst global economic crisis.
    (a) Impededly, flippant
    (b) Relatively, intractable
    (c) Obstructedly, rigid
    (d) Sustainedly, resilient

101. There are different and ______ versions about what happened in the city, but one thing is certain: it is a dastardly act that must be condemned ______.
    (a) Dissimilar, concertedly
    (b) Contrary, obviously
    (c) Conflicting, unequivocally
    (d) Unique, without conflict

102. They ______ their seats away from the curved wall panels to give themselves more space as the flight attendant brought drinks from the gallery, which was ______ with family's favorite snacks and beverages.
    (a) Swiveled, stocked
    (b) Hinged, lacquered
    (c) Pended, embellished
    (d) Retracted, thronged

103. Cairn cannot ______ bring into picture some ______ outsider which has little experience and necessary consents to deal in the oil field.
    (a) Peremptorily, ascribed
    (b) Complaisantly, endorsed
    (c) Democratically, aberrant
    (d) Arbitrarily, unrelated

104. Economic growth is on auto-pilot, unlikely to be derailed by any lapse into ______ and controls or to be ______ by serious policy reforms.
    (a) Growth, blowed
    (b) Boom, berated
    (c) Recession, reduced
    (d) Dirigisme, boosted

2012-14

Directions for questions 105 and 106: Each question below consists of an incomplete sentence. Four words or pharses marked A, B, C and D are given beneath each sentence. Mark the option that best completes the sentence.

105. __________________ made after English settlers came to Jamestown was a map of Virginia by John Smith, the famous adventurer.
    (a) It was the first map
    (b) The first map
    (c) There was a first map
    (d) That the first map

106. The concert this weekend promises to attract __________________ than attended the last one.
    (a) a number of people even larger
    (b) an even larger amount of people
    (c) a group of people even greater
    (d) an even greater number of people

2013-15

Direction for questions 107 and 108: Choose the most appropriate option for filling in the blanks. The sequence of words in the correct option should match the sequence of the sentences in which they should be used.

107. i.   There is so much love.............the two of them.
    ii. I have not seen Aditi...............Friday.
    iii. I started my exam preparations..........January.
    iv. The three sisters did not look for new friends as they were quite happy playing .... themselves.
    v.   I have not seen Mohan...............six months.
    (a) between, from, since, among, for
    (b) among, from, for, between, since
    (c) among, since, for, between, from
    (d) between, since, from, among, for

108. i.   He succeeded...........perserverance and sheer hard work.
    ii. ....the power vested in me, I hereby declare these premises sealed.
    iii. ....his illness he could not finish his work in time.
    iv. ....need, please contact me at the emergency number indicated.
    (a) by virtue of, by dint of, in case of, in consequence of
    (b) by dint of, by virtue of, in consequence of, in case of
    (c) by virtue of, in consequence of, by dint of, in case of
    (d) by dint of, in consequence of, by virtue of, in case of

2014-16

Directions for questions 109 and 110: For each of the questions given below, select the word that fits well in all the four given sentences.

109. (i) The Bill __________ reduction in electoral expenses.

(ii) The plan __________ ten percent growth in production.

(iii) The budget __________ a two-fold increase in this year's turnover.

(iv) The company __________ a good production year due to better harvest.

(a) seeks   (b) envisages

(c) hopes   (d) demands

110. (i) We __________ the room with an electric heater.

(ii) His mother __________ lunch for all his friends.

(iii) The will __________ that each child will receive half of the money.

(iv) He __________ for his family by working overtime.

(a) prepared   (b) equipped

(c) arranged   (d) provided

2015-17

Directions for questions 111 and 112: fill in the blanks with the most appropriate option.

111. Mrs. Kapoor hovered around the patient in a display of great________.

(a) Solictitude   (b) Chivalry

(c) Solicitude   (d) Chivelry

112. Whenever she asked the doctor how long she had left to live, he would dive off into long-winded explanations about the uncertainties inherent in medicine, and eventually tail off as if he had forgotten her original question altogether, it was the worst form of __________ she'd ever come across.

(a) Prevarication

(b) Insinuation

(c) Preambulation

(d) Abrogation

Directions for questions 113 and 114: Fill in the blanks with the word or phrase that completes the idiom correctly in the given sentences.

113. The bigger they come,__________ they fall, or so it is said.

(a) the greater   (b)   the harder

(c) the more   (d)   the less

114. You almost frightened the life __________ me.

(a) from   (b) of

(c) into   (d) out of

2016-18

Directions (Q. 115-116) : *Each of the following questions has a sentence with two blanks. Given below in the options are four pairs of words. Choose the pair that best completes the sentence.*

115. Not for the last time, the British had grossly ______ the toughness of local fighters, and the very ______ kind of terrain from Europe.

(a) misrepresented; mild

(b) underestimated; different

(c) miscalculated; similar

(d) understood; hostile

116. The complicated processes, which often ______ reason, forced us to become very creative in finding ways to work ______ the challenges.

(a) explained; out

(b) reflected; over

(c) defied; around

(d) beyond; about

Directions (Q. 117-118) : *In the following sentences, fill in the blank space with the correct word from the options provided.*

117. During the winter, many deer become; shortage ______ and die because of a food

(a) emancipated   (b) enunciated

(c) elevated   (d) emaciated

118. Though fictional, the story of Shylock is not entirely removed ______ Venetial reality.

(a) of   (b) with

(c) from   (d) through

Directions (Q. 119-121) : *Choose the correct option to fill in the blank spaces in the given sentences*

119. Pipes are not a safer ______ to cigarettes because, though pipe smokers do not inhale, they are still ______ higher rates of lung and mouth cancers than non-smokers.

(a) option .... likely to

(b) answer .... responsible for

(c) alternative .... subject to

(d) preference .... involved with

120. The conspirators met ______ in order to plot a(n) ______ against the oppressive governance of Julius Caesar.

(a) aggressively .... referendum

(b) clandestinely .... revolt

(c) wittily .... upheaval

(d) wickedly .... invocation

121. A part of the following sentence is left unfinished. From the alternatives given to complete the sentence, choose the best alternative.

Although these injuries are not fatal, __________

__________________________________.

   (a) they are not ranked among the top causes of death.

   (b) they are certainly incapacitating and tragic.

   (c) there is no proof of the same.

   (d) they do not get reported.

2017-19

Directions (Q. 122-125) : *In the following passage, fill in the blank spaces with the most appropriate word from the options provided.*

Come October and you are burnt by the mid-day Sun. The storm and the sizzle is particularly **_122_** as it comes after the relatively cool monsoon months. Though it is hot and muggy, that does not prevent people from coming Out on the streets to **_123_** the traditional festivals. And it must be shopping time also, colourfully decorated showrooms are **_124_** the passerby to let his hair down, splurge and take a **_125_** of gifts home for family. After all, the New Year is just around,

122. (a) traumatic   (b) pleasant

   (c) sultry   (d) fantastic

123. (a) herald   (b) moot

   (c) invite   (d) boycott

124. (a) drawing   (b) exhorting

   (c) fascinating   (d) pursuing

125. (a) token   (b) list

   (c) bagful   (d) placement

Directions for questions 126-128: Fill up the blanks with appropriate word (idiom/colloquial) given in the options.

126. Mark is always eager to argue about how this business should be run. He seems to have a real __________ on his shoulder about it.

   (a) Head   (b) Score

   (c) Chip   (d) Bluebird

127. Vishnu thought the last problem on the test was a real _____. It was much harder and more complex than any of the previous problems.

   (a) Doozy   (b) Whooper

   (c) Carp   (d) Snafu

128. I used to be kind of a _____ when I was little, but I lost most of the weight in my teenage years.

   (a) Runt   (b) Beanpole

   (c) Doughboy   (d) Punk

2019-21

Directions (Questions 129-131): Select the most appropriate pair of words from the given option to meaningfully complete sentence(s).

129. Despite being the .... partner in the relationship, the franchiser does not always have all the ....

   (a) sincere .... limitations

   (b) authoritative .... legalities

   (c) dominant .... advantages

   (d) active .... losses

130. With large classes, it is difficult for teachers to.............. regular essay type questions for homework because .... long answers would take too much time.

   (a) consider .... writing

   (b) revalue .... concise

   (c) pursue .... feeling

   (d) handle .... weighing

131. 'Patriotism is the last refuge of scoundrel', says Johnson. In the modern world where the cunning selfish people .... and the hard working, conscientious people .... The quotation holds good.

   (a) dominate .... suppress

   (b) thrive .... suffer

   (c) enjoy .... mutilate

   (d) empower .... subjected

Common Confusables

2012-14

Direction for questions 132 and 133: In the question below, there are two sentences containing underlined homonyms, which may either be *mis-spelt* or *inappropriately used* in the context of the sentence. Select the appropriate answer from the option given below:

132. I.   A vote of <u>censur</u> was passed against the Chairman.

   II.   Before release, every film is passed by the <u>Censor</u> Board.

   (a) only sentence I is correct

   (b) only sentence II is correct

   (c) both sentence I and II are correct

   (d) both sentences I and II are incorrect

133. I.   This behaviour does not <u>compliment</u> his position.

   II.   He thanked his boss for the <u>complement</u>.

   (a) only sentence I is correct

   (b) only sentence II is correct

   (c) both sentences I and II are correct

   (d) both sentences I and II are incorrect

Odd Word Out

Directions for questions 134 and 135: Pick out the odd option.

134. (a) Expiate   (b) Banish
    (c) Expatriate   (d) Exile

135. (a) Brevity   (b) Circumlocution
    (c) Conciseness   (d) Succinctness

Analogy

Directions for Questions 136 and 137: Each question has four analogies from A ... D. Mark all the correct analogies.

136. (a) Murrey : Black   :: Magenta : Red
    (b) Inter : Exhume   :: Piebald : Homogeneous
    (c) Effete : Fructuous :: Chapfallen : Effervescent
    (d) Selenology : Moon :: Epistemology : Knowledge

137. (a) Polyglot : Languages :: Polyphagous : Food
    (b) Escutcheon : Scutcheon :: Fabulist : Liar
    (c) Scurvy : Vitamin C :: Kwashiorkor : Protein
    (d) Apothecary : Drugs :: Cruciverbalist : Crosswords

Directions for Questions 138 and 139:

The following four pairs may have synonymous or antonymous or part-whole relationships or no relationship at all with the pair provided in the question. Select the pair of words which has **the closest relationship** with the numbered pair.

138. COMMUNICATION: MESSAGE::
    (a) Humour: Delight
    (b) Expression: Words
    (c) Clarification: Doubt
    (d) Emission: Cosmic

139. ACTIVATE: DETONATE::
    (a) Deaden: Defuse
    (b) Quicken: Mutilate
    (c) Connect: Detach
    (d) Inform: Deform

Direction for Question 140:

The following four pairs may have synonymous or antonymous or part-whole relationships or no relationship at all with the pair provided in the question. Select the pair of words which has **no relationship** with the numbered pair.

140. PLENTITUDE : ABUNDANCE
    (a) Augury : Divination
    (b) Indurate : Consolidate
    (c) Perspicacity : Transparency.
    (d) Mulct : Muzzle

Direction for questions 141 – 144: Select the option which is having similar analogy vis-à-vis the analogy given in the question.

141. TRAVESTY : PARAGON::
    (a) autonomy : subordination
    (b) disqualification : ineptitude
    (c) sentinel : creed
    (d) conundrum : accountability

142. CONTRITE : OBDURATE ::
    (a) grievous : lamentable
    (b) aphoristic : esoteric
    (c) sophisticated : cultured
    (d) favourable : assenting

143. PECCADILLO : FLAW ::
    (a) clandestine : openness
    (b) nick : score
    (c) forensics : judiciary
    (d) invasion : putsch

144. MUTTER : INDISTINCT ::
    (a) define : easy
    (b) blunder : polished
    (c) articulate : well-spoken
    (d) expedite : completed

Directions for questions 145 and 146: From the given options identify the word pair which is unrelated to the given word pair.

145. IMPUISSANCE: DESECRATE
    (a) Decrepit: Desolate
    (b) Effete: Sacrilege
    (c) Ornery : Contort
    (d) Bedraggled: Profanity

146. INSOUCIANT: GOSSAMER
    (a) Nymphs: Gehenna
    (b) Perfunctory: Diaphanous
    (c) Pococurante: Pellucid
    (d) Nonchalant: Tiffany

Directions for questions 147 to 150: For each of the following questions select the answer pair that expresses a relationship most similar to that expressed in the capitalized pair.

147. OMNISCIENT: KNOWLEDGE::
    (a) Saturnine: energy
    (b) Boundless: expanse
    (c) Inquisitive: science
    (d) Complete: retraction

148. DISQUIETUDE: ANXIOUS ::
    (a) Nonplus: perplexed
    (b) Cupidity: bellicose
    (c) Embellishment: overstated
    (d) Magnitude: unabridged

149. DEVIATE: LECTURE ::
    (a) Meander: drive
    (b) Disown: friend
    (c) Welcome: indifference
    (d) Entreat: solicitation

150. NEBULOUS: FORM ::
    (a) Insincere: misanthrope
    (b) Benevolent: excellence
    (c) Insipid: taste
    (d) Composed: innocence

2013-15

Direction for questions 151 and 152: From the choices provided, identify the pair of words with a relationship similar to that of the given word pair.

151. INDEFATIGABLE: INVETERATE ::
    (a) Tireless: Tired
    (b) Tired: Habitual
    (c) Tireless: Habitual
    (d) Impoverished: Habitual

152. MISANTHROPE: HUMANITY ::
    (a) Chauvinist: Patriot
    (b) Misogynist: Women
    (c) Agnostic: God
    (d) Witch: Magic

2014-16

Directions for questions 153 to 155: Select a word to replace the blank spaces.

153. Alleviate: Aggravate : : Elastic : ___________
    (a) Rigid   (b) Flexible
    (c) Malleable   (d) Strong

154. Benevolent: Kind : : Unclear : ______________
    (a) Bright   (b) Thick
    (c) Luminous   (d) Muddy

2015-17

Directions for questions 155 and 156: Select the option which expresses a relationship similar to the one expressed in the capitalized pair.

155. MUMBLE : INDISTINCT ::
    (a) Swagger : Timid
    (b) Exacerbate : Cure
    (c) Scribble : Illegible
    (d) Drizzle : Downpour

156. RUFFLE : EQUANIMITY ::
    (a) Bewilderment : Confusion
    (b) Disturb : Balance
    (c) Interest : Astound
    (d) Flounce : Turmoil

2016-18

157. The words in the following pair have a certain relationship with each other. Given in the options are four pairs of related words. Select the pair with the same relationship as the given pair.

    Cacophony : Euphony : :
    (a) Belligerent : Serene
    (b) Loneliness : Peace
    (c) Horrific : Sympathetic
    (d) Nocturnal : Diurnal

2018-20

Directions for questions 158-160: *Follow the analogy between the given pair of words in the question (in Capital) and identify the most suitable pair which can represent almost similar relationship*

158. FRET: DISQUIETUDE
    (*a*) Indulge: Vacillation
    (*b*) Inspirit: Confidence
    (*c*) Avian: Fish
    (*d*) Corporeal: Heaven

159. COFFER: VALUABLES
    (*a*) Mountain: Avalanche
    (*b*) Book: Paper
    (*c*) Sea: Waves
    (*d*) Sanctuary: Refuge

160. APOCRYPHAL: CORROBORATION
    (*a*) Sacrilegious: Piety
    (*b*) Tyrannical: Poise
    (*c*) Esoteric: Commonality
    (*d*) Fraudulent: Forgery

2019-21

Directions (Questions 161-162): Choose the correct answer from the options provided below to indicate the most appropriate word to complete the pair.

161. CICERONE : GUIDE :: DRAGOMAN : ....?
    (a) Cavalry officer
    (b) Interpreter
    (c) Hauler
    (d) Turnkey

162. SYLVAN : WOODS :: TERRESTRIAL : ....?
    (a) Urban   (b) Fear
    (c) Earth   (d) Planets

Idioms & Phrase

Directions (Q. 163-164) : *Identify the option which gives the correct meaning of the Idiom/Phrase given below :*

163. To drive home
   - (a) To find one's roots
   - (b) To return to place of rest
   - (c) To lose all money in betting
   - (d) To emphasize

164. To have an axe to grind
   - (a) To have a private end to serve
   - (b) To fail to arouse interest
   - (c) To have no result
   - (d) To work for both sides

Miscellaneous

165. There are four sentences S1, S2, S3, S4 where the underlined word is used either correctly or incorrectly. Choose the option which lists the sentences, where the underlined word is used correctly.
   - S1. Only 22% of the people voted. The rest were totally <u>disinterested</u>.
   - S2. The management and the union asked a completely <u>disinterested</u> party to mediate between them.
   - S3. I don't know why he didn't go to the exhibition. Perhaps he was too busy or just <u>disinterested</u>.
   - S4. France's intervention in the dispute was not entirely <u>disinterested</u>. It gave her increased power and influence in the area.
   - (a) S1, S2, S4.
   - (b) S2, S3, S4.
   - (c) S1, S4.
   - (d) S2, S4

166. There are four sentences S1, S2, S3, S4 where the underlined phrase is used either correctly or incorrectly. Choose the option which lists the sentences. Where the underlined phrase is used correctly.
   - S1. Good Lord, I'm not rich! <u>on the contrary</u>, I'm constantly in debt.
   - S2. She's very intelligent, but <u>on the contrary</u> she's apt to be impatient.
   - S3. Yes, it's a very cosmopolitan city. <u>On the contrary</u>, It's very expensive.
   - S4. I don't think he'll pass the exam. <u>On the contrary</u>, I think he'll almost certainly fail.
   - (a) S1, S2, S4.
   - (b) S2, S4.
   - (c) S1, S4.
   - (d) S2, S3

Directions for questions 167 – 168: Select the right combination of numbers given in A, B, C and D so that letters arranged accordingly form a meaningful word.

167.

D	V	E	O	R	E	A	H
1	2	3	4	5	6	7	8

   - (a) 1 3 5 2 4 6 8 7
   - (b) 8 6 7 1 4 2 3 5
   - (c) 4 2 3 5 8 6 7 1
   - (d) 5 3 7 1 8 4 2 6

168.

P	M	O	I	R	C	T	E	T	O
1	2	3	4	5	6	7	8	9	10

   - (a) 1 5 10 7 8 6   9 4 3 2
   - (b) 6 3 2 1 8 7 4 9 10 5
   - (c) 9 8 5 10 2 4 3 1 7 6
   - (d) 10 6 7 3 1 8 5 4 2 9

Direction for question 169: Match the Latin phrases in column 1 with their appropriate meanings in column 2:

169.

	Column 1		Column 2
a.	ex libris	i.	repeating to the point of boredom
b.	in situ	ii.	approximately
c.	circa	iii.	from the books
d.	ad nauseum	iv.	in its original place

   - (a) a-iv; b-iii; c-i; d-ii
   - (b) a-iii; b-iv; c-ii; d-i
   - (c) a-iv; b-iii; c-ii; d-i
   - (d) a-iii; b-iv; c-i; d-ii

170. Which of the following cannot be termed as an 'oxymoron'?
   - (a) a living death
   - (b) conspicuous by one's absence
   - (c) the sound of music
   - (d) deafening silence

171. Which of the following is a metaphor?
   - (a) He fought like a lion
   - (b) She is as cool as a cucumber
   - (c) Man proposes, God disposes
   - (d) He was a lion in the fight

172. Which of the following is an oxymoron?
   - (a) She accepted it, as the kind cruelty of a surgeon's knife
   - (b) The camel is the ship of the desert
   - (c) Art lies in concealing art
   - (d) Death lays his icy hands on Kings

Direction for questions 173 and 174: Pick the odd word out

173. (a) Perilous   (b) Precarious
(c) Hazardous   (d) Copious

174. (a) Propitiate   (b) Appreciate
(c) Appease   (d) Conciliate

2014-16

175. As busy as a bee is an example of:
(a) an oxymoron   (b) a metaphor
(c) an adage   (d) a simile

2016-18

Directions (Q. 176-178) : *Given below are some French words commonly used in English language. What is the meaning of these French words?*

176. Milieu
(a) Millennium   (b) Century
(c) Social Environment   (d) Feudal

177. Gaffe
(a) Blunder   (b) Loud laughter
(c) Iron hook   (d) House

178. Choose the option closest in meaning to the word 'Qualm'
(a) Concavity   (b) Misgiving
(c) Amplitude   (d) Repute

Directions (Q. 179 and 180) : *Identify the oxymoron*

179. (a) Behave properly   (b) Act naturally
(c) Speak honestly   (d) Drive slowly

180. (a) Original Copy   (b) Small Crowd
(c) Open Secret   (d) All of the Above

2017-19

Directions (Q. 181-183): *Etymological description of the 'word' is given in each question. Identify the origin/source of the 'word'*

181. Debutante (noun)

The origin of the word dates back to early Nineteenth Century . The word is used to describe a female stage actor making her first public performance.
(a) Portuguese   (b) Italian
(c) Greek   (d) French

182. Obvious (adjective)

It means "frequently met with". The origin of the word comes from <u>obvius</u> "that is in the way, presenting itself readily, open, exposed, commonplace," also from <u>obviam</u> (adv.) "in the way", from <u>ob</u> "against" + <u>viam</u>. accusative of <u>via</u> "way", meaning "plain to see, evident" is first recorded in 1630.
(a) Latin   (b) German
(c) Hebrew   (d) Italian

183. Soccer (noun)

The origin of the word dates back to 1889 (<u>socca</u>), later 1891 (<u>socker</u>), 1895 (<u>soccer</u>); originally university slang from a shortened form of <u>Assoc.</u>, abbreviation of Association in Football Association.
(a) French   (b) English
(c) Arabic   (d) Italian

2018-20

184. Match the prefix and suffix with its meaning

Prefix/ Suffix	Meaning
(a) ation	(i) state or process of
(b) trans	(ii) position held
(c) ship	(iii) across
(d) ambi	(iv) full of
(e) ose	(v) both

(*a*) a)-(i), b)-(iii), c)-(ii), d)-(v), e)-(iv)
(*b*) a)-(i), b)-(ii), c)-(iii), d)-(v), e)-(iv)
(*c*) a)-(iv), b)-(v), c)-(iii), d)-(ii), e)-(i)
(*d*) None of the above

2019-21

Directions (Questions 185-188): Identify the origin/ source of the words given below.

185. Auto-da-fè (Noun)

The ceremony for pronouncing judgment by the Inquisition which was followed by the execution of sentence by secular authorities; broadly, the burning of a heretic.
(a) Latin   (b) Italian
(c) Portuguese   (d) French

186. Voracious (Adjective)

To devour
(a) Hebrew   (b) Greek
(c) German   (d) Latin

187. Echt (Adjective)

True, genuine, real and authentic
(a) German   (b) Latin
(c) Italian   (d) Greek

188. Aegis (Noun)

Under the protection of
(a) Russian   (b) Greek
(c) French   (d) Arabic

ANSWERS

1. (a),(b)	**2.** (d)	**3.** (d)	**4.** (a)	**5.** (b)	**6.** (c)	**7.** (d)	**8.** (a)	**9.** (c)	**10.** (b)
11. (c)	**12.** (b)	**13.** (b)	**14.** (d)	**15.** (c)	**16.** (b)	**17.** (c)	**18.** (b)	**19.** (a)	**20.** (c)
21. (d)	**22.** (c)	**23.** (b)	**24.** (d)	**25.** (a)	**26.** (a)	**27.** (c)	**28.** (d)	**29.** (a)	**30.** (d)
31. (d)	**32.** (b)	**33.** (*)	**34.** (d)	**35.** (*)	**36.** (b)	**37.** (a)	**38.** (a)	**39.** (d)	**40.** (c)
41. (a)	**42.** (c)	**43.** (a)	**44.** (c)	**45.** (a)	**46.** (d)	**47.** (b)	**48.** (a)	**49.** (c)	**50.** (d)
51. (c)	**52.** (c)	**53.** (c)	**54.** (d)	**55.** (d)	**56.** (a)	**57.** (b)	**58.** (d)	**59.** (a)	**60.** (a)
61. (b)	**62.** (b)	**63.** (c)	**64.** (d)	**65.** (d)	**66.** (c)	**67.** (c)	**68.** (b)	**69.** (d)	**70.** (a)
71. (b)	**72.** (c)	**73.** (a)	**74.** (d)	**75.** (c)	**76.** (b)	**77.** (a)	**78.** (d)	**79.** (a)	**80.** (b)
81. (a)	**82.** (d)	**83.** (a)	**84.** (c)	**85.** (b)	**86.** (d)	**87.** (c)	**88.** (b)	**89.** (c)	**90.** (a)
91. (a)	**92.** (b)	**93.** (c)	**94.** (d)	**95.** (c)	**96.** (b)	**97.** (a)	**98.** (a)	**99.** (c)	**100.** (d)
101. (c)	**102.** (a)	**103.** (d)	**104.** (d)	**105.** (b)	**106.** (d)	**107.** (d)	**108.** (b)	**109.** (b)	**110.** (d)
111. (c)	**112.** (a)	**113.** (b)	**114.** (d)	**115.** (b)	**116.** (c)	**117.** (d)	**118.** (c)	**119.** (c)	**120.** (b)
121. (b)	**122.** (c)	**123.** (a)	**124.** (b)	**125.** (c)	**126.** (c)	**127.** (a)	**128.** (c)	**129.** (c)	**130.** (d)
131. (b)	**132.** (b)	**133.** (d)	**134.** (a)	**135.** (b)	**136.** (b,c,d)	**137.** (a,b,c,d)		**138.** (b)	**139.** (a)
140. (c)	**141.** (a)	**142.** (b)	**143.** (b)	**144.** (c)	**145.** (*)	**146.** (a)	**147.** (b)	**148.** (a)	**149.** (a)
150. (c)	**151.** (c)	**152.** (b)	**153.** (a)	**154.** (d)	**155.** (c)	**156.** (b)	**157.** (a)	**158.** (b)	**159.** (d)
160. (a)	**161.** (b)	**162.** (c)	**163.** (d)	**164.** (a)	**165.** (d)	**166.** (c)	**167.** (c)	**168.** (b)	**169.** (b)
170. (c)	**171.** (d)	**172.** (a)	**173.** (d)	**174.** (b)	**175.** (d)	**176.** (c)	**177.** (a)	**178.** (b)	**179.** (b)
180. (d)	**181.** (d)	**182.** (a)	**183.** (b)	**184.** (a)	**185.** (c)	**186.** (d)	**187.** (a)	**188.** (b)	

EXPLANATIONS

1. Hypallage and rantipole have been spelt correctly. Correct spelling for (C) is intaglio and for (D) is isagoge.

2. Only panegyric has been spelt correctly. The correct spellings for (A), (B) and (C) are polyphagism, ciguatera and maquette respectively.

3. 'Chalice' refers to a bowl-shaped drinking vessel.

4. 'Vitriolic' refers to a substance, especially a strong acid; highly corrosive.

5. 'Acclivity' means an upward slope or grade.

6. 'Esoteric' which means designed for or understood by the specially initiated alone or requiring or exhibiting knowledge that is restricted to a small group, would give the right synonym for 'pedantic' as used in the sentence. The style of writing in the book being 'esoteric' would be the reason for the book not getting much acclaim. 'Dogmatic' which means characterized by or given to the expression of opinions very strongly or positively as if they were facts, does not fit the context.

7. 'Chagrin' which means disquietude or distress of mind caused by humiliation, disappointment, or failure would be appropriately replaced by 'mortification' (a sense of humiliation and shame caused by something that wounds one's pride or self-respect **or** the cause of such humiliation or shame). Rest of the given words have a positive connotation.

8. 'Genuflect' means lower one's body briefly by bending one knee to the ground. 'Grovel', which means to lie or creep with the body prostrate in token of subservience or abasement is synonyms to 'genuflect'.

9. 'Stentorian' means extremely loud. 'Blaring' (to sound loud and strident) is the correct option.

10. 'Bemused' (to be confused) would be appropriately replaced by 'bewildered', which means to be perplexed or confused as these two are synonyms.

11. 'Predilection' means partiality or biased in favour of something; 'Evanescence' means soon passing out of sight; 'Zephyr' means a soft gentle breeze; 'Diaphanous' means light delicate and translucent; 'Fatuous' means silly, pointless or inane.

12. 'Perspicacity' means to have a ready insight into things; 'Uxorious' means showing excessive fondness for one's wife; 'Nebbish' means someone who is pitifully ineffectual; 'Chicanery' means to use deception or trickery to achieve one's purpose; 'Inchoate' means not fully formed or developed.

13. The correct matching is given in option (B). 'Arrogate' is to claim or seize without justification. 'Chagrin' means disappointment or distress caused due to humiliation.

14. Option (D) gives the correct answer. Candour means 'frankness'. 'Ethereal' is something that is heavenly, not of this world.

15. 'Anthromorphous' means resembling human form. 'Anachronistic' means occurring in the wrong time period. 'Anthology' means a collection of extracts from the writings of various authors. 'Ascension' means to move upwards. Thus, the correct answer is option (C).

16. 'Cacology' refers to poor choice of words. 'Ethology' means the study of human character. 'Misology' refers to the hatred of reasoning. 'Cryology' refers to the study of snow and ice. Therefore, the correct answer is option (B).

17. Endemic means native to a place; Equipoise means a balance of forces; Dogmatic refers to unwillingness to change from fixed 'dogmas'; Emollient is to be conciliatory; encomium means a 'eulogy' or high praise.

18. Encomium means a 'eulogy' or high praise; Espouse is to support.

19. Tedious can mean dreary or tiring; Tenacity is a synonym of doggedness.

20. Emollient means conciliatory; Obloquy means verbal abuse.

21. The jumbled word is HERMETIC. It means "completely sealed or isolated".

22. The jumbled word is ELUCIDATE. It means "enlighten or clarify".

23. The jumbled word is PIQUANT. It means "interesting or exciting".

24. Adonis was the mortal lover of the Greek goddess Aphrodite. He was described as a handsome and attractive man. So, options (B) and (C) are eliminated. Don Juan is a legendary Spaniard who is the proverbial seducer of women. So, option (D) is the correct answer.

25. 'En masse' is an adverb. 'Fetter' is a noun, though it looks like a verb. 'Malinger' is a verb. 'Raspy' is an adjective. So, option (A) is the correct answer.

26. The word is 'Loquacious'. So, 'verbose or talkative' is its synonym.

27. The word is 'Macabre'. So, 'gruesome or violent' is its synonym.

28. The word is 'Pernickety'. It means fussy. So, it is synonym.

29. Repudiate means to reject/deny. It is the opposite of sanction.

30. Grandiloquent (meaning pompous/ pretentious) is the opposite of simple.

31. Veneration means worship. Burlesque is a caricature/ parody.

32. Perspicacious means sagacious. Obtuse means dull-witted.

33. The question is incorrect as none of the options has a word that is opposite in meaning to the given word.

    'Requiem' is a song or hymn of mourning composed or performed as a memorial to a dead person. 'Humility' is the quality or condition of being humble. 'Prerequisite' refers to something required as a prior condition. 'Resolution' means form determination and 'reign' is a period during which something or somebody is dominant or powerful. Hence, there is no correct solution to this question.

34. 'Aspersion' means an abusive attack on a person's character or good name while 'Obeisance' refers to the act of obeying; dutiful or submissive behaviour with respect to another person.

35. The question is incorrect as none of the options has a word that is opposite in meaning to the given word.

    'Stolidity' means impassiveness. 'Posterity' refers to future or succeeding generations. 'Proximity' is closeness. 'Agility' means swiftness and 'sobriety' refers to gravity in bearing, manner, or treatment. Hence, there is no correct solution to this question.

36. The correct antonym for 'specious' (having a false look of truth or genuineness) is 'unfeigned' (genuine).

37. 'Exacting' which means tryingly or unremittingly severe in making demands would be an antonym for insouciant (lighthearted unconcern).

38. 'Levitate' which means to rise or float in or as if in the air especially in seeming defiance of gravitation. So, gravitating is an antonym for levitating.

39. 'Ensnared' means to catch. 'Released' is an antonym for 'ensnared'. Hence option (D) is the correct answer.

40. 'Quagmire' means a difficult, precarious, or entrapping position. 'Tranquility' which means the state of being calm or stable is an antonym for 'quagmire'.

41. Risible means "deserving to be laughed at rather than taken seriously" hence the antonym would be option A 'serious'.

42. Tenebrous means "dark and gloomy" its antonym would be option C 'bright'.

43. 'Puerile' means juvenile or childish. Option (A) i.e. 'adult' is its antonym .

44. 'Prosaic' means dull, unimaginative. 'Interesting' is its correct antonym.

45. 'Apocryphal' means something that is well-known but probably not true. The correct antonym is 'authentic', making option (A) correct.

46. 'Capricious' means inconsistent, making option (D) 'consistent' the correct answer.

47. 'Reverent' refers to a respectful attitude. 'Blasphemous' is exactly the opposite of 'reverent'. 'Blasphemous' means 'disrespectful'. 'Ascetic' refers to a spartan person or a state of abstinence. 'Inferior' refers to something which is not of good quality. 'Blarney' means to cajole or flatter someone. 'Blarney' is a noun.

48. Apogee is the antonym of Nadir; Warranted is the antonym of Unjustified; Epiphany is the antonym of secret; Baleful is the antonym of extrovert.

49. Vexation is the antonym of Happiness, Baleful is the antonym of Benevolent, Recluse is the antonym of Extrovert, Itinerant is the antonym of Static.

50. Recalcitrant

51. Vicissitude

52. Flatulent

53. In option C, the spelling of 'dilettante' is incorrect. The word refers to an admirer or lover of the arts; a person having a superficial interest in an art or a branch of knowledge; dabbler. In option C, the spelling of 'reminiscence' is incorrect. 'Reminiscence' refers to recall to mind a long-forgotten experience or fact.

54. In option D, the correct spellings of words are 'munificent' and pusillanimous'. 'Munificent' means very liberal in giving or bestowing. 'Pusillanimous' means lacking courage and resolution.

55. Even though the IIFT answer key gives option C as the correct answer, the correct spelling is Septuagenarian. It means a person between the age of 70-79.

56. The correct spelling is 'exorbitant'. It means *exceeding the customary or appropriate limits in intensity, quality, amount, or size.*

57. The correct spelling is 'acquiescence'. It means *acceptance without protest.*

58. 'Ammelioration' is the incorrectly spelt word. The correct spelling is 'ameliorate', which means to make something less painful.

59. 'Gazzette' is the incorrectly spelt word. The correct spelling is 'gazette' which means an official journal or a newspaper.

60. The correct spelling is option A, decrepit.

61. The correct spellings are – receive, deceive, perceive and believe. Hence, option B is correct.

62. A few words that can be formed are – latte, late, tale, teal, tele, elate, yale. Therefore, option B is correct.

63. The words that can be formed are – heath, heathen, neat, heat, hate , then, than, eaten, etc. Hence, option C is the answer.

64. The correct spelling is "Danseuse"

65. The correct spelling here is "Acoustic"

66. Option (A) is incorrect because his appears to refer to the President, but the subject of the subordinate clause is the President's Administration, not the President. In option (B), it can refer to either the President's Administration or the budget reduction package. Thus, the reference is ambiguous. Option (D) adds another pronoun, its, but still retains the same flawed reference. Option (C) corrects the flawed reference by removing all pronouns. The answer is (C).

67. The structure of the sentence is that a noun is followed by an adjective, e.g. "war brewing" the third phrase should also follow the same structure and should be "the communication age beginning".

68. Option A is incorrect because the verb "indicate" should be singular. Option C uses 'that' which is not required in the sentence, Option D uses perfect present tense, which makes it incorrect.

69. Option A incorrect as the sentence cannot start with 'due to' in this case. Option B and C do not use the correct tense form in the phrase "will be delayed".

70. To maintain parallelism with the remaining part of the sentence, "marked" is the best way to replace the underlined portion which is unnecessarily verbose.

71. The remaining part of the paragraph is in the active voice. So, option B is the right choice. Otherwise, there will be a parallelism error.

72. The remaining paragraph talks about "art restorers" and not art, the generic topic. So, it should be deleted as it is irrelevant.

73. The other options are grammatically incorrect. So, option A is the correct choice.

74. "however" shows a contradiction. Thematically, no other option fits. So, it should remain unchanged.

75. 'To reducing' is wrong. So, option (d) is eliminated. Option (a) has a parallelism error. 'Improvement' and 'encouragement' don't match with 'reducing'. Option (b) has an unnecessary conjunction 'and' which is redundant. So, option (c) is the correct answer.

76. Option (a) changes the meaning of the sentence. Options (c) and (d) are incorrect and verbose. So, option (b) is the answer.

77. 'Inexorable' means that which cannot be stopped or changed. Option B 'Infallible' means never wrong or never making mistakes. Option C 'Impregnable' means strong and impossible to defeat. Option D 'Inexplicable' means that which cannot be understood or explained.

78. Option A 'Horticulture' is "the study or practice of growing flowers, fruits and vegetables". Option B 'Bonsai' is "a small tree that is grown in a pot and prevented from reaching its normal size". Option C 'Pruning' means "to cut off or remove dead or living parts of a plant to improve shape or growth". Option D 'Topiary' is "the art of cutting bushes into shapes such a s birds or animals".

79. A person who knows or speaks many languages is called a 'Polyglot', making option (A) correct. Option (B) – 'Potable' refers to something that is safe enough to drink, option (C) – 'Plebiscite' is a vote by which the people of a country or region express their opinion for or against an important proposal and option (D) – 'Paramour' refers to an illicit lover.

80. A person deserving blame for an offence or crime is 'Culpable', making option (B) correct. Option (A) – 'Hedonist' is a person who believes that the pursuit of pleasure is the most important thing in life, option (C) – 'Misanthrope' is a person who does not like other people and option (D) – 'Regicide' is the crime of killing a king or queen.

81. 'To have a jaundiced eye' means to be prejudiced. Therefore, option (A) is correct.

82. 'To be uncertain of one's bearings' means to be uncertain of one's position. Hence, the correct answer is option (D).

83. Moribund means dying and is the only word that fits in the context of both the sentences as languages cannot be sycophantic or garrulous.

84. Soporific is a word that can be used both as a noun and as an adverb. In the first sentence it is used as an adverb to qualify the nature of the tone. In the second sentence it is used as a noun to mean a sleep inducing medication.

85. To qualify the pronoun in the first sentence and the noun in the second sentence an adjective is required. Only puerile is an adjective among the given options. 'Puerile' means 'childishly foolish; immature or trivial. The first meaning fits in sentence (ii). The second meaning fits in sentence (i). Hence, option (B) is the correct answer.

86. None of the options fit in both the sentences

87. 'Virulence' (meaning maligning / bitter) is a negative word, so the word 'impudent' (meaning disrespectful) best fits with it. Also, the word 'difficult' in this option makes sense as the sentence talks about the difficulty in circumventing (avoiding).

88. Since we are looking for a type of question that would make someone stutter to the point of suffocation, we need a negative word here. The only negative word available is 'Brusque' (meaning curt / gruff). Also, horribly goes well with the sentence.

89. The sentence goes on to explain how vanity and pride are not the same. Thus, different and dissimilar will be considered. The second part of the first sentence begins with 'though'. 'Synonymously' brings out the needed contrast. Hence, option C is the correct answer.

90. We need an adjective to describe how the leader could refute his opponents' claims. 'Ingeniously' (meaning cleverly / resourcefully) would fit in well. 'Ingenuously' means frankly/naively. The second sentence implies that it was amazing/astonishing how he managed to survive. The word incredible should be used here (difficult to believe) instead of incredulous (one who is disbelieving)

91. 'Malediction' means the act of calling down a curse that invokes evil. It best fits in the context. Other options are out of context.

92. 'Prophesy' is a verb which means to deliver a sermon and 'prophecy' is a noun which means a prediction of future, made under divine inspiration. The pair fits appropriately in the context.

93. 'Embattled' here refers to a person who is surrounded by controversy or is in conflict. Other three options are out of context.

94. 'Trenchant' is an adjective which means distinct and 'winced' is a verb which means to make a face indicating disgust or dislike. Other three options are out of context.

95. The key to solving this question lies in fitting the first blank, on the basis of this we can eliminate options (A) and (B) as ' serendipity or predilection' do not match with the sentence structure. Option (D) can be eliminated as 'conformity' does not fit the second blank.

96. The structure of the sentence is in the format that two events are contrasted. On the basis of this we can eliminate options (A), (C) and (D). The sentence highlights the role of the Himalayas in creating wealth thereby attracting barbarian invaders. Hence option (B) is the correct answer.

97. The key to solve this question lies in filling the second blank. 'Alleviate', 'annihilate' and 'exasperate' do not fit in the context.

98. As the sentence talks about an inherent phenomena. Options (C), (B) and (D) can be eliminated as it would require an external factor for the petition to be 'acceded', 'repudiated' and 'decimated. Since the sentence has a positive tone only option (A) fits both the blanks appropriately.

99. According to the tone of the passage, only 'opportunity' fits well in the second blank 'Curare' means a dried aqueous extract especially of a vine; 'plutocracy' refers to government by the wealthy and 'serendipity' means the faculty or phenomenon of finding valuable or agreeable things not sought for. Hence, option C is the correct answer.

100. The sentence states that growth has been unaffected inspite of the global economic crisis. Hence, 'sustainedly' fits appropriately in the first blank of the sentence and 'resilient' appropriately fits the second blank. Hence, option D is the correct answer.

101. The versions of the happenings in the city are mentioned as different; 'conflicting' fits appropriately in the first blank. Unequivocally' refers to clearly or undoubtedly and fits well in the second blank because the cowardly act should be condemned. Hence, option C is the correct answer.

102. 'Swivel' is a device joining two parts so that one or both can pivot freely (as on a bolt or pin). Thus, 'swiveled' fits well in the first blank of the sentence. Hence, option A is correct.

103. 'Arbitrarily' refers to depending on individual discretion (as of a judge) not fixed by the law. Thus, the sentence states that Cairn cannot bring into picture an unrelated person on his own discretion. Hence, option D is correct.

104. 'Dirigisme' refers to economic planning and control by the state. Thus, it fits well in the first blank of the sentence. The statement talks about the economic growth remaining unaffected by either dirigisme or serious policy reform.

105. A and C can be ruled out because the verb cannot be used twice in this sentence. Also, period at the end of the sentence implies that it is a complete sentence. So, by filling the blank with option D, the sentence won't be complete. Hence, (B)

106. Options A and C are cases of misplaced modifier error. Option B can be ruled out as the correct usage would be 'number of people' instead of 'amount of people'.

107. 'Between' appropriately fits in the first sentence because 'between' *is used to talk about distinct, individual items* (two or more than two) while 'among' is used *to talk about things that aren't distinct items or individuals.* Since, the given sentence refers to two individual people, so the correct preposition to be used here is 'between'. This eliminates options (B) and (D). The word that aptly fits in the second blank is 'since'. 'Since' means *from a certain point in time until now or between then and now* while 'from' *is used before the place, thing, person, etc that is the point at which an action, journey, period of time etc begins.* Hence, 'from' will be used in the second sentence. Thus, option (D) is the correct choice.

108. Option (B) has the correct sequence of words that fit in the given sentences. The only phrase that will make the third sentence meaningful is 'in consequence of' which means *by reason of; as the effect of.* This eliminates options (A), (C) and (D). The phrase ' by dint of' means *as a result of or because of something* and is appropriate in the first sentence. 'By virtue of' aptly fits in the second sentence. It means *because of something; due to something.* 'In case of' means *if a problem occurs; if something happens; in the event that something happens.* It appropriately fits in the fourth sentence.

109. Option (B), 'envisages', meaning to picture something, fits all the blanks appropriately and is thus, the correct answer. 'Seeks' means to search for or to try to discover something, and does not fit into sentences (iii) and (iv). 'Hopes', which means wanting something to happen or to be true, does not fit into the sentences it requires a preposition after it, like for example, China *hopes for* social stability in Ukraine. 'Demands' also will be inappropriate for sentence (iv) because a company cannot 'demand' a good year but rather hope for or envisage it.

110. 'Prepared', meaning to make ready, does not fit into sentence (iii) because "The will prepared that each child..."does not make any sense. The word 'equipped' is incorrect as it does not fit in sentences (ii), (iii) and (iv) because it makes them logically flawed. 'Arranged', though fits in sentences (i), (ii) and (iii); is not the right word to fill the blank in sentence (iv).'Provide' is the correct word as it logically and grammatically fits in all the sentences. Hence, option (D) is the answer

111. Solicitude, which means care or concern for someone or something, is logically correct in the given sentence, rendering option C correct. Solictitude and chivelry are incorrect spellings of the words solicitude and chivalry. Chivalry, which means gallantry or courtliness, does not make sense in this context.

112. To prevaricate means to speak or act in an evasive/ ambiguous/confusing way to mislead the listener. The sentence given here is an example of a doctor talking in an elusive or confusing manner to evade the patient's question of how much time she would live. This renders option A correct. Insinuation refers to an unpleasant hint or suggestion of something bad; preambulation is the wrong spelling of the word perambulation, which means to walk or travel through or round a place; abrogation means abolition or revocation.

113. The phrase 'The bigger they come, the harder they fall' means the more powerful and successful people are, the more they suffer when they experience defeat and disaster. Hence, option B is correct.

114. The phase 'To frighten the life out of someone' means to make someone feel very frightened. Hence, option D is the answer.

115. Only option B correctly fits the blanks. 'Underestimated' makes sense because the British did not expect the local fighters to be tough. Option (C) comes close but the second option 'similar' cannot be the answer.

116. A process which 'defied' reason makes us 'creative'. Hence, option (C) is the answer. 'Reason' cannot be 'reflected'. 'Explained' doesn't make sense in the context of the sentence. So, the other answer choices can be ruled out.

117. 'Emaciated' refers to a state of being very weak or ill. In the context of the sentence, the deer have become very weak or emaciated because of a food shortage. 'Emancipated' refers to a state of being liberated. 'Enunciation' refers to expression or assert. It can also mean pronunciation of words in an articulated manner. 'Elevation' refers to 'height'.

118. The correct preposition should be 'from', option (C). 'Removed from' means 'different from'.

119. Only option (C) correctly fills the two blank spaces. Pipe is an alternative means of smoking. 'Subject to' something means 'prone to' something.

120. A plot can only be 'clandestinely' or secretly' hatched.

121. Since 'although' is used, the correct answer option has to refer to something which is tragic and involves serious injuries. The meaning of the sentence conveys that despite the fact that the injuries were not fatal or life threatening, they were serious in nature. 'Incapacitation' refers to a state of disability. Hence, option (B) is the answer.

122. Sultry applies in this case as the sentence would be idiomatically incorrect with traumatically.

123. Herald is correct as it would apply in the case of people welcoming the celebrations of a traditional festival.

124. Exhorting is the correct choice as the other options would change the tone of the sentence.

125. Bagful is the correct choice in this case list/token wouldn't apply.

126. Chip on shoulder means to have a grievance.

127. Doozy means something unique.

128. Doughboy is used in this case to suggest overweight. The other options all refer to being thin.

129. The clue is 'despite'. So, we need two words which reflect this dichotomy. 'Sincere partner' is not an accepted phrase. It doesn't have a thematic sense. 'Legalities' makes option (B) incorrect. 'Losses' makes option (D) incorrect as it doesn't match the theme. So, option (C) is the correct answer.

130. 'Concise long answers' won't make any sense. So, option (B) is eliminated. Same is the case with 'feeling long answers'. So, option (C) is also eliminated. The sentence talks about the perspective of the teachers. Option (A) talks about the perspective of the students. So, option (D) is the correct answer.

131. Options (A) and (B) are close. Option (A) says 'suppress' which can't describe hard working and conscientious people. They are suppressed as per the theme of the sentence. So, option (B) is the correct answer. Options (C) and (D) don't fit grammatically or thematically.

132. Only sentence II is correct, the word used in sentence I should be 'censure' instead of 'censur' which means strong criticism.

133. Both the sentences are incorrect. 'Compliment' means "a remark that expresses praise or admiration of somebody" and 'complement' means "to add to something in a way that improves it or makes it more attractive".

134. All three words, 'expatriate', 'exile' and 'banish' are synonyms. Therefore, expiate, which means to do something in a way to show that you are sorry about doing something bad, is the odd word out, rendering option A correct.

135. Brevity, succinctness and conciseness are all synonyms. So, circumlocution, which means the use of many words to say something that could be said more clearly and directly by using fewer words, is the odd option and hence the correct answer is option B.

136. Murrey means dark purplish - red colour. Thus a similar relationship cannot be established between murrey and black, like the one between magenta (purplish red) and red. So, A is incorrect. Inter (to bury) and Exhume (to dig out) are opposite actions of each other. Piebald (varied) and Homogeneous (uniform) also share a relationship of being opposites. Effete (barren) and Fructuous (productive) share the same relationship as that of Chapfallen (dejected) and Effervescent (excited) i.e. that of being opposites. Selenology is the study of moon, whereas Epistemology is the study of (human) knowledge. Thus B, C and D are valid analogies.

137. A Polyglot knows several Languages. A Polyphagous feeds on several kind of foods. Hence, there is a relation between them. Escutcheon and Scutcheon are synonyms (both meaning a shield) and so are Fabulist and Liar (both meaning a person concealing the truth). Scurvy is a disease caused by the lack of Vitamin C whereas Kwashiorkor is a disease caused by lack of Protein (caused primarily due to a high carbohydrate diet). Apothecary is a person skilled in manufacturing and/or selling Drugs whereas a Cruciverbalist is a person who is skilled in solving crosswords. Hence all are valid analogies.

138. A message has to be communicated to be passed on and, similarly, words have to be expressed.

139. Activate and detonate are synonymous. So are deaden and defuse.

140. Plentitude and Abundance are synonyms. Indurate means to harden (not the same as consolidate) An Augury is an omen/sign. So is divination. Mulct means 'to punish a person by fine / penalty or 'to deprive of something/cheat'. Muzzle is a snout of an animal (also means to 'gag'.). Perspicacity means insightful, which has no relationship to transparency. Therefore it is the right answer.

141. 'Travesty' means a debased or grotesque likeness and 'paragon' is a perfect embodiment of a concept. The two words have an antonymous relationship. The words in option (A) also have an antonymous relationship. 'Autonomy' is independence and 'subordination' refers to dependency. Hence, option (A) is correct.

142. 'Contrite' and 'obdurate' are antonyms. 'Contrite' is sorrowful and 'obdurate' is relentless. Words in option (b) have a similar relationship. 'Aphoristic' is an adage and 'esoteric' is confined to and understandable by a small group only. Hence, (b) is correct.

143. Both 'Peccadillo' and 'Flaw' mean "a small fault or error". Similarly, 'nick' and 'score' are synonyms. 'Nick' means a shallow notch, cut, or indentation on an edge or a surface.

144. Just as 'Mutter' means to speak indistinctly in low tones, similarly 'articulate' means to be endowed with the power of speech i.e. well spoken.

145. The given question is incorrect. In option (A), 'decrepit' is related to 'impuissance' as both the words mean 'weak'. However, 'desolate' is not related to 'desecrate' (to damage or to treat with disrespect). In option (B), both the words are related to the given pair. In option (C), 'ornery' which means bad tempered is not related to impuissance while 'contort' is related to 'desecrate'. In option (D), 'bedraggled', which means to become wet, dirty or untidy by rain etc., is unrelated to impuissance while 'profanity' is related to 'desecrate'.

146. 'Insouciant' refers to someone who is indifferent or nonchalant. 'Perfunctory', 'pococurante', and 'nonchalant' are synonyms of 'insouciant'. 'Gossamer' refers to something delicate, light, or insubstantial. 'Diaphanous', 'pellucid' and 'tiffany' are synonyms of 'gossamer', Nymphs and Gehenna are unrelated to insouciant and gossamer respectively. Hence, option A is the correct answer.

147. 'Omniscient' has unlimited knowledge. 'Boundless' has unlimited expanse. Hence, they are related to each other.

148. 'Disquietude' is the state of being anxious. 'Nonplus' is the state of being confused. So, there is a relation between these two.

149. One 'deviates' during a 'lecture' and one 'meanders' during a 'drive'. Hence, they are related to each other.

150. 'Nebulous' lacks form. 'Insipid' lacks taste. Hence, there is a relation between these two.

151. 'Indefatigable' means incapable of being fatigued. Tireless is the correct synonym. Inveterate means to be confirmed in a habit. Habitual is the correct synonym. Option (C) is the correct choice.

152. 'Misanthrope' is a person who hates or distrusts humankind, one who is against humanity. A misogynist is a person who is against women. Thus, option (B) gives the correct analogy.

153. The given pair of words have an antonymous relationship with each other. 'Alleviate' means to reduce and 'Aggravate' means to increase. Similarly, 'Elastic' means capable of change, while option (A) 'Rigid 'means incapable of change. Thus, option (A) is correct.

154. 'Benevolent' is synonymous with 'Kind'. Similarly, 'Unclear' is synonymous with 'Muddy'. Thus, option (D) is correct.

155. The relationship between the capitalized pair is – the second word is the characteristic feature of the first word. When a person mumbles, his speech is indistinct. Similarly, when someone scribbles, his writing is illegible. Therefore, option C is the answer.

Swagger (arrogant and self important gait) is not timid. Exacerbate (worsen) and cure are antonyms. Drizzle and downpour are synonyms.

156. Ruffle (upset or disturbed) and Equanimity (calmness; levelheadedness) are antonyms. Similarly, disturb and balance are also antonyms. Hence, option B is the answer. Bewilderment and confusion are synonyms. Interest and astound (shock or surprise) are not antonyms. Flounce (an exaggerated action intended to express annoyance or impatience) and turmoil (disorder or tumult) are not antonyms either.

157. The words given in option (A) are opposites. 'Belligerent' refers to a war like state whereas, 'serene' refers to a state of tranquility or peace.

158. The given pair of words share the relationship of synonyms. Only, option B shows a pair of synonyms.

159. This is an ambiguous question. The logic of the given pair is that "coffers hold or protect valuables". Technically, "sanctuaries protect or hold REFUGEES". The spelling is incorrect in D. It might be a typo. No other option matches the logic.

160. Apocryphal means "of uncertain origin". Corroboration or authentication is the antonym. Options A and C both have pairs of antonyms. However, "commonality" (noun) means "similarity" and "common" (adj.) would have been the antonym of "esoteric" (adj.) which means rare. So, option A is a better choice.

161. Cicerone is a word of Latin origin. It refers to 'a guide who gives information about places of interest to sightseers'. So, the given pair is that of synonyms. Similarly, Dragoman is of Greek origin. It refers to a professional interpreter. So, option (B) is the correct answer.

162. Sylvan is an adjective of 'woods'. It's a literary adjective. It means 'wooded'. Similarly, terrestrial is an adjective of 'Earth'. So, option (C) is the correct answer.

163. 'To drive home' a point refers to emphasising something or stating something in a forceful or effective way.

164. The idiom means 'to have a private reason for doing' or 'being involved in something'.

165. 'Disinterested' means neutral which fits in the context of statement II and IV.

166. In statement II 'but' should not be followed by "on the contrary", as it suggests redundancy. In statement III the meaning of "on the contrary" does not fit the context. Hence, option B is the correct answer.

167. Option A spells out to be "DERVOEHA", option B spells out to be "HEADOVER", option C spells out to be "OVERHEAD", option D spells out to be "READHOVE". Hence, even though the IIFT answer key gives option D as the correct choice, option C is the right answer. 'Overhead' means 'above your head or in the sky'.

168. The IIFT answer key gives option C as the correct answer. But option C spells out to be "TEROMIOPTC", which is not a word. Similarly option A spells out to be "PROTECTIOM", option B spells out to be "COMPETITOR", option D spells out to be "OCTOPERIMT". Hence, option B is the correct answer. 'Competitor' means 'a person or an organization that compete against others especially in business'.

169. 'Ex libris' is a Latin phrase meaning 'from the books'. Similarly 'in situ' means 'in its original place'. 'Circa' means 'approximately' and 'ad nauseum' means 'repeating to the point of boredom'. Only option B shows this combination correctly and is the correct answer. However the IIFT answer key gives option C as the correct answer.

170. An oxymoron is a phrase that combines two words that seem to be complete opposites of each other. Even though the IIFT answer key gives option (b) as the correct answer, 'conspicuous by one absence' is an oxymoron. 'Conspicuous by one's absence' means not present in a situation or place when it is obvious that you should be there for instance; when it came to cleaning up afterwards, Annie was conspicuous by her absence. Option (a) and (d) 'living death' and 'deafening silence' are both an oxymoron. The only option which cannot be termed as an oxymoron is Option (c) 'the sound of music'.

171. A 'metaphor' is a figure of speech in which a word or phrase is applied to an object or action that it does not literally denote in order to imply a resemblance. Hence, option (D) is correct. 'He' designates a 'lion' in the given sentence. Options (A) and (B) are incorrect as they are similies .

172. An 'oxymoron' is a rhetorical figure in which incongruous or contradictory terms are combined. For eg ., a deafening silence and a mournful optimist. 'kind cruelty' in option (A) is an oxymoron.

173. 'Perilous', 'precarious' and 'hazardous' are synonyms. All three words mean *dangerous*. The odd word is 'copious'. It means *abundant*.

174. 'Propitiate', 'appease' and 'conciliate' are synonyms. All the words mean *to satisfy or make peace with.* 'Appreciate' is the odd one as it means *to recognize the quality, significance, or magnitude of something.*

175. A simile is a phrase that uses 'as' or 'like' to describe something by comparing it with something. 'As busy as a bee' is a therefore a simile rendering option (D) correct. An oxymoron is a combination of words that have opposite or very different meanings, a metaphor is a word or phrase for one thing that is used to refer to another thing in order to show or suggest that they are similar and an adage is an old and well-known saying that expresses a general truth.

176. 'Milieu' refers to a cross section of people or the social environment of a person.

177. 'Gaffe' is a blunder or mistake. A gaffe is an unintentional act or remark causing embarrassment to its originator.

178. 'Misgiving' is a synonym of 'qualm'. 'Qualm' can also refer to doubt or reservation. 'Concavity' refers to a concave surface or thing. 'Amplitude' refers to the maximum extent of a vibration or oscillation, measured from the position of equilibrium. 'Repute' refers to 'fame'.

179. 'Act' and 'naturally' are opposites. An act cannot be natural.

180. All the given options are oxymorons. An oxymoron is a figure of speech where two opposite words are juxtaposed. A secret cannot be open. Similarly, 'crowd' refers to a large number of people. 'Copy' cannot be original.

181. Debutante is a French word.

182. Obvious is a latin word.

183. Soccer is an English.

184. "-ation" as a suffix refers to "state or process of" (translation, destination, imagination, rumination). "Trans-" as a prefix means "across" (translate, transgender). "-ship" as a suffix refers to "position held" (friendship, relationship). "Ambi" as a prefix means "both" (ambivert, ambidextrous). "-ose" as a suffix refers to "full of"(verbose, grandiose, bellicose). So, A is the correct choice.

185. 'Auto-da-fe' is of Portuguese origin. It literally means 'act of faith'. It widely refers to the Spanish or Mexican Inquisition.

186. 'Voracious' comes from Latin 'vorax or vorac' meaning 'to devour'. So, option (D) is the correct answer.

187. 'Echt' is of German origin.

188. 'Aegis' is of Greek origin.

Grammar

Sentence Selection

1. Mark the sentence which used the underlined word *incorrectly:*

(a) When Ram started enquiring about the conditions of his business, the <u>childlike</u> directness of his approach left Shyam baffled.

(b) After the huge loss in the new venture, Amol realized that he had been *childish* in his trust and confidence.

(c) The *childlike* gullibility of Bimal has always annoyed Kamal.

(d) When the boss demanded an explanation from Amit for not submitting the project report in time, he burst into a *childish* fit of temper.

2. Mark the *correct* sentence in the following:

(a) Remember,when we tried to sort out the difference over the new project with Mr. Singh, he spoke to you and I as if we were babies?

(b) Was it them who informed you about the music concert yesterday?

(c) The picture on the wall, which was taken years back, doesn't look a little like I.

(d) Was it she you were talking about during the discussion last week?

Directions for Questions 3 and 4:

Mark the ***correct*** sentence in the following:

3. (a) Pele, whom many people consider is the greatest footballer of all times, represented Brazil in four World Cups.

(b) When the news about the decline in the quarterly sales of the product broke out, it was difficult to say who the Company would hold responsible for this disaster.

(c) When the tension with the business partners increased, Mr. Singh decided to visit them personally and talk to whomever is willing to sort the discord.

(d) Who do you think was supposed to meet Mr.Brown from the news bureau, the well-known author, during his week-long visit to Delhi?

4. (a) Returning home from the dinner, we were annoyed to find that the porch light is broke again.

(b) If you keep on losing your composure on minor issues, that isn't going to get you nowhere.

(c) In the meeting, Mr. Mehta informed the executives that they have to fulfill the target regardless of the stringency of the deadline.

(d) The call for the assembly was very disappointing, as we haven't hardly initiated our discussion on a new venture outside the main conference bloc.

IEP

Directions for Questions 5 and 6: Mark the sentences in the options (A ... D) which are grammatically incorrect.

5. (a) The hearing, which had been planned for Monday, December 2, was rescheduled for the following Friday so that all witnesses would be able to attend.

(b) In 1952, Japan's GNP was one third that of France. By the late 1970s, it was larger than the combined GNP of France and Britain.

(c) The Huns who were Mongolian invaded Gaul in 461 A.D.

(d) Because Senator Martin is less interested in the environment than in economic development, she sometimes neglects it.

6. (a) Because strict constructionists recommend fidelity to the Constitution as written, no one objects more than them to judicial reinterpretation.

(b) When a candidate runs for office, they must expect to have their personal life scrutinized.

(c) Einstein, who was a brilliant mathematician, used his ability with numbers to explain the universe.

(d) Despite the cuts, there are services the hospital has, and will continue to provide to doctors.

Directions for questions 7 and 8: Select the correct sentence from the following.

7. (a) He made a blunder mistake.

(b) I have learnt this lesson word by word.

(c) She does not know swimming.

(d) He got his daughter married.

8. (a) The average male investor expects to see all his investment stocks moving up, and they are often disappointed.

   (b) The people in my country are smarter than in other countries.

   (c) The number of failures of product in final quality inspection are increasing every year.

   (d) Before restructuring a firm, the CEO must consider the employees.

2012-14

Directions for questions 9 – 10: Each sentence below has four underlined words or phrases, marked A, B, C and D. Identify the underlined part that must be changed to make the sentence *correct*.

9. Neither the examiner (A) nor his assistant (B) were informed (C) about the cancellation of the examination. No Error (D).

10. Being (A) a short holiday (B) we had to return (C) without visiting many of the places (D).

2013-15

Direction for questions 11 - 12: Each question has five sentences. Identify the sentence which is grammatically correct.

11. (a) Each of the six boys in the class has finished their task.

    (b) One must finish his task in time.

    (c) Either Ram or Shyam will give their book.

    (d) Each of the girls must carry her own bag.

12. (a) The reason why he missed his classes was that he overslept.

    (b) Before the rain would stop, they would have reached home.

    (c) When you will come to see me, we will go to Mumbai.

    (d) I have written both to their branch office and head office.

Word Usage

2007-09

Directions for Questions 13 to 15: There are four options (A ... D) in each question. Each of the options has two sentences and each sentence has one word underlined. Mark those options as correct where the underlined words in both the sentences have been used correctly.

13.

A	i.	Frederica must be as much as sixteen, and ought to know better; but from what her mother insinuates, I am afraid she is a **perverse** girl.
	ii.	For ill, to man's nature, as it stands **perverted**, hath a natural motion, strongest in continuance; but good, as a forced motion, strongest at first.
B	i.	A heavy operator overtaken by a reverse of fortune was bewailing his sudden fall from **effluence** to indigence.
	ii.	The child's own nature had something wrong in it which continually betokened that she had been born amiss – the **affluence** of her mother's lawless passion – and often impelled Hester to ask, in bitterness of heart, whether it were for ill or good that the poor little creature had been born at all.
C	i.	This night she hurried to bed **purposely**, every hair up, one eye on the stranger, who had dropped on a mat in a helpless, hopeless sort of way, all four feet spread out, sighing heavily.
	ii.	The Monkey approached carelessly and was caught in the trap; and on his accusing the Fox of **purposefully** leading him into the snare, she replied, "O Monkey, and are you, with such a mind as yours, going to be King over the Beasts?"
D	i.	All was still; and instead of surrendering to the reasonable exigencies of life he stepped out, with a **rebelling** heart, into the darkness of the house.
	ii.	The matter and manner of his speech were so **revolting** that instinctively Adam's hand wandered to his revolver, and, with his finger on the trigger, he rested satisfied that he was ready for any emergency.

14.

A	i.	But the populace, seeing in that title an **illusion** damaging to Barbicane's project, broke into the auditorium, smashed the benches, and compelled the unlucky director to alter his playbill.
	ii.	Still, whatever the greatness of my **allusion**, the fact remained that the real commander was there, backing up my self-confidence, though invisible to my eyes behind a maple-wood veneered cabin-door with a white china handle.
B	i.	Then he would talk to Philip of the university, quarrels between rival **corps**, the duels, and the merits of this and that professor.
	ii.	The **corps** was dressed in a uniform that once had been blue, but was now faded to a melancholy shade of green.
C	i.	The blows were given by a person of **grisly** aspect, with a head almost bald, sunken cheeks, apparently of the feminine gender, though hardly to be classed in the gentler sex.
	ii.	Also, when the farther arrived to take him away, the cowmen allowed that they would vastly prefer chumming with howling cannibals, glibbering lunatics, cavorting gorillas, **grizzly** bears, and man-eating tigers than with this particular Young college product with hair parted in the middle.
D	i.	I, too, have been foully calumniated by our ancient enemy, the **infamous** falsehood, and I wish to point out that I am made of the fur of the Mustela Maculata, which is dirty from birth.
	ii.	Her neglect of her husband, her encouragement of other men, her extravagance and dissipation, were so gross and **notorious** that no one could be ignorant of them at the time, nor can now have forgotten them.

15.

A	i.	Is it not better to fall into the hands of a murderer, than into the dreams of a **lustful** woman?
	ii.	Instead of representing them as a community of **lusty** savages, who are leading a merry, idle, innocent life, he enters into a very circumstantial and learned narrative of certain unaccoun-table superstitions and practices, about which he knows as little as the islanders themselves.
B	i.	His enticing suggestions I used to **rebel** modestly by the assurance but it was extremely unlikely, as I had not enough experience.
	ii.	His firm step becomes quicker, and the corners of his mouth **repel** against the compression which is meant to forbid a smile.
C	i.	Still, however, he spoke kindly to the lady, and then hastened forth to till his cornfield and set out fruit-trees, or to bargain with the Indians for furs, or perchance to **overlook** the building of a fort.
	ii.	In this way, seeing everything with the utmost vividness, as if he were a spectator of the action, he will discover what is in keeping with it, and be most unlikely to **oversee** inconsistencies.
D	i.	Jennings had been **eager** to see Colonel Brandon well married, ever since her connection with Sir John first brought him to her knowledge.
	ii.	With him went the horse-driving Boeotians, breathing above their shields, and the Locrians who fight hand to hand, and the gallant Phocians **anxious** for war and battle.

Directions for Questions 16 and 17: Each question has four sentences. Mark all the options where the underlined word in the sentence is inappropriately used.

16. (a) There is <u>luxuriant</u> vegetation in the tropics.

(b) Her <u>luxuriant</u> black hair is the most beautiful I have ever seen.

(c) He owns a <u>luxurious</u> yacht.

(d) Coral grows <u>luxuriously</u> on that reef.

17. (a) Do you <u>prophecy</u> a return to war-time prosperity?

(b) He <u>prophesied</u> that the end of the world would come within two weeks.

(c) He is an expert at <u>prophesying</u>.

(d) They made many dire <u>prophecies</u>, none of which ever came true.

2016-18

Directions (Q. 18-19) : *In each of the following options, the same word has been used in different sentences in different ways. Choose the option where the word has been used incorrectly.*

18. (a) He got carried away with the unruly mob and indulged in stone pelting.

(b) She carried on with life in spite of her personal difficulties.

(c) It will be difficult to carry out the plan now.

(d) If they get carried on with their overspending, they will soon be bankrupt.

19. (a) Hang over for a minute, and I will attend to you.

(b) He decided to hang up his boots after his poor form in the last season.

(c) Please do not hang around outside our gate.

(d) She was hanging on to each word I spoke.

Identify the Erroneous Part

2008-10

Directions for Questions 20 and 21:

Mark the option in the following, which contains a *grammatically wrong* sentence:

20. (a) A marvelous stillness pervaded the world, and the stars, together with the serenity of their rays, seemed to shed upon the earth the assurance of everlasting security.

(b) We plowed along bravely for a week or more, and without any conflict of jurisdiction among the captains worth mentioning.

(c) The tulips, concerning whose cultivation Rosa was taught all the mysteries of the art, formed the principal topic of the conversation; but, interesting as the subject was, people cannot always talking about tulips.

(d) She gazed at me as never man's face was scanned yet.

21. (a) Here, a broad, deep, circumvallatory trench, hewn from the solid rock, was defended by a wall of great strength erected upon its inner edge.

(b) I might well say now, indeed, that the latter end of job was better than the beginning.

(c) I really had not yet been able to make up my mind whether I like Uriah or detested him; and I was very doubtful about it still, as I stood looking him in the face on the street.

(d) The Prior had him own reasons, however, for persevring in the course of temperance which he had adopted.

2010-12

Directions for questions 22 – 26: Each of the questions presents a sentence, part of which is underlined. Beneath the sentence you will find four ways of phrasing the underlined part. Follow the requirements of standard written English to choose your answer, paying attention to grammar, word choice, and sentence construction. Select the answer that produces the most effective sentence; your answer should make the sentence clear, exact, and free of grammatical error. It should also minimize awkwardness, ambiguity, and redundancy.

22. When I first became brand manager, we were spending most of our advertising budget to promote our products in the winter. It had worked in North America and Europe, where people caught colds mainly in that season. <u>Our monthly volume data suggested however that stubbornly</u> we were shipping a lot of VapoRub between July and September, the hot monsoon season.

(a) Our monthly volume data suggested however that stubbornly

(b) However, our monthly volume data stubbornly suggested that

(c) However, our volume data suggested stubbornly that monthly

(d) Stubbornly speaks our volume data on a monthly basis, however that

23. The growth rate of companies in several sectors like food, personal care, automobiles, banking and retail in the develop world are flattening. <u>These companies for maintaining their growth rates and margins are looking upon the emerging markets in Asia and Latin America.</u>

(a) These companies for maintaining their growth rates and margins are looking upon the emerging markets in Asia and Latin America.

(b) To maintain their growth rates and margins these companies look at the emerging markets in Asia and Latin America

(c) The emerging markets of Asia and Latin America are looked at by these companies to maintain their growth rates and margins

(d) These companies are looking at the emerging markets in Asia and Latin America for maintaining their growth rates and margins.

24. People <u>who do good work to the corporation wherever they are whatever they do will be assets to the</u> valued corporation.

(a) good work to the corporation wherever they are whatever they do will be assets to the valued corporation.

(b) good work – wherever they are, whatever they do-will be valued assets to the corporation.

(c) whatever good they do the corporation, wherever they are will be valued assets

(d) good to the corporation whatever work they do wherever they are will be valued assets.

25. From what landscapes or flowerbeds would future <u>painters draw their inspiration? Would move poets to craft their symphonies, composers to contemplate the meaning of God, and philosophers write their sonnets.</u>

(a) painters draw their inspiration? Would move poets to craft their symphonies, composers to contemplate the meaning of God, and philosophers write their sonnets.

(b) painters draw their inspiration? Would move poets to write their sonnets, composers to craft their symphonies and philosophers to contemplate the meaning of God

(c) philosophers draw their inspiration? Would move poets to write their sonnets, composers to craft their symphonies, and painters to contemplate the meaning of God

(d) philosophers to contemplate the meaning of God? Would move painters to draw their inspiration, composers to write their sonnets, and poets to craft their symphonies?

26. Car sales in the country rose at an annualized rate of 7.8% in June, helped by a <u>spate of new models and falling borrowing costs bringing new buyers back.</u>

(a) spate of new models and falling borrowing costs bringing new buyers back

(b) luring of new models and falling borrowing costs bringing new buyers back

(c) bringing of new models back, spate in borrowing costs, and falling new buyers

(d) bringing back the borrowing costs, falling in new models, and spate in new models.

2011-13

Directions for questions 27 to 29: Each sentence has a part which is underlined. Beneath the sentence you will find four ways of phrasing the underlined part. Follow the requirements of the standard written English to choose your answer. Selection should make the sentence clear, exact and free of grammatical error. It should minimize awkwardness, ambiguity and redundancy.

27. *__Large and experienced firms are more efficient at acquiring smaller and distressed firms than are large and inexperienced firms__*, and converting them to profitable ventures.

(a) Large and experienced firms are more efficient at acquiring smaller and distressed firms than large and inexperienced firms

(b) Large and experienced firms are more efficient than large and inexperienced firms at acquiring smaller and distressed firms

(c) Large and experienced firms, acquire smaller and distressed firms more efficiently than large and inexperienced firms

(d) Large and experienced firms, more efficient than large and inexperienced firms at acquiring smaller and distressed firms

28. The economic growth increased from 7 to 9 per cent in November 2010, supporting the expectations ***that industrial growth rate in October-December quarter more than doubled that of*** the 4 per cent growth rate in industrial growth for the previous quarter.

    (a) that industrial growth in the October-December quarter more than doubled that of

    (b) of industrial growth in the October- December quarter, that it more than doubled

    (c) of industrial growth in the October-December quarter, that it would more than double that of

    (d) that industrial growth in October-December quarter would more than double

29. As a result of surging financial greed, the international rating agencies upgraded the rating of the credit derivative instruments, and hence analysts recommended a strong buy, ignoring the advice of Warren Buffett ***who warned that these instruments would prove not only dangerous but*** ineffective in the long run.

    (a) who warned that these instruments would prove to be both dangerous and

    (b) warning that these instruments would prove not only dangerous and also

    (c) warning that these instruments would prove itself to be both dangerous and

    (d) who was warning that these instruments would prove not only dangerous but

2013-15

Directions for questions 30 - 31: In each question, a sentence is written in four different ways. Choose the option which gives the most effective and grammatically correct sentence. Pay attention to grammar, word choice and sentence construction.

30. (a) It was thought that freedom and prosperity would spread gradually throughout the world through an orderly process, and it was hoped that tyranny and injustice would continually diminish.

    (b) It was gradually thought that throughout the world, freedom and prosperity would spread through an orderly process, and it was hoped that tyranny and injustice would continually diminish.

    (c) Through an orderly process, it was thought that freedom and prosperity would spread gradually throughout the world, and it was hoped that tyranny and injustice would continually diminish.

    (d) It was thought, through an orderly process that freedom and prosperity would spread gradually throughout the world and it was hoped that tyranny and justice would continually diminish.

31. (a) He must again learn to invoke the energy of growing things and to recognize, that one can be taking from the earth and the atmosphere only so much as one puts back into them, as did the ancient in India centuries ago.

    (b) As did the ancient in India centuries ago, he must again learn to invoke the energy of growing things and to recognize that one can take from the earth and the atmosphere, only so much as they put into them.

    (c) He must again learn to invoke the energy of growing things and to recognize, as did the ancient in India centuries ago, that one can take from the earth and the atmosphere, only so much as one puts back into them.

    (d) He must again learn, as did the ancient in India centuries ago, to invoke the energy of growing things and to recognize, that one can be taking from the earth and the atmosphere only so much as one puts back into them.

2014-16

32. Which of the following statements is grammatically incorrect?

    (a) Will you pay by cash or by demand draft?

    (b) Do you remember that Mr. Mehta made delicious kebabs and that he often held barbeque parties?

    (c) There are, without a doubt, many good dishes to try here.

    (d) The class teacher told Mrs. Kapoor that neither Priya nor Shikha are good dancers.

33. Which of the following statements is grammatically correct?

    (a) Each of the girls living in the orphanage had been ill-treated by her family before they were abandoned.

    (b) Each of the girls living in the orphanage were ill-treated by their family before they were abandoned.

(c) Each of the girls living in the orphanage had been ill-treated by her family before she was abandoned.

(d) Each of the girls living in the orphanage was ill treated by her family before she had been abandoned.

2015-17

Directions for questions 34 and 35: For the underlined part of the given sentence, choose the option that is grammatically correct, effective and reduces ambiguity and redundancy.

34. Many of the workers currently deployed on the assembly line, hope <u>for the exchanging of their routine jobs for new assignments that are interesting</u>.

    (a) for the exchanging of their routine jobs for new assignments that are interesting

    (b) for exchanging routine jobs for new assignments that will interest them

    (c) to exchange their routine jobs for new assignments that will be new and interesting

    (d) to exchange their routine jobs for new and interesting assignments

35. Saundarya's Skin Nourishing cream sold 5 lakh packs last quarter, 20% more than <u>their Face Wash did and nearly five times as much as their Anti-Ageing cream sales</u>.

    (a) their Face Wash did and nearly five times as much as their Anti-Ageing cream sales

    (b) their Face Wash sold and nearly five times as much as Anti-Ageing cream sales

    (c) their Face Wash and nearly five times more than their Anti-Ageing cream

    (d) their Face Wash did and nearly five times what Anti-Ageing cream sales were

Directions for questions 36 and 37: Select the option which is grammatically <u>correct</u>.

36. (a) I forgot that they are coming today.

    (b) I met her more frequently that I meet you.

    (c) This course is challenging and an inspiration.

    (d) She is confident to speak English within six months.

37. (a) The convict escaped from prison and is believed to flee the country

    (b) Did he travel by taxi, train or by plane?

    (c) Visualizing success is not the same as achieving it.

    (d) I would do anything for my friend but not my neighbout.

2019-21

Directions (Questions 38-39): Identify the error in the sentences given below.

38. The job is much worse than expected (a)/if I would have realized (b)/how awful it was going to be (c)/I would not have accepted it (d).

    (a) a   (b) b

    (c) c   (d) d

39. While luminaries of the dance world (a)/has no dearth of opportunities to display their art, (b)/upcoming dancers suffer from (c)/an unfortunate lack of exposure (d).

    (a) a

    (b) b

    (c) c

    (d) d

Miscellaneous

2012-14

Directions for questions 40 – 41: In each of the following questions a sentence is given in "Direct Speech "Identify the right alternative A, B, C or D which best expresses this sentence in "Indirect Speech".

40. He said to her, "Are you coming to the party?"

    (a) He asked her whether she was coming to the party.

    (b) He enquired with her if she was coming to the party.

    (c) He asked her if she was coming to the party.

    (d) He asked her if she will be coming to the party.

41. The teacher said, "Be quiet, boys."

    (a) The teacher ordered that the boys should be quiet.

    (b) The teacher called the boys and ordered them to be quiet.

    (c) The teacher urged the boys to be quiet.

    (d) The teacher commanded the boys that they be quiet.

2014-16

42. Select the option which best changes the given sentence from active to passive voice:

    The invigilator was reading out the instructions.

    (a) The instructions were read by the invigilator.

    (b) The instructions were being read out by the invigilator.

    (c) The instructions had been read out by the invigilator.

    (d) The instructions had been read by the invigilator.

2018-20

Directions for questions 43-46: *Read the sentences below carefully and identify the nature of phrase/clause used in the underlined section of the sentences.*

43. He failed <u>in spite of his best efforts</u>
    - (a) Adjective phrase
    - (b) Adverb phrase
    - (c) Noun Phrase
    - (d) Adverb clause

44. <u>How to find the way to the ruins</u> is the question.
    - (a) Adjective phrase
    - (b) Adverb phrase
    - (c) Noun Phrase
    - (d) Adverb clause

45. <u>Since you have already decided,</u> why do you ask my opinion?
    - (a) Adjective phrase
    - (b) Adverb phrase
    - (c) Noun Phrase
    - (d) Adverb clause

46. The poor debtor intended <u>to pay back every penny of the money.</u>
    - (a) Adjective phrase
    - (b) Adverb phrase
    - (c) Noun Phrase
    - (d) Adverb clause

47. The plan has the virtue <u>of committing us to nothing.</u>
    - (a) Adjective phrase
    - (b) Adverb phrase
    - (c) Noun Phrase
    - (d) Adverb clause

Directions for questions 48-50: *Insert commas wherever necessary in the following sentences and identify the words sequentially after which commas will be inserted*

48. In the old Persian stories Turan the land of darkness is opposed to Iran in the land of light.
    - (a) Turan, darkness, Iran
    - (b) stories, Turan, darkness, opposed, Iran
    - (c) stories, Turan, darkness, Iran
    - (d) stories, darkness, opposed

49. A letter from a young lady, written in most passionate terms,wherein she laments the misfortune of a gentleman her lover, who was lately wounded in a duel has turned my thoughts to that subject and inclined me to examine into the causes which precipitate men into so fatal a folly.
    - (a) terms, lover, wounded, subject,
    - (b) lady, terms, gentleman, lover, duel
    - (c) lady, terms, gentleman, lover, causes
    - (d) lady, terms, lover, duel, men

50. When he was a boy Franklin, who afterward became a distinguished statesman and philosopher learned his trade in the printing office of his brother, who published a paper in Boston.
    - (a) boy, Franklin, philosopher, brother
    - (b) boy, Franklin, afterward, philosopher, brother
    - (c) boy, Franklin, afterward, office, paper
    - (d) boy, Franklin, philosopher, paper

ANSWERS

1. (b)	**2.** (d)	**3.** (c)	**4.** (c)	**5.** (c,d)
6. (a,b,d)	**7.** (d)	**8.** (b)	**9.** (c)	**10.** (a)
11. (d)	**12.** (*a)	**13.** (a,d)	**14.** (b,c,d)	**15.** (a,d)
16. (d)	**17.** (a)	**18.** (d)	**19.** (a)	**20.** (c)
21. (b)	**22.** (b)	**23.** (d)	**24.** (b)	**25.** (b)
26. (a)	**27.** (b)	**28.** (d)	**29.** (a)	**30.** (a)
31. (c)	**32.** (d)	**33.** (c)	**34.** (d)	**35.** (a)
36. (b)	**37.** (c)	**38.** (b)	**39.** (b)	**40.** (*c)
41. (*c)	**42.** (b)	**43.** (b)	**44.** (c)	**45.** (d)
46. (b)	**47.** (a)	**48.** (c)	**49.** (b)	**50.** (a)

EXPLANATIONS

1. The two words – 'childish' and 'childlike' are synonyms but 'childish' also implies being puerile/petty/mentally & physically weak. 'childlike' has a more positive connotation as it implies being artless/innocent/pure/naïve etc. Since sentence B implies that Amol trusted easily, the correct word should be 'childlike'.

2. Option (a) should read "Remember, when we tried to sort out the differences....he spoke to you and me as if we were babies." Option (b) should read "Was it they....?" Option (c) should read "....doesn't look a little like me."

3. Option (a) should read "Pele, ... consider as ...... "Option (b) should read "...... whom the company would ...... "Option (d) should read "...... supposed to meet Mr. Brown, the well known author from the news bureau ......" Option (c) has no error.

4. Option (a) should read "...... the porch light was broken again." Option (b) should read "...... that isn't going to get you anywhere". Option (d) should read "...... we have hardly initiated ......" Option (c) has no error.

5. Sentences C and D are incorrect. In sentence C it should have been "The Huns, who were Mongolian, invaded Gaul in 461 A. D." In D, there is an unclear pronoun reference. The sentence should be "Because of her interest in economic development, Senator Martin sometimes neglects the environment."

6. In sentence A - Pronoun 'they' should be used to refer to the subject of the clause; then is used to refer to the object of the clause. In sentence B 'he' should be used as it refers to only one person. Sentence D is incorrect because of the dangling modifier error.

7. In option A 'mistake' is redundant because 'blunder' and 'mistake' mean the same and are unnecessarily repeated. One does not learn word by word but reads word by word. Option (c) is wrong because it should be 'she does not know how to swim'. Hence, option (d) is the correct answer.

8. Option (a) is incorrect; 'they' has been wrongly used for an investor. Option (b) is correct as it draws a parallel comparison. Option (c) is incorrect as it uses 'are' for 'the number'. 'The number' is always singular. Option (d) is incorrect as in this context the CEO must consult the employees not consider the employees.

9. According to subject verb agreement when two singular subjects are joined by either-or / neither-nor singular form of the verb is used. Hence, 'was informed' is the right usage.

10. Dangling modifier error. The correct sentence should have been "It being a short holiday......".

11. The sentence in option (a) has a pronoun error. 'Each' is singular and must be followed by a singular pronoun 'his' and not 'their'.

12. All the sentences in this question are grammatically incorrect. In option (a), 'why' is redundant when followed by the word 'reason'. Option (b) is incorrect; the correct sentence should be 'Before the rain stops...' Option (c) is also incorrect because 'will' has been used twice in the same sentence; the correct sentence should be 'when you come to see me...' Option (d) is incorrect because 'both' should be used after the infinitive 'to' in the given sentence. However, IIFT is likely to choose option (a) as the correct answer.

13. The words 'perverse' and 'perverted' are correctly used in A. The words 'rebelling' and 'revolting' have also been used correctly in D. This meaning fits in the context of both the sentences. B is incorrect because 'effluence' has been used incorrectly with 'indigence'. C is incorrect because 'purposely' has been misplaced in the sentence.

14. Options (b), (c) & (d) are correct Corps & corpse, 'grisly & grizzly & infamous & notorious have been used correctly. Illusion & allusion have been used incorrectly, fit in accurately when interchanged between options i & ii .

15. Options (a) & (d) are correct. In (b), the usage of the word 'rebel' makes the sentence inconsistent and unclear. In option (c) 'overlook' and 'oversee' make sense only if they are interchanged between options i & ii.

16. Growth cannot be described as luxurious. Hence sentence D contains inappropriate usage of the word 'luxuriously'.

17. Prophecy is a noun and not a verb. Hence, sentence A contains inappropriate usage of the word.

18. The correct expression should have been 'carried away' with something. 'Carried away' refers to 'losing self control'.

19. It should have been 'hang on'. 'Hang on' refers to 'waiting for a short time'.

20. The sentence should read "...... people cannot always talk about tulips." Because a verb is required instead of gerund.

21. The sentence should be "I might as well say this now, that the end of the job was better than the beginning."

22. In the given sentence, 'however' is incorrectly placed. The key to solving this question lies in the semantics of the sentence. The sentence shows a dichotomy that exists between the timing of promotion of the product and the actual timing of shipment. Therefore, the underlined part should start with 'However'. Thus, options (a) and (d) can be eliminated. Out of options (b) and (c), option (c) is incorrect as 'stubbornly' and 'monthly' in option (c) have been incorrectly placed. The correct option should read 'However, our monthly data stubbornly suggested that…'.

23. In the given question, the phrase ' for maintaining their growth rates' is incorrectly placed. The correct sentence should read as ' These companies are looking at the emerging markets in Asia and Latin America for maintaining their growth rates and margins.' Only option (d) gives the correct structure to the sentence.

24. In the question 'good work to the corporation' is incorrect. It should either be 'good work for the corporation' or simply 'good work'. Option (b) structures the sentence correctly. All the other options have a problem of modifier placements.

25. Option (b) appropriately relates the trade and the person who does it. The correct sentence would have been "Painters draw their inspiration? What would move poets to write their sonnets, composers to craft their symphonies and philosophers to contemplate the meaning of God". Also, the preposition 'to' has to follow the noun 'poets'. Hence, option (b) is the correct answer.

26. The given sentence is grammatically correct. Option (d) is incorrect because it changes the meaning and the structure of the sentence by saying that the car sales rose because of " bringing back the borrowing costs". Similar error is encountered in option (c) as it states "spate in borrowing costs". Option (b) is incorrect as it uses "luring of new models incorrectly".

27. The two objects of comparison should be placed one after the other in the sentence i.e. 'large and experienced firms' and 'large and inexperienced firms' are compared in the sentence on the basis of efficiency at acquiring smaller and distressed firms. Hence, option (b) is the correct answer.

28. In the underlined part of the sentence, 'more than doubled that of' is not an idiomatic expression. A mistake of similar kind is repeated in option A. In options (b) and (c), the usage of comma between 'quarter' and 'that' is inappropriate. Hence, option (d) is the correct answer.

29. In the question statement, 'not only' should be followed by 'but also'. A mistake of similar kind is there in option (d). Usage of 'ignoring' and 'warning'

in the same modifier is incorrect. Thereby making options (b) and (c) incorrect.

Hence, A is correct. In option (b) not only 'should be followed by 'but also' not 'and also'.

30. The correct sentence is given in option (a). Option (b) is incorrect because of the placement of the word 'gradually'. The 'spread of freedom and prosperity' was 'gradual', not the 'thought process'. Options (c) and (d) are incorrect. The 'orderly process' has to refer to the spread of freedom and prosperity and not to the 'thought process' as mentioned in options (c) and (d).

31. Options (a) and (d) have a parallelism error; the two verbs in the second part of the sentence (take and put) should both be in the same form- either both ending in –ing or both without it. Option (b) has a pronoun error; 'one can take from the…' should have been followed by 'as much as "one" puts back…' Thus, option (c) gives the correct sentence.

32. Option (d) is grammatically incorrect because 'is' should replace 'are' and 'dancer' should replace 'dancers' for 'neither Priya nor Shikha' warrants the use of a singular verb and not a plural verb.

33. Since 'each of the girls' is singular, 'were' in options (b) and (a) makes them incorrect. The sentence talks about two actions – that of the girls being ill-treated and then being abandoned. In such cases, the past perfect tense is used to show which action happened earlier. Hence, option (c) is the correct answer. Option (d) reverses the tenses and is thus, incorrect.

34. The verb 'hope' should be followed by preposition 'to' and not 'for'. This eliminates options (a) and (b). Option (c) is unnecessarily wordy and therefore option (d) is the answer.

35. Option (c) can be ruled out because the sentence is not comparing Saundarya's Skin nourishing cream with their face Wash and Anti-ageing cream but the sales of the three products. Options (b) and (d) can be eliminated because 'anti-ageing cream' should be preceded by the pronoun 'their'. Since option (a) compares the sales of the three creams and also uses the correct pronoun, it is the correct answer.

36. Option (a): Here the verb 'are' should be replaced by 'were' as the sentence is in simple past tense. The correct sentence is – "I forgot that they were coming today".

Option (b): This sentence is grammatically correct. It means that "I used to meet her more frequently (in the past) than I meet you (in the present)".

Option (c): This sentence has a parallelism error. It uses an adjective (challenging) and a noun (an inspiration) to refer to the same subject (This course). The correct sentence should either be "This course is challenging and inspiring" or "This course is a challenge and an inspiration."

Option (d): The word confident is followed by the preposition 'about/of' and not 'to'. So, the correct statement should be – "She is confident of/about speaking in English within six months."

37. Option (a): Since the action of fleeing has already happened, 'flee' should be replaced by 'have fled'. The correct sentence should therefore be – "The convict escaped from prison and is believed to have fled the country."

    Option (b): This sentence has an error of parallelism. The correct sentence should either be "Did he travel by taxi, train or plane?" or "Did he travel by taxi, by train or by plane?"

    Option (c): This sentence is grammatically correct. It means that to imagine becoming successful is the same as becoming successful.

    Option (d): This sentence also has parallelism error. The correct sentence should be – "I would do anything for my friend but not *for* my neighbor."

38. 'If I would have' is incorrect as the 'would' is redundant while talking about a hypothetical clause. The sentence also needs a punctuation mark after 'expected' to join the two clauses. So, option (b) is the answer.

39. The sentence has a subject-verb agreement error. The subject is 'luminaries' which is a plural noun. So, the verb should be 'have', not 'has'. Hence, option (b) is the answer.

40. Options A and C are both grammatically correct but the IIFT answer key gives option C as the correct answer.

41. IIFT answer key gives option B as the correct answer. However standard grammar books recommend the usage of 'urge' for command or request sentences. Hence, option (C) is the correct answer.

42. When changing a sentence from active to passive, the subject of the sentence becomes the object and the object becomes the subject. Further, if the given sentence is in past continuous tense, 'being' is added while changing it to the passive voice (was/were + being + past participle). Only option (b) follows this rule, making it the correct answer.

43. The underlined phrase acts as an adverb phrase. It is not a clause as it doesn't have a predicate. It also doesn't have a noun and verb. The phrase modifies the verb "failed". So, it is an adverb phrase.

44. The underlined phrase acts as the noun of the sentence. X is the question - In this sentence, X is the noun. The underlined phrase in this sentence can replace X in the sentence. So, it is a noun phrase.

45. The underlined part has a pronoun (you), a verb (decided), and a predicate (have already decided). So, it is a clause. There is only one choice which has the word 'clause' in it. Hence, adverb clause is the correct answer.

46. It's a prepositional phrase. These can act as noun phrases under certain conditions. However, in this sentence, the underlined part modifies the verb 'intended'. Hence, it is an adverb phrase.

47. The underlined part acts as an adjective which qualifies the noun "plan". Hence, it is an adjective phrase.

48. This paragraph has an error. There is a typo. There has to be a comma, instead of the word "in", after Iran. However, we can still answer the question. "the land of darkness" is an additive phrase. So, it has to be covered by comma. So, (c) is the correct choice. There won't be a comma between 'opposed' and 'to' as there is no punctuation needed. And after 'stories' we need a comma to join it with the main clause. Hence, (c) is the correct answer.

49. "written in most passionate terms" is an additive phrase. So there has to be a comma after "lady" and "terms". This eliminates option (a). "who was lately injured in a duel" is an additive phrase too. So, only option (b) can be the possible answer.

50. There can't be a punctuation mark after "afterward" as an adverb can't separated from its corresponding verb. So options (b) and (c) are eliminated. "who published a paper in Boston" is an additive phrase. So, the correct choice is option (a).

Reading Comprehension

Directions for Questions 1 to 8: Read the two passages that follow and answer the questions given at the end of each passage.

Passage 1

From our reading we knew that Gartok was the capital of Western Tibet, and the seat of the Viceroy; our geography books had told us that it was the highest town in the world. When, however, we finally set eyes on this famous place we could hardly help laughing. The first thing we saw were a few nomads' tents scattered about the immense plain, then we caught sight of a few mud-brick huts. That was Gartok. Except for a few stray dogs, there was no sign of life.

We pitched our little tent on the bank of the Gartang-Chu, a tributary of the Indus, At last a few curious individuals came up and we learned from them that neither of the two high officials was in the town and only the "Second Viceroy's" agent could receive us. We decided to submit our petition to this personage at once. Going into his office we had to bend low, for there was no door, only a hole in front of which hung a greasy curtain. We came into dimly-lit room with paper gummed over the windows. When our eyes had grown accustomed to the twilight we discerned a man who looked intelligent and distinguished sitting like a Buddha on the floor before us. From his left ear dangled an ear-ring at least six inches long as a sign of his rank. There was also a woman present, who turned out to be the wife of the absent official. Behind us, pressed a crowd of children and servants who wished to see these peculiar foreigners from close at hand. We were very politely requested to sit down and were immediately offered dried meat, cheese, butter and tea. The atmosphere was cordial and warmed our hearts, and conversation flowed fairly freely with the aid of an English-Tibetan dictionary and supplementary gestures.

Next day, I brought the agent some medicines as a present. He was much pleased and asked me how to use them, whereupon I wrote out directions. At this point, we ventured to ask him if he would grant us a travel permit. He did not directly refuse, but made us await the coming of his chief who was on a pilgrimage to Mount Kailas, but was expected to return in a few days.

In the interval we made good friends with the agent. I gave him a burning-glass, an object of which one can make good use in Tibet. The customary return gift was not long in coming. One afternoon some bearers carried a present of butter, meat and flour to our tents. And not long after came the agent himself, accompanied by a retinue of servants, to return our visit. When he saw how primitively we were lodged in our tents, he could not get over his astonishment that Europeans led such simple lives.

One morning, we heard the sound of bells in the distance as a huge mule-drawn caravan approached the village. Soldiers rode ahead followed by a swarm of male and female servants and after them members of the Tibetan nobility, and mounted, whom we now saw for the first time. The senior of the two Viceroys, whom they call Garpons in Tibet, was arriving. He and his wife wore splendid silk robes and carried pistols in their girdles. The whole village assembled to see the spectacle. Immediately after arriving, the Garpon moved in solemn procession into the monastery to give thanks to the gods for his safe return from the pilgrimage.

Aufschnaiter composed a short letter begging for our audience. As no answer came we set out in the late afternoon to visit the Garpon. His house was not essentially different from that of his agent, but inside it was cleaner and of better quality. The Garpon, a high official, is invested for the duration of his mission with the fourth rank in the hierarchy of the nobles. He is in charge of five districts which are administered by nobles of the fifth, sixth and seventh rank. At last we came into the presence of this potentate. We explained our case to him in all its details and he listened to us with friendly patience. Often he could not refrain from smiling to our defective Tibetan, while his retainers laughed out loud. This merriment added a spice to the conversation and created a friendly atmosphere. The Garpon promised to consider our case carefully to talk it over with the representative of his colleague. At the end of the audience we were hospitably entertained and received tea made in the European fashion. Afterwards, the Garpon sent presents to our tents and we began to hope for a happy issue.

Out next audience was rather more formal but still cordial. It was a regular official meeting. The Garpon sat on a sort of throne and near him on a lower seat was the agent of his colleague. On a low table, lay a file of letters written on Tibetan paper. The Garpon informed us that he could only give us passes and transport for the province of Ngari.

We would in no circumstances be allowed to enter the inner provinces of Tibet. We quickly took counsel together and suggested that he should give us a travel permit to the frontier of Nepal. After some hesitation he promised to communicate our request to the Government in Lhasa, but he explained to us that the answer might not arrive for some months. We were not anxious to wait all that time in Gartok. We had not given up the idea of pushing on the east and were anxious to continue our journey at all costs. As Nepal was a neutral country situated in the direction which we wished to go, we felt that we could be satisfied with the result of the negotiations.

The Garpon then kindly asked us to remain for a few days longer as his guests, as pack-animals and a guide had to be found. After three days, our travel pass was delivered to us. It stipulated that our route should pass through the following places - Ngakhyu, Sersok, Montse, Barkha, Tokchen, Lholung, Shamtsang, Truksum and Gyabnak. It was also laid down that we had the right to requisition two yaks. A very important clause required the inhabitants to sell us provisions at the local prices, and to give us free fuel and servants for the evenings.

We were very glad to have obtained so much in the way of facilities. The Garpon invited us to a farewell dinner. Afterwards, he made us give him our word of honour not to go to Lhasa from his territory. At last, on July 13th, we bade farewell to Gartok and started on our way. Our little caravan, now of decent proportions, consisted of our two yaks with their driver and my small donkey, which was now in good shape and carried no more than a tea-kettle. Then came our guide, a young Tibetan named Norbu, on horseback, while we three Europeans modestly brought up the rear on foot.

The country through which we had been traveling for days had an original beauty. The wide plains were diversified by stretches of hilly country with low passes. We often had to wade through swift-running ice-cold burns. While in Gartok, we had had occasional showers of hail, but now the weather was mainly fine and warm. By this time we all had thick beards, which helped to protect us against the sun. It was long since we had seen a glacier, but as we were approaching the *tasam* at Barkha, a chain of glaciers gleaming in the sunshine came into view. The landscape was dominated by the 25,000-foot peak of the Gurla Mandhata; less striking, but far more famous, was the sacred Mount Kailas, 3000 feet lower, which stands in majestic isolation apart from the Himalaya range. When we first caught sight of it, the Tibetans prostrated themselves and prayed. At the places from which the first sight of the mountain can be obtained are set up heaps of stones, grown through the centuries to giant proportions, expressing the piety of the pilgrims, each of whom, following ancient observance, adds fresh stones to the heaps. We, too, would have liked to travel round the mountain as the pilgrims do, but the unfriendly master of the caravanserai at Barkha prevented us by threatening to stop our future transport facilities unless we continued on our way.

We mountaineers were most strongly attracted to the majestic Gurla Mandhata, mirrored in the waters of Lake Manasarovar, than by the Sacred Mountain. We pitched our tents on the shore of the lake and feasted our eyes on the indescribably beautiful picture of this tremendous mountain, which seemed to grow out of the lake. This is certainly one of the loveliest spots on earth. The lake is held to be sacred and round it one finds many small monasteries in which the pilgrims lodge and perform their devotions. Most of the people we met were traders. The biggest market in the region is that of Gyanyima. Here hundreds of tents from a huge camp given over to buying and selling.

1. Mark all the options from those given below the Lists that correctly match List I items with List II items.

	List I		List II
i	Agent	a	Guide
ii	Garpon	b	Market
iii	Gyanyima	c	Bruning-glass
iv	Norbu	d	Caravan

   (a) i a, ii d, iv c
   (b) i c, ii d, iii b
   (c) ii a, iii c, iv d
   (d) ii d, iii b, iv a

2. Mark all the correct statements

   (a) The author and his friends were not very interested in travelling westwards from the city of Gartok.

   (b) The travel pass for the author was issued immediately after meeting the Garpon.

   (c) The climate of Gartok was moderately warm.

   (d) When the party of the author left Gartok, it consisted of less than seven persons.

3. Mark all the incorrect statements.

   (a) The author and his friends enjoyed the European style tea they had in the agent's office in Gartok.

   (b) When the author and his friends met the Garpon for the second time, he offered the visitors a travel pass up to the town of Gyabnak.

   (c) The viceroy the Gartok was astonished to witness the simplicity in the lifestyle that the author and his friends were following.

   (d) The author and his friends liked the mountain Gurla Mandhata, reflected in the waters of Gartang-Chu, more than Mount Kailas, sacred mountain.

4. Mark all the correct statements.

   (a) The biggest market that the author and his friends witnessed in the region they visited was not located in Ngari.

   (b) While the gifts given by the author and his friends to the Tibetan officials included medicines and burning-glass, the gifts received in return consisted of butter, meat, cheese etc.

   (c) The travel passes received by the author and his friends allowed them to purchase clothes, fuels and foods at local prices.

   (d) The author and his friends came to know that the Garpon, a high official in Gartok, does not administratively control more than four districts.

Passage 2

As the Mongol empire of conquest expanded into an even larger empire of commerce, it became increasingly important for the Mongols to have a smoothly functioning calender that operated according to the same principles throughout the empire. With the need to coordinate activities and regulate social life in places with such varied ways of marking time, Mongols, almost as soon as they conquered an area, created observatories to accurately measure the movement of planets and stars for both practical and religious reasons. They built one immediately near Tabriz, but China needed a series of observatories erected across the land because it was so large. Mongol authorities had specific instructions from the central government to seek out astronomers and astronomical instruments and charts in each newly conquered land. Hulegu sent many of the astronomers captured in the Persian and Arab cities back to his homeland in Mongolia. These included Jamal-ad-Din, who was one of the most brilliant astronomers of the era; he brought with him the blueprints for major astronomical devices and new means of scientific measurement unknown in China.

On a scale that surpassed prior civilizations, the Mongols needed to process and record massive amounts of numerical information in the censuses of people, animals, and buildings. Each year they had to settle the accounts for all the goods sent back and forth, as well as for the movement of herds, soldiers, and merchants. The new forms of agriculture, the demands of astronomy, the system of censuses, and myriad other issues of administration taxed the numerical knowledge and ability of the era. They necessitated new approaches to the handling of numbers. To make the needed calculations quickly and efficiently, the clerks working for the Mongols relied on the abacus, which, with the movement of a few beads, allowed them to calculate large sums mechanically with less mental effort than making the calculations mentally or through writing.

Always fastidious about numerical information and with hundreds of millions of people across the vast Mongol Empire, the Mongols searched for simpler methods, shortcuts, and ways of calculating ever-larger quantities and processing them in every more complex sequences. The larger numbers of calculations required new ways of preserving information through the compilation of complex charts and the coordination of the number systems used in different countries. Mongol administrators found both European and Chinese mathematics too simple and impractical, but they adopted many useful innovations from Arabic and Indian mathematics. The cities of the Khwarizm empire had been a particularly important center for mathematics scholarship; the word algorithm was derived from *al Khwarizm*. The Mongols transported knowledge of these innovations throughout their empire. They quickly discerned the advantages of utilizing columns of numbers or place numbers in the style of Arabic numerals, and they introduced the use of zero, negative numbers, and algebra in China.

Not just in numbers and calendars, but on many levels, life itself in various parts of the empire had to be coordinated in a way that prior history had not required. The writing of history proved too important to allow each civilization to proceed in its own manner and according to the conventions developed in their literary traditions. To control the way that they themselves were presented to their subjects, the Mongols had to make the local standards on writing history correlate and articulate with the Mongol story. Written history was much more than a means of recording information; it served as a tool to legitimize the ruling dynasty and spread propaganda about its great conquests and achievements. For the Mongols, written history also became an important tool in learning about other nations in order to conquer and rule them more efficiently. Khubilai Khan established the National History Office in the 1260s. In keeping with Chinese practices, he commissioned the compilation of complete histories of the Jurched and Khitan kingdoms, as well as the Sung dynasty. The project was probably the most massive history project ever commissioned and took nearly eighty years, until the 1340s, to complete. In Mongol Persia, the Ilkhan Gazan commissioned the first history of the world from Rashid-al-Din, a successor of Juvaini. Rashid-al-Din orchestrated a massive undertaking that employed many different scholars and translators in order to create histories of the Chinese, Turks, and Franks, as the Mongols called the Europeans.

The volume of information produced in the Mongol Empire required new forms of dissemination. Scribes could no longer handle the flow by laboriously hand copying everything that needed to be written. They compiled the records, wrote letters, and sent information to those who needed it, but they did not have time to copy agricultural manuals, medical treatises, atlases, and astronomical tables. Information had to be mass produced for mass dissemination, and for this task, the Mongols turned again to technology, to printing.

The Mongols adopted printing technology very early. Printing with movable letters probably began in China in the middle of the twelfth century, but it was the Mongols who employed it on massive scale and harnessed its potential power to the needs of state administration. Instead of the printing with thousands of characters, as the Chinese did, the Mongols used an alphabet in which the same letters were used repeatedly. Under the Mongols, printers carved out many copies of each letter that could then be arranged into whatever word was needed. Each time the printer wanted a new page of print, instead of carving the whole text, he needed to merely place the right sequence of already carved letters into position, use them, and then wait until the next printing job, when they would be rearranged and the used again.

General literacy increased during the Mongol dynasty, and the volume of literary material grew proportionately. In 1269, Khubilai Khan established a printing office to make government decisions more widely disseminated throughout the population, and he encouraged widespread printing in general by nongovernmental groups as well. This included religious books and novels in addition to government publications. The number of books in print increased so dramatically that their price fell constantly throughout the era of Mongol rule. Presses throughout the Mongol Empire were soon printing agriculture pamphlets, almanacs, scriptures, laws, histories, medical treatises, new mathematical, theories, songs and poetry in many different languages.

In conquering their empire, not only had the Mongols revolutionized warfare, they also created the nucleus of a universal culture and world system. Although never ruled by the Mongols, in many ways Europe gained the most from their world system. The Europeans received all the benefits of trade, technology transfer, and the Global Awakening without paying the cost of Mongol conquest. The Mongols had killed off the knights in Hungary and Germany, but they had not destroyed or occupied the cities.

One technological innovation after another arrived in Europe. The most labor-intensive professions such as mining, milling, and metalwork had depended almost entirely on human and animal labor, but they quickly became more mechanized with the harnessing of water and wind power. The transmission of the technology for improving the blast furnace also arrived in Europe from Asia via the Mongol trade routes, and it allowed metal workers to achieve higher temperatures and thereby improve the quality of metal, an increasingly important material in this new high-technology era. In Europe, as a result of the Mongol Global Awakening, carpenters used the general adze less and adapted more specialized tools for specific functions to make their work faster and more efficient; builders used new types of cranes and hoists. There was quick spread of new crops that required less work to produce or less processing after production; carrots, turnips, cress, buckwheat, and parsnips became common parts of the diet. Labour-intensive cooking was

improved by mechanizing the meat spit to be turned more easily. The new tools, machines, and mechanical devices helped to build everything, from ships and docks to warehouses and canals, faster and better, just as previously the improved Mongol technology of war helped to tear down and destroy quicker with improved cannons and firepower.

5. Mark all the correct statements

   (a) Religious and real world compulsions motivated the Mongols not to delay the construction of observatories in their occupied territories after winning the battle.

   (b) While the Mongols were very impressed with Arabic and Indian mathematical tools and incorporated them in their calculating methods, they adopted Chinese technique for printing purpose.

   (c) Mongol conquest of entire Europe resulted in transmission of knowledge on mining, milling and metalwork.

   (d) In the aftermath of introducing mass production of published materials, the volume of books, both from government and non-government sources, increased with a consequent decline in their price.

6. Mark all the incorrect statements.

   (a) The technique of printing with movable letters was introduced by the Mongols during the twelfth century.

   (b) Numerical knowledge and ability were the main concerns of Mongols.

   (c) According to the article, presses in Mongol days were printing almanacs, scriptures, histories, medical treatises, new astronomical theories, songs, and poetry in many different languages.

   (d) The study of astrology and history during the Mongol period flourished because the Emperors wanted them to serve practical objectives of the ruling regime.

7. Mark all the correct statements.

   (a) Khubilai Khan commissioned compilation of complete histories of Sung period.

   (b) While the available Mongol inventions in Europe aided the advancement of several manufacturing sectors, the agriculture sector also benefited owing to cultivation of new crops.

   (c) The works of Jamal-ad-Din and Rashid-al-Din did not contribute much in the creation of new knowledge during the Mongol regime.

   (d) One of the major inspirations for the Mongols to start looking for advanced yet simpler methods of calculation was the need to effectively document and handle the available figures of military importance as well as those on trade and population.

8. Mark all the options given below the Lists that correctly match List I items with List II items

	List I		List II
i	Astronomy	a	Clerk
ii	Abacus	b	Propaganda
iii	Literacy	c	Tabriz
iv	History	d	Almanc

(a) i c, ii a

(b) i c, iii d

(c) iii d, iv d

(d) i d, ii a

2008-10

The questions in this group are based on the content of the passage. After reading the passage, choose the best answer to each question. Answer all questions following the passage on the basis of what is stated or implied in the passage.

Passage 1:

From the very beginning TCL (Tata Chemicals Ltd.) has successfully grown by meeting consumer requirements in a mutually beneficial way. To determine its benchmark, it uses its own 'Customer Requirements Determination Process (CRDP)' where unit explores present and future customer requirements to enable them to incorporate those in their business offering. This process starts with listening to end-users by exploring various customer listening information sources. This information captures various expectations of customers. Next step starts with identification of segments and matching of segment wise expectations. Outcome of this exercise gives enough guidelines about new business scopes and grey areas of current business practices, After validation of customer expectations through cross checking, TCL matches its internal resources and skill sets with external opportunities and threats to address attractive business avenues. Launch of Tata Kisan Sansar was an outcome to that to offer all sort of end-to end agree solutions of farmers.

Agriculture till today contributes a lot for the development of Indian economy with an employment share of around 69 percent of the work force and with a contribution of near about 24 percent of the GDP of the country. Indian agriculture sector has its importance in economic growth but value addition in this sector in terms of earning capacity is decreasing because of greater income streams form industry and services sectors. The continuous expanding of the gap in per capita income between the agriculture and non-agriculture sectors has huge economic ad social implications and it is almost necessary to empower the farmers financially by enriching the source of income. In this backdrop, one of the motivations for TCL to start 'Tata Kisan Sansar (TKS)' was to ensure business by empowering agri-product producers. again TCL felt that due to its business nature of manufacturing and marketing commodities, it developed an image of a purely product centrie organization. TCL's internal research substantiated its feeling and it recognized a paradigm shift towards a customer centric organization.

TCL first started 'Tata Kisan Kendra' in 1988, executive franchised retail outlets of Tata'with the objective of proving 'one-stop agri input shop' to the farmers. With the marketing function being transferred from Rallis to tata chemicals, TCL used the Tata Kisan Kendras (TKKS) more extensively to market their products. It was understood by the company that the range of offering under the TKKS offered an attractive basket of benefits to the farmers. The business model of the TKKs was base on offering a complete set of inputs to the farmer. Along with this, it also offered extension services and technology inputs to help farmers plan their crops. At that time it dealt more with offering fertilizers and other inputs form those centers. Over the time it realized the job is half done because requirement of a farmer is multi-layered. To offer a more holistic services it changed "Tata Kisan Kendra' as 'Tata Kisan Sansar' and repositioned it as 'one-stop farmers solution shop' by offering entire range of agri services including quality agri input products. Objective was to empower farmers by providing them information about better agronomic practices, facilitating farm credit and providing quality agri inputs from a single source.

9. Which of the following best describes the purpose of the statement in bold (agriculture... income)?

   (a) The emergence of TKS is only because of the rising gap between the income. From the agriculture and non-agriculture sources.

   (b) The farmers income can be enriched through TKS.

   (c) The alternate sector growth can only be curtailed through emphasis on TKS.

   (d) TKS can enhance agriculture's GDP contribution.

10. As a business manager, what **was not** a major motivation behind using 'CRDP' model?

    (a) Ensuring sustainable competitive advantage by knowing customer in a better manner.

    (b) For segmenting the market in heterogeneous group of customers to serve better.

    (c) For estimating of gap analysis of what customer expects and TCL delivers.

    (d) Formulate business offerings and identification of new business scopes.

11. What would have been a **wrong decision** as a manager in the context of 'CRDP' programme of TCL?

    (a) Using external agencies to cross check validity of information.

    (b) Using information to offer readymade solution for different initiatives of TCL.

    (c) Identify external opportunities to explore in a strategically profitable manner.

    (d) Projecting TCL as more customer centric organization.

12. For long term sustainability of TKS as a concept a manager **should not**?

    (a) Project TKS as a corporate social responsibility initiative of TCL.

    (b) Enrich offering of TKS with added facilities and services.

    (c) Position itself as a commodity retailing centre of TCL.

    (d) Focus on return on investment of TKS initiatives.

13. Transition from TKK to TKS was logical for TCL because:

    (a) Conceptually there was a mismatch between skill sets of TCL and TKK.

    (b) TKK lost its acceptability as it became older as a concept and could not leverage first mover advantages.

    (c) Emerging needs sets outmoded existing value proposition of TKK.

    (d) Changing demographics of farmers forced TCL to add new spark in its offer.

Passage 2:

Indian car rental market may be segmented under four broad categories. First, the most popular segment is of a fuel conscious and mileage hungry consumer who prefers a chauffer driven car. To extract maximum benefit from hired car, consumer representing mileage per liter of fuel that he has paid for. Consumer of this segment is very price sensitive and wants maximum value for money even if he may rent an economy car like a Tata Indica or a top end luxury limousine. This segment is dominated by unorganized players. Branded players are lagging behind to lure this segment because of their stringent service condition in comparision to unorganized players. In Indian market, organized car rental industry is crawling for the last couple of years to position itself as a most sought after option to meet segment requirements. Hertz India is also practicing the same. To position itself perfectly in the mind of the targeted segment, it has gone for multiple strategic routes to win over different segments. The major external influencing factors for the consumer in this segment may be the firm's marketing efforts to establish itself as a service provider with value for money. Due to their association with renewed airlines and hotels, Hertz, to a lot many people means faith. This may help Hertz to create an impression in the mind of this segment that they will definitely not be cheated and get their value, even if it means spending a little extra. Further, it is trying to educate this segment about benefits of self-driven car as a medium of hassle-free journey by projecting a premium value for money image and with a fleet mix of compact and luxury cars (such as Ikon, Accent and Esteem).

Second, a sizable amount of people are there who usually use their own compact or three box mid size car but prefer to enjoy the riding thrill of SUV (sports Utility Vehicles) like Ford Endeavor/Honda CRV/GM Chevrolet or a Luxury car like a Mercedes/Camry for a shorter time span. Upcoming new generations or urban executives of large corporate in India with a high disposable income and proactive to enjoy all new things in life and to make it more adventurous and eventful represent this segment. To them renting a self-drive car and driving off to a place of their choice in a Mercedes /SUV gives them an experience similar to that of a foreign holiday. Under this same self-drive segment, another type of consumers are frequent international travelers (including foreign tourists) who prefer their privacy and independence and wish to choose their own routes/car model at the time of exploring destination. They love their freedom & space in life wherever they travel without any barrier like being driven by a chauffer. Equipped with their internationally accepted credit cards, an international driving permit or license, they prefer advance car rental booking by logging on the car rental company's website and thereafter just picking up the keys of their booked car once they enter a new country/city. They are adventurous, driving enthusiast, belonging to the upper-middleclass, have brand loyalty about their car rental agency. In this self-driven segment, Hertz India is trying to position itself as a contemporary service provider by offering both economy cars and SUV's (Scorpio and Tata Safari). To win over occasional self-drivers of SUV type cars and frequent travelers, Hertz uses slogans like "Break free" or "Drive the World's #1" regularly in travel magazines to portrait the quality of its cars,and the range it offers.

Third segment consists of institutional consumers, mainly hotels in big cities and air service providers. *Institutional consumers prefer quality and service assurance to offer maximum possible service to their customers.* In India, all big car rental agencies have contract with star hotels to offer rental service to them. In this segment, Hertz has prominent clienteles like Taj Group of Hotels, Marriott and Jet Airways. Further, they have contract with hotels like Shangrila in Delhi, and Renaissance and JW Marriott in Mumbai to provide all car rental requirements of them.

Their other clients are Carlson Wagonlit, BTI Sita, Thomas Cook and online travel sites like Makemytrip, Indiatimes and Travelguru. According to their deal with Jet Airways, it allows Jet Privilege members to earn 'miles' every time they use Hertz car rental service. For every Rs. 1000/- spent on Hertz rentals, a Jet privilege member earns 100 JP Miles and special discounts are given to platinum, gold and silver card holders.

In recent past 'fleet management' is coming up as a possible fourth target segment for car rental companies in India. _Worldwide cars are not purchased but only leased and this trend is getting its root in Indian market also. It means the management of a fleet of vehicles, using certain tools, to improve operational efficiency and effectiveness. To win over consumers of this segment, services should be professional and a fleet management company should address all the issues a company might deal with pertaining to managing its fleet._ In India, Lease plan Fleet Management India (LPFM), the wholly-owned subsidiary of Leas plan Corporation, Natherlands is pioneer in this field. Orix Auto and Business Solutions, is also present inthis segment. Hertz is focusing more on car rentals than on fleet management. Though it provides chauffeur-driven cars to many companies like IBM, Sony, KPMG, Compaq, there is a huge scope in this segment for future growth. This segment demands customized service in terms of vehicle acquisition, fuel management, vehicle financing and maintenance, resale of the cars at the end of the contract period etc.

14. The primary purpose of this passage is to:

(a) Illustrate how Hertz could plan for the Indian market and maximize profits

(b) Illustrate buying behavior of unorganized sectors offering car rental services

(c) Illustrate segment opportunities for a new entrant in car rental business

(d) Illustrate consumer awareness and views about options available in car-rental business in India.

15. 'Self-Drive' concept may be a lucrative option to a manager to lure Indian consumers because:

(a) Collectivist culture motivates Indian consumers to opt for self drive

(b) Indian roads encourage consumers to experience joy of long drive

(c) Indians may enjoy driving comfort of SUV as they don't have capacity to own it

(d) A sizeable number of Indian consumers aspire to enjoy new things in life

16. As a business manager of a car-rental company, you may popularize 'self-drive' concept to international travelers because:

(a) They know Indian roads and want to explore new places by their own

(b) They dislike concept of chauffeur as Indian chauffeurs are not every professional

(c) Individualistic culture discourages them to travel in group

(d) They can easily book their cars through website of car rental agencies

17. As a business manager of a globally recognized 'car-rental' agency if you like to tap institutional consumers of India, you **should not**:

(a) Bank on your globally recognized 'brand name' to ensure sale

(b) Make a list of your global clientele to impress your prospective consumer

(c) Consider offerings of your competitors to formulate your value proposition

(d) Accept service assurance not as a major influencer behind buying decision

18. As a business manager you think 'fleet management' a profitable segment for organized sector to explore in India because:

(a) Companies want to associate with 'brand name' and unorganized players are lacking here

(b) Their is a huge scope as competition is low in this field

(c) Everywhere in India logistics services are outsourced and companies are focusing on their core business

(d) This business demands gamut of customized services and organized professionals may only offer those

19. If you are to tap "first" segment of "car rental" business as a manager of a branded company, you **should not:**

(a) Advertise your brand name to communicate with consumers

(b) Compare your service conditions vis-a-vis your competitors to influence consumers

(c) Match price of your service with your competitors from organized sector

(d) Cerate unique value proposition to position you away from your competition

Directions for Questions 20-31:

Read the three passages carefully and answer the questions given at the end of each passage:

Passage - 1

The trouble started on May 4, 2004, only days after Google's celebrated coming- out party. Geico, the giant automobile insurer, filed a lawsuit against the search engine for trademark infringement. The insurer claimed the Google's advertising system unlawfully profited form trademarks that Geico owned. Since all of Google's revenue and growth was from advertising, the disclosure of the lawsuit appeared ominous. "We are, and may be in the future, subject to intellectual property right claims, which are costly to defend, could require us to pay damages, and could limit our ability to use certain technologies," Google disclosed in public filing outlining potential risks. Abroad, where Google had promising growth prospects, similar court challenges also arose. "A court in France held us liable for allowing advertisers to select certain trademarked terms as keywords," the company declared. "We have appealed this decision. We were also subject to two lawsuits in Germany on similar matters."

To make matters worse, it turned out that prior to its IPO filing, Google had eased its trademark policy in the U.S., allowing companies to place ads even if they were pegged to terms trademarked and owned by others. That was a significant shift, and one, Google warned could increase the risk of lawsuits against the company. It was also a practice that Yahoo, its search engine rival, did not permit. Google claimed it made the policy change to serve users, but some financial analysts said it appeared designed to pump profits before the IPO.

And there was more. Competition from Yahoo and Microsoft posed a greater challenge to Google following the disclosure about its mammoth profitability. With so much money at stake, the intensity of the competition would heat up. Such competition might be good for computer users searching the Internet, but Google said it posed additional risk for potential shareholders. "If Microsoft or Yahoo are successful in providing similar or better Web search results compared to ours or leverage their platforms to make their Web search services easier to access than ours, we could experience a significant decline in user traffic," the company disclosed. In addition, Google warned that its momentum seemed unsustainable due to competition and "the inevitable decline in growth rates as our revenues increase to a higher level."

Then there was the question of Google's exclusive reliance on advertising, and one particular type of advertising, for all of its revenue. That was potentially quite problematic. If Yahoo or Microsoft gained ground on search, users could flock to their Web sites, and advertisers could follow, "The reduction in spending by; or loss of, advertisers could

seriously harm our business," the company disclosed in its SEC filing.

In the beginning, the firm earned all of its money from ads triggered by searches on Google.com. But now, most of its growth and half of its sales were coming primarily from the growing network of Web sites that displayed ads Google provided. This self-reinforcing network had a major stake in Google's successful future. It gave the search engine, operating in the manner of a television network providing ads and programming to network affiliates, a sustainable competitive advantage. But there was a dark side there too, because of the substantial revenue from a handful of Google partners, notably America Online and the search engine Ask Jeeves. If at any point they left Google and cut a deal with Microsoft or Yahoo, the lost revenue would be immense and difficult to replace. "If one or more of these key relationships is terminated or not renewed, and is not replaced with a comparable relationship, our business would be adversely affected," the company stated.

Google's small, nonintrusive text ads were a big hit. But like major television and cable networks, which were hurt by innovations that enabled users to tune out commercials, the company faced the risk that users could simply turn ads off if new technologies emerged.

Going public also posed a potentially grave risk to Google's culture. Life at the Googleplex was informal. Larry and Sergey knew many people by their first names and still signed off on many hires. With rapid growth and an initial public offering, more traditional management and systems would have to be implemented. No more off-the-shelf software to track revenue on the cheap. Now it was time for audits by major accounting firms. As Google's head count and sales increased, keeping it running without destroying its culture was CEO Eric Schmidt's biggest worry.

Google, the noun that became a verb, had built a franchise and a strong brand name with global recognition based entirely on word of mouth. Nothing like it had been done before on this scale. The Internet certainly helped. But Google's profitability would erode if the company were forced to begin spending the customary sums of money on advertising and marketing to maintain the strength of its brand awareness. Marketing guru Peter Sealey said privately that the advice he gave Google to study consumer perception of the Google brand was rejected by the company and that they were unwilling to spend money on marketing.

20. Which of the following statement is true?

    (a) Google's growing popularity has been a threat to other players operating in that market segment like Yahoo and Ask Jeeves, as Google eroded their market share.

   (b) According to Google its decision to considerably relax its industrial design policy in the US was geared to satisfy its clients.

   (c) One of the major challenges for Peter Sealey has been to expand the Google Empire while keeping its existing internal work culture intact.

   (d) Google's business potential is likely to be threatened seriously if the accessibility and quality of the Web search offered by its competitors like Microsoft or Yahoo becomes superior than the same offered by it.

21. Which of the following Statement is false?

   (a) Google has been potentially vulnerable to external competition owing to its exclusive reliance on advertising for resource generation.

   (b) By writing the "the noun that became a verb", the author indicates the growing popularity of the search engine.

   (c) "non-intrusive" in the current passage refers to the advertisement format that does not directly hamper or distract the flow of operation of the person working in the computer.

   (d) The legal dispute between Google and the automobile giant Geico during May 2004 centered on the advertising system and the trademark policy adopted by the latter.

22. What conclusion can you form about 'Altavista' from the passage?

   (a) It has been a partner of Google.

   (b) It has been a Competitor of Google.

   (c) It can not be concluded from the passage.

   (d) It was a partner of Google initially, but later emerged as a major competitor.

23. Which of the following sentence is false?

   (a) Google has not been keen to undertake any major analysis on the popular impression about the Google brand.

   (b) Google's resolution to provide the search engine and programming to collaborators like America Online ensured significant revnue for both sides involved.

   (c) Google's perceived concern over Intellectual Property issues in the passage has been quoted from a confidential company report.

   (d) With increase in the volume of Google's total annual revenue, it was anticipated by the management that the annual growth rate of their business may decline.

Passage 2

Around the turn of the century; an interesting trend was slowly becoming prominent in retailing across the globe. Department stores were slowly becoming less and less popular with customers. Large department stores offered a wide range of product categories - from apparel, luggage, toys, crockery, to home furnishing - as well as owned and managed the stock of products they sold inside the store and from their warehouses. Industry analysts started questioning whether this could still be the ideal retail model, and whether the changing retail environment marked the end of large department stores as we knew them.

On one side there were the stores that focussed on a particular category - electronics, toys, women's wear or home appliances. Over the years, these had evolved into giant superstores and had become very popular with customers who went shopping for a particular product. On the other hand, there were discounters, hypermarkets and wholesale clubs that served the bargain-hunting customer very well. Department stores were squeezed in between and the new age shoppers found their ambience to be formal and boring.

To keep pace with these trends, some department stores were steadily reinventing themselves. The most prominent among them was UK based Selfridges chain. In 2003, Selfridges launched a new store in Birmingham, England that completely reinvented the idea of the department store. Brands competed with each other within the store but there was no heirarchy of goods: watches competed with each other perfume, and luggage with fashion. In addition the store organised various show stunts and performances through the day and called it, 'shopping entertainment.' Similar stores had come up in various parts of Southeast Asia, Japan and Europe. For customers, these new-age department stores seemed like mall, just that they didn't have the walls that separate the different stores within a mall.

While this trend was becoming more and more apparent abroad, within India too, certain consumer patterns were emerging. Our experience showed that a customer visiting a mall typically walks into four or five stores. That includes a large store and a few smaller brand showrooms. After that fatigue sets in and he or she is unwilling to walk into any more stores at the mall. So we asked ourselves, what would happen if we removed the walls between the different stores in a mall? In that case, a customer would be exposed to multiple brands at the same time, without the necessity of walking in and out of different stores. And along with shopping we could also provide her with other entertainment options.

Within the company itself there was a renewed confidence and an urge to play a larger role in shaping the modern retailing space in India. We had completed more than six years in retailing. With Big Bazaar we had tried and tested our skills at offering a wide range of categories while Pantaloons was firmly positioned in the lifestyle segment. We could now create shopping and entertainment landmarks in the cities in which we had already established a strong presence.

These three insights - the metamorphosis of department stores into developed markets; customer fatigue at the existing shopping malls in India; and the need to create destination malls in Indian cities - formed the genesis of the next format we started working on, Central. The objective was to create a retail format that was much larger and totally different from what India had seen till then. It would offer everything - from multiple brands for shopping, to restaurants, coffee shops, entertainment options and gaming zones - all under one roof. If we were able to deliver on these two fronts, we could attract customers from every part of the city and make it the city's prime shopping destination.

There were a couple of other issues that the Central model addressed quite well. Pantaloons outlets had limited space. We were positioning it as a fashion destination and the business model was based on selling mostly brands that we owned, or what are called private labels. However, with its increasing popularity; we were being approached by multiple foreign and Indian brands to stock these at Pantaloons. Central, being far bigger in size allowed us to open up a lot of space for other brands. However, unlike in any other mall, these brands didn't pay us rent. Instead the brands paid us a certain percentage of their sales in the mall as commission. Based on the performance of these brands, we could decide on which to keep and which to discard.

The first Central mall was launched in Bangalore in May 2004. Measuring 1,20,000 square feet, it was spread over six floors and housed over three hundred brands in categories like apparel, footwear, accessories, home furnishing, music and books. In addition we had coffee shops, food courts, a Food Bazaar, restaurants, pubs and discotheques. A customer could also book tickets for movies and concerts, book travel tickets and make bill payments.

What has primarily made Central the 'destination mall' for Bangalore is its location. It is located in the heart of the city, at M.G. Road, where once Hotel Victoria stood. Moreover, we added a lot of features to further establish it as the focal point of the city. The Central Square located outside the mall building has been made available for art exhibitions, cultural performances, shows and product launches. And in 2005, the vintage car rally was flagged off from the Central flag-point, which has since become the epicenter for many such events. Thus, Central captured in all its glory what we wanted a destination mall to be, and loved up to its tagline of 'Shop, Eat, and Celebrate.'

Soon after the launch of Bangalore Central, we opened the second Central in Hyderabad in November 2004. Once again it was located at the heart of the city on the Punjagutta Cross Road. Here, the roads connecting the city centre with Secunderabad, Jubilee Hills and the old part of the city; converge. It was more than double the size of Bangalore Central. Apart from over hundreds of brands to shop, it had food courts, restaurants, as well as a five-screen multiplex managed by PVR Cinemas. Much like the one Bangalore, Hyderabad Central didn't take much time to become the nerve centre of the city. With an annual retail turnover of around Rs 200 crore it is presently among the largest retail destinations in the country.

24. Which of the following statement is *true*?

    (a) The Central mall in Hyderabad in 2004 occupies more than 2,40,000 square meter in are and currently considered as one of the largest retail destinations in the country with a generated annual retail destinations in the country with a generated annual retail turnover of around Rs. 200 crore.

    (b) It has been observed during the last decade that the hypermarkets are slowing, failing to retain consumers in competition with the department stores.

    (c) The market analysis convinced the company referred in the text that the time is ripe to introduce now shopping and entertainment landmarks in cities, where they already enjoy some market presence.

    (d) While the consumers were able to look for a certain category of products at length in the specialty stores, wholesale clubs allowed them to purchase a number of products at a cheap and negotiable rate.

25. Which of the following statement is *false*?

    (a) The recent consumer response towards department stores led to the quest for a new business Model which may replace it in the coming days.

    (b) Since inauguration the Central Square outside the mall in Hyderabad has been used for various purposes so far including, art exhibitions, cultural shows, product launches etc.

    (c) When the company mentioned in the passage decided to capitalize on the emerging changes in consumer mindset on the retail sales, they already had an experience of nearly six years of operating in this market segment.

    (d) The changing structural framework of the new type of malls became very popular in various European and Southeast Asian countries, owing to their boundary-less arrangement of products, coupled with shopping entertainment options.

26. Which of the following terms has not been mentioned in the above passage?

    (a) Department Stores (b) Hypermarkets

    (c) Wholesale Clubs   (d) Super-speciality stores

27. Which of the following statement is *true*?

    (a) The firm discussed here allowed various foreign and India garment companies to display their products in their show room on the condition that they will pay them either some rent, or a pre-decided percentage of their sales as commission.

    (b) Before going for the Central venture, the firm already had the experience of offering a wide range of product categories through Big Bazaar and in specialized segments through Pantaloons.

    (c) The Central mall in Bangalore provided importance to both goods and services for business development: it displayed around two hundred brands in categories like garments, footwear, music, book etc. on one hand, and ensured eating and entertainment options, ticket-booking for movies and concerts, travel services and bill payments within its premises on the other.

    (d) The reasons behind the losing out of the specialty stores had been multifarious, covering the traditional and unexciting environment, steep price competition from other rivals, inflexibility in operation etc.

28. Which of the following statement is *false*?

    (a) In tune with the changing time, the new store created in Birmingham allowed brand competition within the store without explicit hierarchy of products, and organized various events to ensure lively amusement for the shoppers.

    (b) Since visiting different stores even within a mega shopping complex gets monotonous once the initial excitement is over, the exposure to multiple brands simultaneously with removal of the walls has been a consumer-friendly move.

    (c) The idea behind setting up a mega retail network was to make it city's unique shopping location by ensuring exposure to multiple brands on one hand, and by making it an excellent hang-out option through setting up of entertainment and nourishment options on the other.

    (d) The market analysis by the company described in the passage revealed that a representative buyer to a shopping center goes to at the most four or five stores, selecting large or small showrooms randomly.

Passage 3

In the early 1950s, a plague clouded the American landscape. A mysterious virus stalked the nation's youth like a silent, invisible killer. For generations, it had been devouring young lives. But in the previous three decades the number of its victims had increased dramatically. Those it did not kill, it left hopelessly paralyzed and deformed. Newspaper artists sometimes depicted the disease as a dragon. Its common name was infantile paralysis, or poliomyelitis, or simply polio.

Polio struck every summer, turning strong bodies into crumpled ones, leaving in its wake withered limbs in steel braces and straps. It was simply expected when the children returned to school each fall that a friend or classmate would have been lost to polio over the summer. Everyone knew a victim - if not in their own family, it was the boy down the street or one on the next street. By the early 1950s, some 50,000 cases per year were being reported, and 1952 alone saw 59,000 new cases.

But in April of 1955 a miracle occurred. It came in the form of an announcement that a vaccine had been discovered that could actually prevent polio. With completion of a series of research field tests, the news media hailed it as the most dramatic breakthrought in the history of medical research.

The hero of the day; the man who slew the polio dragon, was a shy young doctor named Jonas Salk. Stories of his heroic effort to perfect his vaccine filled the newspapers. In the months prior to final development of the vaccine, Salk had pushed himself to the limits of human endurance. Realizing he was close to a breakthrough, he worked seven days a week, often up to 20 or 30 hours at a time without sleep. He often skipped meals. the public lionized him for his efforts. But that was not the case among those in the scientific community. Behind the scenes, unknown to the public, Salk was being vilified by his peers. At one point some leading scientists even tried to stop distribution of his life-saving vaccine.

Salk's fellow scientists in biological research considered him an outsider, intruding into their domain. In fact, in order to acquire funds for his research, Salk had to go outside normal channels. When he did so, scientists accused him of being a publicity hound. The research establishment was especially jealous of Salk's relationship with Basil O'Connor, the man who supplied much of his funding. As president of the National Foundation for Infantile Paralysis, O'Connor held the purse strings to millions in research dollars. And he believed in Salk.

Basil O'Connor knew firsthand the devastating effects of the disease. His daughter had been stricken with polio. And when O'Connor was young man, Franklin Roosevelt had been his best friend and law partner, long before becoming president of the United Staes. O'Connor had seen polio turn an athletic young Roosevelt into a man unable to stand without leg braces and walking sticks. In Jonas Salk, O'Connor found someone who shared his outright hatred for the disease.

Viewed in retrospect, one might understand the opposition of biological research scientists to Salk's method. He made many transgressions against traditional research. For one thing, the very efficacy of his vaccine toppled one of the most universally accepted (though erroneous) tenets of orthodox virology - the motion that an active virus could not be checked by its own dead viral bodies. That was precisely the path Salk chose to develop his vaccine.

For decades, traditional biologists had been waging what they considered a deliberate, correct, gentleman's fight against polio with efforts focused on treatment rather than prevention. By contrast, Salk fought the dragon like a man possessed, seeking a final cure. He had grown up on the fringes of poverty and developed an attitude more humanist than scientific, a man unwilling to abide senseless rules in the face of a crisis. He flailed against the disease like a punch-drunk street fighter-and he landed a knockout blow. Finally, his success proved the greatest transgression of all against his fellow scientists. By the 1950s, researching polio was a very big business, and overnight, Salk made further efforts redundant. It was unheard of that an outsider, working independently;could accomplish what the nation's top scientists with their great laboratories and countless millions of dollars could not. They expressed their bitterness in rather petty ways, even refusing to accept Salk into the National Academy of Science. The reason? Salk, they contended, was not really a scientist - only a technician.

The public never knew the depths of his colleagues' resentment. It was almost a decade after his discovery before Salk himself would even discuss it. "The worst tragedy that could have befallen me was my success," he told an interviewer. "I knew right away that I was through, that I would be cast out."

But he was not through. With the polio dragon defeated, he launched a campaign to raise funds to construct the Salk Intitute for Biological Studies at Torrey Pines, California. He worked there, surrounded by bright, young scientists until his death at age eighty. Salk later became obsessed with finding a cure for the human immunodeficiency virus (HIV) that causes AIDS. Also until the day he died, he was trying to catch lightning in a test tube one last time. Perhaps a man is allotted only one miracle in his lifetime.

Today, research scientists work in the laboratories Jonas Salk built, searching for new weapons in the fight against dragons that defy destruction: cancer, AIDS, Alzheimer's, cerebral palsy, multiple sclerosis, and Parkinson's. Among those scientists at Torrey Pines, waging gentlemanly wars against the microscopic enemies of man, perhaps a new maverick will emerge - a stubborn street fighter who will defeat the odds and capture the lightning that eluded Jonas Salk.

29. Which of the following statement is ***true***?

    (a) For a long time the efforts made by traditional biologists in the battle against polio had been a combination of finding cure for the polio patients as well as preventing the newer occurrences.

    (b) Within three years from the menace of polio reaching a new peak, the antidote for the deadly disease was discovered by a relatively lesser known person.

    (c) Basil O'Connor had been a good friend of Theodore Roosevelt and his law partner.

    (d) The scientists at Salk Institute for Biological Studies are currently doing research to invent medicines to ensue permanent cures for diseases like AIDS, cerebral palsy,. multiple stenosis etc.

30. Which of the following statement is ***false***?

    (a) A major proportion of the funds required for the research by Dr. Salk came from National Foundation for Infantile Paralysis, whose president Basil O'Connor ensured the requisite amount for him.

    (b) The extent of the resentment of the colleagues' of Dr. Salk over his achievement was known to the people almost thirty years after the invention of the vaccine against the disease.

    (c) The top scientists of the country did not favour the entry of Dr. Salk into National Academy of Science on the ground of his lack of professional qualification with respect to medical and biological science.

    (d) The driving reason behind the success of Dr Salk was the fact that he did not accept the framework developed by traditional virology research as foolproof, which was a key factor behind his success.

31. Match the following:

	List I		List II
i	Salk	a	Dragon
ii	Polio	b	Breakthrough
iii	Field tests	c	Torrey Pines
iv	HIV Research	d	Vilified

    (a) ii-c, iii-b, iv-a
    (b) 1-c, iii-c, iv-a
    (c) i-d, ii-a, iii-b.
    (d) ii-a, iii-c, iv-b.

2009-11

Directions for Questions 32 – 43: Read the three passages carefully and answer the questions given at the end of each passage:

Passage – 1

We now come to the second part of our journey under the sea. The first ended with the moving scene in the coral cemetery which left a deep impression on my mind. I could no longer content myself with the theory which satisfied Conseil. That worthy fellow persisted in seeing in the Commander of the Nautilus one of those unknown servants who return mankind contempt for indifference. For him, he was a misunderstood genius who, tired of earth's deceptions, had taken refuge in this inaccessible medium, where he might follow his instincts freely. To my mind, this explains but one side of Captain Nemo's character. Indeed, the mystery of that last night during which we had been chained in prison, the sleep, and the precaution so violently taken by the Captain of snatching from my eyes the glass I had raised to sweep the horizon, the mortal wound of the man, due to an unaccountable shock of the Nautilus, all put me on a new track. No; Captain Nemo was not satisfied with shunning man. His formidable apparatus not only suited his instinct of freedom, but perhaps also the design of some terrible retaliation.

That day, at noon, the second officer came to take the altitude of the sun. I mounted the platform, and watched the operation. As he was taking observations with the sextant, one of the sailors of the Nautilus (the strong man who had accompanied us on our first submarine excursion to the Island of Crespo) came to clean the glasses of the lantern. I examined the fittings of the apparatus, the strength of which was increased a hundredfold by lenticular rings, placed similar to those in a lighthouse, and which projected their brilliance in a horizontal plane. The electric lamp was combined in such a way as to give its most powerful light. Indeed, it was produced in vacuum, which insured both its steadiness and its intensity. This vacuum economised the graphite points between which the luminous arc was developed – an important point of economy for Captain Nemo, who could not easily have replaced them; and under these conditions their waste was imperceptible. When the Nautilus was ready to continue its submarine journey, I went down to the saloon. The panel was closed, and the course marked direct west.

We were furrowing the waters of the Indian Ocean, a vast liquid plain, with a surface of 1, 200,000,000 of acres, and whose waters are so clear and transparent that any one leaning over them would turn giddy. The Nautilus usually floated between fifty and a hundred fathoms deep. We went on so for some days. To any one but myself, who had a great love for the sea, the hours would have seemed long and monotonous; but the daily walks on the platform, when I steeped myself in the reviving air of the ocean, the sight of the rich waters through the windows of the saloon, the books in the library, the compiling of my memoirs, took up all my time, and left me not a moment of ennui or weariness.

From the 21st to the 23rd of January the Nautilus went at the rate of two hundred and fifty leagues in twenty-four hours, being five hundred and forty miles, or twenty-two miles an hours. If we recognized so many different varieties of fish, it was because, attracted by the electric light, they tried to follow us; the greater part, however, were soon distanced by our speed, though some kept their place in the waters of the Nautilus for a time. The morning of the 24th, we observed Keeling Island, a coral formation, planted with magnificent cocoas, and which had been visited by Mr. Darwin and Captain Fitzroy. The Nautilus skirted the shores of this desert island for a little distance. Soon Keeling Island disappeared from the horizon, and our course was directed to the north-west in the direction of the Indian Peninsula.

From Keeling Island our course was slower and more variable, often taking us into great depths. Several times they made use of the inclined planes, which certain internal levers placed obliquely to the waterline. I observed that in the upper regions the water was always colder in the high levels than at the surface of the sea. On the 25th of January the ocean was entirely deserted; the Nautilus passed the day on the surface, beating the waves with its powerful screw and making them rebound to a great height. Three parts of this day I spent on the platform. I watched the sea. Nothing on the horizon, till about four o'clock a steamer running west on our counter. Her masts were visible for an instant, but she could not see the Nautilus, being too low in the water. I fancied this steamboat belonged to the P.O. Company, which runs from Ceylon to Sydney, touching at King George's Point and Melbourne.

At five o'clock in the evening, before that fleeting twilight which binds night to day in tropical zones, Conseil and I were astonished by a curious spectacle. It was a shoal of Argonauts traveling along on the surface of the ocean. We could count several hundreds. These graceful molluscs moved backwards by means of their locomotive tube, through which they propelled the water already drawn in. Of their eight tentacles, six were elongated, and stretched out floating on the water, whilst the other two, rolled up flat, were spread to the wing like a light sail. I saw their spiral-shaped and fluted shells, which Cuvier justly compares to an elegant skiff. For nearly an hour the Nautilus floated in the midst of this shoal of molluscs.

The next day, 26th of January, we cut the equator at the eighty-second meridian and entered the northern hemisphere. During the day a formidable troop of sharks accompanied us. They were "cestracio philippi" sharks, with brown backs and whitish bellies, armed with eleven rows of teeth, their throat being marked with a large black spot surrounded with white like an eye. There were also some Isabella sharks, with rounded snouts marked with dark spots. These powerful creatures often hurled themselves at the windows of the saloon with such violence as to make us fell very insecure. But the Nautilus, accelerating her speed, easily left the most rapid of them behind.

About seven o'clock in the evening, the Nautilus, half-immersed, was sailing in a sea of milk. At first sight the ocean seemed lactified. Was it the effect of the lunar rays? No; for the moon, scarcely two days old, was still lying hidden under the horizon in the rays of the sun. The whole sky, though lit by the sidereal rays, seemed black by contrast with the whiteness of the waters. Conseil could not believe his eyes, and questioned me as to the cause of this strange phenomenon. Happily I was able to answer him.

"It is called a milk sea," I explained. "A large extent of white wavelets often to be seen on the coasts of Amboyna, and in these parts of the sea.

"But, sir," said Conseil, "can you tell me what causes such an effect? For I suppose the water is not really turned into milk."

"No, my boy' and the whiteness which surprises you is caused only by the presence of myriads of luminous little worm, gelatinous and without colour, of the thickness of a hair, and whose length is not more than seven-thousandths of an inch. These insects adhere to one another sometimes for several leagues."

"Several leagues!" exclaimed Conseil.

"Yes, my boy; and you need not try to compute the number of these infusoria. You will not be able, for, if I am not mistaken, ships have floated on these milk seas for more than forty miles."

Towards midnight the sea suddenly resumed its usual colour; but behind us, even to the limits of the horizon, the sky reflected the whitened waves, and for a long time seemed impregnated with the vague glimmerings of an aurora borealis.

32. Find the TRUE Sentence:

   (a) According to the narrator, the above-mentioned journey was taking place during full moon period.

   (b) According to Conseil, the Captain of the Nautilus in which they were traveling was really a brilliant person, a fact which had been corroborated by many people.

   (c) It is implied from the passage that although the author was witnessing many interesting events during their journey, he was not always having his way.

   (d) From the chronicle, it is understood that the Nautilus was in the vicinity of the Island of Crespo on the 25th of January.

33. Find the FALSE sentence:

   (a) After entering the Northern Hemisphere, the narrator witnessed several sea creatures, including several varieties of sharks, who kept bumping on the windows of the submarine.

   (b) On 25th January, the second officer of Nautilus came to the platform for measuring the altitude of the sun and for that purpose took observations with the sextant.

   (c) After January 24, Nautilus started travelling at a relatively reduced speed, and some of the time it was going further away from the sea-surface.

   (d) The course of Nautilus took them near the Keeling Island, which had earlier been visited by Mr. Darwin and Captain Fitzroy.

34. Match the following:

1	Molluscs	I	Colourless
2	Sharks	I	Tentacles
3	Infusoria	ii	Coco
4	Coral	iv	Snouts

   (a) 1-ii, 2-iv, 3-i, 4-iii   (b) 1-iii, 2-i, 3-iv, 4-ii

   (c) 1-iv, 2-iii, 3-ii, 4-i   (d) 1-iii, 2-ii, 3-iv, 4-i

35. Find the TRUE statement:

   (a) During 22nd to 24th of January, Nautilus was travelling at the rate of two hundred and fifty leagues in twenty-four hours, which means a speed of twenty-two miles and hour.

   (b) On 26th January for approximately and hour the narrator witnessed a shoal of molluscs, and he enjoyed watching their spiral-shaped and fluted shells.

   (c) On the 25th of January the narrator came across a steamboat, which was owned by P.O. Company, which travels between Ceylon to Sydney.

   (d) The electric lamp of the submarine was an example of efficiency and effective fixture

Passage – 2

Turning the business around involved more than segmenting and pulling out of retail. It also meant maximizing every strength we had in order to boost our profit margins. In reexamining the direct model, we realized that inventory management was not just a core strength; it could be an incredible opportunity for us, and one that had not yet been discovered by any our competitors.

In Version 1.0 of the direct model, we eliminated the reseller, thereby eliminating the markup and the cost of maintaining a store. In Version 1.1, we went one step further to reduce inventory inefficiencies. Traditionally, a long chain of partners was involved in getting a product to the customer. Let's say you have a factory building a PC we'll call model #4000. The system is then sent to the distributor, which sends it to the warehouse, which sends it to the dealer, who eventually pushes it on to the consumer by advertising, "I've got model #4000. Come and buy it." If the consumer says, "But I want model #8000," the dealer replies, "Sorry, I only have model #4000." Meanwhile, the factory keeps building model #4000s and pushing the inventory into the channel.

The result is a glut of model #4000s that nobody wants. Inevitably, someone ends up with too much inventory, and you see big price corrections. The retailer can't sell it at the suggested retail price, so the manufacturer loses money on price protection (a practice common in our industry of compensating dealers for reductions in suggested selling price). Companies with long, multi-step distribution systems will often fill their distribution channels with products in an attempt to clear out older technologies or meet their financial targets. This dangerous and inefficient practice is called "channel stuffing". Worst of all, the customer ends up paying for it by purchasing systems that are already out of date.

Because we were building directly to fill our customers' orders, we didn't have finished goods inventory devaluing on a daily basis. Because we aligned our suppliers to deliver components as we used them, we were able to minimize raw material inventory. Reductions in component costs could be passed on to our customers quickly, which made them happier and improved our competitive advantage. It also allowed us to deliver the latest technology to our customers faster than our competitors.

The direct model turns conventional manufacturing inside out. Conventional manufacturing dictates that you should always have a stockpile of raw materials, because if you run out, your plant can't keep going. But if you don't know what you need to build because of dramatic changes in demand, you run the risk of ending up with terrific amount of excess and obsolete inventory. That is not the goal. The concept behind the direct model has nothing to do with stockpiling and everything to do with information. The quality of your information is inversely proportional to the amount of assets required, in this case excess inventory. With less information about customer needs, you need massive amounts of inventory. So, if you have great information – that is, you know exactly what people want and how much – you need that much less inventory. Less inventory, of course, corresponds to less inventory depreciation. In the computer industry, component prices are always falling as suppliers introduce faster chips, bigger disk drives, and modems with ever-greater bandwidth. Let's say that Dell has six days of inventory. Compare that to an indirect competitor who has twenty-five days of inventory with another thirty in their distribution channel. That's a difference of forty-nine days, and in forty-nine days, the cost of materials will decline about 6 percent.

Then there's the threat of getting stuck with obsolete inventory if you're caught in a transition to a next-generation product, as we were with those memory chips in 1989. As the product approaches the end of its life, the manufacturer has to worry about whether it has too much in the channel and whether a competitor will dump products, destroying profit margins for everyone. This is a perpetual problem in the computer industry, but with the direct model, we have virtually eliminated it. We know when our customers are ready to move on technologically, and we can get out of the market before its most precarious time. We don't have to subsidize our losses by charging higher prices for other products.

And ultimately, our customer wins. Optimal inventory management really starts with the design process. You want to design the product so that the entire product supply chain, as well as the manufacturing process, is oriented not just for speed but for what we call velocity. Speed means being fast in the first place. Velocity means squeezing time out of every step in the process.

Inventory velocity has become a passion for us. To achieve maximum velocity, you have to design your products in a way that covers the largest part of the market with the fewest number of parts. For example, you don't need nine different Disk drives when you can serve 98 percent of the market with only four. We also learned to take into account the variability of low-cost and high-cost components. Systems were reconfigured to allow for a greater variety of low-cost parts and a limited variety of expensive parts. The goal was to decrease the number of components to manage, which increased the velocity, which decreased the risk of inventory depreciation, which increased the overall health of our business system.

We were also able to reduce inventory well below the levels anyone thought possible by constantly challenging and surprising ourselves with the results. We had our internal skeptics when we first started pushing for ever-lower levels of inventory. I remember the head of our procurement group telling me that this was like "flying low to the ground 300 knots." He was worried that we wouldn't see the trees.

In 1993, we had $2.9 billion in sales and $220 million in inventory. Four years later, we posted $12.3 billion in sales ad had inventory of 33 million. We're now down to six days of inventory and we're starting to measure it in hours instead of days. Once you reduce your inventory while maintaining your growth rate, a significant amount of risk comes from the transition from one generation of product to the next. Without traditional stockpiles of inventory, it is critical to precisely time the discontinuance of the older product line with the ramp-up in customer demand for the newer one. Since we were introducing new products all the time, it became imperative to avoid the huge drag effect from mistakes made during transitions. E&O – short for "excess and obsolete" – became taboo at Dell. We would debate about whether our E&O was 30 or 50 cents per PC. Since anything less than $20 per PC is not bad, when you're down in the cents range, you're approaching stellar performance.

In effect, we got stronger with each transition and more competitive with each turn of the crank. We were increasing our productivity and improving our cash flow in a broader range of products in larger and larger markets. Unlike that period in 1993, when every day the news got a little worse, now, finally, every day the news was better and better.

36. Find out the TRUE statement:

(a) According to the passage, the working of the direct model was being heavily exploited by all players in the software business.

(b) Analysis of the supply chain of the product reveals that the product is sent to the warehouse by the dealer, and delay at that stage leads to an obvious increase in cost.

(c) The nature of the computer industry is such that the production decision at factory level is usually undertaken after getting the customer demand feedback from the distributors.

(d) Whenever the production of some old-fashioned model of a product by a company exceeds the existing demand, the market forces create a downward pressure on its prices.

37. Find out the FALSE statement:

(a) The company mentioned in the passage could attain efficiency on raw material inventory management because they were procuring components only in line with their timely requirement.

(b) Generally the more the amount of quality information about the consumer needs and the market a firm possess, the less is its inventory requirement.

(c) In order to serve the market more efficiently, the firm mentioned here reconfigured their computers with increased proportion of low-cost parts and a fewer types of high-priced parts.

(d) The conventional manufacturing system always ensured that no competitor can lower prices to reduce profit margins for everybody.

38. Choose the option which best matches the following sets:

1	Inventory	i	Precarious
2	Conventional Manufacturing	ii	Warehouse
3	Distributor	iii	Stockpile
4	Market	iv	Velocity

(a) 1 – iv, 2 – ii, 3 – I, 4 - iii

(b) 1 – iii, 2 – I, 3 – iv, 4 – ii

(c) 1 – iv, 2 – iii, 3 – ii, 4 – I

(d) 1 – iii, 2 – ii, 3 – iv, 4 – I

39. Find out the FALSE Statement:

(a) A. Having less amount of inventory is better in the computer industry as with time better quality components with enhanced capacity reach the market with lower price.

(b) Before improving the inventory management system under the direct model, the firm first removed the reseller from its marketing model, which contributed in its cost-cutting attempt.

(c) The efficient inventory management allowed the firm to enhance productivity as well as the flexibility to enter or exit a market.

(d) The companies with long distribution network incorporate information – gathering process within their systems which enable them to market products with latest available technologies.

Passage – 3

My comrade and I had been quartered in Jamaica, and from there we had been drafted off to the British settlement of Belize, lying away West and North of the Mosquito coast. At Belize there had been great alarm of one cruel gang of pirates (there were always more pirates than enough in those Caribbean Seas), and as they got the better of our English cruisers by running into out-of-the-way creeks and shallows, and taking the land when they were hotly pressed, the governor of Belize had received orders from home to keep a sharp look-out for them along shore. Now, there was an armed sloop came once a year from Port Royal, Jamaica, to the Island, laden with all manner of necessaries, to eat, and to drink, and to wear, and to use in various ways; and it was aboard of that sloop which had touched at Belize, that I was standing, leaning over the bulwarks.

The Island was occupied by a very small English colony. It had been given the name of Silver-Store. The reason of its being so called, was, that the English colony owned and worked a silver-mine over on the mainland, in Honduras, and used this Island as a safe and convenient place to store their silver in, until it was annually fetched away by the sloop. It was brought down from the mine to the coast on the backs of mules, attended by friendly local people and guarded by white men; from thence it was conveyed over to Silver-Store, when the weather was fair, in the canoes of that country; from Silver-Store, it was carried to Jamaica by the armed sloop once a-year, as I have already mentioned; from Jamaica, it went, of course, all over the world.

How I came to be aboard the armed sloop, is easily told. Four-and-twenty marines under command of a lieutenant – that officer's name was Linderwood – had been told off at Belize, to proceed to Silver-Store, in aid of boats and seamen stationed there for the chase of the Pirates. The Island was considered a good post of observation against the pirates, both by land and sea; neither the pirate ship nor yet her boats had been seen by any of us, but they had been so much heard of, that the reinforcement was sent. Of that party, I was one. It included a corporal and a sergeant. Charker was corporal, and the sergeant's name was Drooce. He was the most tyrannical non-commissioned officer in His Majesty's service.

The night came on, soon after I had the foregoing words with Charker. All the wonderful bright colours went out of the sea and sky in a few minutes, and all the stars in the Heavens seemed to shine out together, and to look down at themselves in the sea, over one another's shoulders, millions deep.

Next morning, we cast anchor off the Island. There was a snug harbour within a little reef; there was a sandy beach; there were cocoa-nut trees with high straight stems, quite bare, and foliage at the top like plumes of magnificent green feathers; there were all the objects that are usually seen in those parts, and I am not going to describe them, having something else to tell about.

Great rejoicings, to be sure, were made on our arrival. All the flags in the place were hoisted, all the guns in the place were fired, and all the people in the place came down to look at us. One of the local people had come off outside the reef, to pilot us in, and remained on board after we had let go our anchor.

My officer, Lieutenant Linderwood, was as ill as the captain of the sloop, and was carried ashore, too. They were both young men of about my age, who had been delicate in the West India climate. I thought I was much fitter for the work than they were, and that if all of us had our deserts, I should be both of them rolled into one. (It may be imagined what sort of an officer of marines I should have made, without the power of reading a written order. And as to any knowledge how to command the sloop--Lord! I should have sunk her in a quarter of an hour!)

However, such were my reflections; and when we men were ashore and dismissed, I strolled about the place along with Charker, making my observations in a similar spirit.

It was a pretty place; in all its arrangements partly South American and partly English, and very agreeable to look at on that account, being like a bit of home that had got chipped off and had floated away to that spot, accommodating itself to circumstances as it drifted along. The huts of the local people, to the number of five-and-twenty, perhaps, were down by the beach to the left of the anchorage. On the right was a sort of barrack, with a South American Flag and the Union Jack, fling from the same staff, where the little English colony could all come together, if they saw occasion. It was a walled square of building, with a sort of pleasure-ground inside, and inside that again a sunken block like a powder magazine, with a little square trench round it, and steps down to the door.

Charker and I were looking in at the gate, which was not guarded; and I had said to Charker, in reference to the bit like a powder magazine, "That's where they keep the silver you see;" and Charker had said to me, after thinking it over, "And silver ain't gold. Is it, Gill?"

40. Find out the FALSE statement:

(a) According to the passage, the silver that was being stored in the place where the author went to was being mined in Honduras.

(b) The narrator noted that the silver was being transported from the mine to the coast on the backs of mules, after which it was being sent to Jamaica in a sloop, from where it was reaching various destinations.

(c) Although the sea-voyage near Belize was being threatened by the presence of one notorious pirate fleet, the captain of the patrolling ship was accompanied by less than thirty soldiers.

(d) The Island the author talks here about was considered to be a good point for surveillance against the pirates both by land and sea.

41. Find out the TRUE statement:

(a) During the time of the narration, the total number of pirates at Belize was much more than the same in the Caribbean Seas.

(b) From the accounts presented here, when the narrator of the passage made the journey he already happened to be an experienced sailor with considerable navigating experiences.

(c) The author and his friends used to consider Drooce as the most authoritarian non-commissioned officer in Her Majesty's service.

(d) While walking with Charker, the narrator came across a barrack like structure where all the English settlers could assemble and stay together. If there was any necessity for doing so.

42. Find out the TRUE statement:

(a) The author was initially staying in Jamaica, which is located in the West and North of the Mosquito coast.

(b) A casual review of the place by the narrator revealed that the store for keeping the silver was heavily guarded, fearing a possible pirate attack anytime.

(c) The narrator and his companion noticed the South American Flag and the Union Jack flying on the port office.

(d) When the ship entered the harbour, both it's Captain and Lieutenant Linderwood was unwell as the West Indian climate was not suiting them.

43. Mark the FALSE statement:

   (a) It was being difficult to capture the pirates because they either used to hide in uncommon waters whenever the patrolling ships were pursuing them or used to disembark and flee whenever severely chased.

   (b) The local canoes were employed by the miners to bring the silver from the coast to the island during favourable climatic condition.

   (c) The lifestyle of the island was no exactly British as it had to adjust itself with the local South American culture, but the same seemed quite delightful for the narrators and his company.

   (d) When Corporal Charker and Sergeant Gill were walking around the harbour, they noticed that the size of the settlement of the local people was not very large.

2010-12

Directions for questions 44 – 58: Read carefully the four passages that follow and answer the questions given at the end of each passage:

Passage I

The most important task is revitalizing the institution of independent directors. The independent directors of a company should be faithful fiduciaries protecting, the long-term interests of shareholders while ensuring fairness to employees, investors, customers, regulators, the government of the land and society. Unfortunately, very often, directors are chosen based on friendship and, sadly, pliability. Today, unfortunately, in the majority of cases, independence is only true on paper.

The need of the hour is to strengthen the independence of the board. We have to put in place stringent standards for the independence of directors. The board should adopt global standards for director-independence, and should disclose how each independent director meets these standards. It is desirable to have a comprehensive report showing the names of the company employees or fellow board members who are related to each director on the board. This report should accompany the annual report of all listed companies.

Another important step is to regularly assess the board members for performance. The assessment should focus on issues like competence, preparation, participation and contribution. Ideally, this evaluation should be performed by a third party. Underperforming directors should be allowed to leave at the end of their term in a gentle manner so that they do not lose face. Rather than being the rubber stamp of a company's management policies, the board should become a true, active partner of the management. For this, independent directors should be trained in their roles and responsibilities. Independent directors should be trained on the business model and risk model of the company, on the governance practices, and the responsibilities of the various committees of the board of the company. The board members should interact frequently with executives to understand operational issues. As part of the board meeting agenda, the independent directors should have a meeting among themselves without the management being present.

The independent board members should periodically review the performance of the company's CEO, the internal directors and the senior management. This has to be based on clearly defined objective criteria, and these criteria should be known to the CEO and other executive directors well before the start of the evaluation period. Moreover, there should be a clearly laid down procedure for communicating the board's review to the CEO and his/her team of executive directors. Managerial remuneration should be based on such reviews.

Additionally, senior management compensation should be determined by the board in a manner that is fair to all stakeholders. We have to look at three important criteria in deciding managerial remuneration-fairness, accountability and transparency. Fairness of compensation is determined by how employees and investors react to the compensation of the CEO. Accountability is enhanced by splitting the total compensation into a small fixed component and a large variable component. In other words, the CEO, other executive directors and the senior management should rise or fall with the fortunes of the company. The variable component should be linked to achieving the long-term objectives of the firm. Senior management compensation should be reviewed by the compensation committee of the board consisting of only the independent directors. This should be approved by the shareholders. It is important that no member of the internal management has a say in the compensation of the CEO, the internal board members or the senior management.

The SEBI regulations and the CII code of conduct have been very helpful in enhancing the level of accountability of independent directors. The independent directors should decide voluntarily how they want to contribute to the company. Their performance should be appraised through a peer evaluation process. Ideally, the compensation committee should decide on the compensation of each independent director based on such a performance appraisal.

Auditing is another major area that needs reforms for effective corporate governance. An audit is the independent examination of financial transactions of any entity to provide assurance to shareholders and other stakeholders that the financial statements are free of material misstatement. Auditors are qualified professionals appointed by the shareholders to report on the reliability of financial statements prepared by the management. Financial markets look to the auditor's report for an independent opinion on the financial and risk situation of a company. We have to separate such auditing from other services. For a truly independent opinion, the auditing firm should not provide services that are perceived to be materially in conflict with the role of the auditor. These include investigations, consulting advice, subcontracting of operational activities normally undertaken by the management, due diligence on potential acquisitions or investments, advice on deal structuring, designing/implementing IT systems, bookkeeping, valuations and executive recruitment. Any departure from this practice should be approved by the audit committee in advance. Further, information on any such exceptions must be disclosed in the company's quarterly and annual reports.

To ensure the integrity of the audit team, it is desirable to rotate auditor partners. The lead audit partner and the audit partner responsible for reviewing a company's audit must be rotated at least once every three to five years. This eliminates the possibility of the lead auditor and the company management getting into the kind of close, cozy relationship that results in lower objectivity in audit opinions. Further, a registered auditor should not audit a company if, during the year preceding the start of the audit, the company's CEO, CFO or chief accounting officer was associated with the auditing firm. It is best that members of the audit teams are prohibited from taking up employment in the audited corporations for at least a year after they have stopped being members of the audit team.

A competent audit committee is essential to effectively oversee the financial accounting and reporting process. Hence, each member of the audit committee must be 'financially literate', Further, at least one member of the audit committee, preferably the chairman, should be a financial expert-a person who has an understanding of financial statements and accounting rules, and has experience in auditing. The audit committee should establish procedures for the treatment of complaints received through anonymous submission by employees and whistleblowers. These complaints may be regarding questionable accounting or auditing issues, any harassment to an employee or any unethical practice in the company. The whistleblowers must be protected.

Any related-party transaction should require prior approval by the audit committee, the full board and the shareholders if it is material. Related parties are those that are able to control or exercise significant influence. These include: parent-subsidiary relationships; entities under common control; individuals who, through ownership, have significant influence over the enterprise and close members of their families; and key management personnel.

Accounting standards provide a framework for preparation and presentation of financial statements and assist auditors in forming an opinion on the financial statements. However, today, accounting standards are issued by bodies comprising primarily of accountants. Therefore, accounting standards do not always keep pace with changes in the business environment. Hence, the accounting standards-setting body should include members drawn from the industry, the profession and regulatory bodies. This body should be independently funded.

Currently, an independent oversight of the accounting profession does not exist. Hence, an independent body should be constituted to oversee the functioning of auditors for independence, the quality of audit and professional competence. This body should comprise a majority of non-practicing accountants to ensure independent oversight. To avoid any bias, the chairman of this body should not have practiced as an accountant during the preceding five years. Auditors of all public companies must register with this body. It should enforce compliance with the laws by auditors and should mandate that auditors must maintain audit working papers for at least seven years.

To ensure the materiality of information, the CEO and CFO of the company should certify annual and quarterly reports. They should certify that the information in the reports fairly presents the financial condition and results of operations of the company, and that all material facts have been disclosed. Further, CEOs and CFOs should certify that they have established internal controls to ensure that all information relating to the operations of the company is freely available to the auditors and the audit committee. They should also certify that they have evaluated the effectiveness of these controls within ninety days prior to the report. False certifications by the CEO and CFO should be subject to significant criminal penalties (fines and imprisonment, if willful and knowing). If a company is required to restate its reports due to material non-compliance with the laws, the CEO and CFO must face severe punishment including loss of job and forfeiting bonuses or equity-based compensation received during the twelve months following the filing.

44. The problem with the independent directors has been that:

   I.   Their selection has been based upon their compatibility with the company management

   II.   There has been lack of proper training and development to improve their skill set

   III.   Their independent views have often come in conflict with the views of company management. This has hindered the company's decision-making process

   IV.   Stringent standards for independent directors have been lacking

   (a) I and II only   (b) I, II, and III only

   (c) II. II, and IV only   (d) I, II, and IV only

45. Which of the following, according to author, does not have an impact on effective corporate governance?

(a) Increased role and importance of independent directors

(b) Increased compensation to independent directors

(c) Not hiring audit firms for other services

(d) Stringent monitoring and control of related party transactions

46. To improve the quality and reliability of the information reported in the financial statements:

I. Accounting standards should keep pace with the dynamic business environment

II. There should be a body of internal auditors to oversee the functioning of external auditors

III. Reports should be certified by key company officials

IV. Accounting standards should be set by a body comprising of practicing accountants only and this body should be funded from a corpus built up from the contributions made by the companies

(a) I, and II   (b) II, and III

(c) I, and III   (d) I, III, and IV

47. Which of the following may not help in improving the accountability of management to the shareholders?

(a) A third party assessment of the performance of independent directors

(b) Rotation of audit partner

(c) Increasing the fixed component in the salary structure of the management

(d) Laying down a proper procedure for handling complaints regarding unethical practices

48. The author of the passage does not advocate:

(a) Increased activism of independent directors

(b) Measures to improve the independence of auditors

(c) Framing the accounting standards in the light of changing business conditions

(d) Active intervention by the regulators in the day-to-day functioning of the company

Passage II

I suggest that the essential character of the trade cycle and, especially, the regularity of time-sequence and of duration which justifies us in calling it a cycle, is mainly due to the way in which the marginal efficiency of capital fluctuates. The trade cycle is best regarded, I think, as being occasioned by a cyclical change in the marginal efficiency of capital, though complicated and often aggravated by associated changes in the other significant short period variables of the economic system.

By a cyclical movement we mean that as the system progresses in, e.g. the upward direction, the forces propelling it upwards at first gather force and have a cumulative effect on one another but gradually lose their strength until at a certain point they tend to be replaced by forces operating in the opposite direction; which in turn gather force for a time and accentuate one another, until they too, having reached their maximum development, wane and give place to their opposite. We do not, however, merely mean by a cyclical movement that upward and downward tendencies, once started, do not persist for ever in the same direction but are ultimately reversed. We mean also that there is some recognizable degree of regularity in the time-sequence and duration of the upward and downward movements. There is, however, another characteristic of what we call the trade cycle which our explanation must cover if it is to be adequate; namely, the phenomenon of the crisis — the fact that the substitution of a downward for an upward tendency often takes place suddenly and violently, whereas there is, as a rule, no such sharp turning-point when an upward is substituted for a downward tendency. Any fluctuation in investment not offset by a corresponding change in the propensity to consume will, of course, result in a fluctuation in employment. Since, therefore, the volume of investment is subject to highly complex influences, it is highly improbable that all fluctuations either in investment itself or in the marginal efficiency of capital will be of a cyclical character.

We have seen above that the marginal efficiency of capital depends, not only on the existing abundance or scarcity of capital-goods and the current cost of production of capital-goods, but also on current expectations as to the future yield of capital-goods. In the case of durable assets it is, therefore, natural and reasonable that expectations of the future should play a dominant part in determining the scale on which new investment is deemed advisable. But, as we have seen, the basis for such expectations is very precarious. Being based on shifting and unreliable evidence, they are subject to sudden and violent changes. Now, we have been accustomed in explaining the 'crisis' to lay stress on the rising tendency of the rate of interest under the influence of the increased demand for money both for trade and speculative purposes. At times this factor may certainly play an aggravating and, occasionally perhaps, an initiating part. But I suggest that a more typical, and often the predominant, explanation of the crisis is, not primarily a rise in the rate of interest, but a sudden collapse in the marginal efficiency of capital. The later stages of the boom are characterized by optimistic expectations as to the future yield of capital goods sufficiently strong to offset their growing abundance and their rising costs of production and, probably, a rise in the rate of interest also. It is of the nature of organized investment markets, under the influence of purchasers largely ignorant of what they are buying and of speculators who are more concerned with forecasting the next shift of market sentiment than with a reasonable estimate of the future yield of capital-assets, that, when disillusion falls upon an over-optimistic and over-bought market, it should fall with sudden and even catastrophic force. Moreover, the dismay and uncertainty as to the future which accompanies a collapse in the marginal efficiency of capital naturally precipitates a sharp increase in liquidity-preference and hence a rise in the rate of interest.

Thus the fact that a collapse in the marginal efficiency of capital tends to be associated with a rise in the rate of interest may seriously aggravate the decline in investment. But the essence of the situation is to be found, nevertheless, in the collapse in the marginal efficiency of capital, particularly in the case of those types of capital which have been contributing most to the previous phase of heavy new investment. Liquidity preference, except those manifestations of it which are associated with increasing trade and speculation, does not increase until after the collapse in the marginal efficiency of capital. It is this, indeed, which renders the slump so intractable.

49. Which of the following does not describe the features of cyclical movement?

    (a) There is a cyclical change in the marginal efficiency of capital

    (b) The movement once starts in upward or downward direction does not get reversed

    (c) The time pattern and the duration of economic movements are recognizable

    (d) It is caused by the economic forces working in opposite direction

50. Marginal efficiency of capital does not depend on which of the following factors?

    (a) Demand and supply of capital goods

    (b) Cost of production of capital goods

    (c) Expectations regarding future return from capital goods

    (d) Availability of capital

51. Which of the following explains the phenomenon of crisis?

    I. A sudden collapse in the marginal efficiency of capital

    II. Increase in the rate of interest causing the decline in investments

    III. A sudden and violent substitution of upward movement by a downward tendency

    IV. Decline in the liquidity preference of the investors

    (a) I & II   (b) I, II, and III

    (c) I, II, and IV   (d) II, III, and IV

Passage III

The broad scientific understanding today is that our planet is experiencing a warming trend-over and above natural and normal variations-that is almost certainly due to human activities associated with large-scale manufacturing. The process began in the late 1700s with the Industrial Revolution, when manual labor, horsepower, and water power began to be replaced by or enhanced by machines. This revolution, over time, shifted Britain, Europe, and eventually North America from largely agricultural and trading societies to manufacturing ones, relying on machinery and engines rather than tools and animals.

The Industrial Revolution was at heart a revolution in the use of energy and power. Its beginning is usually dated to the advent of the steam engine, which was based on the conversion of chemical energy in wood or coal to thermal energy and then to mechanical work-primarily the powering of industrial machinery and steam locomotives. Coal eventually supplanted wood because, pound for pound, coal contains twice as much energy as wood (measured in BTUs, or British thermal units, per pound) and because its use helped to save what was left of the world's temperate forests. Coal was used to produce heat that went directly into industrial processes, including metallurgy, and to warm buildings, as well as to power steam engines. When crude oil came along in the mid 1800s, still a couple of decades before electricity, it was burned, in the form of kerosene, in lamps to make light-replacing whale oil, It was also used to provide heat for buildings and in manufacturing processes, and as a fuel for engines used in industry and propulsion.

In short, one can say that the main forms in which humans need and use energy are for light, heat, mechanical work and motive power, and electricity-which can be used to provide any of the other three, as well as to do things that none of those three can do, such as electronic communications and information processing. Since the Industrial Revolution, all these energy functions have been powered primarily, but not exclusively, by fossil fuels that emit carbon dioxide (CO_2),

To put it another way, the Industrial Revolution gave a whole new prominence to what Rochelle Lefkowitz, president of Pro-Media Communications and an energy buff, calls "fuels from hell" – coal, oil, and natural gas. All these fuels from hell come from underground, are exhaustible, and emit CO_2 and other pollutants when they are burned for transportation, heating, and industrial use. These fuels are in contrast to what Lefkowitz calls "fuels from heaven" – wind, hydroelectric, tidal, biomass, and solar power. These all come from above ground, are endlessly renewable, and produce no harmful emissions.

Meanwhile, industrialization promoted urbanization, and urbanization eventually gave birth to suburbanization. This trend, which was repeated across America, nurtured the development of the American car culture, the building of a national highway system, and a mushrooming of suburbs around American cities, which rewove the fabric of American life. Many other developed and developing countries followed the American model, with all its upsides and downsides. The result is that today we have suburbs and ribbons of highways that run in, out, and around not only America's major cities, but China's, India's and South America's as well. And as these urban areas attract more people, the sprawl extends in every direction.

All the coal, oil, and natural gas inputs for the new economic model seemed relatively cheap, relatively inexhaustible, and relatively harmless-or at least relatively easy to clean up afterward. So there wasn't much to stop the juggernaut of more people and more development and more concrete and more buildings and more cars and more coal, oil, and gas needed to build and power them. Summing it all up, Andy Karsner, the Department of Energy's assistant secretary for energy efficiency and renewable energy, once said to me: "We built a really inefficient environment with the greatest efficiency ever known to man."

Beginning in the second half of the twentieth century, a scientific understanding began to emerge that an excessive accumulation of largely invisible pollutants-called greenhouse gases –was affecting the climate. The buildup of these greenhouse gases had been under way since the start of the Industrial Revolution in a place we could not see and in a form we could not touch or smell. These green house gases, primarily carbon dioxide emitted from human industrial, residential, and transportation sources, were not piling up along roadsides or in rivers, in cans or empty bottles, but, rather, above our heads, in the earth's atmosphere. If the earth's atmosphere was like a blanket that helped to regulate the planet's temperature, the CO_2 buildup was having the effect of thickening that blanket and making the globe warmer.

Those bags of CO_2 from our cars float up and stay in the atmosphere along with bags of CO_2 from power plants burning coal, oil, and gas, and bags of CO_2 released from the burning and clearing of forest, which releases all the carbon stored in trees, plants, and soil. In fact, many people don't realize that deforestation in places like Indonesia and Brazil is responsible for more CO_2 than all the world's cars, trucks, planes, ships, and trains combined – that is, about 20 percent of all global emissions. And when we're not tossing bags of carbon dioxide into the atmosphere, we're throwing up other greenhouse gases, like methane (CH_4) released from rice framing, petroleum drilling, coal mining, animal defecation, solid waste landfill sites, and yes, even from cattle belching.

Cattle belching? That's right-the striking thing about greenhouse gases is the diversity of sources that emit them. A herd of cattle belching can be worse than a

highway full of Hummers. Livestock gas is very high in methane, which, like CO2, is colorless and odorless. And like CO_2, methane is one of those green house gases that, once released into the atmosphere, also absorb heat radiating from the earth's surface. "Molecule for molecule, methane's heat-trapping power in the atmosphere is twenty-one times stronger than carbon dioxide, the most abundant greenhouse gas," reported Science World (January 21, 2002). "With 1.3 billion cows belching almost constantly around the world (100 million in the United States alone). it's no surprise that methane released by livestock is one of the chief global sources of the gas, according to the U.S. Environmental Protection Agency … 'It's part of their normal digestion process,' says Tom Wirth of the EPA. 'When they chew their cud, they regurgitate [spit up] some food to rechew it, and all this gas comes out.' The average cow expels 600 liters of methane a day, climate researchers report."

What is the precise scientific relationship between these expanded greenhouse gas emissions and global warming? Experts at the Pew Center on Climate Change offer a handy summary in their report "Climate Change 101." Global average temperatures, notes the Pew study, "have experienced natural shifts throughout human history. For example, the climate of the Northern Hemisphere varied from a relatively warm period between the eleventh and fifteenth centuries to a period of cooler temperatures between the seventeenth century and the middle of the nineteenth century. However, scientists studying the rapid rise in global temperatures during the late twentieth century say that natural variability cannot account for what is happening now." The new factor is the human factor – our vastly increased emissions of carbon dioxide and other greenhouse gases from the burning of fossil fuels such as coal and oil, as well as from deforestation, large-scale cattle-grazing, agriculture, and industrialization.

"Scientists refer to what has been happening in the earth's atmosphere over the past century as the 'enhanced greenhouse effect,'" notes the Pew study. By pumping man-made greenhouse gases into the atmosphere, human are altering the process by which naturally occurring greenhouse gases, because of their unique molecular structure, trap the sun's heat near the earth's surface before that heat radiates back into space.

"The greenhouse effect keeps the earth warm and habitable; without it, the earth's surface would be about 60 degrees Fahrenheit colder on average. Since the average temperature of the earth is about 45 degrees Fahrenheit, the natural greenhouse effect is clearly a good thing. But the enhanced greenhouse effect means even more of the sun's heat is trapped, causing global temperatures to rise. Among the many scientific studies providing clear evidence that an enhanced greenhouse effect is under way was a 2005 report from NASA's Goddard Institute for Space Studies, Using satellites, data from buoys, and computer models to study the earth's oceans, scientists concluded that more energy is being absorbed from the sun than is emitted back to space, throwing the earth's energy out of balance and warming the globe."

52. Which of the following statements is correct?

    I.   Green house gases are responsible for global warming. They should be eliminated to save the planet

    II. CO_2 is the most dangerous of the greenhouse gases. Reduction in the release of CO_2 would surely bring down the temperature

    III.   The greenhouse effect could be traced back to the industrial revolution. But the current development and the patterns of life have enhanced their emissions

    IV.   Deforestation has been one of the biggest factors contributing to the emission of greenhouse gases

Choose the correct options:

(a) I and III   (b) II and III

(c) II, III, and IV   (d) III, and IV

53. Which of the following statements is incorrect?

(a) Natural and controlled greenhouse effect is good for earth.

(b) As a measure to check global warming, prevention of destruction of forests needs to be given priority over reduction in fuel emission.

(c) Greenhouse gases trap the sun's heat from radiating back into the space making the earth surface warmer.

(d) It is for the first time in human evolution that the global temperatures have started to witness a shift.

54. Increasing warming of earth has been due to:

    I.   Increased manual intervention in the manufacturing process.

    II.   The fallout of mechanization of production.

    III.   Industrial revolution.

    IV.   Over reliance on non-replenishible energy sources.

Choose the correct option:

(a) I, II, and IV   (b) I, III, and IV

(c) I, II, III, and IV   (d) II, III, and IV

55. Which of the following, according to the passage are the features of "fuels from heaven"?

    I.   Replenishability   II. Storability

    III. Cost-effectiveness   IV. Harmlessness

Choose the correct option:

(a) I and II   (b) II and III

(c) III and IV   (d) I and IV

Passage IV

"All raw sugar comes to us this way. You see, it is about the color of maple or brown sugar, but it is not nearly so pure, for it has a great deal of dirt mixed with it when we first get it."

"Where does it come from?" inquired Bob.

"Largely from the plantations of Cuba and Porto Rico. Toward the end of the year we also get raw sugar from Java, and by the time this is refined and ready for the market the new crop from the West Indies comes along. In addition to this we get consignments from the Philippine Islands, the Hawaiian Islands, South America, Formosa, and Egypt. I suppose it is quite unnecessary to tell you young men anything of how the cane is grown; of course you know all that."

"I don't believe we do, except in a general way," Bob admitted honestly. "I am ashamed to be so green about a thing at which Dad has been working for years. I don't know why I never asked about it before. I guess I never was interested. I simply took it for granted."

"That's the way with most of us," was the superintendent's kindly answer. "We accept many things in the world without actually knowing much about them, and it is not until something brings our ignorance before us that we take the pains to focus our attention and learn about them. So do not be ashamed that you do know about sugar raising; I didn't when I was your age. Suppose, then, I give you a little idea of what happens before this raw sugar can come to us."

"I wish you would," exclaimed both boys in a breath.

"Probably in your school geographies you have seen pictures of sugar-cane and know that it is a tall perennial not unlike our Indian corn in appearance; it has broad, flat leaves that sometimes measure as many as three feet in length, and often the stalk itself is twenty feet high. This stalk is joined like a bamboo pole, the joints being about three inches apart near the roots and increasing in distance the higher one gets from the ground."

"How do they plant it?" Bob asked.

"It can be planted from seed, but this method takes much time and patience; the usual way is to plant it from cuttings, or slips. The first growth from these cuttings is called plant cane' after these are taken off the roots send out rations or shoots from which the crop of one or two years, and sometimes longer, is taken. If the soil is not rich and moist replanting is more frequently necessary and it places like Louisiana, where there is annual frost, planting must be done each year. When the cane is ripe it is cut and brought from the field to a central sugar mill, where heavy iron rollers crush from it all the juice. This liquid drips through into troughs from which it is carried to evaporators where the water portion of the sap is eliminated and the juice left; you would be surprised if you were to see this liquid. It looks like nothing so much as the soapy, bluish-gray dish-water that is left in the pan after the dishes have been washed."

"A tempting picture!" Van exclaimed.

"I know it. Sugar isn't very attractive during its process of preparation," agreed Mr. Hennessey. "The sweet liquid left after the water has been extracted is then poured into vacuum pans to be boiled until the crystals form in it, after which it is put into whirling machines, called centrifugal machines that separate the dry sugar from the syrup with which it is mixed. This syrup is latter boiled into molasses. The sugar is then dried and packed in the burlap sacks such as you see here, or in hogsheads, and shipped to refineries to be cleansed and whitened."

"Isn't any of the sugar refined in the places where it grows?" queried Bob.

"Practically none. Large refining plants are too expensive to be erected everywhere; it therefore seems better that they should be build in our large cities, where the shipping facilities are good not only for receiving sugar in its raw state but for distributing it after it has been refined and is ready for sale. Here, too, machinery can more easily be bought and the business handled with less difficulty."

56. Which one of the following is not a essential condition for setting up refining plants?

   (a) Facilities for transportation of machinery

   (b) Facilities for import of raw material

   (c) Facilities for transportation of finished products

   (d) Proximity to the raw material sources

57. Which of the following is the correct sequence of sugar preparation process?

   (a) Cutting – Crushing – Evaporation – Boiling – Whirling.

   (b) Boiling – Crushing – Evaporation – Whirling – Cutting

   (c) Cutting – Boiling – Evaporation – Crushing – Whirling

   (d) Whirling – Crushing – Boiling – Evaporation – Cutting.

58. Which of the following statements, as per the paragraph, is incorrect?

   (a) Sugar in its raw form is brownish in colour due to the presence of dirt

   (b) After evaporation, cane juice looks bluish-gray in colour

   (c) Molasses is obtained as a bye-product from the process of sugar production

   (d) Cane plantation and sugar production process is widely and equally spread across the country.

2011-13

Directions for questions 59 to 73: Read the passage carefully and answer the questions given at the end of each passage.

Passage -1

Kodak decided that traditional film and prints would continue to dominate through the 1980s and that photo finishers, film retailers, and, of course, Kodak itself could expect to continue to occupy their long-held positions until 1990. Kodak was right and wrong. The quality of digital cameras greatly improved. Prices plunged because the cameras generally followed Moore's Law, the famous prediction by Intel co-founder Gordon Moore in the 1960s that the cost of a unit of computing power would fall by 50 percent every eighteen to twenty-four months. Cameras began to be equipped with what the industry called removable media those little cards that hold the pictures - so pictures were easier to print or to move to other devices, such as computers. Printers improved. Their costs dropped, too. The Internet caught the popular imagination, and people began e-mailing each other pictures rather than print them. Kodak did little to ready itself for the onslaught of digital technology because it consistently tried to hold on to the profits from its old technology and underestimated the speed with which the new would take hold. Kodak decided it could use digital technology to enhance film, rather than replace it. Instead of preparing for the digital world, Kodak headed off in a direction that cost it dearly. In 1988, Kodak bought Sterling Drug for $5.1 billion. Kodak had decided it was really a chemicals business, not a photography company. So, Kodak reasoned, it should move into adjacent chemical markets, such as drugs. Well, chemically treated photo paper really isn't that similar to hormonal agents and cardiovascular drugs. The customers are different. The delivery channels are different. Kodak lost its shirt. It sold Sterling in pieces in 1994 for about half the original purchase price. George M. C. Fisher was the new CEO of Kodak in 1993. Fisher's solution was to hold on to the film business as long as possible, while adding a technological veneer to it. For instance, he introduced the Advantix Preview camera, a hybrid of digital and film technology. Users took pictures the way they always had, and the images were captured on film. Kodak spent more than $500 million developing Advantix, which flopped.

Fisher also tried to move Kodak's traditional retail photo-processing systems into digital world and in this regard installed tens of thousands of image magic kiosks. These kiosks came just as numerous companies introduced inexpensive, high-quality photo printers that people could use at home, which, in fact, is where customers preferred to view their images and fiddle with them. Fisher also tried to insert Kodak as an intermediary in the process of sharing images electronically. He formed partnerships that let customers receive electronic versions of their photos bye-mail and gave them access to kiosks that let them manipulate and reproduce old photographs. You don't need Kodak to upload photos to your computer and e-mail them. Fisher also formed a partnership with AOL called "You've Got Pictures." Customers would have their film developed and posted online, where friends and family could view them. Customers would pay AOL $7 for this privilege, on top of the $9 paid for photo processing. However sites like. Snapfish were allowing pictures to be posted online free. Fisher promised early on, that Kodak's digital-photography business would be profitable by 1997. It wasn't. In 1997 Philippe Kahn lead the advent of cell phone camera. With the cell phone camera market growth Kodak didn't just lose out on more prints. The whole industry lost out on sales of digital cameras, because they became just a feature that was given away free on cell phones. Soon cameras became a free feature on many personal computers, too. What had been so profitable for Kodak for so long-capturing images and displaying them-was going to become essentially free.

In 1999 Fisher resigned and Carp became the new CEO. In 2000, Carp's first year as CEO, profit was about flat, at $1.41 billion. Carp, too, retired early, at age fifty-seven. Carp had pursued Fisher's basic strategy of "enhancing" the film business to make it last as long as possible, while trying to figure out some way to get recurring revenue from the filmless, digital world. But the temporizing didn't work any better for Carp than it had for Fisher. Kodak talked, for instance, about getting customers to digitize and upload to the Internet more of the 300 million rolls of film that Kodak processed annually, as of 2000. Instead, customers increasingly skipped the film part. In 2002, sales of digital cameras in the United States passed those of traditional cameras-even though Kodak in the mid-1990s had projected that it would take twenty years for digital technology to eclipse film. The move to digital in the 2000s happened so fast that, in 2004, Kodak introduced a film camera that won a "camera of the year" ward, yet was discontinued by the time Kodak collected the award. Kodak staked out a position as one of the major sellers of digital cameras, but being "one of" is a lot different from owning 70 percent to 80 percent of a market, as Kodak had with film, chemicals, and processing. In 2002 competition in the digital market was so intense that Kodak lost 75 percent of its stock-market value over the past decade, falling to a level about half of what it was when the reporter suggested to Carp that he might sell the company. As of 2005, Kodak employed less than a third of the number who worked for it twenty years earlier. To see what might have been, look at Kodak's principal competitors in the film and paper markets. Agfa temporized on digital technology, then sold its film and paper business to private-equity investors in 2004. The business went into

bankruptcy proceedings the following year, but that wasn't Agfa's problem. It had cashed out at a halfway reasonable price.

59. As per the passage which of the following statement truly reflects the real theme of the passage?

   (a) Moore's law predicted that cost per unit of computing power would exhibit a standard deviation of 25% per annum.

   (b) Popularity of removable media and internet lead to high demand for computers.

   (c) Kodak managers were able to predict the flow of digital technology and their critical value drivers.

   (d) Kodak did not have a vision to plough back the profits from old technology to research and development in new technology.

60. Which of the following statements is not true

   I.   Kodak bought sterling drug as a strategic choice for a chemical business as it was already in the business of chemically treated photo paper

   II. The chemical business was in sync with the existing business of Kodak running across the customer segment, delivery channels and the regulatory environment

   III. Kodak committed a mistake by selling sterling in pieces at a loss of 50%.

   IV. Kodak's diversification attempt with purchase of sterling to strengthen its core business and shift to digital world was a shift from its strategic focus.

   (a) Only I & II   (b) Only II & III

   (c) Only III & IV   (d) Only I, II, III

61. Kodak lost a big piece of its market share to its competitors because of the following best explained reason.

   I.   When Carp became the CEO the digital Technology eclipsed film technology business and further Carp had been with the company for twenty nine years and had no background in technology.

   II. Carp in 2004 introduced a film camera that won camera of the year award, yet it was discontinued by the time Kodak collected the award.

   III. Kodak moved from traditional retail photo processing systems into digital word installing several thousands of image magic kiosks that failed to deliver real benefits to the customers.

   IV. Phillipe Kahn led the advent of cell phone camera and Kodak lost out on the print business and ability to share images became a free feature with no additional charge.

   (a) I & II   (b) II & III

   (c) I & IV   (d) III & IV

62. Arrange the given statements in the correct sequence as they appear in the passage.

I. Kodak lost to its competitors a big pie of its market share.

II. Kodak ventured into chemical business to strengthen its digital technology business.

III. Kodak downsized its workforce drastically.

IV. Kodak tied up with business firms for photo processing.

(a) I , II, III, IV
(b) III, IV, II, I
(c) II, IV, I, IIII
(d) I, III, II, IV

63. Match the following

1. Intel	a. Preview cameras that helped users to immediately see the pictures taken
2. Fisher	b. Photo processing, developing and positing online photos
3. AOL	c. Lead to insolvency of digital technology business
4. Agfa	d. Price of technology product reduces to half every year or two.

(a) 1-d, 2-a, 3-b, 4-c
(b) 1-a, 2-d, 3-c, 4-b
(c) 1-c, 2-b, 3-a, 4-d
(d) 1-d, 2-c, 3-a, 4-b

Passage - 2

People are continually enticed by such "hot" performance, even if it lasts for brief period. Because of this susceptibility, brokers or analysts who have had one or two stocks move up sharply, or technicians who call one turn correctly, are believed to have established a credible record and can readily find market followings. Likewise, an advisory service that is right for a brief time can beat its drums loudly. Elaine Garzarelli gained near immortality when she purportedly "called" the 1987 crash. Although, as the market strategist for Shearson Lehman, her forecast was never published in a research report, nor indeed communicated to its clients, she still received widespread recognition and publicity for this call, which was made in a short TV interview on CNBC. Still, her remark on CNBC that the Dow could drop sharply from its then 5300 level rocked and already nervous market on July 23, 1996. What had been a 40-point gain for the Dow turned into a 40-point loss, a good deal of which was attributed to her comments.

The truth is, market-letter writers have been wrong in their judgments far more often than they would like to remember. However, advisors understand that the public considers short-term results meaningful when they are, more often than not, simply change. Those in the public eye usually gain large numbers of new subscribers for being right by

random luck. Which brings us to another important probability error that falls under the broad rubric of representativeness. Amos Tversky and Daniel Kahneman call this one the "law of small numbers." The statistically valid "law of large numbers" states that large samples will usually be highly representative of the population from which they are drawn; for example, public opinion polls are fairly accurate because they draw on large and representative groups. The smaller the sample used, however (or the shorter the record), the more likely the findings are chance rather than meaningful. Yet the Tversky and Kahneman study showed that typical psychological or educational experimenters gamble their research theories on samples so small that the results have a very high probability of being chance. This is the same as gambling on the single good call of an advisor. The psychologists and educators are far too confident in the significance of results based on a few observations or a short period to time, even though they are trained in statistical techniques and are aware of the dangers.

Note how readily people over generalize the meaning of a small number of supporting facts. Limited statistical evidence seems to satisfy our intuition no matter how inadequate the depiction of reality. Sometimes the evidence we accept runs to the absurd. A good example of the major overemphasis on small numbers is the almost blind faith investors place in governmental economic releases on employment, industrial production, the consumers price index, the money supply, the leading economic indicators, etc. These statistics frequently trigger major stock- and bond-market reactions, particularly if the news is bad. Flash statistics, more times than not, are near worthless. Initial economic and Fed figures are revised significantly for weeks or months after their release, as new and "better" information flows in. Thus, an increase in the money supply can turn into a decrease, or a large drop in the leading indicators can change to a moderate increase. These revisions occur with such regularity you would think that investors, particularly pros, would treat them with the skepticism they deserve. Alas, the real world refuses to follow the textbooks. Experience notwithstanding, investors treat as gospel all authoritative-sounding releases that they think pinpoint the development of important trends. An example of how instant news threw investors into a tailspin occurred in July of 1996. Preliminary statistics indicated the economy was beginning to gain steam. The flash figures showed that GDP (gross domestic product) would rise at a 3% rate in the next several quarters, a rate higher than expected. Many people, convinced by these statistics that rising interest rates were imminent, bailed out of the stock market that month. To the end of that year, the GDP growth figures had been revised down significantly (unofficially, a minimum of a dozen times, and officially at least twice). The market rocketed ahead to new highs to August 1997, but a lot of investors had retreated to the sidelines on the preliminary bad news. The advice of a world champion chess player when asked how to avoid making a bad move. His answer: "Sit on your hands". But professional investors don't sit on their hands; they dance on tiptoe, ready to flit after the least particle of information as if it were a strongly documented trend. The law of small numbers, in such cases, results in decisions sometimes bordering on the inane. Tversky and Kahneman's findings, which have been repeatedly confirmed, are particularly important to our understanding of some stock market errors and lead to another rule that investors should follow.

64. Which statement does not reflect the true essence of the passage

   I.   Tversky and Kahneman understood that small representative groups bias the research theories to generalize results that can be categorized as meaningful result and people simplify the real impact of passable portray of reality by small number of supporting facts.

   II. Governmental economic releases on macroeconomic indicators fetch blind faith from investors who appropriately discount these announcements which are ideally reflected in the stock and bond market prices.

   III. Investors take into consideration myopic gain and make it meaningful investment choice and fail to see it as a chance of occurrence.

   IV. Irrational overreaction to key regulators expressions is same as intuitive statistician stumbling disastrously when unable to sustain spectacular performance.

   (a) Only I   (b) Only IV

   (c) II & III   (d) Only III

65. The author of the passage suggests the anomaly that leads to systematic errors in predicting future. Which of the following statement does not best describe the anomaly as suggested in the passage above.

   I.   The psychological pressures account for the anomalies just like soothsayers warning about the doomsday and natural disasters and market crashes.

   II. Contrary to several economic and financial theories investors are not good intuitive statistician, especially under difficult conditions and are unable to calculate the odds properly when making investments choices.

   III. Investors are swamped with information and they react to this avalanche of data by adopting shortcuts of rules of thumb rather than formally calculating odds of a given outcome.

   IV. The distortions produced by subjectively calculated probabilities are large, systematic and difficult to eliminate even when investors are fully aware of them.

   (a) Only I   (b) Only IV

   (c) I & III   (d) II & IV

66. "Tversky and Kahneman's findings… lead to another rule that investors should follow". Which rule is the author talking about?

   I.   Not to be influenced by short term and occasional record of a money manager, broker, analysts, or advisor, no matter how impressive.

   II. To accept cursory economic or investment news without significant substantiation but supported by statistical evidence even if limited in data sufficiency.

   III. In making decisions we become overly immersed in the details of a particular situation and consider all the outcomes of similar experience in our past.

   IV. None of the above,

   (a) Only IV   (b) Only I

   (c) Only III   (d) I, II & III

67. According to the passage which statement written below is farthest in explaining the meaning of the passage above?

   I.   Market letter writers have been wrong in their judgments many a times but they continue to express their opinion as dramatic predictions and well time call results in huge rewards to analysts, journalists and popular writers.

   II. Public opinion polls are fairly accurate because they are based on randomly selected diminutive representative groups and hence are more meaningful than intuitive statistics of an outcome.

   III. People generally limit the need for hefty statistical evidence as it satisfies their intuition without reflecting the reality.

   IV. None of the above.

   (a) Only IV

   (b) Only II

   (c) II & III

   (d) Only I

Passage 3

When people react to their experiences with particular authorities, those authorities and the organizations or institutions that they represent often benefit if the people involved begin with high levels of commitment to the organization or institution represented by the authorities. First, in his studies of people's attitudes toward political and legal institutions, Tyler found that attitudes after an experience with the institution were strongly affected by prior attitudes. Single experiences influence post-experience loyalty but certainly do not overwhelm the relationship between pre-experience and post-experience loyalty. Thus, the best predictor of loyalty after an experience is usually loyalty before that experience. Second, people with prior loyalty to the organization or institution judge their dealings with the organization's or institution's authorities to be fairer than do those with less prior loyalty, either because they are more fairly treated or because they interpret equivalent treatment as fairer.

Although high levels of prior organizational or institutional commitment are generally beneficial to the organization or institution, under certain conditions high levels of prior commitment may actually sow the seeds of reduced commitment. When previously committed individuals feel that they were treated unfavorably or unfairly during some experience with the organization or institution, they may show an especially sharp decline in commitment. Two studies were designed to test this hypothesis, which, if confirmed, would suggest that organizational or institutional commitment has risks, as well as benefits. At least three psychological models offer predictions of how individuals' reactions may vary as a function of (1) their prior level of commitment and (2) the favorability of the encounter with the organization or institution. Favorability of the encounter is determined by the outcome of the encounter and the fairness or appropriateness of the procedures used to allocate outcomes during the encounter. First, the instrumental prediction is that because people are mainly concerned with receiving desired outcomes from their encounters with organizations, changes in their level of commitment will depend primarily on the favorability of the encounter. Second, the assimilation prediction is that individuals' prior attitudes predispose them to react in a way that is consistent with their prior attitudes.

The third prediction, derived from the group-value model of justice, pertains to how people with high prior commitment will react when they feel that they have been treated unfavorably or unfairly during some encounter with the organization or institution. Fair treatment by the other party symbolizes to people that they are being dealt with in a dignified and respectful way, thereby bolstering their sense of self-identity and self-worth. However, people will become quite distressed and react quite negatively if they feel that they have been treated unfairly by the other party to the relationship. The group-value model suggests that people value the information they receive that helps them to define themselves and to view themselves favorably. According to the instrumental viewpoint, people are primarily concerned with the more material or tangible resources received from the relationship. Empirical support for the group-value model has implications for a variety of important issues, including the determinants of commitment, satisfaction, organizational citizenship, and rule following. Determinants of procedural fairness include structural or interpersonal factors. For example, structural determinants refer to such things as whether decisions were made by neutral, fact-finding authorities who used legitimate decision-making criteria. The primary purpose of the study was to examine the interactive effect of individuals (1) commitment to an organization or institution prior to some encounter and (2) perceptions of how fairly they were treated during the encounter, on the change in their level of commitment. A basic assumption of the group-value model is that people generally value their relationships with people, groups, organizations, and institutions and therefore value fair treatment from the other party to the relationship. Specifically, highly committed members should have especially negative reactions to feeling that they were treated unfairly, more so than (1) less-committed group members or (2) highly committed members who felt that they were fairly treated.

The prediction that people will react especially negatively when they previously felt highly committed but felt that they were treated unfairly also is consistent with the literature on psychological contracts. Rousseau suggested that, over time, the members of work organizations develop feelings of entitlement, i.e., perceived obligations that their employers have toward them. Those who are highly committed to the organization believe that they are fulfilling their contract obligations. However, if the organization acted unfairly, then highly committed individuals are likely to believe that the organization did not live up to its end of the bargain.

68. The hypothesis mentioned in passage tests atleast one of the following ideas.

    (a) People continue to show loyalty only if they were initially committed to the organization.

    (b) Our experiences influence post-experience loyalty but certainly underwhelm the relationship between pre-experience and post-experience loyalty.

    (c) Pre-experience commitment always has inverse relationship with the post-experience commitment.

    (d) None of these ideas are being tested by the hypothesis.

69. There is only one term in the left column which matches with the options given in the second column. Identify the correct pair from the following table:

a. Instrumental	1. Better outcome leads to more commitment.
b. Assimilation	2. Prior belief is instrumental in deciding about the post encounter commitment.
c. Group-value	3. Sense of value gets jeopardized that leads to negative attitude.
d. Institutional	4. Deals mainly with tangible outcomes.

(a) a-1 and 4
(b) b-3 and 4
(c) c-2 and 4
(d) d-1 only

70. For summarizing the passage, which of the following is most appropriate:

(a) The study explored how citizens' commitment to legal authorities changed as a function of their initial level of commitment and their perceptions of how fairly they were treated in their recent encounters with legal authorities.

(b) The influence of individuals' prior commitment to an institution on their reactions to the perceived fairness of decisions rendered by the institution was examined.

(c) Given the generally positive consequences to organizations of having committed employees, it may be that unfair managerial practices would begin to alienate the very employees that the organization would least wish to alienate.

(d) The passage aims at understanding how people define happiness and these definitions include instrumental view-points.

Passage 4

In the annals of investing, Warren Buffett stands alone. Starting from scratch, simply by picking stocks and companies for investment, Buffett amassed one of the epochal fortunes of the twentieth century. Over a period of four decades more than enough to iron out the effects of fortuitous rolls of the dice, Buffett outperformed the stock market, by a stunning margin and without taking undue risks or suffering a single losing year. Buffett did this in markets bullish and bearish and through economies fat and lean, from the Eisenhower years to Bill Clinton, from the 1950s to the 1990s, from saddle shoes and Vietnam to junk bonds and the information age. Over the broad sweep of postwar America, as the major stock averages advanced by 11 percent or so a year, Buffett racked up a compounded annual gain of 29.2 percent. The uniqueness of this achievement is more significant in that it was the fruit of old-fashioned, long-term investing. Wall Street's modern financiers got rich by exploiting their control of the public's money: their essential trick was to take in and sell out the public at opportune moments. Buffett shunned this game, as well as the more venal excesses for which Wall Street is deservedly famous. In effect, he rediscovered the art of pure capitalism, a cold-blooded sport, but a fair one. Buffett began his career, working out his study in Omaha in 1956. His grasp of simple verities gave rise to a drama that would recur throughout his life. Long before those pilgrimages to Omaha, long before Buffett had a record, he would stand in a corner at college parties, baby-faced and bright-eyed, holding forth on the universe as a dozen or two of his older, drunken fraternity brothers crowded around. A few years later, when these friends had metamorphosed into young associates starting out on Wall Street, the ritual was the same. Buffett, the youngest of the group, would plop himself in a big, broad club chair and expound on finance while the others sat at his feet. On Wall Street, his homespun manner made him a cult figure. Where finance was so forbiddingly complex, Buffett could explain it like a general-store clerk discussing the weather. He never forgot that underneath each stock and bond, no matter how arcane, there lay a tangible, ordinary business. Beneath the jargon of Wall Street, he seemed to unearth a street from small-town America. In such a complex age, what was stunning about Buffett was his applicability. Most of what Buffett did was imitable by the average person (this is why the multitudes flocked to Omaha). It is curious irony that as more Americans acquired an interest in investing. Wall Street became more complex and more forbidding than ever. Buffett was born in the midst of depression. The depression cast a long shadow on Americans, but the post war prosperity eclipsed it. Unlike the modern portfolio manager, whose mind-set is that of a trader, Buffett risked his capital on the long term growth of a few select businesses. In this, he resembled the magnates of a previous age, such as J P Morgan Sr.

As Jack Newfield wrote of Robel1 Kennedy, Buffett was not a hero, only a hope; not a myth, only a man. Despite his broad wit, he was strangely stunted. When he went to Paris, his only reaction was that he had no interest in sight-seeing and that the food was better in Omaha. His talent sprang from his unrivaled independence of mind and ability to focus on his work and shut out the world, yet those same qualities exacted a toll. Once, when Buffett was visiting the publisher Katharine Graham on Martha's Vineyard, a friend remarked on the beauty of the sunset. Buffett replied that he hadn't *focused* on it, as though it were necessary for him to exert a deliberate act of concentration to "focus" on a sunset. Even at his California beachfront vacation home, Buffett would work every day for weeks and not go near the water. Like other prodigies, he paid a price. Having been raised in a home with more than its share of demons, he lived within an emotional fortress. The few people who shared his office had no knowledge of the inner man, even after decades. Even his children could scarcely recall a time when he broke through his surface calm and showed some feeling. Though part of him is a showman or preacher, he is essentially a private person. Peter Lynch, the mutual-fund wizard, visited Buffett in the 1980s and was struck by the tranquility in his inner sanctum. His archives, neatly alphabetized in metal filing cabinets, looked as files had in another era. He had no armies of traders, no rows of electronic screens, as Lynch did. Buffett had no price charts, no computer-only a newspaper clipping from 1929 and an antique ticker under a glass dome. The two of them paced the floor, recounting their storied histories, what they had bought, what they had sold. Where Lynch had kicked out his losers every few weeks, Buffett had owned mostly the same few stocks for years and years. Lynch felt a pang, as though he had traveled back in time. Buffett's one concession to modernity is a private jet. Otherwise, he derives little pleasure from spending his fabulous wealth. He has no art collection or snazzy car, and he has never lost his taste for hamburgers. He lives in a commonplace house on a tree-lined block, on the same street where he works. His consuming passion-and pleasure-is his work, or, as he calls it, his canvas. It is there that he revealed the secrets of his trade, and left a self-portrait.

71. "Saddle shoes and Vietnam", as expressed in the passage, refers to:

    I. Dernier cri and Vietnam war

    II. Growth of leather footwear industry and Vietnam shoe controversy

    III. Modern U.S. population and traditional expatriates

    IV. Industrial revolution and Vietnam Olympics

    V. Fashion and Politics

    (a) I & V   (b) II & IV

    (c) III & V   (d) II & III

72. Identify the correct sequence:

    I. Depression -> Eisenhower -> Microsoft

    II. California -> New York -> Omaha

    III. J.P. Morgan -> Buffett -> Bill Gates

    IV. Mutual funds -> Hedge funds -> Brokers

    (a) I & II   (b) I & III

    (c) II & IV   (d) III & IV

73. Choose the most appropriate answer: according to the author, Warren Buffett was

    I. Simple and outmoded

    II. Against planned economy and technology

    III. Deadpan

    IV. Spiritually raw

    (a) I & IV   (b) II & IV

    (c) III & IV   (d) I & III

Directions for questions 74 – 77: Read the following passage carefully and answer the questions given at the end.

Passage 1

Before the internet, one of the most rapid changes to the global economy and trade was wrought by something so blatantly useful that it is hard to imagine a struggle to get it adopted: the shipping container. In the early 1960s, before the standard container became ubiquitous, freight costs were 10 per cent of the value of US imports, about the same barrier to trade as the average official government import tariff. Yet in a journey that went halfway round the world, half of those costs could be incurred in two ten-mile movements through the ports at either end. The predominant 'break-bulk' method, where each shipment was individually split up into loads that could be handled by a team of dockers, was vastly complex and labour-intensive. Ships could take weeks or months to load, as a huge variety of cargoes of different weights, shapes and sizes had to be stacked together by hand. Indeed, one of the most unreliable aspects of such a labour-intensive process was the labour. Ports, like mines, were frequently seething pits of industrial unrest. Irregular work on one side combined with what was often a tight-knit, well - organized labour community on the other.

In 1956, loading break-bulk cargo cost $5.83 per ton. The entrepreneurial genius who saw the possibilities for standardized container shipping, Malcolm McLean, floated his first containerized ship in that year and claimed to be able to shift cargo for 15.8 cents a ton. Boxes of the same size that could be loaded by crane and neatly stacked were much faster to load. Moreover, carrying cargo in a standard container would allow it to be shifted between truck, train and ship without having to be repacked each time.

But between McLean's container and the standardization of the global market were an array of formidable obstacles. They began at home in the US with the official Interstate Commerce Commission,

which could prevent price competition by setting rates for freight haulage by route and commodity, and the powerful International Longshoremen's Association (ILA) labour union. More broadly, the biggest hurdle was achieving what economists call 'network effects': the benefit of a standard technology rises exponentially as more people use it. To dominate world trade, containers had to be easily interchangeable between different shipping lines, ports, trucks and railcars. And to maximize efficiency, they all needed to be the same size. The adoption of a network technology often involves overcoming the resistance of those who are heavily invested in the old system. And while the efficiency gains are clear to see, there are very obvious losers as well as winners. For containerization, perhaps the most spectacular example was the demise of New York City as a port.

In the early 1950s, New York handled a third of US seaborne trade in manufactured goods. But it was woefully inefficient, even with existing break-bulk technology: 283 piers, 98 of which were able to handle ocean-going ships, jutted out into the river from Brooklyn and Manhattan. Trucks bound' for the docks had to fight through the crowded, narrow streets of Manhattan, wait for an hour or two before even entering a pier, and then undergo a laborious two-stage process in which the goods were first unloaded into a transit shed and then loaded onto a ship. 'Public loader' work gangs held exclusive rights to load and unload on a particular pier, a power in effect granted by the ILA, which enforced its monopoly with sabotage and violence against competitors. The ILA fought ferociously against containerization, correctly foreseeing that it would destroy their privileged position as bandits controlling the mountain pass. On this occasion, bypassing them simply involved going across the river. A container port was built in New Jersey, where a 1500-foot wharf allowed ships to dock parallel to shore and containers to be liifed on and off by crane. Between 1963-4 and 1975-6, the number of days worked by longshoremen in Manhattan went from 1.4 million to 127,041.

Containers rapidly captured the transatlantic market, and then the growing trade with Asia. The effect of containerization is hard to see immediately in freight rates, since the oil price hikes of the 1970s kept them high, but the speed with which shippers adopted; containerization made it clear it brought big benefits of efifciency and cost. The extraordinary growth of the Asian tiger economies of Singapore, Taiwan, Korea and Hong Kong, which based their development strategy on exports, was greatly helped by the container trade that quickly built up between the US and east Asia. Ocean-borne exports from South Korea were 2.9 million tons in 1969 and 6 million in 1973, and its exports to the US tripled.

But the new technology did not get adopted all on its own. It needed a couple of pushes from government - both, as it happens, largely to do with the military. As far as the ships were concerned, the same link between the merchant and military navy that had inspired the Navigation Acts in seventeenth-century England endured into twentieth-century America. The government's first helping hand was to give a spur to the system by adopting it to transport military cargo. The US armed forces, seeing the efficiency of the system, started contracting McLean's company Pan-Atlantic, later renamed Sea-land, to carry equipment to the quarter of a million American soldiers

stationed in Western Europe. One of the few benefitsof America's misadventure in Vietnam was a rapid expansion of containerization. Because war involves massive movements of men and material, it is often armies that pioneer new techniques in supply chains.

The government's other role was in banging heads together sufficiently to get all companies to accept the same size container. Standard sizes were essential to deliver the economies of scale that came from interchangeability - which, as far as the military was concerned, was vital if the ships had to be commandeered in case war broke out. This was a significant problem to overcome, not least because all the companies that had started using the container had settled on different sizes. Pan-Atlantic used 35-foot containers, because that was the maximum size allowed on the highways in its home base in New Jersey. Another of the big shipping companies, Matson Navigation, used a 24-foot container since its biggest trade was in canned pineapple from Hawaii, and a container bigger than that would have been too heavy for a crane to lift. Grace Line, which largely traded with Latin America, used a 17-foot container that was easier to truck around winding mountain roads.

Establishing a US standard and then getting it adopted internationally took more than a decade. Indeed, not only did the US Maritime Administration have to mediate in these rivalries but also to fight its own turf battles with the American Standards Association, an agency set up by the private sector. The matter was settled by using the power of federal money: the Federal Maritime Board (FMB), which handed out to public subsidies for shipbuilding, decreed that only the 8 x 8-foot containers in the lengths of 10, 20, 30 or 40 feet would be eligible for handouts.

74. Identify the *correct* statement:

  (a) The freight costs accounted for around 10 per cent of the value of imports in general during early 1960s, given the labour-intensive 'break-bulk' cargo handling.

  (b) As a result of growing adoption of containerized trade during 1969-73, while the ocean-borne exports from South Korea in general more than doubled, the same to the US tripled.

  (c) The outbreak of the Vietnam war functioned as a major positive force towards rapid expansion of containerization, as American imports from the country increased heavily.

  (d) In the early days of container trade development, a major shipping firm Matson Navigation used a 24-foot container since a bigger container was not suitable for its trucks.

75. Identify the *false* statement:

(a) In the pre-containerization days, trucks bound for the New York docks had to pass through the narrow streets, wait for an hour or two before even entering a pier, and then undergo a laborious three-stage process for loading onto a ship.

(b) Once satisifed with the effectiveness of containerized trade, the US military engaged the company of Malcolm McLean to transport equipments for their soldiers stationed in Western Europe.

(c) Cargo loading during 1960s usually took a long period, as it involved manual handling of huge variety of cargoes of different weights, shapes and sizes.

(d) The issue of standardization of the containers created led to a debate .between the US government and American Standards Association, but the question was finally sorted through public subsidy programme by Federal Maritime Board.

76. The emergence of containerization technology in early seventies resulted in:

(a) Immediate adoption of the containerized export route by private companies, in their own accord.

(b) An instant sharp reduction in freight costs expressed as a percentage of imports across countries.

(c) Spectacular growth in exports from the East Asian tiger economies, which were reliant on an export-oriented growth strategy.

(d) All of the above

77. Match the following set of words:

Set A	Set B
a. ILA	i. New Jersey
b. FMB	ii. Mountain roads
c. Grace Line	iii. Dockers
d. McLean	iv. Standardization

(a) a - i; b - iv, c - ii; d - iii

(b) a - iii; b - i, c - iv; d - ii

(c) a - iv; b - i, c - ii; d - iii

(d) a - iii; b - iv, c - ii; d - i

Directions for questions 78 – 81: Read the following passage carefully and answer the questions given at the end.

Passage 2

I have tried to introduce into the discussion a number of attributes of consumer behaviour and motivations, which I believe are important inputs into devising a strategy for commercially viable financial inclusion. These related broadly to the (i) the sources of livelihood of the potential consumer segment for financial inclusion (ii) how they spend their money, particularly on non-regular items (iii) their choices and motivations with respect to saving and (iv) their motivations for borrowing and their ability to access institutional sources of finance for their basic requirements. In discussing each of these sets of issues, I spent some time drawing implications for business strategies by financial service providers. In this section, I will briefly highlight, at the risk of some repetition, what I consider to be the key messages of the lecture.

The first message emerges from the preliminary discussion on the current scenario on financial inclusion, both at the aggregate level and across income categories. The data suggest that even savings accounts, the most basic financial service, have low penetration amongst the lowest income households. I want to emphasize that we are not talking about Below Poverty Line households only; Rs. 50,000 per year in 2007, while perhaps not quite middle class, was certainly quite far above the official poverty line. The same concerns about lack of penetration amongst the lowest income group for loans also arise. To reiterate the question that arises from these data patterns: is this because people can't access banks or other service providers or because they don't see value in doing so? This question needs to be addressed if an effective inclusion strategy is to be developed.

The second message is that the process of financial inclusion is going to be incomplete and inadequate if it is measured only in terms of new accounts being opened and operated. From the employment and earning patterns, there emerged a sense that better access to various kinds of financial services would help to increase the livelihood potential of a number of occupational categories, which in turn would help reduce the income differentials between these and more regular, salaried jobs. The fact that a huge proportion of the Indian workforce is either self-employed and in the casual labour segment suggests the need for products that will make access to credit easier to the former, while offering opportunities for risk mitigation and consumption smoothing to the latter.

The third message emerges from the analysis of expenditure patterns is the significance of infrequent, but quantitatively significant expenditures like ceremonies and medical costs. Essentially, dealing with these kinds of expenditures requires either low-cost insurance options, supported by a correspondingly low-cost health care system or a low level systematic investment plan, which allows even poor households to create enough of a buffer to deal with these demands as and when they arise. As has already been pointed out, it is not as though such products are not being offered by domestic financial service providers. It is really a matter of extending them to make them accessible to a very large number of lower income households, with a low and possibly uncertain ability to maintain regular contributions.

The fourth message comes strongly from the motivations to both save and borrow, which, as one might reasonably expect, significantly overlap with each other. It is striking that the need to deal with emergencies, both financial and medical, plays such an important role in both sets of motivations. The latter is, as has been said, amenable to a low-cost, mass insurance scheme, with the attendant service provision. However, the former, which is a theme that recurs through the entire discussion on consumer characteristics, certainly suggests that the need for some kind of income and consumption smoothing product is a signiifcant one in an effective financial inclusion agenda. This, of course, raises broader questions about the role of social safety nets, which offer at least some minimum income security and consumption smoothing. How extensive these mechanisms should be, how much security they should offer and for how long and how they should be financed are fundamental policy questions that go beyond the realm of the financial sector. However, to the extent that risk mitigation is a significant financial need, it must receive the attention of any meaningful financial inclusion strategy, in a way which provides practical answers to all these three questions.

The fifth and final message is actually the point I began the lecture with. It is the critical importance of the principle of commercial viability. Every aspect of a financial inclusion strategy - whether it is the design of products and services or the delivery mechanism - needs to be viewed in terms of the business opportunity that it offers and not as a deliverable that has been imposed on the service provider. However, it is also important to emphasize that commercial viability need not necessarily be viewed in terms of immediate cost and profitability calculations. Like in many other products, financial services also offer the prospect of a life-cycle model of marketing. Establishing a relationship with first-time consumers of financial products and services offers the opportunity to leverage this relationship into a wider set of financial transactions as at least some of these consumers move steadily up the income ladder. In fact, in a high growth scenario, a high proportion of such households are likely to move quite quickly from very basic financial services to more and more sophisticated ones. In other words, the commercial viability and profitability of a financial inclusion strategy need not be viewed only from the perspective of immediacy. There is a viable investment dimension to it as well.

78. Which of the following statements is *incorrect*?

    (a) In order to succeed, financial inclusion has to be commercially viable.

    (b) Savings account is one of the basic vehicles for financial inclusion.

    (c) Savings accounts have low penetration amongst "Below Poverty Line" households only.

    (d) There is lack of penetration for loans amongst the lowest income group.

79. Which of the following statements is *correct*?

    (a) Financial inclusion is exclusively measured in terms of new accounts being opened and operated.

    (b) There is a felt need for better access to credit products for the self-employed.

    (c) It is felt that financial inclusion could be proiftable from day one if a commercially viable strategy is devised.

    (d) Financial Institutions must deliver social service through financial inclusion.

80. Identify the *correct* statement from the following:

    (a) Casual labour segment may not require risk mitigation products like insurance as their expenditures on consumption are high relative to their incomes.

    (b) Income of upto Rs. 60,000 per year is the benchmark for official Poverty Line.

    (c) Financial sector should also look into their role of broadening social safety nets.

    (d) Risk mitigation of casual labour must receive attention in any meaningful financial inclusion strategy.

81. Identify the *wrong* statement from the following:

    (a) High expenditures on ceremonies and medical costs can be met through a low - level Systematic Investment Plan.

    (b) Given the high growth scenario of the country, only few of the consumers are expected to move up the income ladder.

    (c) Financial and medical emergencies motivate one to save and borrow.

    (d) There is an opportunity for banks to cross-sell their products to the bottom of the pyramid.

Directions for questions 82 – 85: Read the following passage carefully and answer the questions given at the end.

Passage 3

When Ratan Tata moved the Supreme Court, claiming his right to privacy had been violated, he called

Harish Salve. The choice was not surprising. The former solicitor general had been topping the legal charts ever since he scripted a surprising win for Mukesh Ambani against his brother Anil. That dispute set the gold standard for legal fees. On Mukesh's side were Salve, Rohinton Nariman, and Abhishek Manu Singhvi. The younger brother had an equally formidable line-up led by Ram Jethmalani and Mukul Rohatgi.

The dispute dated back three-and-a-half years to when Anil filed case against his brother for reneging on an agreement to supply 28 million cubic metres of gas per day from its Krishna-Godavari basin fields at a rate of $ 2.34 for 17 years. The average legal fee was Rs. 25 lakh for a full day's appearance, not to mention the overnight stays at Mumbai's five-star suites, business class travel, and on occasion, use of the private jet. Little wonder though that Salve agreed to take on Tata's case pro bono. He could afford philanthropy with one of India's wealthiest tycoons.

The lawyers' fees alone, at a conservative estimate, must have cost the Ambanis at least Rs. 15 crore each. Both the brothers had booked their legal teams in the same hotel, ifrst the Oberoi and, after the 26/11 Mumbai attacks, the Trident. It's not the essentials as much as the first that raise eyebrows. The veteran Jethmalani is surprisingly the most modest in his fees since he does not charge rates according to the strength of the client's purse. But as the crises have multiplied, lawyers'fees have exploded.

The 50 court hearings in the Haldia Petrochemicals vs. the West Bengal Government cost the former a total of Rs. 25 crore in lawyer fees and the 20 hearings in the Bombay Mill Case, which dragged on for three years, cost the mill owners almost Rs. 10 crore. Large corporate firms, which engage star counsels on behalf of the client, also need to know their quirks. For instance, Salve will only accept the first brief. He will never be the second counsel in a case. Some lawyers prefer to be paid partly in cash but the best are content with cheques. Some expect the client not to blink while picking up a dinner tab of Rs.1.75 lakh at a Chennai five star. A lawyer is known to carry his home linen and curtains with him while travelling on work. A firm may even have to pick up a hot Vertu phone of the moment or a Jaeger-LeCoutre watch of the hour to keep a lawyer in good humour.

Some are even paid to not appear at all for the other side - Aryama Sundaram was retained by Anil Ambani in the

gas feud but he did not fight the case. Or take Raytheon when it was fighting the Jindals. Raytheon had paid seven top lawyers a retainer fee of Rs. 2.5 lakh each just to ensure that the Jindals would not be able to make a proper case on a taxation issue. They miscalculated when a star lawyer fought the case at the last minute. "I don't take negative retainers", shrugs Rohatgi, former additional solicitor general. "A Lawyer's job is to appear for any client that comes to him. It's not for the lawyers to judge if a client is good or bad but the court". Indeed. He is, after all, the lawyer who argued so famously in court that B. Ramalinga Raju did not 'fudge any account in the Satyam Case. All he did was "window dressing".

Some high proifle cases have continued for years, providing a steady source of income, from the Scindia succession battle which dates to 1989, to the JetLite Sahara battle now in taxation arbitration to the BCCI which is currently in litigation with Lalit Modi, Rajasthan Royals and Kings XI Punjab.

Think of the large law firms as the big Hollywood studios and the senior counsel as the superstar. There are a few familiar faces to be found in most of the big ticket cases, whether it is the Ambani gas case, Vodafone taxation or Bombay Mills case. Explains Salve, "There is a reason why we have more than one senior advocate on a case. When you're arguing, he's reading the court. He picks up a point or a vibe that you may have missed." Says Rajan Karanjawala, whose firm has prepared the briefs for cases ranging from the Tata's recent right to privacy case to Karisma Kapoor's divorce, "The four jewels in the crown today are Salve, Rohatgi, Rohinton Nariman and Singhvi. They have replaced the old guard of Fali Nariman, Soli Sorabjee, Ashok Desai and K.K. Venugopal." He adds, "The one person who defies the generational gap is Jethmalani who was India's leading criminal lawyer in the 1960s and is so today."

The demand for superstar lawyers has far outstripped the supply. So a one-man show by, say, Rohatgi can run up billings of Rs. 40 crore, the same as a mid-sized corporate law firm like Titus and Co that employs 28 juniors. The big law firms such as AZB or Amarchand & Mangaldas or Luthra & Luthra have to do all the groundwork for the counsel, from humouring the clerk to ensure the A-lister turns up on the hearing day to sourcing appropriate foreign judgments in emerging areas such as environmental and patent laws. "We are partners in this. There are so few lawyers and so many matters," points out Diljeet Titus.

As the trust between individuals has broken down, governments have questioned corporates and corporates are questioning each other, and an array of new issues has come up. The courts have become stronger. "The lawyer," says Sundaram, with the flourish that has seen him pick up many Dhurandhares and Senakas at pricey art auctions, "has emerged as the modern day purohit." Each purohit is head priest of a particular style. Says Karanjawala, "Harish is the closest example in today's bar to Fali Nariman; Rohinton has the best law library in his brain; Mukul is easily India's busiest lawyer while Manu Singhvi is the greatest multi-tasker." Salve has managed a fine balancing act where he has represented Mulayam Singh Yadav and Mayawati, Parkash Singh Badal and Amarinder Singh, Lalit Modi and Subhash Chandra and even the Ambani brothers, of course in different cases. Jethmalani is the man to call for anyone in trouble. In judicial circles he is known as the first resort for the last resort. Even Jethmalani's junior Satish Maneshinde, who came to Mumbai in I993 as a penniless law graduate from Karnataka, shot to fame (and wealth) after he got bail for Sanjay Dutt in 1996. Now he owns a plush office in Worli and has become a one-stop shop for celebrities in trouble.

82. Which of the following is *not* true about Ram Jethmalani?

    (a) In judicial circles, he is known as the first resort for the last resort first

    (b) He is the most modest in his fees

    (c) He has been India's leading criminal lawyer since 1960s

    (d) None of his juniors have done well in their careers

83. Match the following:

	Lawyer		Distinguishing Quality
a.	Harish Salve	i.	India's busiest lawyer
b.	Rohinton	ii.	Today's Fali Nariman
c.	Mukul Rohatgi	iii.	Greatest multi - tasker
d.	Abhishek Manu Singhvi	iv.	Best Law library in his brain

    (a) a-ii; b-iii; c-iv; d-i

    (b) a-ii; b-iv; c-i; d-iii

    (c) a-iii; b-iv; c-i; d-ii

    (d) a-iii; b-ii; c-iv; d-i

84. What does a 'negative retainer' refer to?

    (a) Giving a lawyer only his fees and not the frills

    (b) Paying a lawyer to not fight a case for the other side

    (c) Having more than one senior advocate on a case

    (d) Reimbursing law firms for doing groundwork for the counsel

85. What does the phrase 'pro bono' mean?

    (a) Charged according to the client's purse

    (b) Done without compensation for the public good

    (c) Carried out in the prescribed form

    (d) Taken up from the beginning

Directions for questions 86 – 88: Read the following passage carefully and answer the questions given at the end.

Passage 4

The second issue I want to address is one that comes up frequently - that Indian banks should aim to become global. Most people who put forward this view have not thought through the costs and benefits analytically; they only see this as an aspiration consistent with India's growing international profile. In its 1998 report, the Narasimham (II) Committee envisaged a three tier structure for the Indian banking sector: 3 or 4 large banks having an international presence on the top, 8-10 mid-sized banks, with a network of branches throughout the country and engaged in universal banking, in the middle, and local banks and regional rural banks operating in smaller regions forming the bottom layer. However, the Indian banking system has not consolidated in the manner envisioned by the Narasimham Committee. The current structure is that India has 81 scheduled commercial banks of which 26 are public sector banks, 21 are private sector banks and 34 are foreign banks. Even a quick review would reveal that there is no segmentation in the banking structure along the lines of Narasimham II.

A natural sequel to this issue of the envisaged structure of the Indian banking system is the Reserve Bank's position on bank consolidation. Our view on bank consolidation is that the process should be market-driven, based on profitability considerations and brought about through a process of mergers & amalgamations (M&As). The initiative for this has to come from the boards of the banks concerned which have to make a decision based on a judgment of the synergies involved in the business models and the compatibility of the business cultures. The Reserve Bank's role in the reorganisation of the banking system will normally be only that of a facilitator.

It should be noted though that bank consolidation through mergers is not always a totally benign option. On the positive side are a higher exposure threshold, international acceptance and recognition, improved risk management and improvement in financials due to economies of scale and scope. This can be achieved both through organic and inorganic growth. On the negative side, experience shows that consolidation would fail if there are no synergies in the business models and there is no compatibility in the business cultures and technology platforms of the merging banks.

Having given that broad brush position on bank consolidation let me address two speciifc questions:

(i)   can Indian banks aspire to global size?; and

(ii)   should Indian banks aspire to global size?

On the first question, as per the current global league tables based on the size of assets, our largest bank, the

State Bank of India (SBI), together with its subsidiaries, comes in at No.74 followed by ICICI Bank at No. 145 and Bank of Baroda at 188. It is, therefore, unlikely that any of our banks will jump into the top ten of the global league even after reasonable consolidation.

Then comes the next question of whether Indian banks should become global. Opinion on this is divided. Those who argue that we must go global contend that the issue is not so much the size of our banks in global rankings but of Indian banks having a strong enough, global presence. The main argument is that the increasing global size and influence of Indian corporates warrant a corresponding increase in the global footprint of Indian banks. The opposing view is that Indian banks should look inwards rather than outwards, focus their efforts on financial deepening at home rather than aspiring to global size.

It is possible to take a middle path and argue that looking outwards towards increased global presence and looking inwards towards deeper financial penetration are not mutually exclusive; it should be possible to aim for both. With the onset of the global financial crisis, there has definitely been a pause to the rapid expansion overseas of our banks. Nevertheless, notwithstanding the risks involved, it will be opportune for some of our larger banks to be looking out for opportunities for consolidation both organically and inorganically. They should look out more actively in regions which hold out a promise of attractive acquisitions.

The surmise, therefore, is that Indian banks should increase their global footprint opportunistically even if they do not get to the top of the league table.

86. Identify the *correct* statement from the following:
    (a) Large banks having an international presence should not be engaged in universal banking.
    (b) Some people expect all banks to become global in coming years, in line with globalization.
    (c) Indian banking system has not consolidated as was foreseen by the Narasimham Committee.
    (d) Reserve Bank of India envisages the role of a facilitator for itself in the direction of bank consolidation.

87. Identify the *correct* statement from the following:
    (a) Indian banks should not go for global inorganic expansion as there is no compatibility in business cultures.
    (b) Indian banks do not aspire to be global.
    (c) Indian banks cannot be global even after reasonable consolidation.
    (d) After the onset of the global financial crisis, some regions hold out a promise of attractive acquisitions for banks.

88. Identify the *wrong* statement from the following:
    (a) Bank consolidation through mergers increases the merged entity's ability to take higher exposures.
    (b) There is still scope for Indian banks to expand internally.
    (c) None of the Indian banks presently are global.
    (d) Global financial crisis has increased the risks of overseas expansion.

2013-15

Direction for questions 89 - 104: Read the following passages carefully and answer the questions at the end of each passage

Passage 1

Asked what a business is, the typical businessman is likely to answer, "An organisation to make a profit." The typical economist is likely to give the same answer. This answer is not only false, it is irrelevant.

The prevailing economic theory of the mission of business enterprise and behaviour, the maximization of profit – which is simply a complicated way of phrasing the old saw of buying cheap and selling dear – may adequately explain how Richard Sears operated. But it cannot explain how Sears, Roebuck or any other business enterprise operates, or how it should operate. The concept of profit maximization is, in fact, meaningless. The danger in the concept of profit maximization is that it makes profitability appear a myth.

Profit and profitability are, however, crucial – for society even more than for the individual businesses. Yet profitability is not the purpose of, but a limiting factor on business enterprise and business activity. Profit is not the explanation, cause, or rationale of business behaviour and business decisions, but rather the test of their validity. If archangels instead of businessmen sat in directors' chairs, they would still have to be concerned with profitability, despite their total lack of personal interest in making profits.

The root of the confusion is the mistaken belief that the motive of a person – the so-called profit motive of the businessman – is an explanation of his behaviour or his guide to right action. Whether there is such a thing as a profit motive at all is highly doubtful. The idea was invented by the classical economists to explain the economic reality that their theory of static equilibrium could not explain. There has never been any evidence for the existence of the profit motive, and we have long since found the true explanation of the phenomena of economic change and growth which the profit motive was first put forth to explain.

It is irrelevant for an understanding of business behaviour, profit, and profitability, whether there is a profit motive or not. That Jim Smith is in business to make a profit concerns only him and the Recording Angel. It does not tell us what Jim Smith does and how he performs. We do not learn anything about the work of a prospector hunting for uranium in the Nevada desert by being told that he is trying to make his fortune. We do not learn anything about the work of a heart specialist by being told that he is trying to make a livelihood, or even that he is trying to benefit humanity. The profit motive and its offspring maximization of profits are just as irrelevant to the function of a business, the purpose of a business, and the job of managing a business.

In fact, the concept is worse than irrelevant: it does harm. It is a major cause of the misunderstanding of the nature of profit in our society and of the deep –seated hostility to profit, which are among the most dangerous diseases of an industrial society. It is largely responsible for the worst mistakes of public policy – in this country as well as in Western Europe – which are squarely based on the failure to understand the nature, function, and purpose of business enterprise. And it is in large part responsible for the prevailing belief that there is an inherent contradiction between profit and a company's ability to make a social contribution. Actually, a company can make a social contribution only if it is highly profitable.

To know what a business is, we have to start with its purpose. Its purpose must lie outside of the business itself. In fact, it must lie in society since business enterprise is an organ of society. There is only one valid definition of business purpose: to create a customer.

Markets are not created by God, nature, or economic forces but by businesspeople. The want a business satisfies may have been felt by the customer before he or she was offered the means of satisfying it. Like food in a famine, it may have dominated the customer's life and filled all his waking moments, but it remained a potential want until the action of business people converted it into effective demand. Only then is there a customer and a market. The want may have been unfelt by the potential customer; no one knew that he wanted a Xerox machine or a computer until these became available. There may have been no want at all until business action created it – by innovation, by credit, by advertising, or by salesmanship. In every case, it is business action that creates the customer.

89. The author of this passage is of the opinion that profits and profitability are:
    (a) The purpose of setting up a business
    (b) The sole goal and responsibility of a businessman
    (c) The test of validity of business existence
    (d) The guiding factor for a businessman's actions and decisions

90. This passage highlights that the theory of profit maximisation and profit motive
    (a) Is largely responsible for the worst mistakes in public policy
    (b) Is a synchronised goal with a company's ability to make a social contribution
    (c) Is the main purpose and job of managing a business
    (d) Was an idea not invented by classical economists

91. As stated in this passage, the purpose of a business is to
    (a) Make profits   (b) Increase wants
    (c) Create customers   (d) Manage Demand

92. According to the author of this passage, what comes first?
    (a) Want   (b) Market
    (c) Demand   (d) Customers

Passage 2

The first thing I learned at school was that some people are idiots; the second thing I learned was that some are even worse. I was still too young to grasp that people of breeding were meant to affect innocence of this fundamental distinction, and that the same courtesy applied to any disparity that might rise out of religious, racial, sexual class, financial and (latterly) cultural difference. So in my innocence I would raise my hand every time the teacher asked a question, just to make it clear I knew the answer.

After some months of this, the teacher and my classmates must have been vaguely aware I was a good student, but still I felt the compulsion to raise my hand. By now the teacher seldom called on me, preferring to give other children a chance to speak, too. Still my hand shot up without my even willing it, whether or not I knew the answer. If I was putting on airs, like someone who even in ordinary clothes, adds a gaudy piece of jewellery, it's also true that I admired my teacher and was desperate to cooperate.

Another thing I was happy to discover at school was the teacher's 'authority'. At home, in the crowded and disordered Pamuk Apartments, things were never so clear; at our crowded table, everyone talked at the same time. Our domestic routines, our love for one another, our conversations, meals and radio hours; these were never debated - they just happened. My father held little obvious authority at home, and he was often absent. He never scolded my brother or me, never even raised his eyebrows in disapproval. In later years, he would introduce us to his friends as 'my two younger brothers', and we felt he had earned the right to say so. My mother was the only authority I recognised at home. But she was hardly a distant or alien tyrant: her power came from my desire to be loved by her. And so I was fascinated by the power my teacher wielded over her twenty-five pupils.

Perhaps I identified my teacher with my mother, for I had an insatiable desire for her approval. 'Join your arms together like this and sit down quietly,' she would say, and I would press my arms against my chest and sit patiently all through the lesson. But gradually the novelty wore off; soon it was no longer exciting to have every answer or solve an arithmetic problem ahead of everyone else or earn the highest mark; time began to flow with painful slowness, or stop flowing altogether.

Turning away from the fat, half-witted girl who was writing on the blackboard, who gave everyone-teachers, school caretakers and her classmates - the same vapid, trusting smile, my eyes would float to the window, to the upper branches of the chestnut tree that I could just see rising up between the apartment buildings. A crow would land on a branch. Because I was viewing it from below, I could see the little cloud floating behind it - as it moved, it kept changing shape: first a fox's nose, then a head, then a dog. I didn't want it to stop looking like a dog, but as it continued its journey it changed into one of the four-legged silver sugar bowls from my grandmother's always-locked display case, and I'd long to be at home. Once I'd conjured up the reassuring silence of the shadows of home, my father would step out from them, as if from a dream, and off we'd go on a family outing to the Bosphorus. Just then, a window in the apartment building opposite would open, a maid would shake her duster and gaze absentmindedly at the street that I could not see from where I was sitting. What was going down there? I'd wonder. I'd hear a horse cart rolling over the cobblestones, and a rasping voice would cry out 'Eskiciiiiiii! The maid would watch the junk dealer make his way down the street before pulling her head back inside and shutting the window behind her, but then, right next to that window, moving as fast as the first cloud but going in the opposite direction, I'd see a second cloud. But now my attention was called back to the classroom, and seeing all the other raised hands, I would eagerly raise my hand too: long before I worked out from my classmates' responses what the teacher had asked us, I was foggily confident I had the answer.

It was exciting, though sometimes painful, to get to know my classmates as individuals, and to find out how different they were from me. There was that sad boy who, whenever he was asked to read out loud in Turkish class, would skip every other line; the poor boy's mistake was as involuntary as the laughter it would elicit from the class. In first grade, there was a girl who kept her red hair in a ponytail, who sat next to me for a time. Although her bag was a slovenly jumble of half-eaten apples, simits, sesame seeds, pencils and hairbands, it always smelled of dried lavender around her, and that attracted me; I was also drawn to her gift for I speaking so openly about the little taboos of daily life, and if I didn't see her at the weekend, I missed her, though there was another girl so tiny and delicate that I was utterly entranced by her as well. Why did that boy keep on telling lies even knowing no one was going to believe him? How could that girl be so indiscreet about the goings-on in her house? And could this other girl be shedding real tears as she read that poem about Atatürk?

Just as I was in the habit of looking at the fronts of cars and seeing noses, so too did I like to scrutinise my classmates, looking for the creatures they resembled. The boy with the pointed nose was a fox and the big one next to him was, as everyone said, a bear, and the one with the thick hair was a hedgehog ... I remember a Jewish girl called Mari telling us all about Passover - there were days when no one in her grandmother's house was allowed to touch the light switches. Another girl reported that one evening, when she was in her room, she turned around so fast she glimpsed the shadow of an angel - a fearsome story that stayed with me. There was a girl with very long legs who wore very long socks and always looked as if she was about to cry; her father was a government minister and when he died in a plane crash from which Prime Minister Menederes emerged without a scratch, I was sure she'd been crying because she had known in advance what was going to happen. Lots of children had problems with their teeth; a few wore braces. On the top floor of the building that housed the lycée dormitory and the sports hall, just next to the infirmary, there was rumoured to be a dentist, and when teachers got angry they would often threaten to send naughty children there. For lesser infractions pupils were made to stand in the corner between the blackboard and the door with their backs to the class, sometimes one leg, hut because we were all so curious to see how long someone could stand on one leg, the lessons suffered, so this particular punishment was rare.

93. The synonym for the term 'vapid' is

    (a) Lively   (b) Original

    (c) Lacklustre   (d) Spicy

94. Who is the least talked about character in this passage?

    (a) Mother   (b) Classmates

    (c) Grandmother   (d) Teacher

95. Which among the following cannot be concluded from this passage?

    (a) The author was a good student but sometimes felt bored in class

    (b) The author got along fairly well with his classmates

    (c) The author came from a very authoritarian home environment

    (d) The author had an imaginative mind

96. What did the teachers do when they got angry?

   (a) Sent the students to the infirmary

   (b) Denied them a chance to answer questions

   (c) Made them join their hands together and sit quietly

   (d) Threatened to send them to the dentist

Passage 3

Not many people saw it coming. It had seemed that the time for Kaun Banega Crorepati had come and gone. This column argued as much a few years ago, when Shah Rukh Khan took over the reigns of the show. He did well enough, but it still seemed that the time for the genteel game of knowledge had passed. There was too much blood in reality television, and KBC simply did not have enough platelets for it. It had no backbiting intrigue, it lacked a cast of almost-losers and missed the low-life loquaciousness of other reality shows, and nothing ever needed to be beeped out on it, a sure sign that it was out of touch with the times.

And yet, not only is KBC back, but it is back in a very real sense not just as a TV show that gets good ratings, but as an idea that connects with something deep and real in our lives. What makes this particularly interesting is that not very much has changed in the show. Its focus has shifted to smaller towns and an 'aadmi' more 'aam', and the prize money has gone up over the years, but these are minor adjustments, not major departures. The format is pretty much the same and the return of Amitabh Bachchan restores to the show both the gravitas and the empathy that has been its hallmark.

Perhaps KBC works because it reconciles many competing ideas for us. For a show that bestows undreamt of wealth on people who win, and does so with reasonable regularity, KBC manages somehow to rise above the money it throws around. By locating money squarely in the context of small dreams, family and community, KBC shows us a face of money that is ennobling. The money of KBC is treated not as a jackpot but as a 'vardaan', a gift from divinity that comes for one's persistent effort, a prize for the penance called ordinary life. The images that surround the winners are not big cars and fancy brands, but houses made 'pukka' and IAS dreams pursued. The winners have been remarkable ambassadors for the show, focussing not what the money buys them but what it enables them to work at in the future. Money speaks in the language of responsibility, not indulgence and steeps a larger collective in its pleasing warmth.

The format of the show ensures that we see people as they are, rather than the usual sight of raw innocents losing their transparent naiveté in a haze of hair dye and exfoliation. On other reality shows, fame and money are insistent in transforming those that they favour and what they tell us is that success must put distance between destination and source, between who we are and what we must become. On KBC, it is the innocence that is spoken to and as an audience it is this quality we respond to. When a Sushil Kumar describes his life and attributes his success to his wife, who in turn is quick to shyly shrug off the credit, we see, for once, something that smacks of the real on a reality show.

As the reality show evolved, it found reality too boring and vapid. It was so much for fun to manufacture it by making people act in unpleasant ways, and say unsavoury things to each other. Now, no reality show can really bring us reality; any act of representation and framing creates its own version of reality in many different ways – by aestheticizing it, emotionalising moments, dramatising revelations, withholding information selectively, or by imbuing some moments with significance, while ignoring others and even KBC uses these techniques. The difference is that it uses these to drive us towards the central premise of the show rather than see those as individual 'masala' elements. In a world where television is racked by anxiety about itself, and where every new season is an exercise in renewed desperation, KBC stands apart by continuing to tell a human story about dreams and their fulfilment and doing so without trying too hard.

There is no question that KBC rests on the persona of Amitabh Bachchan for he reconciles for us the ideas of fame and humility, of achievement and empathy in the way he treats the participants. He has a special ability to look into the ordinary and find something special and the humility to be awed by it. He is simultaneously The Amitabh Bachchan, the wax God who we touch and squeal when we find out that it is real and a fellow sympathiser and co-traveller on the journey called life. As a carrier of life-altering destiny, he underplays his role to perfection, acknowledging the enormity of what winning means for the participant while revealing the wisdom that knows that it is only money. Under his steerage money is no longer cold with acquisitive urgency but warm with unfolding possibility.

KBC shows us, close-up and in slow motion, the act of a miracle colliding with a dream. In doing so, it tells us that money can change things for the better, when it finds the right home. By applying good fortune to good intention, it keeps the miracle alive, well after the moment of impact. As the winners no doubt find out, one can never have enough money, and that relative scale makes everyone a relative pauper. In the final analysis, Kaun Banega Crorepati reveals both the nobility and the eventual poverty of money, no matter if it comes in eight figures.

97. According to the author's opinion a few years before writing this article, which of the following appeared to be in store for KBC?

   (i)   The show's time was over

   (ii) The show was too refined to compete with other reality shows

   (iii) Shah Rukh Khan as the show host would take it to new heights

   (iv) The show's viciousness was leading it to its end

   (a) (i) only   (b) (i) and (ii)

   (c) (ii) and (iii)   (d) (i) and (iv)

98. Unlike most reality shows, KBC has gained viewership on television by

   (a) Using glamorous participants on the show

   (b) Getting participants to say unpleasant things about the truth of life

   (c) Making major adjustments to its format time and again

   (d) Connecting with the depth and reality of lives of people

99. According to the author, KBC presents the prize money as

   (a) a means for indulgence

   (b) a jackpot

   (c) a reward for relentless work

   (d) a reason for changing the real person

100. In what context does the author use the phrase "a relative pauper"?

   (a) No one can ever have enough money

   (b) Money can change who we are

   (c) Money is cold and has materialistic importance

   (d) Money can change things for better only if it finds the right home

Passage 4

Babur's head was throbbing with the persistent ache that dogged him during the monsoon. The warm rain had been falling for three days now but the still, heavy air held no promise of relief. The rains would go on for weeks, even months. Lying back against silken bolsters in his bedchamber in the Agra fort, he tried to imagine the chill, thin rains of Ferghana blowing in over the jagged summit of Mount Beshtor and failed. The *punkah* above his head hardly disturbed the air. It was hard even to remember what it was like not to feel hot. There was little pleasure just now even in visiting his garden - the sodden flowers, soggy ground and overflowing water channels only depressed him.

Babur got up and tried to concentrate on writing an entry in his diary but the words wouldn't come and he pushed his jewel-studded inkwell impatiently aside. Maybe he

would go to the women's apartments. He would ask Maham to sing. Sometimes she accompanied herself on the round-bellied, slender-necked lute that had once belonged to Esan Dawlat. Maham lacked her grandmother's gift but the lute still made a sweet sound in her hands.

Or he might play a game of chess with Humayun. His son had a shrewd, subtle mind - but so, he prided himself, did he and he could usually beat him. It amused him to see Humayun's startled look as he claimed victory with the traditional cry *shah mat* - 'check-mate', 'the king is at a loss'. Later, they would discuss Babur's plans to launch a campaign when the rains eased against the rulers of Bengal. In their steamy jungles in the Ganges delta, they thought they could defy Moghul authority and deny Babur's overlordship.

'Send for my son Humayun and fetch my chessmen,' Babur ordered a servant, Trying to shake off his lethargy he got up and went to a casement projecting over the riverbank to watch the swollen, muddy waters of the Jumna rushing by. A farmer was leading his bony bullocks along the oozing bank.

Hearing footsteps Babur turned, expecting to see his son, but it was only the white-tunicked servant.

'Majesty, your son begs your forgiveness but he is unwell and cannot leave his chamber.'

What is the matter with him?'

'I do not know, Majesty.'

Humayun was never ill. Perhaps he, too, was suffering from the torpor that came with the monsoon, sapping the energy and spirit of even the most vigorous.

'I will go to him.' Babur wrapped a yellow silk robe around himself and thrust his feet into pointed kidskin slippers. Then he hurried from his apartments to Humayun's on the opposite side of a galleried courtyard, where water was not shooting, as it should, in sparkling arcs from the lotus-shaped marble basins of the fountains but pouring over the inundated rims.

Humayun was lying on his bed, arms thrown back, eyes closed, forehead beaded with sweat, shivering. When he heard his father's voice he opened his eyes but they were bloodshot, the pupils dilated. Babur could hear his heavy wheezing breathing. Every scratchy intake of air seemed an effort which hurt him.

'When did this illness begin?'

'Early this morning, Father.'

'Why wasn't I told?' Babur looked angrily at his son's attendants. 'Send for my *hakim immediately*!' Then he dipped his own silk handkerchief into some water and wiped Humayun's brow. The sweat returned at once - in fact, it was almost running down his face and he seemed to be shivering even more violently now and his teeth had begun to chatter.

'Majesty, the *hakim* is here.'

Abdul-Malik went immediately to Humayun's bedside, laid a hand on his forehead, pulled back his eyelids and felt his pulse. Then, with increasing concern, he pulled open Humayun's robe and, bending, turned his neatly turbaned head to listen to Humayun's heart.

'What is wrong with him?'

Abdul-Malik paused. 'It is hard to say, Majesty. I need to examine him further.'

'Whatever you require you only have to say ... '

'I will send for my assistants. If I may be frank, it would be best if you were to leave the chamber, Majesty. I will report to you when I have examined the prince thoroughly - but it looks serious, perhaps even grave. His pulse and heartbeat are weak and rapid.' Without waiting for Babur's reply, Abdul-Malik turned back to his patient. Babur hesitated and, after a glance at his son's waxen trembling face, left the room. As attendants closed the doors behind him he found that he, too, was trembling.

A chill closed round his heart. So many times he had feared for Humayun. At Panipat he could have fallen beneath the feet of one of Sultan Ibrahim's war elephants. At Khanua he might have been felled by the slash of a Rajput sword. But he had never thought that Humayun - so healthy and strong - might succumb to sickness. How could he face life without his beloved eldest son? Hindustan and all its riches would be worthless if Humayun died. He would never have come to this sweltering, festering land with its endless hot rains and whining, blood- sucking mosquitoes if he had known this would be the price.

101. Babur was feeling depressed because ...

    (a) the rulers of Bengal were defying Moghul authority

    (b) he could not usually beat Humayun at chess

    (c) he did not like the warm rains and the heaviness of monsoon air

    (d) Maham could not play the lute as well as her grandmother.

102. Which among the following things did Babur not consider doing to relieve himself of depression?

    (a) Go to the women's apartments

    (b) Visit his garden

    (c) Playa game of chess with Humayun

    (d) Listen to Maham sing

103. What was it that Babur currently feared for Humayun?

    (a) Humayun could fall beneath the feet of war elephants

    (b) Humayun could be felled by the slash of a sword

    (c) Humayun may not be treated properly by the Hakim

    (d) Humayun might succumb to sickness

104. According to this passage, which of the following has not been used to describe Humayun?

    (a) Shrewd and subtle minded

    (b) Healthy and strong bodied

    (c) Neatly turbaned head

    (d) Father's beloved

2014-16

Directions for questions 105 to 120: Read the following passages carefully and answer the questions at the end of each passage.

Passage 1

Much remained a mystery about Bernie Madoff's crime, even after he pleaded guilty in March 2009. But one thing, it seemed, that everybody knew was true was this: his wife and sons were guilty too. From the first weeks after his arrest, unidentified "former prosecutors" and "criminal lawyers who have followed the case" and "legal sources" were repeatedly quoted in various media outlets asserting that Ruth, Mark, and Andrew Madoff were under investigation and would soon be indicted. Glossy magazine articles would speculate carefully; garish Internet blogs would accuse recklessly; television commentators would wink and nod knowingly. All that fierce, smug certainty about their guilt-unsupported by any cited facts-effectively drove Madoff's immediate family into exile.

In an era of hypermedia, with mobile phone paparazzi and self-defined Internet commentators constantly on the alert for ways to attract attention, it is worth noting that these attacks on the Madoff family were a sharp departure from the typical public reaction to cases of white-collar crime, going back more than a century.

Of course, such criminals-confidence men, embezzlers, crooked politicians, fraudsters of all kinds-were attacked savagely by the press and the public when their crimes came to light. But their wives and children were almost never included in those attacks; rather they were almost always ignored or, at the very least, quickly left alone. There were a few exceptions where criminal charges were actually filed against a close relative, who was then pulled to the whipping post of public attention. In general, however, even the wives and children of executed murderers were left to rebuild their lives in relative obscurity, unless they sought the spotlight themselves.

The treatment over the years of organized-crime defendants is instructive. Despite widespread fascination with the murderous escapades of so-called "Mafia dons" and crime-family "capos", it was extremely rare for any attention to fall on the elderly Mrs. Mafia Don or the capos' children-even though a realist might have wondered how much they knew about why their husband or father had asked all his closest buddies to wear guns and sleep on mattresses in the garage. On rare occasions, a mobster's relatives actively courted publicity. But those who didn't were routinely ignored by the media and certainly were never publicly and repeatedly accused of complicity in their husbands' or fathers' crimes.

Yet the public outcry against Ruth Madoff and her sons began almost from the instant of Madoff's arrest and did not cease. By the time he pleaded guilty, it was deafening.

From the beginning, however, there were facts in the Madoff case that just didn't seem to be consistent with the family's guilt. First, there was the fact that none of them fled the country. Perhaps Bernie Madoff, seventy years old at the time of his confession, felt too old and tired to leave as a wealthy fugitive; and perhaps Ruth, even if she were guilty and faced arrest and a lifelong imprisonment, would not leave without him. But his two sons, if they were guilty, had the opportunity, the means, and the motive to flee. The end was clearly in sight weeks in advance, there was still a princely sum in the bank, and they and their families were relatively young and portable. Surely, Madoff, before turning himself in, would have handed his sons the keys to the company jet and enough cash to let them live comfortably beyond the reach of the law for the rest of their lives. After all, if they were his accomplices, their only other option would have been to stay and go to prison.

And yet Madoff did not flee- and neither did his wife or sons.

Then, there was his confession. Some hostile theorists immediately argued that Madoff and his guilty sons staged his confession so they could turn him in and thereby deflect suspicion from themselves. But this would have been a worthless gesture unless they all could have been absolutely sure that no incriminating evidence would surface later and none of their other low-level accomplices would finger the sons in a bid for leniency-assumptions that were not remotely realistic if the sons were actually guilty. Moreover, if Madoff truly believed anyone could be insulated from suspicion simply by turning himself in, wouldn't he have arranged for that to be Ruth?

Logic aside, assumptions about the family's guilt began to run up against the fact that, as the Madoff investigation progressed, the predicted arrests of his wife and sons simply did not happen.

105. According to the author, why did the wife and sons of Madoff not flee the country?

(a) Because Bernie Madoff had already pleaded guilty

(b) Because they did not have the opportunity and means to flee

(c) Because they had deflected suspicion from themselves by turning Bernie Madoff in

(d) None of the above

106. How did the family of Bernie Madoff react to media frenzy declaring them guilty?

(a) They launched counter publicity to prove they were not guilty

(b) They sued the media for defamation

(c) They stayed away from public eye

(d) They approached the media to confess their crime

107. What is the point the author has highlighted in the given passage?

(a) That the Madoff crime came to light because of the dynamism of hypermedia

(b) That the treatment over the years of organized-crime defendants has changed

(c) That media tends to run parallel trials to the court

(d) That families of criminals must also be indicted

108. Which of the following sentences is incorrect?

(a) It was the facts about the Madoff case that indicated that his family was guilty

(b) Madoff had been arrested following his confession

(c) Media has always shown extensive interest in the exploits of mafia dons and other criminals

(d) Madoff had committed a white-collar crime

Passage 2

Many years ago, one mustard dominated the supermarket shelves: French's. It came in a plastic bottle. People used it on hot dogs and bologna. It was yellow mustard, made from ground white mustard seed with turmeric and vinegar, which gave it a mild, slightly metallic taste. If you looked hard in the grocery store, you might find something in the speciality-foods section called Grey Poupon, which was Dijon mustard, made from the more pungent brown mustard seed. In the early seventies, Grey Poupon was no more than a hundred-thousand-dollar-a-year business. Few people knew what it was or how it tasted, or had any particular desire for an alternative to French's or the runner-up, Gulden's. Then one day, the Heublein Company, which owned Grey Poupon, discovered something remarkable: if you gave people a mustard taste test, a significant number had only to try Grey Poupon once to switch from yellow mustard. In the food world that almost never happens; even among the most successful food brands, only about one in a hundred has that kind of conversion rate. Grey Poupon was magic.

So Heublein put Grey Poupon in a bigger glass jar, with an enamelled label and enough of a whiff of Frenchness to make it seem as if it were still being made in Europe (it was made in Hartford, Connecticut, from Canadian mustard seed and white wine). The company ran tasteful print ads in upscale food magazines. They put the mustard in little foil packets and distributed them with airplane meals – which was a brand-new idea at the time. Then they hired the Manhattan ad agency Lowe Marschalk to do something, on a modest budget, for television. The agency came back with an idea: A Rolls-Royce is driving down a country road. There's a man in the backseat in a suit with a plate of beef on a silver tray. He nods to the chauffeur, who opens the glove compartment. Then comes what is known in the business world as the *reveal*. The chauffeur hands back ajar of Grey Poupon. Another Rolls Royce pulls up alongside. A man leans his hand out of the window. "Pardon me. Would you have any Grey Poupon?"

In the cities where the ads ran, sales of Grey Poupon leaped 40 to 50 percent, and whenever Heublein bought airtime in new cities sales jumped 40 to 50 percent again. Grocery stores put Grey Poupon next, to French's and Gulden's. By the end of the 1980's Grey Poupon was the most powerful brand in mustard. "The tagline in the commercial was that this was one of life's finer pleasures." Larry Elegant, who wrote the original Grey Poupon spot, says, "and that, along with the Rolls Royce, seemed to impart to people's minds that this was something truly different and superior."

The rise of Grey Poupon proved that the American supermarket shopper was willing to pay more – in this case $3.99 instead of $1.49 for eight ounces – as long as what they were buying carried with it an air of sophistication and complex aromatics. Its success showed, furthermore, that the boundaries of taste and custom were not fixed: that just because mustard had always been yellow didn't mean that customers would use only yellow mustard. It is because of Grey Poupon that the standard American supermarket today has an entire mustard section. And it is because of Grey Poupon that a man named Jim Wigon decided, four years ago, to enter the ketchup business.

Isn't the ketchup business today exactly where mustard was thirty years ago? There is Heinz and, far behind, Hunt's and Del Monte and a handful of private label brands. Jim Wagon wanted to create the Grey Poupon of ketchup.

Wigon is from Boston. He runs his ketchup business-under the brand World's Best Ketchup-out of the catering business of his partner, Nich Schiarizzi, in Norwood, Massachusetts. He starts with red peppers, Spanish onions, garlic, and a high-end tomato paste. Basil is chopped by hand, because the buffalo chopper bruises the leaves. He uses maple syrup, not corn syrup, which gives him a quarter of the sugar of Heinz. He pours his ketchup into a clear ten-ounce jar, and sells its for three times the price of Heinz, and for the past few years he has crisscrossed the country, peddling World's Best in six flavours- regular, sweet, dill, garlic, caramelized onion,

and basil - to speciality grocery stores and supermarkets. If you were in Zabar's on Manhattan's Upper West Side a few months ago, you would have seen him at the front of the store, in the spot between the sushi and the gefilte fish. In front of him, on a small table, was a silver tureen filled with miniature chicken and beef meatballs, a box of toothpicks, and a dozen or so open jars of his ketchup. "Try my ketchup!" Wigon said, over and over, to anyone who passed. "If you don't try it, you're doomed to eat Heinz the rest of your life."

In the same aisle at Zabar's that day two other demonstrations were going on, so that people were starting at one end with free chicken sausage, sampling a slice of prosciutto, and then pausing at the World's Best stand before heading for the cash register. They would look down at the array of open jars, and Wigon would impale a meatball on a toothpick, dip it in one of his ketchups, and hand it to them with a flourish. The ratio of tomato solids to liquid in World's Best is much higher than in Heinz, and the maple syrup gives it an unmistakable sweet kick. Invariably, people would close their eyes, just for a moment, and do a subtle double take. Some of them would look slightly perplexed and walk away, and others would nod and pick up a jar. "You know why you like it so much?" he would say, in his broad Boston accent, to the customers who seemed most impressed. "Because you have been eating bad ketchup all your life!" Jim Wigon had a simple vision: build a better ketchup - the way Grey Poupon built a better mustard - and the world will beat a path to your door.

109. Why has the author termed Grey Poupon as "magic"?

    (a) It had a different taste and was seen as belonging to speciality-foods division

    (b) It was made from Dijon mustard

    (c) It commanded a conversion rate uncommon in the food world

    (d) It came in a bigger glass jar than French's

110. How many years did it take for Grey Poupon to grow from a hundred-thousand dollar a year brand to the most powerful brand in mustard?

    (a) Less than 5 years

    (b) About 5-10 years

    (c) About 15-20 years

    (d) More than 25 years

111. What kind of audience was Grey Poupon reaching out to through its ads?

    (a) Frequent Flyers

    (b) Those who did not like the taste of French's

    (c) Buyers of large quantities of mustard

    (d) Rich and sophisticated customers

112. Which of the following statements is correct?

    (a) World's Best Ketchup was cheaper than Heinz

    (b) Wigon claimed that people will be doomed if they tried Heinz Ketchup

    (c) World's Best Ketchup was thicker than Heinz

    (d) People who were perplexed with the taste tended to pick up the jar of World's Best Ketchup

Passage 3

To equate 'capitalism' with 'greed' is a mistake. We tend to confuse self-interest in the marketplace with selfishness or greed. At the heart of capitalism is the idea of exchange between ordinary, self-interested human beings, who seek to advance their interests peacefully in the marketplace. Adam Smith called this 'rational self-interest'. It is the same motive that gets one to jump out of bed in the morning or makes one carry an umbrella if it rains—nothing selfish about that. To be human is to be self-interested, and this is what exchange in the market place entails.

Greed or selfishness, on the other hand, is an excess of self interest and often transgresses on the rights of others. It is present in all of us, but we find it easier to see it in others and difficult to see it in ourselves. Greed can motivate theft, entail himsa—hurting another whose opposite, ahimsa, is a virtue that Mahatma Gandhi extolled. But the other side of greed is ambition, a positive thing, and when rightly directed, is life-affirming. Herein lies the conundrum of human existence: that the same inner forces that result in a vice can just as easily become virtues that can motivate the well-being of our species.

Those who believe that capitalism has been forced on us by the imperial West are also wrong. Friedrich Hayek, the Noble laureate, called the market a spontaneous order—it is natural for human beings to exchange goods and services, and this is how every society evolved money, laws, conventions and morals to guide behaviour in the marketplace. These are natural products of human endeavour. Competing and cooperating in the marketplace existed in India before the West was imperial or modern.

Whether we like it or not, India is headed in the direction of some sort of democratic capitalism. After two decades of reforms, hardly anyone in India wants state ownership of production, where the absence of competition corrodes the character even more, as we know too well from the dark days of the 'license raj'. Our animus against capitalism has diminished after communism's fall as people increasingly believe that markets do deliver greater prosperity, but most think that capitalism is not a moral system. They continue to believe that morality must depend on religion.

Although the market is neither moral nor immoral, human self-interest usually brings about good behaviour in the marketplace. A seller who does not treat his customers with fairness and civility will lose market share. A company that markets defective products will lose customers. A firm that does not promote the most deserving employees will lose talent to its competitors. A buyer who does not respect the market price will not survive. Lying and cheating will ruin a firm's image, making it untouchable to creditors and suppliers. Hence, free markets offer powerful incentives for ethical conduct, but they must be backed by state institutions that enforce contracts and punish criminal behaviour. If the market has an inbuilt morality, why are there so many crooks in the marketplace? The answer is that there are crooked people in every society, and this is why we need effective regulators, policemen and judges. We should design our institutions to catch crooks and not harass innocent people as we do so often.

The other cause of our grief is to mistake being 'pro-market' with being 'pro-business'. To be 'pro-market' is to believe in competitive markets which help to keep prices low and gradually raise the quality of products. Competition also means that some businesses will die because they are poorly managed and cannot compete. Kingfisher Airlines and Air India should be allowed to die and not be bailed out by the government. Thus, being pro-market leads to 'rules-based capitalism'; 'pro-business' often leads to 'crony capitalism'. Not to have explained this difference has been the great mistake of our reformers and this has led to the false impression that the reforms only make the rich richer. Crony capitalism exists in India today because of the lack of reforms in sectors such as mining and real estate. To get rid of crony capitalism we need more rather than less reform.

The doom-mongers, who claim that we are now resigned to live in an age of decaying moral standards, are also wrong. Yes, the new Indian middle class is permissive and indulges enthusiastically in harmless pleasures. Yes, it is materialistic, consumerist and capitalistic. But these impulses are not to be mistaken for greed. Only when one's pleasure hurts another does it become a matter of the law and then, of course, it must be punished. The shared imagination of the new India with its harmless pleasure and victimless vice should not be condemned. Think of ours as a society in transition. Mass wealth is profoundly disturbing but once there is enough, India might again return to its old character of renunciation.

Instead of religious rules, young Indians are motivated by duties to fellow human beings rather than to gods. Those who accuse them of shallow materialism ignore the injustices that prevailed when religion held a monopoly on morality. They overlook real ethical progress with regard to sexual and caste equality that our secular society has begun to deliver. So, the next time Kejriwal makes an expose and the TV screams 'greed', do not fall into the trap of believing capitalist culture is morally sick or that we should return to a moral order rooted in socialism or religion.

113. Which of the following statement correctly reflects the views of the author?

    (a) Greed entails both himsa and ahimsa

    (b) Self interest does not necessarily lead to selfish behavior

    (c) Being pro market lead to the rich becoming richer

    (d) Both B and D

114. Which of the following options most closely explains what the author wants to say, in the sentence beginning with: "Herein lies the conundrum of human existence:...."

    (a) The enigma of human existence is that vices and virtues can result from the same inner forces.

    (b) The bane of human existence is that vices and virtues can result from the same inner forces.

    (c) The boon of human existence is that the same inner forces can lead to vices and virtues.

    (d) The solution for human existence is that the same inner forces can lead to vices and virtues.

115. As wealth spreads in society, what is likely to happen according to the author?

    (a) India will have to resign itself to decaying moral standards

    (b) India may once again embrace renunciation

    (c) The moral order in India will become deeply rooted in religion

    (d) None of the above

116. Which of the following statements does not reflect the views given in this passage?

    (a) Indian society is undergoing a change and the middle class is emerging

    (b) Crony capitalism exists in India today because of the governments' pro- market policies.

    (c) The Indian youth is motivated' driven by moral duties rather than religious diktats.

    (d) Free markets need the oversight of state institutions for defeating crooks and criminals

Passage 4

Brazil is a top exporter of every commodity that has seen dizzying price surges - iron ore, soybeans, sugar - producing a golden age for economic growth. Foreign money-flows into Brazilian stocks and bonds climbed heavenward, up more than tenfold, from $5 billion a year in early 2007 to more than $50 billion in the twelve months through March 2011.

The flood of foreign money buying up Brazilian assets has made the currency one of the most expensive in the world, and Brazil one of the most costly, over hyped economies. Almost every major emerging-market currency has strengthened against the dollar over the last decade, but the Brazilian *Real* is on a path alone, way above the pack, having doubled in value against the dollar.

Economists have all kinds of fancy ways to measure the real value of a currency, but when a country is pricing itself this far out of the competition, you can feel it on the ground. In early 2011 the major Rio paper, *O Globo,* ran a story on prices showing that croissants are more expensive than they are in Paris, haircuts cost more than they do in London, bike rentals are more expensive than in Amsterdam, and movie tickets sell for higher prices than in Madrid. A rule of the road: if the local prices in an emerging market country feel expensive even to a visitor from a rich nation, that country is probably not a breakout nation.

There is no better example of how absurd it is to lump all the big emerging markets together than the frequent pairing of Brazil and China. Those who make this comparison are referring only to the fact that they are the biggest players in their home regions, not to the way the economies actually run. Brazil is the world's leading exporter of many raw materials, and China is the leading importer; that makes them major trade partners - China surpassed the United States as Brazil's leading trade partner in 2009 - but it also makes them opposites in almost every important economic respect: Brazil is the *un-China,* with interest rates that are too high, and a currency that is too expensive. It spends too little on roads and too much on welfare, and as a result has a very un-China-like growth record.

It may not be entirely fair to compare economic growth in Brazil with that of its Asian counterparts, because Brazil has a per capita income of $12,000, more than two times China's and nearly ten times India's. But even taking into account the fact that it is harder for rich nations to grow quickly, Brazil's growth has been disappointing. Since the early 1980s the Brazilian growth rate has oscillated around an average of 2.5 percent, spiking only in concert with increased prices for Brazil's key commodity exports.

While China has been criticized for pursuing "growth at any cost," Brazil has sought to secure "stability at any cost." Brazil's caution stems from its history of financial crises, in which overspending produced debt, humiliating defaults, and embarrassing devaluations, culminating in a disaster that is still recent enough to be fresh in every Brazilian adult's memory: the hyperinflation that started in the early 1980s and peaked in 1994, at the vertiginous annual rate of 2,100 percent.

Wages were pegged to inflation but were increased at varying intervals in different industries, so workers never really knew whether they were making good money or not. As soon as they were paid, they literally ran to the store with cash to buy food, and they could afford little else, causing nonessential industries to start to die. Hyperinflation finally came under control in 1995, but it left a problem of regular inflation behind. Brazil has battled inflation ever since by maintaining one of the highest interest rates in the emerging world. Those high rates have attracted a surge of foreign money, which is partly why the Brazilian *Real* is so expensive relative to comparable currencies.

There is a growing recognition that China faces serious "imbalances" that could derail its long economic boom. Obsessed until recently with high growth, China has been pushing too hard to keep its currency too cheap (to help its export industries compete), encouraging excessively high savings and keeping interest rates rock bottom to fund heavy spending on roads and ports. China is only now beginning to consider a shift in spending priorities to create social programs that protect its people from the vicissitudes of old age and unemployment.

Brazil's economy is just as badly out of balance, though in opposite ways. While China has introduced reforms relentlessly for three decades, opening itself up to the world even at the risk of domestic instability, Brazil has pushed reforms only in the most dire circumstances, for example, privatizing state companies when the government budget is near collapse. Fearful of foreign shocks, Brazil is still one of the most closed economies in the emerging world -total imports and exports account for only 15 percent of GDP - despite its status as the world's leading exporter of sugar, orange juice, coffee, poultry, and beef.

To pay for its big government, Brazil has jacked up taxes and now has a tax burden that equals 38 percent of GDP, the highest in the emerging world, and very similar to the tax burden in developed European welfare states, such as Norway and France. This heavy load of personal and corporate tax on a relatively poor country means that businesses don't have the money to invest in new technology or training, which in turn means that industry is not getting more efficient. Between 1980 and 2008 Brazil's productivity grew at an annual rate of about 0.2 percent, compared to 4 percent in China. Over the same period, productivity grew in India at close to 3 percent and in South Korea and Thailand at close to 2 percent.

117. According to the passage, the major concern facing the Brazil economy is:
    (a) Despite being a major exporter of several key primary commodities, the openness of the economy has not improved.
    (b) High tax incidence on the household and company incomes, which restricts the ability of the firms to facilitate innovation and skill formation.
    (c) Insufficient spending of budgetary resources on infrastructure augmentation, which hurts economic interests.
    (d) All of the above

118. Brazil's quest for stability in its economy has originated from:
    (a) The bitter experience of financial crisis and hyperinflation in the nineties
    (b) The need to maintain steady supply of commodity exports from its economy
    (c) The urge to enhance economic growth further
    (d) All of the above

119. Identify the false statement:
    (a) The Brazilian government in the past has shown lesser inclination towards quick implementation of reform measures.
    (b) The inflow of foreign currency in Brazil has increased by around US $ 45 Billion over the four-year period starting from 2007.
    (c) The annual productivity growth rate in China during 1980-2008 is found to be 20 times higher than the corresponding figure experienced by Brazil.
    (d) The current inflation management practice of Brazil has provided its economy a significant edge vis-a-vis other countries.

120. According to the passage, Brazil does not seem to be an exporter of which commodity combination?
    (a) Poultry and beef
    (b) Iron ore and soybeans
    (c) Croissants and bikes
    (d) Sugar, orange juice and coffee

2015-17

Directions for questions 121 to 125: Read the following passage carefully and answer the questions given at the end.

Passage 1

No club in the English Premier League generated less money than Wigan Athletic. No club in the Premier League had so little history, or so few Fans. Ever sires 2005, when they won promotion to the top flight for the first time in their existence, Wigan started the season listening to prophecies of doom. 2013 was the year that football gravity finally caught up with them and they returned to their 'rightful' place among the also-rans. Even as the naysayers and doubters were ignoring seven years of wrong forecasts and congratulating themselves for seeing Wigan's fate, this little David took out one last Goliath, Manchester City, in the FA Cup final.

In their book *Why England Lose*, the football journalist Simon Kuper and the economist Stefan Szymanski found that money matters a great deal for the success of football clubs. According to their calculations. 92 per cent of the differences in English Football clubs' league position can be explained by a club's relative wage bill. It might not be the case that the team with the highest wage bill finishes top each and every season, but over the long term, the correlation is uncanny. At the other end of the table, it seems inevitable that, eventually, in football poverty will drag you down.

For Wigan, this was unfortunate. The annual reports into football's finances prepared by the accountants Deloitte must have made miserable reading for anyone who followed the club: their turnover, wages and attendance were all fractions of the Premier League's giants. And yet Wigan managed to avoid relegation for seven years. It was almost pathological. They defied he laws of football economics. They disobeyed the laws of football gravity.

Part of the reason Wigan managed to survive so long in the rarefied air of the Premier League is Dave Whelan, the local magnate who owns the club. Wigan's average attendance was just 17,000 - they rarely sold out their home ground, the DW Stadium, its initials a (self-awarded) tribute to the club's benefactor - on a par with the likes of Vitesse Arnhem or the average German second-division side, but half the Premier League's average. That's a considerable shortfall in revenue. It's the same when we look at television and commercial earnings: in 2010-11, they earned £50.5 million from all of these streams - a tidy sum, to be sure, but half what the average Premier League team took. Only because of Whelan's enduring generosity did the club avoid sinking into the red. In 2011-12, he wrote off a £48 million loan to the club to balance the books. Financially, Wigan could not compete. And yet on the pitch they did.

In truth, Wigan did not dramatically outperform their wage bill, the gauge - for Kuper and Szymanski - of a manager's true: impact. From 2006 to 2011, they finished eighteenth, Fifteenth, fifteenth, sixteenth and sixteenth in the salary league, not far off their finishes in the actual division. Yet Wigan's continued survival was still, as the respected financial blog The Swiss Ramble had it. 'a minor modern miracle'. To explain why, we have to consider the odds that - given their spending on wages - Wigan would have been relegated well before the final axe fell in 2013. To do that properly, we need to calculate the odds of relegation as a function of a club's payroll.

The notional odds of relegation from the Premier League in any given season, for any team, are 15 per cent: three sides out of twenty endure the pain of demotion every year. But of course those three clubs are not simply drawn out of a hat: money does mater. More specifically, when we examined twenty years of club finances with the help of data from Deloitte, we found that a club's odds of relegation are 7.2 per cent if its wage spends is greater than average. In other words, you can halve the chances of being relegated just by spending a little more on your salaries than the average side. But for clubs that spend less, the odds of relegation shoot up from 15 to 21 per

cent. For a team that spends as little as Wigan or less, these odds can even be as high as 44 per cent in any given season.

Spending less isn't death sentence, but you are flirting with the chair. And spending less than the average year after year means the odds of relegation accumulate. For Wigan, the odds that they would be relegated at some point over the five Premier League seasons to 2012 were 95 per cert. It was, both mathematically and financially, almost a certainty. With wage bills four, two, and one and a half times Wigan's £40 million, Manchester United, Aston Villa and Fulham faced odds of demotion of 0, 31 and 69 per cent, respectively.

All this suggests that Wigan's continued survival was more than just good luck, and it was not simply attributable to their individual wage spending in any given year: the numbers were squarely against them. So Wigan's story is not just about money, but also how that money is put to use. By any standard measure Wigan had been a mediocre team for a long time. They conceded more goals than they scored in every season they were in the Premier League. They tended to have more possession than most of their peers at the wrong end of the table, but much of that came from the sterile domination of their own half. Roberto Martinez's team, though, had been doing more than just passing the ball around at the back and getting lucky.

With the help of Ramzi Ben Said, a student at Cornell University, and the performance chalkboards published online by the British newspaper the *Guardian* in conjunction with Opta Sports, we tried to establish how Wigan went about scoring their goals in the 2010-11 season. Ramzi collected and coded a year's worth of data of attacking production (how each Premier League club scored their goals that season).

The data showed that the vast majority - 66 per cent - of the 1.4 goals a team scored in the average match that year came from open play. By far the smallest proportion of goals came from direct free kicks: just 2.8 per cent team, per match. The average team produced one goal a game from open play, but needed to take thirty-five direct free kicks before finding the net that way.

But Martinez's Wigan was not your typical club. In 2010-11, they created goals in extremely unusual ways. They relied much less on traditional open-play goals than most, and did not bother with anything that resembled a patient build-up. In half their games they failed to score from open play at all. When they did, they tended to come from what are known among analysts as fast breaks' - lightning-quick counter-attacks. And the rest of their goals came from free kicks. Their output in both these categories was exceptional. They scored twice as many goals on the break as the average side. And they scored almost four times as many goals from free kicks.

Rather than choosing one or the other, Martinez as a manager seemed to have forsaken both high frequency - not scoring from the most common source of goals - as well as good odds - trying to score from low probability shots (free kicks) - as a way to win matches. Martinez was not trying to fight his opponents in a conventional way. Instead, he was beating them any way he could. Albert Larcada, an analyst at ESPN's Stats & Information Group, filled in the picture further. Using Opta's master file of play-by-play data, Larcada discovered Wigan were unusual in a number of other ways.

Not only did they score from fast breaks and free kicks, but when Larcada calculated the average distances from which Premier League clubs attempted shots that season, Wigan were the overall league leaders. Their average shooting distance was some twenty-six yards. This looked deliberate: their goals came from a longer distance than any of their peers - an average of 18.5 yards, way ahead of second-placed Tottenham, while their players Charles N'Zogbia and Hugo Rodallega both finished in the top five scorers from distance in the Premier League in 2010-11.

Martinez was thinking outside the box in the most literal fashion. Indeed, his team had the lowest number of goals scored from inside the penalty area of any side in the league - just twenty-eight, compared to Manchester United's sixty-nine. This sounds very defensive - hitting teams on the break, relying on set pieces and long-range shots - but Wigan's formations told a more nuanced story. Martinez's strategy relied on highly accurate long-range shooting, firing from distance - allowing his team to recover their defensive shape more easily - and persistence. He did not place any emphasis on corners - Wigan scored just one goal from a corner in the entire 2010-11 season - because it meant allowing his troop out of hiding and into open sight, leaving them vulnerable. Martinez was playing guerrilla football. He had his team lie in wait for their opponents and then punish them on the counter-attack. He employed sharpshooters, to let fly from distance, and snipers, to hit free kicks. His team were adaptable, unpredictable.

121. Identify the <u>correct</u> statement:

   (a) In tams of salary payments to the staff, Wigan was ranked fifteenth during the 2009-10 season.

   (b) According to the article, the wage bill of Manchester United is two times the corresponding figure for Aston Villa.

   (c) According to the article, the research of Kuper and Szymanski revealed that if a football club is successful in including a number of highly paid footballers in its team, the club is more likely to win all major European tournaments.

   (d) For analyzing the performance of the teams in English Premier League the above article has used the performance chalkboards published by The Guardian in its daily newspaper in conjunction with ESPN Sports.

122. As per the research conducted by the ESPN's Stats & information Group, the average distances from which Wigan Athletic attempted shots during 2010-11 was:

   (a) 22 yards   (b) 20 yards

   (c) 26 yards   (d) 18.5 yards

123. Match the Following:

	Name		Occupation
i	Hugo Rodallega	a	Student at Cornell University
ii	Ramzi Ben said	b	Manager of Wigan Athletic
iii	Roberto Martinez	c	Analyst at ESPN
iv	Albert Larcada	d	Player of Wigan Athletic

   (a) i-c, ii-b, iii-d, iv-a

   (b) i-d, ii-c, iii-a, iv-b

   (c) i-b, ii-a, iii-c, iv-d

   (d) i-d, ii-a, iii-b, iv-c

124. Wigan's playing style has been termed as 'guerrilla football' because:

   (a) Instead of deciding to play with a team full of superstars, they were relying mainly on junior players with less professional experience, which resulted into poorer performance of the team.

   (b) The team was among the lowest scoring teams in the English Premier League in all the years they played.

   (c) Instead of attacking style of playmaking the team played a counter-attack based game, and depended heavily on goals scored from distance and through free kicks, and getting back to defensive positions quickly.

   (d) All of the above

125. Identify the <u>incorrect</u> statement:

   (a) The data on club finances, collected by Deloitte in the last decade alone, indicates that the odds of relegation of an English Premier League team are 7.2 per cent if the club's spending on wage is greater than average.

   (b) The Article suggests that in 2010-11, an average English Premier League team earned around £101 million through television and commercial earnings.

   (c) The average attendance in Wigan's matches was around 17,000 and their home matches were held at DW Stadium, named after Dave Whelan, the magnate and owner of the club.

   (d) During 2010-11, the goals scored by Wigan from free kicks were as high as almost four times as the goals scored by an average English Premier league team.

Directions for questions 126 to 129: Read the following passage carefully and answer the questions given at the end.

Passage 2

The tight calendar had calmed him, as did the constant exertion of his authority as a judge. How he relished his power over the classes that had kept his family pinned under their heels for centuries - like the stenographer, for example, who was a Brahmin. There he was, now crawling into a tiny tent to the side, and there was Jemubhai reclining like a king in a bed carved out of teak, hung with mosquito netting.

"Bed tea", the cook would shout "Baaad tee".

He would sit up to drink.

6.30: he'd bathe in water that had been heated over the fire so it was redolent with the smell of wood smoke and flecked with ash. With a dusting of powder, he graced his newly washed face, with a daub of pomade, his hair. Crunched up toast like charcoal from having been toasted upon the flame, with marmalade over the burn.

8.30: he rode into the fields with the local officials and everyone else in the village going along for fun. Followed by an orderly holding an umbrella over his head to shield him from the glare, he measured the fields and checked to make sure his yield estimate matched the headman's statement. Farms were growing less than ten maunds an acre of rice or wheat, and at two rupees a maund, every single man in a village, sometimes, was in debt to the *bania*, (Nobody knew that Jemubhai himself was noosed, of course, that long ago in the little town of Piphit in Gujarat, money-lenders had sniffed out in him a winning combination of ambition and poverty... that they still sat waiting cross-legged on a soiled mat in the market, snapping their toes, cracking their knuckles in anticipation of repayment ....)

2.00: after lunch, the judge sat at his desk under a tree to try cases, usually in a cross mood, for he disliked the informality, hated the splotch of leaf shadow on him imparting an untidy mongrel look. Also, there was a worse aspect of contamination and corruption: he heard cases in Hindi, but they were recorded in Urdu by the stenographer and translated by the judge into a second record in English, although his own command of Hindi and Urdu was tenuous; the witnesses who couldn't read at all put their thumbprints at the bottom of "Read Over and Acknowledged Correct", as instructed. Nobody could be sure how much of the truth had fallen between languages, between languages and illiteracy; the clarity that justice demanded was nonexistent. Still, despite the leaf shadow and language confusion, he acquired a fearsome reputation for his speech that seemed to belong to no language at all, and for his face like a mask that conveyed something beyond human

fallibility. The expression and manner honed here would carry him, eventually, all the way to the high court in Lucknow where, annoyed by lawless pigeons shuttlecocking about those tall, shadowy halls, he would preside, white powdered wig over white powdered face, hammer in hand.

His photograph, thus attired, thus annoyed, was still up on the wall, in a parade of history glorifying the progress of Indian law and order.

4:30: tea had to be perfect, drop scones made in the frying pan. He would embark on them with forehead wrinkled, as if angrily mulling over something important, and then, as it would into his retirement, the draw of the sweet took over, and his stern work face would hatch an expression of tranquillity.

5:30: out he went into the countryside with his fishing rod or gun. The countryside was full of game; lariats of migratory birds lassoed the sky in October; quail and partridge with lines of babies strung out behind whirred by like nursery toys that emit sound with movement; pheasant - fat foolish creatures, made to be shot - went scurrying through the bushes. The thunder of gunshot rolled away, the leaves shivered, and he experienced the profound silence that could come only after violence. One thing was always missing, though, the proof of the pudding, the prize of the action, the manliness in manhood, the partridge for the pot, because he returned with - *Nothing!*

He was a terrible shot.

8:00: the cook saved his reputation, cooked a chicken, brought it forth, proclaimed it "roast bastard", just as in the Englishman's favourite joke book of natives using incorrect English. But sometimes, eating that roast bustard, the judge felt the joke might also be on him, and he called for another rum, took a big gulp, and kept eating feeling as if he were eating himself, since he, too, was (was he?) part of the fun ...

9:00: sipping Ovaltine, he filled out the registers with the day's gleanings. The Petromax lantern would be lit - what a noise it made - insects fording the black to dive - bomb him with soft flowers (moths), with iridescence (beetles). Lines, columns, and squares. He realized truth war best looked at in tiny aggregates, for many baby truths could yet add up to one big size unsavory lie. Last, in his diary also to be submitted to his superiors, he recorded the random observations of a cultured man, someone who was observant, schooled in literature as well as economies; and he made up hunting triumphs: two partridge ... one deer with thirty- inch horns ...

11:00: he had a hot water bottle in winter, and, in all seasons, to the sound of the wind buffeting the trees and the cook's snoring, he fell asleep.

126. Which of the following statements is <u>incorrect</u>?

    (a) The judge used to visit the countryside to shoot game

    (b) The judge was not a Brahmin

    (c) The judge had good command over Hindi and Urdu

    (d) The judge owed money to moneylenders in Piphit

127. What always happened when the judge went to the countryside?

    (a) He could not hear any noise and there was only profound silence

    (b) He could not manage to hit a single bird

    (c) He could not get the proof that the pudding was made from the Patridge

    (d) He could not see lariats of migratory birds

128. People were in debt to the "bania" because:

    (a) Yield per acre did not appear to be very good.

    (b) Moneylenders in Piphit were asking all villagers for repayment.

    (c) People in the village spent too much time on hunting,

    (d) The fields were spoiled when the judge rode around to take measurement.

129. Which is the odd one out:

    (a) Lariat   (b) Brood

    (c) Flock   (d) flight

Directions for questions 130 to 134: Read the following passage carefully and answer the questions given at the end.

Passage 3

The movement to expel the Austrians from Italy and unite Italy under a republican government had been gaining momentum while Garibaldi was away. There was a growing clamour, not just from Giuseppe Mazzini's republicans, but from moderates as well, for a General capable of leading Italy to independence. Even the King of Piedmont, for whom Garibaldi was still an outlaw under sentence of death, subscribed to an appeal for a sword for the returning hero. Meanwhile, the 'year of revolutions', 1848, had occurred in which Louis Philippe had been toppled from the French throne. In Austria, an uprising triggered off insurrections in Venice and Milan, and the Austrian garrisons were forced out. The King of Piedmont Charles Albert ordered his troops to occupy these cities. There had also been insurrections in Sicily, causing the King Ferdinand II, to grant major constitutional freedoms in 1849, prompting both the Pope and Charles Albert to grant further concessions.

Meanwhile, largely ignorant of these developments, Garibaldi was approaching Italy at a leisurely pace, arriving at Nice on 23 June 1848 to a tumultuous reception. The hero declared himself willing to fight and lay down his life for Charles Albert, who he now regarded as a bastion of Italian nationalism.

Mazzini and the republicans were horrified, regarding this as outright betrayal: did it reflect Garibaldi's innate simple-mindedness, his patriotism in the war against Austria, or was it part of a deal with the monarchy? Charles Albert had pardoned Garibaldi, but to outward appearances, he was still very wary of the General and the Italian Legion he had amassed of 150 'brigands'. The two men met near Mantus, and the King appeared to dislike him instantly. He suggested that Garibaldi's men should join his army and that Garibaldi should go to Venice and captain a ship as a privateer against the Austrians.

Garibaldi, meanwhile, met his former hero Mazzini for the first time, and again the encounter was frosty. Seemingly rebuffed on all sides, Garibaldi considered going to Sicily to fight King Ferdinand II of Naples, but changed his mind when the Milanese offered him the post of General - something they badly needed when Charles Albert's Piedmontese army was defeated at Custoza by the Austrians. With around 1,000 men, Garibaldi marched into the mountains at Varese, commenting bitterly; 'The King of Sardinia may have a crown that he holds on to by dint of misdeeds and cowardice, but my comrades and I do not wish to hold on to our lives by shameful action'.

The King of Piedmont offered an armistice to the Austrians and all the gains in northern Italy were lost again. Garibaldi returned to Nice and then across to Genoa, where he learned that, in September 1848, Ferdinand II had bombed Messina as a prelude to invasion - an atrocity which caused him to be dubbed 'King Bomba'. Reaching Livorno he was diverted yet again and set off across the Italian peninsula with 350 men to come to Venice's assistance, but on the way, in Bologna, he learned that the Pope had taken refuge with King Bomba. Garibaldi promptly altered course southwards towards Rome where he was greeted once again as a hero. Rome proclaimed itself a Republic. Garibaldi's Legion had swollen to nearly 1,300 men, and the Grand Duke of Tuscany fled Florence before the advancing republican force.

However, the Austrians marched southwards to place the Grand Duke of Tuscany back on his throne. Prince Louis Napoleon of France dispatched an army of 7,000 men under General Charles Oudinot to the port of Civitavecchia to seize the city. Garibaldi was appointed as a General to defend Rome.

The republicans had around 9,000 men, and Garibaldi was given control of more than 4,000 to defend the Janiculum Hill, which was crucial to the defence of Rome, as it commanded the city over the Tiber. Some 5,000 well-equipped French troops arrived on 30 April 1849 at Porta Cavallegeri in the old walls of Rome, but failed to get through, and were attacked from behind by Garibaldi, who led a baton charge and was grazed by a bullet slightly on his side. The French lost 500 dead and wounded, along with some 350 prisoners, to the Italians, 200 dead and wounded. It was a famous victory, wildly celebrated by the Romans into the night, and the French signed a tactical truce.

However, other armies were on the march: Bomba's 12,500-strong Neapolitan army was approaching from the south, while the Austrians had attacked Bologna in the north. Garibaldi took a force out of Rome and engaged in a flanking movement across the Neapolitan army's rear at Castelli Romani; the Neapolitans attacked and were driven *off,* leaving 50 dead, Garibaldi accompanied the Roman General, Piero Roselli, in an attack on the retreating Neapolitan army. Foolishly leading a patrol of his men right out in from of his forces, he tried to stop a group of his cavalry retreating and fell under their horses, with the enemy slashing at him with their sabres. He was rescued by his legionnaires, narrowly having avoided being killed, but Roselli had missed the chance to encircle the Neapolitan army.

Garibaldi boldly wanted to carry the fight down into the Kingdom of Naples, but Mazzini, who by now was effectively in charge of Rome, ordered him back to the capital to face the danger of Austrian attack from the north. In fact, it was the French who arrived on the outskirts of Rome first, with an army now reinforced by 30,000. Mazzini realized that Rome could not resist and ordered a symbolic stand within the city itself, rather than surrender, for the purposes of international propaganda and to keep the struggle alive, whatever the cost. On 3 June, the French arrived in force and seized the strategic country house, Villa Pamphili.

Garibaldi rallied his forces and fought feverishly to retake the villa up narrow and steep city streets, capturing it, then losing it again. By the end of the day, the sides had 1,000 dead between them. Garibaldi once again had been in the thick of the fray, giving orders to his troops and fighting, it was said, like a lion. Although beaten off for the moment, the French imposed a siege in the morning, starving the city of provisions and bombarding its beautiful centre.

On 30 June, the French attacked again in force, while Garibaldi, at the head of his troops, fought back ferociously. But there was no prospect of holding the French off indefinitely, and Garibaldi decided to take his men out of the city to continue resistance in the mountains. Mazzini fled to Britain while Garibaldi remained to fight for the cause. He had just 4,000 men, divided into two legions, and faced some 17,000 Austrians and Tuscans in the north, 30,000 Neapolitans and Spanish in the south, and 40,000 French in the west. He was being directly pursued by 8,000 French and was approaching Neapolitan and Spanish divisions of some 18,000 men. He stood no chance whatever. The rugged hill country was ideal, however, for his style of irregular guerrilla warfare, and he manoeuvred skilfully, marching and counter-marching in different directions, confounding his pursuers before finally aiming for Arena in the north. But his men were deserting in droves and local people were hostile in his army: he was soon reduced to 1500 men who struggled across the high mountain passes to San Marino where he found temporary refuge.

The Austrians, now approaching, demanded that he go into exile in America. He was determined to fight on and urged the ill and pregnant Anita, his wife, to stay behind in San Marino, but she would not hear of it. The pair set off with 200 loyal soldiers along the mountain tracks to the Adriatic coast, from where Garibaldi intended to embark for Venice, which was still valiantly holding out against the Austrians. They embarked aboard 13 fishing boats anti managed to sail to within 50 miles of the Venetian lagoon before being spotted by an Austrian flotilla and fired upon.

Only two of Garibaldi's boats escaped. He carried Anita through the shallows lo a beach and they moved further inland. The ailing Anita was placed in a cart and they reached a farmhouse, where she died. Her husband broke down into inconsolable wailing and she was buried in a shallow grave near the farmhouse, but was transferred to a churchyard a few days later. Garibaldi had no time to lose; he and his faithful companion Leggero escaped across the Po towards Ravenna.

At last Garibaldi was persuaded to abandon his insane attempts to reach Venice by sea and to return along less guarded routes on the perilous mountain paths across the Apennines towards the western coast of Italy. He visited his family in Nice for an emotional reunion with his mother and his three children - but lacked the courage to tell them what had happened to their mother.

130. Find the <u>correct</u> statement:

(a) Garibaldi had a sore relationship with King Charles Albert before 1849, which however greatly improved in the subsequent period.

(b) Garibaldi's wife Anita Garibaldi passed away at a farmhouse, after their journey to Venice was interrupted by a Spanish flotilla.

(c) After defeat of the republican army in the battle of Rome, a total of 80000 foreign soldiers were moving in Italy across all directions, while Garibaldi was being directly pursued by 8000 French forces.

(d) When Garibaldi and his wife left San Marino after threat from the Austrians, they were accompanied by 200 soldiers who were still loyal to him.

131. Which of the following statements can be deduced from the passage?

    (a) King of Naples was given the name 'King Bombe', when he bombed Milan before the invasion that he was planning.

    (b) During the defence of Rome from the attack of Austrian troops, Garibaldi positioned his army near the Janiculum Hill.

    (c) While Garibaldi was fighting in Italy for unification of the country, his children stayed at Nice.

    (d) At the time when Garibaldi returned to meet King Charles Albert at Mantua, Giuseppe Mazzini was a major leader of the Italian moderates.

132. Match the Following:

	Name		Place
i	Charles Albert	a	Naples
ii	Ferdinand II	b	Tuscany
iii	Louis Philippe	c	Piedmont
iv	Grand Duke	d	France

    (a) i-c, ii-a, iii-d, iv-b   (b) i-c, ii-b, iii-a, iv-d

    (c) i-a, ii-c, iii-d, iv-b   (d) i-b, ii-a, iii-d, iv-c

133. After his failure to reach Venice, Garibaldi left towards _____ with _____.

    (a) Arezzo, Oudinot   (b) Ravenna, Leggera

    (c) Livorno, Anita   (d) Varese, Roselli

134. Find the <u>incorrect</u> statement:

    (a) In 1848, when the battle for unification of Italy was going on, the Pope had taken refuge with the King of Piedmont.

    (b) When the news of Garibaldi's decision to return to Italy and fight under King Charles Albert reached the republicans, they initially suspected his ulterior motive.

    (c) After the fighting at Castelli Romani, Garibaldi's intention was to fight down into the Kingdom of Naples, a decision which was not approved by Mizzini.

    (d) Around the time Rome was declared a Republic, a French army under the command of General Oudinot were dispatched to Civitavecchia by Prince Louis Napoleon.

Directions for questions 135 to 137: Read the following passage carefully and answer the questions given at the end.

Passage 4

Public sector banks (PSBs) are pulling back on credit disbursement to lower rated companies, as they keep a closer watch on using their own scarce capital and the banking regulator heightens its scrutiny on loans being sanctioned.

Bankers say the Reserve Bank of India has started strictly monitoring how banks are utilizing their capital. Any big-ticket loan to lower rated companies is being questioned. Almost all large public sector banks that reported their first quarter results so far have showed a contraction in credit disbursal on a year-to-date basis, as most banks have shifted to a strategy of lending largely to government-owned "Navratna" companies and highly rated private sector companies. On a sequential basis too, banks have grown their loan book at an anaemic rate.

To be sure, in the first quarter, loan demand is not quite robust. However, in the first quarter last year, banks had healthier loan growth on a sequential basis than this year. The country's largest lender State Bank of India grew its loan book at only 1.21% quarter-on-quarter. Meanwhile, Bank of Baroda and Punjab National Bank shrank their loan book by 1.97% and 0.66% respectively in the first quarter on a sequential basis.

Last year, State Bank of India had seen sequential loan growth of 3.37%, while Bank of Baroda had seen a smaller contraction of 0.22%. Punjab National Bank had seen a growth of 0.46% in loan book between the January-March and April-June quarters last year.

On a year-to-date basis, SBI's credit growth fell more than 2%, Bank of Baroda's credit growth contracted 4.71% and Bank of India's credit growth shrank about 3%. SBI chief Arundhati Bhattacharya said the bank's year-to-date credit growth fell as the bank focused on 'A' rated customers. About 90% of the loans in the quarter were given to high-rated companies. "Part of this was a conscious decision and part of it is because we actually did not get good fresh proposals in the quarter," Bhattacharya said.

According to bankers, while part of the credit contraction is due to the economic slowdown, capital constraints and reluctance to take on excessive risk has also played a role, "Most of the PSU banks are facing pressure on capital adequacy. It is challenging to maintain 9% core capital adequacy. The pressure on monitoring capital adequacy and maintaining capital buffer is so strict that you cannot grow aggressively," said Rupa Rege Nitsure, chief economist at Bank of Baroda.

Nitsure said capital conservation pressures will substantially cut dawn "irrational expansion of loans" in some smaller banks, which used to grow at a rate much higher than the industry average. The companies coming to banks, in turn, will have to make themselves more creditworthy for banks to lend. "The conservation of capital is going to inculcate a lot of discipline in both bankes and borrowers," she said.

For every loan that a bank disburses, some amount of money is required to he set aside as provision. Lower the credit rating of the company, riskier the loan is perceived to be. Thus, the bank is required to set aside more capital for a lower rated company than what it otherwise would do for a higher rated client. New international accounting norms, known as Base III norms, require banks to maintain higher capital and higher liquidity. They also require a bank to set aside "buffer" capital to meet contingencies. As per the norms, a bank's total capital adequacy ratio should be 12% at any time, in which tier-I, or the core capital, should be at 9%. Capital adequacy is calculated by dividing total capital by risk-weighted assets. If the loans have been given to lower rated companies, risk weight goes up and capital adequacy falls.

According to bankers, all loan decisions are now being assessed on the basis of the capital that needs to be set aside as provision against the loan and as a result, loans to lower rated companies are being avoided. According to a senior banker with a public sector bank, the capital adequacy situation is so precarious in some banks that if the risk weight increases a few basis points, the proposal gets cancelled. The banker did not wish to be named. One basis point is one hundredth of a percentage point. Bankers add that the Reserve Bank of India has also started strictly monitoring how banks are utilising their capital. Any big-ticket loan to lower rated companies is being questioned.

In this scenario, banks are looking for safe bets. Even if it means that profitability is being compromised. "About 25% of our loans this quarter was given to Navratna companies, who pay at base rate. This resulted in contraction of our net interest margin (NIM)," said Bank of India chairperson V.R. Iyer, while discussing the bank's first quarter results with the media. Bank of India's NIM, or the difference between yields on advances and cost of deposits, a key gauge of profitability, fell in the first quarter to 2.45% from 3.07% a year ago, as the bank focused on lending to highly rated customers.

Analysts, however, say the strategy being followed by banks is short-sighted. "A high rated client will take loans at base rate and will not give any fee income to a bank. A bank will never be profitable that way. Besides, there are only so many PSU companies to chase. All banks cannot be chasing them all at a time. Fact is, the banks are badly hit by NPA and are afraid to lend now to big projects. They need capital, true, but they have become risk-averse," said a senior analyst with a local brokerage who did not wish to be named.

Various estimates suggest that Indian banks would require more than Rs 2 trillion of additional capital to have this kind of capital adequacy ratio by 2019. The central government, which owns the majority share of these banks, has been cutting down on its commitment to recapitalize the banks. In 2013-14, the government infused Rs 14,000 crore in its banks. However, in 2014-15, the government will infuse just Rs 11.200 crore.

135. Which of the following statements is <u>correct</u> according to the passage?

  (a) Last year banks had recorded a healthier loan growth in the first quarter over the preceding quarter, as compared to this year.

  (b) Risk level of loans move in the same direction as the credit ratings of a company.

  (c) Bank of Baroda shrank its loan book by less than 1% in the first quarter this year as compared to the preceding quarter.

  (d) Punjab National Bank recorded a decline in its loan books by less than 1% in the first quarter this year as compared to the same quarter last year.

136. Which of the following <u>cannot</u> be concluded from the passage?

  (a) Banks' loan books have shown a weak rate of growth in the first quarter this year.

  (b) According to Basel III norms total capital adequacy ratio should be 12%.

  (c) SBI received many good fresh proposals in the first quarter this year.

  (d) The shrinking credit is partly caused by economic slowdown.

137. Based on the information given in the passage, which of the following is a likely outcome of lending to highly rated customers?

  (a) Narrowing gap between yields on advances and cost of deposit

  (b) Lower risk for the bank

  (c) Easier meeting of capital adequacy norms

  (d) All of the above

2016-18

Directions (Q. 138-153) : *Read the following passages carefully and answer the questions given at the end of each passage.*

PASSAGE 1

Because of the critical role played by steel in economic development, the steel industry is often considered, especially by the governments, which traditionally owned it, to be an indicator of economic prowess. World production has grown exponentially, but there were big highs and equally big lows all through the 1900s and up to 2002. Recovery from the two World Wars and the Great Depression of the 1930s caused massive disruption and lay-offs. Over-capacity and low steel prices continued to play havoc through the 1970s and 1980s and politicians began to lose their belief that the wealth of a nation was directly coupled to its steel production.

This led to a wave of privatisations, as state-owned enterprises shed their financial liabilities to hungry capitalists. A whole new breed of steel-makers came into being using a new technology, the mini-mill. This used a smaller electric-arc furnace fed that just melts down 'cold' scrap. It was a cheaper process than the traditional 'hot metal integrated mills' with their mountains of ore and coal and monumental machinery, but it was used almost exclusively for lower-grade building and other 'long' products.

By the beginning of 2005, the world steel industry was on a high, after decades of moving from apocalypse to break-even and then back to apocalypse. Since 2003, when a staggering 960 million tonnes were produced - compared to 21.9 million tonnes for aluminium - there had been unprecedented demand, mainly from China and India. China was both the biggest producer, the first country to exceed 200 million tonnes of crude steel in a year, and also its biggest consumer at 244 million tonnes. The global economy was also booming, but this was creating production bottlenecks for all steel-makers and by 2004 steel had for the first time hit an average of $650 per tonne shipped. Profit margins were better, but where was the growth to come from? In tandem, the costs of essential raw materials for steel-making - iron ore and coking coal - had gone through the roof, along with bulk shipping costs. The key to future growth was to secure plants in emerging markets where ore and coal were close to production sites, labour costs were much lower and where technology and investment could spur greater savings.

But the central issue was that globally the industry remained a very fragmented one. No single company was producing 100 million tonnes a year, or 10 per cent of total world production. The name of the game was consolidation into fewer, bigger players. With this would come the chance for steel-makers to gain greater pricing power, increasing their profitability and the value of their shares.

Two groups had begun to move ahead of the pack. One was Mittal Steel with its operational headquarters in London's prestigious Berkeley Square. Mittal Steel was the world's biggest producer of 'long' products. It was young, aggressive, fast, and a big risk-taker, fuelled by its founder Lakshmi Mittal's visionary zeal to consolidate the industry. It's nearest rival, Arcelor - the world's most profitable steel company, focusing on 'flat' products - was headed by the Frenchman Guy Dolle, and was a combination of three former state-owned European steel plants: Arbed of Luxembourg, Usinor from France and Spain's Aceralia. These three were now merged, restructured and administered from the grandiose, chateau-like former Arbed headquarters in Luxembourg's Avenue de la Liberte.

Both groups were passionate about steel. Mittal, already dubbed 'the Carnegie from Calcutta', had a clearer vision of the need to streamline steel, but Arcelor was determined to become the biggest as well as the best. Dominating the market would enable either firm to increase its pricing position with customers, the car-makers, ship-builders and construction firms, as well as chasing growth in the new markets of Asia, South America and Eastern Europe.

Guy Dolle could hear the clump of Mittal's feet marching ahead, and it hurt. Arcelor was Europe's reigning steel champion and was arrogantly proud of it. It had a commanding market share of the specialised high-strength steel supplied to European car-makers and a total overall production approaching 50 million tonnes a year, all with state-of-the-art technology. The group had repaired its consolidated balance sheet, ravished by decades of downturns and continual restructuring costs. It had invested heavily in the quest for best technology and had also acquired companies in Brazil, set up joint ventures in Russia, Japan and China and now was eagerly eyeing gateways to the North American car market. And to its long-suffering shareholders, starved of decent dividends, Arcelor was at last moving in the right direction, after the blood, sweat and tears of shifting from public to private sector. The Luxembourg group was clearly on a wake-up call, gunning to overtake Mittal Steel and keep it at bay.

By 2005, the battle for supremacy had begun to heat up. Two projected state sell-offs by public auction, in Turkey and Ukraine, were particularly attractive commercially. Both auctions were taking place in October, within three weeks of each other. The first, in Turkey, was for the 46.3 percent of government-owned shares in Erdemir, a steel-maker producing 3.5 million tonnes a year for car-makers and other industrial clients in a country of seventy million people shaping up to join the European Union. Mittal and Arcelor both already owned minority stakes in the Turkish company and were eager to get majority control.

138. Which of the following statements is true?

   (a) In 2003, China consumed more steel than it produced

   (b) Mittal Steel was the world's most profitable steel company in mid 2000s

   (c) Arcelor was a bigger producer of steel than Mittal

   (d) All of the above

139. Which among the following is the common objective both Mittal and Arcelor had for aspiring to become bigger steel-makers?

   (a) To consolidate the rather fragmented steel industry

   (b) To facilitate privatisation initiatives of the government

   (c) To have 10% of the industry share

   (d) To increase pricing position with customers

140. From the above passages, it clearly emerges that:

   (a) Arcleor had delivered good returns to its shareholders

   (b) Mittal Steel-was Arcelor's nearest competitor

   (c) By 2005, steel industry was in recession

   (d) A nation's steel production continues to be a good indicator of its wealth

141. What are the plausible reasons for privatisation in steel industry?

   (a) Slow growth in world production

   (b) Lobbying by the capitalists

   (c) Havoc played by over-capacity and falling steel prices

   (d) Introduction of the 'mini-mill'

PASSAGE 2

In the decades that Otlet's papers had sat gathering dust, his dream of a universal knowledge of network had found a new expression across the Atlantic, where a group of engineers and computer scientists laid the groundwork for what would eventually become the Internet. Beginning during the Cold War, the United States poured money into a series of advanced research projects that would eventually lead to the creation of the technologies underpinning the present-day Internet. In the 1990s, the World Wide Web appeared and quickly attracted a widespread audience, eventually establishing itself as the foundation of a global knowledge-sharing network much like the one that Otlet envisioned. Today, the emergence of that network has triggered a series of dramatic – perhaps even "axial" – transformations. In 2011, the world's population generated more than 1.8 zettabytes of data, including documents, images, phone calls, and radio and television signals. More than a billion people now use Web browsers, and that number will almost certainly increase for years to come. In an era when almost anyone with a mobile phone can press a few keys to search the contents of the world's libraries, when millions of people negotiate their personal relationships via online social networks, and when institutions of all stripes find their operations disrupted by the sometimes wrenching effects of networks, it scarcely seems like hyperbole – and has even become cliche - to suggest that the advent of the Internet ranks as an event of epochal significance.

While Otlet did not by any stretch of imagination "invent" the Internet – working as he did in an age before digital computers, magnetic storage, or packet-switching networks – nonetheless his vision looks nothing short of prophetic. In Otlet's day, microfilm may have qualified as the most advanced information storage technology, and the closest thing anyone had ever seen to a database was a drawer full of index cards. Yet despite these analog limitations, he envisioned a global network of interconnected institutions that would alter the flow of information around the world, and in the process lead to profound social, cultural, and political transformations,

By today's standards, Otlet's proto-Web was a clumsy affair, relying on a patchwork system of index cards, file cabinets, telegraph machines, and a small army of clerical workers. But in his writing he looked far ahead to a future in which networks circled the globe and data could travel freely. Moreover, he imagined a wide range of expression taking shape across the network: distributed encyclopaedias, virtual classrooms, three-dimensional information spaces, social networks, and other forms of knowledge that anticipated the hyperlinked structure of today's Web. He saw these developments as fundamentally connected to a larger Utopian project that would bring the world closer to a state of permanent and lasting peace and toward a state of collective spiritual enlightenment.

The conventional history of the Internet traces its roots through an Anglo-American lineage of early computer scientists like Charles Babbage, Ada Lovelace, and Alan Turing; networking visionaries like Vinton G. Cerf and Robert E. Kahn; as well as hypertext seers like Vannevar Bush, J.C.R. Licklider, Douglas Engelbart, Ted Nelson, and of course Tim Berners-Lee and Robert Cailliau, who in 1991 released their first version of the World Wide Web. The dominant influence of the modern computer industry has placed computer science at the centre of this story.

Nonetheless Otlet's work, grounded in an age before microchips and semiconductors, opened the door to an alternative stream of thought, one undergirding our present-day information age even though it has little to do with the history of digital computing. Well before the first Web servers started sending data packets across the Internet, a number of other early twentieth-century figures were pondering the possibility of a new, networked society: H.G. Wells, the English science fiction writer and social activist, who dreamed of building a World Brain, Emanuel Goldberg, a Russian Jew who invented a fully functional mechanical search engine in 1930s Germany before fleeing the Nazis; Scotland's Patrick Geddes and Austria's Otto Neurath, who both explored new kinds of highly designed, propagandists museum exhibits designed to foster social change; Germany's Wilhelm Ostwald, the Nobel Prize-winning chemist who aspired to build a vast new 'brain of humanity'; the sculptor Hendrik Andersen and the architect Le Corbusier, both of whom dreamed of designing a World City to house a new, one-world government with a networked information repository at its epicentre. Each shared a commitment to social transformation through the use of available technologies. They also each shared a direct connection to Paul Otlet, who seems to connect a series of major turning points in the history of the early twentieth-century information age, synthesizing and incorporating their ideas along with his own, and ultimately coming tantalizingly close to building a fully integrated global information network.

142. What is the remark that the author of this passage considers a defensible one, rather than a hyperbole?

    (a) That the number of people who will use Internet will increase for the years to come

    (b) That the advent of the Internet is an event of epochal significance

    (c) That millions of people negotiate their personal relationships via online social networks

    (d) That more than a billion people now use web browsers

143. In the above passage, Otlet is being credited with

    (a) Inventing the Internet

    (b) Co-developing the Internet

    (c) Prophesising the Internet

    (d) All of the above

144. What has been said as the common commitment shared by the early twentieth-century figures who imagined and worked for a networked society?

    (a) Designing a World City with a networked information repository at its epicentre

    (b) Achieving social transformation through the use of available technologies

    (c) Building a vast new "Brain of Humanity"

    (d) Bringing world peace through online social networks

145. Otlet's original idea of the network can be described as:

    (a) Futuristic   B. Visionary

    (c) Utopian   D. All of the above

PASSAGE 3

Every loan has a lender and a borrower; both voluntarily engage in the transaction. If the loan goes bad, there is at least a prima facie case that the lender is as guilty as the borrower. In fact, since lenders are supposed to be sophisticated in risk analysis and in making judgements about a reasonable debt burden, they should perhaps bear even more culpability.

Does it make a difference if we say there is over-lending rather than over-borrowing? The difference in where we see the problem affects where we seek the solution. Is the problem more on the side of the lenders, that they are not exercising due diligence in judging who is creditworthy? Or on the borrowers, being profligate and irresponsible? If we consider the problem to be over borrowing, then we naturally think of making it more difficult for borrowers to discharge their debts; on the contrary, if the problem is over lending, we focus on strengthening incentives for lenders to exercise due diligence.

The political economy of over-borrowing is easy to understand. The current borrowing government benefits and later governments have to deal with the consequences. But why have sophisticated, profit maximizing lenders so often over-lent? Lenders encourage indebtedness because it is profitable. Developing country governments are sometimes even pressured to over-borrow. There may be kickbacks in loans, or even more frequently in the projects that they finance. Even without corruption, it is easy to be influenced by Western businessmen and financiers. They wine and dine those responsible for borrowing as they sell their loan packages, and tell them why this is a good time to borrow, why their particular package is attractive, why this is the right time to restructure debt? Countries that are not sure that borrowing is worth the risk are told how important it is to establish a credit rating: borrow even if you really don't need the money.

Excessive borrowing increases the chance of a crisis, and the costs of a crisis are borne not just by lenders but by all of society. In recent years, IMF programs may have resulted in significant further distortions in lenders' incentives. When crisis occurred, the IMF lent money in what was called a 'bail-out'- but the money was not really a bail-out for the country; it was a bail out for Western banks. In both East Asia and Latin America, bail-outs provided money to repay foreign creditors, thus absolving creditors from having to bear the costs of their mistaken lending. In some instances, governments even assumed private liabilities, effectively socializing private risk. The creditors were left off the hook, but the IMF's money wasn't a gift, just another loan- and the developing country was left to pay the bill. In effect, the poor country's taxpayers paid for rich country's lending mistakes.

The bail-outs give rise to the famous 'moral hazard' problem. Moral hazard arises when a party does not bear all the risks associated with his action and as a result does not do everything he can to avoid risk. The term originates in the insurance literature; it was deemed immoral for an individual to take less care in preventing a fire simply because he had insurance coverage. It is, of course, simply a matter of incentives: those with insurance may not set their houses on fire deliberately, but their incentive to avoid a fire is still weakened. With loans, the risk is default, with all of its consequences; lenders can reduce that risk simply by lending less. If they perceive a high likelihood of a bail-out, they lend more than they otherwise would.

Lending markets are also characterized by, in the famous words of former chairman of the U.S. Federal Reserve Alan Greenspan, 'irrational exuberance', as well as irrational pessimism. Lenders rush into a market in a mood of optimism, and rush out when the mood changes. Markets move in fads and fashions, and it is hard to resist joining the latest fad. If only one firm were affected by a mood of irrational optimism, it would have to bear the cost of its mistake; but when large numbers share the same mood, in a fad, there are macro-economic consequences, potentially affecting everyone in the country.

146. The author is trying to find the underlying cause of:

(a) Financial crisis in the economy

(b) Under development in the developing world

(c) Bargaining power asymmetry between lenders and borrowers

(d) Inequalities in the world economy

147. The 'moral hazard' arises because:

(a) The insured takes less precaution to avoid a risk because the risk is covered by insurance

(b) The insured takes less precaution to avoid a risk because he is unaware about the risk

(c) The insured takes less precaution to avoid risk because he tends to benefit from the risk

(d) The amount spent on insurance is seen as a waste because the risk is unlikely or minimum

148. According to the author the IMF bail-outs for the countries in crisis have been in effect:

(a) The bail-out for the governments of the borrowing countries

(b) The bail-out for the banks in the borrowing country

(c) The bail-out for the lending foreign banks

(d) The bail out for the governments of the countries of the creditors

149. The author believes that the cost of the crisis is ultimately borne by:

(a) The lending banks

(b) The IMF

(c) The tax payers of the borrowing country

(d) The rich countries

PASSAGE 4

The mass media have been recognized as politically significant since the advent of mass literacy and the popular press in the late nineteenth century. However, it is widely accepted that, through a combination of social and technological changes, the media have become increasingly more powerful political actors and, in some respects, more deeply enmeshed in the political process. Three developments are particularly noteworthy. First, the impact of the so-called 'primary' agents of political socialization, such as the family and social class, has declined. Whereas once people acquired, in late childhood and adolescence in particular, a framework of political sympathies and leanings that adult experience tended to modify or deepen, but seldom radically transformed, this has been weakened in modern society by greater social and geographical mobility and by the spread of individualist and consumerist values. Abiding political allegiances and habitual voting patterns have thus given way to a more instrumental approach to politics, in which people make political choices according to a calculation of personal self-interest based on the issues and policy positions on offer. This, in turn, widens the scope for the media's political influence, as they are the principal mechanism through which information about issues and policies, and therefore political choices, is presented to the public.

Second, the development of mass television audience from the 1950s onwards, and more recently the proliferation of channels and media output associated with the 'new' media, has massively increased the mass media's penetration into people's everyday lives. This means that the public now relies on the mass media more heavily than ever before: for instance, television is a much more important source of news and current affairs information than political meetings; many more people watch televised sport than participate in it; and even shopping is increasingly being carried out through shopping channels and the internet.

Third, the media have become more powerful economic actors. Not only have major media corporations become more powerful global players, but also a series of mergers has tended to incorporate the formerly discrete domains of publishing, television, film, music, computers and telecommunications into a single massive 'infotainment' industry. Media businesses such as Microsoft, AOL-Time Warner, Disney and Rupert Murdoch's News Corporation have accumulated so much economic and market power that no government can afford to ignore them.

Few commentators doubt the media's ability to shape political attitudes and values or, at least, to structure political and electoral choice by influencing public perceptions about the nature and importance of issues and problems, thereby. However, there is considerable debate about the political significance of this influence. A series of rival theories offer contrasting views of the media's political impact.

The *pluralist model* of the mass media portrays the media as an ideological marketplace in which wide range of political views are debated and discussed. While not rejecting the idea that the media can affect political views and sympathies, this nevertheless suggests that their impact is essentially neutral in that they reflect the balance of forces within the society at large. The pluralist view nevertheless portrays the media in strongly positive terms. In ensuring the 'informed citizenry', the mass media both enhance the quality of democracy and guarantee that government power is checked, This 'watchdog' role was classically demonstrated in the 1974 *Washington Post* investigation into the Watergate scandal, which led to the resignation of Richard Nixon as US President. Some, moreover, argue that the advent of the 'new' media, and particularly the Internet, has strengthened pluralism and political competition by giving protest groups a relatively cheap and highly effective means of disseminating information and organizing campaigns.

The *dominant ideology model* portrays media as a politically conservative force that is aligned to the interests of economic and social elites, and serves to promote compliance or passivity amongst the masses. The ownership ultimately determines the political and other views that the mass media disseminate, and ownerships are increasingly concentrated in the hands of a small number of global media corporations.

The *elite-values model* shifts attention away from the ownership of media corporations to the mechanism through which media output is controlled. This view suggests that editors, journalists and broadcasters enjoy significant professional independence, and that even the most interventionist of media moguls is able only to set a broad political agenda but not the day-to-day editorial decision-making. The media's political bias therefore reflects the values of groups that are disproportionally represented amongst its senior professionals.

The *market model* of the mass media differs from the other models in that it dispenses with the idea of media bias: it holds that newspaper and television reflect, rather than shape, the views of general public. This occurs because, regardless of the personal views of media owners and senior professionals, private media outlets are first and foremost businesses concerned with profit maximization and thus with extending market share. The media therefore give people 'what they want', and cannot afford to alienate existing or potential viewers and readers by presenting political viewpoints with which they may disagree.

150. Which of the following is the most appropriate title for the passage?

(a) Mass media and political communication

(b) Mass media and economic development

(c) Mass media and social development

(d) Mass media and cultural development

151. Who, according to the author, are the primary agents of political socialization?

(a) Media moguls

(b) Political parties

(c) The family and social class

(d) Journalists

152. According to the author the mass media is a powerful political actor because:

(a) The impact of primary agents of socialization has reduced

(b) The technology has increased the penetration of mass media in everyday life

(c) Infotainment industry has emerged as a big economic force

(d) All of the above reasons

153. Which of the following rival theories discussed in the passage portrays the media in a more positive light in terms of its role in the society?

(a) The Market Model

(b) The Elite Values Model

(c) The Pluralist Model

(d) The Dominant Ideology Model

2017-19

Directions (Q. 154-169): *Read the following passages carefully and answer the questions given at the end of each passage.*

PASSAGE - 1

In a study of 150 emerging nations looking back fifty years, it was found that the single most powerful driver of economic booms was sustained growth in exports especially of manufactured products. Exporting simple manufactured goods not only increases income and consumption at home, it generates foreign revenues that allow the country to import the machinery and materials needed to improve its factories without running up huge foreign bills and debts. In short, in the case of manufacturing, one good investment leads to another. Once an economy starts down the manufacturing path, its momentum can carry it in the right direction for some time. When the ratio of investment to GDP surpasses 30 percent, it tends to stick at the level for almost nine years (on an average). The reason being that many of these nations seemed to show a strong leadership commitment to investment, particularly to investment in manufacturing. Today various international authorities have estimated that the emerging world need many trillions of dollars in investment on these kinds of transport and communication networks. The modern outlier is India where investment as a share of the economy exceeded 30 percent of GDP over the course of the 2000s, but little of that money went into factories. Indian manufacturing had been stagnant for decades at around 15 percent of GDP. The stagnation stems from the failures of the state to build functioning ports and power plants and to create an environment in which the filles governing labour, land and capital are designed and enforced in a way that encourages entrepreneurs to invest, particularly in factories. India has disappointed on both counts creating labour friendly rules and workable land acquisition norms. Between 1989 and 2010 India generated about ten million new jobs in manufacturing, but nearly all those jobs were created in enterprises that are small and informal and thus better suited to dodge India's bureaucracy and its extremely restrictive rules regarding firing workers. It is commonly said in India that the labour laws are so onerous that it is practically impossible to comply with even half of them without violating the other half. Informal shops, many of them one man operations, now account for 39 percent of

India's manufacturing workforce, up from 19 percent in 1989 and they are simply too small to compete in global markets. Harvard economist Dani Rodrik calls manufacturing the "automatic escalator" of development, because once a country finds a niche in global manufacturing, productivity often seems to start rising automatically. During its boom years India was growing in large part on the strength of investment in technology service industries, not manufacturing. This was put forward as a development strategy. Instead of growing richer by exporting even more advanced manufactured products, India could grow rich by exporting the services demanded in this new information age. These arguments began to gain traction early in the 2010s. In new research on the "service escalator", a 2014 working paper from the World Bank made the case that the old growth escalator in manufacturing was already giving way to a new one in service industries. The report argued that while manufacturing is in retreat as a share of the global economy and is producing fewer jobs, services are still growing, contributing more to growth in output and jobs for nations rich and poor. However, one basic problem with the idea of the service escalator is that in the emerging world most of the new service jobs are still in very traditional ventures. A decade on, India's tech sector is still providing relatively simple IT services mainly in the same back office operations it started with and the number of new jobs it is creating is relatively small. In India only about two million people work in IT services, or less than 1 percent of the workforce. So far the rise of these service industries has not been big enough to drive the mass modernisation of rural farm economies. People can move quickly from working in the fields to working on an assembly line, because both rely for the most part on manual labour. The leap from the farm to the modern service sector is much tougher since those jobs often require advanced skills. Workers who have moved into IT service jobs have generally come from a pool of relatively better educated members of the urban middle class, who speak English and have atleast some facility with computers. Finding jobs for the underemployed middle class is important but there are limits to how deeply it can transform the economy, because it is a relatively small part of the population. For now, the rule is still factories first, not services first.

154. According to the information in the above passage, manufacturing in India has been stagnant because there is

    (a) Lack of availability of skilled and educated manpower particularly in rural areas

    (b) Lack of investment in required infrastructure, labour friendly rules and land acquisition norms

    (c) Lack of investment in primary and higher education and women empowerment

    (d) Lack of investment in technology, telecommunications and IT, and service sector in general

155. In India, nearly all jobs created were primarily in the small and informal sector because

    (a) They are more innovative and can produce better products suited for export markets

    (b) They are able to hire less number of workers and have to pay less taxes

    (c) They are better suited to handle the bureaucratic procedures followed in India and the difficult labour laws with regard to dismissal of workers

    (d) They do not require good infrastructure and are able to manage better in the Indian conditions

156. According to the opinion expressed in the above excerpt, growth in services is not as impactful on the economy as manufacturing because

    (a) Companies in services sector focus only on technology and not on overall infrastructure such as power and ports

    (b) Services sector can create jobs only for a small percent of the population who are English speaking and have access to better education

    (c) Manufacturing leads to increase in export led income which benefits the whole economy

    (d) Manufacturing leads to creation of better infrastructure, health facilities and educational institution

157. In the passage, sustained growth in exports of manufactured products has been identified as the most powerful driver of economic boom because

    (a) It leads to an increase in building of functioning ports and power plants and also improvement in rriining and shipping sectors

    (b) It leads to an increase in foreign investment, domestic income generation and consumption

    (c) It leads to increase in transportation and communication network and also leads to increase in education

    (d) It leads to modernisation of rural farm economies and also improvement of the Agriculture sector

PASSAGE - 2

The company will tackle this problem much more readily if reverse innovation is part of its repertoire. And yet until recently PepsiCo took a glocalisation approach. The company developed products for the US and then sold and distributed substantially similar products throughout the world. As a result PepsiCo's growth particularly in emerging markets hit a wall. The company's brands bumped up against local needs, tastes and habits that could not be satisfied by lowest-common-denominator global products. Under the glocalisation scenario, what first appears to be promising momentum hits a wall - often sooner than later. The renown of even the most potent global brands wear thin when the ottered product is neither designed expressly for local markets nor priced for local means. These days PepsiCo is finding ways to address sharp differences across borders by designing products with local tastes and consumer needs in mind and is capturing a greater share of the opportunity in emerging economies. But that's not all. PepsiCo is finding that its innovations in emerging markets have the potential to have impact and deliver performance with purpose all over the world. For example, PepsiCo is finding that some long popular ingredients in emerging economies such as lentils in India have healthy profiles that suggest new dimensions for snacking across geographies. The company's approach to reverse innovation combines local product development efforts, strong support from global resources, plus efforts to ensure that the raw material of PepsiCo's innovations - ideas, flavours, ingredients, marketing expertise, packaging materials, manufacturing methods and so on can flow in any direction within the organisation. Concerns about childhood and adult obesity are on the rise. It's not news that snack foods are not commonly associated with health and wellness. Nonetheless, PepsiCo saw that there was enormous opportunity for impact in creating options for healthier snacking. "Consumers interact with our products on three levels; the neurological level, the gut level and the metabolic level." Traditionally food and beverage companies have focussed only on the first. The neurological level is where brands, marketing and sensory payloads operate. Looking at the problems of emerging markets it is important to also understand what PepsiCo's products do to the person's gut? What do they do to their body chemistry? If those effects are ignored then it is indulgence without any balance. As PepsiCo geared up for its efforts to develop Aliva, it wondered whether there were any examples in which PepsiCo had already practised successful reverse innovation. There was one such example in India. It was a lentil and rice based snack called Kurkure. Introduced more than a decade ago, it had grown to be Frito Lay India's top selling product. PepsiCo had learnt a lot from the Kurkure experience. Once emerging nations aspired to have access to rich world products. But these days they want rich world quality baked into products with local origins. It exemplified the idea that innovations shouldn't simply be handed down from on high.

158. According to the above excerpt, most MNCs face problems in emerging countries because they interpret the concept of 'glocalisation' as

   (a) Offering global products with minimal changes leading to a mismatch between the requirements of the local markets with regard to its usage as well as the pricing

   (b) Offering global products with minimal changes that are useful for local markets but not priced appropriately

   (c) Offering global products with minimal changes that are not useful for local markets but are priced appropriately

   (d) Offering global products with changes leading to a match between the requirements of the local markets with regard to its utility as well as the pricing

159. According to the author, snack food companies traditionally focus on the

   (a) Sensory level   (b) Gut level

   (c) Neurological level   (d) Digestive level

160. The passage suggests that MNCs should replace glocalistion with

   (a) Market Research   (b) Reverse Engineering

   (c) Globalisation   (d) Reverse Innovation

161. What is the learning for PepsiCo from Indian experience

   (a) Innovation should be governed from the top and use global quality

   (b) Snack food is driven by indulgence only

   (c) Snack food should use global quality and healthy local ingredients

   (d) Snack food should be priced cheaply as per local affordability

PASSAGE - 3

Typically women participate in the labour force at a very high rate in poor rural countries. The participation rate then falls as countries industrialise and move, into the middle income class. Finally, if the country grows richer still, more families have the resources for higher education for women and from there they often enter the labour force in large numbers. Usually, economic growth goes hand in hand with emancipation of women. Among rich countries according to a 2015 study, female labour force participation ranges from nearly 80 percent in Switzerland to 70 percent in Germany and less than 60 percent in the United States and Japan. Only 68 percent of Canadian women participated in the workforce in 1990; two decades later that increased to 74 percent largely due to reforms including tax cuts for second earners and new childcare services. In Netherlands the female labour participation rate doubled since 1980 to 74 percent as a result of expanded parental leave policies and the spread of flexible, part time working arrangements. In a 2014 survey of 143 emerging countries, the World Bank found that 90 percent have at least one law that limits the economic opportunities available to women. These laws include bans or limitations on women owning property, opening a bank account, signing a contract, entering a courtroom, travelling alone, driving or controlling family finances. Such restrictions are particularly prevalent in the Middle East and South Asia with the world's lowest female labour force participation, 26 and 35 percent respectively. According to data available with the International Labour Organization (ILO), between 2004 and 2011, when the Indian economy grew at a healthy average of about 7 percent, there was a decline in female participation in the country's labour force from over 35 percent to 25 percent. India also posted the lowest rate ot female participation in the workforce among BRICS countries. India's performance in female workforce participation stood at 27 percent, significantly behind China (64 percent), Brazil (59 percent), Russian Federation (57 percent), and South Africa (45 percent). The number of working women in India had climbed between 2000 and 2005, increasing from 34 percent to 37 percent, but since then the rate of women in the workforce has fallen to 27 percent as of 2014, said the report citing data from the World Bank. The gap between male and female workforce participation in urban areas in 2011 stood at 40 percent, compared to rural areas where the gap was about 30 percent. However, in certain sectors like financial services, Indian women lead the charge. While only one in 10 Indian companies are led by women, more than half of them are in the financial sector. Today, women head both the top public and private banks in India. Another example is India's aviation sector, 11.7 percent of India's 5,100 pilots are women, versus 3 percent worldwide. But these successes only represent a small section of women in the country. India does poorly in comparison to its neighbours despite a more robust economic growth. In comparison to India, women in Bangladesh have increased their participation in the labour market, which is due to the growth of the ready-made garment sector and a push to rural female employment. In 2015, women comprised of 43 percent of the labour force in Bangladesh. The rate has also increased in Pakistan, albeit from a very low starting point, while participation has remained relatively stable in Sri Lanka. Myanmar with 79 percent and Malaysia with 49 percent are also way ahead of India. Lack of access to higher education, fewer job opportunities, the lack of flexibility in working conditions, as well as domestic duties are cited as factors behind the low rates. Marriage significantly reduced the probability of women working by about 8 percent in rural areas and more than twice as much in urban areas, said an Assocham report. ILO attributes this to three factors: increasing educational enrolment, improvement in earnings of male workers that discourages women's economic participation, and the lack of employment opportunities at certain levels of skills and qualifications discouraging women to seek work. The hurdles to working women often involve a combination of written laws and cultural norms. Cultures don't change

overnight but laws can. The IMF says that even a small step such as countries granting women the right to open a bank account can lead to substantial increase in female labour force participation over the next seven years. According to the United Nations Economic and Social Commission for Asia and the Pacific (ESCAP), even a 10 percent increase in women participating in the workforce can boost gross domestic product (GDP) by 0.3 percent. The OECD recently estimated that eliminating the gender gap would lead to an overall increase in GDP of 12 percent in its member nations between 2015 and 2030. The GDP gains would peak close to 20 percent in both Japan and South Korea and more than 20 percent in Italy. A similar analysis by Booz and Company showed that closing the gender gap in emerging countries could yield even larger gains in GDP by 2020, ranging from a 34 percent gain in Egypt to 27 percent in India and 9 percent in Brazil.

162. According to the above passage, though there are many reasons for low female labour force participation, the most important focus of the passage is on

  (a) Women do not like to work after marriage

  (b) Laws and cultural norms limiting economic opportunities available to women

  (c) Lack of access to higher education resulting in lack of skills and qualifications

  (d) Preference for child rearing and household work amongst women

163. Identify the sentence that most accurately summarizes the message of the above excerpt

  (a) Compared to other countries India has the lowest female labour force participation

  (b) Richer the nation, higher the female labour force participation, therefore nations have to become rich to increase the female labour force participation

  (c) Emerging countries are lagging behind developed countries with regard to the female labour force participation

  (d) Increasing the female labour force participation can have a positive impact on not just the social indicators but also economic growth

164. According to the IMF what small step can lead to larger impact on increasing female labour force participation

  (a) Providing access to higher education

  (b) Improving childcare services

  (c) Allowing women to open bank accounts

  (d) Providing a safe work environment

165. According to the information in the above passage between 2004 to 2011, when the Indian economy grew at a healthy average of about 7 percent

    (a) There was a steady increase in female participation in the country's labour force from over 25 percent to 35 percent

    (b) There was no change in female participation in the country's labour force and remained at 35 percent

    (c) There was a decline in female participation in the country's labour force from 35 percent to 25 percent

    (d) There was a similar increase in female participation in the country's labour force from 7 percent to 15 percent

PASSAGE - 4

The Cyclopses according to mythology were a race of bad tempered and rather stupid one eyed giants. Not perhaps a great portend for a new generation of robots. But Andrew Davison a computer scientist at Imperial College, London, thinks one eye is enough for a robot, provided its brain can think fast enough. For a robot to work autonomously it has to understand its environment. Stereoscopic vision, integrating the images from two eyes looking at the same thing from different angles is one approach to achieve this, but it involves a lot of complicated computer processing. The preferred method these days therefore is Simultaneous Localisation and Mapping (SLAM) which uses sensors such as laser based range finders that see by bouncing beams of light off their surroundings and timing the return. Dr. Davison however wants to replace the range finders which are expensive and fiddly with a digital camera, which is small, cheap and well understood. With this in mind he is developing ways to use a single moving video camera to create continually updated 3D maps that can guide even the most hyperactive robots on its explorations. His technique involves collecting and integrating images taken from different angles as the camera goes on its travels. The trick is to manage to do this in real time, at frame rates of 100-1,000 per second. The shape of the world pops out easily from laser data because it represents a direct contour map of the surrounding area. A camera captures this geometry indirectly and so needs more (and smarter) computation if it is to generate something good enough for a self-directing robot. The answer is a form of triangulation, tracking features such as points and edges from one frame to the next. With enough measurements of the same set of features from different viewpoints, it is possible if you have a fast enough computer program to estimate their positions and thus by inference the location

of the moving camera. However, developing such a program is no mean feat. In the milliseconds between successive frames, relevant information from each fresh image must be extracted and fused with the current map to produce an updated version. The higher the frame rate, the less time there is to do this work.

166. What is the main message of the above passage?

    (a) To explain the technique of SLAM

    (b) To discuss techniques for increasing efficiency of self-guided robots

    (c) To advocate the use of digital cameras

    (d) To highlight the work of the scientist in the area of robotics

167. What message is the author conveying by drawing attention to a mythical figure and a one eyed robot?

    (a) A robot is uglier than the mythical figure and also less efficient

    (b) Unlike the robot, the mythical figure is uglier but more efficient than the robot because it is one eyed

    (c) Unlike the mythical figure, having one eye does not affect the performance of the robot

    (d) Having both eyes will make the mythical figure less uglier and stupid than the robot

168. Laser based range finders are more effective than digital cameras because (select the right option)?

    i. Laser based range finders directly capture the contour map of the surroundings which enables faster processing

    ii. Digital cameras are expensive

    iii. Laser based range finders are easier to use

    iv. Digital cameras are easy to use but require more computation

    (a) i & ii

    (b) ii & iii

    (c) i & iv

    (d) ii & iv

169. It is possible to improve the performance of digital camera

    (a) by using images from laser based range finders along with images from digital cameras

    (b) by collecting images from different viewpoints and a computer program for faster processing

    (c) by combining the methodology of SLAM along with images from digital camera

    (d) by calculating the measurements of different contour points and measuring the distance

Directions for questions 170-185: *Read the following passages carefully and identify most appropriate answer to the questions given at the end of each passage.*

PASSAGE 1

Groupon is one of the fastest-growing companies of all time. Its name comes from "group coupons," an ingenious idea that has spawned an entire industry of social commerce imitators. However, it didn't start out successful. When customers took Groupon up on its first deal, a whopping twenty people bought two-for-one pizza in a restaurant on the first floor of the company's Chicago offices-hardly a world-changing event. In fact, Groupon wasn't originally meant to be about commerce at all. The founder, Andrew Mason, intended his company to become a "collective activism platform" called The Point. Its goal was to bring people together to solve problems they couldn't solve on their own, such as fund-raising for a cause or boycotting a certain retailer. The Point's early results were disappointing, however, and at the end of-2008 the founders decided to try something new. Although they still had grand ambitions, they were determined to keep the new product simple. They built a minimum viable product. Does this sound like a billion-dollar company to you? Mason tells the story: "We took a Word Press Blog and we skinned it to say Groupon and then every day we would do a new post. It was totally ghetto. We would sell T-shirts on the first version of Groupon. We'd say in the write-up, "This T-shirt will come in the colour red, size large. If you want a different colour or size, e-mail that to us." We didn't have a form to add that stuff. It was just so cobbled together. It was enough to prove the concept and show that it was something that people really liked. The actual coupon generation that we were doing was all FileMaker. We would run a script that would e-mail the coupon PDF to people. It got to the point where we'd sell 500 sushi coupons in a day, and we'd send 500 PDFs to people with Apple Mail at the same time. Really until July of the first year it was just a scrambling to grab the tiger by the tail. It was trying to catch up and reasonably piece together a product." Handmade PDFs, a pizza coupon, and a simple blog were enough to launch Groupon into record-breaking success; it is on pace to become the fastest company in history to achieve $ 1 billion in sales. It is revolutionizing the way local businesses find new customers, offering special deals to consumers in more than 375 cities worldwide. A minimum viable product (MVP) helps entrepreneurs start the process of learning as quickly as possible." It is not necessarily the smallest product imaginable, though; it is simply the fastest way to get through the Build-Measure-Leam feedback loop with the minimum amount of effort. Contrary to traditional product development, which usually involves a long, thoughtful incubation period and strives for product perfection, the goal of the MVP is to begin the process of learning', not end it. Unlike a prototype or concept test, an MVP is designed not just to answer product design or technical questions. Its goal is to test fundamental business hypotheses.

Early adopters use their imagination to fill in what a product is missing. They prefer that state of affairs, because what they care about above all is being the first to use or adopt a new product or technology. In consumer products, it's often the thrill of being the first one on the block to show off a new basketball shoe, music player, or cool phone. In enterprise products, it's often about gaining" a competitive advantage by taking a risk with something new that competitors don't have yet. Early adopters are suspicious of something that is too polished if it's ready for everyone to adopt, how much advantage cart one get by being early? As a result, additional features or polish beyond what early adopters demand is a form of wasted resources and time. This is a hard truth for many entrepreneurs to accept. After all, the vision entrepreneurs keep in their heads is of a high-quality mainstream product that will change the world, not one used by a small niche of people who are willing to give it a shot before it's ready. That world-changing product is polished, slick, and ready for prime time. It wins awards at trade shows and, most of all, is something you can proudly show Mom and Dad. An early, buggy, incomplete product feels like an unacceptable compromise. How many of us were raised with the expectation that we would put our best work forward? As one manager put it to me recently, "I know for me, the MVP feels a little dangerous- in a good way-since 1 have always been such a perfectionist." Minimum viable products range in complexity from extremely simple smoke tests (little more than an advertisement) to actual early prototypes complete with problems and missing features. Deciding exactly how complex an MVP needs to be cannot be done formulaically. It requires judgment. Luckily, this judgment is not difficult to develop: most entrepreneurs and product development people dramatically over estimate how many features are needed in an MVP. When in doubt simplify. For example, consider a service sold with a one-month free trial. Before a customer can use the service, he or she has to sign up for the trial. One obvious assumption, then, of the business model is that customers will sign up for a free trial once they have a certain amount of information about the service. A critical question to consider is whether customers will in fact signup for the free trial given a certain number of promised features (the value hypothesis). Somewhere in the business model, probably buried in a single cell in a spreadsheet, it specifies the "percentage of customers who see the free trial offer who then sign up." Maybe in our projections we say that this number should be 10 percent. If you think about it, this is a leap-of-faith question. It really should be represented in giant letters in a bold red font: WE ASSUME 10 PERCENT OF CUSTOMERS WILL SIGN UP.

Most entrepreneurs approach a question like this by building the product and then checking to see how customers react to it. I consider this to be exactly backward because it can lead to a lot of waste. First, if it turns out that we're building something nobody wants, the whole exercise will be an avoidable expense of time and money. If customers won't sign up for the free trial, they'll never get to experience the amazing features that await them. Even if they do sign up, there are many other opportunities for waste. For example, how many features do we really need to include to appeal to early adopters? Every extra feature is a form of waste, and if we delay the test for these extra features, it comes with a tremendous potential cost in terms of learning and cycle time. The lesson of the MVP is that any additional work beyond what was required to start learning is waste, no matter how important it might have seemed at the time.

170. What is the central idea of the passage?

    (a) Entrepreneurs should strive to make complete polished products ready for everyone to adopt

    (b) Entrepreneurs should start with a simple idea or product to avoid wastage, learn from user experience and build on it

    (c) Entrepreneurs should concentrate on saving cost and not spend time and energy on quality

    (d) Entrepreneurs should make world changing products that users want and which have many features

171. According to the Author, what do early adopters want?

    (a) Early adopters want products that are readily available at low cost and high visibility

    (b) Early adopters want high quality, polished products that are ready to use

    (c) Early adopters want products with free trials with certain number of promised features

    (d) Early adopters want products that are new, incomplete and offer competitive advantage

172. What does the author seek to imply by quoting "I know for me, the MVP feels a little dangerous-in a good way-since I have always been such a perfectionist."?

    (a) It implies more value for people as the entrepreneur works towards perfecting the quality of products which reduces the danger for the. consumer

    (b) It implies that there is a risk associated with the product which enables entrepreneurs to achieve perfection in the product

    (c) It implies that the incomplete nature is associated with a certain amount of risk drawing entrepreneurs out of their comfort zone

    (d) It implies that if entrepreneurs make products that are less than perfect it is dangerous for the consumer

173. What is the function of MVP?

    (a) To enable entrepreneurs to reach out to as many consumers as possible in the fastest possible time with their product

    (b) To enable entrepreneurs to continuously improve their product in the fastest time with least amount of time and cost

    (c) To enable entrepreneurs to develop products that are of high quality and have many features

    (d) To enable entrepreneurs to create world changing products that can win awards in trade shows

PASSAGE 2

I wear a variety of professional hats-university professor, literacy consultant to districts, author of several books related to comprehension. To keep myself honest (and humble), I spend a lot of time in classrooms watching kids and teachers at work. During the past decade, I've observed a transformation in the teaching of reading from an approach that measured readers' successful, understanding of text through lengthy packets of comprehension questions to one that requires students to think about their thinking, activating their "good reader" strategies. Close reading is deep analysis of how a literary text works; it is both a reading process and something you include in a literary analysis paper, though in a refined form. Fiction writers and poets build texts out of many central components, including subject, form, and specific word choices. Essentially, close reading means reading to uncover layers of meaning that lead to deep comprehension. "Close, analytic reading stresses engaging with a text of sufficient complexity directly and examining meaning thoroughly and methodically, encouraging students to read and reread deliberately. Directing student attention on the text itself empowers students to understand the central ideas and key supporting details. It also enables students to reflect on the meanings of individual words and sentences; die order in which sentences unfold; and the development of ideas over the course of the text, which ultimately leads students to arrive at an understanding of the text as a whole." Reread the definition of close reading- closely-to extract key concepts. You might identify these ideas: examining meaning thoroughly and analytically; directing attention to the text, central ideas, and supporting details; reflecting on meanings of individual words and sentences; and developing ideas over the course of the text. Notice that reader reflection is still integral to the process. But close reading goes beyond that: The best thinkers do monitor and assess their thinking, but in the context of processing the thinking of others (Paul & Elder, 2008).

When you close read, you observe facts and details about the text. You may focus on a particular passage, or on the text as a whole. Your aim may be to notice all striking features of the text, including rhetorical features, structural elements and cultural references; or, your aim may be to notice only selected features of the text-for instance, oppositions and correspondences, or particular historical references. Either way, making these observations constitutes the first step in the process of close reading. The second step is interpreting your observations. What we're basically talking about here is inductive reasoning: moving from the observation of particular facts and details to a conclusion, or interpretation, based on those observations. And, as with inductive reasoning, close reading requires carefully gathering of data (your observations) and careful thinking about what these data add up to. Literary analysis involves examining these Components, which allows us to find in small parts of the text clues to help us understand the whole. For example, if an author writes a novel in the form of a personal journal about a character's daily life, but that journal reads like a series of lab reports, what do we learn about that character? What is the effect of picking a word like "tome" instead of "book"? In effect, you are putting the author's choices under a microscope. The process of close reading should produce a lot of questions. It is when you begin to answer these questions that you are ready to participate thoughtfully in class discussion or write a literary analysis paper that makes the most of your close reading work. Close reading sometimes feels like overanalyzing, but don't worry. Close reading is a process of finding as much information as you can in order to form as many questions as you can. When it is time to write your paper and formalize your close reading, you will sort through your work to figure out what is most convincing and helpful to the argument you hope to make and, conversely, what seems like a stretch. It's our responsibility as educators to build students' capacity for independently comprehending a text through close reading. Teaching is about transfer. The goal is for students to take what they learn from the study of one text and apply it to the next text they read. How can we ensure that students both reap the requisite knowledge from each text they read and acquire skills to pursue the meaning of other texts independently? I suggest we coach students to ask themselves four basic questions as they reflect on a specific portion of any text, even the shortest: What is the author telling me here? Are there any hard or important words? What does the author want me to understand? How does the auther play, with language to add to meaning? If students take time to ask themselves these questions while reading and become skillful at answering them, there'll be less need for the teacher to do all the asking. For this to happen, we must develop students' capacity to observe and analyze. First things first: See whether students have noticed the details of a passage and can recount those details in their own words. Note that the challenge here isn't to be brief (as-in a summary); it's to be accurate, precise, and clear.

The recent focus on finding evidence in a text has sent students (even in primary grades) scurrying back to their books to retrieve a quote that validates their opinion. But to paraphrase what that quote means in a student's own language, rather than the author's, is more difficult than you might think. Try it with any paragraph. Expressing the same meaning with different words often requires going back to that text a few times to get the details just right. Paraphrasing is pretty low on Bloom's continuum- of lower- to higher-order thinking, yet many students stumble even here. This is the first stop along the journey to close reading. If students can't paraphrase the basic content of a passage How can they dig for its deeper meaning? The second basic question about hard of. important words encourages students to zoom in on precise meaning. When students are satisfied that they have a basic grasp of what the author is telling them, they're ready to move on to analyzing the fine points of content. If students begin their analysis by asking themselves the third question. What does the author want me to understand in this passage? they'll be on their way to making appropriate inferences, determining what the author is trying to show without stating it directly.

We can also teach students to read carefully with the eye of a writer, which means helping them analyze craft. How a text is written is as important as the content itself in getting the author's message across. Just as a movie director focuses the camera on a particular detail to get you to view the scene the way he or she wants you to, authors play with words to get you to see a text their way. Introducing students to some of the tricks authors use opens students' minds to an entirely new realm in close reading.

174. In the above passage the author has used the term 'Rhetoric features'. What does it mean?

    (a) Any characteristics of a text that are repetitive in nature and is interesting

    (b) Any characteristics of a text that improves the grammar of the literary text

    (c) Any characteristic of a text that helps convince reader of a certain point of view

    (d) Any characteristic of the text that provides solutions to questions for the readers

175. According to the author what is inductive reasoning with regard to Close Reading?

    (a) Observing the characteristics and features of the text and moving to conclusions

    (b) Understanding the overall theme and gathering evidence from the text to support it

    (c) Understanding the text and preparing lot of questions

    (d) Observing the nuances of the text and preparing a suitable analysis for class discussion

176. According to the passage, what is the importance of 'paraphrasing' for students?

    (a) It is part of higher order learning and improves the speed of reading of students

    (b) It leads to a deeper understanding of the text by improving the accuracy and clarity

    (c) It accelerates the understanding of the text and enables students to be brief

    (d) It enables students to reproduce the text exactly as it is without confusion

177. With reference to the above passage, what responsibility, according to the author, do educators have?

    (a) To build skills of close reading so that students can independently improve their knowledge of English grammar and translate the meaning from one English text to another

    (b) To build skills of close reading so that students can by themselves apply the knowledge they have gained through analysis and understanding of one English text to another

    (c) To build skills of close reading amongst students to improve their ability to paraphrase from one of English text to another

    (d) To build skills of close reading so that students can independently analyse one English text and prepare for class discussions

PASSAGE 3

As someone said, this crisis was too valuable to waste. I, for one, learnt many lessons on crisis management and leadership. By far the most important lesson I learnt is that the primary focus of a central bank during a crisis has to be on restoring confidence in the markets, and what this requires is swift, bold and decisive action. This is not as obvious as it sounds because central banks are typically given to agonizing over every move they make out of anxiety that failure of their actions to deliver the intended impact will hurt their creditability and their policy effectiveness down the line. There is a lot to be said for such deliberative action in normal times. In crisis time's though, it is important for them to take more chances without being too mindful of whether all of their actions are going to be fully effective or even mildly successful. After all, crisis management is a percentage game and you do what you think has the best chance of reversing the momentum. Oftentimes, it is the fact of the action rather than the precise nature of the action that bolsters confidence. Take the Reserve Bank's measure I wrote about earlier of instituting exclusive lines of credit for augmenting the liquidity of NBFCs and mutual funds (MFs) which came under redemption pressure. It is simply unthinkable that

the Reserve Bank would have done anything like this in normal times. In the event of a liquidity constraint in normal times, the standard response of the Reserve Bank would be to ease liquidity in the overall system and leave it to the banks to determine how to use that additional liquidity.

But here, we were targeting monetary policy at a particular class of financial institutions-the MFs and NBFCs-a decidedly unconventional action. This departure from standard protocol pushed some of our senior staff beyond their comfort zones. Their reservations ranged from: 'this is not how monetary policy is done' to 'this will make the Reserve Bank vulnerable to pressures to bail out other sectors'. After hearing them out, I made the call to go ahead. Market participants applauded the new facility and saw it as the Reserve Bank's willingness to embrace unorthodox measures to address Specific areas of pressure in the system. In the event, these facilities were not significantly tapped. In normal times, that would have been seen as a failure of policy. From the crisis perspective though, it was a success inasmuch as the very existence of the central bank backstop restored confidence in the NBFCs and MFs, and smoothed pressures in the financial system. Similarly, the cut in the repo rate of one full percentage point that I effected in October 2008 was a non-standard action from the perspective of a central bank used to cutting the interest rate by a maximum of half a percentage point (50 basis points in the jargon) when it wanted to signal strong action. Of course, we deliberated the advisability of going into uncharted waters and how it might set expectations for the future. For example, in the future, the market may discount a 50 basis-point cut as too tame. But considering the uncertain and unpredictable global environment and the imperative to improve the flow of credit in a stressed situation, I bit the bullet again and decided on a full percentage-point cut.

Managing the tension between short-term pay-offs and longer-term consequences is a constant struggle in all central bank policy choices as indeed it is in all public policy decisions. This balance between horizons shifts in crisis times, as dousing the fires becomes an overriding priority even if some of the actions taken to do that may have some longer-term costs. For example, in 2008, we saw massive infusion of liquidity as the best bet for preserving the financial stability of our markets. Indeed, in uncharted waters, erring on the side of caution meant providing the system with more liquidity than considered adequate. This strategy was effective in the short-term, but with hindsight, we know that excess liquidity may have reinforced inflation pressures down the line. But remember, we were making a judgement call in real time. Analysts who are criticizing us are doing so with the benefit of hindsight. Another lesson we leant is that even in a global crisis, central banks have to adapt their responses to domestic conditions. I am saying this because all through the crisis months, whenever another central bank, especially an advanced economy central bank, announced any measure, there was immediate pressure that the Reserve Bank too should institute a similar measure. Such straightforward copying of measures of other central banks without first examining their appropriateness for the domestic situation can often do more harm than good. Let me illustrate. During the depth of the crisis, fearing a run on their banks, the UK authorities had extended deposit insurance across board to all deposits in the UK banking system. Immediately, there were commentators asking that the Reserve Bank too must embrace such an all-out measure. If we had actually done that, the results would have been counterproductive if not outright harmful. First, the available premium would not have been able to support such a blanket insurance, and the markets were aware of that.

If we had glossed over that and announced a blanket cover anyway, that action would have clearly lacked credibility. Besides, any such move would be at odds with what we had been asserting-that our banks and our financial systems were safe and sound. The inconsistency between our walk and talk would have confused the markets; instead of reassuring them, any blanket insurance of the UK type would have scared the public and sown seeds of doubt about the safety of their bank deposits, potentially triggering a run on some vulnerable banks. Finally, an important lesson from the crisis relates to the imperative of the government and the regulators speaking and acting in unison. It is possible to argue that public disclosure of differences within closed doors of policymaking could actually be helpful in enhancing public understanding on how policy might evolve in the future. For example, a 6-6 vote conveys a different message from a 12-0 vote. During crisis times, though, sending mixed signals to fragile markets can do huge damage. On the other hand, the demonstration of unity of purpose would reassure markets and yield great synergies. The experience of the crisis from around the world, and our own experience too, showed that coordination could be managed without compromising regulatory autonomy. Merely synchronizing policy announcements for exploiting the synergistic impact need not necessarily imply that regulators were being forced into actions they did not own.

178. What 'crisis' is the author referring to, in the above passage?

    (a) Financial crisis of 2008

    (b) Currency crisis of 1997

    (c) Balance of Payment crisis of 1991

    (d) De-monetization crisis of 2016

179. According to the author, what is the typical response of central banks in times of crisis?

Answer with reference to the passage.

    (a) Central banks are proactive in their approach and are quick to respond to crisis

    (b) Central banks take risks and are aggressive in their response to crisis

    (c) Central banks are deliberate in their approach and respond cautiously to crisis

    (d) Central banks analyse different policy issues and then respond to crisis

180. Why does the author say "...even in a global crisis, central banks have to adapt their responses to domestic conditions"? Answer with reference to passage.

    (a) Central banks do not have sufficient knowledge or expertise with regard to global conditions and cannot apply them to domestic conditions

    (b) Only World bank has the information and expertise to deal with global conditions and help countries deal with domestic conditions

    (c) Domestic conditions are typical to every country and applying solutions from other countries creates confusion

    (d) Central bank policies are different for different countries and government permission is required to apply them in domestic conditions

181. With reference to the above passage, what is the role of government and regulators in times of crisis? Select the most appropriate response with reference to information provided in the passage.

    (a) In times of crisis the government and regulators play the role of check, and balance to provide safety to financial systems of a country

    (b) In times of crisis regulators have to become more strict with government to prevent misuse of power and compromising regulatory anatomy

    (c) In times of crisis the government has to exercise control on the regulators so that they do not become too powerful and exploit the financial systems

    (d) In times of crisis the government and the regulators have to work on common ground and avoid any conflicts to prevent instability and confusion

PASSAGE 4

Any company can generate simple descriptive statistics about aspects of its business-average revenue per employee, for example, or average order size. But analytics competitors look well beyond basic statistics. These companies use predictive modelling to identify the most profitable customers-plus those with the greatest profit potential and the ones most likely to cancel their accounts. They pool data generated in-house and data acquired from outside sources (which they analyze more deeply than do their less statistically savvy competitors) for a comprehensive understanding of their customers. They optimize their supply chains and can thus determine the impact of an unexpected constraint, simulate alternatives and route shipments around problems. They establish prices in real time to get the highest yield possible from each of their customer transactions. They create complex models of how their operational costs relate to their financial performance. Leaders in analytics also use sophisticated experiments to measure the overall impact or "lift" of intervention strategies and then apply the results to continuously improve subsequent analyses. Capital One, for example, conducts more than 30,000 experiments a year, with different interest rates, incentives, direct-mail packaging, and other variables. Its goal is to maximize the likelihood both that potential customers will sign up for credit cards and that they will pay back Capital One.

Analytics competitors understand that most business functions- even those, like marketing, that have historically depended on art rather than science-can be improved with sophisticated quantitative techniques. These organizations don't gain advantage from one killer app, but rather from multiple applications supporting many parts of the business-and, in a few cases, being rolled out for use by customers and suppliers. UPS embodies the evolution from targeted analytics user to comprehensive analytics competitor. Although the company is among the world's most rigorous practitioners of operations research and industrial engineering, its capabilities were, until fairly recently, narrowly focused. Today, UPS is wielding its statistical skill to track the movement of packages and to anticipate and influence the actions of people- assessing the likelihood of customer attrition and identifying sources of problems. The UPS Customer Intelligence Group, for example, is able to accurately predict customer defections by examining usage patterns and complaints.

When the data point to a potential defector, a salesperson contacts that customer to review and resolve the problem, dramatically reducing the loss of accounts. UPS still lacks the breadth of initiatives of a full-bore analytics competitor, but it is heading in that direction. Analytics competitors treat all such activities from all provenances as a single, coherent initiative, often massed under one rubric, such as "information-based strategy" at Capital One or "information- based customer management" at Barclays

Bank. These programs operate not just under a common label but also under common leadership and with common technology and tools. In traditional companies, "business intelligence" (the term IT people use for analytics and reporting processes and software) is generally managed by departments; number-crunching functions select their own tools, control their own data warehouses, and train their own people. But that way, chaos lies. For one thing, the proliferation of user-developed spreadsheets and databases inevitably leads to multiple versions of key indicators within an organization.

Furthermore, research has shown that between 20% and 40% of spreadsheets contain errors; the more spreadsheets floating around a company, therefore, the more fecund the breeding ground for mistakes. Analytics competitors, by contrast, field centralized groups to ensure that critical data and other resources are well managed and that different parts of the organization can share data easily, without the impediments of inconsistent formats, definitions, and standards. Some analytics competitors apply the same enterprise approach to people as to technology. Procter & Gamble, for example, recently created a kind of uberanalytics group consisting of more than 100 analysts from such functions as operations, supply chain, sales, consumer research, and' marketing. Although most of the analysts are embedded in business operating units, the group is centrally managed. As a result of this consolidation, P&G can apply a critical mass of expertise to its most pressing issues. So, for example, sales and marketing analysts supply data on opportunities for growth in existing markets to analysts who design corporate supply networks. The supply chain analysts, in turn, apply their expertise in certain decision-analysis techniques to such new areas as competitive intelligence. The group at P&G also raises the visibility of analytical and data based decision making within the company. Previously, P&G's crack analysts had improved business processes and saved the firm money; but because they were squirreled away in dispersed domains, many executives didn't know what services they offered or how effective they could be. Now those executives are more likely to tap the company's deep pool of expertise for their projects. Meanwhile, masterful number crunching has become part of the story P&G tells to investors, the press and the public.

A companywide embrace of analytics impels changes in culture, processes, behaviour, and skills for many employees. And so, like any major transition, it requires leadership from executives at the very top who have a passion for the quantitative approach. Ideally, the principal advocate is the CEO. Indeed, we found several chief executives who have driven the shift to analytics at their companies over the past few years, including Loveman of Harrah's, Jeff Bezos of Amazon, and Rich Fairbank of Capital One. Before he retired from the Sara Lee Bakery Group, former CEO Barry Beracha kept a sign on his desk that summed up his personal and organizational philosophy: "In God we trust. All others bring data!' We did come across some companies in which a single functional or business unit leader was trying to push analytics throughout the organization, and a few were making some progress. But we found that these lower-level people lacked the clout, the perspective, and the cross-functional scope to change the culture in any meaningful way. CEOs leading the analytics charge require both an appreciation of and a familiarity with the subject.

A background in statistics isn't necessary, but those leaders must understand the theory behind various quantitative methods so that they recognize those methods' limitations-which factors are being weighed and which ones aren't. When the CEOs need help grasping quantitative techniques, they turn to experts who understand the business and how analytics can be applied to it. We interviewed several leaders who had retained such advisers, and these executives stressed the need to find someone who can explain things in plain language and be trusted not to spin the numbers. A few CEOs we spoke with had surrounded themselves with very analytical people-professors, consultants, MIT graduates and the like. But that was a personal preference rather than a necessary practice. Of course, not all decisions should be grounded in analytics - atleast not wholly so. Research shows that human beings can make quick, surprisingly accurate assessments of personality and character based on simple observations. For analytics minded leaders then the challenge boils down to knowing when to run with the numbers and when-to run with their guts.

182. With reference to the above passage what does the phrase "uberanalytic group" mean?

   (a) A centralized homogeneous group comprising of experts in analytics within the organization who provide their expertise to all

   (b) A centralized group that draws upon expertise from multifunctional areas within the organization and provides their expertise to all

   (c) A centralized group consisting of data analytics experts from within the organization who provide their expertise to all

   (d) A powerful centralized group of crack analysts within the organisation who provide their expertise to all

183. Replace the phrase 'more fecund the breeding ground for mistakes' from the passage by selecting the most appropriate phrase without changing the meaning.

   (a) An unsuitable environment where mistakes are bound to happen

   (b) Fructiferous environment for mistakes

   (c) A highly fertile ground for producing more errors

   (d) Creating a high possibility of inaccuracy

184. According to the author, what is the leadership challenge for analytics minded leaders?

   (a) The analytics minded leader has to be well versed in statistics and quantitative analysis in order to be effective

   (b) The analytics minded leader should have experts in data analysis from top institutes such as MIT etc. to advise him

   (c) The analytics minded leader should be able to strike a balance between data driven decisions and intuition

   (d) The analytics minded leader should be able to lead teams of cross-functional experts

185. In the above passage, how does the author differentiate between 'Analytics competitors' and 'traditional companies' with regard to their strategy towards data management?

   (a) Analytics competitors have a centralised, multi-functional approach to data management and encourage data sharing whereas traditional companies have a departmental, multiple databases approach

   (b) Traditional companies surround themselves with very analytical people from academia, consultants, and pass outs from institutes like MITs but Analytics competitors hire the best analytical minds

   (c) Analytics competitors use predictive modelling to identify the most profitable options whereas traditional companies use basic statistics

   (d) Traditional companies appoint leaders with data management expertise but Analytics competitors train all employees in data analytics

2019-21

Directions (186-201). This section consists of 5 passages followed by questions. Read each passage carefully. Answer the questions by selecting the most appropriate option (with reference to the passage).

PASSAGE 1

We use the word culture quite casually when referring to a variety of thoughts and actions. I would like to begin my attempt to define cultures by a focus on three of its dictionary meanings that 1 think are significant to our understanding of the general term-culture. We often forget that it's more essential usage is as a verb rather than as a noun, since the noun follows from the activities involved in the verb. Thus the verb, to culture, means to cultivate. This can include at least three activities: to artificially grow microscopic organisms; to improve and refine the customs, manners and activities of one's life; to give attention to the mind as part of what goes into the making of what we call civilization, or what was thought to be the highest culture. In short, one might argue that culture is the intervention of human effort in refining and redefining that which is natural, but that it gradually takes on other dimensions in the life of the individual, and even more in the interface between the individual and society. When speaking of society, this word also requires defining. Society, it has been said, is what emerges from a network of interactions between people that follow certain agreed upon and perceptible patterns. These are determined by ideas of status, hierarchy and a sense of community governing the network. They are often, but not invariably, given a direction by those who control the essentials in how a society functions, as for instance, its economic resources, its technology and its value systems. The explanation and justification for who controls these aspects of a society introduces the question of its ideology and often its form.

The resulting patterns that can be differentiated from segment to segment of the society are frequently called its cultures. Most early societies register inequalities. The access of their members to wealth and status varies. The idea of equality therefore has many dimensions. All men and women may be said to be equal in the eyes of God, but may at the same time be extremely differentiated in terms of income and social standing, and therefore differentiated in the eyes of men and women. This would not apply to the entire society. There may be times when societies conform to a greater degree of equality, but such times may be temporary. It has been argued that on a pilgrimage, the status of every pilgrim is relatively similar but at the end returns to inequalities. Societies are not static and change their forms and their rules of functioning. Cultures are reflections of these social patterns, so they also change My attempt in this introduction is to explain how the meaning of a concept such as culture has changed in recent times and has come to include many more facets than it did earlier. What we understand as the markers of culture have gone way beyond what we took them to be a century or two ago. Apart from items of culture, which is the way in which culture as heritage was popularly viewed, there is also the question of the institutions and social codes that determine the pattern of living, and upon which pattern a culture is constructed. Finally, there is the process of socialization into society and culture through education. There is a historical dimension to each of these as culture and history are deeply intertwined. There is also an implicit dialogue between the present and the past reflected in the way in which the readings of the past changed over historical periods.

Every society has its cultures, namely, the patterns of how the people of that society live. In varying degrees this would refer to broad categories that shape life, such as the environment that determines the relationship with the natural world, technology that enables a control over the natural world, political-economy that organizes the larger vision of a society as a community or even as a state, structures of social relations that ensure its networks of functioning, religion that appeals to aspirations and belief, mythology that may get transmuted into literature and philosophy, that teases the mind and the imagination with questions. The process of growth is never static therefore there are mutations and changes within the society. There is communication and interaction with other societies through which cultures evolve and mutate. There is also the emergence of subcultures that sometimes take the form of independent and dominant cultures or amoeba-like breakaway to form new cultures. Although cultures coincide with history and historical change, the consciousness of a category such as culture, in the emphatic sense in which the term is popularly used these days, emerges in the eighteenth century in Europe. The ideal was the culture of elite groups, therefore sometimes a distinction is made between what came to be called 'high culture' that of the elite, and 'low culture' that of those regarded as not being of the elite, and sometimes described as 'popular'. Historical records of elite cultures in forms such as texts and monuments for instance, received larger patronage and symbolized the patterns of life of dominant groups. They were and are more readily available as heritage than the objects of the socially lower groups in society whose less durable cultural manifestations often do not survive. This also predisposed people to associate culture as essentially that of the elite.

186. What is the central idea of the passage?

   (a) The author has explained the importance of religion and equality before God

   (b) The author has defined culture and its sub-elements

   (c) The author has explained the social inequalities existing in a society

   (d) The author has explained the contextual metamorphosis of culture in different contexts

187. According to the author what are the characteristics of 'Society'?

   (a) Society consists of rich and poor

   (b) Society consists of relationships between people who have agreed to follow certain social norms

   (c) Society consists of inequalities between people who have access to and control over resources

   (d) Society consists of people who go on pilgrimage together

188. With reference to the above passage, what are the important elements of 'Culture'?

   (a) Social inequalities, wealth, status, social norms

   (b) High culture elite and low culture popular

   (c) History, education, religion, beliefs, social patterns

   (d) Growth, civilisation, communication, texts and monuments

PASSAGE 2

Today, we have specialists in various professions, but many among them are unconcerned with the world beyond their own specialization. It is sometimes said that they are replacing the public intellectual. But the two are not identical. There are many more academics, for instance, than existed before. But it seems that most refer not to confront authority even if it obstructs the path of free thought. Is this because they wish to pursue knowledge undisturbed, or because they are ready to discard knowledge should authority require them to do so? Or does association with national or international agencies require that critical assessments of social thought and action remain sotto voce? Today, as always, the public intellectual is expected to take a position independent of those in power, enabling him or her to question debatable ideas, irrespective of who propagates them. Reasoned critiques are often the essential starting point. The public intellectual has to see himself or herself as a person who is as close to being autonomous as is possible, and more than that, be seen by others as such.

An acknowledged professional status makes it somewhat easier to be autonomous. Such status brings with it another kind of authority, conceded, even if grudgingly, by professional peers and this does make some small impact on the non-professional world. The public Intellectual of today, in addition to being of such a status, has to have at the same time a concern for what constitutes the rights of citizens, particularly on issues of social justice, and further, there should be a readiness to raise these matters as public policy. The combination of drawing upon the professional respect that a person has garnered, together with a concern for society, can sometimes establish the moral authority of that person and ensure public support. This is a conceded qualification and not a tangible one. In the past it was those who had distanced themselves somewhat from society who were believed not to have a vested interest in the changes they were suggesting. Although this was not always so, we know that close associations, such as formal affiliation to a political party, can inhibit free-thinking and prescriptions for action, even if it has the advantage of providing a certain leverage to the suggestions being made. As an attitude of mind, autonomy is more readily expected of the professional specialist or the academic. Such persons, and they are not the only ones, can suggest alternative ways of thinking, even about problems of the larger society. Their thinking should emerge from reasoned, logical analyses. Yet academics today are hesitant to defend even the right to make what might be broadly called alternative, if not rational interpretations, however sensitively they may be expressed. This is evident from the ease with which books are banned and pulped, or demands made that they be burned, and syllabuses changed under pressure from religious or political organizations, or the intervention of the state. Why do such actions provoke so little reaction among many academics and professionals? The answer that is usually given is that they fear the instigators who are persons with the backing of political authority. But is this the only answer?

Is it assumed that opinions about governance and society must hinge on ideologies linked to political parties and as a result there can be no thinking about how to configure society in a manner that is independent of a necessary commitment to political parties? Surely in this day and age, it is possible to be an independent liberal in this country with ideological commitments that are not determined solely by political parties? Being a liberal is an attitude of mind that determines the fight for space in a society when that society resists ethics and reasoned thinking. The understanding of what one is battling for assumes an ideological direction but this does not require association with a political party. And there should also be the freedom to choose one's position on an issue and this position need not be in conformity with the ideological take of a particular political party on every occasion. The public intellectual has, by definition, to be liberal, that is, to insist that there be space to present varying perspectives and that wherever possible, reason and ethics should have primacy in whatever debates are taking place. This is not a new definition and has been a recognizable part of the interface between knowledge and society since earliest times. Approximations to orthodoxy and orthopraxy have always been contested by similar approximations to heterodoxy although those leading the charge do not always have or need to have the same social identity. This is apparent among people and situations in the Indian past yet we have often ignored it or failed to recognize it. How an intellectual even without being a public intellectual, requires a more than average knowledge in his/her professional specialization and beyond that a familiarity with the context of that knowledge: how did it come about and what are the implications for the people who use that knowledge. To be a technician (or be technically accomplished) in a specialization, however good, is not sufficient. An intellectual perspective requires that the specialized knowledge one possesses should be related to social concerns where required and to other branches of knowledge as well. Added to this it helps if that knowledge can be contextualized in an accessible way for a wider range of people to understand facets of the variegated world in which we live, and to which understanding the specialization contributes. The public intellectual uses such foundations in his/her thinking in order to extend the understanding of the world we inhabit, and to do so by insisting on space for debate and the right to informed opinion.

189. According to the author, 'Public Intellectual' is one who

(a) is very knowledgeable, possesses a postgraduate or higher degree and is a specialist in his field

(b) is liberal minded, considers varying perspectives, takes an independent position and is concerned for greater good

(c) has a professional status, works with national and international agencies and is an expert in specific domain

(d) has the backing of political authority, speaks and writes sensitively about various issues and is concerned about social policy

190. How does the author differentiate between Public Intellectuals of the past and today?

(a) Public intellectuals of the past were merely academicians and idealists. Public intellectuals of today are more learned and specialists in their own field

(b) Public intellectuals of the past were not concerned about matters of social policy or social concerns. Public intellectuals of today are technically accomplished and believe in reasoned critiques.

(c) Public intellectuals of the past were more concerned with rational thought. Public intellectuals of today are more sensitive to different perspectives

(d) Public intellectuals of the past were distanced from vested interests, liberal in thought and spoke up about issues concerning society. Public intellectuals of today are concerned about being politically correct while expressing views

191. With reference to the above passage, explain the relationship between Orthodoxy, Orthopraxy and Heterodoxy as proposed by the author as applicable to the 'Public Intellectual'

(a) The 'Public Intellectual' can be both orthodox and orthoprax but not heterodox

(b) The 'Public Intellectual' can be heterodox but not orthodox and orthoprax

(c) The 'Public Intellectual' can be both orthoprax and heterodox but not orthodox

(d) The 'Public Intellectual' can be orthodox but not heterodox and orthoprax

PASSAGE 3

We love information. Especially in times of crisis. Have you ever noticed your tendency to become glued to the television or Internet when disaster strikes? It is human nature to try togather as much information as possible, to make sense and create meaning when we don't understand what is happening. We seek information for another reason too, control. We operate under the illusion that if we can gain more information, we will not only understand what is happening, we might just be able to control it. I am not suggesting that there is no value to information or to clearly defined reporting and accountability relationships for routine business operations. I am instead calling out the temptation that an information-centred approach to agility offers: there's a desire to settle into the illusion that information will give you control, when in many situations it is simply not possible to gather or process enough information to be effective when it counts.

Recognizing that there are many situations that you not only cannot control but cannot predict is a radical mind-set and practice shift for most. It requires that you decide whether your goal is to reduce the perception of uncertainty or to actually become more effective in its midst. It also involves more than a simple reconfiguration of the organisation chart and job descriptions. It require relinquishing the illusion of control that lies at the very foundation of most management training and business practice. This shift is being made in one of the most hierarchal, command-and-control organizations in the country, the United States military. Recognizing the insidious nature of information age strategies and their tendency to lead to either analysis paralysis or the false security of convenient stories, the U.S. military has begun to make a fundamental shift in its approach to VUCA (volatility, uncertainty, complexity, and ambiguity), a shift from information to interactions. This change does not begin with restructuring and redeployments but with a fundamental shift in mind-set. In fact, the term. VUCA was first coined by the U.S. Army War College to describe increasingly complex and unpredictable combat conditions." VUCA has become shorthand for the reality of life in the twenty-first century. Most business approaches to VUCA focus on strategies to reduce uncertainty. These strategies tend to centre around gaining greater control, including amassing more and better information, minimizing risk, and improving planning and analysis. While risk and uncertainty reduction are valid strategies, they do not necessarily make an organization more agile, for two reasons: (1) collecting more and better information takes time and may foster the illusion of control and comfort when, in reality, it is impossible to gather all available information in complex, changing contexts, let alone fully analyze and make meaning of, it and (2) planning and analysis are dependent on relatively stable contexts. Another liability of information-centred approaches is that they typically lead to more questions and the need to gather more information to reduce the uncertainty created by the information already collected. There is an even more significant liability of the information-centred approach to agility: our preconceptions lead us to filter out information that does not align with our expectations. Under the stress of an unexpected challenge or opportunity, our ability to access our higher thinking capacity can be reduced, leading us to fall back on the version of the story we expected. Warnings of terrorist threats before 9/11 and potential malfunctions of crucial components prior to the Challenger space shuttle disaster went unheeded because they did not fit the narrative that was co-constructed by leaders during years of experience and expectation. Agile leaders, teams and organizations know they cannot afford to get caught up in a story. They are instead learning how they might be more effective by focusing on their interactions with one another and with the available information in the dynamic present moment.

Let me emphasize that this is a shift away from an overreliance on information. I am not suggesting you curtail important industry and market data analysis, or take this as encouragement to blindly make decisions when further investigation is warranted. I am encouraging you to shift away from the false comfort such information can offer, and toward the relational context in which you make sense of it, decide and act. When we make the shift from information to interaction, we may be called to shift more than our relationship to external information; we may need to shift the way we perceive ourselves as well. The agility shift requires that we value our capacity to connect and build relationships over-or at least as much' as-our hard-won expertise. Years of experience, training and credentials are, of course, still valuable. But their value is minimal without the networks to which the skills, knowledge, experience, and resource awareness are linked. In other words, separating, the process of "knowing what" and "knowing how" from the process of "knowing who" significantly diminishes agility capacity. The shift from information to interaction values the human system in which all meaning and action take place. Rather than problematizing this system as non- objective or messy, the agility shift embraces it and engages it more fully. You may not be able to control or predict what happens, but with a conscious, continuous commitment to interacting within your web of relationships and resources, you will be more effective than you ever imagined. The agility shift is first and foremost a shift in mind-set. This mind-set values interactions within the dynamic present moment. It is also a shift from the false comfort of "a plan" to achieving a state of readiness to find opportunity in the unexpected.

192. With reference to the above passage what is the author's stand with regard to 'information'?

(a) The author considers information as important in order to reduce risk and uncertainty while taking decisions

(b) The author considers information as important for human beings as they love information

(c) The author considers information as necessary but an obstacle in taking quick decisions by organisation leaders

(d) The author considers that there is an over reliance on information leading to complacency in decision making

193. According to the author what causes 'analysis-paralysis'?

(a) Today's leaders are not able to take decisions because of lack of policy thereby causing paralysis of policy

(b) Today's leaders have access to lot of information and spend more time on analysing rather than acting upon it

(c) Today's leaders are not able to take decisions because they do not have the skills to analyse information

(d) Today's leaders are paralysed because they do not have networking with other leaders

194. With reference to the above passage, 'agility shift' is

(a) the uncertainty reduction mind set of leaders to gather more information in order to take effective decisions

(b) the mind set of leaders towards using the VUCA approach in order to take effective decisions

(c) the mind set of leaders to reduce over reliance on information and move to interaction in order to take effective decisions

(d) the mind set of leaders to seek more information and analysis in order to take effective decisions

195. According to the author, why do we 'love' information?

(a) Today the internet and television provide us with easy access to lot of information and entertainment

(b) Information helps us in anticipating and preventing crisis like 9/11.

(c) Information provides us with an illusion of control and we remain in our comfort zone.

(d) Information helps us in getting more knowledge and enhancing expertise

PASSAGE 4

While majoring in computer science isn't a requirement to participate in the Second Machine Age, what skills do liberal arts graduates specifically possess to contribute to this brave new world? Another major oversight in the debate has been the failure to appreciate that a good liberal arts education teaches many skills that are not only valuable to the general world of business, but are in fact vital to innovating the next wave of breakthrough tech-driven products and services. Many defenses of the value of a liberal arts education have been launched, of course, with the emphasis being on the acquisition of fundamental thinking and communication skills, such as critical thinking, logical argumentation, and good communication skills. One aspect of liberal arts education that has been strangely neglected in the discussion is the fact that the humanities and social sciences are devoted to the study of human nature and the nature of our communities and larger societies. Students who pursue degrees in the liberal arts disciplines tend to be particularly motivated to investigate what makes us human: how we behave and why we behave as we do. They're driven to explore how our families and our public institutions-such as our schools and legal systems-operate, and could operate better, and how governments and economies work, or as is so often the case, are plagued by dysfunction. These students learn a great deal from their particular courses of study and apply that knowledge to today's issues, the leading problems to be tackled, and various approaches for analyzing and addressing those problems.

The greatest opportunities for innovation in the emerging era are in applying evolving technological capabilities to finding better ways to solve human problems like social dysfunction and political corruption; finding ways to better educate children; helping people live healthier and happier lives by altering harmful behaviors; improving our working conditions; discovering better ways to tackle poverty; Improving healthcare and making it more affordable; making our governments more accountable, from the local level up to that of global affairs; and finding optimal ways to incorporate intelligent, nimble machines into our work lives so that we are empowered to do more of the work that we do best, and to let the machines do the rest. Workers with a solid liberal arts education have a strong foundation to build on in pursuing these goals. One of the most immediate needs in technology innovation is to invest products and services with more human qualities, with more sensitivity to human needs and desires. Companies and entrepreneurs that want to succeed today and in the future must learn to consider in all aspects of their product and service creation how they can make use of the new technologies to make them more humane.

Still, many other liberal arts disciplines also have much to provide the world of technological innovation. The study of psychology, for example, can help people build products that are more attuned to our emotions and ways of thinking. Experience in Anthropology can additionally help companies understand cultural and individual behavioural factors that should be considered in developing products and in marketing them. As technology allows for more machine intelligence and our lives become increasingly populated by the Internet of things and as the gathering of data about our lives and analysis of it allows for more discoveries about our behaviour, consideration of how new products and services can be crafted for the optimal enhancement of our lives and the nature of our communities, workplaces and governments will be of vital importance. Those products and services developed with the keenest sense of how they can serve our human needs and complement our human talents will have a distinct competitive advantage. Much of the criticism of the liberal arts is based on the false assumption that liberal arts students lack rigor in comparison to those participating in the STEM disciplines and that they are 'soft' and unscientific whereas those who study STEM fields learn the scientific method. In fact the liberal arts teach many methods of rigorous inquiry and analysis such as close observation and interviewing in ways that hard science adherents don't always appreciate. Many fields have long incorporated the scientific method and other types of data driven scientific inquiry and problem solving.

Sociologists have developed sophisticated mathematical models of societal networks. Historians gather voluminous data on centuries-old household expenses, marriage and divorce rates, and the world trade, and use data to conduct statistical analyses, identifying trends and contributing factors to the phenomena they are studying. Linguists have developed high-tech models of the evolution of language, and they've made crucial contributions to the development of one of the technologies behind the rapid advance of automation-natural language processing, whereby computers are able to communicate with the, accuracy and personality of Siri and Alexa. It's also important to debunk the fallacy that liberal arts students who don't study these quantitative analytical methods have no 'hard' or relevant skills. This gets us back to the arguments about the fundamental ways of thinking, inquiring, problem solving and communicating that a liberal arts education teaches.

196. What is the central theme of the passage?

   (a) A combination of STEM skills as well as skills of liberal arts are required by Companies in order to develop products that are most relevant today

   (b) Companies need to develop products that are technologically sophisticated and use lot of data driven technology

   (c) The Second machine Age is causing disruption and is going to require a higher number of workers specialised in STEM

   (d) Students with liberal arts background will be able to solve all the social problems as they are experts in the use of quantitative analytical methods

197. How can companies gain an edge in today's era of technological innovation?

   (a) By creating products and services that are technologically sophisticated which can perform a wide range of functions using scientific methods

   (b) By creating products and services that are affordable, humane and do the work that humans don't want to do

   (c) By creating products and services that are technologically advanced and are endowed with human qualities that can be used to solve variety of social problems

   (d) By creating products and services that are similar to human beings and use data based problem solving methodologies

198. What is the author's opinion with regard to the contribution of students of liberal arts and those of STEM, in this new technological age?

    (a) Students of liberal arts have good soft skills but are not skilled with quantitative analytical methods, while STEM students possess both of these

    (b) Students of STEM can contribute effectively by applying rational decision making algorithms. Liberal Arts students provide understanding of social issues but cannot contribute to the development of technological innovations

    (c) Students of STEM are better positioned to participate in the Second machine Age as they have technical skills and understand machine language. Liberal Arts students are not suitable as they do not have degrees in computer science

    (d) Students of Liberal Arts because of their knowledge of human nature can contribute effectively to technological innovations with human qualities. STEM students can contribute to technological innovations but not to human aspects

PASSAGE 5

For policy makers to this day, GDP remains the definitive yardstick for economic performance, permitting them to assess the health and progress of a nation's economy and, by extension, people's lives. Yet GDP's dominance has brought criticism. It fails to capture changes to an economy's structure, such as the shifts to a service-led or technology-based economy. Some have protested that it fails to capture the unofficial or black market economy. Others have asserted that any purely economic indicator by itself may be inadequate to truly measure society's progress, it is therefore no surprise that over the last several decades, economists, sociologists, and other academics have devised other metrics for tracking happiness, wellbeing, and social progress, some of which have garnered a substantial following. Implicit in these metrics is a challenge to GDP as the dominant measure of human progress-despite the fact that these measures sometimes themselves rely on GDP or some variance of GDP and come with limitations of their own. Even so, GDP remains a compelling measure of economic as well as social progress in as much as improvements in economic GDP translate into social progress. Policymakers have nevertheless become interested in these alternative measures, which, even if they do not displace GDP as the most prominent measure of economic growth, have value in complementing GDP in future assessments for economic and living standard progress. Furthermore, these proposed additions to GDP remind us that the endgame for public policy is progress and improved living standards rather than GDP growth for growth's sake. Nonetheless, these rankings reveal that consistently richer Countries (in terms of GDP) rank at the top of the indices and poorer ones at the bottom. For example, happiness indices reflect a demand that happiness be recognized as a criterion for government policy. First published in 2012, the *World Happiness Report* measures happiness by indexing GDP per capita alongside social support, life expectancy, freedom, generosity, and the absence of corruption. Of the 155 Countries collated in the 2017 *World Happiness Report*, the ten happiest countries, in descending order, are Norway, Denmark, Iceland, Switzerland, Finland, the Netherlands, Canada, New Zealand, Australia, and Sweden. The ten least happy countries, beginning with the least happy, are the Central African Republic, Burundi, Tanzania, Syria, Rwanda, Togo, Guinea, Liberia, South Sudan, and Yemen. While the United States is the largest country in GDP terms, it ranks fourteenth on the 2017 happiness index. A more traditional measure that goes beyond GDP alone is the United Nations' Human Development Index (HDI). First published in 1990, the HDI assesses longevity, education, and income across each nation's population, on the premise "that people and their capabilities should be the ultimate criteria for assessing the development of a country, not economic growth alone." The HDI reveals how two countries with the same level of gross national income (GNI)-that is, the total domestic output (GDP) plus foreign GDP generated by citizens abroad, minus domestic output created by foreigners-can end up with such different outcomes. In this way, it allows observers to compare the relative effectiveness of different policy choices and capital investments. In this index, Norway, Australia, and Switzerland rank at the top, with GNIs above US$40,000, and the Central African Republic, Niger, and Chad are at the bottom of the index, all with GNIs of less than US$2,000 per capita. Some of these measures move beyond individuals and attempt a holistic assessment of the health of society. Since its founding in 2012, the Social Progress Imperative has offered a Social Progress Index that examines a range of social and environmental indicators beyond GDP, from access to electricity to religious tolerance, to measure three distinct dimensions of social progress: Basic Human Needs, Foundations of Wellbeing, and Opportunity. The 2017 Social Progress Index covers 133 countries and 94 percent of the world's population. The world as a whole would score 64.85 in Social Progress based on an average of all countries. On average, the top cluster of fourteen countries ranked as having "very high social progress"-including Denmark, Finland, Iceland, Norway, and Switzerland among others-scores 94.92 on Basic Human Needs, Foundations of Wellbeing, and Opportunity. The cluster of seven countries described as having "very low social progress" include the Central African Republic, Afghanistan, Chad, Angola, Niger, Guinea, and

Yemen. For this cluster the average dimension scores of Basic Human Needs, Foundations of Wellbeing, and Opportunity are 42.67, 45.42, and 27.74. What can we learn from these various indices? While noneconomic factors such as health, well-being, and quality of life matter to humanity, economic measures such as GDP generally correlate to success in the other areas, with a small amount of variation among those who are awarded the top spot. In a nutshell, economic growth underpins all else; a country needs economic growth to achieve happiness, well-being, and ultimately human progress. To be sure, GDP estimates provide a snapshot of GDP at a single point in time, but nothing more. A large GDP can indicate that a country is rich yet mask that its economy might be struggling and scarcely growing.

199. What is the author's opinion regarding GDP as a measure for economic performance of a country?

(a) GDP is the yardstick for measuring economic growth of a country

(b) GDP provides policy makers with definitive steps to be taken for improving economic performance

(c) GDP provides accurate but incomplete information of an economy at a single point of time

(d) GDP is the only reliable measure that can be used for framing economic policy

200. What are the characteristics of non GDP measures?

(a) Non GDP measures are subjective in nature and cannot be relied upon

(b) Non GDP measures are not standardized and not universally accepted across countries

(c) Non GDP measures provide data regarding living standards, development, and social progress

(d) Non GDP measures cannot contribute to public policy making

201. According to the passage, what is the difference between using just GDP measures and using non GDP measures in policy making?

(a) Economic measures such as GDP generally correlate to success in other areas and lead to social progress but non GDP measures do not

(b) GDP measure contribute effectively towards policy making as they provide objective and actionable inputs but non GDP measures are open to interpretation

(c) Non GDP measures are able to provide information on gaps in public policy making whereas GDP provides information only on economic performance

(d) Non GDP measures are not accepted by most countries but GDP measures are accepted universally

ANSWERS

1. (b,d)	2. (a,d)	3. (a,b,c,d)	4. (a)	5. (a,b,d)	6. (a,b,c,d)	7. (a,b,d)	8. (a,b,c)	9. (b)	10. (a)
11. (a)	12. (c)	13. (c)	14. (a)	15. (d)	16. (c)	17. (d)	18. (b)	19. (c)	120. (d)
21. (d)	22. (c)	23. (c)	24. (d)	25. (b)	26. (d)	27. (b)	28. (d)	29. (b)	30. (b)
31. (c)	32. (c)	33. (b)	34. (a)	35. (d)	36. (d)	37. (d)	38. (c)	39. (d)	40. (b)
41. (d)	42. (d)	43. (d)	44. (d)	45. (b)	46. (c)	47. (c)	48. (d)	49. (b)	50. (d)
51. (b)	52. (d)	53. (d)	54. (d)	55. (d)	56. (d)	57. (a)	58. (d)	59. (d)	60. (b)
61. (d)	62. (c)	63. (a)	64. (b)	65. (b)	66. (b)	67. (b)	68. (d)	69. (a)	70. (b)
71. (a)	72. (b)	73. (d)	74. (b)	75. (a)	76. (c)	77. (d)	78. (c)	79. (b)	80. (d)
81. (b)	82. (d)	83. (b)	84. (b)	85. (b)	86. (*)	87. (*d)	88. (c)	89. (c)	90. (a)
91. (c)	92. (a)	93. (c)	94. (c)	95. (c)	96. (d)	97. (b)	98. (d)	99. (c)	100. (a)
101. (c)	102. (b)	103. (d)	104. (c)	105. (d)	106. (c)	107. (b)	108. (*a)	109. (c)	110. (c)
111. (d)	112. (c)	113. (b)	114. (a)	115. (b)	116. (b)	117. (d)	118. (a)	119. (d)	120. (c)
121. (b)	122. (c)	123. (d)	124. (c)	125. (a)	126. (c)	127. (b)	128. (a)	129. (a)	130. (d)
131. (c)	132. (a)	133. (b)	134. (a)	135. (a)	136. (c)	137. (d)	138. (a)	139. (d)	140. (b)
141. (c)	142. (b)	143. (c)	144. (b)	145. (d)	146. (a)	147. (a)	148. (c)	149. (c)	150. (a)
151. (c)	152. (d)	153. (c)	154. (b)	155. (c)	156. (b)	157. (b)	158. (a)	159. (c)	160. (d)
161. (c)	162. (b)	163. (d)	164. (c)	165. (c)	166. (b)	167. (c)	168. (c)	169. (b)	170. (b)
171. (d)	172. (c)	173. (b)	174. (c)	175. (a)	176. (b)	177. (b)	178. (b*)	179. (a*)	180. (c)
181. (d)	182. (c)	183. (c)	184. (c)	185. (a)	186. (d)	187 (b)	188. (c)	189. (b)	190. (d)
191. (b)	192. (c)	193. (b)	194. (c)	195. (c)	196. (a)	197 (c)	198. (d)	199. (c)	200. (c)
201. (c)									

EXPLANATIONS

1. The correct combinations are

Agent	Burning-Glass
Garpon	Caravan
Gyanyima	Market
Norbu	Guide

   Hence the correct choices are B and D

2. From the passage only statements A and D are correct. Statement B is incorrect because the pass was delivered to them after 3 days.

3. Satement A is not mentioned in the passage. It only states that the visitors received tea made in European fashion. Statement B is incorrect because the passage mentions that during the second visit 'the Garpon' insisted the visitors to stay put for a few more days. C is an incorrect statement because it was the agent who was astonished to witness the simplicity in the lifestyle of the author and his friends. (paragraph 4). The last paragraph reveals that mountain Gurla Mandhata was reflected in the waters of Lake Mansarovar. Hence, all four statements are incorrect.

4. Statement A is the only correct statement. The last lines of the passage reveal that "the biggest market ....Gyanyima." Statement B is incorrect because the return gift included flour and not cheese. Statement C is not mentioned in the passage. Statement D is incorrect as the Garpon administers five districts. Hence, only A is correct.

5. There is no mention of Statement C in the passage. The remaining statements are correct.

6. Paragraph 6 reveals that "Printing with movable letters began in China in the middle of the 12th century" So, A is incorrect. It cannot be inferred that 'numerical knowledge and ability' , were the main concerns. There were other concerns like co-ordination, history, printing, war, technology etc. So, B is incorrect. C is incorrect because paragraph 7 mentions "new mathematical theories". D is not mentioned in the passage. So, all the statements are incorrect.

7. A and B are clearly mentioned in the passage. D can be inferred from paragraph 2.

8. The combinations are

Astronomy	Tabriz
Abacus	Clerk
Literacy	Almanac
History	Propaganda

Thus the correct answers are A, B, C.

9. It can be inferred directly from the given lines (Agriculture....income)The line after that mentions 'empowering agri-product producers.'

10. Nothing in the passage has been mentioned which talks about getting a competitive advantage from knowing the customers better. Hence, option (a) is the correct answer.

11. It has been mentioned in the passage that TCL relies on its 'CRDP' model which is not an external agency.

12. Sentence 25 mentions that TCL felt that it was being viewed as purely product centric. So, positioning itself as a commodity retailing center may not be good for its long term sustainability.

13. Sentences 35-40 mention that the requirements of farmers were multi-layered and TCL had to reinvent itself to meet those requirements.

14. The entire passage talks about Hertz and its present and possible operations. Hence, option (a) is the correct answer.

15. As mentioned in line 28-29 the Indian population with high disposable income is looking to enjoy all new things in life. Hence, option (d) is the correct answer.

16. Sentences 32-33 mention international travellers' disposition to drive alone. It is not mentioned that they know Indian roads or the chauffeurs are unprofessional. Option (d) is not the reason for self-drive. It is just a related sentence.

17. The underlined sentence 47-48 mentions the importance of service assurance as an important element for institutional consumers.

18. It is mentioned in line 69 of the passage that there is a huge scope in this segement for future growth.

19. Option (a) is not mentioned in the passage. Option (c) would be a wrong practice because paragraph 1 mentions that the organized sector is viewed as being a superior service provider than the unorganized sector. So, matching the price with them will not be the right move as the consumer will expect better quality for that price which he will find in the organized sector.

20. Refer to the line "But there was a dark ... the company stated." All other options are false.

21. Geico is a 'giant automobile insurer' as mentioned in the second sentence of the passage. It is not an automobile giant.

22. 'Altavista' is not mentioned in the passage. Hence, option (c) is the correct answer.

23. Refer to the line "We are, and may be .... outlining potential risks." Hence, option (c) is the correct answer.

24. In sentence A the catch is that the unit of measurement mentioned in the passage is square feet. In the option it is square meter. B is not mentioned in the passage. In C the error is 'market analysis' the 5th para mentions that there was a growing confidence within the company. D is mentioned in para 2.

25. The details mentioned are about the mall in Bangalore. Hence, option (b) is the correct answer.

26. The passage does not mention anything about the term 'Super- speciality stores'

27. The monetary agreement given in A is wrong. In C 'about 200 brands' is incorrect. D is not given in the passage. Hence, option (b) is the correct answer.

28. The passage states that 'experience' (not market analysis) tells the company that a buyer visits around 4 or 5 stores (not at the most 4 or 5 stores) and that they go to a large store and a few smaller brand showrooms (not necessarily selected at random). Hence, option (d) is the correct answer.

29. The passage mentions that 1952 saw 59,000 new cases (the most ever) This is considered the peak. In 1955 a vaccine was discovered. 'A' wrongly mentions that traditional biologists were interested in cure and prevention whereas paragraph 8 mentions cure rather than prevention. 'C' wrongly mentions Theodore Roosevelt instead of Franklin Roosevelt. 'D' wrongly mentions multiple stenosis instead of sclerosis. Hence, option (b) is the correct answer.

30. In paragraph 9 it is mentioned that after a decade of his discovery Salk started talking about his colleagues' resentment. The option says 'almost 30 years later'. 'B' is implied in the last sentence of paragraph 8. Hence, option (b) is the correct answer.

31. Salk was vilified by the scientists, field tests resulted in breakthrough and polio is referred to as dragon in the passage. Hence, option (c) is the correct answer.

32. Please refer to the lines "Indeed, the mystery of that …on a new track." given in the 1st paragraph. From this it is clearly implied that he was involuntarily put on a new track. Option (d) is wrongly stated as there is no mention of Crespo Island and Nautilus being in its vicinity on 25th January.

33. All other options are mentioned in the passage. The incident explained in option (b) has no reference to 25th January.

34. Refer to the 6th paragraph where the relation between "Molluscs" and "Tentacles" has been explicitly mentioned. The relation between "Sharks" and "Snouts" has been mentioned in the seventh paragraph. .The relation between "Infusoria" and " Colourless" can be established from the last four paragraphs of the passage. The relation between "coral" and "coco" is mentioned in the fourth paragraph. Hence, Option (a) as the correct option.

35. Only option (d) can be inferred from the passage; it is mentioned in the second paragraph. The rest of the options are not true according to the passage.

36. Option (d) can be inferred from the line "in the computer industry….with ever greater bandwidth" given in the 5th paragraph. Options (a), (b) and (c) are not correct as per the passage.

37. All other options are mentioned in the passage except option (d). There is no reference for reduction in profit margins.

38. Refer to the starting 2 lines in the 5th paragraph "The direct model……keep going." Conventional manufacturing has a direct linkage with "stockpile". Only option (c) matches the above-mentioned relationship.

39. Option (d) is false because the passage mentions that "Companies with long…meet their financial targets" whereas the option contradicts this information making it the only false statement. The rest of the options are mentioned in the passage.

40. The passage talks about the transportation of silver from the mine to the coast on mule backs in the 2nd paragraph.

41. Option (d) is clearly mentioned in the ninth paragraph where the author describes the "barracks". Rest of the options are not mentioned in the passage.

42. The first and the second sentences of the seventh paragraph state the reasons for the Captain of the ship and the Lieutenant of the marines falling ill. The rest of the options are factually incorrect.

43. According to the passage the name of the sergent was Drooce and not Gill. This makes option (d) the false statement.

44. Statements I, II and IV have been mentioned in the first two paragraphs of the passage. III is not a part of the passage.

    ***Option (c) in the given question is incorrect because of the repetition of statement II.**

45. Except for option (b) the rest of the options have an impact on effective corporate governance according to the passage.

46. Only statements I and III would improve the quality and reliability of the information reported in the financial statement. II is distorted as it mentions that internal auditors should oversee the functioning of the external auditors whereas the passage mentions that an independent body should monitor the functioning of auditors. Statement IV is contradictory to the facts mentioned in the passage. The passage clearly states that "accounting-standards setting body should include members drawn from the industry, the profession and regulatory bodies. This body should be independently funded".

47. The passage mentions that an increase in the variable component in tandem with the achievement of the long-term objectives of the firm would enhance accountability of the directors. This makes option (c) correct.

48. Except for option (d) all the other options are mentioned in the passage.

49. Options (a), (c) and (d) describe the features of cyclical movement. Refer to the lines, "By a cyclical movement…ultimately reversed". Option (b) is contrary to what is mentioned in the passage.

50. Refer to the first five lines of the third paragraph. Marginal efficiency of capital depends upon all the factors except for option (d).

51. Statements I, II and III are mentioned as an explanation of the phenomenon of crisis in the third paragraph. Option IV is contrary to what is mentioned in the passage.

52. Statement III is mentioned in the first paragraph. Refer to the line, "The broad…tools and animals". Statement IV is mentioned in the eight paragraph. Refer to the lines, "in fact…global emissions". The second part of statement I is distorted. According to the passage methane is more dangerous than carbon di-oxide. This negates statements I and II.

53. Option (d) is contrary to what is mentioned in the passage. The third last paragraph clearly mentions, " global average temperatures, notes the Pew study," have experienced natural shifts throughout human history…that natural variability cannot account for what is happening now.""

54. The passage clearly mentions II, III and IV as reasons for warming of the earth. I has not been mentioned as a reason for the same. Hence, option (d) is the correct answer.

55. Refer to the fourth paragraph, I and IV are clearly mentioned as the characteristics of " fuels from heaven".

56. D is not mentioned in the last paragraph, which gives the essential criteria for setting up sugar refining plants.

57. In the ninth paragraph, the author describes the sequence of sugar preparation process as given in option (a). Hence, option (a) is the correct answer.

58. Option (d) is not mentioned anywhere in the passage. Options (a), (b) and (c) are mentioned in the first, ninth and tenth paragraphs of the passage respectively.

59. Option (a) is incorrect as Moore predicted that the cost of a unit of computing power would fall by 50%, not 25%, every 18 to 24 months. Option B is incorrect as "high demand for computers" is not mentioned. Popularity of removable media and internet lead to easy and cost effective ways to print and transfer photographs. Option (c) is also incorrect. Hence, option (d) is the correct answer.

60. Statement I and IV are correct. Refer to the line "Kodak had decided it was really a chemicals business…" given in the first paragraph.

    Statement II & III are incorrect. Refer to lines "Well, chemically treated … original purchase price." given in the first paragraph. It clearly states that customers and delivery channels are different for the two businesses. Hence, correct answer is option (b).

61. The second part of statement I is incorrect as the passage is silent on number of years that Carp had spent in the company. Statement II is correct according to the passage but is not a reason for Kodak loosing its market share. Hence, correct option is (d).

62. Statement II – 1988 (1st paragraph)

    Statement III – 2005 (3rd paragraph)

    Statement I – 2002 (3rd paragraph)

    Statement IV – 1993 (2nd paragraph)

    Correct option is (c).

63. Intel–Price of technology products reduces to half every year or two (1st paragraph). Fisher–Preview cameras that helped users to immediately see the pictures taken (1st paragraph). AOL–Photo processing, developing and posting online photos (2nd paragraph). Correct option is (a).

64. Statement IV hasn't been discussed anywhere in the passage. All the other statements reflect ideas author uses in order to explain how, why and which errors are committed by investors.

65. Statement IV hasn't been discussed anywhere in the passage. Passage clearly states that investors follow popular trends and don't consider probabilities while deciding how to invest.

66. Author implies that the investors must not be swayed by the advice of so called experts as their judgements have only slim chance of being able to predict market trends. Hence, option (b) is the correct answer.

67. Statement II is incorrect as the passage clearly states that public opinion polls have large not diminutive samples. Statement III is correct as per the passage.

68. Option (a) can be negated because of the 'only if' condition present in the option. Option (c) is incorrect only option (b) is close but can be negated because "<u>Single experiences</u> influence post experience loyalty but certainly <u>do not over whelm</u> the relationship between pre-experience and post experience loyalty".

   Hence option (d) is the correct option.

69. 'Institutional prediction' has not been mentioned in the passage. So, option (d) is negated. Only the instrumental prediction deals with the tangible outcomes. Hence, option (a) is the correct option.

70. Option (a) deals only with legal authorities and can be negated. Option (d) is out of the scope of the passage. Option (c) does not provide an adequate summary. Option (b) is the best possible summary amongst the given options.

71. "Dernier cri" means newest fashion. Passage States that Buffett outperformed the stock market in all kinds of economic periods. Saddle shoes represent fashion and Vietnam refers to war and politics. Hence, option (a) is the correct answer.

72. Refer to lines "Unlike the modern … such as J.P. Morgan Sr." given in 1st paragraph. It clearly states that Buffet resembled magnates of a previous age. Such as J.P. Morgan. Hence, sequence III is the correct sequence. Option II is incorrect as Buffet was in Omaha in 1956. He went to California later. Hence, option (b) is the correct answer.

73. Refer to 2nd paragraph, It states that Buffet is a private person and did not show emotions easily. It also states he lived a very simple life. Hence, option (d) is the correct answer.

74. The last sentence of the fifth paragraph clearly mentions that "Ocean-borne exports ……………the US tripled". This implies that option (b) is the correct answer.

75. The statement in option (a) is false. The passage talks about a two-stage process and not a three-stage process. Refer to the line "Trucks bound …..onto a ship." given in the fourth paragraph.

76. Statement C follows from "The extraordinary growth… East Asia." given in the fifth paragraph.

77. The correct option is (d). The ILA is related to dockers. FMB helped in the standardization of shipping containers. Grace Line used a container that was easier to truck around mountain roads. New Jersey has been mentioned as the home base of Pan-Atlantic (McLean's company).

78. The passage only states that savings accounts have low penetration amongst the lowest income households. The author makes it clear that he/she is not talking exclusively about BPL households.

79. Only option (b) is correct. Refer to the lines "The fact that a huge proportion… make access to credit easier to the former".

80. Only option (d) is correct. Option (a) is wrong because the passage does not suggest that casual labour segment may not require risk mitigation. Option B gives an incorrect benchmark for the official poverty line. Option (c) is incorrect because the author clearly states that broadening social safety nets requires fundamental policy decisions which go beyond the realm of the financial sector.

81. Statement B is incorrect based on the line "In fact, in a high growth scenario, a high proportion … sophisticated ones." given in the last paragraph. Hence, option (b) is the correct answer.

82. The passage gives the example of Jethmalani's junior Satish Maneshinde who has done well for himself as a lawyer. Hence, option (d) is the correct answer.

83. Last paragraph clearly mentions "Harish is the…multi-tasker". Hence, option (b) is the correct answer.

84. Refer to the fifth paragraph-"Some are even paid to not appear at all for the other side…"

85. 'Pro Bono' means being, involving, or doing professional and especially legal work donated especially for the public good. A clue here is the mention of "philanthropy" in the last line of the second paragraph.

86. Statement D follows from the second paragraph of the passage. "A natural sequel … of a facilitator."

87. Option (d) is the most appropriate answer. According to the passage "they should look out more actively…attractive acquisitions". However, this does not necessarily imply that some regions hold out a promise of attractive acquisition for banks. But rest of the options are incorrect. Thus, option (d) is better than the other options.

88. Statement C does not follow from the passage. The passage only states (in the fifth paragraph) that none of the Indian banks will jump into the top ten of the global league even after reasonable consolidation.

89. The third paragraph states that "Profit is not the explanation, cause, or rationale of business behavior and business decisions, but rather the test of their validity." This leads us to the opinion that profits and profitability are the test of validity of business existence.

90. The sixth paragraph states that the concept of profit maximisation and profit motive is largely responsible for the worst mistakes of public policy. Hence, option (a) is the correct answer.

91. The correct answer is option (c) which can be inferred from the last line of the seventh paragraph, "There is only one definition of business purpose: to create a customer."

92. The last paragraph states that a potential want may have dominated a customer's life for a long time before being converted into a demand by the actions of business people. It is only after want and demand that there is a customer and a market. Thus we can clearly deduce that 'want' comes before the remaining options.

93. The adjective 'vapid' means *tasteless* or *dull*. 'lacklusture' which means *dull* or *lacking in liveliness* is the correct synonym.

94. The least talked about character in the passage is the 'Grandmother'. The author mentions her only once when he compares a cloud's shape to his grandmother's four-legged silver sugar bowl.

95. All statements except for (c) can be inferred from the passage. The third paragraph states that the author's father was barely present at home and his mother was the only form of authority that he recognized. However, she could barely be called authoritative or tyrannical. Thus, we cannot conclude that the author came from a very authoritative home environment.

96. The last paragraph states that on the top floor, next to the infirmary, there was supposedly a dentist. Whenever the teachers got angry, they would threaten to send the naughty students to this dentist. So option (d) is the correct answer.

97. The first paragraph states that people thought that the time for the genteel game of knowledge, Kaun Banega Crorepati had passed. It lacked the backbiting intrigue and low-life loquaciousness of other reality shows. Thus we can say that both statements (i) and (ii) are correct.

98. The correct answer is option (d). It can be inferred from the second paragraph where the author states that KBC is an idea that connects with something deep and real in our lives.

99. The third paragraph states that the prize money of KBC is not a jackpot or means of indulgence, but a reward or gift from the divine for the winner's persistent efforts. Hence, option (c) is the correct answer.

100. The last paragraph states that eventually the winners of KBC realize that relative scales make everyone a relative pauper because no one can never have enough money. So option (a) is the correct answer.

101. The opening paragraph mentions that the monsoon season was prevailing and warm rains and monsoon air made the weather so hot and humid that even a fan above Babur's head gave him no respite. There was no pleasure in visiting the garden because he was depressed to see the sodden flowers and the soggy ground. Hence, we can say that the warm rains and monsoons made him feel depressed.

102. The first paragraph states that given the monsoon weather, sodden flowers and soggy ground, Babur would find little pleasure in visiting his garden. Hence, he did not consider visiting it. On the other hand, second and third passages state that he considered the other options. Therefore, option (b) is the correct answer.

103. The last paragraph states that during the war of Panipat, Babur had feared that Humayun would fall beneath the feet of the war elephants. At Khanua he feared that Humayun would be killed by a slash of the Rajut sword. However, currently he feared that Humayun might succumb to his illness/ sickness and leave Babur forever. So option (d) is the correct answer.

104. The words 'neatly turbaned head' have been used to describe the Hakim that came to treat Humayun.

105. The author nowhere mentions the reason why Ruth Madoff and her sons did not flee. Bernie Madoff's pleading guilty has no bearing on the fact that his family did not flee. In fact, the passage says that 'the public outcry against Ruth Madoff and her sons began almost from the instant of Madoff's arrest and did not cease. By the time he pleaded guilty, it was deafening' which means that the public still considered the family guilty even after Bernie had made a formal admission. Hence, option (a) is incorrect. The author also mentions in the passage that the Madoff family had the means to flee. Further, in the penultimate paragraph the author himself disproves the theory that Bernie Madoff turned him in to save his family. This makes options (b) and (c) incorrect as well. Therefore, the correct answer is option (d).

106. The last line of the first paragraph states that all the media frenzy surrounding the Madoff family drove them into exile. In other words, this means that the family stayed away from the public eye. Therefore, option (c) is the correct answer.

107. While the author mentions that traditionally media did not target the families of mafia and dons, the Madoff case highlighted a marked departure from that tradition when the media pointed fingers at the Madoff family. Thus, the treatment of the organized-crime defendants has changed over the years.

108. The first line of the sixth paragraph states that "the facts in the Madoff case did not seem to be consistent with the family's guilt", meaning that the facts did not point to the family of Bernie Madoff as guilty. This makes option (a) the correct answer. However, in the same paragraph, the sentence "Surely, Madoff, before turning himself in, would have handed his sons the keys to the company jet..." and the second sentence in the penultimate paragraph implies that Bernie Madoff was arrested following his confession. This makes option (b) correct too. But then, option (a) is more likely to be deemed correct by IIFT.

109. The 'Grey Poupon' has been termed as 'magic' because the number of people who converted to it from normal mustard, after tasting this mustard, was unheard of. Therefore, option (c) is the correct answer.

110. The author talks of 'Grey Poupon' as small business in the early seventies. Later, he mentions that 'Grey Poupon' had become the most powerful brand in mustard by the end of the 1980's. This constitutes a time of roughly 15-20 years and hence, option (c) is the correct answer.

111. The author mentions the advertisement that Grey Poupon used in order to increase its sales – an ad which included a chauffeur driven Rolls-Royce. Also, the last line of the third paragraph states that with the image of the Rolls-Royce in the advertisement, Grey Poupon seemed to project something that was 'truly different and superior'. Hence, it can be understood that the brand was trying to reach out to the rich and sophisticated people. Therefore, option (d) is the correct answer.

112. In the last paragraph of the passage, the author mentions that the ratio of tomato solids to liquid in World's Best Ketchup was much higher than that of Heinz, which means that Worlds' Best Ketchup was thicker than Heinz. Hence, option (c) is the correct answer.

113. In the second paragraph, the author mentions that greed entails himsa, but does not mention ahimsa to be entailed by greed. Hence, option (a) is incorrect. Option (c) is again incorrect because the author only says that to be pro-market means to believe in competitive markets but he does not talk of it as a means of becoming richer. The author mentions in the passage that self-interest, only when in excess can breed selfishness, while rational self-interest is healthy. Thus, option (b) is the correct answer.

114. A 'conundrum' is a confusing situation, and can be used interchangeably with the word 'enigma'. By the given sentence, the author means to say that the enigma of the human existence is that vices and virtues can result from the same inner forces. Hence, option (a) is the correct answer.

115. The last line of the penultimate paragraph of the passage states that once there is enough wealth in India, the country "might again return to its old character of renunciation". Therefore, option (b) is the correct answer.

116. The author clearly mentions in the sixth paragraph that "being pro-market leads to 'rules-based capitalism'; 'pro-business' often leads to 'crony capitalism'". Hence, option (b) goes against the views expressed in the passage and is thus, the correct answer. Options (a), (c) and (d) have all been mentioned in the passage. Thus, option (b) is the correct answer.

117. The author mentions in the penultimate paragraph that inspite of being the world's leading exporter of a number of products, Brazil is still one of the most closed economies in the world. In the last paragraph, he states that due to heavy taxes, skill formation in Brazil is suffering. In the last line of the fourth paragraph, the author talks of little spending on infrastructure by Brazil, resulting "in un-China like growth". Thus, options (a), (b) and (c) are correct. Hence, option (d) is the correct answer.

118. Refer to the sixth paragraph of the passage. There, the author clearly says Brazil's quest for "stability at any cost" stems from its history of financial crisis and the hyperinflation that had started in the 1980s and peaked in the 1990s. Hence, option (a) is the correct answer. Option (c) is incorrect as the urge for enhancing economic growth further has been mentioned in the context of China and not Brazil.

119. In the seventh paragraph of the passage, the author mentions that Brazil has constantly been battling inflation ever since hyperinflation came under control in 1995. Therefore, option (d) is a false statement. All other options find mention in the passage. Hence, option (d) is the correct answer.

120. The author mentions sugar, orange juice, coffee, poultry and beef as Brazil's exports in the penultimate paragraph of the passage. Iron ore and soybeans are also mentioned by the author as Brazil's exports in the first paragraph. Only croissants and bikes have not been mentioned as Brazilian exports in the passage, making option (c) the correct answer.

121. Option (a): Refer to the following lines from the fifth paragraph, "... Wigan did not dramatically outperform their wage bill...From 2006 to 2011, they finished eighteenth, fifteenth, fifteenth, sixteenth and sixteenth in the salary league ..." So, accordingly, in terms of salary payments of the staff, Wigan ranked sixteenth and not fifteenth in the year 2009-10, rendering option (a) incorrect.

    Option B: Refer to the following line from the seventh paragraph, "With the wage bills four, two and one and a half times Wigan's £ 40 million, Manchester United, Aston Villa and Fulham faced odds of demotion of 0, 31 and 69 per cent, respectively." From this we can infer option (b).

    Option (c): The second paragraph of the passage states that according to Simon Kuper and the economist Stefan Szymanski it "might not be the case that the team with the highest wage bill finishes top each and every season, but over the long term, the correlation is uncanny". Since the results in the long term are uncanny, we cannot infer option (c).

    Option (d): The passage uses the performance chalkboards published by The Guardian in conjunction with Opta Sports and not ESPN sports. This renders option (d) incorrect.

122. According to the following statement from the penultimate paragraph, "when Larcada calculated the average distances from which Premier league clubs attempted shots that season, Wigan were the overall league leaders. Their average shooting distance was some twenty-six yards...their goals came from a longer distance from any of their peers – an average of 18.5 yards..." This makes option (c) correct.

123. As per the passage, Hugo Rodallega is a player of the Wigan Atheletic, Ramzi Ben Said is a student at Cornell University, Roberto Martinez is the manager of Wigan Athletic and Albert Larcada is an analyst at ESPN. Hence, option (d) is correct.

124. The author in the last paragraph describes the characteristics of the unique game played by Wigan Athletic - highly accurate long range shots, recovering to their defensive shape easily and reliance on counter attack instead of attacking. This he touts is the Guerilla football style, rendering option (c) correct. Options (a) and (b) are factually incorrect.

125. Option (a) is incorrect. The sixth paragraph of the passage gives the data of the club finances collected by Deloitte in the last "twenty years" and not "the last decade alone".

    Option (b) can be inferred from the following statement of the fourth paragraph, "It's the same when we look at television and commercial earnings: in 2010-11, they earned £ 50.5 million ... but half what the average Premier League team took.

    Option (c) can be inferred from the following lines of the fourth paragraph, "Part of the reason Wigan managed to survive so long in the rarefied air of the Premier League is Dave Whelan, the local magnate who owns the club. Wigan's average attendance was just 17000 – they rarely sold out their home ground, the DW stadium, its initials a (self-awarded) tribute to the club's benefactor..."

    Option (d): The fourth-last paragraph while comparing the scores of Wigan Athletic (made by free kicks) with that scored by the other teams of the Premier League in the year 2010-11, states that Wigan "scored as many goals on the break as the average side, and they scored almost four times as many goals from free kicks". From this, we can infer option (d).

126. Option (c) is incorrect because the following line from the fourth paragraph states that the Judge's command of "Hindi and Urdu was tenuous (weak)". Hence, option (c) is the answer. All other statements are correct.

127. The third last paragraph of the passage states that one thing that always happened on the Judge's return from the countryside was that "he returned with – *Nothing!*". This renders option (b) as the answer. All other options are factually incorrect.

128. Refer to the following line from the third paragraph, "Farms were growing less than ten mounds an acre of rice and wheat, and at two rupees a mound, every single man in the village sometimes was in debt to the bania. This makes option (a) as the correct answer. All other options are factually incorrect.

129. All the words 'brood', 'flock' and 'flight' are collective nouns that describe a group of birds. Only lariat, which means 'like a rope', is the odd word and also the correct option.

130. Option (a): The author in the third paragraph states that in 1948, after Garibaldi arrived in Italy, "Charles Albert had pardoned Garibaldi, but to outward appearances he was still very wary of the general". This reference renders option (a) incorrect.

Option (b): is incorrect because the penultimate paragraph states that Garibaldi's wife died after they were attacked by the "Austrian flotilla" and not "Spanish flotilla".

Option (c): can be eliminated because the passage makes no reference to the defeat of the republican army. Also, Rome at one point was attacked by 60,000 foreign soldiers and not 80,000.

Option (d): From the third-last and the fourth-last paragraphs, we can infer option (d), which makes it the answer.

131. Option (a): This option is factually incorrect. According to the fifth paragraph, King of Naples, Ferdinand II was dubbed 'King Bomba' after bombing "Messina" and not "Milan".

Option (b): The seventh paragraph of the passage states that Garibaldi defended "Janiculum Hill, which was crucial to the defense of Rome", but does not state that Garibaldi positioned his army near that Hill to protect it. It is possible that he stationed the army very far off from the hill on the enemy's route towards the Hill. Additionally, it cannot be inferred that he was protecting Rome from the attack of Austrian troops. So, this option cannot be inferred.

Option (c): The last paragraph states that Garibaldi, after the various wars he fought, came back to Nice to 'reunite' with his family. So, this option appears to be the best of all the other options and hence is the answer.

Option (d): Mazzini was a leader of the republicans.

132. According to the passage Charles Albert is the King of Piedmont, Ferdinand II is the King of Naples, Louis Philippe was the King of France and Grand Duke belongs to Tuscany. This makes option (a) correct.

133. The second-last and the third-last paragraphs state that after they failed to reach Venice, "Garibaldi had no time to lose; he and his faithful companion Leggero escaped across the Po towards Ravenna." Therefore, the correct answer is option (b).

134. Option (a) is incorrect because it is stated in the end of the fifth paragraph that the Pope had taken refuge with King Bomba and not the King of Piedmont. Therefore, option (a) is the answer.

Option (b) can be inferred from the third paragraph of the passage.

Option (c): Refer to the ninth paragraph of the passage, "Garibaldi wanted to carry the fight down into the Kingdom of Naples, but Mazzini, who by now was effectively in charge of Rome, ordered him back to the capital..." From this, we can infer option (c).

Option (d): The fifth paragraph states that that "Rome declared itself a republic". After that, "Prince Louis Napoleon of France dispatched an army of 7000 men under General Charles Oudinot to the port of Civitavecchia to seize the city." From this, we can infer option (d).

135. Option (a): Refer to the following line from the third paragraph, "However, in the first quarter last year, banks had healthier loan growth on a sequential basis then this year." Therefore, option (a) is correct and also the answer.

Option (b): Refer to the following line from the eighth paragraph, "Lower the credit rating of the company, riskier the loan is perceived to be." According to this, the risk level of loans is inversely proportional to the credit ratings of a company. So, option (b) is incorrect.

Option (c): This is factually incorrect. The third paragraph states that "Bank of Baroda and Punjab National Bank shrank their loan book by 1.97% and 0.66% respectively in the first quarter on a sequential basis."

Option (d): The passage makes no reference to it, rendering this option incorrect.

136. Option (a): Refer to the following line from the third paragraph, "However, in the first quarter last year, banks had healthier loan growth on a sequential basis then this year." From this, we can infer option (a).

Option (b): can be inferred from the following line in the ninth paragraph, "As per the norms (Basel III norms), a bank's total capital adequacy ratio should be 12% at any time..."

Option (c): The last line of the fifth paragraph states that SBI did not get many fresh proposals that year. So, it is the correct answer.

Option (d): can be inferred from the sixth paragraph which states that "part of the credit contraction is due to the economic slowdown".

137. The passage states that Banks are now looking for safe bets by preferring highly rated customers to lower rated companies. This ensures that the risk taken by the bank is low ("Lower the credit rating of the company, riskier the loan is perceived to be."). Also, it decreases profitability or the difference between yields on advances and cost of deposits narrows ("...the difference between yields on advances and cost of deposits, a key gauge of profitability, fell...as the bank focused on lending to highly rated customers."). Moreover, capital adequacy increases which can then be easily met by the banks ("If loans have been given to lower rated companies, risk weight goes up and capital adequacy falls.") This renders option (d) as the correct answer.

138. China produced over 200 million of steel and consumed over 244 million. Although, over 200 can also mean over 244 million (and hence there can be no correct answer), this indicates that A is the most probable answer.

139. Option (b) is incorrect as the author states that consolidation of the fragmented steel industry is the name of the game. This can mean that this consolidation was the most important part of the activity they were undertaking to achieve their objective. But the real question here is why did these two companies wanted to become big by consoliating the fragmented industry. This was because becoming big will give them greater pricing power.

140. Refer to 5th Paragraph. The passage states - "it's nearest rival".

141. Refer to paragragh 1 , last line. The passage states that - "Over capacity and low stell prices continued to play havoc".

142. The answer is given in last line of the second paragrapgh. It states that - "......scarcely seems like hyperbole—and has even become cliche—*to suggest that the advent of the Internet ranks as an event of epochal* significance.....".

143. The passage states that we cannot credit Otlet with inventing the internet. Otlet envisioned a knowledge network long before the technology was available to make it a reality. Hence Otlet prophesised the internet.

144. Towards the end of the passage the author states that each of these people mentioned shared a commitment to social transformation through the use of available technology.

145. Otlet was a visionary and his view of the knowledge network was futuristic. The author also states at the end of the fourth paragraph that Otlet saw the developments as fundamentally connected to a large utopian projectthat would bring the world closer.

146. The author talks about why lenders lend more and borrowers borrow more and what adverse affect this over lending (or borrowing) has on economy and the financial condition. Although it is mentioned that lenders may want for people/contries to borrow more

and lure them accordingly, this does not indicate bargaining power assymetry. The passage also talks about how developing world/countries fall into a debt cycle, but the main idea of the passage does not revolve around this.

147. The passage states that - "The *moral hazard arises when a party does not bear all the risks associated with his action* and as a result does not do everything he can do to avaoid risk". Hence, the insured takes less care to avaoid fire if he is covered.

148. In the fourth paragraph, the author states that the 'bail-out' package is not really a bail-out option for the borrower but for the western banks.

149. The last lines of the fourth paragraph states that- "In effect, the poor country's taxpayers paid for rich country's lending mistakes"

150. The passage is focused to discuss how media affects political communication and if media affects public opinion (on political issues and situations).

151. Paragraph one states that - ".... so called 'primary' agents of political socialization, such as the family and social class, has declined"

152. Statement A is correct as paragraph one states that - ".... so called 'primary' agents of political socialization, such as the family and social class, has declined". Hence, The impact of primary agents of socialization has reduced. Statement B is correct as paragraph two states that the proliferation of channels and media output has massively increased. Statement C is correct as paragraph three states that media (infotainment industry) has become more powerful economic actor.

153. Pluralist view potrays media in positive termsand suggest that its effect on society is neutral in that they reflect the balances of forces within the society.

154. The passage is about how India has not developed its manufacturing sector. This makes Option (b) the correct choice. Option (a) and (c) are not mentioned in the passage. Option (d) is a criticism of the Indian approach to development (excessive focus on tech services).

155. Options (a) and (b) extend beyond the scope of the passage. Option (d) is incorrect as it says 'do not require good infrastructure'. Option (c) has been directly mentioned in the passage.

156. Option (a) and (d) are incorrect because of the usage of the phrase 'only' and 'better'. Option (b) is correct as the Services sector can create jobs for limited people only. Option (c) is incorrect as it is a general vague statement.

157. Option (b) has been clearly stated in the passage. Option (a) is incorrect as it mentions mining and shipping which hasn't been mentioned in the passage.

158. Option (b) is too narrow as it does not address the mismatch and it wrongly says 'useful for local markets'. Option (c) is extends beyond the scope of the passage. Option (a) is correct as can be seen from the fourth sentence of the passage.

159. Option (c) is correct as it is clearly mentioned in the passage—"traditionally food and beverage companies have focused only on the first".

160. Option (d) is mentioned in the first sentence of the passage.

161. Option (c) has been mentioned in the passage and has been illustrated using the example of Kurkure.

162. Option (b) is correct because it is mentioned in the passage as a central reason behind participation of women in the workforce. Options (a), (c) and (d) extend beyond the scope of the passage.

163. Option (d) is the correct choice. Option (a) (b) are too narrow in their focus and Option (c) makes it an emerging countries vs developing countries debate which not what the passage is essentially about.

164. Option (c) has been clearly mentioned in the passage.

165. Option (c) has been clearly mentioned in the passage.

166. Option (b) is the correct choice. Option (a) is close but is invalidated based upon the fact that the passage expands further the idea of SLAM.

167. Option (c) is the correct answer as it is mentioned in the passage that having one eye is not a disadvantage to a robot.

168. Only statements i and iv are mentioned in the passage.

169. Option (a) is incorrect as it is nowhere mentioned in the passage. Option (c) and (d) are incorrect as they extend beyond the scope of the passage. Option (b) is mentioned in the passage in the sentence 'enough measurements....'.

170. The paragraph explains via the example of MVP that entrepreneurs should not strive for a perfect product. They must learn from their mistakes and try to improve their products. Options (a), (c), and (d) go against this theme. Option (c) is also factually contradicted by the passage. So, (b) is the correct choice.

171. Refer to the first three sentences of the second paragraph. It clearly shows option (d) to be the answer. The other options are factually contradicted by these lines.

172. The line in question comes in the 15th line of the second paragraph. It basically talks about the author's apprehension regarding the risk factor involved in an unfinished product. Option (c) is the clear answer.

173. Refer to the last sentence of the passage. Option (c) and (d) go beyond the spirit of MVP as it doesn't focus on polished or finished products. Option (a) is incomplete. MVP not only caters to the customers but it also provides a valuable learning curve to the companies. So, option (b) is the correct choice.

174. "Rhetoric" means usage of words to convince or persuade the listeners or readers. So, option (c) is the obvious answer.

175. Refer to the lines in the second paragraph, "What we're basically talking about here is inductive reasoning: moving from the observation...the observations." The clear answer is option (a) as only this option talks about the essence of this reasoning.

176. The answer to this question can be located in paragraph 3. It doesn't talk about improving speed reading, enabling students to be brief, or reproducing the text in exact terms. So, option (b) is the correct answer as the paragraph talks about "clarity and accuracy of understanding."

177. The author of the passage focuses on improving the understanding and close reading of the texts. He doesn't talk about translation or the ability to translate. Option (a) is, thus, eliminated. Similarly option (c) is eliminated as it is distorted. They are not being taught to literally paraphrase. Similarly, option (d) is distorted because "preparing students for class discussions" is not the focus of the educators. So, option (b) is the right answer keeping in mind the essence of the passage.

178. As per the theme of the passage, the crisis has to have happened before 2008. Logically, option (a) can't be the answer but that looks like a really good choice keeping in mind the other options. Logically the best option is (b) as options (c) and (d) don't deal with liquidity crisis. So, both options (a) and (b) can be the answer.

179. This question was vague. The passage talks about theoretically what the banks should do. It remains quiet on how they "typically" deal with crisis. Option (c) is surely not the answer as it is the typical reaction during normal times. Option (d) is irrelevant. The problem is between options (a) and (b). Both appear to be correct. However, option (a) looks like a better option because of the word "quick to respond". Though, option (b) might turn out to be the official answer.

180. This sentence appears in the penultimate paragraph. Refer to the two lines before and after. Option B is eliminated because of the word "only" and it talks about World Bank. This is irrelevant. Option (a) is twisted because "not having sufficient knowledge" is not mentioned in the passage as a reason for the quotation under question. Option (d) incorrectly attributes the reason to requirement of "permission". Option (c) is the correct answer as it is the reason the author gives in the passage.

181. Refer to the last three lines of the passage. It clearly refers to option (d) as the answer as it is the clearest of the given options.

182. The phrase can be located in paragraph 4 when the author talks about Procter and Gamble. The first thing to note is that all these analysts are from different functional areas. These analysts also provide a huge pool of expertise. The group is not homogeneous. So, option (a) is eliminated. Option (d) uses the term "crack analysts" in a vague way and it distorts the tone of the passage. Option (b) mistakenly states that this group derives expertise from other areas. This group has analysts who themselves come from diverse areas. So, option (c) is the correct answer.

183. Refer to the lines that flank the given line. Fecund means fertile. So, it is not an unsuitable environment. Hence, option (a) is eliminated. Fructiferous is a misleading term. Option (d) says "high probability" but the passage focuses on possibility or certainty. So, option (c) is the correct answer.

184. Refer to the last sentence of the passage. It clearly refers to option (c) as the answer.

185. This question is related to the central theme of the passage. Option (b) wrongly talks about the educational background of the leaders as the distinguishing factor. It is not supported by the passage. MIT is given as an example only. Option (c) is too narrow. Option (d) is irrelevant. Option (a) is the closest to the main theme of the passage. Hence, it is the correct answer.

186. In this passage, the author talks about the concept of culture. Refer to the second line of the first paragraph. It clearly states the main aim of the author. Out of the four choices, options (a) and (c) are clearly too narrow. So, these two can be eliminated. Option (b) comes close but 'sub-elements' is a vague term. Option (d) is clearer and, hence, it is the correct answer.

187. The author has defined society in the first paragraph. Refer to the line, "Society, it has been said, is what emerges from a network of interactions between people that follow certain agreed upon and perceptible patterns." So, option (b) is the clear answer. Options (a) and (d) are too narrow and irrelevant. Option (c) has an overtly negative connotation. The concept of 'control' has not been highlighted by the author.

188. This is a tricky question. Option (b) and (c) are both correct. However, to answer this question, we need to focus on the last paragraph as a whole. In the last paragraph, the author defines the different elements of culture. Option (b) is subtly highlighted as the most important element of culture. However, the question asks us to identify all the important elements. So, option (c) is a better choice. All the elements mentioned in option (c) are there in the final paragraph.

189. This is a fact based question. The answer can be found in the second half of the first paragraph. Refer to the line, "Today, as always, the public intellectual is expected to take a position independent of those in power." Refer to the next few lines too. The question asks us to define a public intellectual in the generic sense. The other options focus on a public intellectual in today's age. So, option (b) is the correct answer.

190. This is actually an inference based question. We need to pay close attention to the last two paragraphs. The author portrays the public intellectuals of today in a mildly negative light. The clue is the phrase 'politically correct'. This is mentioned in the line, 'Yet academics today are hesitant...' in the second paragraph. Options (a), (b), and (c) are factually incorrect. So, option (d) is the correct answer.

191. This is a tough question. The author merely hints at the definitions of orthodoxy, orthopraxy, and heterodoxy in two lines of the final paragraph. Read the given lines carefully. One this is clear. The public intellectual has to follow heterodoxy as it constitutes the basic definition of 'liberal ideas'. So, options (a) and (d) are eliminated. 'Orthodox' and 'heterodox' are contradictory terms. One can't be both. So, option (c) is eliminated. Option (b) is the correct answer.

192. The answer can be located in the first paragraph. The main idea of the first paragraph is that 'information is useful'. The author clearly states that he is not 'suggesting that there is no value to information...' So, we can eliminate option (d). Option (b) is distorted. Option (A) goes beyond the scope of the paragraph. So, option (c) is the correct answer.

193. Refer to the line, "Recognizing the insidious nature of information age strategies and their tendency to lead to either analysis paralysis..." in the second

paragraph. This part defines the reason why leaders today face the threat of analysis paralysis. The lack of agility to take a decision has been highlighted by the author. So, option (b) is the correct answer.

194. Refer to the lines, "When we make the shift from information…The agility shift requires that we value…" in the last paragraph. Option (a) is wrong because of the word 'uncertainty' which is incorrect. Option (b) is too narrow and distorted. Option (d) is factually the opposite of what the author mentions. So, option (c) is the correct answer.

195. This is an easy question. Refer to the first paragraph. Option (c) best describes the main idea of the first paragraph. So, it is the clearest option and the best choice.

196. The author, in the passage, focuses on STEM skills and how liberal arts can help people acquire skills suitable to the current technologically advanced scenario. Option (b) is vague and doesn't focus on the skills. Option (c) is too narrow. Option (d) is too extreme because of the phrase 'all the social problems'. So, option (a) is the correct answer.

197. The answer can be located in the second paragraph. The author advises companies to focus on technological enhancement as well as human values. Option (a) only talks about the 'scientific' side. So, it is incomplete. Option (b) focuses only on what humans want. So, this is wrong. Option (d) talks about 'similar to human beings', which is distorted. So, option (c) is the correct answer.

198. This question can be answered if we understand the main idea of the passage. Option (a) is wrong as the author clearly mentions that liberal arts can help students become analytical. Option (b) is wrong because of the second part. The author mentions that students of liberal arts can help in the technical field. Option (c) unnecessarily compares the two types of students and says that students of STEM are better prepared to face the new age challenges. The passage states the opposite. So, option (d) is the correct answer.

199. Refer to the first four lines of the passage. The author talks about both the pros and cons of relying on GDP as a measure for economic performance of a country. Option (a) is partially correct. Option (b) is wrong as the author doesn't mention that it is 'definitive'. Option (d) is wrong because of the word 'only'. Option (c) is the correct answer.

200. Refer to the portions where the author talks about HDI and Social Progress Index. Then we need to eliminate the incorrect options. Option (a) mentions non-GDP measures in a negative light. The author, in fact, subtly supports these non-GDP measures. Option (b) is similarly negative and wrong. Option (d) is wrong as the author doesn't state this. So, option (c) is the correct answer.

201. Refer to the second half of the passage. Option (c) is the only correct answer. The other options are irrelevant or wrong.

Quantitative Aptitude

Number System

Property

2008-10

1. If $u_1 = \sqrt{3}$, $u_2 = \sqrt{3\sqrt{3}}$, $u_3 = \sqrt{3\sqrt{3\sqrt{3}}}$, etc., $u_{10} : u_9$ is:

(a) $\sqrt{3}$

(b) $3^{\frac{1}{10}}$

(c) $3^{\frac{1}{20}}$

(d) None of these

2. The value of the expression $7777 + 7777 \times 7777 \times (5 \div 77) \times (11 \div 35)$ is:

(a) 1234321

(b) 2344321

(c) 7^{7777}

(d) None of these

2009-11

3. $2 - \dfrac{\sqrt{6407522209}}{\sqrt{3600840049}} =$

(a) 0.666039

(b) 0.666029

(c) 0.666009

(d) None of the above

2011-13

4. The smallest perfect square that is divisible by 7!

(a) 44100

(b) 176400

(c) 705600

(d) 19600

2012-14

5. $\left(\sqrt{\dfrac{225}{729}} - \sqrt{\dfrac{25}{144}} \right) \div \sqrt{\dfrac{16}{81}} = ?$

(a) $\dfrac{5}{16}$

(b) $\dfrac{7}{12}$

(c) $\dfrac{3}{8}$

(d) None of these

6. There are four prime numbers written in ascending order of magnitude. The product of the first three is 7429 and last three is 12673. Find the first number.

(a) 19

(b) 17

(c) 13

(d) None of the above

2013-15

7. If k is an integer and 0.0010101×10^k is greater than 1000, what is the least possible value of k?

(a) 4

(b) 5

(c) 6

(d) 7

8. The value of $\sqrt{7 + \sqrt{7 - \sqrt{7 + \sqrt{7 - \cdots\infty}}}}$ is

(a) 1

(b) 2

(c) 3

(d) 4

2014-16

9. If the product of the integers a, b, c and d is 3094 and if $1 < a < b < c < d$, what is the product of b and c?

(a) 26

(b) 91

(c) 133

(d) 221

10. Mrs Sonia buys Rs. 249.00 worth of candies for the children of a school. For each girl she get a strawberry flavoured candy priced at Rs. 3.30 per candy; each boy receives a chocolate flavoured candy priced at Rs. 2.90 per candy.

How many candies of each type did she buy?

(a) 21, 57

(b) 57, 21

(c) 37, 51

(d) 27, 51

11. If the product of n positive integers is n^n, then their sum is

(a) a negative integer

(b) equal to n

(c) equal to $n + \dfrac{1}{n}$

(d) never less than n^2

2015-17

12. In a school, students were called for the Flag Hoisting ceremony on August 15. After the ceremony, small boxes of sweets were distributed among the students. In each class, the student with roll no. I got one box of sweets, student with roll number 2 got 2 boxes of sweets, student with roll no. 3 got 3 boxes of sweets and so on. In class III. a total of 1200 boxes of sweets were distributed, By mistake one of the students of class III got double the sweets he was entitled to get, Identify the roll number of the student who got twice as many boxes of sweets as compared to his entitlement.

(a) 22

(b) 24

(c) 28

(d) 30

2017-19

13. What is the sum of the integers 54 through 196 inclusive?

(a) 28,820

(b) 24,535

(c) 20,250

(d) 17,875

14. The highest number amongst $\sqrt{2}$, $\sqrt[3]{3}$ and $\sqrt[4]{4}$ is

(a) $\sqrt{2}$

(b) $\sqrt[3]{3}$

(c) $\sqrt[4]{4}$

(d) All are equal

HCF and LCM

2008-10

15. IBM-Daksh observes that it gets a call at an interval of every 10 minutes from Seattle, at every 12 minutes from Arizonia, at the interval of 20 minutes from New York and after every 25 minutes it gets the call from Newark. If in the early morning at 5:00 a.m. it has received the calls simultaneously from all the four destinations, then at which time it will receive the calls at a time from all places on the same day?

(a) 10:00 a.m.

(b) 3:00 a.m.

(c) 5:00 a.m.

(d) both A. and B.

2014-16

16. A rod is cut into 3 equal parts. The resulting are then cut into 12, 18 and 32 equal parts, respectively. If each of the resulting portions have integer length, the minimum length of the rod is

(a) 6912 units

(b) 864 units

(c) 288 units

(d) 240 units

Miscellaneous

2007-09

17. Which of the following is obtained after rationalization of the expression $\dfrac{1}{\left(\sqrt{5}+\sqrt{6}+\sqrt{11}\right)}$

(a) $\dfrac{5\sqrt{6}+6\sqrt{5}-\sqrt{330}}{60}$

(b) $\dfrac{6\sqrt{5}-5\sqrt{6}-\sqrt{330}}{30}$

(c) $\dfrac{5\sqrt{6}+6\sqrt{5}+\sqrt{330}}{60}$

(d) $\dfrac{6\sqrt{5}+5\sqrt{6}-\sqrt{330}}{60}$

2008-10

18. Mr. Bedi's family members went on a picnic. There were two grandfathers and four fathers and two grandmothers and four mothers in the group. There was at least one grandson or a granddaughter present in this group. There were two husband-wife pairs in this group. The single grandfather (Whose wife was not present) had two grandsons and a son present in the party. The single grandmother (Whose husband was not present) had two granddaughters present. A grandfather or a grandmother present with their spouses did not have any grandson or granddaughter present.

What was the minimum number of people present in this picnic group?

(a) 14

(b) 10

(x) 12

(d) 16

19. The value of $\displaystyle\sum_{r=1}^{n}\frac{{}^{n}P_{r}}{r!}$ is:

(a) 2^{n}

(b) $2^{n}-1$

(c) 2^{n-1}

(d) $2^{n}+1$

20. If the complex number z_1 and z_2 are such that $|z_1|=12$ and $|z_2-3-4i|=5$, then the minimum value of $|z_1-z_2|$ is:

(a) 0

(b) 2

(c) 7

(d) None of these

2010-12

21. Kartik's mother asked him to get the vegetables, milk and butter from the market and gave him the money in the denomination of 1 Rupee, 2 Rupee and 5 Rupee coins. Kartik first goes to the grocery shop to buy vegetables. At the grocery shop he gives half of his 5 Rupee coins and in return receives the same number of 1 Rupee coins. Next he goes to a dairy shop to buy milk and butter and gives all 2 Rupee coins and in return gets thirty 5 Rupee coins which increases the number of 5 Rupee coins to 75% more than the original number. If the number of 1 Rupee coins now is 50, the number of 1 Rupee and 5 Rupee coins originally were:

(a) 10, 60

(b) 10, 70

(c) 10, 80

(d) None of the above.

2011-13

22. A small confectioner bought a certain number of pastries flavoured pineapple, mango and black-forest from the bakery, giving for each pastry as many rupees as there were pastry of that kind; altogether he bought 23 pastries and spent Rs. 211; find the number of each kind of pastry that he bought, if mango pastry are cheaper than pineapple pastry and dearer than black-forest pastry.

(a) (10, 9, 4)

(b) (11, 9, 3)

(c) (10, 8, 5)

(d) (11, 8, 4)

23. In a Green view apartment, the houses of a row are numbered consecutively from 1 to 49. Assuming that there is a value of 'x' such that the sum of the numbers of the houses preceding the house numbered 'x' is equal to the sum of the numbers of the houses following it. Then what will be the value of 'x'?

(a) 21   (b) 30

(c) 35   (d) 42

2012-14

24. While preparing for a management entrance examination, Romit attempted to solve three papers namely Mathematics, Verbal English and Logical Analysis, each of which have the full marks of 100. It is observed that one-third of the marks obtained by Romit in Logical Analysis is greater than half of his marks obtained in Verbal English by 5. He has obtained a total of 210 marks in the examination and 70 marks in Mathematics. What is the difference between the marks obtained by him in Mathematics and Verbal English?

(a) 40   (b) 10

(c) 20   (d) 30

2013-15

25. The unit digit in the product of $(8267)^{153} \times (341)^{72}$ is

(a) 1   (b) 2

(c) 7   (d) 9

26. Z is the product of first 31 natural numbers. If $X = Z + 1$, then the numbers of primes among $X + 1$, $X + 2$, ..., $X + 29$, $X + 30$ is

(a) 30

(b) 2

(c) Cannot be determined

(d) None of the above

2015-17

27. The sum of $1 - \dfrac{1}{6} + \dfrac{1}{6} \times \dfrac{1}{4} - \dfrac{1}{6} \times \dfrac{1}{4} \times \dfrac{5}{18} + ...$ is :

(a) $\dfrac{2}{3}$ (b) $\dfrac{2}{\sqrt{3}}$

(c) $\sqrt{\dfrac{2}{3}}$ (d) $\dfrac{\sqrt{3}}{2}$

2018-20

28. If $10^{67} - 87$ is written as an integer in base 10 notation, what is the sum of digits in that integer?

(a) 683   (b) 489

(c) 583   (d) 589

ANSWERS

1. (d)	**2.** (d)	**3.** (a)	**4.** (b)	**5.** (a)	**6.** (b)	**7.** (c)	**8.** (c)	**9.** (b)	**10.** (b)
11. (d)	**12.** (b)	**13.** (d)	**14.** (b)	**15.** (a)	**16.** (b)	**17.** (a)	**18.** (c)	**19.** (b)	**20.** (b)
21. (d)	**22.** (b)	**23.** (c)	**24.** (c)	**25.** (c)	**26.** (d)	**27.** (d)	**28.** (d)		

EXPLANATIONS

1. Given, $u_1 = \sqrt{3} = 3^{\frac{1}{2}}$.

$$u_2 = \sqrt{3\sqrt{3}} = 3^{\frac{3}{4}} = 3^{\frac{2^2-1}{2^2}}$$

$$u_3 = \sqrt{3\sqrt{3\sqrt{3}}} = 3^{\frac{7}{8}} = 3^{\frac{2^3-1}{2^3}}$$

...   .

$$\Rightarrow \frac{u_{10}}{u_9} = \frac{3^{\frac{2^{10}-1}{2^{10}}}}{3^{\frac{2^9-1}{2^9}}} = 3^{\frac{1}{2^{10}}}$$

Hence, (d) is the correct option.

2. $7777 + 7777 \times 7777 \times (5 \div 77) \times (11 \div 35)$

$$= 7777 + 7777 \times 7777 \times \frac{5}{77} \times \frac{11}{35}$$

$$= 1242098.$$

Hence, (d) is the correct option.

3. The given expression

$$2 - \frac{\sqrt{6407522209}}{3600840049} = 2 - (1.333961) = 0.666039$$

4. $\lfloor 7 = 1 \times 2 \times 3 \times 4 \times 5 \times 6 \times 7$

$$= 2^4 \times 3^2 \times 5^1 \times 7^1$$

The smallest perfect square divisible by $\lfloor 7$ is

$$2^4 \times 3^2 \times 5^2 \times 7^2 = 176400.$$

5. $\left(\sqrt{\frac{225}{729}} - \sqrt{\frac{25}{144}} \right) \div \sqrt{\frac{16}{81}}$

$$= \left(\frac{15}{27} - \frac{5}{12} \right) \div \frac{4}{9}$$

$$= \frac{5}{36} \times \frac{9}{4} = \frac{5}{16}.$$

6. The factorisation of numbers can be done with the help of options.

The four prime numbers are 17, 19, 23 and 29.

(Since, $17 \times 19 \times 23 = 7429$ and $19 \times 23 \times 29 = 12673$)

7. We have,

$$0.0010101 \times 10^k > 1000$$

$$\Rightarrow k \geq 6$$

Hence, the least value of k is 6.

8. Let $y = \sqrt{7 + \sqrt{7 - \sqrt{7 + ...}}}$

$$\Rightarrow y^2 - 7 = \sqrt{7 - \sqrt{7 + ...}}$$

$$\Rightarrow (y^2 - 7)^2 = 7 - y$$

Putting y = 1, 2, 3, 4, only y = 3 satisfies the equation.

Alternate Method:

$$\sqrt{7} < \sqrt{7 + \sqrt{7 - \sqrt{7}}} \, ... < \sqrt{7 + \sqrt{7}}$$

$$\Rightarrow 2.64 < \sqrt{7} < \sqrt{7 + \sqrt{7 - \sqrt{7}}} \, ... < \sqrt{7 + 2.64}$$

$$\Rightarrow 2.64 < \sqrt{7 + \sqrt{7 - \sqrt{7}}} \, ... < \sqrt{9.64}$$

$\therefore$ From options, $\sqrt{7 + \sqrt{7 - ...}} = 3.$

9. According to the question,

$a \times b \times c \times d = 3094 = 2 \times 7 \times 13 \times 17$

Since $1 < a < b < c < d$, b = 7 and c = 13.

Hence, $b \times c = 7 \times 13 = 91$.

10. Let the number of girls be x and the number of boys be y.

$$\therefore \quad 3.3x + 2.9y = 249$$

Option (b) satisfies this equation.

Hence, Mrs. Sonia bought 57 strawberry flavoured and 21 chocolate flavoured candies.

11. The product of n positive numbers is n^n.

For the sum to be the minimum, all the numbers must be equal to n.

Hence, the minimum value of the sum is $(n \times n)$ i.e. n^2.

12. Let the number of students in the class be 'N' and the number of chocolate was to be given to the student who got twice as many chocolates as he was entited to be 'X'.

According to the question,

$$(1 + 2 + 3 + ... + N) + X = 1200$$

As we know that 'N' and 'X' are integers, we can find the required quantity with the help of options. The option that gives an integer value of X, will be the correct answer. Going by the options, we get N = 48 and X = 24.

13. We have $54 + 55 + 56 + ... + 196$

$$= \frac{143}{2} [54 + 196] = 17875.$$

14. We have $2^{\frac{1}{2}}, 3^{\frac{1}{3}}, 4^{\frac{1}{4}} = 2^{\frac{1}{2} \times 12}, 3^{\frac{1}{3} \times 12}, 4^{\frac{1}{4} \times 12}$

$$= 2^6, 3^4, 4^3$$

$$= 64, 81, 64.$$

As 81 is the largest number among the above numbers so $3^{\frac{1}{3}}$ is the highest number.

15. IBM – Daksh will get calls from all the places simultaneously after an interval of time given by the LCM of 10, 12, 20 and 25 which is 300. So the next simultaneous calls will be received after 300 minutes or after 5 hours i.e., at 10:00 a.m. Hence, (A) is the correct option.

16. For the total length to be the minimum, the length of each part should be the LCM of 12, 18 and 32, i.e. 288.

Hence, the required length of the rod = 3 × 288 = 864 units.

17. $\dfrac{1}{\sqrt{5}+\sqrt{6}+\sqrt{11}}$

$$= \frac{1}{\left(\sqrt{5}+\sqrt{6}\right)+\sqrt{11}} \times \frac{\left(\sqrt{5}+\sqrt{6}\right)-\sqrt{11}}{\left(\sqrt{5}+\sqrt{6}\right)-\sqrt{11}}$$

$$= \frac{\sqrt{5}+\sqrt{6}-\sqrt{11}}{2\sqrt{30}}$$

$$= \frac{\left(\sqrt{5}+\sqrt{6}-\sqrt{11}\right)\times\sqrt{30}}{2\left(\sqrt{30}\right)^2}$$

$$= \frac{5\sqrt{6}+6\sqrt{5}-\sqrt{330}}{60}$$

Option (a) is correct

***Note that option (d) is similar to (a), so this question has two correct solutions.**

18. There are 4 fathers out of which 2 are grandfathers. Also, there are 4 mothers out of which 2 are grandmothers. So in all 8 persons are there. Now, there are also 2 grandsons and 2 grand-daughters present in the picnic. So, in all there is a minimum of 12 persons present at the picnic.

One of the possible family tree is as follows:

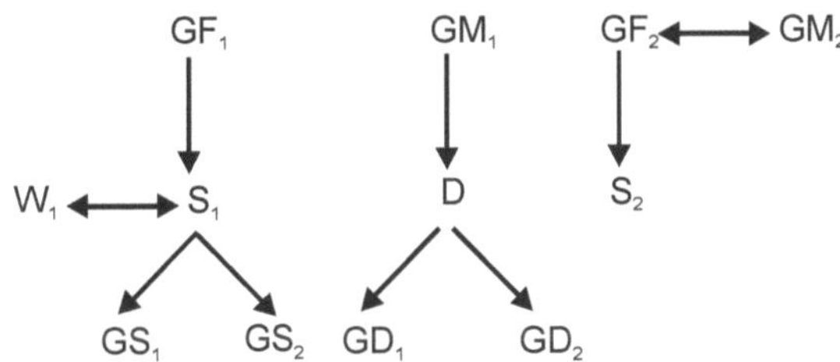

Here, GF_1, GF_2, S_1 and S_2 are fathers, where S_2's children are not present in the picnic. GM_1, GM_2, W_1 and D are the mothers present in the picnic.

Hence, the correct option is (c).

19. $\displaystyle\sum_{r=1}^{n}\frac{{}^{n}P_r}{r!}=\sum_{r=1}^{n}\frac{\frac{n!}{(n-r)!}}{r!}=\sum_{r=1}^{n}{}^{n}C_r=\left(\sum_{r=0}^{n}{}^{n}C_r\right)-{}^{n}C_0=2^n-1.$

Hence, (b) is the correct answer.

20. $|z_1|=12$ ...(i)

$|z_2-(3+4i)|=5$ ...(ii)

Using Triangular Inequality in (ii) we get.

$$|z_2-(3+4i)|\geq \big||z_2|-(3+4i)\big|$$

$$\Rightarrow 5\geq \big||z_2|-|3+4i|\big|$$

$$\Rightarrow 5\geq |z_2|-|3+4i|\geq -5$$

$$\Rightarrow 10\geq |z_2|\geq 0$$

Now, $|z_1-z_2|\geq \big||z_1|-|z_2|\big|=|12-10|=2$

21. Let the initial number of 1 Rupee, 2 Rupee and 5 Rupee coins be a, b and c.

At the grocery shop,

The number of 5 Rupee coin left

$$=\frac{c}{2}$$

New count of 1 Rupee coin

$$=a+\frac{c}{2}$$

At the dairy shop,

New count of 5 Rupee coins

$$=\frac{c}{2}+30$$

Also, according to the condition,

$$\frac{c}{2}+30=1.75c \qquad \text{...(i)}$$

$$a+\frac{c}{2}=50 \qquad \text{...(ii)}$$

From (i), c = 24 and putting this value in equation (ii), we get, a = 38.

Therefore, original count of 1 Rupee and 5 Rupee coins is 38 and 24 respectively.

Hence, option (d) is the correct choice.

22. Let the number of pastries of pineapple, mango and black forest be p, m and b respectively. Then,

$$p^2 + m^2 + b^2 = 211,$$

where p, m, b are natural numbers.

Now, p + m + b = 23.

Using options, since 11 + 9 + 3 = 23

and $11^2 + 9^2 + 3^2 = 211,$

(b) is the correct option.

23. Sum of the house numbers of the houses preceding

$$x=\frac{(x-1)x}{2}.$$

Also sum of the house numbers of the houses following

$$x = \frac{49.50}{2} - \frac{x(x+1)}{2}$$

According to the question,

$$\frac{(x-1)x}{2} = \frac{49.50}{2} - \frac{x(x+1)}{2}$$

$$\Rightarrow\quad 2x^2 = 49 \times 50$$

$$\Rightarrow\quad x^2 = 49 \times 25$$

Hence, $x = 35$.

24. Let the marks obtained by Ronit in Logical Reasoning and Verbal Ability be $3a$ and $2b$ respectively.

According to the question,

$$a = b + 5 \qquad\qquad\qquad \ldots(i)$$

Also, $3a + 2b + 70 = 210 \qquad\qquad \ldots(ii)$

From equations (i) and (ii), required difference = 20.

25. Unit digit of $(8267)^{153} \times (341)^{72}$

$$= \ldots\, 7^1 \times \ldots\, 1^2 = 7.$$

26. $X = Z + 1 = 31! + 1$

∴ The values of $X + 1$, $X + 2$ ... $X + 30$ are $31! + 2$, $31! + 3$ ... $31! + 30$

Hence, none of the numbers $X + 1$, $X + 2$, ... $X + 30$ is prime.

27. On the basis of the given terms in the sequence, it does not seem possible to find the next term of the sequention. One more thing that needs to be noted is the answer has to be a rational number, but none of options except A is a rational number, which cannot be the answer as the approximate value of the expression is 0.85.

Out of the given options, the value of option D is approximately 0.85.

28. $10^{67} - 87$

As in 10^{67} we have total 67 zeros $- 87$

We get last 2 digits 13 and 65 9's.

So $65 \times 9 + 1 + 3 = 589$

Hence option (d)

1. Percentages and Fraction

2008-10

1. At the end of the year 2002, Rajoria Institute of Management (RIM) had conducted 108 Management Development Programmes (MDP). Henceforth, every year the institute added p% of the MDP topics at the beginning of the year and discarded q% of the outdated MDP topics at the end of the year, where $p > 0$ and $q > 0$. If RIM scheduled 108 MDP programmes at the end of the year 2006, which one of the following is true?

(a) $p = q$ (b) $p < q$

(c) $p > q$ (d) $p = \dfrac{q}{2}$

2. Ashok a master adulterator cum grosser sells haldi powder (turmeric powder), which contains five percent saw dust. What quantity of pure haldi should be added to two kilos of haldi (containing five percent saw dust) so that the proportion of saw dust becomes four percent?

(a) 1 kg.   (b) 23 kgs

(c) 0.5 kg.   (d) None of these

2010-12

3. Bennett distribution company, a subsidiary of a major cosmetics manufacturer Bavlon, is forecasting the zonal sales for the next year. Zone I with current yearly sales of Rs.193.8 lakh is expected to achieve a sales growth of 7.25%; Zone II with current sales of Rs.79.3 lakh is expected to grow by 8.2%; and Zone III with sales of Rs. 57.5 lakh is expected to increase sales by 7.15%. What is the Bennett's expected sales growth for the next year?

(a) 7.46%   (b) 7.53%

(c) 7.88%   (d) 7.41%

2011-13

4. A Techno company has 14 machines of equal efficiency in its factory. The annual manufacturing costs are Rs. 42,000 and establishment charges are Rs.12,000. The annual output of the company is Rs. 70,000. The annual output and manufacturing costs are directly proportional to the no. of machines. The share holders get 12.5% profit, which is directly proportional to the annual output of the company. If

7.14% machines remain closed throughout the year, then the percentage decrease in the amount of profit of the share holders would be:

(a) 12%   (b) 12.5%

(c) 13.0%   (d) None of these

2012-14

5. Mr. Sinha received a certain amount of money by winning a lottery contest. He purchased a new vehicle with 40 percent of the money received. He then gave 20 percent of the remaining amount to each of his two sons for investing in their business. Thereafter, Mr. Sinha spent half of the remaining amount for renovation of his house. One-fourth of the remaining amount was then used for purchasing a LCD TV and the remaining amount - Rs. 1,35,000/- was deposited in a bank. What was the amount of his cash prize?

(a) Rs. 10,00,000/-   (b) Rs. 9,00,000/-

(c) Rs. 8,00,000/-   (d) None of the above

2014-16

6. If decreasing 70 by X percent yields the same result as increasing 60 by X percent, then X percent of 50 is

(a) 3.84

(b) 4.82

(c) 7.10

(d) The data is insufficient to answer the question

2015-17

7. A pharmaceutical company, manufactures 6000 strips of prescribed diabetic drugs for Rs. 8,00,000 every month. In July 2014, the company supplied 600 strips of free medicines to doctors at various hospitals. Of the remaining medicines, it was able to sell 4/5th of the strips at 25 percent discount and the balance at the printed price of Rs. 250. Assuming vendor's discount at the rate of a uniform 30 percent of the total revenue, the approximate percentage profit / loss of the pharmaceutical company in July 2014 is:

(a) 5.5 percent (profit)

(b) 4 percent (loss)

(c) 5.5 percent (loss)

(d) None of the above

8. The pre-paid recharge of Airtel gives 21% less talktime than the same price pre-paid recharge of Vodafone. The post-paid talktime of Airtel is 12% more than its pre-paid recharge, having the same price. Further, the post-paid talktime of same price of Vodafone is 15% less than its pre-paid recharge. How much percent less / more talktime can one get from the Airtel post-paid service compared to the post-paid service of Vodafone?

   (a) 3.9% more   (b) 4.7% less

   (c) 4.7% more   (d) 2.8% less

9. Garima had only Rs. 200, Rs. 500 and Rs. 2000 notes in her wallet. She goes to Shoppers Stop, purchases some dresses and gives half of her Rs. 2000 notes & in turn receives same number of Rs. 200 notes. She then goes to a restaurant and gives all her Rs. 500 notes and receives thirty Rs. 2000 notes, which increases the number of Rs. 2000 notes she had by 75%. If now she has fifty Rs. 200 notes, what were the original number of Rs.. 2000 and Rs. 200 notes she had at the start?

   (a) 60, 10

   (b) 60, 15

   (c) 80,10

   (d) 80, 15

2. Profit, Loss and Discount

10. Joshi has purchased a small shop in a city by paying an amount of Rs. 20,000. He decides to decorate the shop before starting business for which he spends Rs. 8,000 in the first month and Rs. 2,000 in the next month. However, at the beginning of the third month, he gets a good offer from Wadhwa and sells the shop to him at a profit of 20 percent. Wadhwa shortly afterwards decides that he will be better off by doing business in another location and decides to sell the shop back to Joshi. Given this, mark <u>all</u> the correct options.

   (a) If Wadhwa loses a total of Rs. 7,200, his loss is not more than 20%.

   (b) If Joshi had originally purchased the shop at Rs. 14,000, then by selling the shop to Wadhwa at the same price, he could have made a profit of 50%.

   (c) If Joshi had sold the shop to Wadhwa at a profit of 40%, his monetary gain would have been Rs. 12,000.

   (d) If Joshi had sold the shop to Wadhwa at a profit of 40%, and Wadhwa sold the shop back to him at a loss of 40%, then Joshi would have acquired the shop with a net investment of Rs. 13,200.

11. A small and medium enterprise imports two components A and B from Taiwan and China respectively and assembles them with other components to for a toy. Component A contributes to 10% of production cost. Component B contributes to 20% of the production cost. Usually the company sells this toy at 20% above the production cost. Due to increase in the raw material and labour cost in both the countries, component A became 20% costlier and component B became 40% costlier. Owing to these reasons the company increased its selling price by 15%. Considering that cost of other components does not change, what will be the profit percentage, if the toy is sold at the new price?

   (a) 15.5%   (b) 25.5%

   (c) 35.5%   (d) 40%

12. Shyam, Gopal and Madhur are three partners in a business. Their capitals are respectively Rs 4000, Rs 8000 and Rs 6000. Shyam gets 20% of total profit for managing the business. The remaining profit is divided among the three in the ratio of their capitals. At the end of the year, the profit of Shyam is Rs 2200 less than the sum of the profit of Gopal and Madhur. How much profit, Madhur will get?

   (a) Rs.1600   (b) Rs. 2400

   (c) Rs. 3000   (d) Rs. 5000

13. Sujoy, Mritunjoy and Paranjoy are three friends, who have worked in software firms *Z Solutions, G Software's and R Mindpower* respectively for decade. The friends decided to float a new software firm named *XY Infotech* in January 2010. However, due to certain compulsions, Mritunjoy and Paranjoy were not able to immediately join the start-up in the appointed time. It was decided between friends that Sujoy will be running the venture as the full time director during 2010, and Mritunjoy and Paranjoy will be able to join the business only in January 2011. In order to compensate Sujoy for his efforts, it was decied that he will receive 10 percent of the profits and in the first year will invest lesser amount as compared to his friends. The remaining profit will be

distributed among the friends in line with their contribution. Sujoy invested Rs.35,000/- for 12 months, Mritunjoy invested Rs.1,30,000/- for 6 months and Paranjoy invested Rs.75,000/- for 8 months. If the total profit earned during 2010 was Rs. 4,50,000/-, then Paranjoy earned a profit of:

(a) Rs.1,75,500 (b) Rs.1,35,500

(c) Rs.1,39,500 (d) None of the above

14. In March 2011, *EF Public Library* purchased a total of 15 new books published in 2010 with a total expenditure of Rs.4500. Of these books, 13 books were purchased from *MN Distributors*, while the remaining two were purchased from *UV Publishers*. It is observed that one-sixth of the average price of all the 15 books purchased is equal to one-fifth of the average price of the 13 books obtained from *MN Distributors*. Of the two books obtained from *UV Publishers*, if one-third of the price of one volume is equal to one-half of the price of the other, then the price of the two books are:

(a) Rs.900/- and Rs.600/-

(b) Rs.600/- and Rs.400/-

(c) Rs.750/- and Rs.500/-

(d) None of the above

15. Rohit bought 20 soaps and 12 toothpastes. He marked-up the soaps by 15% on the cost price of each, and the toothpastes by Rs. 20 on the cost price of each. He sold 75% of the soaps and 8 toothpastes and made a profit of Rs. 385. If the cost of a toothpaste is 60% the cost of a soap and he got no return on unsold items, what was his overall profit or loss?

(a) Loss of Rs. 355 (b) Loss of Rs. 210

(c) Loss of Rs. 250 (d) None of the above

16. As a strategy towards retention of customers, the service centre of a split AC machine manufacturer offers discount as per the following rule: for the second service in a year, the customer can avail of a 10% discount; for the third and fourth servicing within a year, the customer can avail of 11 % and 12% discounts respectively of the previous amount paid. Finally, if a customer gets more than four services within a year, he has to pay just 55% of the original servicing charges. If Rohan has availed 5 services from the same service centre in a given year, the total percentage discount availed by him is approximately:

(a) 16.52 (b) 20.88

(c) 22.33 (d) 24.08

17. A firm is thinking of buying a printer for its office use for the next one year. The criterion for choosing is based on the least per-page printing cost. It can choose between an inkjet printer which costs ₹ 5000 and a laser printer which costs ₹ 8000. The per-page printing cost for an inkjet is ₹ 1.80 and that for a laser printer is ₹ 1.50. The firm should purchase the laser printer, if the minimum number of pages to be printed in the year exceeds

(a) 5000 (b) 10000

(c) 15000 (d) 18000

18. Seema has joined a new Company after the completion of her B.Tech from a reputed engineering college in Chennai. She saves 10% of her income in each of the first three months of her service and for every subsequent month, her savings are ₹ 50 more than the savings of the immediate-previous month. If her joining income was ₹ 3000, her total savings from the start of the service will be ₹ 11400 in:

(a) 6 months (b) 12 months

(c) 18 months (d) 24 months

19. Sailesh is working as a sales executive with a reputed FMCG Company in Hyderabad. As per the Company's policy, Sailesh gets a commission of 6% on all sales upto ₹ 1,00,000 and 5% on all sales in excess of this amount. If Sailesh remits ₹ 2,65,000 to the FMCG company after deducting his commission, his total sales were worth:

(a) ₹ 1,20,000 (b) ₹ 2,90,526

(c) ₹ 2,21,054 (d) ₹ 2,80,000

20. In a local shop, as part of promotional measures, the shop owner sells three different varieties of soap, one at a loss of 13 percent, another at a profit of 23 percent and the third one at a loss of 26 percent. Assuming that the shop owner sells aU three varieties of soap at the same price, the approximate percentage by which average cost price is lower or higher than the selling price is

(a) 10.5 higher (b) 12.5 lower

(c) 14.5 lower (d) 8.5 higher

3. Ratio and Proportion

21. If $\dfrac{x}{y} = \dfrac{7}{4}$, find the value of $\dfrac{x^2 - y^2}{x^2 + y^2}$

(a) $\dfrac{27}{49}$ (b) $\dfrac{43}{72}$

(c) $\dfrac{33}{65}$ (d) None of the above

22. An old lady engaged a domestic help on the condition that she would pay him Rs.90 and a gift after service of one year. He served only 9 months and received the gift and Rs. 65. Find the value of the gift.

(a) Rs.10

(b) Rs.12

(c) Rs.15

(d) None of the above

23. The ratio of number of male and female journalists in a newspaper office is 5 : 4. The newspaper has two sections, political and sports. If 30 percent of the male journalists and 40 percent of the female journalists are covering political news, what percentage of the journalists (approx.) in the newspaper is currently involved in sports reporting?

(a) 65 percent (b) 60 percent

(c) 70 percent (d) None of the above

2013-15

24. A sum of Rs. 1400 is divided amongst A, B, C and D such that A's share : B's share = B's share : C's share = C's share : D's share = $\dfrac{3}{4}$. How much is C's share?

(a) Rs. 72 (b) Rs. 288

(c) Rs. 216 (d) Rs. 384

2015-17

25. Ravindra and Rekha got married 10 years ago, their ages were in the ratio of 5:4. Today Ravindra's age is one sixth more than Rekha's age. After marriage, they had 6 children including a triplet and twins. The age of the triplets, twins and the sixth child is in the ratio of 3:21. What is the largest possible value of the present total age of the family?

(a) 79 (b) 93

(c) 101 (d) 107

2016-18

26. If p, q and r are three unequal numbers such that p, q and r are in A.P., and p, r-q and q-p are in G.P., then p : q : r is equal to:

(a) 1 : 2 : 3 (b) 2 : 3 : 4

(c) 3 : 2 : 1 (d) 1 : 3 : 4

2018-20

27. A mobile company that sells two models ACN-I and ACN-II of mobile, reported that revenues from ACN-I in 2016 were down 12% from 2015 and revenue from ACN-II sales in 2016 were up by 9% from 2015. If the total revenues from sales of both the mobile models ACN-I and ACN-II in 2016 were up by 3% from 2015, what is the ratio of revenue from ACN-I sales in 2015 to revenue from ACN-II sales in 2015?

(a) 5:2

(*b*) 2:5

(c) 3:4

(*d*) None

4. Average

2009-11

28. The mean salary in ICM Ltd. was Rs. 1500, and the standard deviation was Rs. 400. A year later each employee got a Rs. 100 raise. After another year each employee's salary (including the above mentioned raise) was increased by 20%. The standard deviation of the current salary is:

(a) 460 (b) 480

(c) 580 (d) None of the above

2010-12

29. M/s. Devi Radiograms, a shop which sells electronic gadgets, marks its merchandise 35% above the purchase price. Until four months ago, purchase price of one Philips DVD player was Rs.3000. During the last four months M/s. Devi Radiograms has received four monthly consignments of Philips DVD player at the purchase price of Rs.2750, Rs.2500, Rs.2400, and Rs.2250. The average rate of decrease in the purchase price of DVD player during these four months is:

(a) 7.51% (b) 8.20%

(c) 6.94% (d) 7.03%

2011-13

30. In a B-School there are three levels of faculty positions i.e. Professor, Associate Professor and Assistant Professor. It is found that the sum of the ages of all faculty present is 2160, their average age is 36; the average age of the Professor and Associate Professor is 39; of the Associate Professor and Assistant Professor is $32\dfrac{8}{11}$; of the Professor and Assistant Professor is $36\dfrac{2}{3}$. Had each Professor been 1 year older, each Associate Professor 6 years older, and each Assistant Professor 7 years older, then their average age would increase by 5 years. What will be the number of faculty at each level and their average ages?

(a) (16, 24, 20 : 45, 35, 30 years)

(b) (18, 24, 20 : 42, 38, 30 years)

(c) (16, 20, 24 : 50, 30, 30 years)

(d) None of these

2012-14

31. 2 years ago, one-fifth of Amita's age was equal to one-fourth of the age of Sumita, and the average of their age was 27 years. If the age of Paramita is also considered, the average age of three of them declines to 24. What will be the average age of Sumita and Paramita 3 years from now?

(a) 25 years   (b) 26 years

(c) 27 years   (d) cannot be determined

2013-15

32. At a reputed Engineering College in India, total expenses of a trimester are partly fixed and partly varying linearly with the number of students. The average expense per student is Rs. 400 when there are 20 students and Rs. 300 when there are 40 students. When there are 80 students, what is the average expense per student?

(a) Rs. 250   (b) Rs. 300

(c) Rs. 330   (d) Rs. 350

2014-16

33. The average of 7 consecutive numbers is P. If the next three numbers are also added, the average shall

(a) remain unchanged   (b) increase by 1

(c) increase by 1.5   (d) increase by 2

2017-19

34. Two farmers were cultivating wheat on their respective agricultural land in a village. Farmer A had an average production of 20 bushels from a hectare. Farmer B, who had 15 hectares of more land dedicated to wheat cultivation, had an output of 30 bushels of wheat from a hectare. If farmer B harvested 530 bushels of wheat more than farmer A, how many bushels of wheat did farmer A cultivate?

(a) 50   (b) 80

(c) 160   (d) 200

Simple Interest and Compound Interest

2008-10

35. Mr. Jeevan wanted to give some amount of money to his two children, so that although today they may not be using it, in the future the money would be of use to them. He divides a sum of Rs. 18,750/- between his two sons of age 10 years and 13 years respectively in such a way that each would receive the same amount at 3% p.a. compound interest when he attains the age of 30 years. What would be the original share of the younger son?

(a) 8959.80   (b) 8559.80

(c) 8969.80   (d) 8995.80

36. Pawan retires at the age of 60 years and his employer gives him a pension of Rs. 3600/- a year paid in half yearly installments for the rest of his life. Assuming life expectancy in India is 70 years and interest is 6% per annum payable half yearly, determine the present value of the pension. [Given, $(103)^{-20} = 0.55362$].

(a) 26,728.50

(b) 27,782.80

(c) 26,744.40

(d) 26,782.80

2010-12

37. In 2006, Raveendra was allotted 650 shares of Sun Systems Ltd in the initial public offer, at the face value of Rs.10 per share. In 2007, Sun Systems declared a bonus at the rate of 3:13. In 2008, the company again declared the bonus at the rate of 2:4. In 2009, the company declared a dividend of 12.5%. How much dividend does Raveendra get in 2009 as the percentage of his initial investment?

(a) 24.5%   (b) 23.9%

(c) 24.1%   (d) 23%

2011-13

38. To start a new enterprise, Mr. Yogesh has borrowed a total of Rs. 60,000 from two money lenders with the interest being compounded annually, to be repaid at the end of two years. Mr. Yogesh repaid Rs. 38,800 more to the first money lender compared to the second money lender at the end of two years. The first money lender charged an interest rate, which was 10% more than what was charged by the second money lender. If Mr. Yogesh had instead borrowed Rs. 30,000 from each at their respective initial rates for two years, he would have paid Rs. 7,500 more to the first money lender compared to the second. Then money borrowed by Mr. Yogesh from first money lender is?

(a) 20,000   (b) 35,000

(c) 40,000   (d) 42,000

2012-14

39. Aniket and Animesh are two colleagues working in *PQ Communications*, and each of them earned an investible surplus of Rs.1,50,000/- during a certain period. While Animesh is a risk-averse person, Aniket prefers to go for higher return opportunities. Animesh uses his entire savings in Public Provident Fund (PPF) and National Saving Certificates (NSC). It is observed that one-third of the savings made by Animesh in PPF is equal to one-half of his savings in NSC. On the other hand, Aniket distributes his investible funds in share market, NSC and PPF. It is observed that his investments in share market exceeds his savings in NSC and PPF by Rs.20,000/- and Rs.40,000/- respectively. The difference between the amount invested in NSC by Animesh and Aniket is:

(a) Rs.25,000/-   (b) Rs.15,000/-

(c) Rs.20,000/-   (d) Rs.10,000/-

2013-15

40. The annual production in cement industry is subject to business cycles. The production increases for two consecutive years consistently by 18% and decreases by 12% in the third year. Again in the next two years, it increases by 18% each year and decreases by 12% in the third year. Taking 2008 as the base year, what will be the approximate effect on cement production in 2012?
    (a) 24% increase   (b) 37% decrease
    (c) 45% increase   (d) 60% decrease

41. Mr. Mishra invested Rs. 25,000 in two fixed deposits X and Y offering compound interest @ 6% per annum and 8% per annum respectively. If the total amount of interest accrued in two years through both fixed deposits is Rs. 3518, the amount invested in Scheme X is
    (a) Rs. 12,000   (b) Rs. 13,500
    (c) Rs. 15,000   (d) Cannot be determined

2014-16

42. Three years ago, your close friend had won a lottery of Rs. 1 crore. He purchased a flat of Rs. 40 lakhs, a car for Rs. 20 lakhs and shares worth Rs. 10 lakhs. He put the remaining money in a bank depost that pays compound interest @12 percent per annum. If today, he sells off the flat, the car and the shares at certain percentage of their original value and withdraws his entire money from the bank, the total gain in his assets is 5%. The closest approximate percentage of the original value at which he sold off the tree items is
    (a) 60 percent   (b) 75 percent
    (c) 90 percent   (d) 105 percent

2015-17

43. Eight year's after completion of your MBA degree, You start a business of your own. You invest INR 30,00,00 in the business that is expected to give you a return of 6%, compounded annually. If the expected number of years by which your investment shall double is 72/r, where r is the percent interest rate, the approximate expected total value of investment (in INR) from your business 48 years later is:
    (a) 2, 40, 00,000   (b) 3, 60, 00, 000
    (c) 4, 80, 40, 000   (d) None of the above

2018-20

44. Swarn a SME enterprise borrowed a sum of money from a nationalized bank at 10% simple interest per annum and the same amount at 8% simple interest per annum from a microfinance firm for the same period. It cleared the first loan 6 months before the scheduled date of repayment and repaid the second loan just at the end of the scheduled period. If in each case it had to pay Rs. 62100 as amount then how much money and for what time period did it borrow?
    (a) Rs. 55750,2 years
    (b) Rs. 52500, 2 years
    (c) Rs. 51750,2.5 years
    (d) Rs. 55750,2.5 years

2019-21

45. A Business Group has 3 Companies X, Y, Z and a Trust P which is engaged in charitable activities. Each group company has to donate 5% of its own funds to the Trust, excluding the loan which the company has taken from other companies of the group. X has given a loan to Y which is equivalent to 10% of the funds of Y. After receiving the loan, Y has funds which are 2 times the funds of Z. If Z gave Rs. 10,000 as donation to the Trust P, how much is the approximate contribution of Y to the Trust P?
    (a) Rs. 17,000   (b) Rs. 18,000
    (c) Rs. 19,000   (d) Rs. 20,000

6. Mixture and Solutions

2007-09

46. A trader forms a mixture of cement and sand weighing 40 kgs. In the mixture, cement and sand are in the ratio of 4 : 1 in weight terms. Later, when he adds more sand to the mixture, the new ratio becomes 4 : 3. Given this, mark <u>all</u> the correct statements.
    (a) The second mixture formed is one and a half times heavier than the original mixture.
    (b) In order to arrive at the second mixture, the trader had to add a quantity of sand weighing 16 kg.
    (c) Had the original mixture been in the ratio of 8 : 3, the weight of the sand in the original mixture would have been 12 kg.
    (d) If the trader sells 7 kg of the second mixture formed by him, and adds 11 kg of a new mixture of cement and sand in the ratio 7 : 4 to the residual, then the new ratio of cement to sand will become 7 : 5.

2008-10

47. Sumit works as a state contractor for PWD and supplies bitumen mix for road construction. He has two varieties of bitumen, one at Rs. 42 per kg and the other at Rs. 25 per kg. How many kg of first variety must Sumit mix with 25 kg of second variety, so that he may, on selling the mixture at 40 kg, gain 25% on the outlay?
    (a) 30   (b) 20
    (d) 25   (d) None of these

48. The ratio of 'metal 1' and 'metal 2' in Alloy 'A' is 3 : 4. In Alloy 'B' same metals are mixed in the ratio 5 : 8. If 26 kg of Alloy 'B' and 14kg of Alloy 'A' are mixed then find out the ratio of 'metal 1' and 'metal 2' in the new Alloy.

(a) 3 : 2   (b) 2 : 5

(c) 2 : 3   (d) None of the above

49. A 10 litre cylinder contains a mixture of water and sugar, the volume of sugar being 15% of total volume. A few litres of the mixture is released and an equal amount of water is added. Then the same amount of the mixture as before is released and replaced with water for a second time. As a result, the sugar content becomes 10% of total volume. What is the approximate quantity of mixture released each time?

(a) 1 litre   (b) 1.2 litres

(c) 1.5 litres   (d) 2 litres

50. Two alloys of aluminium have different percentages of aluminium in them. The first one weighs 8 kg and the second one weighs 16 kg. One piece each of equal weight was cut off from both the alloys and first piece was alloyed with the second alloy and the second piece alloyed with the first one. As a result, the percentage of aluminium became the same in the resulting two new alloys.

What was the weight of each cut-off piece?

(a) 3.33 kg   (b) 4.67 kg

(c) 5.33 kg   (d) None of the above

51. X and Y are the two alloys which were made by mixing Zinc and Copper in the ratio 6:9 and 7:11 respectively. If 40 grams of alloy X and 60 grams of alloy Y are melted and mixed to form another alloy Z, what is the ratio of Zinc and Copper in the new alloy Z?

(a) 6:9   (b) 59:91

(c) 5:9   (d) 59:90

52. A milk vendor soils 10 litre of milk from a can containing 40 litres of pure milk to the 1st customer. He then adds 10 litres of water to the milk can. Again he sells 10 litres of mixture to the 3rd customer and then adds 10 litres of water to the can and so on. What amount of pure milk will the 5th customer receive?

(a) $\dfrac{510}{128}$ litres   (b) $\dfrac{505}{128}$ litres

(c) $\dfrac{410}{128}$ litres   (d) $\dfrac{405}{128}$ litres

53. There are two alloys P and Q made up of silver, copper and aluminium. Alloy P contains 45% silver and rest aluminium. Alloy Q contains 30% silver, 35% copper and rest aluminium. Alloys P and Q are mixed in the ratio of 1 : 4.5. The approximate percentages of silver and copper in the newly formed alloy is:

(a) 33% and 29%   (b) 29% and 26%

(c) 35% and 30%   (d) None of the above

54. A Pharmaceutical company produces two chemicals X and Y, such that X consists of 5% salt A and 10% salt B and Y consists of 10% salt A and 6% salt B. For producing the chemicals X and Y, the company requires at least 7 gm of Salt A and at least 7 gm of Salt B. If chemical X costs Rs. 10.50 per gm and chemical Y costs Rs, 7.80 per gm, what is the minimum cost at which the company can meet the requirement by using a combination of both types of chemicals?

(a) Rs. 810   (c) Rs. 850

(c) Rs. 537   (d) None

55. The Drizzle Pvt. Ltd., a squash company has 2 cans of juice. The first contains 25% water and the rest is fruit pulp. The second contains 50% water and rest is fruit pulp. How much juice should be mixed from each of the containers so as to get 12 litres of juice such that the ratio of water to fruit pulp is 3:5?

(a) 6 litres, 6 litres   (b) 4 litres, 8 litres

(c) 5 litres, 7 litres   (d) 9 litres, 3 litres

7. Time, Speed and Distance

56. Laxman and Bharat decide to go from Agra to Delhi for watching a cricket match and board two different trains for that purpose. While Laxman takes the first train that leaves for Delhi, Bharat decides to wait for some time and take a faster train. On the way, Laxman sitting by the window-seat noticed that the train boarded by Bharat crossed him in 12 seconds. Now the faster train can travel 180 km in three hours, while the slower train takes twice as much time to do it. Given this, mark <u>all</u> the correct options.

(a) If the faster train has taken 30 seconds to cross the entire length of the slower train, the difference between the lengths of the two trains is 50 m.

(b) If the faster train had been running twice as much faster, it would have taken 10 seconds to overtake the slower train.

(c) Had the faster train taken 24 seconds to cross the entire length of the slower train, the length of the slower train would have been 100 m.

(d) If the slower train had been running at one and a half times of its current speed, the faster train would have taken 24 seconds to overtake Laxman.

2008-10

57. The Ghaziabad-Hapur-Meerut EMU and the Meerut-Hapur-Ghaziabad EMU start at the same time from Gahaziabad and Meerut and proceed towards each other at 16 km/hr and 21 km/hr respectively. When they meet, it is found that one train has traveled 60 km more than the other. The distance between two stations is:

(a) 445 km   (b) 444 km

(c) 440 km   (d) 450 km

2009-11

58. A boat goes 30 km upstream and 44 km downstream in 10 hours. In 13 hours, it can go 40 km upstream and 55 km downstream. The speed of the boat in still water is:

(a) 3 km/hour   (b) 4 km/hour

(c) 8 km/hour   (d) None of the above

2010-12

59. Two motorists Anil and Sunil are practicing with two different sports cars: Ferrari and Maclarun, on the circular racing track, for the car racing tournament to be held next month. Both Anil and Sunil start from the same point on the circular track. Anil completes one round of the track in 1 minute and Sunil takes 2 minutes to complete a round. While Anil maintains same speed for all the rounds, Sunil halves his speed after the completion of each round. How many times Anil and Sunil will meet between the 6th round and 9th round of Sunil (6th and 9th round is excluded)? Assume that the speed of Sunil remains steady throughout each round and changes only after the completion of that round.

(a) 260   (b) 347

(c) 382   (d) None of the above

Directions for questions 60 – 61: Read the following information carefully and answer the questions

A warship and a submarine (completely submerged in water) are moving horizontally in a straight line. The Captain of the warship observes that the submarine makes an angle of depression of 30º, and the distance between them from the point of observation is 50 km. After 30 minutes, the angle of depression becomes 60º.

60. Find the distance between them after 30 min from the initial point of reference.

(a) $\dfrac{50}{\sqrt{3}}$ km   (b) 25 km

(c) $\dfrac{25}{\sqrt{3}}$ km   (d) $25\sqrt{3}$ km

61. If both are moving in the same direction and the submarine is ahead of the warship in both the situations, then the speed of the warship, if the ratio of the speed of warship to that of the submarine is 2:1, is:

(a) $\dfrac{100}{\sqrt{3}}$ km / hr.   (b) $100\sqrt{3}$ km / hr.

(c) $200\sqrt{3}$ km / hr.   (d) $\dfrac{200}{\sqrt{3}}$ km / hr.

62. Sukriti and Saloni are athletes. Sukriti covers a distance of 1 km in 5 minutes and 50 seconds, while Saloni covers the same distance in 6 minutes and 4 seconds. If both of them start together and run at uniform speed, by what distance will Sukriti win a 5 km mini marathon:

(a) 150 m   (b) 200 m

(c) 175 m   (d) 225 m.

2011-13

63. Mukesh, Suresh and Dinesh travel from Delhi to Mathura to attend Janmasthmi Utsav. They have a bike which can carry only two riders at a time as per traffic rules. Bike can be driven only by Mukesh. Mathura is 300km from Delhi. All of them can walk at 15Km/hr. All of them start their journey from Delhi simultaneously and are required to reach Mathura at the same time. If the speed of bike 60Km/hr then what is the shortest possible time in which all three can reach Mathura at the same time.

(a) $8\dfrac{2}{7}$ Hrs   (b) $9\dfrac{2}{7}$ Hrs

(c) 10 Hrs   (d) None of these

2012-14

64. Mandeep and Jagdeep had gone to visit Ranpur, which is a seaside town and also known for the presence of the historical ruins of an ancient kingdom. They stayed in a hotel which is exactly 250 meters away from the railway station. At the hotel, Mandeep and Jagdeep learnt from a tourist information booklet that the distance between the sea-beach and the gate of the historical ruins is exactly 1 km. Next morning they visited the sea-beach to witness sunrise and afterwards decided to have a race from the beach to the gate of the ruins. Jagdeep defeated Mandeep in the race by 60 meters or 12 seconds. The following morning they had another round of race from the railway station to the hotel. How long did Jagdeep take to cover the distance on the second day?

(a) 53 seconds   (b) 47 seconds

(c) 51 seconds   (d) 45 seconds

2013-15

65. It takes 15 seconds for a train travelling at 60 km/hour to cross entirely another train half its length and travelling in opposite direction at 48 km/hour. It also passes a bridge in 51 seconds. The length of the bridge is

(a) 550 m   (b) 450 m

(c) 500 m   (d) 600 m

66. The Howrah-Puri express can move at 45 km/hour without its rake, and the speed is diminished by a constant that varies as the square root of the number of wagons attached. If it is known that with 9 wagons, the speed is 30 km/hour, what is the greatest number of wagons with which the train can just move?

(a) 63   (b) 64

(c) 80   (d) 81

2014-16

67. It was a rainy morning in Delhi when Rohit drove his mother to a dentist in his Maruti Alto. They started at 8.30 AM from the home and Rohit maintained the speed of the vehicle at 30 km/hr. However, while returning from the doctor's chamber, rain intensified and the vehicle could not move due to severe water logging. With no other alternative, Rohit kept the vehicle outside the doctor's chamber and returned home along with his mother in a rickshaw at a speed of 12 km/hr. They reached home at 1.30 PM. If they stayed at the doctor's chamber for the dental check-up for 48 minutes, the distance of the doctor's chamber from Rohit's house is

(a) 15 km   (b) 30 km

(c) 36 km   (d) 45 km

2015-17

68. A ferry carries passengers to Rock of Vivekananda and back from Kanyakumari. The distance of Rock of Vivekananda from Kanyakumari is 100km. One day, the ferry started for Rock of Vivekananda with passengers on board, at a speed of 20 km per hour. After 90 minutes, the crew realized that there is a hole in the ferry and 15 gallons of sea water had already entered the ferry. Sea water is entering the ferry at the rate of 10 gallons per hour. It requires 60 gallons of water to sink the ferry. At what speed should the driver now drive the ferry so that it can reach the Rock of Vivekananda and return back to Kanyakumari just in time before the ferry sinks? (Current of the sea water from Rock of Vivekananda to Kanyakumari is 2km per hour.)

(a) 40 km/hr towards the Rock & 39 km/hr while returning to Kanyakumari

(b) 41 km/hr towards the Rock & 38 km/hr while returning to Kanyakumari

(c) 42 km/hr towards the Rock & 36 km/hr while returning to Kanyakumari

(d) 35 km/hr towards the Rock & 39 km/hr while returning to Kanyakumari

2016-18

69. A chartered bus carrying office employees travels everyday in two shifts – morning and evening. In the evening, the bus travels at an average speed which is 50% greater than the morning average speed; but takes 50% more time than the amount of time it takes in the morning. The average speed of the chartered bus for the entire journey is greater / less than its average speed in the morning by:

(a) 18% less   (b) 30% greater

(c) 37.5% greater   (d) 50% less

2017-19

70. A child, playing at the balcony of his multi-storied apartment, drops a ball from a height of 350 m. Each time the ball rebounds, it rises 4/5th of the height it has fallen through. The total distance travelled by the ball before it comes to rest is

(a) 2530 m   (b) 2800 m

(c) 3150 m   (d) 3500 m

71. Shruti and Krishna left Delhi for Noida at the same time. While Shruti was driving her car, Krishna, an environmentalist by profession, was traveling on his bicycle. Having reached Noida, Shruti turned back and met Krishna an hour after they started. Krishna continued his journey to Noida after the meeting, while Shruti turned back and also headed for Noida. Having reached Noida, Shruti again turned back and met Krishna 30 minutes after their first meeting. The time taken by Krishna to cover the distance between Delhi and Noida is

(a) 2 hours   (b) 2.5 hours

(c) 3 hours   (d) None of the above

2018-20

72. Ramesh and Sohan start walking away from each other from a point P at an angle of 120°. Ramesh walks at a speed of 3 km/hour while Sohan walks at a speed of 4 km/hour. What is the distance between them after 90 minutes?

(a) 9.89 km   (*b*) 10.56 km

(c) 9.12 km   (*d*) 12.42 km

2019-21

73. Joseph diametrically crosses a semi-circular playground and takes 48 seconds less than if he crosses the playground along the semi-circular path. If he walks 50 metres in one minute, the diameter of playground is

   (a) 54 metres   (b) 70 metres

   (c) 85 metres   (d) 35 metres

8. Time and Work

2007-09

74. A contractor takes up an assignment that 20 men can complete in 10 days. The same assignment could be finished by 15 women in 20 days. The contractor decides to employ 10 men and 10 women for the project. Given this, mark <u>all</u> the correct options.

   (a) If the wage rate for men and women are Rs. 50 and Rs. 45 respectively, the total wage bill for the project will be Rs. 11,400.

   (b) If the wage rate for men and women are Rs. 45 and Rs. 40 respectively, the total wage bill for the project will be Rs. 10,200.

   (c) If the wage rate for men and women are equal at Rs. 40, the total wage bill for the project will be Rs. 9,100.

   (d) If the contractor decides to employ 20 men and 30 women for the project and the wage rate for men and women are Rs. 40 and Rs. 35 respectively, the total wage bill for the project will be Rs. 9,250.

75. Pavan builds an overhead tank in his house, which has three taps attached to it. While the first tap can fill the tank in 12 hours, the second one takes one and a half times more than the first one to fill it completely. A third tap is attached to the tank which empties it in 36 hours. Now, one day, in order to fill the tank, Pavan opens the first tap and after two hours opens the second tap as well. However; at the end of the sixth hour, he realizes that the third tap has been kept open right from the beginning and promptly closes it. What will be the total time required to fill the tank?

   (a) 8 hours 48 minutes

   (b) 9 hours 12 minutes

   (c) 9 hours 36 minutes

   (d) 8 hours 30 minutes

2008-10

76. The digging work of the DMRC on the Adchini-Andheriamore stretch requires Twenty-four men to complete the work in sixteen days. As a part of the task if DMRC were to hire Thirty-two women, they can complete the same work in twenty-four days. Sixteen men and sixteen women started working and worked for twelve days. Due to time bound schedule the work had to be completed in remaining 2 days, for which how many more men are to be employed?

   (a) 48   (b) 24

   (c) 36   (d) 16

2010-12

77. Aditya, Vedus and Yuvraj alone can do a job in 6 weeks, 9 weeks and 12 weeks respectively. They work together for 2 weeks. Then Aditya leaves the job. Vedus leaves the job a week earlier to the completion of the work. The job would be completed in:

   (a) 4 weeks   (b) 5 weeks

   (c) 7 weeks   (d) None of the above.

78. Cylindrical overhead tank is filled by two pumps – P1 and P2. P1 can fill the tank in 8 hours while P2 can fill the tank in 12 hours. There is a pipe P3 which can empty the tank in 8 hours. Both the pumps are opened simultaneously. The supervisor of the tank, before going out on a work, sets a timer to open P3 when the tank is half filled so that tank is exactly filled up by the time he is back. Due to technical fault P3 opens when the tank is one third filled. If the supervisor comes back as per the plan what percent of the tank is still empty?

   (a) 25% tank   (b) 12% tank

   (c) 10% tank   (d) None of the above

2011-13

79. Three Professors Dr. Gupta, Dr Sharma and Dr. Singh are evaluating answer scripts of a subject. Dr. Gupta is 40% more efficient than Dr. Sharma, who is 20% more efficient than Dr. Singh. Dr. Gupta takes 10 days less than Dr. Sharma to complete the evaluation work. Dr. Gupta starts the evaluation work and works for 10 days and then Dr. Sharma takes over. Dr. Sharma evaluates for next 15 days and then stops. In how many days, Dr. Singh can complete the remaining evaluation work.

   (a) 7.2 days   (b) 9.5 days

   (c) 11.5 days   (d) None of these

80. Three pipes, A, B and C are connected to a tank. These pipes can fill the tank separately in 5 hrs, 10 hrs and 15 hrs respectively. When all the three pipes were opened simultaneously, it was observed that pipes A and B were supplying water at 3/4th of their normal rates for the first hour after which they supplied water at the normal rate. Pipe C supplied water at 2/

3rd of its normal rate for first 2 hours, after which it supplied at its normal rate. In how much time, tank would be filled.

(a) 1.05 Hrs   (b) 2.05 Hrs

(c) 3.05 Hrs   (d) None of these

2012-14

81. In Bilaspur village, 12 men and 18 boys completed construction of a primary health center in 60 days, by working for 7.5 hours a day. Subsequently the residents of the neighbouring Harigarh village also decided to construct a primary health center in their locality, which would be twice the size of the facility built in Bilaspur. If a man is able to perform the work equal to the same done by 2 boys, then how many boys will be required to help 21 men to complete the work in Harigarh in 50 days, working 9 hours a day?

(a) 45 boys   (b) 48 boys

(c) 40 boys   (d) 42 boys

82. A contract is to be completed in 56 days and 104 men are set to work, each working 8 hours a day. After 30 days, 2/5th of the work is finished. How many additional men may be employed so that work may be completed on time, each man now working 9 hours per day?

(a) 56 men   (b) 65 men

(c) 46 men   (d) None of the above

2013-15

83. 12 men can complete a work in ten days. 20 women can complete the same work in twelve days. 8 men and 4 women started working and after nine days 10 more women joined them. How many days will they now take to complete the remaining work?

(a) 2 days   (b) 5 days

(c) 8 days   (d) 10 days

2014-16

84. A mother along with her two sons is entrusted with the task of cooking Biryani for a family get-together. It takes 30 minutes for all three of them cooking together to complete 50 percent of the task. The cooking can also be completed if the two sons start cooking together and the elder son leaves after 1 hour and the younger son cooks for further 3 hours. If the mother needs 1 hour less than the elder son to complete the cooking, how much cooking does the mother complete in an hour?

(a) 33.33%   (b) 50%

(c) 66.67%   (d) None of the above

85. Capacity of tap Y is 60% more than that of X .If both the taps are opened simultaneously, they take 40 hours to fill the tank. The time taken by Y alone to fill the tank is

(a) 60 hours   (b) 65 hours

(c) 70 hours   (d) 75 hours

2015-17

86. The student fest in an Engineering College is to be held in one month's time and no sponsorship has yet been arranged by the students. Finally the General Secretary (GS) of the student body took the initiative and decided to go alone for sponsorship collection. In fact, he is the only student doing the fund raising job on the first day. However, seeing his enthusiasm, other students also joined him as follows: on the second day, 2 more students join him; on the third day, 3 more students join the group of the previous day; and so on. In this manner, the sponsorship collection is completed in exactly 20 days. If an MBA student is twice as efficient as an Engineering student, the number of days which 11 MBA students would take to do the same activity, is:

(a) 70   (b) 80

(c) 90   (d) 100

2016-18

87. A tank is connected with both inlet pipes and outlet pipes. Individually, an inlet pipe can fill the tank in 7 hours and an outlet pipe can empty it in 5 hours. If all the pipes are kept open, it takes exactly 7 hours for a completely filled-in tank to empty. If the total number of pipes connected to the tank is 11, how many of these are inlet pipes?

(a) 2   (b) 4

(c) 5   (d) 6

88. Three carpenters P, Q and R are entrusted with office furniture work. P can do a job in 42 days. If Q is 26% more efficient than P and R is 50% more efficient than Q, then Q and R together can finish the job in approximately:

(a) 11 days   (b) 13 days

(c) 15 days   (d) 17 days

2017-19

89. In the marketing management course of an MBA programme, you and your roommate can complete an assignment in 30 days. If you are twice as efficient as your roommate, the time required by each to complete the assignment individually is

(a) 45 days and 90 days

(b) 30 days and 60 days

(c) 40 days and 120 days

(d) 45 days and 135 days

2018-20

90. Somesh, Tarun and Nikhil can complete a work separately in 45, 60 and 75 days. They started the work together but Nikhil left after 5 days of start and Somesh left 2 days before the completion of the work. In how many days will the work be. completed?

(a) $25\dfrac{1}{7}$

(b) $50\dfrac{1}{7}$

(c) $35\dfrac{5}{7}$

(d) $40\dfrac{5}{7}$

91. An overhead tank, which supplies water to a settlement, is filled by three bore wells. First two bore wells operating together fill the tank in the same time as taken by third bore well to fill it. The second bore well fills the tank 10 hours faster than the first one and 8 hours slower than the third one. The time required by the third bore well to fill the tank alone is:

(a) 9 hours

(b) 12 hours

(c) 18 hours

(d) 20 hours

2019-21

92. Ram, Ravi and Ratan can alone finish an assignment in 9 days, 12 days and 15 days respectively. They decide to complete a work by working in turns. Ram works alone on Monday, Ravi does the work alone on Tuesday, followed by Ratan working alone on Wednesday & so on. What proportion of the complete work is done by Ravi?

(a) $\dfrac{2}{9}$

(b) $\dfrac{12}{47}$

(c) $\dfrac{1}{3}$

(d) $\dfrac{4}{9}$

93. Nitin installed an overhead tank on the roof of his newly constructed house. Three taps are connected to the tank: 2 taps A and B to fill the tank and one tap C to empty it. Tap A alone can fill the tank in 12 hours, while tap B alone takes one and a half times more time than tap A to fill the tank completely. Tap C alone can empty a completely filled tank in 36 hours. Yesterday, to fill the tank, Nitin first opened tap A, and then after 2 hours opened tap B also. However after 6 hours he realised that tap C was open from the very beginning. He quickly closes tap C. What will be the total time required to fill the tank?

(a) 8 hours 48 minutes

(b) 8 hours 30 minutes

(c) 9 hours 12 minutes

(d) 9 hours 36 minutes

9. Miscellaneous

2008-10

94. For constructing the working class consumer price index number of a particular town, the following weights corresponding to different group of items were assigned:

Food - 55, Fuel - 15, Clothing - 10, Rent - 8 and Miscellaneous - 12

It is known that the rise in food prices is double that of fuel and the rise in miscellaneous group prices is double that of rent. In October 2006, the increased D.A. by a factory of that town by 182% fully compensated for the rise in prices of food and rent but did not compensate for anything else. Another factory of the same locality increased D.A. by 46.5% which compensated for the rise in fuel and miscellaneous groups.

Which is the correct combination of the rise in prices of food, fuel, rent and miscellaneous groups?

(a) 320.14, 159.57, 95.64, 166.82

(b) 317.14, 158.57, 94.64, 189.28

(c) 311.14, 159.57, 90.64, 198.28

(d) 321.14, 162.57, 84.46, 175.38

95. The following data represent the age of husband (Y) and wife (X) for 10 couples:

X	18	20	20	24	22	24	27	24	21	25
Y	22	24	26	26	27	27	28	28	29	30

(I) What is the predicted age of husband when age of wife is 23?

(II) What is the predicated age of wife when age of husband is 35?

(a) 35.735 and 29.389

(b) 31.76 and 31.334

(c) 37.223 and 29.389

(d) None of these

2010-12

96. Because of economic slowdown, a multinational company curtailed some of the allowances of its employees. Rashid, the marketing manager of the company whose monthly salary has been reduced to Rs.42000 is unable to cut down on his expenditure. He finds that there is a deficit of Rs.2000 between his earnings and expenses in the first month. This deficit, because of inflationary pressure, will keep on increasing by Rs.500 every month. Rashid has a saving of Rs.60000 which. will be used to fill this deficit. After his savings get exhausted, Rashid would start borrowing from his friends. How soon will he start borrowing?

(a) 10th month

(b) 11th month

(c) 12th month

(d) 13th month

2012-14

97. Mr. and Mrs. Gupta have three children - Pratik, Writtik and Kajol, all of whom were born in different cities. Pratik is 2 years elder to Writtik. Mr. Gupta was 30 years of age when Kajol was born in Hyderabad, while Mrs. Gupta was 28 years of age when Writtik was born in Bangalore. If Kajol was 5 years of age when Pratik was born in Mumbai, then what were the ages of Mr. and Mrs. Gupta respectively at the time of Pratik's birth?

    (a) 35 years, 26 years   (b) 30 years, 21 years

    (c) 37 years, 28 years   (d) None of the above

98. A petrol tank at a filling station has a capacity of 400 litres. The attendant sells 40 litres of petrol from the tank to one customer and then replenishes it with kerosene oil. This process is repeated with six customers. What quantity of pure petrol will the seventh customer get when he purchases 40 litres of petrol?

    (a) 20.50 litres   (b) 21.25 litres

    (c) 24.75 litres   (d) 22.40 litres

2013-15

99. In 2011, Plasma - a pharmaceutical company - allocated Rs. 4.5×10^7 for Research and Development. In 2012, the company allocated Rs. 60,000,000 for Research and Development. If each year the funds are evenly divided among 2×10^2 departments, how much more will each department receive this year than it did last year?

    (a) Rs. 2.0×10^5 (b) Rs. 7.5×10^5

    (c) Rs. 7.5×10^4 (d) Rs. 2.5×10^7

2016-18

100. In 2004, Rohini was thrice as old as her brother Arvind. In 2014, Rohini was only six years older than her brother. In which year was Rohini born?

    (a) 1984   (b) 1986

    (c) 1995   (d) 2000

ANSWERS

1. (c)	**2.** (c)	**3.** (a)	**4.** (*b)	**5.** (a)	**6.** (a)	**7.** (c)	**8.** (a)	**9.** (c)	**10.** (a,b,c,d)
11. (b)	**12.** (b)	**13.** (b)	**14.** (c)	**15.** (a)	**16.** (b)	**17.** (b)	**18.** (c)	**19.** (d)	**20.** (a)
21. (c)	**22.** (a)	**23.** (a)	**24.** (d)	**25.** (d)	**26.** (a)	**27.** (b)	**28.** (b)	**29.** (*c)	**30.** (a)
31. (b)	**32.** (a)	**33.** (c)	**34.** (c)	**35.** (a)	**36.** (d)	**37.** (d)	**38.** (c)	**39.** (d)	**40.** (c)
41. (c)	**42.** (c)	**43.** (c)	**44.** (c)	**45.** (b)	**46.** (b,d)	**47.** (d)	**48.** (c)	**49.** (d)	**50.** (c)
51. (b)	**52.** (d)	**53.** (a)	**54.** (a)	**55.** (a)	**56.** (a,c,d)	**57.** (b)	**58.** (c)	**59.** (c)	**60.** (a)
61. (d)	**62.** (b)	**63.** (b)	**64.** (b)	**65.** (a)	**66.** (c)	**67.** (c)	**68.** (c)	**69.** (b)	**70.** (c)
71. (a)	**72.** (c)	**73.** (b)	**74.** (a,b,d)	**75.** (b)	**76.** (b)	**77.** (a)	**78.** (c)	**79.** (a)	**80.** (c)
81. (d)	**82.** (a)	**83.** (a)	**84.** (b)	**85.** (b)	**86.** (a)	**87.** (d)	**88.** (b)	**89.** (a)	**90.** (a)
91. (b)	**92.** (c)	**93.** (c)	**94.** (b)	**95.** (d)	**96.** (d)	**97.** (a)	**98.** (b)	**99.** (c)	**100.** (c)

EXPLANATIONS

1. In any given year, the number of programmes conducted remain the same. The number of programmes added at the beginning of every year must be equal to the number of programmes that are discarded at the end of every year. We must have:

$$108 \times \left(\frac{p}{100}\right) = 108 \times \left(1 + \frac{p}{100}\right) \times \left(\frac{q}{100}\right).$$

After simplifying, we get the relation $p = q + \frac{pq}{100}$. Clearly, $p > q$. Hence, (c) is the correct option.

2. Pure haldi has 0% saw dust and the adulterated sample has 5% saw dust in it. By adding appropriate amount of pure haldi, the concentration of saw dust, in the 5% sample, can be reduced to 4%. Applying allegation, we have

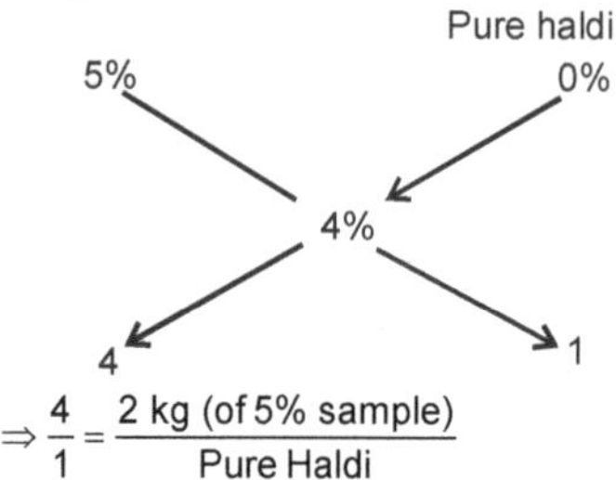

$$\Rightarrow \frac{4}{1} = \frac{2 \text{ kg (of 5\% sample)}}{\text{Pure Haldi}}$$

$\Rightarrow$ Pure haldi = 0.5 kg

Hence, (c) is the correct option.

3. For zone I, Rs.193.8 lakh is expected to achieve a sales growth of 7.25%.

Similarly, for zone II and zone III, expected sales growth are 8.2% and 7.15%.

Hence, Bennett's expected sales growth will be

$$= \frac{(193.8 \times 7.25) + (79.3 \times 8.2) + (57.5 \times 7.15)}{193.8 + 79.3 + 57.5} = 7.46\%$$

4. **Language of the question is very ambiguous.**
So, the likely solution is as follows:

$$\left.\begin{array}{l}\text{Manufacturing cost} = \text{Rs.42000} \\ \text{Establishment charges} = \text{Rs.12000}\end{array}\right] \text{Total charges} = \text{Rs.54,000}$$

Annual output = Rs.70,000

$\Rightarrow$ Profit = 70000 – 54000

$= $ Rs.16,000

Now, 1 out of 14 machines is not working

$$\left.\begin{array}{l}\text{Manufacturing cost} = \text{Rs.42000} \times \dfrac{13}{14} = \text{Rs.39000} \\ \text{Establishment charges} = \text{Rs.12000}\end{array}\right] = \text{Rs.51,000}$$

and annual output $= \dfrac{70000}{14} \times 13 = \text{Rs.65,000}$

Profit = Rs.14,000

Percentage decrease in profit $= \dfrac{2000}{16000} \times 100 = 12.5\%$

5. Let the amount of his cash prize be Rs. 100x.
Amount spent on:

Purchase of vehicle = Rs. 40x

Sons for business = 0.2 × 60x × 2 = Rs. 24x

Renovation of house = 0.5 × 36x = Rs. 18x

Purchase of LCD TV $= $ Rs. $\dfrac{18x}{4}$

According to the question,

$$\frac{3}{4} \times 18x = 1{,}35{,}000 \text{ or } 100x = 10{,}00{,}000.$$

6. According to the question,

$$\frac{70}{100}(100 - X) = \frac{60}{100}(100 + X)$$

$$\Rightarrow 7(100 - X) = 6(100 + X)$$

$$\Rightarrow 13X = 100 \Rightarrow X = 7.69$$

Now, X percent of 50 $= \dfrac{X}{100} \times 50 = \dfrac{X}{2} = \dfrac{7.69}{2} = 3.84$.

7. Cost price of 6000 strips = Rs. 8,00,000

Free Medicine = 600 strips

Remaining medicine = 5400 srips

Revenue generated by selling 5400 strips

$$= \frac{4}{5} \times 5400 \times 250 \times 0.75 + \frac{1}{5} \times 5400 \times 250 = 10{,}80{,}000$$

Revenue after discount given to vendor

$= 1080000 \times 0.7 = 756000$

The required percentage loss

$$= \frac{800000 - 756000}{800000} \times 100 = 5.5.$$

8. Let the vodafone gives ₹ 100 talktime on ₹ 100 Prepaid recharge.

	Airtel	Vodafone
Talktime on Prepaid	100 – 21 = 79	100
Talktime on Pospaid	79 × 1.12 = 88.48	100 – 15 = 85

Required Percentage $= \dfrac{88.48 - 85}{85} \times 100 = 4.1\%$.

9. Garima had x notes of Rs. 2000. She gave $\dfrac{x}{2}$ notes of Rs. 2000. She is left with $x - \dfrac{x}{2} = \dfrac{x}{2}$ notes.

$$\frac{x}{2} + 30 = 1.75\frac{x}{2} \Rightarrow x = 80$$

So she remains $\dfrac{80}{2} = 40$ rs. 200 notes

So, she must be having 50 – 40 = 10 Rs. 200 notes.

10. Joshi's total cost price = 20,000 + 8,000 + 2,000

$$= Rs.30,000$$

Joshi's selling price = Wadhwa's cost price

$$= 30,000\left(1+\frac{20}{100}\right) = Rs.36,000$$

And then Wadhwa sells it back to Joshi.

Option (a): Wadhwa lost Rs.7200 while selling the shop back to Joshi.

$$\Rightarrow \quad \text{Wadhwa's loss} = \frac{7200}{36000} = 20\%$$

$\therefore$ Option (a) is correct.

Option (b): Joshi's new total cost price

$$= 14000 + 8000 + 2000$$

$$= Rs.24,000$$

Joshi's selling price is still the same = Rs.36,000

$$\Rightarrow \quad \text{Joshi's profit \%} = \frac{36000 - 24000}{24000} \times 100$$

$$= 50\%$$

$\therefore$ Option (b) is correct.

Option (c): At a profit of 40% on his total cost price of Rs. 36,000, Joshi's monetary gain is

$$= 30000 \times \frac{40}{100} = Rs\ 12,000$$

$\therefore$ Option (c) is correct.

Option (d): If Joshi sold the shop to Wadhwa at 40% profit, then Wadhwa's cost price = Rs.42,000

Wadhwa sells it back to Joshi at a loss of 40% i.e., at a price

$$= 42000 \times \left(1 - \frac{40}{100}\right)$$

$$= Rs.\ 25,200.$$

As Joshi had a monetary gain of Rs. 12,000 in selling the same shop to Wadhwa earlier, his net investment in taking the shop back = 25200 − 12000 = Rs.13,200

$\Rightarrow$ Option (d) is correct.

Hence, all the 4 options are correct.

11. Let the production cost be Rs.100

Contribution of A = Rs.10

Contribution of B = Rs.20

Selling price = Rs.120

Now, cost of A = Rs.12

and cost of B = Rs.28

Hence, the new production cost = Rs.110 (since cost of other components are fixed)

New selling price = 1.15 × 120 = Rs.138

$\therefore$ Profit percentage $= \frac{28}{110} \times 100 \approx 25.5\%.$

12. Let total profit be x.

Shyam gets 0.2x for managing the business Remaining 0.8x is divided among Shyam, Gopal and Madhur in the ratio 2 : 4 : 3 respectively.

Out of this, share of Shyam $= \frac{2}{9} \times 0.8x = \frac{1.6}{9}x$

and share of Gopal $= \frac{4}{9} \times 0.8x = \frac{3.2x}{9}$

and share of Madhur $= \frac{3}{9} \times 0.8x = \frac{2.4x}{9}$

Share of Shyam from total profit $= 0.2x + \frac{1.6}{9}x = \frac{3.4}{9}x$

And shares of Gopal and Madhur $= \frac{3.2x}{9} + \frac{2.4x}{9} = \frac{5.6x}{9}$

$\therefore \frac{5.6x}{9} - \frac{3.4x}{9} = 2200 \Rightarrow x = 9000$

$\therefore$ Share of Madhur $= \frac{2.4}{9} \times 9000 = Rs.2400.$

13. 10% of Rs. 4,50,000 i.e. Rs. 45,000 will be given to Sujoy for his efforts.

Remaining profit = Rs. 4,05,000

Ratio of sharing by Sujoy, Mritunjoy and Paranjoy

$$= 35,000 \times 12 : 1,30,000 \times 6 : 75,000 \times 8$$

$$= 7 : 13 : 10$$

Profit share of Paranjoy

$$= \frac{10}{30} \times 4,05,000 = Rs.1,35,000$$

14. Average price of 15 books $= \frac{4500}{14} = 300$

Let the average price of 13 books be Rs. x

According to the question,

$$\frac{300}{6} = \frac{x}{5} \text{ or } x = 250$$

Total price of 13 books = 250 × 13 = Rs. 3,250

Total price of two books = Rs. 1,250

Therefore, the two books cost Rs. 750 and Rs. 500.

15.

	Soap	Toothpaste
Total quantity	20	12
CP	x	0.6x
Total cost	20x	7.2x
Quantity sold at profit	75% of 20 = 15	8
Profit	15% of 15x = 2.25x	8 × 20 = 160
SP	17.25x	8×.06x = 4.8x + 160

Profit from selling these items = 2.25x + 160 = 385

$\Rightarrow \qquad x = 100$

Total CP = 20x + 7.2x = 2720

Total SP = 17.25x + 4.8x + 160 = 2365

Hence, total loss = 2720 − 2365 = Rs.355.

16. Let the amount paid for first service be ₹ 100

Amount paid for second service = 90

Discount offered for third service = $\dfrac{90 \times 11}{100} = 9.9$

Amount paid for third service = $90 - 9.9 = 80.1$

Amount paid for fourth service = $80.1 - 80.1 \times \dfrac{12}{100}$

$$= 70.49$$

Amount paid for fifth service = ₹ 55

Total amount paid for five services

$$= 100 + 90 + 80.1 + 70.49 + 55$$
$$= 395.59$$

Total discount offered = $500 - 395.56$

$$= 104.41$$

Total amount that need to be paid without discount

$$= ₹\ 500$$

Percentage discount = $\dfrac{104.41}{500} \times 100 = 20.88\%$

17. Let the minimum number of Pages to be printed be x.

Total Cost in inkjet Printer = $5000 + 1.80x$

Total Cost in Laser Printer = $8000 + 1.50x$

According to the questions;

$$5000 + 1.80x > 8000 + 1.50x$$
$$\Rightarrow \qquad x > 10000$$

Hence, required answer = 10000.

18. Total savings in first 3 months

$$= 3000 \times \dfrac{10}{100} \times 3 = 900.$$

According to the questions;

$$350 + 400 + 450 + \ldots\ldots + n \text{ terms}$$
$$= 11400 - 900 = 10500$$
$$\Rightarrow \dfrac{n}{2}\big[700 + (n-1)50\big] = 10500$$
$$\Rightarrow \qquad n = 15$$

Total required time = $3 + 15 = 18$ months.

19. Let total Sales be ₹ x.

$$x - \left[100000 \times \dfrac{6}{100} + (x - 100000) \times \dfrac{5}{100}\right] = 2,65,000$$

$$\Rightarrow x - \left[6000 + \dfrac{x}{20} - 5000\right] = 265000$$

$$\Rightarrow x - \dfrac{x}{20} = 266000$$

$$\therefore x = \dfrac{266000 \times 20}{19} = ₹\ 2,80,000.$$

20. Let SP of each article be Rs. 100

Thus, $CP_1 = \dfrac{100}{87} \times 100 = 115, CP_2 = \dfrac{100}{123} \times 100 = 81.3$

$CP_3 = \dfrac{100}{74} \times 100 = 135.1$

Hence, total CP = 331.4.

Percentage by which CP is lower/higher than SP

$$= \dfrac{331.4 - 300}{300} \times 100 = 10.5\% \text{ higher.}$$

21. Let x be 7a and y be 4a.

According to the question,

$$\dfrac{49a^2 - 16a^2}{49a^2 + 16a^2} = \dfrac{33}{65}.$$

22. Let the cost of gift be Rs. x.

According to the question,

$$\dfrac{90 + x}{65 + x} = \dfrac{12}{9} \text{ or } x = 10$$

Therefore, cost of gift is Rs. 10.

23. Let the total number of journalist be 90x.

Number of male journalist = 50x

Number of female journalist = 40x

Number of journalist covering political news

$$= 0.3 \times 50x + 0.4 \times 40x = 31x$$

Number of journalist covering sports news

$$= 90x - 31x = 59x$$

Required percentage

$$= \dfrac{59}{90} \times 100 \approx 65.5\%.$$

24. Let A's share, B's share, C's share and D's share be A, B, C and D respectively.

$$\dfrac{A}{B} = \dfrac{B}{C} = \dfrac{C}{D} = \dfrac{3}{4}$$

$$\Rightarrow A : B : C : D = 27 : 36 : 48 : 64$$

$$\therefore \quad \text{The C's share} = \dfrac{1400 \times 48}{27 + 36 + 48 + 64}$$

$$= \dfrac{48 \times 1400}{175}$$

$$= \text{Rs. } 384.$$

25. Ten years ago, let the age of Ravindra be 5x years and the age of Rekha be 4x years.

At present:

The age of Ravindra = $(5x + 10)$ years

The age of Rekha = $(4x + 10)$ years

$$\therefore (5x + 10) = \dfrac{7}{6}(4x + 10) \Rightarrow x = 5$$

The the presemt age of each child belonging to triplets, that of to twins and that of the sixt child be A, B and C respectively.

Present age of parents and six children

$$= (25 + 10) + (20 + 10) + 3A + 2B + C$$
$$= 35 + 30 + 9A' + 6B' + C'$$

In order to maximise the maximise the total age of family, the value of A, B and C have to be 9, 6, 3 years respectively.

$$\text{Total age} = 35 + 30 + 9 \times 3 + 6 \times 2 + 3 \times 1$$
$$= 65 + 27 + 12 + 3$$
$$= 107 \text{ years.}$$

26. Go through options:-

    only option (a) justifies she given condition.

27. Decrease of 12% in ACNI I

    Increase of 9% in ACN II

    Final Increase of 3% in all

    Using Alligation:

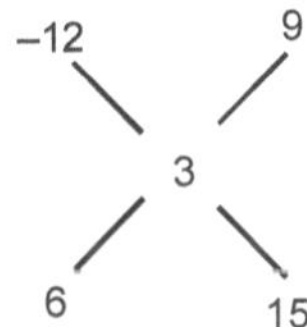

    Ratio becomes 2 : 5

28. When a constant value is added to all the numbers of a set, then there is no effect on standard deviation. But, if we multiply all the terms by any constant factor standard deviation of the resulting numbers also get, multiplied by that factor.

    Hence, by increasing the salary by 20%, standard deviation will also increase by 20%.

    Therefore, the new standard deviation will be $1.2 \times 400 = 480$.

29. Four monthly consignments received by Philips DVD player are at the purchase price of Rs. 2750, Rs. 2500, Rs. 2400 and Rs. 2250. The corresponding rate of decrease in purchase are 8.33%, 9.09%, 4% and 6.25%.

    Now, the required average rate of decrease

    $$= \frac{8.33 + 9.09 + 4 + 6.25}{4} = 6.94\%$$

    ***There is ambiguity in the language of the question. The options suggest that the question should be: "The average of rates of decrease in the purchase price of DVD player during these four months is".**

30. Let the number of Professors, Associate Professors and Assistant Professors be a, b and c respectively. Let their average ages be x, y and z years respectively.

    Given, $ax + by + cz = 2160 = 36(a + b + c)$

    $$\frac{ax + by}{a+b} = 39; \quad \frac{by + cz}{b+c} = \frac{360}{11}; \quad \frac{cz + ax}{c+a} = \frac{110}{3}$$

    Also, $a(x + 1) + b(y + 6) + c(z + 7)$
    $$= 41(a + b + c) = 2460$$

    Solving these equations, we get

    $a = 16$, $b = 24$, $c = 20$ and $x = 45$, $y = 35$, $z = 30$.

    Alternate Method:

    The best way to do this question is by using the options. Option B and C doesnot give the sum of the ages of all faculty positions as 2160. Option A satisfies all other conditions.

31. Let the age (in years) of Amita and Sumita be x and y respectively.

    According to the question,

    $$\frac{x - 2}{5} = \frac{y - 2}{4} \text{ or } 5y - 4x = 2 \qquad \ldots (i)$$

    Also, $\dfrac{x - 2 + y - 2}{2} = 27$ or $x + y = 58 \qquad \ldots (ii)$

    From equations (i) and (ii), we get $x = 32$ and $y = 26$

    Let the age of Paramita be p years, therefore,

    $$\frac{32 + 26 + p}{3} = 24 \text{ or } p = 14$$

    Required average $= \dfrac{35 + 17}{2} = 26$ years

32. Let the fixed cost (in Rs.) F and variable cost per student(in Rs.) be V.

    $$F + 20V = 20 \times 400$$
    $$F + 30V = 30 \times 300$$
    $$\Rightarrow \qquad V = 200 \text{ and } F = 4000.$$

    When there are 80 students, total expense
    $$= \text{Rs.}20,000$$

    $\therefore$ Average expense per student = Rs.250.

33. The average of 7 consecutive numbers will be the 4th number in the sequence.

    Let the 4th number be x.

    When the next 3 numbers are also added, the average will be the mean of the 5th and the 6th of the sequence,

    $$\therefore \quad \frac{(x + 1) + (x + 2)}{2} = \frac{2x + 3}{2} = x + 1.5$$

    Hence, the average shall increase by 1.5.

34. Let farmer A has 'x' hectare land.

$\therefore$ Total production of A = 20x

Farmer B has x + 7 hectare land

$\therefore$ Total production of B = (x + 15) × 30

Given that (x + 15) × 30 − 20x = 530

$\Rightarrow$ 30x + 450 − 20x = 530

$\Rightarrow$ 10x = 80

$\Rightarrow$ x = 8.

$\therefore$ Production of farmer

$$A = 20x$$
$$= 20 × 8$$
$$= 160 \text{ bushels.}$$

35. Let the amount given to younger son be Rs. x and the amount given to older son be Rs.(18750 − x). The younger son turns 30, after 20 years and the older turns 30 after 17 years. As each of them will receive the same amount, we must have:

$$x\left(1+\frac{3}{100}\right)^{20} = (18750 - x)\left(1+\frac{3}{100}\right)^{17}$$

$\Rightarrow$ $x(1.03)^3 = (18750 - x)$

$\Rightarrow$ $1.092727x = 18750 - x$

$\Rightarrow$ $2.092727\,x = 18750$

$\Rightarrow$ x = Rs. 8959.60 is the share of the younger son.

Hence, (A) is the correct option.

36. The present value of the pension is the principal amount of money which after interests for different time intervals, will sum up to make 20 installments of Rs.1800 each, which is Pawan's pension. So the present value of pension is equal to

$$\frac{1800}{1.03}+\frac{1800}{(1.03)^2}+...+\frac{1800}{(1.03)^{20}}$$

$$= 1800 \times \frac{1}{1.03} \frac{\left[1-\dfrac{1}{(1.03)^{20}}\right]}{1-\dfrac{1}{1.03}}$$

$$= \frac{1800}{0.03}\left[1-0.55362\right] = 26782.80$$

Hence, (d) is the correct option.

37. Raveendra was allotted 650 shares with face value of Rs.10 per share. So, the value of investment = Rs.6500.

In year 2007, since the bonus is at the rate of 3:13. So for 650 shares, the bonus shares will be 150, making the total number of share equal to 800.

Similarly, for the year 2008, the total number of shares become 1200.

$\therefore$ Dividend in 2007 $= \dfrac{1}{8}\times10\times1200$

$\therefore$ Required percentage $= \dfrac{\dfrac{1}{8}\times10\times1200}{6500} = \dfrac{3}{13} \approx 23\%$

38. Let the interest rates charged by the first money lender and the second money lender (r + 10)% and r% respectively.

According to the question,

$$30000\left(1+\frac{r+10}{100}\right)^2 = 30000\left(1+\frac{r}{100}\right)^2 + 7500$$

On solving the above equation, we get r = 20%

Also, let Rs. x be the amount borrowed from the first lender.

Therefore,

$$x\left(1+\frac{30}{100}\right)^2 = (60000 - x)\left(1+\frac{20}{100}\right)^2 + 38800$$

On solving, we get, x = Rs.40,000.

39. The distribution of savings (in Rs.) made by Animesh and Aniket is as follows:

Savings Type	Share Market	PPF	NSC
Animesh	-	90,000	60,000
Aniket	70,000	30,000	50,000

Required difference is Rs. 10,000.

40. Let the production in 2008 be x.

$\therefore$ The production in 2012

$$= x × 1.18 × 1.18 × 0.88 × 1.18 \approx 1.45x$$

Hence, the approximate effect on cement production in 2012 will be 45% (increase).

41. The average percentage return

$$= \frac{3518}{25000} \times 100 = 14.072$$

The percentage return from deposit in Scheme X

$$= 6 + 6 + \frac{6^2}{100} = 12.36$$

The percentage return from deposit in Scheme Y

$$= 8 + 8 + \frac{8^2}{100} = 16.64$$

Using alligation,

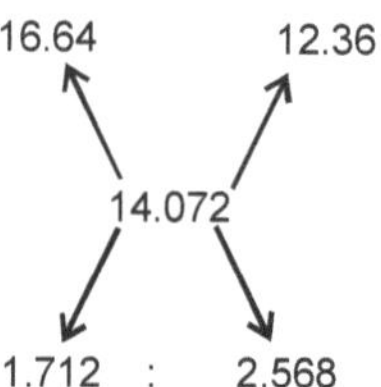

$\Rightarrow$ 2 : 3

Hence, the amount invested $= \dfrac{3}{5}\times 25000 = $ Rs.15000.

42. The total amount of money spent in buying flat, car and hares

$$= \text{Rs. } 70 \text{ lakhs}$$

Money invested in bank = Rs. 30 lakhs

Total amount withdrawn from the bank after 3 years

$$= 3000000\left(1+\frac{12}{100}\right)^3 = 3000000\left(\frac{28}{25}\right)^3$$

$$= \text{Rs. } 4214784$$

Let the present net value of flat, car and shares be Rs. x.

The increase in the value of assets is 5%.

$$\therefore 4214784 + x = \frac{105}{100} \times 10000000$$

$$\Rightarrow \qquad x = 6285216$$

$$\Rightarrow \text{ The required percentage} = \frac{6285216}{7000000} = 89.8$$

$$= 90 \text{ (approx.)}.$$

43. The investment will become double in 72/6 = 12 years. As the return compounds annually, the amount will getting doubled in every 12 years. Therefore, in 48 years, it will become 16 times i.e. 16 × 3000000 i.e. 48000000.

44. Let T be The Same Time Period

As per the question

$$10\% \times T = 8\%\left[T + \frac{1}{2}\right]$$

$$10\,T = 8\left[\frac{2T+1}{2}\right]$$

$$10T = 8T + 4$$

$$10T - 8T = 4$$

$$T = \frac{4}{2} = 2 \text{ years}$$

As he cleared the first loan 6 months before the period. So time = 2.5 years

$$\text{Also} \Rightarrow \frac{62100}{1.2} = \frac{621000}{12} = \text{Rs. } 51750$$

Hence option c.

45. We have 5% of total z = 10000

$$\therefore \qquad \text{total of z} = \text{Rs. } 200000$$

$$\therefore \qquad \text{total of y} = \text{Rs. } 400000$$

Let the funds of y is 'a'

$$\therefore \qquad 1.1a = 100000$$

$$\Rightarrow \qquad a = \text{Rs. } 363636$$

$$\therefore \quad \text{Contribution of y} = 5\% \text{ of } 363636$$

$$= \text{Rs. } 18181 \approx \text{Rs. } 18000$$

46. Initial mixture = 40 kg

S and (S): Cement (C) = is 1 : 4

$$\Rightarrow \qquad S \text{ (by weight)} = \frac{1}{5} \times 40 = 8 \text{ kg}$$

$$\text{and C (by weight)} = \frac{4}{5} \times 40 = 32 \text{ kg}$$

Let he mixes x kg of sand to the 40 kg mixture. Then,

$$\frac{8+x}{40+x} = \frac{3}{7} \Rightarrow x = 16 \text{ kg}$$

$$\Rightarrow \quad \text{He mixed 16 kg of sand to the 40 kg mixture.}$$

Option (a): Weight of second mixture = 40 + 16 = 56 kg which is $\frac{56}{40} = 1.4$ times heavier and not 1.5 times.

Hence, (a) is incorrect.

Option (b): Correct. x = 16 kg, as solved above.

Option (c): If the original mixture was in 8 : 3 ratio, then weight of sand would have been

$$\frac{3}{8+3} \times 40 = 10.9 \text{ kg} \neq 12 \text{ kg}$$

Hence, (c) is incorrect.

Option (d): The mixture weighs 56 kg. After selling 7 kg of it, he is left with 49 kg of the mixture. In 11 kg of new mixture (7 : 4 ratio),

$$\text{Sand is } \frac{4}{7+4} \times 11 = 4 \text{ kg}$$

$$\text{and Cement is } \frac{7}{7+4} \times 11 = 7 \text{ kg}$$

In the final mixture,

$$\text{Cement} = \frac{4}{7} \times (49) + 7 = 28 + 7 = 35 \text{ kg}$$

$$\text{Sand } \frac{3}{7} \times (49) + 4 = 25 \text{ kg}$$

$$\text{Cement : Sand ratio} = \frac{35}{25} = \frac{7}{5}$$

$$\therefore \quad \text{(d) it is correct.}$$

Hence, options (b) and (d) are correct.

47. The problem statement misses the word "*per*".

The last sentence should have had "*....mixture at Rs. 40 per kg ...*"

$$\text{Cost price of the mixture} = \frac{40}{1.25} = \text{Rs. } 32/\text{kg}$$

Let the required ratio be x : y.

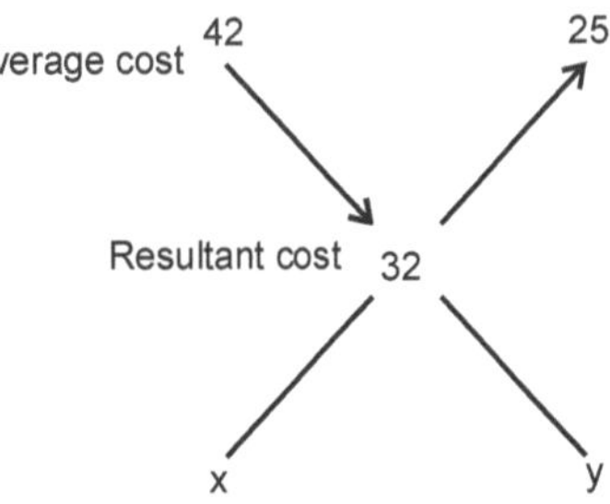

Now applying alligation, we have

$$\frac{42-32}{32-25} = \frac{y}{x} \Rightarrow \frac{x}{y} = \frac{7}{10} = \frac{x}{25} \Rightarrow x = \frac{35}{2}$$

48. Fraction of 'metal 1' in Alloy A = $\dfrac{3}{7}$

Fraction of 'metal 1' in Alloy B = $\dfrac{5}{13}$

Quantity of 'Metal 1' in mixture of Alloy A and B

$$= 14 \times \dfrac{3}{7} + 26 \times \dfrac{5}{13} = 16 \text{ kg}$$

Required ratio $= \dfrac{16}{40-16} = \dfrac{2}{3}$ i.e. $2:3$.

49. Let the quantity removed from the vessel be 'a' litres.

$$\dfrac{10}{100} = \dfrac{15}{100}\left(1-\dfrac{a}{10}\right)^2$$

$$\Rightarrow \dfrac{2}{3} = \left(1-\dfrac{a}{10}\right)^2$$

$$\Rightarrow \quad a = 2 \text{ litres.}$$

50. Let the percentage of Aluminium in alloy of weight 8 and 16 kg be 'a' and 'b' respectively, the weight of the piece cut be 'x' kg and the percentage of Aluminium in the resulting alloy (in both cases) be 'm'.

$$\therefore \dfrac{ax + b(16 - x)}{x + 16 - x} = m \qquad \qquad \ldots(i)$$

and $\dfrac{bx + a(8 - x)}{x + 8 - x} = m \qquad \qquad \ldots(ii)$

From (i) & (ii), we get,

$$ax + b(16 - x) = 2[bx + a(8 - x)]$$

$$\Rightarrow \qquad 3ax - 3bx = 16a - 16b$$

$$\Rightarrow x = \dfrac{16(a-b)}{3(a-b)} = \dfrac{16}{3} = 5.33.$$

51. Alloy X contains:

Zn = 16 grams

Cu = 24 grams

Alloy Y 60 contains:

Zn = 70/3 gram

Cu = 110/3 gram

Alloy Z contains:

Zn = $16 + \dfrac{70}{3} = \dfrac{118}{3}$ gram

Cu = $24 + \dfrac{110}{3} = \dfrac{182}{3}$ gram

Hence, the required ratio = $59 : 91$.

52. By using the concept of replacement continuously, the required quantity of milk comes out to be

$$40\left(1-\dfrac{10}{40}\right)^5 = \dfrac{405}{128} \text{ litres.}$$

53. Let the total quantity of Alloy P be 20 gm and that of alloy Q be 90 gm.

Quaintly of Silver in New Alloy

$$= \dfrac{45}{100} \times 20 + \dfrac{30}{100} \times 90 = 36 \text{ gm}$$

Percentage of silver in new Alloy

$$= \dfrac{36}{110} \times 100 \approx 33\%$$

Percentage of Copper in new Alloy

$$= \dfrac{32.5}{110} \times 100 \approx 29\%$$

54. A.T.Q.

$$0.05x + 0.10y \geq 7 \Rightarrow 5x + 10y \geq 700$$

$$0.1x + 0.06y \geq 7 \Rightarrow 10x + 6y \geq 700$$

By solving $x = 40$, $y = 50$ [As for minimum]

Now total cost $= 10.5x + 7.8y$

$$= 10.5 \times 40 + 7.8 \times 50$$

$$= \text{Rs. } 810$$

Hence option (a).

55. We have

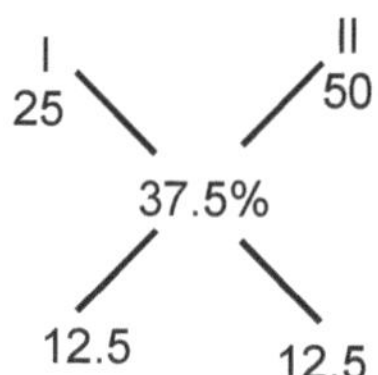

$\therefore$ 6 litres each of both juices should be mixed

56. Laxman takes the first train which is the slower one. Bharat takes the faster train. Let the trains be A and B respectively. Speed of the faster train, B is V_B

$$= \dfrac{180 \text{ km}}{3 \text{ hr}} = 60 \text{ km/hr.}$$

Since, train A takes double time, $V_A = 30 \text{ km/hr}$.

Speed of the train B, w.r.t. Laxman (when he is sitting in the train A) is $(60 - 30) = 30$ km/hr.

Laxman observes the train B that passes by him in 12 seconds. If L_B was the length of the faster train, then

$$30 \text{ km/hr} = \dfrac{L_B}{12 \text{ seconds}}$$

$$\Rightarrow L_B = 30 \times \dfrac{5}{18} \times 12 = 100 \text{m}$$

Option (a): $30 \text{ km/hr} = \dfrac{L_A + L_B}{30 \text{ seconds}}$

$\{L_A = \text{Length of the slower train}\}$

$$\Rightarrow L_A + L_B = 30 \times \dfrac{5}{18} \times 30 = 250 \text{m}$$

$$\Rightarrow L_A = (250 - 100) \text{m}$$

$$\therefore \quad L_A = 150 \text{ m}$$

So $L_A - L_B = 50$ m. Option (A) is correct.

Option (b): If $V_B = 60 \times 2 = 120$ km/hr

$V_A = 30$ km/hr, as before.

To overtake train A, train B has to cover its length, L_A. As we cannot determine the length of the slower train, we cannot find the time taken to overtake. Hence, option (b) is not correct.

Option (c): $V_A = 30$ km/hr

$V_B = 60$ km/hr

$$30\,\text{km/hr} = \frac{L_A + L_B}{24}$$

$$\Rightarrow L_A + (100) = 30 \times \frac{5}{18} \times 24$$

$$\therefore \quad L_A = 200 - 100 = 100 \text{ m.}$$

Option (c) is correct.

Option (d): $V_A = 30 \times \frac{3}{2} = 45$ km/hr and $V_B = 60$ km/hr

$$\Rightarrow 15\,\text{km/hr} = \frac{L_B}{t} = \frac{100}{t}\,\text{m}$$

$$\Rightarrow \quad t = 24 \text{ seconds.}$$

Hence, option (d) is correct.

57. The two trains start simultaneously. Let they meet after time 't'.

The train that has covered 60 km more must be the faster of the two. Hence,

$$60 = (21 - 16) \times t$$

$$\Rightarrow \qquad t = 12 \text{ hours.}$$

Since they are traveling towards each other, total distance is the sum of the distances travelled by the two trains individually.

$$\text{Total distance} = 16 \times 12 + 21 \times 12 = 444 \text{ km}$$

Hence, (b) is the correct option.

58. Let B = speed of boat in still water and

R = speed of stream.

Then as per the question,

$$\frac{30}{B-R} + \frac{44}{B+R} = 10 \qquad\qquad \text{...(i)}$$

$$\frac{40}{B-R} + \frac{55}{B+R} = 13 \qquad\qquad \text{...(ii)}$$

Equation (i) x 4 – Equation (ii) x 3

$$\frac{120}{B-R} + \frac{176}{B+R} - \frac{120}{B-R} - \frac{165}{B+R} = (40 - 39)$$

$$\Rightarrow \frac{176}{B+R} - \frac{165}{B+R} = 1$$

$$\Rightarrow (B + R) = 11$$

Similarly, $(B - R) = 5$

Solving these two equations, we get B = 8 km/hr.

59. According to the question, Sunil's time to cover a round is 2 min and the speed keeps getting halved after completion of each round while Anil maintains his initial speed and the time taken by him 1 min.

Till 6th round, Sunil's time to cover a round = 2^6

During 7th and 8th round, time taken by Sunil will be 2^7 and 2^8 minutes

Since Anil maintains his speed and time as 1 minute, so they will meet $(128 + 256) - 2 = 382$ times between the 6th round and 9th round.

Note: Subtraction of 2 indicates the exclusion of 6th and 9th round.

Hence, option (c) is the correct choice.

60. Let A be the initial point of observation of the captain of warship and D and C be the initial and final positions of the submarine.

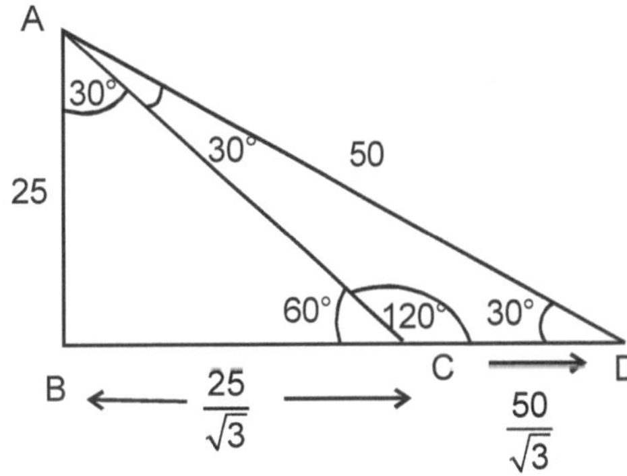

In $\triangle ACD$, applying the sine rule, we have

$$\frac{CD}{\sin 30°} = \frac{50}{\sin 120°}$$

$$\therefore CD = \frac{50}{\sqrt{3}}$$

Now since $\angle ADC = \angle CAD$,

$$AC = CD = \frac{50}{\sqrt{3}}\,\text{km.}$$

Hence, option (a) is the correct choice.

61. As per the condition given in the question, we can draw the following figure.

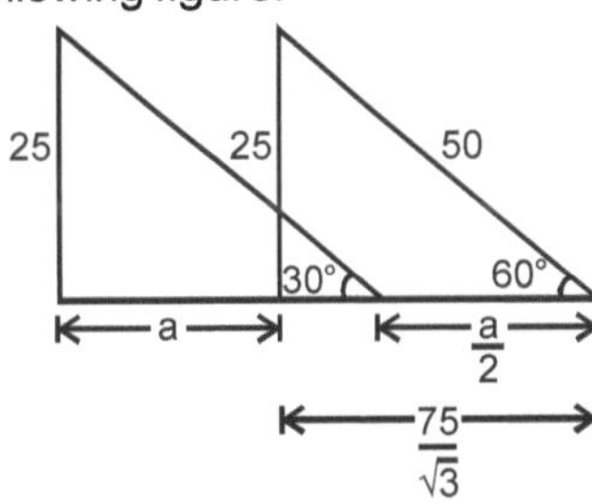

Here, $25\cot 60° = \dfrac{75}{\sqrt{3}} - \dfrac{a}{2}$

$$\frac{25}{\sqrt{3}} = \frac{75}{\sqrt{3}} - \frac{a}{2} \Rightarrow a = \frac{100}{\sqrt{3}}$$

$\therefore$ Required speed of the warship $= \dfrac{200}{\sqrt{3}}$ km/hr.

62. Speed of Sukriti $= \dfrac{1000}{350}$ m/sec

Distance to be covered = 5000 m

Time taken by Sukriti $= \dfrac{5000 \times 350}{1000} = 1750$ sec

Distance covered by Saloni in the same time $= \dfrac{1000}{364} \times 1750$

$\therefore$ The distance by which Sukriti will win

$$5000 - \dfrac{1000}{364} \times 1750 \approx 200 \text{ m}$$

Hence, the correct option is (b).

63.

```
        B       A
|-------|-------|-------|
Delhi                 Mathura
  <------ 300 kms ------>
```

To minimize the distance they will follow the following strategy.

Two of them (let's say Mukesh and Suresh) will start on bike and Dinesh will start walking. Suresh will get down at point A and start walking towards Mathura, whereas the other person will come back on bike to pick Dinesh from B and will turn back so that they all reach Mathura at same time.

Dinesh travelled 300 kms, partly on bike and partly walking, whereas Suresh also did the same, both of them taking the same time. Hence, their walking stretches should be of equal length i.e. Delhi to B = A to Mathura = x (say)

$\therefore$ Delhi To A + AB = 4x

(speed of bike is 4 times walking speed)

$\therefore$ $AB = \dfrac{4 \times -x}{2} = 1.5x$

$x + 1.5x + x = 300$

$\Rightarrow 3.5x = 300$ kms

$\therefore$ Total time taken $= \dfrac{x}{15} + \dfrac{2.5x}{60}$

$$= \dfrac{300}{3.5 \times 15} + \dfrac{2.5 \times 300}{3.5 \times 60} = 9\dfrac{2}{7} \text{ hours.}$$

64. Distance between sea beach and gate of ruins = 1000 m

By the time Jagdeep covered 1000 m, Mandeep had covered 940 m.

Let the speed (in m/s) of Jagdeep and Mandeep be 50x and 47x.

Let the time taken by Jagdeep be 't' sec.

According to the question,

$\dfrac{47x}{50x} = \dfrac{t}{t+12}$ or $t = 47 \times 4$ sec.

Speed of Jagdeep $= \dfrac{1000}{47 \times 4} = \dfrac{250}{47}$ m/s

Therefore, time taken by Jagdeep to cover 250 m

$$= 47 \text{ sec.}$$

65. Let the length of one train be 'l' metre.

Therefore, length of the other train = 2l meters.

When both the train are crossing each other, their relative

speed $= 60 + 48 = 108$ km/hr

As per the given information,

$$(2l + l) = 108 \times \dfrac{5}{18} \times 15 \Rightarrow l = 150 \text{ m}$$

Since the train having length 300 m crosses the bridge in 51 seconds, total distance traveled by it in 51 seconds = 850 m.

Hence, length of the bridge = 850 – 300 = 550 m.

66. Let the number of bogies be x.

Since $\sqrt{9} \propto 15$

Then $\dfrac{3}{\sqrt{x}} = \dfrac{15}{45} \Rightarrow x = 81$

When 81 bogies are attached, speed will be reduced by 45 km/hr. Hence, maximum of 80 boggies can be attached.

67. Let the distance (in km) of Rohit's home from the doctor's chamber be x.

Total time (in hours) taken by Rohit to take his mother from home to doctor's chamber $= \dfrac{x}{30}$

Total time (in hours) taken by Rohit to take his mother from doctor's chamber to home $= \dfrac{x}{12}$

Total time taken in travelling

$$= \dfrac{x}{12} + \dfrac{x}{30} = \dfrac{7x}{60} \text{ hours} = 7x \text{ minutes}$$

According to the question,

$$7x = 5 \times 60 - 48$$
$$\Rightarrow \qquad 7x = 252$$
$$\Rightarrow \qquad x = 36.$$

68. By the time the crew came to know about the hole, the boat has travelled 27 km (at the rate of 18 km/hr as the current of water is 2km/hr). Now the boat has to travel 73 km towards Vivekanand rock and then100 km back to KanyaKumari in 4 ½ hours.

Let the speeds(in km/hr) of boat towards Vivekanandrock and that of towards kanyakumari be x and y respectively.

$$\dfrac{73}{x-2} + \dfrac{100}{y+2} = 4\dfrac{1}{2}$$

Among the given options, option C satisfies the above equation.

69. Let the speed of bus in morning shift be 1 km/hr and time taken be 1 hour.

Distance covered in morning shift = 1 × 1 = 1 km

Speed of bus in the evening shift = $1 \times \dfrac{3}{2} = \dfrac{3}{2}$ km/hr

Time taken in the evening shift = $1 \times \dfrac{3}{2} = \dfrac{3}{2}$ km/hr

Distance covered in evening shift = $\dfrac{3}{2} \times \dfrac{3}{2} = \dfrac{9}{4}$ km

Average speed for the entire journey

$$= \dfrac{1 + \dfrac{9}{4}}{1 + \dfrac{3}{2}} = \dfrac{13}{4} \times \dfrac{2}{5} = \dfrac{13}{10} \text{ km/hr.}$$

Required percentage = $\dfrac{\dfrac{13}{10} - 1}{1} \times 100 = 30\%.$

70. Taking the first term (a) to be 280 $\left(350 \times \dfrac{4}{5}\right)$ and applying the formula for infinite G.P.

$$\Rightarrow \quad \dfrac{a}{1-r} = \dfrac{280}{1 - \dfrac{4}{5}} = 1400 \text{ m.}$$

Now since the ball travels any distance twice, up and down, we take $2 \times (1400) = 2800$ m.

Hence, total distance will be 2800 + 350 (as the ball was thrown from a height of 350 m initially and only this distance is covered once) = 3150 m.

71.

Delhi d A   B $\dfrac{d}{2}$ Noida

Let the distance between Delhi and Noida be x km.

Let they first meet at point A after one hour.

Distance covered by Shruti = $(2x - d)$ km

Distance covered by Krishna = d km

∴ Ratio of speeds of Shrutit and Krishna

$$= 2x - d : d \qquad \ldots(i)$$

Let they meet next at B after half an hour. As Krishna covered distance 'd' in one hour, so he will cover distance $\dfrac{d}{2}$ in half an hour.

∴ AB = $\dfrac{d}{2}$

Distance covered by Shruti in second meeting

$$= x - d + \left(x - \dfrac{3d}{2}\right) = 2x - \dfrac{5d}{2}$$

∴ Ratio of speeds of Shruti and Krishna is

$$2x - \dfrac{5d}{2} : \dfrac{d}{2} \qquad \ldots(ii)$$

Now Krishna covered distance 'd' in one hour, so he will cover distance x in 2 hours.

72.

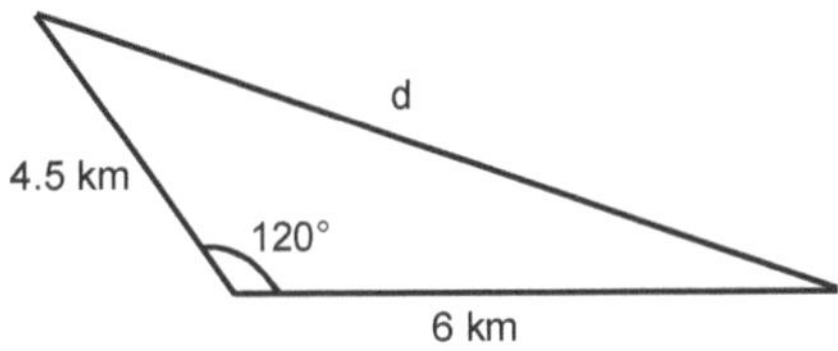

Distance covered by Sohan = $4 \times \dfrac{3}{2} = 6$ km

Distance covered by Ramesh = $3 \times \dfrac{3}{2} = 4.5$ km

A.T. Cosine formula

$$\cos 120° = \dfrac{(4.5)^2 + 6^2 - d^2}{2 \times 4.5 \times 6}$$

$$-\dfrac{1}{2} = \dfrac{20.25 + 36 - d^2}{54} \Rightarrow d = \sqrt{83.25} = 9.12 \text{ km}$$

Hence option (c)

73. So $\qquad \pi x - 2x = 40$

$$x\left(\dfrac{22}{7} - 2\right) = 40$$

$$x = 35$$

Diameter = 35 × 2 = 70

74. 20 men can complete a work in 10 days

∴ 10 men can complete the work in 20 days

Similarly, 10 women can complete the work in 30 days.

⇒ 10 men + 10 women can complete the work in

$$\dfrac{1}{\dfrac{1}{30} + \dfrac{1}{20}} = 12 \text{ days.}$$

Option (a): Total wages for men = 12 × 50 × 10 = Rs.6,000

Total wages for women = 12 × 10 × 45 = Rs.5,400

∴ Total wages bill = Rs.11,400

Hence, option (a) is correct.

Option (b): Total wages for men = 12 × 10 × 45 = Rs.5,400

Total wages for women = 12 × 10 × 40 = Rs.4,800

∴ Total wages bill = Rs.10,200

Hence, option (b) is correct.

Option (c): Total wages for men = 12 × 10 × 40 = Rs.800

Total wage for women = 12 × 10 × 40 = Rs.4,800

∴ Total wages bill = Rs.9,600

Hence, option (c) is incorrect.

Option (d): If 20 men and 30 women are employed then, together they will finish the work in

$$\dfrac{1}{\dfrac{1}{10} + \dfrac{1}{10}} = 5 \text{ days.}$$

Total wages for men = 5 × 20 × 40 = Rs.4,000

Total wages for women = 5 × 30 × 35 = Rs.5,250

∴ Total wages bill = Rs.9,250

Hence, option (d) is correct.

75. After 6 hours, part of the tank filled by the three pipes

$$= \frac{6}{12} + \frac{4}{18} - \frac{6}{36} = \frac{1}{2} + \frac{2}{9} - \frac{1}{6} = \frac{9+4-3}{18} = \frac{10}{18} = \frac{5}{9}$$

Remaining part $= 1 - \frac{5}{9} = \frac{4}{9}$

This part is to be filled by A and B together. Further, A and B together can fill in one hour

$$= \left(\frac{1}{12} + \frac{1}{18}\right) \text{part} = \frac{5}{36}^{th} \text{ part.}$$

$\therefore \frac{4}{9}^{th}$ part will be filled by A and B together in time $= 3\frac{1}{5}$ h.

$\therefore$ Total time required = 6h + 3h + 12 min

$$= 9 \text{ hrs and 12 min.}$$

Hence, option (b) is correct.

76. From the given data, we can write that the total work is equivalent to (24 × 16) Man-Days which in turn is equivalent to (32 × 24) Woman-Days.

Hence, 1 Man-Day is equivalent to 2 Woman-Days.

Let x be the number of additional men required for the last two days' work.

Total work ≡ 24 × 16

≡ (16 Men + 16 Women) × 12-Days

$\qquad$ + (16 Men + 16 Women) × 2-Days

$\equiv \left(16 \text{ Men} + \frac{16}{2} \text{ Men}\right) × 12\text{-Days} + \{(16 + x) \text{ Men}$

$$+ \frac{16}{2} \text{ Men)} \} × 2\text{-Days}$$

Therefore, 24 × 16 = 24 × 12 + (24 + x) × 2

$\Rightarrow$ x = 24.

Hence, (b) is the correct option.

77. Aditya, Vedus and Yuvraj alone can do a job in 6 weeks, 9 weeks and 12 weeks respectively.

Work done for 2 weeks $= \frac{2}{6} + \frac{2}{9} + \frac{2}{12} = \frac{13}{18}$

Now, Work left $= \frac{5}{18}$

Let y weeks more is required to complete the job.

So we can write, $\frac{y-1}{9} + \frac{y}{12} = \frac{5}{18}$

$\Rightarrow$ y = 2 weeks

$\therefore$ Required weeks = 2 + 2 = 4 weeks.

Therefore, the job would be completed in 4 weeks.

Hence, option (a) is the correct choice.

78. P1 → 8 hr; P2 → + 12 hrs; P3 = –8 hrs

P1 and P2 can fill the tank in

$\frac{8-12}{8+12} = \frac{24}{5} = 4.8$ hr.

So timer is to start after 2.4 hrs.

When P3 is opened then P1 and P2 together become

ineffective. P2 can fill the whole tank in 12 hr, so half will be fixed in 6 hr. He was supposed to comes after 2.4 + 6 = 8.4 hr.

But the P3 opens when the tank was $\frac{1}{3}$rd full.

i.e., in the 1.6 hr. Now P2 is supposed to fill $\frac{2}{3}$rd of tank in 8 hrs. But the supervisor will come after 8.4 – 1. 6 = 6.8 hr. So 1.2 hr of work remains incomplete. Therefore, 10% of the tank is empty if the supervisor comes back as per the plan.

79. Let efficiency of Gupta, Sharma and Singh are x, y, z respectively and the time taken by them be t_g, t_s and t_h respectively.

x = 1.4y, y = 1.2z

$$t_s - t_g = 10 \Rightarrow \frac{W}{y} - \frac{W}{1.4y} = 10 \Rightarrow \frac{W}{y} = 35 = t_s.$$

$\Rightarrow$ t_g = 35 – 10 = 25 days

and t_h = 35 × 1.2 = 42 days

$$\frac{W}{25} × 10 + \frac{W}{35} × 15 + \frac{W}{42} × t'_h = W$$

$$\frac{t'_h}{42} = 1 - \left(\frac{2}{5} + \frac{3}{7}\right) = 1 - \left(\frac{14+15}{35}\right) = \frac{6}{35}$$

$$\Rightarrow t'_h = \frac{6}{35} × 42 = 7.2 \text{ days}$$

80. Let the work done by 3 pipes per hour be T_A, T_B and T_C.

$$T_A = \frac{1}{5}, \ T_B = \frac{1}{10}, \ T_C = \frac{1}{15}$$

For 1st hour,

$$= \frac{3}{4}\left[\frac{1}{5} + \frac{1}{10}\right] + \frac{2}{3} × \frac{1}{15} = \frac{3}{4} × \frac{3}{10} + \frac{2}{45} = \frac{9}{40} + \frac{2}{45} = \frac{97}{360}$$

For 2nd hour $= \frac{1}{5} + \frac{1}{10} + \frac{2}{3} × \frac{1}{15} = \frac{3}{10} + \frac{2}{45} = \frac{31}{90}$

For 3rd hour $= \frac{1}{5} + \frac{1}{10} + \frac{1}{15} = \frac{11}{30}$

$\therefore$ Work left $= 1 - \left(\frac{97}{360} + \frac{31}{90} + \frac{11}{30}\right) = \frac{7}{360}$

It can be completed in another $\dfrac{\frac{7}{360}}{\frac{11}{30}} = 0.05$ hours

$\therefore$ Total time = 3 + 0.05 = 3.05 hours.

81. Let the amount of work done by a man and a boy in an hour be 'm' units and '$\frac{m}{2}$' units respectively.

Let the number of boys who joins 21 men be 'x'.

$$\left(21m + x × \frac{m}{2}\right) × 50 × 9 = 2 × \left(12m + \frac{18m}{2}\right) × 60 × 7.5$$

$\Rightarrow$ x = 42.

82. Let the total work be 5x units.

Work completed in 30 days = 2x units

Let the number of men working for next 26 days be 'n'.

According to the question,

$$\frac{104 \times 8 \times 30}{2x} = \frac{n \times 9 \times 26}{3x} \text{ or } n = 160$$

Number of additional men required = $160 - 104 = 56$.

83. Let the total work be 240 units

Work done by a man in one day = 2 units

Work done by a woman in one day = 1 unit

Total work done in 9 days = $9 \times (2 \times 8 + 1 \times 4) = 180$ units.

Remaining 60 units will be done in $= \left(\frac{60}{16+14}\right)$ i.e. 2 days

84. Let the time (in hours) taken to complete cooking by the mother alone be A, that by the elder son be B, and that by the younger son be C.

Cooking together, they can complete cooking in 1 hour.

$$\therefore \frac{1}{A} + \frac{1}{B} + \frac{1}{C} = 1 \qquad \qquad ...(i)$$

Also, $\dfrac{1}{C} + \dfrac{1}{B} + \dfrac{3}{C} = 1$

$$\Rightarrow \frac{4}{C} + \frac{1}{B} = 1$$

$$\Rightarrow \frac{4}{C} + \frac{1}{B} = \left(\frac{1}{A} + \frac{1}{B} + \frac{1}{C}\right)$$

$$\rightarrow \frac{3}{C} = \frac{1}{A} \rightarrow \frac{1}{C} = \frac{1}{3A} \qquad \qquad ...(ii)$$

The time taken by elder son to complete cooking is 1 hour more than the mother.

$$\therefore \quad B = A + 1$$

$$\Rightarrow \quad \frac{1}{B} = \frac{1}{A+1} \qquad \qquad ...(iii)$$

Putting the values of $\dfrac{1}{B}$ and $\dfrac{1}{C}$ in equation (i), we get

$$\frac{1}{A} + \frac{1}{A+1} + \frac{1}{3A} = 1 \Rightarrow A = 2$$

Hence the total work done by the mother in 1 hour is 50%.

85. Let x be the amount of work done by tap X in 1 hour and y be the amount of work done by tap Y in 1 hour.

$$\therefore \frac{y}{x} = \frac{8}{5}$$

The part of the tank filled by both of tanks in 1 hour

$$= \frac{1}{40}$$

$$\therefore x + \frac{8x}{5} = \frac{1}{40}$$

$$\Rightarrow x = \frac{5}{520} \Rightarrow y = \frac{8}{5} \times \frac{5}{520} = \frac{1}{65}$$

$\therefore$ The total time taken by Y alone to fill the tank

$$= 65 \text{ hours.}$$

86. From the information given in the question, it can be noted that nth of the sequence is the sum of the first n terms.

$$\therefore T_n = \frac{n(n+1)}{2}$$

$$\therefore S_n = \sum T_n = \frac{1}{2}\sum N^2 + \frac{1}{2}\sum N = \frac{n(n+1)(2n+1)}{12} + \frac{n(n+1)}{4}$$

Putting n = 20, we get

$$S_n = 1540$$

An MBA students is twice as efficient as an Engeneering student.

Hence, the required number of days $= \dfrac{1540}{2 \times 11} = 70.$

87. Let the total work be 1 unit and number of inlet pipes and outlet pipes be x and y respectively.

Work done by an inlet pipe in an hour $= \dfrac{1}{7}$ unit

Work done by an outlet pipe in an hour $= -\dfrac{1}{5}$ unit

When all the pipes are kept open, then work done in

1 hour $= -\dfrac{1}{7}$ unit

According to the question: $x \times \dfrac{1}{7} - y \times \dfrac{1}{5} = \dfrac{-1}{7}$

After solving,

we get $\qquad \qquad x = 6$

and $\qquad \qquad y = 5.$

Hence, the number of inlet pipes = 6.

88. Let P can do 10 units in a day.

So, total work = $42 \times 10 = 420$ units

Work done by Q in a day = 12.6 units

Work done by R in a day = $12.6 \times \dfrac{3}{2} = 18.9$

Required number of days

$$= \frac{420}{12.6 + 18.9} = \frac{420 \times 2}{63} = 13 \text{ days.}$$

89. If I do 2 units per day, my roommate will do 1 unit per day.

Together we do 3 units per day.

Now, I will take 45 days for 90 units and my roommate will take 90 days for the same.

90. Time taken by Somesh, Tarun and Nihkil is 45, 60 and 75 days respectively. Let Tarun completes the work in x days. Then according to question Somesh completed in (x – 2) days & Nikhil in 5 days.

So eq. is $\dfrac{x-2}{45} + \dfrac{x}{60} + \dfrac{5}{75} = 1$

On solving above eq. x = $25\dfrac{1}{7}$ days.

Hence option (a).

91. Let the second borewell B taken x hours

∴ The first borewell A will take x + 10 hours and the third C will take x − 8 horus

It is given that the first two borewells A and B takes same time as the third C

$$\therefore \frac{1}{x+10} + \frac{1}{x} = \frac{1}{x-8} \Rightarrow \frac{x+x+10}{x^2+10x} = \frac{1}{x-8}$$

$\Rightarrow$ (2x + 10)(x − 8) = x² + 10x

$\Rightarrow$ 2x² − 6x − 80 = x² + 10x

$\Rightarrow$ x² − 16x − 80 = 0

$\Rightarrow$ (x − 20)(x + 4) = 0

$\Rightarrow$ x = 20

∴ The third borewell will take 20 − 8 = 12 hrs

92. Ram = 9 days   Ravi = 12 days

Ratan = 15 days   Let total work = 180 unit

Ram = 20 units / day Ravi = 15 units / day

Ratan = 12 units / day

They work alone for one day each. If they work in this way, Ravi will work alone for 4 days. Ravi will do 4 × 15 = 60 units.

$$\text{So } \frac{60}{180} = \frac{1}{3}$$

93. A = 12 hrs to fill; B = 18 hrs to fill; C = 36 hrs to empty

Total capacity = 180

A = 15 units /hr; B = 10 units/hr; C = -5 units/hr

Both A and C work for the first 6 hrs. B works only for 4 hrs in the first 6 hrs

A = 15 × 6 = 90; B = 10 × 4 = 40; C = - 5 × 6 = -30

90 + 40 − 30 = 100 units

Remaining 80 will be filled by A and B in $\frac{80}{25}$ hrs = 3hr 12 min.

So total hrs = 6 + 3hr 12 min = 9hr 12 min

94. The rise in food prices is double that of fuel prices and the rise in miscellaneous groups prices is double that of rent. Only option (B) satisfies the above criteria, Hence, it is correct.

95. Looking at the data, we can easily observe that if the wife's age is 23 years, then the age of the husband is likely to be in the range of 22 - 30 years. This doesn't satisfy options (a), (b) and (c).

96. As per the question, we can write here

S= 2000 + 2500 + ... + n

or $S = \frac{n}{2}\left[4000 + (n-1)500\right]$

For n = 12, S = 57000.

Therefore, 13 month onwards, Rashid would start borrowing.

Hence, option (d) is the correct choice.

97. When Writtik was born, age of Mrs. Gupta = 28 years

Therefore, when Pratik was born age of Mrs. Gupta = 26 years

(Since, Pratik is 2 years elder to Writtik)

When Kajol was born, age of Mr. Gupta = 30 years

Therefore, when Pratik was born, age of Mr. Gupta = 35 years

(Since, Pratik is 5 years younger to Kajol)

98. Let 'x' be the initial volume which is 400 litres and 'a' be the volume replaced.

After sixth operation, we have $= \left(\frac{x-a}{x}\right)^6 = \left(\frac{400-40}{400}\right)^6$

∴ The quantity of pure petrol received by seventh customer $= \left(\frac{400-40}{400}\right)^6 40 = \left(\frac{9}{10}\right)^6 40 = 21.25$

99. Amount receive by every department in

$$2011 = \frac{4.5 \times 10^7}{2 \times 10^2} = 2.25 \times 10^5$$

Amount receive by every department in

$$2012 = \frac{6 \times 10^7}{2 \times 10^2} = 3 \times 10^5$$

Therefore, each department has received, 7.5 × 10⁴ more as compared to last year

100. Let the age of Rohini's brother in 2004 be x years.

Age of Rohini in 2004 = 3x

In 2014; Rohini's age = 3x + 10

Rohini's brother's age = x + 10

According to the question;

3x + 10 = x + 10 + 6

$\Rightarrow$ x = 3 years.

In 2004, Rohini was 9 years old.

It means Rohini was born in the year 1995. i.e. (2004-9).

Triangle

2007-09

1. In the right-angled triangle QPR given below, PS is the altitude to the hypotenuse. The figure is followed by three possible inferences.

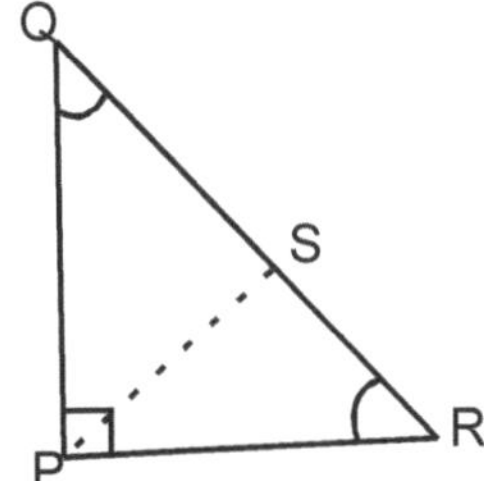

   I.   Triangle PQS and Triangle RPS are similar.

   II. Triangle PSQ and Triangle RSP are congruent.

   III. Triangle PSQ and Triangle RPQ are similar.

   Mark the correct option

   (a) I and II are correct
   (b) I and III are incorrect
   (c) Only III is correct
   (d) All three are correct

2009-11

2. A ladder 25 meters long is placed against a wall with its foot 7 meters away from the foot of the wall. How far should the foot be drawn out so that the top of the ladder may come down by half the distance of the total distance if the foot is drawn out?

   (a) 6 meters
   (b) 8 meters
   (c) 8.75 meters
   (d) None of the above

3. If D is the midpoint of side BC of a triangle ABC and AD is the perpendicular to AC then:

   (a) $3AC^2 = BC^2 - AB^2$
   (b) $3BC^2 = AC^2 - 3AB^2$
   (c) $BC^2 + AC^2 = 5AB^2$
   (d) None of the above

2011-13

4. The area of a triangle is 6, two of its vertices are (1,1) and (4,-1), the third vertex lies on y = x + 5. Find the third vertex.

   (a) $\left(\dfrac{2}{5}, \dfrac{27}{5}\right)$
   (b) $\left(-\dfrac{3}{5}, \dfrac{22}{5}\right)$
   (c) $\left(\dfrac{3}{5}, \dfrac{28}{3}\right)$
   (d) None of these

5. In a triangle ABC the length of side BC is 295. If the length of side AB is a perfect square, then the length of side AC is a power of 2, and the length of side AC is twice the length of side AB. Determine the perimeter of the triangle.

   (a) 343
   (b) 487
   (c) 1063
   (d) None of these

2013-15

6. The perimeter of a right-angled triangle measures 234 m and the hypotenuse measures 97 m. Then the other two sides of the triangle are measured as

   (a) 100m and 37m
   (b) 72m and 65m
   (c) 80m and 57m
   (d) None of the above

2014-16

7. There is a triangular building (ABC) located in the heart of Jaipur, the Pink City. The length of the one wall in east (BC)direction is 397 feet. If the length of south wall (AB)is perfect cube, the length of southwest wall (AC)is a power of three, and the length of side AB, determine the perimeter of this triangular building.

   (a) 3209 feet
   (b) 3213 feet
   (c) 3773 feet
   (d) 3313 feet

2019-21

8. In the triangle PQR, S is the midpoint of QR. X is any point on PR. T is the point on QR such that PT || SX. If the area of triangle PQR is 5.8 sq. cm, then the area of triangle RTX is

   (a) 2.9 sq. cm
   (b) 3.2 sq. cm
   (c) 5.8 sq. cm
   (d) 2.45 sq. cm

Quadrilaterals

2010-12

9. If there is threefold increase in all the sides of a cyclic quadrilateral, then the percentage increase in its area will be:

   (a) 81%
   (b) 9%
   (c) 900%
   (d) None of the above

2018-20

10. A rectangular plank $\sqrt{10}$ metre wide, is placed symmetrically along the diagonal of a square of side 10 metres as shown in the figure. The area of the plank is:

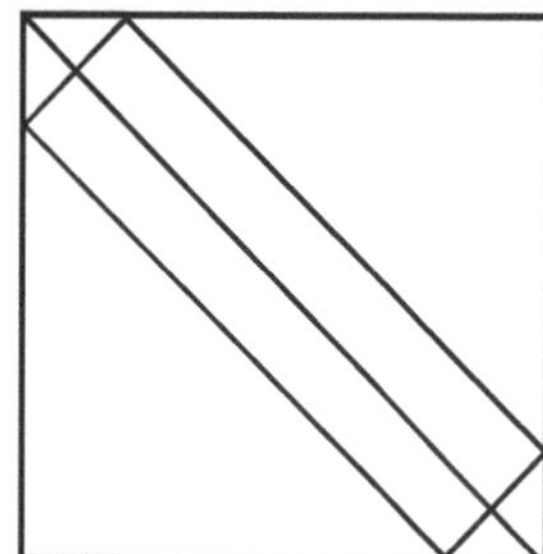

(a) $10\sqrt{20}$ 1 sq.mt.

(b) $10\sqrt{5}$ 1 sq.mt.

(c) $10\sqrt{20} - 1$ sq.mt.

(d) None

Polygons

2009-11

11. The interior angles of a polygon are in Arithmetic Progression. If the smallest angle is 120° and common difference is 5°, then number of sides in the polygon is:

(a) 7

(b) 8

(c) 9

(d) None of the above

2010-12

12. Mohan was playing with a square cardboard of side 2 metres. While playing, he sliced off the corners of the cardboard in such a manner that a figure having all its sides equal was generated. The area of this eight sided figure is:

(a) $\dfrac{4\sqrt{2}}{(\sqrt{2}+1)}$

(b) $\dfrac{4}{(\sqrt{2}+1)}$

(c) $\dfrac{2\sqrt{2}}{(\sqrt{2}+1)}$

(d) $\dfrac{8}{(\sqrt{2}+1)}$

13. Find the ratio of shaded area to unshaded area.

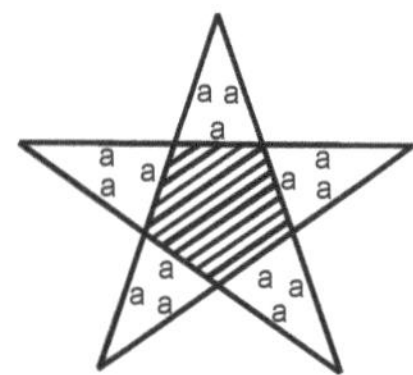

(a) $\dfrac{1}{5}(\sqrt{21}-2)$

(b) $\dfrac{1}{5}(3\sqrt{7}-2)$

(c) $\dfrac{1}{5}(3\sqrt{7}-2\sqrt{3})$

(d) None of the above

2011-13

14. In a square of side 2 meters, isosceles triangles of equal area are cut from the corners to form a regular octagon. Find the perimeter and area of the regular octagon.

(a) $\dfrac{16}{2+\sqrt{2}}$; $\dfrac{4\left(1+\sqrt{2}\right)}{3+2\sqrt{2}}$

(b) $\dfrac{8}{2+\sqrt{2}}$; $\dfrac{2\left(1+\sqrt{2}\right)}{3+2\sqrt{2}}$

(c) $\dfrac{16}{1+\sqrt{2}}$; $\dfrac{3\left(1+\sqrt{2}\right)}{3+2\sqrt{2}}$

(d) none of these

2015-17

15. ABCDEF is a regular hexagon and PQR is an equilateral triangle of side a. The area of the shaded portion is X and CD: PQ: 2:1. Find the area of the circle circumscribing the hexagon in terms of X.

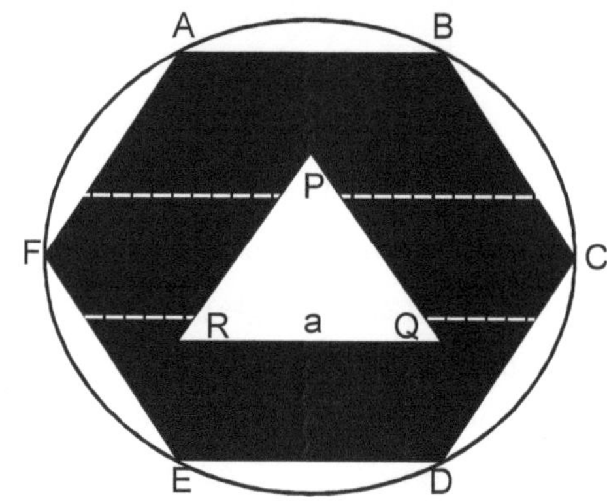

(a) $\dfrac{16\pi}{23\sqrt{3}}X$

(b) $\dfrac{42\pi}{5\sqrt{3}}X$

(c) $\dfrac{2\pi}{3\sqrt{3}}X$

(d) $2\sqrt{3}\pi X$

2017-19

16. Let PQRSTU be a regular hexagon. The ratio of the area of the triangle PRT to that of the hexagon PQRSTU is

(a) 0.3

(b) 0.5

(c) 1

(d) None of the above

2018-20

17. A pest control person uses a particular machine for his job, it moves along the circumference of a circular hall of radius 49 metres in 148 minutes to finish the pest control. How many minutes more will it take him to move along the perimeter of a hexagon of side 54 metres?

(a) 7.69 minutes

(c) 14.36 minutes

(c) 14.00 minutes

(d) 4.28 minutes

Circle

18. A spiral is made up of 13 successive semicircles, with center alternately at A and B, starting with center at (a) The radii of semicircles, thus developed, are 0.5 cm, 1.0 cm, 1.5 cm, and 2.0 cm and so on. The total length of the spiral is:

(a) 144 cm   (b) 143 cm

(c) 147 cm   (d) None of the above

19. A pole has to be erected on the boundary of a circular park of diameter 13 meters is such a way that the difference of its distances from two diametrically opposite fixed gates A and B on the boundary is 7 meters. The distance of the pole from one of the gates is:

(a) 8 meters   (b) 8.25 meters

(c) 5 meters   (d) None of the above

20. Let A_1 be a square whose side is 'a' metres. Circle C_1 circumscribes the square A_1 such that all its vertices are on C_1. Another square A_2 circumscribes C_1. Circle C_2 circumscribes A_2 and A_3 circumscribes C_2, and so on. If D_N is the area between the square A_N and the circle C_N, where N is a natural number, then the ratio of the sum of all D_N to D_1 is:

(a) 1   (b) $\dfrac{\pi}{2} - 1$

(c) Infinity   (d) None of the above

21. An arc AB of a circle subtends an angle 'x' radian at the center O of the circle. If the area of the sector AOB is equal to the square of the length of the arc AB, then x is:

(a) 0.5   (b) 1.0

(c) 0.75   (d) None of the above

22. What is the value of c^2 in the given figure, where the radius of the circle is 'a' unit.

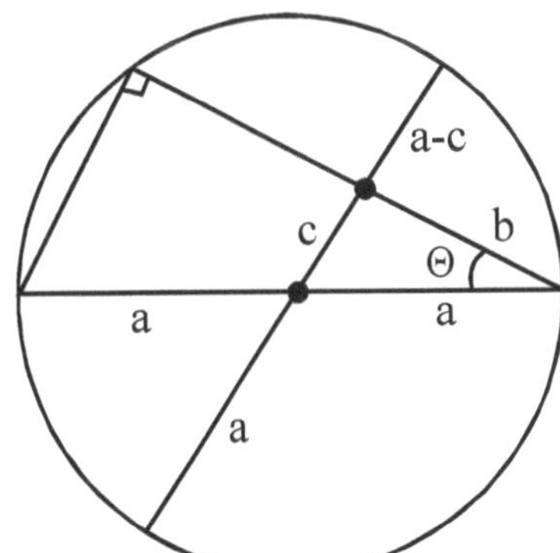

(a) $c^2 = a^2 + b^2 - 2ab\cos\theta$

(b) $c^2 = a^2 + b^2 - 2ab\sin\theta$

(c) $c^2 = a^2 - b^2 + 2ab\cos\theta$

(d) None of these

23. In a circle, the height of an arc is 21 cm and the diameter is 84 cm. Find the chord of 'half of the arc'.

(a) 45 cm

(b) 40 cm

(c) 42 cm

(d) None of the above

24. If in the figure below, angle XYZ = 90° and the length of the arc XZ = 10π, then the area of the sector XYZ is:

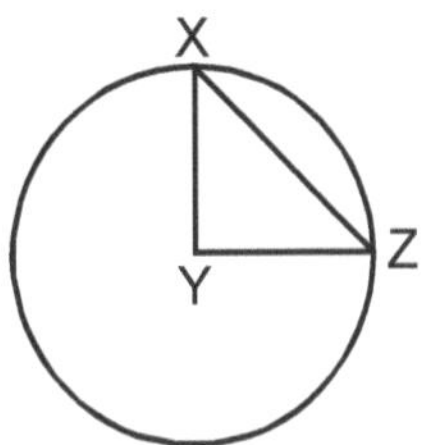

(a) 10π

(b) 25π

(c) 100π

(d) None of the above

25. A chord AB of length 24 cm is drawn in a circle of radius 13 cm. Find the area of the shaded portion AP(b)

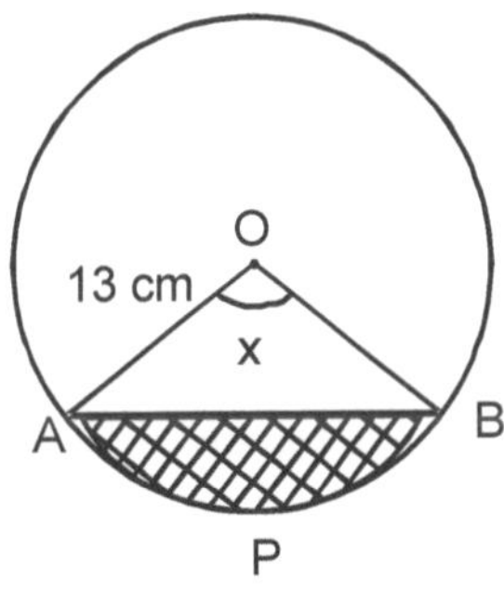

(a) $13\pi x$ cm^2

(b) $\dfrac{13\ x}{180}$ cm^2

(c) $\dfrac{169\ x}{360}\ 60$ cm^2

(d) $\dfrac{169\ x}{180}\ 60$ cm^2

26. Two tangents are drawn from a point P on the circle with centre at O, touching the circle at point Q and T respectively. Another tangent AB touches the circle at point S. If angle QPT = 55°, find the angle AOB = ?

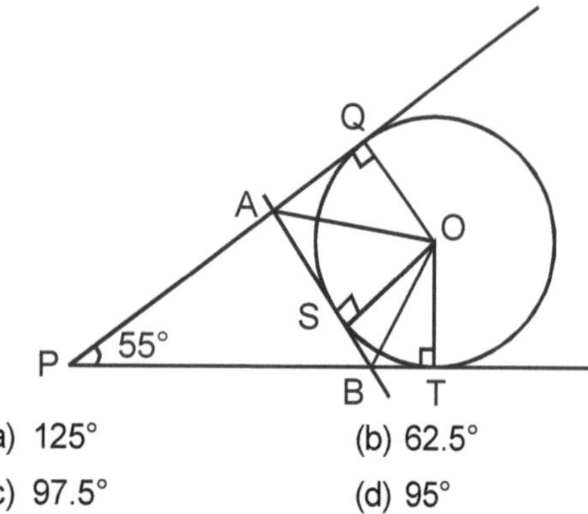

(a) 125°

(b) 62.5°

(c) 97.5°

(d) 95°

Mensuration

27. Madan is going from Mumbai to Delhi in order to join a new job there. He has a glass memento of right circular conic shape under his possession and he does not want it to break during transportation. So, he purchases a cubic metal box from the market spending Rs. 500. The cone is exactly fitted in the metal cube in such a way that while the edges of the base of the cone are touching the edges of all the sides of the cube, the vertex of it touches the opposite face of the cube. After inserting the memento in the box, he packed the metal box from outside with wallpaper costing Rs. 1.5 per sq cm. Given that the volume of the glass memento is $718\,\frac{2}{3}$ cc mark <u>all</u> the correct statements.

(a) Madan had incurred total expenditure of Rs. 2,264 on the metal box.

(b) Madan had incurred an expenditure of Rs. 1,754 on packing the metal box.

(c) The area of any one side of the metal box is 196 sq. cm

(d) The volume of the metal box is 2,644 cc.

28. A wire, if bent into a square, encloses an area of 484 cm². This wire is cut into two pieces; with the bigger piece having a length three-fourth of the original wire's length. Now, if a circle and a square are formed with the bigger and the smaller piece respectively, what should be the area enclosed by the two pieces?

(a) 464cm²

(b) 544.25 cm²

(c) 376.75 cm²

(d) 424.25cm²

29. A cylinder, a hemisphere and a cone stand on the same base and have the same heights. The ratio of the areas of their curved surface is:

(a) $2:2:1$

(b) $2:\sqrt{2}:1$

(c) $2:\sqrt{2}:1$

(d) None of the above

30. A right circular cone is enveloping a right circular cylinder such that the base of the cylinder rests on the base of the cone. If the radius and the height of the cone is 4 cm and 10 cm respectively, then the largest possible curved surface area of the cylinder of radius r is:

(a) $20\pi r^2$

(b) $5\pi r(4-r)$

(c) $5\pi r(r-4)$

(d) $5\pi r(2-r)$

31. Radius of a spherical balloon, of radii 30 cm, increases at the rate of 2 cm per second.

Then its curved surface area increases by:

(a) 120π

(b) 480π

(c) 600π

(d) None of the above

32. In a rocket shape firecracker, explosive powder is to be filled up inside the metallic enclosure. The metallic enclosure is made up of a cylindrical base and conical top with the base of radius 8 centimeter. The ratio of height of cylinder and cone is 5 : 3. A cylindrical hole is drilled through the metal solid with height one third the height of metal solid. What should be the radius of the hole, so that volume of the hole (in which gun powder is to be filled up) is half of the volume of metal solid after drilling?

(a) $4\sqrt{3}$ cm

(b) 4.0 cm

(c) 3.0 cm

(d) None of these

33. A rectangular piece of paper is 22 cm. long and 10 cm. wide. A cylinder is formed by rolling the paper along its length. Find the volume of the cylinder.

(a) 175 cm³

(b) 180 cm³

(c) 185 cm³

(d) None of the above

34. Consider the volumes of the following objects and arrange them in *decreasing* order:

   i. A parallelepiped of length 5 cm, breadth 3 cm and height 4 cm.

   ii. A cube of each side 4 cm.

   iii. A cylinder of radius 3 cm and length 3 cm.

   iv. A sphere of radius 3 cm.

   (a) iv, iii, ii, i   (b) iv, ii, iii, i

   (c) iv, iii, i, ii   (d) None of the above

35. In a circular field, there is a rectangular tank of length 130 m and breadth 110 m. If the area of the land portion of the field is 20350 m^2, then the radius of the field is

   (a) 85 m   (b) 95 m

   (c) 105 m   (d) 115 m

36. A hemispherical bowl is filled with hot water to the brim. The contents of the bowl are transferred into a cylindrical vessel whose radius is 50% more than its height. If diameter of the bowl is the same as that of the vessel, the volume of the hot water in the cylindrical vessel is

   (a) 60% of the cylindrical vessel

   (b) 80% of the cylindrical vessel

   (c) 100% of the cylindrical vessel

   (d) None of the above

37. Your friend's cap is in the shape of right circular cone of base radius 14 cm and height 26.5 cm. The approximate area of the sheet required to make 7 such caps is

   (a) 6750 sq cm   (b) 7280 sq cm

   (c) 8860 sq cm   (d) 9240 sq cm

38. In an engineering college there is a rectangular garden of dimensions 34 m by 21 m. Two mutually perpendicular walking corridors of 4 m width have been made in a central part and flowers have been grown in the rest of the garden.

   The area under the flowers is

   (a) 320 sq m   (b) 400 sq m

   (c) 510 sq m   (d) 630 sq m

39. A ladder just reaches a window that is 8 metres high above the ground on one side of street. Keeping one end of the ladder at the same place, the ladder is moved to the other side of the street so as to reach a 12 metre high window. If the ladder is 13 metres long, what is the width of the street?

   (a) 14.6 metres.   (b) 15.8 metres.

   (c) 15.2 metres.   (d) 15.5 metres.

40. A right circular cylinder has a radius of 6 and a height of 24. A rectangular solid with a square base and a height of 20, is placed in the cylinder such that each of the corners of the solid is tangent to the cylinder wall. If water is then poured into the cylinder such that it reaches the rim, the volume of water is:

   (a) 288(π - 5)   (b) 288(2π - 3)

   (c) 288 (3π - 5)   (d) None of the above

41. If a right circular cylinder of height 14 is inscribed in a sphere of radius 8, then the volume of the cylinder is:

   (a) 110   (b) 220

   (c) 440   (d) 660

42. A right circular cylinder has a height of 15 and a radius of 7. A rectangular solid with a height of 12 and a square base, is placed in the cylinder such that each of the corners of the solid is tangent to the cylinder wall. Liquid is then poured into the cylinder such that it reaches the rim. The volume of the liquid is

   (a) 147(5π − 8)   (b) 180(π − 5)

   (c) 49(5π − 24)   (d) 49(15π − 8)

43. A bucket contains 200cc of liquid. A solid ball is dropped in the bucket resulting in the rise of liquid level to 1.3 times of its original level. If the radius of the base of the bucket is 3 cm and the radius of the surface of the liquid level is 1cm more than the radius of the base of the bucket before the ball is dropped. Find the volume of the solid metal ball.

   (a) 68cc   (b) 80cc

   (c) 92cc   (d) Can't be determined

44. In the given figure, PA = QB and PRQ is the arc of the circle, centre of which is O such that angle POQ = 90°. If AB= 25 $\sqrt{2}$ cm and the perpendicular distance of AB from centre O is 30cm. Find the area of the shaded region?

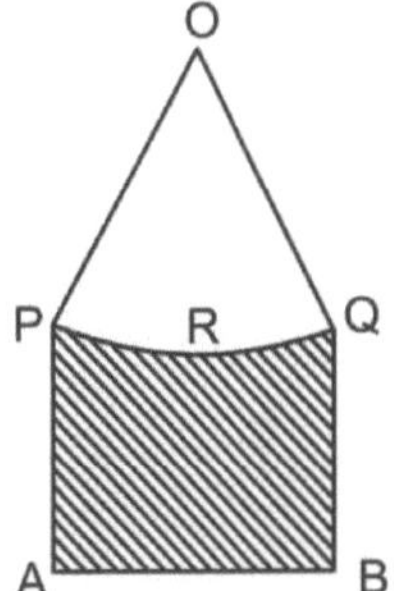

(a) $625\sqrt{2}$ sq. cm

(b) $625\left(\dfrac{1}{2}+\dfrac{\pi}{4}\right)$ sq. cm

(c) $750\sqrt{2}-625\left(\dfrac{1}{2}+\dfrac{\pi}{4}\right)$ sq.cm

(d) None

45. A metallic solid is made up of a solid cylindrical base with a solid cone on its top. The radius of the base of the cone is 5 cm. and the ratio of the height of the cylinder and the cone is 3 : 2. A cylindrical hole is drilled through the solid with height equal to 2/3rd of the height of solid. What should be the radius (in cm)of the hole so that the volume of the hole is 1/3rd of the volume of the metallic solid after drilling?

(a) $\sqrt{\dfrac{45}{8}}$ (b) $\sqrt{\dfrac{35}{8}}$

(c) $\sqrt{\dfrac{65}{8}}$ (d) $\sqrt{\dfrac{55}{8}}$

Co-ordinate Geometry

2007-09

46. Find the solution set of the shaded region in the diagram below

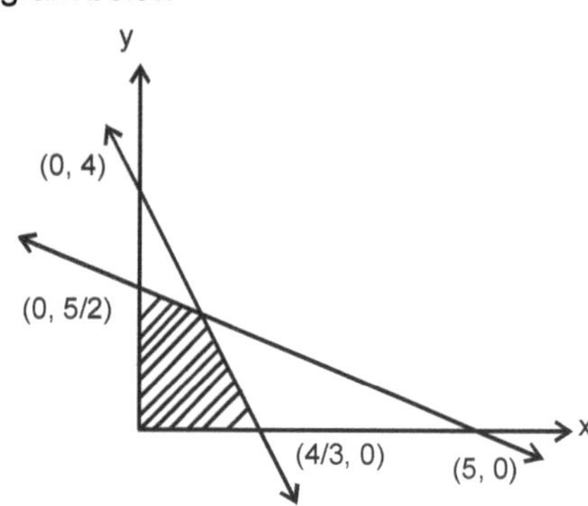

(a) $3x + y \le 4,\ x + 5y \le 5,\ x \ge 0,\ y \ge 0$

(b) $x + y \le 3,\ x + 4y \le 5,\ x \ge 0,\ y \ge 0$

(c) $3x + y \le 4,\ x + 2y \le 5,\ x \ge 0,\ y \ge 0$

(d) $3x + 2y \le 2,\ x + 2y \le 5,\ x \ge 0,\ y \ge 0$

2018-20

47. The coordinates of a triangle ABC are A(1, 5), B(-2, 3), and C(0,-4); find the equation of the median AD?

(a) $7x - 3y + 8 = 0$

(b) $5x - 4y + 15 = 0$

(c) $x + 3y - 16 = 0$

(d) $11x - 4y + 9 = 0$

Trigonometry

2007-09

48. Vijay has been invited for dinner in a club. While walking through the garden path towards the club, he observes that there is an electric rod on the top of the building. From the point where he is standing, the angles of elevation of the top of the electric rod and the top of the building are ϕ and θ respectively. If the heights of the electric rod and the building are p and q respectively, mark <u>all</u> the correct statements.

(a) The height of the tower is $\dfrac{p\tan\theta}{\tan\phi-\tan\theta}$

(b) The height of the electric rod is $\dfrac{q\tan\theta}{(\tan\theta-\tan\phi)}$

(c) The height of the tower is $\dfrac{p\tan\phi}{\tan\theta-\tan\phi}$

(d) The height of the electric rod is $\dfrac{q(\tan\phi-\tan\theta)}{\tan\theta}$

49. The area of an isosceles triangle is 12 sq. cm. If one of the equal sides is 5 cm long, mark <u>all</u> the options which can give the length of the base.

(a) 4 cm   (b) 6 cm

(c) 8 cm   (d) 9 cm

50. Ranjan goes to a countryside lake for a boat ride. Standing at the ferry counter, he looked at the opposite bank and observed a tall tower on a hill downstream, the angle of elevation being 45°. Ranjan comes to know from the bystanders that the tower is a historical ruin and decides to visit it. The boat takes him directly to the opposite bank, from where the angle of elevation to the top of the tower becomes 60°. While exploring the site, he comes to know that the combined height of the tower and the hill is 300 m. If the speed of the boat by which Ranjan travelled was 2 km/hr in still waters, mark <u>all</u> the correct observations.

(a) It took Ranjan $3\sqrt{6}$ minutes to cross the lake by the boat.

(b) The breadth of the lake is $100\sqrt{6}$ m.

(c) It took Ranjan $4\sqrt{3}$ minutes to cross the lake by the boat.

(d) If the combined height of the hill and the tower was 450 m and the speed of the boat was 1 km/hr (the angles of elevation remaining unchanged), the time taken by Ranjan to cross the lake by boat would have been $9\sqrt{6}$ minutes.

51. If $\sin\alpha + \sin\beta = a$, $\cos\alpha + \cos\beta = b$, $\tan\left(\dfrac{\alpha}{2}\right) * \tan\left(\dfrac{\beta}{2}\right) = c$, and $a \neq b \neq c \neq 0$, $c \neq 1$, $\dfrac{1-c}{1+c}$ is equal to

(a) $\dfrac{b}{a^2 + b^2}$

(b) $\dfrac{2a}{a^2 + b^2}$

(c) $\dfrac{2b}{a^2 + b^2}$

(d) $\dfrac{a}{a^2 + b^2}$

52. If $a \sin^{-1} x - b \cos^{-1} x = c$, then find the value of $\dfrac{a}{b} \sin^{-1} x + \dfrac{b}{a} \cos^{-1} x$ (Assume $-1 \leq x \leq 1$).

(a) 0

(b) $\dfrac{\pi}{4}$

(c) $\dfrac{\pi\, ab + 2c\,(a - b)}{2ab}$

(d) $\dfrac{\pi\, ab + 2c\,(b - a)}{2ab}$

53. If $\dfrac{2\sin\theta}{1 + \sin\theta + \cos\theta} = k$, then $\dfrac{1 - \cos\theta + \sin\theta}{1 + \sin\theta}$ is equal to

(a) k

(b) k + 1

(c) $\dfrac{1}{k}$

(d) None of the above

2008-10

54. If α, β, γ and δ be four angles of a cyclic quadrilateral, then the value of $\cos\alpha + \cos\beta + \cos\gamma + \cos\delta$ is:

(a) –1

(b) 0

(c) 1

(d) None of these

2009-11

55. $\mathrm{Cot}^{-1}\left[\dfrac{\sqrt{1 - \sin a} + \sqrt{1 + \sin a}}{\sqrt{1 - \sin a} - \sqrt{1 + \sin a}}\right] =$

(a) $2\pi - a$

(b) $\pi - \dfrac{1}{2}a$

(c) $\dfrac{1}{2}a - 3\pi$

(d) None of the above

56. If $\mathrm{Tan}\, x + \mathrm{Tan}\,(x + \dfrac{\pi}{3}) + \mathrm{Tan}\,(x + \dfrac{2\pi}{3}) = 3$ then which of the following is correct?

(a) Tan x = 1

(b) Tan 2x = 1

(c) Tan 3x = 1

(d) None of the above

2011-13

57. If each α, β, γ is a positive acute angle such that $\sin\,(\alpha + \beta - \gamma) = 1/\sqrt{2}$, $\mathrm{cosec}\,(\beta + \gamma - \alpha) = 2/\sqrt{3}$ and $\tan\,(\gamma + \alpha - \beta) = 1/\sqrt{3}$. What are the values of α, β, γ?

(a) $\left(37\dfrac{1}{2}, 52\dfrac{1}{2}, 45\right)$

(b) $(37, 53, 45)$

(c) $\left(45, 37\dfrac{1}{2}, 52\dfrac{1}{2}\right)$

(d) $\left(34, \dfrac{1}{2}, 55\dfrac{1}{2}, 45\right)$

58. The minimum value of $3^{\sin x} + 3^{\cos x}$ is

(a) 2

(b) $2\left(3^{-1/\sqrt{2}}\right)$

(c) $3^{1 - 1/\sqrt{2}}$

(d) None of these

2013-15

59. There are two buildings, one on each bank of a river, opposite to each other. From the top of one building – 60 m high, the angles of depression of the top and the foot of the other building are 30° and 60° respectively. What is the height of the other building?

(a) 30 m

(b) 18 m

(c) 40 m

(d) 20 m

2015-17

60. A boat is being rowed away in still water, from a 210 metres high cliff at the speed of 3 km/hr. What is the approximate time taken for the angle of depression of the cliff at the boat to change from 60 deg, to 45 deg?

(a) 5 min

(b) 4 min

(c) 1 min

(d) 2 min

2016-18

61. A ladder of 7.6 m long is standing against a wall and the difference between the wall and the base of the ladder is 6.4 m. If the top of the ladder now slips by 1.2 m, then the foot of the ladder shifts by approximately:

(a) 0.4 m

(b) 0.6 m

(c) 0.8 m

(d) 1.2 m

2018-20

62. A flag pole on the top of a mall building is 75 m high. The height of the mall building is 325 m. To an observer at a height of 400 m, the mall building and the pole subtend equal angle θ. If the horizontal distance of the observer from the pole is 'x', then what is the value of x?

(a) $20\sqrt{10}$ m

(b) $30\sqrt{10}$ m

(c) $25\sqrt{5}$ m

(d) None

2019-21

63. At the foot of the mountain, the angle of elevation of the summit at the top of the mountain is 45°. After ascending 100 metres, at a slope of 30° up the mountain towards the summit, the angle of elevation of the summit is 60°. Find the height of the summit.

(a) $50(\sqrt{3}+1)$ metres

(b) $50(\sqrt{5}+1)$ metres

(c) $50(\sqrt{3}+2)$ metres

(d) $50\sqrt{3}$ metres

ANSWERS

1. (b)	**2.** (b)	**3.** (a)	**4.** (a)	**5.** (c)	**6.** (b)	**7.** (*)	**8.** (a)	**9.** (d)	**10.** (a)
11. (c)	**12.** (d)	**13.** (*)	**14.** (d)	**15.** (a)	**16.** (b)	**17.** (a)	**18.** (b)	**19.** (c)	**20.** (c)
21. (a)	**22.** (a)	**23.** (c)	**24.** (c)	**25.** (c)	**26.** (b)	**27.** (a,c)	**28.** (c)	**29.** (d)	**30.** (b)
31. (b)	**32.** (a)	**33.** (a)	**34.** (a)	**35.** (c)	**36.** (c)	**37.** (d)	**38.** (c)	**39.** (c)	**40.** (c)
41. (d)	**42.** (a)	**43.** (b)	**44.** (c)	**45.** (d)	**46.** (c)	**47.** (d)	**48.** (a,d)	**49.** (b,c)	**50.** (a,b,d)
51. (c)	**52.** (c)	**53.** (a)	**54.** (b)	**55.** (b)	**56.** (c)	**57.** (a)	**58.** (b)	**59.** (c)	**60.** (d)
61. (b)	**62.** (b)	**63.** (a)							

EXPLANATIONS

1. 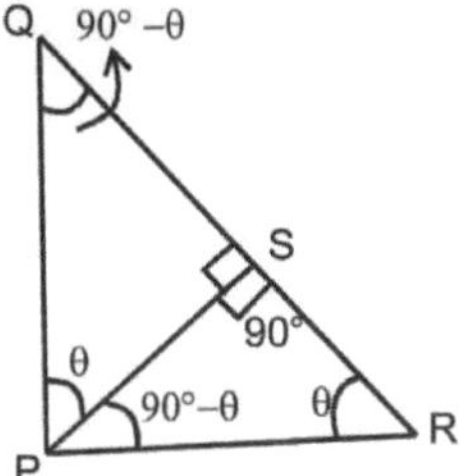

Statement I: In $\triangle PQS$,

$\angle P = \theta$, $\angle Q = 90° - \theta$, and $\angle S = 90°$

In $\triangle RPS$, $\angle R = \theta$, $\angle P = 90° - \theta$ and $\angle S = 90°$

Since all the corresponding angles are equal,

$\therefore \triangle PQS \sim \triangle RPS$.

Hence, statement I is correct.

Statement II: In $\triangle PSQ$, $\angle P = \theta$, $\angle S = 90°$ and $\angle Q = 90° - \theta$

In $\triangle RSP$, $\angle R = \theta$, $\angle S = 90°$ and $\angle P = 90° - \theta$

$\Rightarrow \triangle PSQ \sim \triangle RSP$

But, $\triangle PSQ \not\cong \triangle RSP$ (not necessary)

Hence, statement II is incorrect.

Statement III:

In $\triangle PSQ$, $\angle P = \theta$, $\angle S = 90°$ and $\angle Q = 90° - \theta$

In $\triangle RPQ$, $\angle R = \theta$, $\angle P = 90°$ and $\angle Q = 90° - \theta$

$\therefore \triangle PSQ \sim \triangle RPQ$

Hence, statement III is correct.

Hence, statements I and III are correct.

***Option (b) in the given question has been mistyped. It should be 'I and II are correct'.**

2. Initial position of the ladder: If x is the height at which top of the ladder is above the ground.

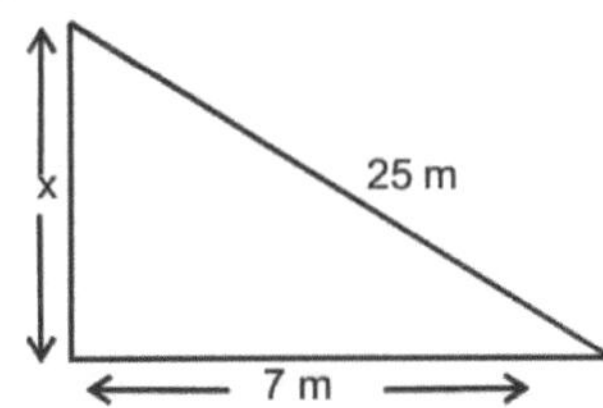

$\Rightarrow x = \sqrt{25^2 - 7^2} = 24$ meters

Final position of the ladder: Let ladder moves away y meters from the wall.

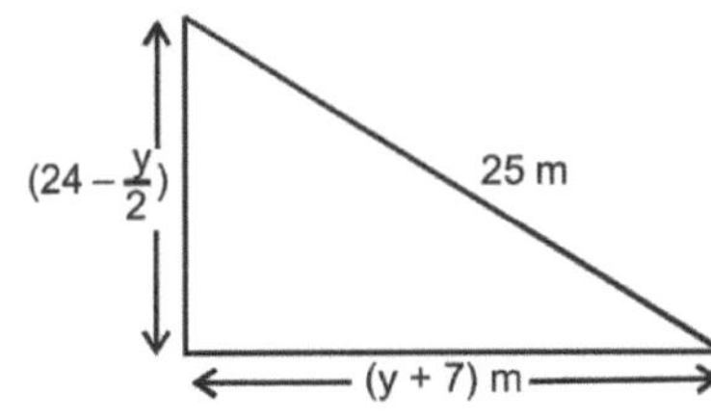

$(25)^2 = (y + 7)^2 + \left(24 - \dfrac{y}{2}\right)^2$

$\Rightarrow y = 8$ meters

3. As per the data given in the question, following figure can be drawn:

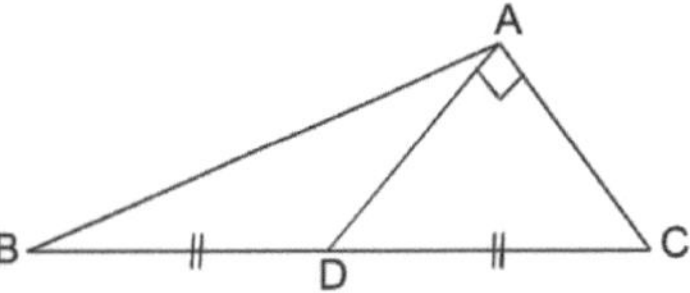

Using Pythagoras Theorem, we get

$AD^2 + AC^2 = CD^2$ ...(i)

Using Apollonius Theorem, we get

$AB^2 + AC^2 = 2AD^2 + 2CD^2$ ...(ii)

$\Rightarrow AB^2 + AC^2 = 2AD^2 + \dfrac{BC^2}{2}$

$\Rightarrow AB^2 + AC^2 = 2(CD^2 - AC^2) + \dfrac{BC^2}{2}$

$\Rightarrow AB^2 + AC^2 = 2\left(\dfrac{BC^2}{4} - AC^2\right) + \dfrac{BC^2}{2}$

$\Rightarrow 3AC^2 = BC^2 - AB^2$

4. Let the third vertix be $(x_1, x_1 + 5)$

$$\text{Area of triangle} = 6 = \frac{1}{2}\begin{Vmatrix} 1 & 1 & 1 \\ 4 & -1 & 1 \\ x_1 & x_1 + 5 & 1 \end{Vmatrix} = \frac{1}{2}$$

$\Rightarrow \dfrac{1}{2}|5x_1 + 10| = 6$

$\Rightarrow |5x_1 + 10| = 6 \times 2 \Rightarrow 5x_1 + 10 = \pm 12$

$\Rightarrow 5x_1 = +2, -22$

$\Rightarrow x_1 = \dfrac{+2}{5}, \dfrac{-22}{5}$

$\therefore y = x_1 + 5 = \dfrac{27}{5}, \dfrac{3}{5}$

$\therefore$ The coordinates of the point could be

$\left(\dfrac{2}{5}, \dfrac{27}{5}\right), \left(\dfrac{-22}{5}, \dfrac{3}{5}\right)$

5. Let $AC = 2^x$, where x is any natural number.

$\therefore AB = \dfrac{1}{2} AC = 2^{x-1}$; but AB is a perfect square

$\Rightarrow x - 1$ is even $\Rightarrow x$ is odd.

Sum of two sides of a $\triangle$ is greater than the third side

$\Rightarrow AB + AC > BC$

$\Rightarrow 3AB > 295$

$\Rightarrow AB > 98.33$

$\Rightarrow 2^{x-1} > 98.33$ ...(i)

Also, $AC - AB < BC$

$\Rightarrow 2^x - 2^{x-1} < 295$

$\Rightarrow 2^{x-1} < 295$ ...(ii)

The only satisfying value for equations (i) and (ii) is $x = 9$

$\therefore AB = 2^8 = 256$ and $AC = 2^9 = 512$

$\therefore$ Perimeter $= 256 + 512 + 295 = 1063$.

6. Given hypotenuse = 97 m

$\therefore$ Sum of other two sides of the right angled triangle
= 234 − 97 = 137 m

Let a be the one of the other two sides,

$a^2 + (137 − a)^2 = 97^2$

$\Rightarrow 2a^2 − 274a + 9360 = 0$

$\Rightarrow a^2 − 137a + 4680 = 0$

$\Rightarrow a = \dfrac{137 \pm \sqrt{(137)^2 − 4 \times 4680}}{2 \times 1}$

$\Rightarrow a = \dfrac{137 \pm \sqrt{49}}{2}$

$\Rightarrow a = \dfrac{137 \pm 7}{2} \Rightarrow a = 65,\ 72$

Hence, the other two sides are 65 m and 72 m.

7. Data inconsistent

8. The area of triangle RTX is 2.9 sq cm

9. Area of a cyclic quadrilateral is given as

$$A = \sqrt{(s − a)(s − b)(s − c)(s − d)}\,,$$

where 's' is the semi-perimeter and a, b, c and d are the sides of a quadrilateral. Now if there is threefold increase in all the sides, we have A' = 9A.

$\therefore$ Percentage increase = 800%.

Hence, option (d) is the correct choice.

10. Width of bank = $\sqrt{10}$ m

Side of the sq. = 10

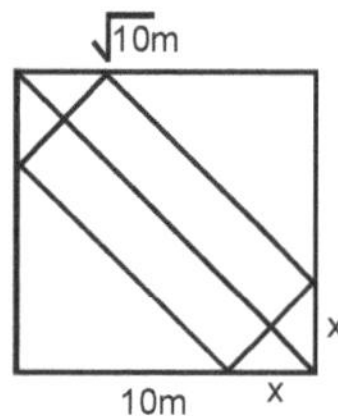

From above diagram

$x^2 + x^2 = \left(\sqrt{10}\right)^2$

$2x^2 = 10$

$x = \sqrt{5}$

Area of sq. = 10 × 10 = 100 m²

Area of the blank = $100 − \left[\left(10 − \sqrt{5}\right)^2 \dfrac{1}{2} \times 2 + \dfrac{1}{2}\left(\sqrt{5}\right)^2 \times 2\right]$

$= 100 − \left\{105 − 20\sqrt{5} + 5\right\}$

$= 100 − \left[110 − 20\sqrt{5}\right]$

$= 20\sqrt{5} − 10 = 10\left(2\sqrt{5} − 1\right)$

$= 10\left(\sqrt{20} − 1\right)$

Hence option (a).

11. We know:

(I) Sum of any interior and exterior angles of a polygon is always 180°.

(II) Sum of all the exterior angles of a polygon is 360°.

If the smallest interior angle is 120°, then largest exterior angle = 60°.

$\Rightarrow$ Second largest exterior angle = 55°

$\Rightarrow$ (60° + 55° + 50° +...+ n terms) = 360°

$\Rightarrow$ n = 9.

12.

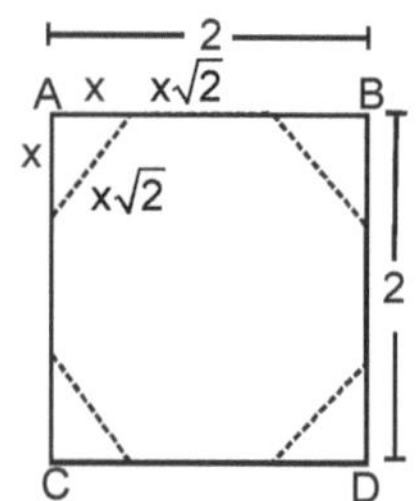

Now, for the side of the square, we can write

$x\sqrt{2} + 2x = 2$

$\Rightarrow x = \dfrac{2}{2 + \sqrt{2}}$

Reduced area = Area (ABCD) − (Area of sum of four right triangles at the corner)

$= 4 − \left(4 \times \dfrac{1}{2} \times \dfrac{4}{(2 + \sqrt{2})^2}\right) = \dfrac{4 − 8}{(2 + \sqrt{2})^2}$

Solving and rationalizing the above expression, we get $= \dfrac{8}{\sqrt{2} + 1}$ sq. units

13. The given diagram is

In the above diagram, please note that $\angle AIG = 60°$ which makes $\angle GIJ = 120°$.

This is not possible since GIJFH is a regular pentagon whose internal angle is always 108°.

Hence, **the question is inconsistent.**

14.

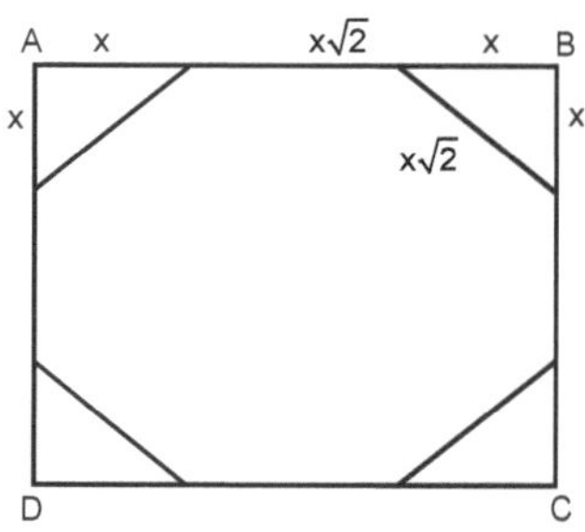

Let the equal sides of the isosceles triangles be x metres each. Hence, each side of the regular octagon is $x\sqrt{2}$ metres.

$$x + x\sqrt{2} + x = 2$$

$$\Rightarrow x = \frac{2}{2+\sqrt{2}} = \frac{\sqrt{2}}{\sqrt{2}+1} = 2 - \sqrt{2}$$

Perimeter of the octagon

$$= 8 \times x\sqrt{2} = 8\sqrt{2}\left(2 - \sqrt{2}\right) = 16\sqrt{2} - 16$$

$$= \frac{16}{\sqrt{2}+1}\text{metres}$$

Area of the octagon = (Area of square ABCD) − 4 (Area of each triangle)

$$= 4 - 4 \times \frac{1}{2}.\left(2 - \sqrt{2}\right)^2$$

$$= 8\sqrt{2} - 8 \text{ square metres.}$$

15. Side of hexagon = 2a.

$$X = 6 \times \frac{\sqrt{3}}{4} \times (2a)^2 - \frac{\sqrt{3}}{4} \times a^2 \Rightarrow a^2 = \frac{4X}{23\sqrt{3}}$$

Radius of the circle = 2a

The area of the circle = $\pi(2a)^2 = 4\pi a^2 = \frac{16\pi}{23\sqrt{3}}X.$

16.

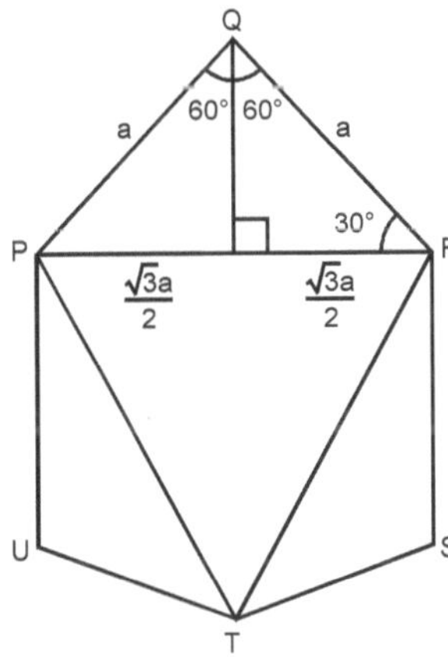

The side of triangle PRT = $\sqrt{3}a$

$$\therefore \text{ Area of } \Delta PRT = \frac{\sqrt{3}}{4} \times \left(\sqrt{3}a\right)^2 = \frac{3\sqrt{3}}{4}a^2.$$

$$\therefore \text{ Required ratio is } \frac{3\sqrt{3}}{4}a^2 \times \frac{4}{6\sqrt{3}a^2} = \frac{3}{6} = \frac{1}{2} = 0.5$$

17. Here circumference = $2\pi r = 2 \times \frac{22}{7} \times 49 = 308\text{ m}$

$\therefore$ Time taken = 148 min

$\therefore$ Speed = $\dfrac{\text{circumference}}{\text{time}} = \dfrac{308}{148}\text{ m/min}$

The side of hexagon = 54 m.

$\therefore$ The total distance to be travelled = 54 × 6 = 324 m

Extra distance to travel = 324 m − 308 m = 16 m

$$\Rightarrow \text{ Extra time taken} = \frac{16 \times 48}{308} \approx 7.69$$

18. As per the question, there are 13 successive semicircles with radii 0.5 cm, 1.0 cm, 1.5 cm, and so on.

$\therefore$ Total length of the spiral

$$= \pi \times 0.5 + \pi \times 1.0 + ... + \pi \times 6.5$$

$$= \pi(0.5 + 1.0 + ... + 6.5)$$

We assume, $\pi = \dfrac{22}{7}$

Required total length = $\dfrac{22}{7} \times \dfrac{7}{2} \times 13 = 143$ cm

19. As per the question, the following figure can be drawn with 'O' as the center of the circle.

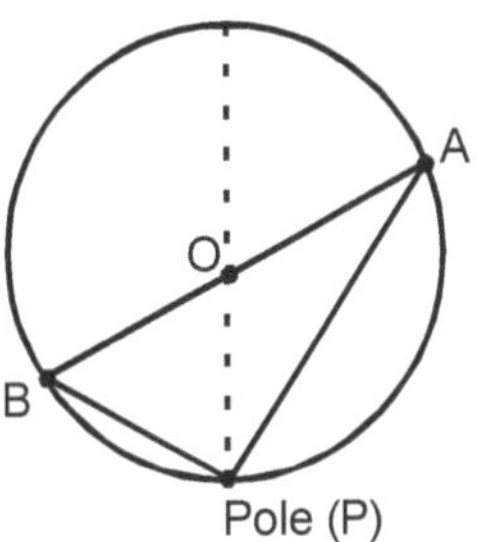

PA − PB = 7

As AB is the diameter,

$$\Rightarrow AB^2 = PA^2 + PB^2 \quad ...(i)$$

$$13^2 = PA^2 + PB^2 \quad ...(ii)$$

Solving equation (i) and (ii)

PA = 12 meters

PB = 5 meters

$\therefore$ Option (c) is the correct choice.

20.

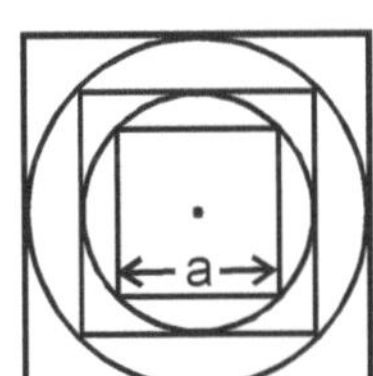

From the above figure,

Radius of the circle, $C_1 = \dfrac{a}{\sqrt{2}}$ metres

$$D_1 = \frac{\pi a^2}{2} - a^2 \qquad ...(i)$$

For A_2 and C_2

$$A_2 = \pi a^2 \text{ and } c_2 = 2a^2$$

$$D_2 = \pi a^2 - 2a^2 = 2\left(\frac{\pi}{2}a^2\right) = 2D_1$$

Also, $D_3 = 4D_1$ and so on.

Therefore, $D_N = 2^{N-1}D_1$

Required ratio $= \dfrac{D_1 + D_2 + D_3 + ... + D_N}{D_1}$

$$= \frac{D_1 + 2D_1 + 4D_1 + ... + 2^{N-1}D_1}{D_1}$$

$$= (1 + 2 + 4 + ... + 2^{N-1}) = 1 \cdot \frac{2^N - 1}{2 - 1} = 2^N - 1$$

$$\to \infty \text{ as } N \to \infty$$

Hence, option (c) is the correct choice.

21. Let the radius of the circle be 'r'.

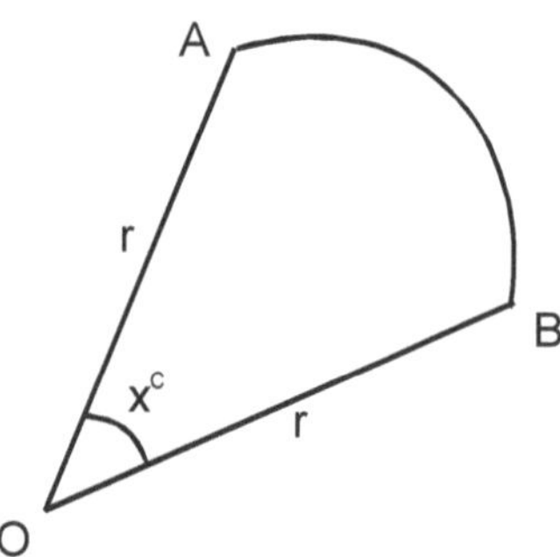

$\therefore$ Area of the sector = (Angle in radius) πr^2

$$= \frac{x}{2\pi} \times \pi r^2 = \frac{\pi r^2}{2}$$

and length of the arc = rx

Square of the length of arc = $x^2 r^2$

According to the given condition,

$$\frac{x r^2}{2} = x^2 r^2 \Rightarrow x = \frac{1}{2} = 0.5$$

22. Using Cosine rule,

$$\cos\theta = \frac{a^2 + b^2 - c^2}{2ab}$$

Hence, $c^2 = a^2 + b^2 - 2ab\cos\theta$

23. In the figure below, CBD is the arc and AB is the height of the arc. We have to find length of chord BC.

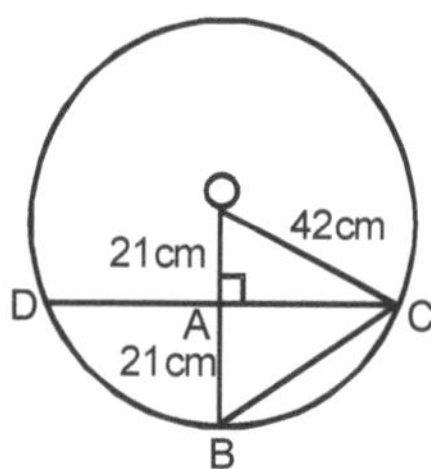

In triangle OAB,

$$\frac{OA}{OC} = \frac{21}{42} = \sin\angle ACO$$

Therefore, $\angle ACO = 30°$ and hence $\angle AOC = 60°$

Also, $\angle OBC = \angle OCB$

(Since, OB = OC = radius)

Therefore, $\triangle OBC$ is an equilateral triangle and length of chord BC = 42 cm.

24. Let the radius of the Circle be r.

$$\frac{2\pi r}{4} = 10\pi$$

$$\Rightarrow \qquad r = 20$$

Area of sector xyz $= \frac{1}{4} \times \pi r^2$

$$= \frac{1}{4} \times \pi.(20)^2$$

$$= 100\pi.$$

25. Area of segment $= \frac{\pi r^2 \theta}{360°} - 2\left(\frac{1}{2} \times 5 \times 12\right)$

$$= \frac{\pi \times 169 \times x}{360°} - 60 \text{ cm}^2$$

Hence option (c)

26. $\triangle AQQ \sim \triangle OSA \sim \triangle BTO$

$\angle QOA = \angle AOS = x$ (let)

and $\angle SOB = \angle BOT = y$ (let)

So, $2(x + y) = 180° - 55° = 125°$

$\Rightarrow x + y = \angle AOB = \frac{125}{2} = 62.5°$

27. Here, height of the cone = diameter of the cone = side of the cube.

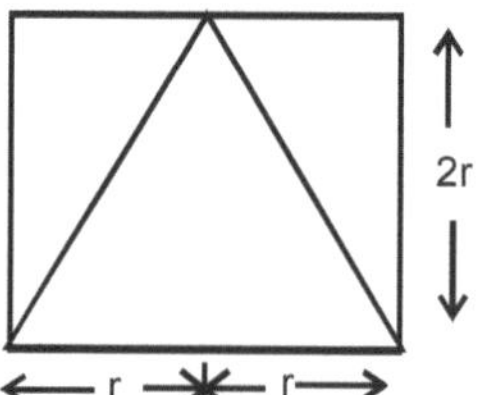

Volume of the memento $= 718\frac{2}{3}$ cc (given)

$$\Rightarrow \frac{1}{3} \times \pi \times r^2 (2r) = 718\frac{2}{3}$$

$\Rightarrow r = 7$ cm and side of cube = 14 cm.

Now, surface area of the box = 6 × (14)² = 1176 cm²

and expenditure on packing = 1176 × 1.5 = Rs.1764

Option (a): Madan's total expenditure on the box

= (Cost of the box) + (Expenditure in the covering)

= 500 + 1764 = Rs.2264.

Hence, option (a) is correct.

Option (b): Wrong, as expenditure was Rs.1764.

Option (c): Correct, as area of any one side of the box = (14)² = 196 cm².

Option (d): Volume of the box = (14)³ = 2744 cc

Hence, option (d) is incorrect.

Hence, only options (a) and (c) are correct.

28. Side of the square $= \sqrt{484}$ cm $= 22$ cm

$\therefore$ Length of the wire $= 4 \times (22) = 88$ cm.

After cutting, longer part $= \dfrac{3}{4} \times 88 = 66$ cm

shorter part $= 88 - 66 = 22$ cm.

Radius of the circle thus formed $= \dfrac{66}{2\pi} = \dfrac{21}{2}$ cm .

Side of the square formed $= \dfrac{22}{4} = \dfrac{11}{2}$ cm

$\therefore$ Area of the circle $= \pi \left(\dfrac{21}{2}\right)^2 = \dfrac{693}{2}$ cm^2

and area of the square $= \left(\dfrac{11}{2}\right)^2 = \dfrac{121}{4}$ sq. cm

Therefore, total area enclosed by both

$= \left(\dfrac{693}{2} + \dfrac{121}{4}\right)$ sq cm $= 376.75$ cm^2

Hence, option (c) is correct.

29. Let the three solids have base radius and height of x units. The curved surface areas of the three solids are:

Cylinder: $2\pi x \times x = 2\pi x^2$

Hemisphere: $2\pi x^2$

Cone: $\pi \cdot x \times (\text{Slant height}) = \pi \cdot x \times (\sqrt{2}\, x)$

The ratio of curved surface areas is $\sqrt{2} : \sqrt{2} : 1$

30. Let DE and AD be the radius and height of the right circular cone and 'h' and 'r' be the height and radius of the cylinder.

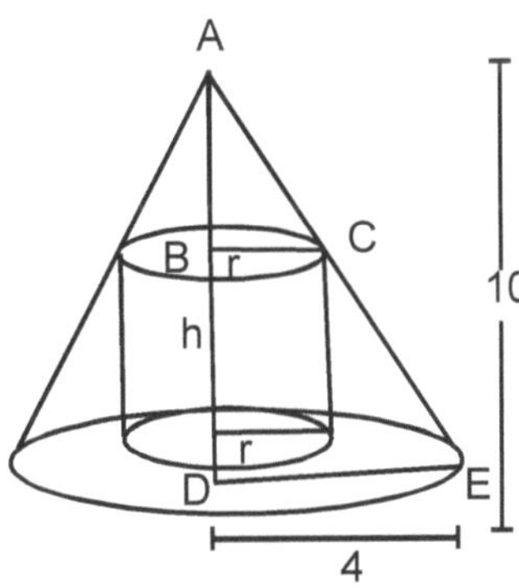

Applying similarity in $\triangle$ABC and $\triangle$ADE, we have

$\dfrac{10 - h}{r} = \dfrac{10}{4} = \dfrac{5}{2}$

$\Rightarrow 20 - 2h = 5r$

$\Rightarrow h = \dfrac{20 - 5r}{2}$

Now, Curved surface area of cylinder of radius r

$= 2\pi r h = 2\pi r \left(\dfrac{20 - 5r}{2}\right) = 5\pi r (4 - r)$

Hence, option (b) is the correct choice.

31. The curved surface area of sphere $= 4\pi r^2$

It is given that $\dfrac{dr}{dt} = 2$ cm per second and $r = 30$ cm.

Now we have $s = 4\pi r^2$

$\Rightarrow \dfrac{ds}{dt} = 4\pi \cdot 2r \cdot \dfrac{dr}{dt} = 8\pi r \dfrac{dr}{dt} = 8\pi (30) \times (2) = 480\,\pi$

Hence, option (b) is the correct choice.

32. Let the height of cylinder and cone be 5h and 3h respectively.

Volume of the metal solid $= \pi . 8^2 . 5h + \dfrac{1}{3} . \pi . 8^2 . 3h = 384\pi h$

Height of the drilled cylinder $= \dfrac{8}{3} h$

Let radius of the drilled cylinder = r cm

So, $\pi . r^2 \times \dfrac{8}{3} h = \dfrac{1}{2} \left[384\pi h - \pi r^2 \times \dfrac{8}{3} h \right]$

Solving, we get $r = 4\sqrt{3}$ cm.

33. Circumference of the base of the cylinder

$= 2\pi r = 10$ or $r = \dfrac{5}{\pi}$

Height of the cylinder = 22 cm

Volume $\pi r^2 h = \dfrac{22}{7} \times \left(\dfrac{5}{\pi}\right)^2 \times 22 = 175$ cm^2

34. i. Volume of parallelepiped = Area of base × height

Area of base $\leq 5 \times 3$

$\therefore$ volume ≤ 60 cm^3

ii. Volume of cube $= 4 \times 4 \times 4 = 64$ cm^3

iii. Volume of cylinder $= \pi r^2 h = 27\pi$ cm^2

iv. Volume of sphere $= \dfrac{4}{3}\pi r^3 = 36\pi$ cm^3

Therefore, iv > iii > ii > i.

35. Let the radius of the circular field be R metre

Total area of circular field = Land Area + Area of Tank

$\pi R^2 = 20350 + 110 \times 130$

$\Rightarrow \dfrac{22}{7} \times R^2 = 34650$

$\Rightarrow R^2 = 34650 \times \dfrac{7}{22} \Rightarrow R = 105$m

Hence, option (c) is the correct answer.

36. Let the radius of the bowl and of the vessel be R. Let the height of the vessel be H.

Since radius of the cylindrical vessel is 50% more than height, $R = \dfrac{3}{2} H$ or $H = \dfrac{2}{3} R$

Volume of water = Volume of bowl $= \dfrac{2}{3}\pi R^3$

Volume of vessel $= \pi R^2 H = \pi R^2 \times \dfrac{2}{3} R = \dfrac{2}{3}\pi R^3$

So cylindrical vessel must be filled to the brim.

37. Radius of the cap = 14 cm

Height of the cap = 26.5 cm

Slant height = 30 cm.

Surface area of the cap $= \pi r l = \dfrac{22}{7} \times 14 \times 30$

= 1320 sq.cm

Hence, the required area = 7 × 1320 = 9240 sq cm.

38. Area of the garden = 34 × 21 = 714 sq m

Area covered by the corridors = (4 × 34) + (4 × 21) − (4 × 4)

= 136 + 84 −16

= 204 sq. m.

Hence, the area under the flowers = 714 − 204 = 510 sq. m.

39. The required width $= 5 + \sqrt{13^2 - 8^2} = 15.2$.

40. Volume of the cylinder $= \pi \times 6^2 \times 24 = 864\pi$

Diameter of the Base = 12

Side of the rectangular solid $= 6\sqrt{2}$

Volume of rectangular solid $= (6\sqrt{2})^2 \times 20 = 1440$.

Required amount of water

$= 864\pi - 1440 = 288(3\pi - 5)$.

41. Cross section of sphere and cylinder:

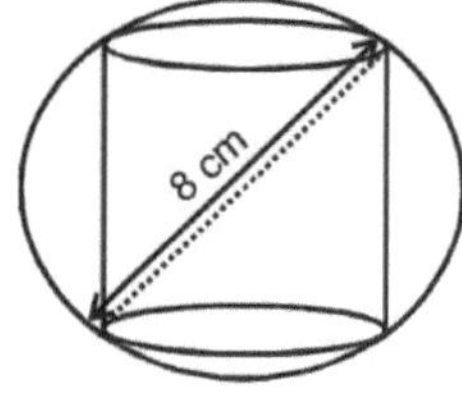

(Diameter of sphere)^2

$\quad$ = (Diameter of base of Cylinder)^2

$\qquad\qquad\qquad$ + (height of Cylinder)^2

$\Rightarrow$ Radius of base of cylinder $= \dfrac{\sqrt{16^2 - 14^2}}{2} = \sqrt{15}$

Volume of the cylinder $= \pi\left(\sqrt{15}\right)^2 .14$

$\qquad = \dfrac{22}{7} \times 15 \times 14 = 660$.

42. The Volume of Cylinder $= 15 \times 49\pi$

The rectangle solid is placed in cylinder such that each of the corners of solid is tangent to walls of cylinder. Hence, the diameter of cylinder will be diagonal to the square base.

As the diameter of cylinder is 14, so diagonal of square is 14 and hence side of square is $7\sqrt{2}$.

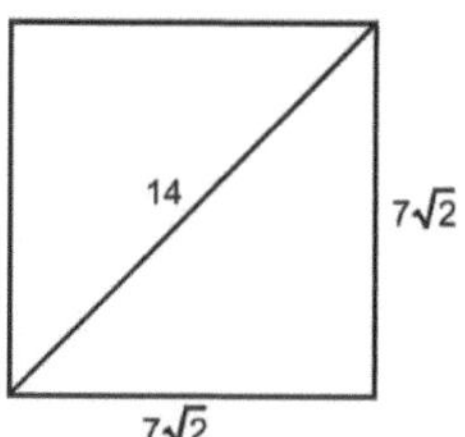

The volume of solid $= 7\sqrt{2} \times 7\sqrt{2} \times 12 = 98 \times 12$

$\therefore$ The volume of the liquid = 15 × 49π − 98 × 12

$\qquad\qquad = 147\,(5\pi - 8)$.

43. Given bucket having liquid is in the shape of a frustum having radius of 3 cm and 4 cm of liquid level before the ball is dropped.

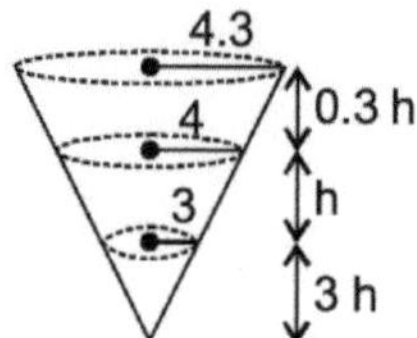

Now Volume of liquid before ball dropped

$= \dfrac{1}{3}(\pi \times 4^2 \times 4h) - \dfrac{1}{3}(\pi \times 3^2 \times 3h) = 200$

Volume of ball = volume of increased liquid level

$= \dfrac{1}{3}(\pi \times (4.3)^2 \times 4.3h) - \dfrac{1}{3}(\pi \times 4^2 \times 4h) = X$

Dividing both the equations, we get

$\dfrac{(64 - 27)h}{(79.507 - 64)h} = \dfrac{200}{X}$

This implies, X = 83 ∼ 80 (from the given options)

44. $AB = 25\sqrt{2}$

$PQ = 25\sqrt{2}$

$OP = \angle OPQ = \angle OQP$

$x\sqrt{2} = 25\sqrt{2}$

$x = 25$

In triangle OPR

$\dfrac{OR}{OP} = \sin 45$

$OR = \dfrac{25}{\sqrt{2}}$

$AP = 30 - \dfrac{25}{\sqrt{2}}$

Area of shaded region = Area of rectangle − (Area of quadrant − Area of triangle OPQ)

$= 25\sqrt{2}\left(30 - \dfrac{25}{\sqrt{2}}\right) - \left(\dfrac{\pi(25)^2}{4}\right) - \dfrac{1}{2} \times 25\sqrt{2} \times \dfrac{25}{\sqrt{2}}$

$= 750\sqrt{2} - 625\left(\dfrac{1}{2} + \dfrac{\pi}{4}\right)$

45. Let radius of hale = r

Radius of cone = 5

Height of cone = 2x

Height of cylinder = 3x

Volume of hole = $\dfrac{1}{3}$ (volume of solid − volume of hole)

$$\dfrac{4}{3} \times \pi \times r^2 \times \dfrac{2}{3} \times 5x$$

$$\dfrac{1}{3\pi\left(\dfrac{25}{3} \times 2x + 25 \times 3\right)}$$

Solving this $r = \sqrt{\dfrac{55}{8}}$ option (d)

46.

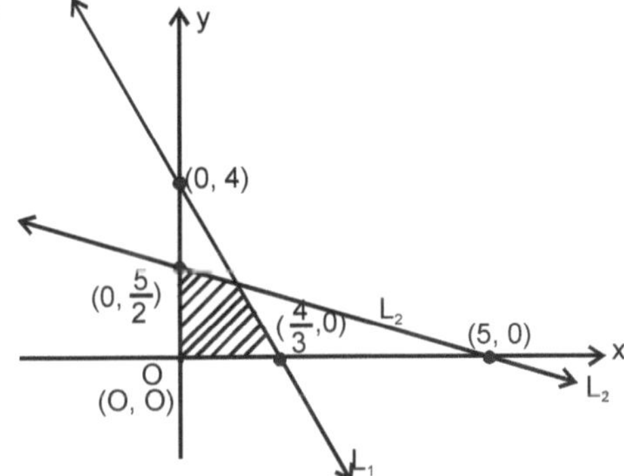

Line L_1 passes through (0, 4) and $\left(\dfrac{4}{3}, 0\right)$.

Its equation is $\dfrac{x}{\dfrac{4}{3}} + \dfrac{y}{4} = 1$

$\Rightarrow 3x + y - 4 = 0$ ...(i)

and the equation of line L_2 is

$x + 2y - 5 = 0$ ...(ii)

The shaded region includes x-axis (y = 0) and y-axis (i.e. x = 0) as its boundaries and bounds only the positive quadrant of the x-y plane.

$\Rightarrow x \geq 0$ and $y \geq 0$ ...(iii)

For the shaded region,

$y + 3x - 4 \leq 0$ ...(iv)

and $x + 2y - 5 \leq 0$ ...(v)

The bounded region is given by

$3x + y \leq 4,\ x + 2y \leq 5,\ x \geq 0,\ y \geq 0$

Hence, option (c) is correct.

47.

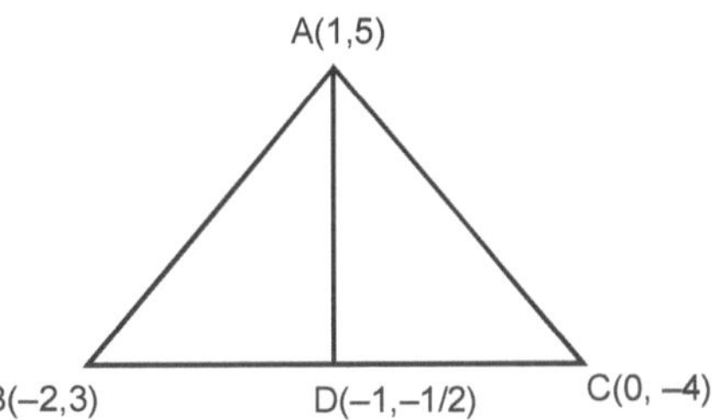

Here AD is the median, so D is the midpoint of BC

$\therefore D\left(-1, -\dfrac{1}{2}\right)$

The equation of AD is

$$y - 5 = \dfrac{\dfrac{-1}{2} - 5}{-1 - 1}(x - 1)$$

$$\Rightarrow y - 5 = \dfrac{11}{4}(x - 1)$$

$$\Rightarrow 4y - 20 = 11x - 11$$

$$\Rightarrow 11x - 4y + 9 = 0$$

48.

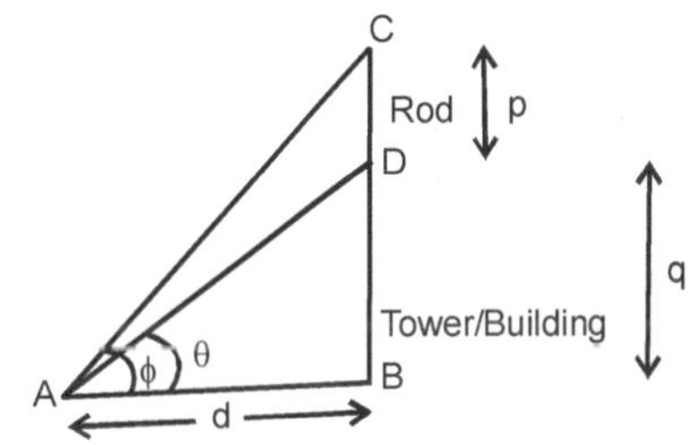

$\dfrac{p + q}{d} = \tan\phi$ ...(i)

and $\dfrac{q}{d} = \tan\theta$ ...(ii)

Dividing (i) by (ii), we get

$\Rightarrow \dfrac{p}{q} + 1 = \dfrac{\tan\phi}{\tan\theta}$

$\Rightarrow \dfrac{p}{q} = \dfrac{\tan\phi - \tan\theta}{\tan\theta}$

Height of the tower is $q = \dfrac{p\tan\theta}{\tan\phi - \tan\theta}$ and

Height of the rod is $p = q\dfrac{(\tan\phi - \tan\theta)}{\tan\theta}$

So (a) and (d) are the only correct options.

49.

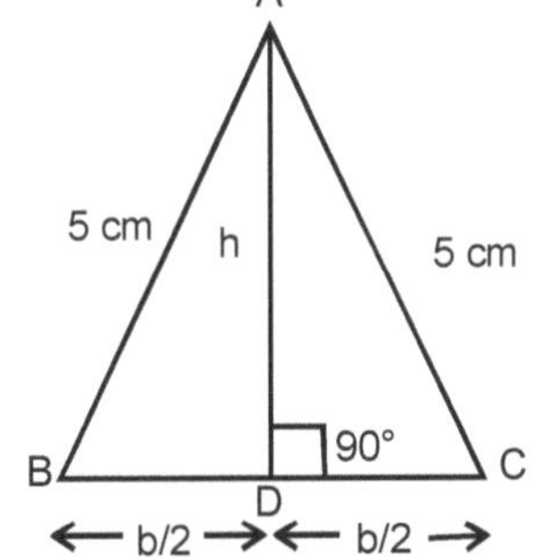

$$\text{Area}(\triangle ABC) = \frac{1}{2} \times b \times h = 12 \text{ sq. cm}$$

$$\Rightarrow b \times h = 24 \qquad \qquad \dots(i)$$

Also, in right triangle ABD,

$$(5)^2 = \left(\frac{b}{2}\right)^2 + h^2$$

$$\Rightarrow b^2 + 4h^2 = 100 \qquad \qquad \dots(ii)$$

$$\Rightarrow b^2 + \left(\frac{48}{b}\right)^2 = 100 \qquad \qquad \dots(iii)$$

b = 6 and 8, are the roots of the above equation.

Hence, only options (b) and (c) are correct.

50.

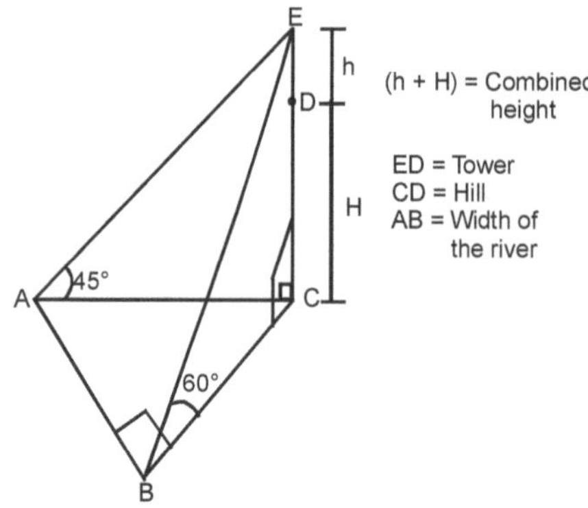

Water does not move in the lake.

In right triangle ACE, $\angle A = 45°$

$$\Rightarrow EC = AC = (h + H) = 300 \text{ m} \qquad \dots(i)$$

In right triangle BCE, $\angle B = 60°$

$$\Rightarrow \frac{EC}{BC} = \tan 60° = \sqrt{3} \qquad \qquad \dots(ii)$$

And in right triangle ABC,

$$AC^2 = AB^2 + BC^2 \qquad \qquad \dots(iii)$$

Speed of the boat = 2 km/hr.

Option (a): AC = 300 m

$$\frac{EC}{BC} = \sqrt{3} \Rightarrow BC = \frac{300 \times \sqrt{3}}{3} = 100\sqrt{3}\text{m}$$

$$\Rightarrow AB = \sqrt{AC^2 - BC^2}$$

$$\therefore AB = 100\sqrt{6} \text{ m} \text{ is the breadth of the river.}$$

Time taken by boat to move from A to B,

$$\text{Time}_{A \to B} = \frac{100\sqrt{6} \times 60}{2 \times 1000} = 3\sqrt{6} \text{ minutes.}$$

$\therefore$ Option (a) is correct.

Option (b): The breadth of the river is $100\sqrt{6}$m,

Option (c): Incorrect, as Rajan took $3\sqrt{6}$ minutes.

Option (d): h + H = 450 m

Speed of boat = 1 km/hr

As all the angles remain the same, we will get 3 new right triangles which are correspondingly similar to the earlier ones.

$$\text{Breadth of the river} = \frac{450}{300} \times (100\sqrt{6}) \text{ m} = 150\sqrt{6} \text{ m}$$

$$\therefore \text{Time taken} = \frac{150\sqrt{6}\text{m}}{1\text{km/hr}} = 9\sqrt{6} \text{ minutes}$$

$\Rightarrow$ Option (d) is correct.

Hence, only options (a), (b) & (d) are correct.

51.
$$\frac{1-c}{1+c} = \frac{1 - \tan\left(\frac{\alpha}{2}\right) \times \tan\left(\frac{\beta}{2}\right)}{1 + \tan\left(\frac{\alpha}{2}\right) \times \tan\left(\frac{\beta}{2}\right)}$$

$$= \frac{\cos\left(\frac{\alpha}{2}\right)\cos\left(\frac{\beta}{2}\right) - \sin\left(\frac{\alpha}{2}\right) \times \sin\left(\frac{\beta}{2}\right)}{\cos\left(\frac{\alpha}{2}\right)\cos\left(\frac{\beta}{2}\right) + \sin\left(\frac{\alpha}{2}\right) \times \sin\left(\frac{\beta}{2}\right)}$$

$$= \frac{\cos\left(\frac{\alpha+\beta}{2}\right)}{\cos\left(\frac{\alpha-\beta}{2}\right)} \qquad \qquad \dots(i)$$

Since $\sin\alpha + \sin\beta = a$ and $\cos\alpha + \cos\beta = b$,

squaring and adding up both equations, we get

$$\sin^2\alpha + \sin^2\beta + 2\sin\alpha\sin\beta = a^2$$

and $\cos^2\alpha + \cos^2\beta + 2\cos\alpha\cos\beta = b^2$

Adding both the equations, we get,

$$1 + 1 + 2(\cos\alpha\cos\beta + \sin\alpha\sin\beta) = a^2 + b^2$$

$$\Rightarrow 2 + 2\{\cos(\alpha-\beta)\} = a^2 + b^2$$

$$\Rightarrow 1 + \cos(\alpha-\beta) = \frac{a^2 + b^2}{2} \qquad \dots(ii)$$

Since $\cos\alpha + \cos\beta = b$, $\qquad \qquad \dots(iii)$

dividing equation (iii) by (ii), we get

$$\frac{\cos\alpha + \cos\beta}{1 + \cos(\alpha-\beta)} = \frac{2b}{a^2 + b^2}$$

$$\Rightarrow \frac{2\cos\frac{(\alpha+\beta)}{2} \times \cos\frac{(\alpha-\beta)}{2}}{2\cos^2\frac{(\alpha-\beta)}{2}} = \frac{2b}{a^2 + b^2}$$

$$\Rightarrow \frac{\cos\frac{(\alpha+\beta)}{2}}{\cos\frac{(\alpha-\beta)}{2}} = \frac{2b}{a^2 + b^2}$$

From equation (i), we get

$$\Rightarrow \frac{1-c}{1+c} = \frac{2b}{a^2 + b^2}$$

$\therefore$ Option (c) is correct.

52. We know,

$$\sin^{-1}x + \cos^{-1}x = \frac{\pi}{2} \qquad \qquad \dots(a)$$

Since $a\sin^{-1}x = c + b\cos^{-1}x$ $\qquad$ (given)

$$\Rightarrow \frac{a}{b}\sin^{-1}x = \frac{c}{b} + \cos^{-1}x \qquad \dots(i)$$

$$\Rightarrow b\cos^{-1}x = a\sin^{-1}x - c$$

$$\Rightarrow \frac{b}{a}\cos^{-1}x = \sin^{-1}x - \frac{c}{a} \qquad \dots(ii)$$

Adding equation (i) and (ii), we get

$$\frac{a}{b}\sin^{-1}x + \frac{b}{a}\cos^{-1}x = (\sin^{-1}x + \cos^{-1}x) + \frac{c}{b} - \frac{c}{a}$$

$$= \left(\frac{\pi}{2}\right) + c\left\{\frac{1}{b} - \frac{1}{a}\right\} \dots \text{(Using A)}$$

$$= \left(\frac{\pi}{2}\right) + \frac{c(a-b)}{ab}$$

$$= \frac{\pi ab + 2c(a-b)}{2ab}$$

Hence, option (c) is the correct answer.

53. $\dfrac{2\sin\theta}{1+\sin\theta+\cos\theta} = \dfrac{4\sin\frac{\theta}{2}\cos\frac{\theta}{2}}{1+2\sin\frac{\theta}{2}\cos\frac{\theta}{2}+2\cos^2\frac{\theta}{2}-1}$

$$= \frac{4\sin\frac{\theta}{2}\cos\frac{\theta}{2}}{2\cos\frac{\theta}{2}\left\{\sin\frac{\theta}{2}+\cos\frac{\theta}{2}\right\}}$$

$$\Rightarrow k = \frac{2\sin\frac{\theta}{2}}{\left(\sin\frac{\theta}{2}+\cos\frac{\theta}{2}\right)} \qquad \dots(i)$$

Now, $\dfrac{1-\cos\theta+\sin\theta}{1+\sin\theta} = \dfrac{1-1+2\sin^2\frac{\theta}{2}+2\sin\frac{\theta}{2}\cos\frac{\theta}{2}}{\left(\sin\frac{\theta}{2}+\cos\frac{\theta}{2}\right)^2}$

$$= \frac{2\sin\frac{\theta}{2}\left(\sin\frac{\theta}{2}+\cos\frac{\theta}{2}\right)}{\left(\sin\frac{\theta}{2}+\cos\frac{\theta}{2}\right)^2} = \frac{2\sin\frac{\theta}{2}}{\left(\sin\frac{\theta}{2}+\cos\frac{\theta}{2}\right)} \qquad \dots(ii)$$

As equation (i) and (ii) are same, the value is equal to k Hence, option (a) is correct.

54. Let (α,β) and (γ,δ) be the two pairs of opposite angles in the cyclic quadrilateral. Then, we have $(\alpha + \beta) = 180°$ and $(\gamma + \delta) = 180°$. Now,

$\cos\alpha + \cos\beta + \cos\gamma + \cos\delta = \cos\alpha + \cos(180° - \alpha) + \cos\gamma + \cos(180° - \gamma)$

$= \cos\alpha - \cos\alpha + \cos\gamma - \cos\gamma = 0$

Hence, (b) is the correct option.

55. $\cot^{-1}\left\{\dfrac{\sqrt{1-\sin a}+\sqrt{1+\sin a}}{\sqrt{1-\sin a}-\sqrt{1+\sin a}}\right\}$

$= \cot^{-1}\left\{\dfrac{\left(\sqrt{1-\sin a}+\sqrt{1+\sin a}\right)^2}{\left(\sqrt{1-\sin a}\right)^2-\left(\sqrt{1+\sin a}\right)^2}\right\} = \cot^{-1}\left\{\dfrac{2+2\cos a}{-2\sin a}\right\}$

$= \cot^{-1}\left\{\dfrac{1+\cos a}{-\sin a}\right\} = \cot^{-1}\left\{\dfrac{2\cos^2\frac{a}{2}}{-2\sin\frac{a}{2}.\cos\frac{a}{2}}\right\}$

$= \cot^{-1}\left\{-\cot\left(\dfrac{a}{2}\right)\right\} = \pi - \dfrac{1}{2}$

56. The given equation can be written as:

$$\tan x + \frac{\tan x + \tan \pi/3}{1-\tan x\tan\pi/3} + \frac{\tan x + \tan 2\pi/3}{1-\tan x\tan 2\pi/3} = 3$$

$$\Rightarrow \tan x + \frac{\tan x + \sqrt{3}}{1-\sqrt{3}\tan x} + \frac{\tan x - \sqrt{3}}{1+\sqrt{3}\tan x} = 3$$

$$\Rightarrow \tan x + \frac{(\tan x+\sqrt{3})(1+\sqrt{3}\tan x)+(1-\sqrt{3}\tan x)(\tan x-\sqrt{3})}{1-3\tan^2 x} = 3$$

$$\Rightarrow \tan x + \frac{8\tan x}{1-3\tan^2 x} = 3 \Rightarrow \frac{\tan x(1-3\tan^2 x)+8\tan x}{1-3\tan^2 x} = 3$$

$$\Rightarrow \frac{3(3\tan x-\tan^3 x)}{1-3\tan^2 x} = 3 \Rightarrow 3\tan 3x = 3 \Rightarrow \tan 3x = 1$$

57. $\sin(\alpha+\beta-\gamma) = \dfrac{1}{\sqrt{2}} \Rightarrow \alpha+\beta-\gamma = 45°$

$\operatorname{cosec}(\beta+\gamma-\alpha) = \dfrac{2}{\sqrt{3}} \Rightarrow \beta+\gamma-\alpha = 60°$

$\tan(\gamma+\alpha-\beta) = \dfrac{1}{\sqrt{3}} \Rightarrow \gamma+\alpha-\beta = 30°$

$\Rightarrow \alpha = 37\dfrac{1}{2}°, \ \beta = 52\dfrac{1}{2}°, \ \gamma = 45°$

58. We know $A.M. \geq G.M.$

$$\Rightarrow \frac{3^{\sin x}+3^{\cos x}}{2} \geq \sqrt{3^{\sin x}.3^{\cos x}}$$

$$\Rightarrow 3^{\sin x}+3^{\cos x} \geq 2\sqrt{3^{\sin x+\cos x}}$$

Now minimum value of six x + cos x is at

$$x = \frac{5\pi}{4} \Rightarrow \sin x + \cos x = -\sqrt{2}$$

$$\therefore 3^{\sin x}+3^{\cos x} \geq 2\sqrt{3^{-\sqrt{2}}} = 2.3^{\frac{-\sqrt{2}}{2}} = 2\left(3^{\frac{-1}{\sqrt{2}}}\right)$$

59. Let AB and DC be the two buildings where AB = 60 m.

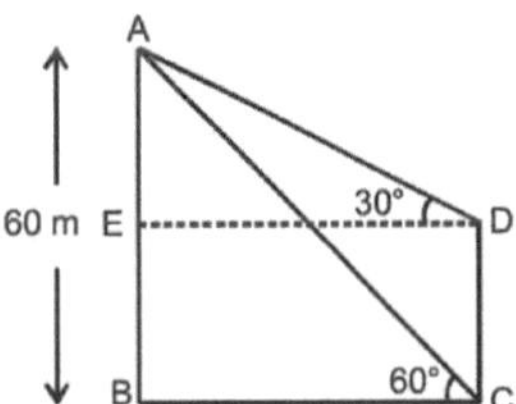

As per the given information,

$$\tan 60° = \frac{AB}{BC} \Rightarrow BC = \frac{60}{\sqrt{3}}$$

$$\tan 30° = \frac{AE}{ED} = \frac{AE}{BC} \Rightarrow AE = 20$$

$\therefore$ EB = 40 m.

Hence, height of the other building = 40 m.

60. Distance covered

$$= 210\left(1-\frac{1}{\sqrt{3}}\right) = 210\left(\frac{\sqrt{3}-1}{\sqrt{3}}\right) = 70(3-\sqrt{3}) \approx 89\text{ m}$$

Speed = 3km/hr = 3000 meter/hr = 50 meters/ min

The required time $= \dfrac{89}{50} \approx 2\text{min.}$

61.

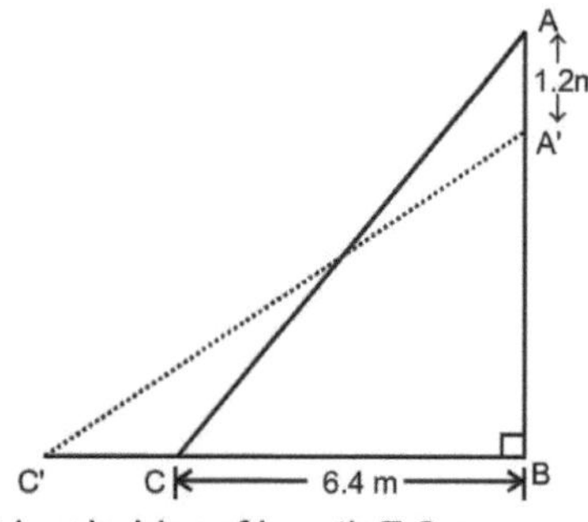

AC is a ladder of length 7.6m.

Now, AC is Slipped, in this care

$$DE = 7.6m.$$

IN $\triangle ABC$, $\quad (7.6)^2 = AB^2 + (6.4)^2$

$$AB \approx 4.1\ m$$

In $\triangle A'BC'$,

$$A'B^2 + BC'^2 = 7.6^2$$

$$\Rightarrow \quad (4.1 - 1.2)^2 + BC'^2 = 7.6^2$$

$$\Rightarrow \quad BC' = 7.02\ m \approx 7\ m$$

Required length $= 7.6 - 7 = 0.6\ m.$

62.

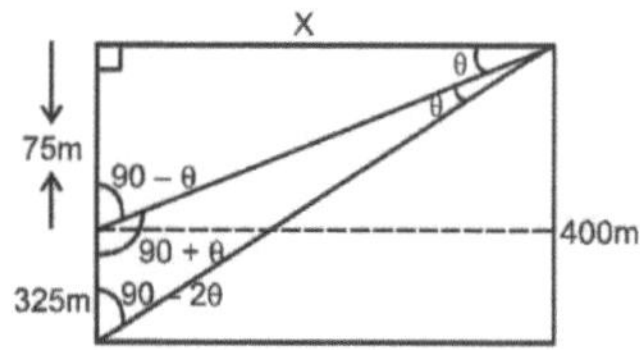

$$\frac{75}{x} = \tan\theta$$

$$\frac{400}{x} = \tan 2\theta = \frac{2\tan\theta}{1-\tan^2\theta} \quad \Rightarrow \quad \frac{400}{x} = \frac{2\times\dfrac{75}{x}}{1-\left(\dfrac{75}{x}\right)^2}$$

$$400 = \frac{150}{1-\dfrac{5625}{x^2}}$$

$$\frac{400}{150} = \frac{x^2}{x^2 - 5625}$$

On solving above equation we get $x^2 = 9000$,

so x is $= 30\sqrt{10}$

Hence option (b).

63.

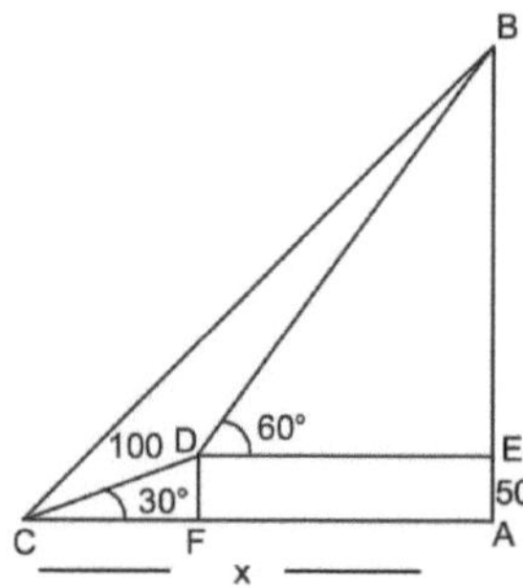

Let AB is the summit

Here $\angle BCA = 45° \Rightarrow AB = AC = x$(say)

Now CD $= 100\ m \Rightarrow DF = 50m$ & CF $= 50\sqrt{3}m$

$\Rightarrow FA = DE = \left(x - 50\sqrt{3}m\right)m$ and BE x $-$ 50

In $\triangle BDE$,

$$x - 50\sqrt{3}\left(x - 50\sqrt{3}\right)$$

$$\Rightarrow x - 50 = \sqrt{3}x - 150$$

$$\Rightarrow \sqrt{3}x - x = 100 \Rightarrow \left(\sqrt{3} - 1\right)\times 100$$

$$\Rightarrow \frac{100}{\sqrt{3} - 1} = \frac{100}{\sqrt{3} - 1}\times\frac{\sqrt{3} + 1}{\sqrt{3} + 1} = \frac{100\left(\sqrt{3} + 1\right)}{2}$$

$$\Rightarrow x = 50\left(\sqrt{3} + 1\right)m$$

Modern Maths

Permutation and Combination

2007-09

1. Sunil goes to a small city in Europe on vacation, where he enjoys walking along the streets in the afternoon. He observes that there are 6 parallel roads running East - West and 5 parallel roads running North-South in the city. In order to observe the landmarks in the city, he takes different routes every time he goes out. He also observed that the distance between every consecutive pair of roads is equal. Given this, mark <u>all</u> the correct options.

   (a) The number of shortest possible routes that Sunil can take to travel from one corner of the city to the other diagonal end is 126.

   (b) The total number of possible routes that Sunil can take to travel from one corner of the city to the other diagonal end is 196.

   (c) The number of rectangles that can be formed with their sides along the roads is 150.

   (d) If the number of parallel roads running East-West and North - South increase by one each, the number of shortest possible routes that Sunil can take to travel from one corner of the city to the other diagonal end would go up by 336.

2. Three business entities X Ltd, Y Ltd. and Z Ltd, with 4, 3 and 5 employees respectively, merged into XYZ Ltd in order to jointly raise the capital for setting up a new modern production plant in Jaipur. After two years, on the question of management decisions on the new venture at Jaipur, the employees started adopting differing viewpoints and began to quarrel among themselves. Given the fact that there is no quarrel among the employees of the erstwhile X Ltd, Y Ltd and Z Ltd, what could be the maximum number of quarrels that can take place within XYZ Ltd?

   (a) 31   (b) 53

   (c) 47   (d) 41

2009-11

3. If $^{n+2}C_8 : {}^{n-2}P_4 = 57 : 16$, then n =

   (a) 20   (b) 22

   (c) 15   (d) None of the above

4. The number of ways in which a mixed double tennis game can be arranged amongst 9 married couples if no husband and wife play in the same game is:

   (a) 1514   (b) 1512

   (c) 3024   (d) None of the above

5. While packing for a business trip Mr. Debashis has packed 3 pairs of shoes, 4 pants, 3 half-pants, 6 shirts, 3 sweater and 2 jackets. The outfit is defined as consisting of a pair of shoes, a choice of "lower wear" (either a pant or a half-pant), a choice of "upper wear" (it could be a shirt or a sweater or both) and finally he may or may not choose to wear a jacket. How many different outfits are possible?

   (a) 567   (b) 1821

   (c) 743   (d) None of the above

2011-13

6. How many positive integers 'n' can we form using the digits 3, 4, 4, 5, 6, 6, 7 if we want 'n' to exceed 6,000,000?

   (a) 320   (b) 360

   (c) 540   (d) 720

7. In how many ways can four letters of the word 'SERIES' be arranged?

   (a) 24   (b) 42

   (c) 84   (d) 102

2012-14

8. A five digit number divisible by 3 is to be formed using the numerals 0, 1, 2, 3, 4 and 5 without repetition. The total number of ways in which this can be done is:

   (a) 220   (b) 600

   (c) 240   (d) None of the above

2013-15

9. A student is required to answer 6 out of 10 questions in an examination. The questions are divided into two groups, each containing 5 questions. She is not allowed to attempt more than 4 questions from each group. The number of different ways in which the student can choose the 6 questions is

   (a) 100   (b) 160

   (c) 200   (d) 280

10. Eight points lie on the circumference of a circle. The difference between the number of triangles and the number of quadrilaterals that can be formed by connecting these points is

(a) 7 (b) 14

(c) 32 (d) 84

2014-16

11. Out of 8 consonants and 5 vowels, how many words can be made, each containing 4 consonants and 3 vowels?

(a) 700 (b) 504000

(c) 3528000 (d) 7056000

12. In a sports meet for senior citizens organized by the Rotary Club in Kolkata, 9 married couples participated in Table Tennis mixed double event. The number of ways in which the mixed double team can be made, so that no husband and wife play in the same set, is

(a) 1512 (b) 1240

(c) 960 (d) 640

2015-17

13. The total number of eight-digit landline telephone numbers that can be formed having at least one of their digits repeated is:

(a) 98185600

(b) 97428800

(c) 100000000

(d) None of the above

14. In an Engineering College in Pune, 8 males and 7 females have appeared for Student Cultural Committee selection process, 3 males and 4 females are to be selected. The total number of ways in which the Committee can be formed, given that Mr. Raj is not to be included in the Committee if Ms. Rani is selected, is;

(a) 1960

(b) 2840

(c) 1540

(d) None of the above

2016-18

15. During 'the essay writing stage of MBA admission process in a reputed B-School, each group consists of 10 students. In one such group, two students are batchmates from the same IIT department. Assuming that the students are sitting in a row, the number of ways in which the students can sit so that the two batchmates are not sitting next to each other, is:

(a) 3540340 (b) 2874590

(c) 2903040 (d) None of the above

16. In the board meeting of a FMCG Company, everybody present in the meeting shakes hand with everybody else. If the total number of handshakes is 78, the number of members who attended the board meeting is:

(a) 7 (b) 9

(c) 11 (d) 13

2017-19

17. Which of the following statements regarding arrangement of the word 'RIYADH' is/are true:

(i) Two vowels can be arranged together in 120 ways

(ii) Vowels do hot occur together in 240 ways

Which of the above statements are true?

(a) Statement (i) only

(b) Statement (ii) only

(c) Both statements (i) and (ii)

(d) None of the above

18. A reputed paint company plans to award prizes to its top three salespersons, with the highest prize going to the top salesperson, the next highest prize to the next salesperson and a smaller prize to the third-ranking salesperson. If the company has 15 salespersons, how many different arrangements of winners are possible (Assume there are no ties)?

(a) 1728 (b) 2730

(c) 3856 (d) 1320

19. A multi-storied office building has a total of 17 rows of parking spaces. There are 20 parking spaces in the first row and 21 parking spaces in the second row. In each subsequent row, there are 2 more parking spaces than in the previous row. The total number of parking spaces in the office building is

(a) 380 (b) 464

(c) 596 (d) 712

20. In an MBA entrance examination, a minimum is to be secured in each of the 6 sections to qualify the cut-offs. In how many ways can a candidate fail to secure the cut-offs?

(a) 60 (b) 61

(c) 62 (d) 63

2019-21

21. P . . . . . Q

R . . . . . S

T . . . . . U

V . . . . . W

Using 5 dots in each of the lines PQ, RS, TU and VW as the vertices, how many triangles can be drawn such that the base is on any one of the above lines?

(a) 120 (b) 150

(c) 200 (d) 600

Probability

22. Ankit is appearing in an entrance examination for a professional course. In the General Knowledge section, the students are asked to match certain years in which the soccer world cup was held with the name of the champion team in that particular year. The information given was as follows:

Champion	Year
West Germany	1966
Italy	1982
France	1990
England	1998

Now, Ankit not being a football fan, does the matching randomly. If X denotes the number of correct answers his random matching generates, mark <u>all</u> the correct probabilities.

(a) $P\left(X \geq 1\right) = \dfrac{5}{8}$ (b) $P\left(X = 1\right) = \dfrac{1}{4}$

(c) $P\left(X = 3\right) = 0$ (d) $P\left(X = 4\right) = \dfrac{1}{24}$

23. In a pizza stall, Ajay and Mohan, being the lucky customers, were given the option of drawing tickets from a pot containing x number of tickets for the knife-throwing show and y number of tickets for the talking-doll show. Both Ajay and Mohan being excited about the knife-throwing show, start drawing tickets from the pot until they get one for the show, replacing any drawn ticket for the talking-doll show in the pot. Ajay draws the ticket first, followed by Mohan. Given this, mark <u>all</u> the correct options.
(a) If the probability of Ajay first getting a ticket for the knife-throwing show is four times that for Mohan, the ratio between x and y is 3 : 1
(b) If the probability of Ajay first getting a ticket for the knife-throwing show is five times that for Mohan, the ratio between y and x is 1 : 4
(c) If the probability of Ajay first getting a ticket for the knife-throwing show is two times that for Mohan, the ratio between x and y is 1 : 1
(d) If the probability of Mohan first getting a ticket for the knife-throwing show is six times that for Ajay, the ratio between x and y is 5 : 1

24. Amit, Sumit and Pramit go to a seaside town to spend a vacation there and on the first day everybody decides to visit different tourist locations. After breakfast, each of them boards a different tourist vehicle from the nearest bus-depot. After three hours, Sumit who had gone to a famous sea-beach, calls on the mobile of Pramit and claims that he has observed a shark in the waters. Pramit learns from the local guide that at that time of the year, only eight sea-creatures (including a shark) are observable and the probability of observing any creature is equal. However, Amit and Pramit later recall during their discussion that Sumit has a reputation for not telling the truth five out of six times. What is the probability that Sumit actually observed a shark in the waters?

(a) $\dfrac{1}{36}$ (b) $\dfrac{1}{30}$

(c) $\dfrac{5}{36}$ (d) $\dfrac{1}{24}$

25. x_1, x_2, x_3... x_{50} are fifty real numbers such that $x_r < x_{r+1}$ for r = 1, 2, 3... 49. Five numbers out of these are picked up at random. The probability that the five numbers have x_{20} as the middle is:(Note: The expression in bold has been corrected.)

(a) $\dfrac{^{20}C_2 \times ^{30}C_2}{^{50}C_3}$ (b) $\dfrac{^{30}C_2 \times ^{19}C_2}{^{50}C_5}$

(c) $\dfrac{^{19}C_2 \times ^{31}C_2}{^{50}C_5}$ (d) None of these

26. The game of "chuck-a-luck" is played at carnivals in some parts of Europe. Its rules are as follows: if you pick a number from 1 to 6 and the operator rolls three dice. If the number you picked comes up on all three dice, the operator pays you €3; if it comes up on two dice, you are paid €2; and if it comes up on just one die, you are paid €1. Only if the number you picked does not come up at all, you pay the operator €1. The probability that you will win money playing in this game is:

(a) 0.52 (b) 0.753

(c) 0.42 (d) None of the above

27. McDonald's ran a campaign in which it gave game cards to its customers. These game cards made it possible for customers to win hamburgers, French fries, soft drinks, and other fast-food items, as well as cash prizes. Each card had 10 covered spots that could be uncovered by rubbing them with a coin. Beneath three of these spots were "No Prize" signs. Beneath the other seven spots were names of prizes, two of which were identical. For example, one card might have two pictures of a hamburger, one picture of a Coke, one of French fires, one of a milk shake, one of $5, one of $1000, and three "No Prize" signs. For this card the customer could win a hamburger. To win on any card, the customers had to uncover the two matching spots (which showed the potential prize for that card) before uncovering a "No Prize"; any card with a "No Prize" uncovered was automatically void. Assuming that the two matches and the three "No Prize" signs were arranged randomly on the cards, what is the probability of a customer winning?

(a) 0.10   (b) 0.15

(c) 0.12   (d) None of the above

28. A medical clinic tests blood for certain disease from which approximately one person in a hundred suffers. People come to the clinic in group of 50. The operator of the clinic wonders whether he can increase the efficiency of the testing procedure by conducting pooled tests. In the pooled test, the operator would pool the 50 blood samples and test them altogether. If the pooled test was negative, he could pronounce the whole group healthy. If not, he could then test each person's blood individually. The expected number of tests the operator will have to perform if he pools the blood samples are:

(a) 47   (b) 25

(c) 21   (d) None of the above

2010-12

29. A card is drawn at random from a well shuffled pack of 52 cards.

X: The card drawn is black or a king

Y: The card drawn is a club or a heart or a jack.

Z: The card drawn is an ace or a diamond or a queen.

Then which of the following is correct?

(a) $P(X) > P(Y) > P(Z)$ (b) $P(X) >= P(Y) = P(Z)$

(c) $P(X) = P(Y) > P(Z)$ (d) $P(X) = P(Y) = P(Z)$

30. Mr. Raheja, the president of Alpha Ltd., a construction company, is studying his company's chances of being awarded a Rs.1000 crore bridge building contract in Delhi. In this process, two events interest him. First, Alpha's major competitor Gamma Ltd, is trying to import the latest bridge building technology from Europe, which it hopes to get before the deadline of the award of contract. Second, there are rumors that Delhi Government is investigating all recent contractors and Alpha Ltd is one of those contractors, while Gamma Ltd is not one of those. If Gamma is able to import the technology and there is no investigation by the Government, then Alpha's chance of getting the contract is 0.67. If there is investigation and Gamma Ltd is unable to import the technology in time, the Alpha's chance is 0.72. If both the events occur, then Alpha's chance of getting the contract is 0.58 and if none events occur, its chances are 0.85. Raheja knows that the chance of Gamma Ltd being able to complete the import of technology before the award date is 0.80. How low must the probability of investigation be, so that the probability of the contract being awarded to Alpha Ltd is alteast 0.65? (Assume that occurrence of investigation and Gamma's completion of import in time is independent to each other.)

(a) 0.44   (b) 0.57

(c) 0.63   (d) 0.55

31. A doctor has decided to prescribe two new drugs D1 and D2 to 200 heart patients such that 50 get drug D1, 50 get drug D2 and 100 get both. The 200 patients are chosen so that each had 80% chance of having a heart attack if given neither of the drugs. Drug D1 reduces the probability of a heart attack by 35%, while drug D2 reduces the probability by 20%. The two drugs when taken together, work independently. If a patient, selected randomly from the chosen 200 patients, has a heart attack then the probability that the selected patient was given both the drugs is:

(a) 0.42   (b) 0.49

(c) 0.56   (d) 0.40

2011-13

32. Sun Life Insurance Company issues standard, preferred, and ultra-preferred policies. Among the company's policy holders of a certain age, 50% are standard with a probability of 0.01 of dying in the next year, 30% are preferred with a probability of 0.008 of dying in the next year, and 20% are ultra-preferred with a probability of 0.007 of dying in the next year. If a policy holder of that age dies in the next year, what is the probability of the deceased being a preferred policy holder?

(a) 0.1591   (b) 0.2727

(c) 0.375   (d) None of these

2012-14

33. A bag contains 8 red and 6 blue balls. If 5 balls are drawn at random, what is the probability that 3 of them are red and 2 are blue?

(a) 80/143

(b) 50/143

(c) 75/143

(d) None of the above

34. Ashish is studying late into the night and is hungry. He opens his mother's snack cupboard without switching on the lights, knowing that this mother has kept 10 packets of chips and biscuits in the cupboard. He pulls out 3 packets from the cupboards, and all of them turn out to be chips. What is the probability that the snack cupboard contains 1 packet of biscuits and 9 packets of chips?

(a) 6/55   (b) 12/73

(c) 14/55   (d) 7/50

35. The answer sheets of 5 engineering students can be checked by any one of 9 professors. What is the probability that all the 5 answer sheets are checked by exactly 2 professors?

(a) 20/2187

(b) 40/2187

(c) 40/729

(d) None of the above

36. The probability that in a household LPG will last 60 days or more is 0.8 and that it will last at most 90 days is 0.6. The probability that the LPG will last 60 to 90 days is

(a) 0.40   (b) 0.50

(c) 0.75   (d) None of the above

37. Suppose there are 4 bags. Bag 1 contains 1 black and $a^2 - 6a + 9$ red balls, bag 2 contains 3 black and $a^2 - 6a + 7$ red balls, bag 3 contains 5 black and $a^2 - 6a + 5$ red balls and bag 4 contains 7 black and $a^2 - 6a + 3$ red balls. A ball is drawn at random from a randomly chosen bag. The maximum value of probability that the selected ball is black, is

(a) $16/a^2 - 6a + 10$

(b) $20/a^2 - 6a + 10$

(c) 1/16

(d) None of the above

38. Two trains P and Q are scheduled to reach New Delhi railway station at 10.00 AM. The probability that train P and train Q will be late is 7/9 and 11/27 respectively. The probability that train Q will be late, given that train P is late, is 8/9. Then the probability that neither train will be late on a particular day is

(a) 40/81

(b) 41/81

(c) 77/81

(d) 77/243

39. A survey was conducted to test relative aptitudes in quantitative and logical reasoning of MBA applicants. It is perceived (prior to the survey) that 80 percent of MBA applicants are extremely good in logical reasoning, while only 20 percent are extremely good in quantitative aptitude. Further, it is believed that those with strong quantitative knowledge are also sound in data interpretation, with conditional probability as high as 0.87. However, some MBA applicants who are extremely good in logical reasoning can be also good in data interpretation, with conditional probability 0.15. An applicant surveyed is found to be strong in data interpretation. The probability that the applicant is also strong in quantitative aptitude is

(a) 0.4   (b) 0.6

(c) 0.8   (d) 0.9

40. In the MBA Programme of a B-School, there are two sections A and B 1/4th of the students in Section A and 4/9th of the students in section B are girls. If two students are chosen at random, one each from section A and Section B as class representative, the probability that exactly one of the students chosen is a girl, is:

(a) 23/72   (b) 11/36

(c) 5/12   (d) 17/36

41. The internal evaluation for Economics course in an Engineering programme is based on the score of four quizzes. Rahul has secured 70, 90 and 80 in the first three quizzes. The fourth quiz has ten True-False type questions, each carrying 10 marks. What is the probability that Rahul's average internal marks for the Economics course is more than 80, given that he decides to guess randomly on the final quiz?

(a) 12/1024   (b) 11/1024.

(c) 11/256   (d) 12/256

42. In a reputed engineering college in Delhi, students are evaluated based on trimesters. The probability that an Engineering student fails in the first trimester is 0.08. If he does not fail in the first trimester, the probability that he is promoted to the second year is 0.87. The probability that the student will complete the first year in the Engineering College is approximately:

(a) 0.8   (b) 0.6

(c) 0.4   (d) 0.7

2017-19

43. The student mess committee of a reputed Engineering College has n members. Let P be the event that the Committee has students of both sexes and let Q be the event that there is at most one female student in the Committee. Assuming that each committee member has probability 0.5 of being female, the value of n for which the events A and B are independent is

(a) 2

(b) 3

(c) 4

(d) None of the above

2018-20

44. Witrex Brown, an E-commerce company gives home delivery of its valuable products after receiving final order on their website by different modes of transportation like bike, scooter, tempo and truck. The probabilities of using bike, scooter, tempo and truck are respectively 2/9, 1/9, 4/9 and 2/9. The probabilities of his delivering the product late to the destination by using these modes of transport are 3/5, 2/5, 1/5 and 4/5. If the product reach to the destination in time, find the probability that he has used scooter to reach the office.

(a) 1/10

(b) 4/25

(c) 3/25

(d) None

2019-21

45. A physical therapist of Russian football team knows that the team will play 40% of its matches on artificial turf, this season. Because of his vast experience, he knows that a football player's chances of incurring a knee injury is 50% higher if he is playing on artificial turf instead of grass. If the player's chances of a knee injury on artificial turf is 0.42, what is the probability that a football player with knee injury, incurred the injury while playing on grass?

(a) 0.28

(b) 0.336

(c) 0.5

(d) None of the above

Set Theory

2011-13

46. A survey shows that 61%, 46% and 29% of the people watched "3 idiots", "Rajneeti" and "Avatar" respectively. 25% of people watched exactly two of the three movies and 3% watched none. What percentage of people watched all the three movies?

(a) 39%

(b) 11%

(c) 14%

(d) 7%

47. How many subsets of {1, 2, 3, ... 11}contain at least one even integer?

(a) 1900

(b) 1964

(c) 1984

(d) 2048

2015-17

48. The business consulting division of TCS has overseas operations in 3 locations: Singapore, New York and London. The Company has 22 analysts covering Singapore, 28 covering New York and 24 covering London, 6 analysts cover Singapore and New York but not London, 4 analysis cover Singapore and London but not New York, and 8 analysts cover New York and London but not Singapore. If TCS has a total of 42 business analysts covering at least one of the three locations: Singapore, New York and London, then the number of analysts covering New York alone is:

(a) 14

(b) 28

(c) 5

(d) 7

2016-18

49. In a certain village, 22% of the families own agricultural land, 18% own a mobile phone and 1600 families own both agricultural land and a mobile phone. If 68% of the families neither own agricultural land nor a mobile phone, then the, total number of families living in the village is:

(a) 20000

(b) 10000

(c) 8000

(d) 5000

2017-19

50. 290 students of MBA (International Business) in a reputed Business School have to study foreign language in Trimesters IV and V. Suppose the following information are given

(i) 120 students study Spanish

(ii) 100 students study Mandarin

(iii) At least 80 students, who study a foreign language, study neither Spanish nor Mandarin

Then the number of students who study Spanish but not Mandarin could be any number from

(a) 80 to 170

(b) 80 to 100

(c) 50 to 80

(d) 20 to 110

2018-20

51. A premier B-school, which is in process of getting an AACSB accreditation, has 360 second year students. To incorporate sustainability into their curriculum, it has offered 3 new elective subjects in the second year namely Green Supply Chain, Global Climate Change & Business and Corporate Governance. Twelve students have taken all the three electives, and 120 students have taken Green Supply Chain. There are twice as many students who study Green Supply Chain and Corporate Governance but not Global Climate Change & Business, as those who study both Green Supply Chain and Global Climate Change & Business but not the Corporate Governance, and 4 times as many who study all the three. 124 students study Corporate Governance. There are 72 students who could not muster up the courage to take up any-of these subjects. The group of students who study both Green Supply Chain and Corporate Governance but not Global Climate Change & . Business is exactly the same as the group made up of the students who study both Global Climate Change & Business and Corporate governance. How many students study Global Climate Change & Business only?

(a) 176 (b) 104
(c) 152 (d) 188

2019-21

52. In a survey on the viewership of the TV channels, 73% of those surveyed viewed at least one of the three Channels: Star Plus, Sab TV, and Sony. 38% of those surveyed viewed Star Plus, 39% viewed Sony, and 23% viewed Sab TV. 11% of all those surveyed viewed all the three channels. What percentage of those surveyed, viewed more than one of the three TV channels?

(a) 16 (b) 38
(c) 27 (d) Data Inadequate

ANSWERS

1. (a,c,d)	**2.** (c)	**3.** (d)	**4.** (b)	**5.** (d)	**6.** (c)	**7.** (d)	**8.** (d)
9. (c)	**10.** (b)	**11.** (c)	**12.** (a)	**13.** (a)	**14.** (c)	**15.** (c)	**16.** (d)
17. (d)	**18.** (b)	**19.** (c)	**20.** (d)	**21.** (d)	**22.** (a,c,d)	**23.** (a,b,c)	**24.** (a)
25. (b)	**26.** (c)	**27.** (a)	**28.** (c)	**29.** (c)	**30.** (b)	**31.** (a)	**32.** (b)
33. (d)	**34.** (c)	**35.** (b)	**36.** (a)	**37.** (d)	**38.** (b)	**39.** (b)	**40.** (d)
41. (b)	**42.** (a)	**43.** (b)	**44.** (c)	**45.** (c)	**46.** (d)	**47.** (c)	**48.** (d)
49. (a)	**50.** (d)	**51.** (b)	**52.** (a)				

EXPLANATIONS

1.

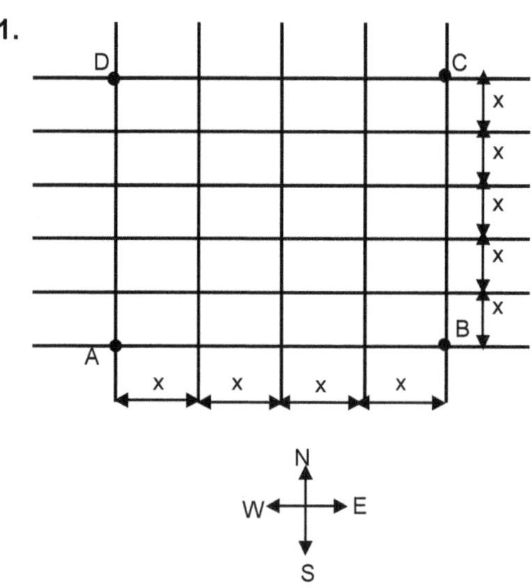

Option (A): Sunil has to go from A to C. There are 4 x's horizontally and 5 x's vertically which have to be arranged in order to reach C, from A. The total number

of routes $= \dfrac{9!}{4!\ 5!} = 126$.

Option (B): The total number of ways includes the shortest possible routes as well. There can be infinitely possible routes as retracing of the paths will not be restricted. Hence, (B) is wrong.

Option (C): A square is a special case of rectangle. To form a rectangle, we have to choose 2 N-S lines from the given 5 and 2 W-E lines, out of 6. Hence, the total number of rectangles $= {}^6C_2 \times {}^5C_2 = 150$.

$\therefore$ Option (C) is correct.

Option (D): As in option (A), we have 11 objects now, out of which 5 are of one kind and 6 are of another

kind. Total number of routes $= \dfrac{11!}{5! \times 6!} = 336$.

$\therefore$ Option (D) is correct.

Hence, only options, (A), (C) and (D) are correct.

2. Before the merger,

X Ltd. had number of employees = 4

Y Ltd. had number of employees = 3

Z Ltd. had number of employees = 5

After the merger, there are quarrels amongst the employees of the erstwhile X Ltd, Y Ltd, & Z Ltd. An employee does not quarrel with any of the employees from his parent company.

Company	X	Y	Z
Employees	4	3	5

Maximum possible number of quarrels of any employee of X Ltd. with the employees of Y Ltd. & Z Ltd. as given by:

$$1 \times 3 + 1 \times 5.$$

Since there are 4 employees in the merged company, who came from X, the total number of quarrels involving employees of X company

$$= 4 \times (1 \times 3 + 1 \times 5)$$
$$= 4 \times 8 = 32 \text{ quarrels} \qquad \text{...(i)}$$

Further, employees of Y Ltd. & Z Ltd. will be involved in quarrels with each other. The total number of such quarrels $\quad = 3 \times (1 \times 5)$

$$= 5 \times (1 \times 3) = 15 \text{ quarrels} \qquad \text{...(ii)}$$

From (i) and (ii),

total number of quarrels between the employees of three erstwhile companies is = 32 + 15 = 47 quarrels.

Hence, option (C) is correct.

3. $\dfrac{{}^{n+2}C_8}{{}^{n-2}P_4} = \dfrac{57}{16}$

$\Rightarrow \dfrac{(n+2)(n+1)(n)(n-1)}{8 \cdot 7 \cdot 6 \cdot 5 \cdot 4 \cdot 3 \cdot 2 \cdot 1} = \dfrac{57}{16}$

$\Rightarrow (n+2)(n+1)(n)(n-1) = 57 \times 7 \times 6 \times 5 \times 4 \times 3$

$$= 21 \times 20 \times 19 \times 18$$

$\Rightarrow \qquad n = 19$

4. As per the question, there are 9 married couples and no husband and wife should play in the same game.

We know that in a mixed double match there are two males and two females.

Step I: Two male members can be selected in

$${}^9C_2 = 36 \text{ ways}$$

Step II: Having selected two male members, 2 female members can be selected

in ${}^7C_2 = 21$ ways

Step III: Two male and two female members can be played a particular game in 2 ways.

Total number of arrangements = 36 × 21 × 2

$$= 1512 \text{ ways.}$$

5. Number of ways in which a pair of shoes can be selected $= {}^3C_1 = 3$ ways

   Number of ways in which "lower wear" can be selected $= (3 + 4) = 7$ ways

   Number of ways in which "upper wear" can be selected $= 3 + 6 + 3 \times 6 = 27$ ways

   Number of ways in which jacket can be chosen or not chosen $= 3$ ways

   {No jacket, 1st jacket, 2nd jacket)

   $\Rightarrow$ Total number of different outfits

   $= 3 \times 7 \times 27 \times 3$

   $= 1701.$

6. The number of numbers between 6000000 and 6999999 that can be formed from the given digits is

   $$\underline{6}\_\_\_\_\_\_ \rightarrow \frac{6!}{2!} = 360$$

   The number of numbers greater than 7000000 that can be formed from the given digits is

   $$\underline{7}\_\_\_\_\_\_ \rightarrow \frac{6!}{2!2!} = 180$$

   So the total number of numbers greater than 6000000 that can be formed from the given digits is 540.

7. We have, $S \rightarrow 2, E \rightarrow 2, R \rightarrow 1, I \rightarrow 1$

   Case I: All alphabet are different

   Number of ways $= 4! = 24$

   Case II: 2 alike and remaining 2 diff.

   Number of ways $= {}^2C_1 \times {}^3C_2 \times \dfrac{4!}{2!} = 72$

   Case III: 2 alike and 2 alike. SSEE

   Number of ways $= \dfrac{4!}{2!2!} = 6$

   Total number of ways $= 24 + 72 + 6 = 102$

8. Let the five-digit number be ABCDE.

   As the number is divisible by 3, possible combinations are:

   (0, 1, 2, 3, 5) and (1, 2, 3, 4, 5)

   Total possible numbers $= 4 \times 4! + 5! = 216.$

9. Let the groups be G_1 and G_2. The possible cases can be tabulated as below

$G_1(5)$	$G_2(5)$
2	4
3	3
4	2

   Hence, the number of ways

   $= {}^5C_2 \times {}^5C_4 + {}^5C_3 \times {}^5C_3 + {}^5C_4 \times {}^5C_2 = 200.$

10. The number of triangles $= {}^8C_3 = 56$

    The number of quadrilaterals $= {}^8C_4 = \dfrac{8!}{4!4!} = 70$

    Hence, the difference $= 70 - 56 = 14.$

11. The required number of words

    $= \left({}^8C_4 \times {}^5C_3\right) \times 7! = 5040 \times 700 = 3528000.$

12. Number of ways of selecting two men and two women who are not couples $= {}^9C_1 \times {}^8C_1 \times {}^7C_1 \times {}^6C_1 = 3024$

    Hence, the required number of ways $= \dfrac{3024}{2} = 1512.$

13. The Required Number = The total number of 8-digit number – Number of 8-digit number with no digits repeated

    $= 10^8 - 10 \times 9 \times 8 \times 7 \times 6 \times 5 \times 4 \times 3$

    $= 981885600.$

14. Required no. of ways = The number of committees that has Rani but not Raj + The number of committees that has Raj but not Rani + The number of committees that has neither Raj nor Rani

    $= {}^6C_3 \times {}^7C_3 + {}^6C_4 \times {}^7C_2 + {}^6C_2 \times {}^7C_4$

    $= 20 \times 35 + 15 \times 21 + 15 \times 35$

    $= 700 + 315 + 525 = 1540.$

15. Required number of ways $= 10! - 2! \times 9!$

    $= 9! (10 - 2)$

    $= 362880 \times 8$

    $= 2903040.$

16. Let the total no. of members be n.

    Total hand shaker $= {}^nC_2$

    ${}^nC_2 = 78$

    $\Rightarrow \quad n = 13.$

17. There are two vowels I and A in RIYADH

    (i) Consider these two vowels IA as one unit.

    $\therefore$ Number of ways in which 2 vowels can be arranged together $= 5! \times 2! = 240$

    Hence, statement (i) is false

    (ii) Total number of arrangements $= 6! = 720.$

    Number of ways in which vowels do not occur together $= 720 - 240 = 480.$

    Hence, statement (ii) is false.

18. The total number of arrangement

    $= {}^{15}P_3 = \dfrac{15!}{12!} = 15 \times 14 \times 13 = 2730.$

19. The number of parking spaces

$$= 20 + 21 + 23 + \ldots$$

$$= 20 + \left[\frac{16}{2}[2 \times 21 + 15 \times 2]\right]$$

$$= 20 + [8[72]]$$

$$= 20 + 576 = 596.$$

20. Number of ways in which a candidate can fail to secure cut offs.

$$= {}^6C_0 + {}^6C_1 + {}^6C_2 + \ldots {}^6C_5$$

$$= 2^6 - 1 = 63.$$

21. One of the lines can be chosen in $4C_1$ ways. Then the 2 points for the base can be chosen in $5C_2$ ways. Remaining 1 point can be chosen in 15 ways.

So $4C_1 \times 5C_2 \times 15 = 600$

22. The correct option will have exactly one country assigned (or matched) to a single year out of the four given. Total number of ways of randomly answering (randomly matching) the question are

$$= 4 \times 3 \times 2 \times 1 = 24 \text{ ways.}$$

Option (D):

$$P(X = 4) = P(\text{All four matches are correct})$$
$$= P(\text{Answer is marked correctly})$$

$$= \frac{1}{24}$$

Hence, (D) is correct.

Option (C): $P(X = 3) = P$(Exactly three matches are correct & fourth is not correct)

If 3 countries are matched correctly, fourth must be correct as well.

So $\quad\quad$ $P(X = 3)$ event will never occur.

Hence, $\quad\quad$ $P(X = 3) = 0$ is also correct.

Option (B): $\quad$ $P(X = 1)$

Let's assume that the match given in the question is the correct match. We have to count, all the possible ways of matches where exactly one is correct and the rest three are wrong.

Lets say, Italy $\rightarrow$ 82 is a correct match. For a wrong match, WG can be 90 or 98 and F $\rightarrow$ 98 or 66 and E $\rightarrow$ 90 or 66.

Case 1: When F is 98; only one way of assignment is (E $\rightarrow$ 66 & WG $\rightarrow$ 90).

Case 2: When F is 66; only one way of assignment is (E $\rightarrow$ 90 & WG $\rightarrow$ 98).

So if the only correct match is that of Italy, there are

exactly two ways of marking the other countries, wrongly.

$$\Rightarrow P(X = 1) = \frac{4 \times (2)}{24} = \frac{8}{24} = \frac{1}{3}.$$

$$\Rightarrow P(X = 1) = \frac{1}{3}.$$

Hence, option (B) is wrong.

Option (A): $P(X \geq 1)$

$$= P(X = 1) + P(X = 2) + P(X = 3) + P(X = 4)$$

$P(X = 2)$ going as in option (B)

$$P(X = 2) = \frac{({}^4C_2 \times 1)}{24} = \frac{6}{24} = \frac{1}{4}$$

$$\Rightarrow P(X \geq 1) = \frac{1}{3} + \frac{1}{4} + 0 + \frac{1}{24} = \frac{15}{24}. \quad P(X \geq 1) = \frac{5}{8}$$

$\Rightarrow$ Option(A) is correct.

Hence, options (A), (C) & (D) are correct.

23. In the pot, there are 'x' tickets of the Knife throwing game and 'y' tickets of the Talking Dolls game. Starting from Ajay, one ticket out of a total of (x + y) is drawn. If the ticket is one of the x tickets for the Knife throwing game, the drawing of tickets is stopped. If a Talking Dolls ticket is drawn, it is put back in the pot.

Probability that Ajay got the first knife throwing ticket (P_A) = (Ajay gets it in first draw)

$$+ \text{(Ajay gets it in third draw)}$$
$$+ \text{(Ajay gets it in fifth draw)} + \ldots\ldots \infty$$

$$P_A = \frac{x}{x + y} + \left(\frac{y}{x + y}\right)^2 \times \left(\frac{x}{x + y}\right)$$
$$+ \left(\frac{y}{x + y}\right)^4 \times \left(\frac{x}{x + y}\right) \ldots \infty$$

$$P_A = \frac{\dfrac{x}{x + y}}{1 - \left(\dfrac{y}{x + y}\right)^2} = \frac{x + y}{x + 2y}$$

$$\Rightarrow P_A = \frac{x + y}{x + 2y}$$

Probability that Mohan got the first Knife throwing ticket (P_M)

$$= \text{(Mohan gets it in second draw)}$$
$$+ \text{(Mohan gets it in fourth draw)}$$
$$+ \text{(Mohan gets it in sixth draw)}$$
$$+ \ldots\ldots \infty$$

$$P_M = \left(\frac{y}{x+y}\right) \times \left(\frac{x}{x+y}\right) + \left(\frac{y}{x+y}\right)^3 \left(\frac{x}{x+y}\right)$$

$$+ \left(\frac{y}{x+y}\right)^5 \times \left(\frac{x}{x+y}\right) + \ldots \infty$$

$$= \frac{\dfrac{xy}{(x+y)^2}}{1 - \left(\dfrac{y}{x+y}\right)^2}$$

$$\therefore P_M = \frac{y}{x+2y}$$

Option (A): Given, $P_A = 4 P_M$

i.e., $\dfrac{x+y}{x+2y} = \dfrac{4y}{x+2y} \Rightarrow \dfrac{x}{y} = \dfrac{3}{1}$

Hence, (A) is correct.

Option (B): Given, $P_A = 5 P_M \Rightarrow \dfrac{x}{y} = \dfrac{4}{1}$

Hence, (B) is correct.

Option (C): $P_A = 2 P_M \Rightarrow \dfrac{x}{y} = \dfrac{1}{1}$

Hence, (C) is correct.

Option (D): $P_M < P_A$ always. $\{\because y < (x+y)\}$

Here, (D) cannot be a valid statement.

Hence, only options (A), (B) and (C) are correct.

24. Probability that Sumit actually sees a Shark, given that he claimed to have seen one,

$$= \frac{P(\text{He actually sees the shark \& reports truth})}{P(\text{He claims of seeing a shark})}$$

$$= \frac{P(\text{sees the shark}) \times P(\text{reports truth})}{\left(\begin{array}{c} P(\text{sees the shark}) \times P(\text{reports truth}) \\ + P(\text{doesn't see}) \times P(\text{reports false}) \end{array}\right)}$$

$$= \frac{\dfrac{1}{8} \times \dfrac{1}{6}}{\dfrac{1}{8} \times \dfrac{1}{6} + \dfrac{7}{8} \times \dfrac{5}{6}} = \frac{\dfrac{1}{48}}{\dfrac{36}{48}} = \frac{1}{36}$$

Hence, option (A) is correct.

25. There is a typographical error in the problem statement. Please read $x_r < x_{r=1}$ as $x_r < x_{r+1}$.

This means, $x_1 < x_2 < x_3 \ldots < x_{50}$. Hence, each of the 19 numbers $x_1, x_2, x_3 \ldots, x_{19}$ is less than the number x_{20} and each of the 30 numbers $x_{21}, x_{22}, x_{23} \ldots, x_{50}$ is greater than x_{20}. Out of the five numbers that are randomly picked, when two numbers are picked from the set $\{x_1, x_2, x_3 \ldots, x_{19}\}$ and two others are picked from the set $\{x_{21}, x_{22}, x_{23} \ldots, x_{50}\}$, the number x_{20} will always be in the middle, when the five numbers are arranged in an order. Total number of ways of selecting such five numbers is $^{30}C_2 \times {}^{19}C_2$. As the total number of ways of selecting a set of any five numbers out of given 50 is $^{50}C_5$, therefore, the required probability is $\dfrac{^{30}C_2 \times {}^{19}C_2}{^{50}C_5}$.

26. If one picks up a number out of the six numbers, then the only case in which he/she will lose money is when none of the three dice shows the picked number on the top surface.

$\Rightarrow$ Required probability of losing the game

$$= \frac{5}{6} \times \frac{5}{6} \times \frac{5}{6} = \frac{125}{216}$$

$\therefore$ Probability of winning the game

$$= \left(1 - \frac{125}{216}\right) = \frac{91}{216} = 0.42$$

27. As per the question there are 10 cover spots out of which

(i) Three spots are there with no prize (identical)

(ii) Two spots of the same sign (Prize)

(iii) Five other spots which are distinct

Let three spots of no prize are (x, x, x), two spots of same sign are (P, P) and five other spots are (A, B, C, D, E).

Total number of cases without restriction $= \dfrac{10!}{3!2!}$

Total number of favourable cases happen in the following ways which shows sequence of can covering

Case I: Second uncovering is 'P'

$$\underline{P}\ \underline{P}\ \_\ \_\ \_\ \_\ \_\ \_\ \_\ \_ \qquad = {}^8C_3 \times 5! \times 1$$

Case II: $\_\ \_\ \underline{P}\ \_\ \_\ \_\ \_\ \_\ \_\ \_$

Number of ways $= {}^7C_3 \times 5! \times 2$

Case III: $\_\ \_\ \_\ \underline{P}\ \_\ \_\ \_\ \_\ \_\ \_$

Number of ways $= {}^6C_3 \times 5! \times 3$

Case IV: $\_\ \_\ \_\ \_\ \underline{P}\ \_\ \_\ \_\ \_\ \_$

Number of ways $= {}^5C_3 \times 5! \times 4$

Case V: $\_\ \_\ \_\ \_\ \_\ \underline{P}\ \_\ \_\ \_\ \_$

Number of ways $= {}^4C_3 \times 5! \times 5$

Case VI: $\_\ \_\ \_\ \_\ \_\ \_\ \underline{P}\ \_\ \_\ \_$

Number of ways $= {}^3C_3 \times 5! \times 6$

Total number of favourable cases

$$= \frac{\left(\begin{array}{l} ^{8}C_3 \times 5! + {}^{7}C_3 \times 5! \times 2 + {}^{6}C_3 \times 5! \times 3 + \\ {}^{5}C_3 \times 5! \times 4 + {}^{4}C_3 \times 5! \times 5 + {}^{3}C_3 \times 5! \times 6 \end{array} \right)}{\left(\dfrac{10!}{3!2!} \right)} = 0.10$$

28. $P(\text{one person is unhealthy}) = \dfrac{1}{100}$

In a group of 50, number of unhealthy persons can be 0, 1, 2, 3, …. or 50.

Their probabilities are:

$P(0 \text{ unhealthy}) = (0.99)^{50}$

$P(1 \text{ unhealthy}) = {}^{50}C_1 \times (0.01) \times (0.99)^{49}$

$P(2 \text{ unhealthy}) = {}^{50}C_2 \times (0.01)^2 \times (0.99)^{48}$

….

$P(50 \text{ unhealthy}) = {}^{50}C_{50} \times (0.01)^{50}$

When no person is unhealthy, the polled test will be negative and hence, in a single test the group shall be declared healthy. In all the other cases, one pool test + 50 individual tests (i.e. 51 tests) are conducted to ascertain the status of health.

∴ $P(\text{one test is required}) = (0.99)^{50} \approx 0.60$ and $P(51$ tests are required$) = 1 - 0.60 = 0.40$

∴ Required expectation = 1 × 0.60 + 51 × 0.40 = 21

29. We have, $P(X) = \dfrac{26 + 2}{52} = \dfrac{28}{52}$

$$P(Y) = \dfrac{13 + 13 + 2}{52} = \dfrac{28}{52}$$

$$P(Z) = \dfrac{3 + 13 + 3}{52} = \dfrac{19}{52}$$

∴ $P(X) = P(Y) > P(Z)$

30. Let the probability of investigation be 'p'.

Given that the probability of Gamma Ltd. being able to complete the import of technology before the award date = 0.8

There are four possible cases:

Case I: Gamma is able to import the technology and there is no investigation by the government. Probability of occurrence of Case I = 0.8(1 – p)

Case II: Gamma is unable to import the technology and there is investigation by the government. Probability of occurrence of Case II = 0.2p

Case III: Gamma is able to import the technology and there is investigation by the government. Probability of occurrence of Case III = 0.8p

Case IV: Gamma is unable to import the technology and there is no investigation by the government. Probability of occurrence of Case II = 0.2(1 – p)

Probability of contract being awarded to Alpha Ltd.

$$= 0.67 \times 0.8(1 - p) + 0.72 \times 0.2p$$
$$+ 0.58 \times 0.8p + 0.85 \times 0.2(1 - p)$$
$$= 0.706 - 0.098p.$$

For the probability of contract being awarded to Alpha Ltd. to be at least 0.65:

$$0.706 - 0.098p \geq 0.65$$

$$\Rightarrow \quad 0.056 \geq 0.098p$$

$$\Rightarrow \quad p \leq 0.57$$

For $p \leq 0.57$, the probability of contract being awarded to Alpha is at least 0.65.

*There is ambiguity in the question. Going by the options, the question should have been:

"How high must the probability of investigation be, so that the probability of the contract being award to Alpha Ltd. is attest 0.65?".

Hence, the correct option is (B).

31. Probability of a person getting a heart attack,

$$P(H) = \dfrac{80}{100} = 0.8$$

Here, $P(D1) = \dfrac{50}{200} = \dfrac{1}{4}$,

$$P(D2) = \dfrac{50}{200} = \dfrac{1}{4}$$

and $P(D1 \cap D2) = \dfrac{100}{200} = \dfrac{1}{2}$

Probability of a person getting a heart attack, if drug D1 is given,

$$P(H / D1) = (1 - 0.35) \times 0.8$$

$$= \dfrac{65}{100} \times \dfrac{80}{100} = \dfrac{52}{100}$$

Probability of a person getting a heart attack, if drug D2 is given,

$$P(H / D2) = (1 - 0.20) \times 0.8$$

$$= \dfrac{80}{100} \times \dfrac{80}{100} = \dfrac{64}{100}$$

Probability of a person getting a heart attack, if both D1 and D2 are given,

$P(H / D1 \cap D2) = (1 - 0.35) \times (1 - 0.20) \times 0.8$

$$= \frac{65}{100} \times \frac{80}{100} \times \frac{80}{100} \approx \frac{42}{100}$$

Applying Baye's Theorem,

$$P(D1 \cap D2 / H) = \frac{P(H/ D1 \cap D2)\, P(D1 \cap D2)}{\begin{array}{c} P(H/ D1 \cap D2)\, P(D1 \cap D2) + \\ P(H / D1)\, P(D1) + P(H /D2)\, P(D2) \end{array}}$$

$$= \frac{\dfrac{42}{100} \times \dfrac{1}{2}}{\dfrac{42}{100} \times \dfrac{1}{2} + \dfrac{52}{100} \times \dfrac{1}{4} + \dfrac{64}{100} \times \dfrac{1}{4}} = \frac{42}{100} = 0.42$$

32.

Standard	Preferred	Ultra – preferred
50%	30%	20%

Probability	0.01	0.008	0.007
P(dying)	0.5%	0.24%	0.14%

$$\text{Required probability} = \frac{P(\text{preferred})}{P(\text{dying})} = \frac{0.24}{0.88}$$

$$= \frac{3}{11} = 0.2727.$$

33. Number of ways of selecting 3 red balls $= {}^{8}C_3$

Number of ways of selecting 2 blue balls $= {}^{6}C_2$

Number of ways of selecting 5 balls $= {}^{14}C_5$

$$\text{Required probability} = \frac{{}^{8}C_3 \times {}^{6}C_2}{{}^{14}C_5} = \frac{60}{143}.$$

34. There could have been 3 or 4 or 5 or $\cdots$ or 9, or 10 packets of chips.

Since the favorable case is that of 9 packets of chips, total number of favourable cases $= {}^{9}C_3 = 84$

Total number of cases

$$= {}^{3}C_3 + {}^{4}C_3 + {}^{5}C_3 + {}^{6}C_3 + {}^{7}C_3 + {}^{8}C_3 + {}^{9}C_3 + {}^{10}C_3$$
$$= 330$$

Required probability

$$= \frac{\text{Number of favourable case}}{\text{Total number of cases}} = \frac{14}{55}.$$

35. The number of ways in which the answer sheets of 5 engineering students can be checked by any one of 9 professor

$$= 9 \times 9 \times 9 \times 9 \times 9 = 9^5$$

The number of ways in which answer sheets of 5 students can be checked by exactly 2 professors

$$= (2 \times 2 \times 2 \times 2 \times 2 - 2) \times {}^{9}C_2$$
$$= 30 \times 36 = 1080 \text{ ways.}$$

We need to subtract two cases, as either of the professors cannot check all the five sheets.

The probability that all the 5 answer sheets are checked by exactly two professors $= \dfrac{1080}{9^5} = \dfrac{40}{2187}.$

36. The probability in a household LPG will last 60 days or more $= 0.8$

Therefore, the probability in a household LPG will last less than 60 days $= 0.2$

The probability LPG will last at most 90 days $= 0.6$

Therefore, the probability LPG will last 60 to 90 days is $= 0.6 - 0.2 = 0.4$

37. Total number of black balls $= 16$

Total number of red balls $= 4a^2 - 24a + 24$

Total number of balls $= 4a^2 - 24a + 40$

Probability that a ball selected is black

$$= \frac{16}{4a^2 - 24a + 40} = \frac{4}{a^2 - 6a + 10}$$

For the probability to be the maximum, the number of red balls in bag 4 should be 0 i.e. $a^2 - 6a + 3 = 0$.

Hence, the required probability $= \dfrac{4}{7}.$

38. Probability that train P will be late $= P(P) = \dfrac{7}{9}$

Probability that train Q will be late $= P(Q) = \dfrac{11}{27}$

Probability of Q will be late in case P is late

$$= P\left(\frac{Q}{P}\right) = \frac{P(P \cap Q)}{P(P)} \quad \text{[Using conditional probability]}$$

$$\Rightarrow \frac{7}{9} \times \frac{8}{9} = P(P \cap Q) \Rightarrow P(P \cap Q) = \frac{56}{81}$$

Probability of either P or Q or both being late

$$= P(P) + P(Q) - P(P \cap Q)$$

$$= \frac{7}{9} + \frac{11}{27} - \frac{56}{81} = \frac{40}{81}$$

Hence, the probability that neither of the trains will be late $= 1 - \dfrac{40}{81} = \dfrac{41}{81}.$

39. Probability that an applicant is good in Logical reasoning = P(LR) = 0.8

Probability that an applicant is good in Quantitative aptitude = P(QA) = 0.2

Probability that an applicant is good in Data interpretation given that he is good in Quantitative aptitude $= P\left(\dfrac{DI}{QA}\right) = 0.87$

Probability that an applicant is good in Data interpretation given that he is good in Logical reasoning $= P\left(\dfrac{DI}{LR}\right) = 0.15$

Probability that an applicant is good in Data interpretation given that he is good in Quantitative aptitude

$$= P\left(\dfrac{DI}{LR}\right) = \dfrac{P(QA) \times P\left(\dfrac{DI}{QA}\right)}{P(QA) \times P\left(\dfrac{DI}{QA}\right) + P(LR) \times P\left(\dfrac{DI}{LR}\right)}$$

$$= P\left(\dfrac{DI}{LR}\right) = \dfrac{0.2 \times 0.87}{0.2 \times 0.87 + 0.8 \times 0.15} \approx 0.6.$$

40. The two students can be selected in two ways: girl from section A and boy from Section B; boy from section A and girls from Section B.

The required probability $= \dfrac{1}{4} \times \dfrac{5}{9} + \dfrac{3}{4} \times \dfrac{4}{9} = \dfrac{17}{36}$.

41. Since, Rahul's average internal marks should be more than 80, therefore He must score more than 320 (80 × 4) marks in four quizzes together.

Total score in three quizzes = 70 + 90 + 80 = 240

How, he should score 90 or 100 marks in the fourth quiz.

To score 90 marks, he should correct 9 questions out of 10 questions, which is possible in $^{10}C_9 = 10$ ways.

To score 100 marks he should correct all the ten questions, which is possible in only one way.

Total number of required ways = 10 + 1 = 11

Total number of possible ways in which he can attempt 10 questions

$$= 2 \times 2 \times 2 \times 2 \times 2 \times 2 \times 2 \times 2 \times 2 \times 2$$
$$= 2^{10} = 1024.$$

Required probability $= \dfrac{11}{1024}$.

42. Required Probability = (1 − 0.08) × 0.87 = 0.8.

43. $P(P) = 1 - \dfrac{1}{2^n}$ (when all males) $- \dfrac{1}{2^n}$ (when all females)

$P(Q) = \dfrac{1}{2^n}$ (when all males) $+ \dfrac{n \times 1}{2} \times \dfrac{1}{2^{n-1}}$ (when one female and rest males)

$P(P \cap Q) =$ exactly one female $= n \times \dfrac{1}{2} \times \dfrac{1}{2^{n-1}}$

For independent events
$P(P \cap Q) = P(P) \times P(Q)$

$$\dfrac{n}{2^n} = \left(1 - \dfrac{1}{2^n} - \dfrac{1}{2^n}\right)\left(\dfrac{1}{2^n} + \dfrac{n}{2^n}\right)$$

Solving we get n = 3.

44. Prob. of delivery product on time by scooter

$$= \dfrac{1}{9} \times \dfrac{3}{5} = \dfrac{3}{45}$$

Prob. of delivery product on there by all means

$$= \dfrac{2}{9} \times \dfrac{2}{5} + \dfrac{1}{9} \times \dfrac{3}{5} + \dfrac{4}{9} \times \dfrac{4}{5} + \dfrac{2}{9} \times \dfrac{1}{5} = \dfrac{25}{45}$$

$$\therefore \dfrac{\text{Prob. of (on time by scooter)}}{\text{On time by all means}} = \dfrac{\dfrac{3}{45}}{\dfrac{25}{45}} = \dfrac{3}{25}$$

Hence option (C)

45. 40% matches on artificial turf

60% matches on grass.

Chances of knee injury on Artificial turf = 0.42

Chance of knee injury on Grass = .28

Probability of injury = (0.4 × 0.42) + (0.6 × 0.28)
$$= .336$$

Required probability $= \dfrac{.6 \times .28}{.3.36} = .5$

46. Let A, B and C are the number of people who watched exactly one, exactly two and exactly three movies respectively.

$$A + B + C = 97\% \ (\text{i.e. } 100\% \text{-}3\%)$$
$$A + 2B + 3C = 136\%$$

Here $\qquad B = 25\%$,

$\therefore \qquad A + C = 72\%$

and $\qquad A + 3C = 86\%$

On solving, we get, C = 7%.

47. Total number of subsets $= 2^{11}$

Total number of subsets having no even element 2^6 (i.e. using (1, 3, 5, 7, 11, 13)

Hence, answer $= 2^{11} - 2^6 = 1984$

48. Let the number of analyst covering all the three locations be x.

$\therefore 42 = 22 + 28 + 24 - (6 + x) - (8 + x) - (4 + x) + x$

$\Rightarrow x = 7$

Hence, the no. employees covering New York alone

$= 28 - (6 + 8 + 7) = 7.$

49.

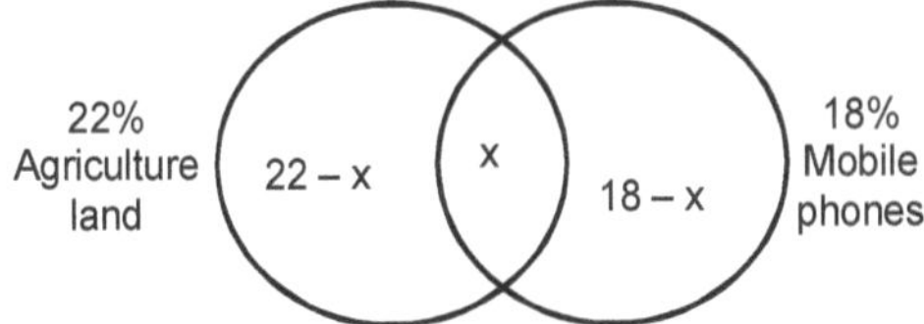

Percentage families having either agriculture land or Mobile phones

$$= 100 - 68 = 32\%$$

$$32 = 22 - x + x + 18 - x$$

$$\Rightarrow \quad x = 8\%$$

Since, 8% is equal to 1600;

Hence total number of families

$$= \frac{1600}{18} \times 100$$

$$= 20000.$$

50. Total students = 290.

Let 80 students do not study either Spanish or Mandarin.

$\therefore$ Number of students who study Spanish or Mandarin or both = 290 – 80 = 210.

$\therefore \quad n(S \cup M) = n(S) + n(M) - n(S \cap M)$

$\Rightarrow \quad 210 = 120 + 100 - n(S \cap M)$

$\Rightarrow \quad n(S \cap M) = 10$

$\therefore$ Number of students who study Spanish but not Mandarin $= 120 - 10$

$\qquad\qquad = 110.$

51.

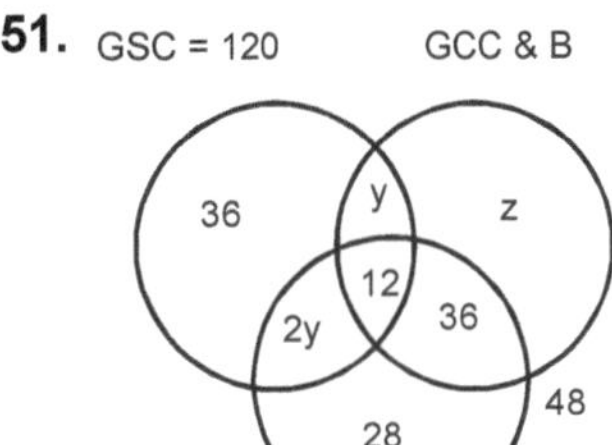

Here $\quad y = 24, 2y = 48$

$36 + 24 + z + 48 + 1 + 36 + 28 = 288$

$\qquad 184 + z = 288$

$\qquad\qquad z = 288 - 184 = 104$

Hence option (B)

52. Let total surveyed = 100

$\qquad$ Star plus = 38

$\qquad\qquad$ Sony = 39

$\qquad\qquad$ Sab TV = 23

Let x, y, z be the no. of people who viewed exactly 1, exactly 2 and exactly 3 channel respectively

$\qquad x + 2y + 32 = 38 + 39 + 23$

$\Rightarrow 100$

$\qquad x + 2y + 32 = 100 \dots\dots (1)$

$\qquad x + y + z = 73 \dots\dots\dots (2)$

on solving (1) and (2) y + 2z = 27

Now $\qquad\qquad z = 11$, so y = 5

Answer 11 + 5 = 16

Equations, Polynomials & Inequations

2007-09

1. If the sum of the roots of the quadratic equation $px^2 + qx + r = 0$ is equal to the sum of the square of their reciprocals, mark <u>all</u> the correct statements.

   (a) r/p, p/q and q/r are in (a)P.

   (b) p/ r, q/p and r/q are in G. P.

   (c) p/r, q/p and r/q are in H. P.

   (d) p/r, q/p and r/q are in (a)P.

2. The square root of the harmonic mean of the roots of the equation

   $$\left(5 + \sqrt{2}\right)x^2 - \left(4 + \sqrt{5}\right)x + 8 + 2\sqrt{5} = 0 \text{ is.}$$

   (a) ± 3

   (b) ± 4

   (c) $\sqrt{2}$

   (d) None of these

3. If one root is the square of the other root in the equation $x^2 + px + q = 0$, mark the correct relationship in the following options.

   (a) $p^3 - q(3p + 1) + q^2 = 0$

   (b) $p^3 - q(3p - 1) + q^2 = 0$

   (c) $p^3 + q(3p - 1) + q^2 = 0$

   (d) $p^3 - q(3p - 1) - q^2 = 0$

4. If α, β are the roots of the quadratic equation $x^2 + mx + 1 = 0$ and γ, δ are the roots of the equation $x^2 + nx + 1 = 0$, then the value of $(\alpha - \gamma)(\beta - \gamma)(\alpha + \delta)(\beta + \delta)$ is equal to

   (a) $n^2 - m^2$.

   (b) $m^2 - n^2$.

   (c) $2 m^2 - n^2$.

   (d) None of the above

2008-10

5. Suppose q is the number of workers employed by Simplex Ltd. for one of its projects. The average cost of production c is given by

   $$c = \frac{1}{3}q^2 + \frac{5}{2}q - 150 + \frac{75}{q}.$$ In the interest of the company, it should employ __________ workers.

   (a) 5

   (b) 4

   (c) 7

   (d) None of these

6. LG Electronics finds that it can sell x television per week at Rs. p each where $p = 2\left(100 - \frac{x}{4}\right)$. The cost of production of x television per week is Rs. $\left(120x + \frac{x^2}{2}\right)$. Find it's maximum profit per week.

   (a) 1200

   (b) 1700

   (c) 1600

   (d) 1000

2009-11

7. DSBO Company produces Z units of output at a total cost of Rs. R, where

   $$R = \frac{1}{10}Z^3 - 5Z^2 + 10Z + 5.$$ At what level of output will the average variable cost attain its minimum?

   (a) 20

   (b) 33

   (c) 25

   (d) None of the above

8. If one root of the equation $ax^2 + bx + c = 0$ is double of the other, then $2b^2 =$

   (a) 9ca

   (b) $c\sqrt{2}a$

   (c) $2\sqrt{3}ac$

   (d) None of the above

2010-12

9. The number of distinct terms in the expansion of $(X + Y + Z + W)^{30}$ are:

   (a) 4060

   (b) 5456

   (c) 27405

   (d) 46376

10. The coefficient of x^7 in the expansion of $(1 - x^2 + x^3)(1 + x)^{10}$ is:

   (a) 75

   (b) 78

   (c) 85

   (d) None of the above

2011-13

11. Find the root of the quadratic equation $bx^2 - 2ax + a = 0$

   (a) $\dfrac{\sqrt{b}}{\sqrt{b} \pm \sqrt{a - b}}$

   (b) $\dfrac{\sqrt{a}}{\sqrt{b} \pm \sqrt{a - b}}$

   (c) $\dfrac{\sqrt{a}}{\sqrt{a} \pm \sqrt{a - b}}$

   (d) $\dfrac{\sqrt{a}}{\sqrt{a} \pm \sqrt{a + b}}$

12. Find the coefficient of x^{12} in the expansion of $(1-x^6)^4$ $(1-x)^{-4}$

(a) 113

(b) 119

(c) 125

(d) 132

2012-14

13. If x satisfies the inequality $|x-1|+|x-2|+|x-3| \geq 6$, then:

(a) $0 \leq x \leq 4$

(b) $x \leq 0$ or $x \geq 4$

(c) $x \leq -2$ or $x \geq 3$

(d) None of the above

2013-15

14. The equation $7^{x-1} + 11^{x-1} = 170$ has

(a) no solution

(b) one solution

(c) two solution

(d) three solutions

2014-16

15. If $x^2 + 3x - 10$ is a factor of $3x^4 + 2x^3 - bx - a + b - 4$, then the closest approximate values of a and b are

(a) 25, 43

(b) 52, 43

(c) 52, 67

(d) None of the above

16. If x is real, the smallest value of the expression $3x^2 - 4x + 7$ is:

(a) 2/3

(b) 3/4

(c) 7/9

(d) None of the above

2016-18

17. The value of x for which the equation $\sqrt{4x-9} + \sqrt{4x+9} = 5 + \sqrt{7}$ will be satisfied, is:

(a) 1

(b) 2

(c) 3

(d) 4

18. The simplest value of the expression

$$\left\{ \frac{4^{p+\frac{1}{4}} \times \sqrt{2 \times 2^p}}{2 \times \sqrt{2^{-p}}} \right\}^{1/p}$$

(a) 4

(b) 8

(c) 4

(d) 8

2017-19

19. The smallest integer x for which the inequality $\dfrac{x-7}{x^2+5x-36} > 0$ is given by

(a) −12

(b) 9

(c) −9

(d) −8

2019-21

20. Given $P(x, y) = x^2 + xy + y^2$; $Q(x, y) = x^2 - xy + y^2$. Find the value of $P(7, Q(9, 4))$

(a) 4169

(b) 4197

(c) 4089

(d) 4127

21. The roots of quadratic equation $y^2 - 8y + 14 = 0$ are α and β. Find the value of $(1 + \alpha + \beta^2)(1 + \beta + \alpha^2)$

(a) 419

(b) 431

(c) $485 + 3\sqrt{22}$

(d) $453 + \sqrt{22}$

22. The square root of $1 + x^2 + \sqrt{1 + x^2 + x^4}$ is

(a) $\dfrac{1}{\sqrt{2}}\left[\sqrt{1+x+x^2} + \sqrt{1-x+x^2} \right]$

(b) $\dfrac{1}{\sqrt{2}}\left[\sqrt{1+x+x^2} - \sqrt{1-x+x^2} \right]$

(c) $\dfrac{1}{\sqrt{2}}\sqrt{\left(1+x^2+x^4+x^8\right)}$

(d) None of the above

Functions

2007-09

23. The domain of definition of the function

$$y = \frac{1}{\{\log_{10}(3-x)\}} + \sqrt{x+7} \text{ is}$$

(a) $[-7, 3) \sim \{0\}$

(b) $[-7, 3] \sim \{0\}$

(c) $(-7, 3) \sim \{0\}$

(d) $(-7, 3] \sim \{0\}$

2010-12

24. Fortuner, the latest SUV by Toyota Motors, consumes diesel at the rate of $\dfrac{1}{400}\left\{ \left[\dfrac{1000}{x} \right] + x \right\}$ litres per km, when driven at the speed of x km per hour. If the cost of diesel is Rs.35 per litre and the driver is paid at the rate of Rs.125 per hour then find the approximate optimal speed (in km per hour) of Fortuner that will minimize the total cost of the round trip of 800 kms.

(a) 49

(b) 55

(c) 50

(d) 53

2011-13

25. A Metro train from Mehrauli to Gurgaon has capacity to board 900 people. The fare charged (in Rs.) is defined by the function $f = \left(54 - \dfrac{x}{32}\right)^2$ where 'x' is the number of the people per trip. How many people per trip will make the marginal revenue equal to zero?

(a) 1728   (b) 576

(c) 484   (d) 364

2014-16

26. The duration of the journey from your home to the College in the local train varies directly as the distance and inversely as the velocity. The velocity varies directly as the square root of the diesel used per km., and inversely as the number of carriage in the train. If, in a journey of 70 km. in 45 minutes with 15 carriages, 10 litres of diesel is required, then the diesel that will be consumed in a journey of 50 km. in half an hour with 18 carriages is

(a) 2.9 litres   (b) 11.8 litres

(c) 15.7 litres   (d) None of the above

2018-20

27. If $f(x) = \dfrac{1}{1 \ x}$, then find the value of $f[f\{f(x)\}]$, at x=5

(a) 7/9

(b) 7/13

(c) 5/13

(d) 5/9

28. In a certain sequence the term x_n is given by formula

$$X_n = 5x_{n-1} - \frac{3}{4}X_{n-2} \text{ for } n \geq 2.$$

What is the value of x_3, if $x_0 = 4$ and $x_1 = 2$?

(a) 67/2   (b) 37/2

(c) 123/4   (d) None

29. Suntex Company plans to manufacture a new product line of Razor next year and sell it at a price of Rs. 12 per unit. The variable costs per unit in each production run is estimated to be 50% of the selling price, and the fixed costs for each production run is estimated to be Rs. 50,400. Based on their estimated. costs how many units of the new product will company Suntex need to manufacture and sell in order for their revenue to be equal to their total costs for each production run?

(a) 5400   (b) 4200

(c) 8400   (d) 2100

2019-21

30. Land Cruiser Prado, the latest SUV from Toyota Motors, consumes diesel at the rate of $\dfrac{1}{400}\left\{\dfrac{100}{x} + x\right\}$ litres per Km, when travelling at the speed of x km/hr. The diesel costs Rs. 65 per litre and the driver is paid Rs. 50 per hour. Find the steady speed that will minimize the total cost of a 1000 km trip?

(a) 33 km/hr   (b) 36 km/hr

(c) 39 km/hr   (d) 52 km/hr

Logarithm and Exponents

2007-09

31. If $\dfrac{\log x}{b - c} = \dfrac{\log y}{c - a} = \dfrac{\log z}{a - b}$, mark all the correct options

(a) $xyz = 1$ (b) $x^a y^b z^c = 1$

(c) $x^{b+c} y^{c+a} z^{a+b} = 1$ (d) $x^{b+c} y^{c+a} z^{a+b} = 0$

2009-11

32. If three positive real numbers a, b and c (c > a) are in Harmonic Progression, then Log $(a+c) + $ Log $(a - 2b + c)$ is equal to:

(a) $2 \log (c - b)$ (b) $2 \log (c - c)$

(c) $2 \log (c - a)$ (d) Log a + Log b + Log c

2010-12

33. If $\text{Log}_2 x . \text{Log}_{\frac{x}{64}} 2 = \text{Log}_{\frac{x}{16}} 2$. Then x is

(a) 2   (b) 4

(c) 16   (d) 12

2011-13

34. Find the sum of the following series;

$$\frac{2}{1!} + \frac{3}{2!} + \frac{6}{3!} + \frac{11}{4!} + \frac{18}{5!} + \dots$$

(a) 3e–1   (b) 3(e–1)

(c) 3(e+1)   (d) 3e + 1

35. What is the value of $\sqrt{\dfrac{a}{b}}$, If $\log_4 \log_4 4^{a-b}$

$$= 2\log_4 \left(\sqrt{a} - \sqrt{b}\right) + 1$$

(a) –5/3   (b) 2

(c) 5/3   (d) 1

36. $\log_5 2$ is

(a) An integer   (b) A rational number

(c) A prime number   (d) An irrational number

2012-14

37. Find the value of x from the following equation: $\log_{10}3 + \log_{10}(4x+1) = \log_{10}(x+1)+1$

(a) 2/7   (b) 7/2

(c) 9/2   (d) None of the above

2013-15

38. If $\log 3$, $\log(3^x-2)$ and $\log(3^x+4)$ are arithmetic progression, then x is equal to

(a) 8/3   (b) $\log_3 8$

(c) $\log_2 3$ (d) 8

2014-16

39. If $\log_{10} x - \log_{10} \sqrt[3]{x} = 6\log_x 10$, then the value of x is

(a) 10   (b) 30

(c) 100   (d) 1000

40. If $\log_{13}\log_{21}\left\{\sqrt{x+21}+\sqrt{x}\right\} = 0$, then the value of x is

(a) 21   (b) 13

(c) 81   (d) None of the above

2015-17

41. The value of $\log_7 \log_7 \sqrt{7(\sqrt{(7\sqrt{7})})}$ is equal to:

(a) 7   (b) $\log_7 2$

(c) $1 - 3\log_2 7$ (d) $1 - 3\log_7 2$

2016-18

42. If $\log_{25}5 = a$ and $\log_{25}15 = b$, then the value of $\log_{25}27$ is:

(a) $3(b+a)$ (b) $3(1-b-a)$

(c) $3(a+b-1)$ (d) $3(1-b+a)$

2017-19

43. Find the value of x which satisfies the following equation

$$4\log_7(x-8) = \log_3 81$$

(a) 8   (b) 18

(c) 20   (d) None of the above

2018-20

44. $(1+5)\log_e 3 + \dfrac{1}{2!}5^2(\log_e 3)^2 + \dfrac{1}{3!}5^3(\log_e 3)^3 + \ldots$

(a) 12   (b) 244

(c) 243   (d) 245

2019-21

45. $\dfrac{1}{\log_x yz + 1} + \dfrac{1}{\log_y xz + 1} + \dfrac{1}{\log_z xy + 1} = ?$

(a) 0

(b) 1

(c) xyz

(d) $\dfrac{\log xyz}{\log xyz + 1}$

46. $\log_2 x \cdot \log_{\frac{x}{64}} 2 = \log_{\frac{x}{16}} 2$; then x = ?

(a) 2   (b) 4

(c) 12   (d) 16

Progressions

2007-09

47. The inverse of the sum of the following series up to n terms can be written as $\dfrac{3}{4} + \dfrac{5}{36} + \dfrac{7}{144} + \ldots$

(a) $\dfrac{(n-1)^2}{n^2+2n}$ (b) $\dfrac{n^2+2n}{(n-1)^2}$

(c) $\dfrac{n^2+2n}{(n+1)^2}$ (d) $\dfrac{(n+1)^2}{n^2+2n}$

48. If $\alpha \neq n\pi$ and $\tan\alpha$ is the GM of $\sin\alpha$ and $\cos\alpha$, determine the square of the expression

$$2 - 4\sin^2\alpha + 3\sin^4\alpha - \sin^6\alpha.$$

(a) 1   (b) 4

(c) $\dfrac{1}{4}$ (d) None of these

2009-11

49. If $H_1, H_2, H_3, \ldots, H_n$, are n Harmonic means between 'a' and 'b' $(\neq a)$, then value of $\dfrac{H_1+a}{H_1-a} + \dfrac{H_n+b}{H_n-b}$ is equal to:

(a) $n+1$ (b) $2n$

(c) $2n+3$ (d) $n-1$

50. Suppose a, b and c are in Arithmetic Progression, and a^2, b^2 and c^2 are in Geometric Progression.

If $a < b < c$ and $a+b+c = \dfrac{3}{2}$ then the value a =

(a) $\dfrac{1}{2\sqrt{2}}$ (b) $\dfrac{1}{2\sqrt{3}}$

(c) $\dfrac{1}{2} - \dfrac{1}{\sqrt{3}}$ (d) $\dfrac{1}{2} - \dfrac{1}{\sqrt{2}}$

51. Sum of the series $1^2 - 2^2 + 3^2 - 4^2 + \ldots\ldots\ldots +2001^2 - 2002^2 + 2003^2$ is:
    (a) 2007006
    (b) 1005004
    (c) 200506
    (d) None of the above

52. If the positive real numbers a, b and c are in Arithmetic Progression, such that $abc = 4$, then minimum possible value of b is:
    (a) $2^{\frac{3}{2}}$
    (b) $2^{\frac{2}{3}}$
    (c) $2^{\frac{1}{3}}$
    (d) None of the above

2010-12

53. The sum of the series is:
$$\frac{1}{1.2.3} + \frac{1}{3.4.5} + \frac{1}{5.6.7} + \ldots\ldots$$
    (a) $e^2 - 1$
    (b) $\log_e 2 - 1$
    (c) $2\log_{10} 2 - 1$
    (d) None of the above

54. A ping pong ball is dropped from a 45 meters high multi-storey building. The ball bounces back three fifth of the distance each time before coming to rest. The total distance traversed by the ball is:
    (a) 150m
    (b) 180m
    (c) 175m
    (d) None of the above

2011-13

55. If [x] is the greatest integer less than or equal to 'x' then find the value of the following series.
$$[\sqrt{1}] + [\sqrt{2}] + [\sqrt{3}] + [\sqrt{4}] + \ldots + [\sqrt{361}]$$
    (a) 4389
    (b) 4839
    (c) 3498
    (d) 3489

2012-14

56. If 2, a, b, c, d, e, f and 65 form an arithmetic progression, find out the value of 'e'.
    (a) 48
    (b) 47
    (c) 41
    (d) None of the above

2014-16

57. A tennis ball is initially dropped from a height of 180 m. After striking the ground, it rebounds $(3/5)^{th}$ of the height from which it has fallen. The total distance that the ball travels before it comes to rest is
    (a) 540 m
    (b) 600 m
    (c) 720 m
    (d) 900 m

2015-17

58. A bouncing tennis ball is dropped from a height of 32 metre. The ball rebounds each time to a height equal to half the height of the previous bounce. The approximate distance travelled by the ball when it hits the ground for the eleventh time, is.
    (a) 64 metre
    (b) 96 metre
    (c) 128 metre
    (d) 150 metre

59. Let P_1 be the circle of radius r. A square Q_1 is inscribed in P_1 such that all the vertices of the square Q_1 lie on the circumference of P_1. Another circle P_2 is inscribed in Q_1. Another Square Q_2 is inscribed in the circle P_2. Circle P_3 is inscribed in the square Q_2 and so on. If S_N is the area between Q_N and P_{N+1}, where N represents the set of natural numbers, then the ratio of sum of all such S_N to that of the area of the square Q_1 is:
    (a) $\dfrac{4 - \pi}{2}$
    (b) $\dfrac{2\pi - 4}{\pi}$
    (c) $\dfrac{\pi - 2}{2}$
    (d) None of the above

2017-19

60. The sum of $4 + 44 + 444 + \ldots$ upto n terms is
    (a) $\dfrac{40}{81}(8^n - 1) - \dfrac{5n}{9}$
    (b) $\dfrac{40}{81}(8^n - 1) - \dfrac{4n}{9}$
    (c) $\dfrac{40}{81}(10^n - 1) - \dfrac{4n}{9}$
    (d) $\dfrac{40}{81}(10^n - 1) - \dfrac{5n}{9}$

2019-21

61. Let S_1 be a square of side 4 cm. Circle C_1 circumscribes the square S_1 such that all its corners are on C_1. Another square S_2 circumscribes the circle C_1. Circle C_2 circumscribes the square S_2, and square S_3 circumscribes circle C_2, & so on. If A_N is the area between the square S_N and the circle C_N, where N is the natural number, then the ratio of sum of all A_N to A_1 is
    (a) 1
    (b) $\dfrac{\pi}{2} - 1$
    (c) Can't be determined
    (d) None of the above

Matrix and Determinants

2008-10

62. Let $\omega = -\dfrac{1}{2} + \dfrac{\sqrt{3}}{2}i$, then the value of the determinant

$$\begin{vmatrix} 1 & 1 & 1 \\ 1 & -1-\omega^2 & \omega^2 \\ 1 & \omega^2 & \omega^4 \end{vmatrix} \text{ is:}$$

(a) 3ω

(b) $3\omega(\omega-1)$

(c) $3\omega^2$

(d) $3\omega(1-\omega)$

63. There are 2 men, 3 women and 1 child in Pradeep's family and 1 man, 1 woman and 2 children in Prabhat's family. The recommended calorie requirement is- Men: 2400, Women: 1900, Children: 1800 and for proteins is: Men: 55 gm, Woman: 45 gm, children: 33 gm. Calculate the total requirement of calories and proteins for each of the two families.

(a) $\begin{matrix} A \\ B \end{matrix}\begin{bmatrix} 12300 & 278 \\ 7900 & 166 \end{bmatrix}$

(b) $\begin{matrix} A \\ B \end{matrix}\begin{bmatrix} 12400 & 300 \\ 8000 & 167 \end{bmatrix}$

(c) $\begin{matrix} A \\ B \end{matrix}\begin{bmatrix} 12300 & 278 \\ 6600 & 200 \end{bmatrix}$

(d) $\begin{matrix} A \\ B \end{matrix}\begin{bmatrix} 8000 & 278 \\ 7900 & 166 \end{bmatrix}$

Miscellaneous

2007-09

64. a and b are two vectors and the angle between a and b is θ. If (a + 3b). (7a – 5b) = 0 and (a – 4 b). (7a – 2b) = 0, then the value of tan θ is

(a) $\sqrt{3}$

(b) 1

(c) $\dfrac{1}{\sqrt{3}}$

(d) None of the above

2017-19

65. A playschool contains 4 boys and y girls. On every Wednesday during winter, five students, of which at least three are boys, go to Zoological Garden, a different group being sent every week. At the Zoological Garden, each boy in the group is given a ball. If the total number of balls distributed is 368, then the value of y is

(a) 5

(b) 6

(c) 7

(d) 8

66. Suppose the two sides of a square are along the straight lines 6x – 8y = 15 and 4y – 3x = 2. Then the area of the square is

(a) 2.52 Sq. units

(b) 3.61 Sq. units

(c) 4.33 Sq. units

(d) None of the above

ANSWERS

1. (a,c)	2. (d)	3. (b)	4. (a)	5. (d)	6. (c)	7. (c)	8. (a)	9. (b)	10. (b)
11. (c)	12. (c)	13. (b)	14. (b)	15. (c)	16. (d)	17. (d)	18. (b)	19. (d)	20. (b)
21. (b)	22. (a)	23. (a)	24. (a)	25. (b)	26. (b)	27. (b)	28. (a)	29. (c)	30. (b)
31. (a,b,c)	32. (c)	33. (b)	34. (b)	35. (c)	36. (d)	37. (b)	38. (b)	39. (d)	40. (d)
41. (d)	42. (c)	43. (d)	44. (b)	45. (b)	46. (b)	47. (d)	48. (a)	49. (b)	50. (d)
51. (a)	52. (b)	53. (d)	54. (b)	55. (a)	56. (b)	57. (c)	58. (b)	59. (a)	60. (c)
61. (c)	62. (b)	63. (a)	64. (a)	65. (d)	66. (b)				

EXPLANATIONS

1. Let the roots be α and β. Then,

$$\alpha + \beta = \frac{-q}{p} \text{ and } \alpha \times \beta = \frac{r}{p} \qquad \ldots(i)$$

Now, $\dfrac{1}{\alpha^2} + \dfrac{1}{\beta^2} = \dfrac{\alpha^2 + \beta^2}{(\alpha\beta)^2} = \dfrac{(\alpha+\beta)^2 - 2(\alpha\beta)}{(\alpha\beta)^2}$

$$= \frac{\left(\frac{-q}{p}\right)^2 - 2\left(\frac{r}{p}\right)}{\left(\frac{r}{p}\right)^2}$$

(From (i)), According to the question,

$$\frac{-q}{p} = \frac{\left(\frac{-q}{p}\right)^2 - 2\left(\frac{r}{p}\right)}{\left(\frac{r}{p}\right)^2}$$

$\Rightarrow 2p^2 r = pq^2 + qr^2$

$\Rightarrow \dfrac{2p^2 r}{pqr} = \dfrac{p.q^2}{pqr} + \dfrac{qr^2}{pqr}$ (dividing by pqr)

$\Rightarrow \dfrac{2p}{q} = \dfrac{q}{r} + \dfrac{r}{p}$

Option (a): Clearly $\dfrac{r}{p}, \dfrac{p}{q}$ and $\dfrac{q}{r}$ are in arithmetic progression. (a) is correct.

Option (b): As $\dfrac{q^2}{p^2} \neq \left(\dfrac{p}{r}\right) \times \left(\dfrac{r}{q}\right) = \dfrac{p}{q}$, (b) is incorrect.

Option (c): As $\dfrac{r}{p}, \dfrac{p}{q}$ and $\dfrac{q}{r}$ are in arithmetic progression, their reciprocals are in harmonic progression.

Option (d): It is wrong as these terms as in harmonic progression, not in arithmetic progression.

Hence, only options (a) and (c) are correct.

2. $(5 + \sqrt{2})x^2 - (4 + \sqrt{5})x + (8 + 2\sqrt{5}) = 0$

Let the roots be α, β and H be their harmonic mean.

$$\therefore \frac{2}{H} = \frac{1}{\alpha} + \frac{1}{\beta} = \frac{\alpha + \beta}{\alpha\beta} = \frac{\frac{4+\sqrt{5}}{5+\sqrt{2}}}{\frac{8+2\sqrt{5}}{5+\sqrt{2}}} = \frac{4+\sqrt{5}}{8+2\sqrt{5}}$$

$\Rightarrow \dfrac{2}{H} = \dfrac{1}{2}$

$\Rightarrow H = 4$

$\Rightarrow \sqrt{H} = \pm 2$

Hence, option (d) is correct.

3. Let the roots be α and α^2.

Given, $\alpha + \alpha^2 = -p$ and $(\alpha) \times (\alpha^2) = q$

$\Rightarrow \alpha + \alpha^2 = -p$ and $\alpha^3 = q$

$\Rightarrow \left(\alpha + \alpha^2\right)^3 = (-p)^3$

$\Rightarrow (\alpha)^3 + (\alpha^2)^3 + 3(\alpha)^2 \times (\alpha^2) + 3(\alpha)(\alpha^2)^2 = -p^3$

$\Rightarrow p^3 - q(3p - 1) + q^2 = 0$

Hence, option (b) is correct.

4. For $x^2 + mx + 1 = 0$, the roots are α and β.

$\Rightarrow \alpha + \beta = -m$ and $\alpha.\beta = 1$

For $x^2 + nx + 1 = 0$, roots are γ and δ

$\Rightarrow \gamma + \delta = -n$ and $\gamma.\delta = 1$

Given expression $= (\alpha - \gamma)(\beta - \gamma)(\alpha + \delta)(\beta + \delta)$

$= (\alpha - \gamma)(\beta + \delta)(\beta - \gamma)(\alpha + \delta)$

$= [\alpha\beta + \alpha\delta - \gamma\beta - \gamma\delta][\alpha\beta + \beta\delta - \gamma\alpha - \gamma\delta]$

$= [1 + \alpha.\delta - \gamma\beta - 1][1 + \beta\delta - \gamma\alpha - 1]$

$= (\alpha.\delta - \gamma\beta)(\beta\delta - \gamma\alpha)$

$= 1.\delta^2 - \alpha^2.1 - \beta^2.1 + \gamma^2.1 = \left(\delta^2 + \gamma^2\right) - \left(\alpha^2 + \beta^2\right)$

$= \left[(\delta + \gamma)^2 - 2\delta.\gamma\right] - \left[(\alpha + \beta)^2 - 2\alpha\beta\right]$

$= \left[(-n)^2 - 2.1\right] - \left[(-m)^2 - 2.1\right] = n^2 - m^2$

Hence, option (a) is correct.

5. The average cost of production c is a function of a single variable q, the number of workers employed. Hence, the total cost of production is given by $c \times q$ = T, say:

$$T = c \times q = \frac{1}{3}q^3 + \frac{5}{2}q^2 - 150q + 75$$

When the cost of production is minimum, $\dfrac{d}{dq}(T) = 0$.

$\Rightarrow \dfrac{d}{dq}(T) = q^2 + 5q - 150 = 0$

$\Rightarrow (q + 15)(q - 10) = 0$

$\Rightarrow q = 10$.

$\therefore$ 10 workers should be employed.

Hence, (d) is the correct option.

6. Cost of production of x televisions $= \left[120x + \dfrac{x^2}{2}\right]$

Revenue by selling x televisions

$= x \times 2\left[100 - \dfrac{x}{4}\right] = \left[200x - \dfrac{x^2}{2}\right]$

Net Profit $= \left[200x - \dfrac{x^2}{2}\right] - \left[120x + \dfrac{x^2}{2}\right]$

$= (80x - x^2) = 1600 - (x - 40)^2$

For maximum profit, x = 40 and the corresponding profit = Rs.1600. Hence, (c) is the correct option.

7. Total cost = R = $\left(\dfrac{Z^3}{10} - 5Z^2 + 10Z + 5\right)$

Total variable cost = $\left(\dfrac{Z^3}{10} - 5Z^2 + 10Z\right)$

['5' is a constant value]

Average variable cost (AV) = $\dfrac{\left(\dfrac{Z^3}{10} - 5Z^2 + 10Z\right)}{Z}$

$= \dfrac{1}{10}\left(Z^2 - 50Z + 100\right) = \dfrac{1}{10}\left\{(Z - 25)^2 - 525\right\}$

∴ At Z = 25, average variable cost is minimum.

8. The given equation: $ax^2 + bx + c = 0$ If one of the root = α

⇒ The other root = 2α

Sum of roots:

$\alpha + 2\alpha = \dfrac{-b}{a}$

$3\alpha = \dfrac{-b}{a}$ ...(i)

Product of roots:

$2\alpha^2 = \dfrac{c}{a}$ ...(ii)

Equating the value of α^2, we get

$\dfrac{b^2}{9a^2} = \dfrac{c}{2a} \Rightarrow 2b^2 = 9ac.$

9. The given expression is $(x + y + z + w)^{30}$.

Now, the number of distinct terms in the expansion of above expression is equivalent to finding the number of whole number solution for the equation

$a + b + c + d = 30$ ...(i)

The required number of whole number solutions

$= {}^{30+4-1}C_{4-1} = {}^{33}C_3 = 5456.$

(Here, n = 30 and r = 4).

10. Given expression is $(1 - x^2 + x^3)(1 + x)^{10}$

$= (1 - x^2 + x^3)(1 + {}^{10}C_1 x + {}^{10}C_2 x^2 + {}^{10}C_3 x^3 + {}^{10}C_4 x^4$
$+ ...+ {}^{10}C_7 x^7 + ...+ x^{10})$

∴ Coefficient of $x^7 = {}^{10}C_7 - {}^{10}C_5 + {}^{10}C_4$

$= \dfrac{10.9.8}{3.2.1} - \dfrac{10.9.8.7.6}{5.4.3.2.1} + \dfrac{10.9.8.7}{4.3.2.1} = 78.$

11. $x = \dfrac{2a \pm \sqrt{4a^2 - 4ab}}{2b} = \dfrac{a \pm \sqrt{a^2 - ab}}{b}$

$= \dfrac{\sqrt{a}\left(\sqrt{a} \pm \sqrt{a-b}\right)}{b} \times \dfrac{\left(\sqrt{a} \mp \sqrt{a-b}\right)}{\left(\sqrt{a} \mp \sqrt{a-b}\right)} = \dfrac{\sqrt{a}}{\sqrt{a} \pm \sqrt{a-b}}$

12. $\left(1 - x^6\right)^4 = 1 - 4.x^6 + 6x^{12} - 4x^{18} + x^{24}$

$(1 - x)^{-4} = 1 - 4(-x) + \dfrac{-4 \times -5}{2 \times 1}(-x)^2 + \cdots\infty$

x^{12} will come in 3 cases:

Case I: x^0 from $(1 - x^6)^4$ and x^{12} from $(1 - x)^{-4}$.
In the case the coefficient will be

$(1)\left(\dfrac{-4 \times -5 \times -6 \times \cdots -13 \times -14 \times -15}{12 \times 11 \times 10 \cdots \times 2 \times 1}\right) = 1 \times {}^{15}C_3 = 455$

Case II: x^6 from $(1 - x^6)^4$ and x^6 from $(1 - x)^{-4}$
In the case the coefficient will be

$(-4)\left(\dfrac{-4 \times -5 \times -6 ...... \times -9}{6 \times 5 \times 4 \times .....1}\right) = -4 \times {}^9C_3 = -336$

Case III: x^{12} from $(1 - x^6)^4$ and x^0 from $(1 - x)^{-4}$
In the case the coefficient will be $6 \times 1 = 6$

Hence, required coefficient = 455 − 336 + 6 = 125.

13. I. x < 1

⇒ $1 - x + 2 - x + 3 - x \geq 6$ or $x \leq 0$.

Hence, this case is possible.

II. $1 \leq x < 2$

⇒ $x - 1 + 2 - x + 3 - x \geq 6$ or $x \leq -2$

Hence, this case is not possible.

III. $2 \leq x < 3$

⇒ $x - 1 + x - 2 + 3 - x \geq 6$ or $x \geq 6$

Hence, this case is not possible.

IV. $x \geq 3$

⇒ $x - 1 + x - 2 + x - 3 \geq 6$ or $x \geq 4$

Hence, this case is possible.

Therefore, required solution set is $x \leq 0$ and $x \geq 4$.

14. Let $y_1 = 7^{x-1} + 11^{x-1}$ and $y_2 = 170$. The graphs of the functions can be drawn as shown below.

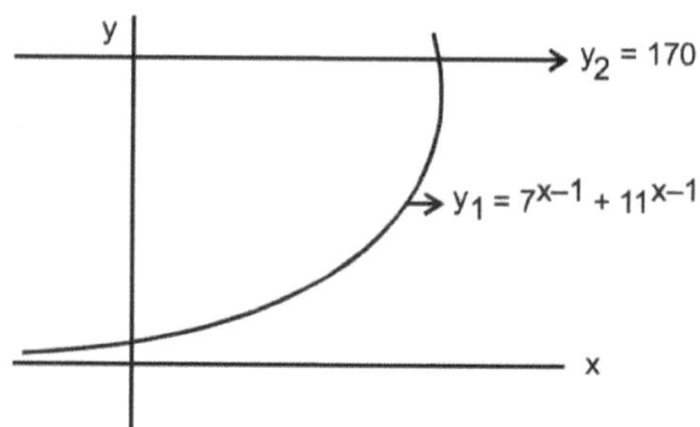

From the graph, it is obvious that y_1 and y_2 intersect at only one point. Hence, the number of solution is one.

15. $x^2 + 3x - 10 = (x + 5)(x - 2)$

Let $p(x) = 3x^4 + 2x^3 - ax^2 + bx - a + b - 4$

(x + 5) is a factor of p(x).

∴ $p(-5) = 3(-5)^4 + 2(-5)^3 - a(-5)^2 + b(-5) - a$

$+ b - 4 = 0$

$\Rightarrow 1875 - 250 - 25a - 5b - a + b - 4 = 0$

$\Rightarrow 26a + 4b = 1621$ ... (i)

$(x - 2)$ is also a factor of $p(x)$.

$p(2) = 3(2)^4 + 2(2)^3 - a(2)^2 + b(2) - a + b - 4 = 0$

$\Rightarrow 48 + 16 - 4a + 2b - a + b - 4 = 0$

$\Rightarrow 5a - 3b = 60$ ...(ii)

From (i) and (ii), we get, $a \simeq 52$ and $b \simeq 67$.

16. $3x^2 - 4x + 7 = (\sqrt{3}x)^2 - 2.\sqrt{3}x.\dfrac{2}{\sqrt{3}} + \dfrac{4}{3} + \dfrac{17}{3}$

$= \left(\sqrt{3}x - \dfrac{2}{\sqrt{3}}\right)^2 + \dfrac{17}{3}$

Hence, the minimum value of the expression $= \dfrac{17}{3}$

17. $\sqrt{4x - 9} + \sqrt{4x + 9} = 5 + \sqrt{7}$

It is clear that

$$\sqrt{4x + 9} = 5$$

and $\sqrt{4x - 9} = \sqrt{7}$

Which is Possible at $x = 4$.

18. For the sake of Simplicity.

Put $P = 1$

$$\left\{\dfrac{4^{1+\frac{1}{4}}\sqrt{2.2^1}}{2\sqrt{2^{-1}}}\right\}^1 = \dfrac{2^{\frac{10}{4}}.2.\sqrt{2}}{2.1}$$

$$= 2.^{\frac{10}{4}+\frac{1}{2}} = 2^3 = 8.$$

19.

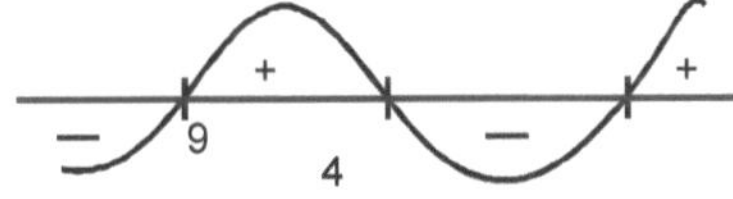

We have $\dfrac{x - 7}{x^2 + 5x - 36} > 0$

$\dfrac{x - 7}{(x + 9)(x - 4)} > 0$

The solution set is $(-9, 4) \cup (7, \infty)$

The least integral value of x is -8.

20. $Q(9, 4) = 9^2 - 9 \times 4 + 4^2 = 61$

$P(7, 61) = 61^2 + 7^2 + 7 \times 61 = 4197$

21. $Y^2 - 8y + 14 = 0$

So $\alpha + \beta = 8$, $\alpha\beta = 14$

$(1 + \alpha + \beta^2)(1 + \beta + \alpha^2)$

$1 + \alpha + \beta + \alpha^2 + \beta^2 + \alpha^3 + \beta^3 + \alpha\beta + \alpha^2\beta^2$

Just put the values, so 431

22. Put $x = 1$ only option A satisfies

23. $y = \dfrac{1}{\{\log_{10}(3 - x)\}} + \sqrt{x + 7}$

y is defined it:

(i) $\log_{10}(3 - x) \neq 0$

     $\Rightarrow 3 - x \neq 1 \Rightarrow x \neq 2$

(ii) $3 - x > 0 \Rightarrow x < 3$

(iii) $x + 7 \geq 0 \Rightarrow x \geq -7$

From (i), (ii) and (iii), we get the domain as

$-7 \leq x < 3$, $x \neq 2$

i.e., $x \in [-7, 3) \sim \{2\}$

24. Given that the diesel consumption is at the rate

$= \dfrac{1}{400}\left\{\left(\dfrac{1000}{x}\right) + x\right\}$ litres per km

Cost of diesel $=$ Rs.35 per litre

Payment to the driver $=$ Rs.125 per hour

Also given that the SUV is driven at the speed of x km per hour

Total cost (C)

$= \dfrac{1}{400}\left\{\left(\dfrac{1000}{x}\right) + x\right\} \times 800 \times 35 + \dfrac{800 \times 125}{x}$

$\Rightarrow C = \dfrac{70000}{x} + 70x + \dfrac{100000}{x}$

Now, differentiating both sides of the above equation with respect to x, we get

$\dfrac{dC}{dx} = \dfrac{-70000}{x^2} + 70 - \dfrac{100000}{x^2}$

For minimum total cost, $\dfrac{dC}{dx} = 0$. Therefore, we have

$\dfrac{-70000}{x^2} + 70 - \dfrac{100000}{x^2} = 0$

$\Rightarrow \dfrac{170000}{x^2} = 70$

$\Rightarrow x \simeq 49$ km per hour

Hence, option (a) is the correct choice.

25. Revenue, $g(x) = x\left(54 - \dfrac{x}{32}\right)^2$

$= x\left[54^2 - 2 \times 54 \times \dfrac{x}{32} + \left(\dfrac{x}{32}\right)^2\right]$

$\therefore g'(x) = 54^2 - \dfrac{4 \times 54x}{32} + \dfrac{3x^2}{(32)^2}$

For zero marginal revenue, $g'(x) = 0$

$\Rightarrow 3x^2 - 4 \times 32 \times 54x + (54 \times 32)^2 = 0$

On solving, we get

$x = 576, 1728$

Since $x < 900$, 573 is the required number of people per trip.

26. Let the duration, distance, velocity, number of carriages and diesel used per km be 't', 'd', 'v', 'C' and 'D' respectively.

$$\therefore \ t \ \alpha \ \frac{d}{v} \ \text{and} \ v \ \alpha \ \frac{\sqrt{D}}{C}$$

$$\Rightarrow t = k\frac{d}{v} \ \text{and} \ v = m\frac{\sqrt{D}}{C}$$

$$\Rightarrow t = k\frac{d}{m\dfrac{\sqrt{D}}{C}}$$

$$\Rightarrow t = \frac{kdC}{m\sqrt{D}} \Rightarrow \frac{k}{m} = \frac{t\sqrt{D}}{dC}$$

Putting the values,

$$\Rightarrow \frac{3}{4} = \frac{k(70)15}{m\sqrt{10/70}} \Rightarrow \frac{k}{m} = \frac{\sqrt{10/70}}{1400} = \frac{1}{1400\sqrt{7}}$$

Let the required amount of diesel consumed be 'x'.

$$\therefore \ \sqrt{x} = \left(\frac{50 \times 18}{\dfrac{1}{2}}\right) \times \frac{1}{1400\sqrt{7}}$$

$$\Rightarrow x \approx 11.8.$$

27. $f(x) = \dfrac{1}{1+x}$

$$f\big[f\{f(x)\}\big] = f\left[f\left\{\frac{1}{1+x}\right\}\right] = f\left[\frac{1}{1+\dfrac{1}{1+x}}\right] = f\left[\frac{1+x}{2+x}\right]$$

$$= \frac{1}{1+\dfrac{1+x}{2+x}} = \frac{2+x}{2+x+1+x} = \frac{2+x}{3+2x}$$

Put $x = 5$

$$\Rightarrow \frac{2+5}{3+5\times 2} = \frac{7}{13}$$

Hence option (b).

28. $x_n = 5x_{n-1} - \dfrac{3}{4}x_{n-2}; \ n \geq 2$

$x_0 = 4, \ x_1 = 2$

Put $n = 2$ in above equation

$$x_2 = 5x_1 - \frac{3}{4}x_0 = 10 - \frac{3}{4} \times 4 = 7$$

Put $x = 3$

$$\Rightarrow x_3 = 5x_2 - \frac{3}{4}x_1 = 5 \times 7 - \frac{3}{4}x_2 = 35 - 1.5 = \frac{67}{2}$$

Hence option is (a)

29. Total production cost = Fixed + variable cost

$$= 50400 + x \times 50\% \ (SP)$$

$$= 50400 + x \times \frac{1}{2} \times 12$$

$$= 50400 + 6x$$

But $x = 8400$

$$\therefore \ \text{Total cost} = 50400 + 8400 \times 6 = 100800$$

Total SP = 12 × 8400 = 100800

∴ No profit no loss

Hence option (c)

30. Total Cost $= \left[\dfrac{1}{400}\left(\dfrac{100}{x} + x\right) \times 100 \times 65\right] + \left(\dfrac{1000}{x} \times 50\right)$

With the help of option: when $x = 36$ will give minimum total cost.

31. $\dfrac{\log x}{b-c} = \dfrac{\log y}{c-a} = \dfrac{\log z}{a-b} = k,$ say.

Let B be the base.

Then, $\log_B x = k(b - c) \Rightarrow x = B^{k(b-c)}$ and

$y = B^{k(c-a)}$ and $z = C^{k(a-b)}$.

Option (a): $xyz = 1$, is correct.

$B^{k(b-c)} \times B^{k(c-a)} \times B^{k(a-b)}$

$= B^{k(b-c+c-a+a-b)} = B^{k\times 0} = 1$

Option (b): $x^a . y^b . z^c$

$$= \left[B^{k(b-c)}\right]^a \times \left[B^{k(c-a)}\right]^b \times \left[B^{k(a-b)}\right]^c$$

$$= B^{k[a(b-c)+b(c-a)+c(a-b)]}$$

$$= B^{k(0)} = B^0 = 1$$

∴ Option (b) is correct.

Option (c); $x^{b+c} . y^{c+a} . z^{a+b}$

$$= \left[B^{k(b+c)(b-c)}\right] \times \left[B^{k(c+a)(c-a)}\right] \times \left[B^{k(a+b)(a-b)}\right]$$

$$= B^{k\left[(b^2-c^2)+(c^2-a^2)+(a^2-b^2)\right]} = B^0 = 1$$

∴ Option (c) is correct.

Option (d) is wrong.

Hence, options (a), (b) and (c) are correct.

32. As a, b and c are in harmonic progression, therefore,

$$b = \frac{2ac}{a+c}.$$

As per the question,

$\log(a + c) + \log(a + c - 2b) = \log[(a + c)(a + c - 2b)]$

$$= \log\left[(a+c) \times \frac{(a+c)^2 - 4ac}{(a+c)}\right]$$

$$= \log[(a-c)]^2$$

Since $a < c$, instead of expressing the given expression as $\log[(a - c)^2]$, we should express it as $\log[(c - a)^2]$

$= 2\log(c - a)$.

33. Given that $\log_2 x . \log_{\frac{x}{64}} 2 = \log_{\frac{x}{16}} 2$

Putting $x = 4$ in LHS we have

$$(2\log_2 2)\left(\log_{\frac{1}{16}} 2\right) = \frac{2\log_2 2}{(-4)\log_2 2} = \frac{-1}{2}$$

Similarly, in RHS $= \log_{\frac{1}{4}} 2 = -\frac{1}{2}$

Hence, option (b) is the correct choice.

34. Let $S = \dfrac{2}{1!} + \dfrac{3}{2!} + \dfrac{6}{3!} + \dfrac{11}{4!} + \dfrac{18}{5!} + ...$

Also, $e = 1 + \dfrac{1}{1!} + \dfrac{1}{2!} + \dfrac{1}{3!} + \dfrac{1}{4!} + \dfrac{1}{5!} + ...$

Let T_n be the nth term of S.

$$T_n = \frac{n^2 - 2n + 3}{n!} = \frac{n^2}{n!} - \frac{2n}{n!} + \frac{3}{n!}$$

$$S = \sum_{n=1} T_n = \sum_{n=1} \frac{n^2}{n!} - \sum_{n=1} \frac{2n}{n!} + \sum_{n=1} \frac{3}{n!}$$

Now, $\displaystyle\sum_{n=1} \frac{n^2}{n!} = \sum_{n=1} \frac{n}{(n-1)!} = \sum_{n=1} \frac{n-1+1}{(n-1)!}$

$$= \sum_{n=1} \frac{n-1}{(n-1)!} + \sum_{n=1} \frac{1}{(n-1)!}$$

$$= \sum_{n=2} \frac{1}{(n-2)!} + \sum_{n=1} \frac{1}{(n-1)!} = e + e = 2e$$

Also, $\displaystyle\sum_{n=1} \frac{2n}{n!} = 2\sum_{n=1} \frac{1}{(n-1)!} = 2e$

and, $\displaystyle\sum_{n=1} \frac{3}{n!} = 3e - 3$

$\Rightarrow S = 2e - 2e + 3e - 3 = 3(e - 1)$

35. $\log_4 \log_4 4^{a-b} = \log_4 \left(\sqrt{a} - \sqrt{b}\right)^2 + \log_4 4.$

$\Rightarrow (a - b) = 4\left(a + b - 2\sqrt{ab}\right) = 4a + 4b - 8\sqrt{ab}$

$\Rightarrow 3a + 5b - 8\sqrt{ab} = 0$

$\Rightarrow 3\left(\sqrt{\dfrac{a}{b}}\right)^2 - 8\sqrt{\dfrac{a}{b}} + 5 = 0$

Let $\sqrt{\dfrac{a}{b}} = x.$

Then, $3x^2 - 8x + 5 = 0.$

$\Rightarrow x = 1, \dfrac{5}{3}$

But $a - b \neq 0 \Rightarrow x = \sqrt{\dfrac{a}{b}} = \dfrac{5}{3}$

36. Let $\log_5 2 = p \Rightarrow 2 = 5^p$

This is possible only if p is irrational.

37. $\log_{10} 3 + \log_{10}(4x + 1) = \log_{10}(x + 1) + \log_{10} 10$

$3 \times (4x + 1) = (x + 1) \times 10$

$2x = 7$ or $x = \dfrac{7}{2}$

38. As $\log 3$, $\log(3^x - 2)$ and $\log(3^x + 4)$ are in A. P., therefore

$2\log(3^x - 2) = \log 3 + \log(3^x + 4)$

$\Rightarrow (3^x - 2)^2 = 3(3^x + 4)$

Let $3^x = y$

$\therefore (y - 2)^2 = 3(y + 4)$

$\Rightarrow y^2 - 7y - 8 = 0$

$\Rightarrow y = 8, -1$

$\therefore 3^x = 8$ or -1

$\Rightarrow x = \log_3 8$ or $\log_3(-1)$

$\log_3(-1)$ is not acceptable. Hence, $x = \log_3 8$.

39. $\log_{10} x - \log_{10} \sqrt[3]{x} = 6\log_x 10$

$\Rightarrow \log_{10} \dfrac{x}{\sqrt[3]{x}} = 6\log_x 10$

$\Rightarrow \log_{10} x^{\frac{2}{3}} = 6\log_x 10$

$\Rightarrow \dfrac{2}{3}\log_{10} x = 6\log_x 10$

$\Rightarrow \log_{10} x = 9\log_x 10$

$\Rightarrow \log_{10} x = \dfrac{9}{\log_{10} x}$

$\Rightarrow \left(\log_{10} x\right)^2 = 9$

$\Rightarrow \log_{10} x = \pm 3$

$\Rightarrow x = 10^3$ or 10^{-3}

$\Rightarrow x = 1000.$

40. $\log_{13} \log_{21} \left\{\sqrt{x + 21} + \sqrt{x}\right\} = 0$

$\Rightarrow \log_{21} \left\{\sqrt{x + 21} + \sqrt{x}\right\} = 13^0$

$\Rightarrow \sqrt{x + 21} + \sqrt{x} = 21^1$

$\Rightarrow \sqrt{x + 21} = 21 - \sqrt{x}$

$\Rightarrow x + 21 = 441 + x - 42\sqrt{x}$

$\Rightarrow 42\sqrt{x} = 420 \Rightarrow \sqrt{x} = 10$

$\Rightarrow x = 100.$

41. $\log_7 \log_7 \left(\sqrt{7\sqrt{7\sqrt{7}}}\right) = \log_7 \log_7 \left(7^{\frac{1}{2} + \frac{1}{4} + \frac{1}{8}}\right)$

$= \log_7 7 - \log_7 8 = 1 - 3\log_7 2$

42. $\log_{25} 5 = a = 0.5$

$\log_{25} 15 = b = 0.8$ (approx)

$\log_{25} 27 = 3\log_{25} 3 = 3\left[\log_{25} 15 - \log_{25} 5\right]$

$= 3(0.8 - 0.5) = 0.9.$

Option (c) :

$3(a + b - 1) = 3(0.5 + 0.8 - 1) = 0.9.$

Hence, option (c) is Correct.

43. We have $4\log_7(x - 8) = \log_3 81$

$\Rightarrow 4\log_7(x - 8) = \log_3 3^4$

$\Rightarrow 4\log_7(x - 8) = 4$

$\Rightarrow \log_7(x - 8) = 1 \Rightarrow x - 8 = 7 \Rightarrow x = 15.$

44. $(1+5)\log_e 3 + \dfrac{(1+5^2)}{2!}(\log_e 3)^2 + \left(\dfrac{1+5^3}{3!}\right)(\log_e 3)^3 + \ldots$

$= \left(\log_3 3 + \dfrac{(\log_e 3)^2}{2!} + \dfrac{(\log_e 3)^3}{3!} + \ldots\right)$

$\quad + \left(5\log_e 3 + \dfrac{5^2(\log_e 3)^2}{2!} + \dfrac{5^3(\log_e 3)^3}{3!} + \ldots\right)$ ... (1)

Now $e^x = 1 + x + \dfrac{x^2}{2!} + \dfrac{x^3}{3!} + \ldots$

$\Rightarrow e^x - 1 = x + \dfrac{x^2}{2!} + \dfrac{x^3}{3!} + \ldots$

Put $x = \log_e 3$

$\therefore e^{\log_e 3} - 1 = \log_e 3 + \dfrac{(\log_e 3)^2}{2!} + \dfrac{(\log_e 3)^3}{3!} + \ldots$

$2 = \log_e 3 + \dfrac{(\log_e 3)^2}{2!} + \dfrac{(\log_e 3)^3}{3!} + \ldots$

Also $a^y = 1 + y\log_e a + \dfrac{y^2(\log_e a)^2}{2!} + \dfrac{y^3(\log_e a)^3}{3!} + \ldots$

$\Rightarrow a^y - 1 = y\log_e a + \dfrac{y^2(\log_e a)^2}{2!} + \dfrac{y^3(\log_e a)^3}{3!} + \ldots$

Put $a = 3$, $y = 3$

$3^5 - 1 = 5\log_e 3 + 5^2 \cdot \dfrac{(\log_e 3)^2}{2!} + 5^3 \cdot \dfrac{(\log_e 3)^3}{3!} + \ldots$

$\Rightarrow 242 = 5\log_e 3 + \dfrac{5^2(\log_e a)^2}{2!} + \dfrac{5^3(\log_e 3)^3}{3!} + \ldots$

Eq. (i)

$\Rightarrow 242 + 2 = 244$

So answer is option (b).

45. $\dfrac{1}{\log_x yz + 1} + \dfrac{1}{\log_y xz + 1} + \dfrac{1}{\log_z xy + 1}$

$\dfrac{\log x}{\log yz + \log x} + \dfrac{\log y}{\log xz + \log y} + \dfrac{\log z}{\log xy + \log z}$

$\dfrac{\log xyz}{\log xyz} = 1$

46. $\log_2 x \times \dfrac{1}{\log_2 \frac{x}{64}} = \dfrac{1}{\log_2 \frac{x}{16}}$

$\Rightarrow \log_2 x \times \log_2 \dfrac{x}{16} = \log_2 \dfrac{x}{64}$

$\Rightarrow \log_2 x\{\log_2 x - 4\} = \log_2 x - 6$

$\Rightarrow y(y-4) = y - 6$

$\Rightarrow y^2 - 4y - y + 6 = 0$

$\Rightarrow y^2 - 5y + 6 = 0$

$\Rightarrow (y-2)(y-3) = 0$

$\Rightarrow y = 2, 3 \Rightarrow \log_2 x = 2, 3$

$\Rightarrow x = 4, 8$

47. $S = \dfrac{3}{4} + \dfrac{5}{36} + \dfrac{7}{144} + \ldots$

$S = \left(\dfrac{1}{1^2} - \dfrac{1}{2^2}\right) + \left(\dfrac{1}{2^2} - \dfrac{1}{3^2}\right) + \left(\dfrac{1}{3^2} - \dfrac{1}{4^2}\right)$

$\quad + \ldots + \left(\dfrac{1}{(n)^2} - \dfrac{1}{n+1)^2}\right)$

$\Rightarrow S = \left(1 - \dfrac{1}{2^2} + \dfrac{1}{2^2} - \dfrac{1}{3^2} + \dfrac{1}{3^2} + \ldots + \left(\dfrac{1}{n^2} - \dfrac{1}{(n+1)^2}\right)\right)$

$= 1 - \dfrac{1}{(n+1)^2} = \dfrac{(n+1)^2 - 1}{(n+1)^2}$

$\Rightarrow S = \dfrac{n^2 + 2n}{(n+1)^2}$

$\therefore \dfrac{1}{S} = \dfrac{(n+1)^2}{n^2 + 2n}$

Hence, option (d) is the correct answer.

48. Given, $\tan\alpha$ is the G.M. of $\sin\alpha$ and $\cos\alpha$

$\Rightarrow (\tan\alpha)^2 = (\sin\alpha)(\cos\alpha)$

$\Rightarrow (\sin\alpha) = (\cos\alpha)^3$

$\Rightarrow (\sin\alpha)^2 = \left[(\cos\alpha)^3\right]^2$

$\Rightarrow \sin^2\alpha = (1)^3 + (-\sin^2\alpha)^3 + 3(1)^2(-\sin^2\alpha)$
$\qquad\qquad + 3(1)(-\sin^2\alpha)^2$

$\Rightarrow \sin^2\alpha = 1 - \sin^6\alpha - 3\sin^2\alpha + 3\sin^4\alpha$

$\Rightarrow 1 - 4\sin^2\alpha + 3\sin^4\alpha - \sin^6\alpha = 0$

Adding 1 on both sides, we get

$2 - 4\sin^2\alpha + 3\sin^4\alpha - \sin^6\alpha = 1$

Hence, option (a) is correct.

49. Consider the following harmonic progression.

$1, \dfrac{1}{2}, \dfrac{1}{3}, \dfrac{1}{4}, \dfrac{1}{5}$

Here, $a = 1$, $b = \dfrac{1}{5}$ and $n = 3$, harmonic means between a and b are such that $H_1 = \dfrac{1}{2}$, $H_2 = \dfrac{1}{3}$ and

$H_3 = \dfrac{1}{4}$

Now, $\dfrac{H_1 + a}{H_1 - a} + \dfrac{H_n + b}{H_n - b}$ is same as

$\dfrac{\frac{1}{2} + 1}{\frac{1}{2} - 1} + \dfrac{\frac{1}{4} + \frac{1}{5}}{\frac{1}{4} - \frac{1}{5}} = 6 = 2 \times 3$

Only option (b) satisfies the condition and hence, it is the correct option.

50. As per the question, a^2, b^2, c^2 are in geometric progression

$\Rightarrow \dfrac{b^2}{a^2} = \dfrac{c^2}{b^2} \Rightarrow b^2 = \pm ac$ ...(i)

It is given that a, b and c are in arithmetic progression. If we take 'd' as the common difference then a = b − d and c = b + d

It is given that $a + b + c = \dfrac{3}{2}$.

$\Rightarrow (b - d) + b + (b + d) = \dfrac{3}{2}$

$\Rightarrow b = \left(\dfrac{1}{2}\right)$

$\therefore a = \left(\dfrac{1}{2} - d\right)$ and $c = \left(\dfrac{1}{2} + d\right)$

From equation (i),

$\left(\dfrac{1}{2}\right)^2 = \pm\left(\dfrac{1}{2} - d\right)\left(\dfrac{1}{2} + d\right)$

$\Rightarrow d = 0, \ \pm\left(\dfrac{1}{\sqrt{2}}\right)$

Since $a < b < c$, $d = \dfrac{+1}{\sqrt{2}}$

$\therefore a = b - d = \left(\dfrac{1}{2} - \dfrac{1}{\sqrt{2}}\right)$

51. $1^2 - 2^2 + 3^2 - 4^2 + \ldots 2001^2 - 2002^2 + 2003^2$

$= (1^2 + 3^2 + 5^2 + \ldots + 2003^2) - (2^2 + 4^2 + 6^2 + \ldots 2002^2)$

$= (1^2 + 2^2 + 3^2 + 4^2 + \ldots + 2003^2) - 2(2^2 + 4^2 + 6^2 + \ldots 2002^2)$

$= (1^2 + 2^2 + \ldots + 2003^2) - 8(1^2 + 2^2 + \ldots + 1001^2)$

We know, sum of squares of first n natural numbers

$= \dfrac{n(n + 1)(2n + 1)}{6}$

Sum of the series

$= \left(\dfrac{2003 \times 2004 \times 4007}{6}\right) - \left(\dfrac{8 \times 1001 \times 1002 \times 2003}{6}\right)$

$= \dfrac{2003 \times 1002}{6}(8014 - 8008)$

$= \dfrac{2003 \times 1002 \times 6}{6} = 2007006$.

52. It is given that abc = 4.

We know, (a + b + c) will be minimum when a, b, c are constants and a = b = c.

As a, b, c are in arithmetic progression,

$\Rightarrow a + b + c = 3b$

This will be minimum when a = b = c, $b^3 = 4$.

$\Rightarrow b = 4^{1/3} = 2^{2/3}$

53. $S = \dfrac{1}{1.2.3} + \dfrac{1}{3.45} + \dfrac{1}{5.6.7} + \ldots$

Here $T_n = \dfrac{1}{(2n - 1).\,2n.\,(2n + 1)} = \dfrac{1}{2}\left[\dfrac{1}{2n - 1} - \dfrac{2}{2n} + \dfrac{1}{2n + 1}\right]$

$\therefore T_1 = \dfrac{1}{2}\left[\dfrac{1}{1} - \dfrac{2}{2} + \dfrac{1}{3}\right]$

$T_2 = \dfrac{1}{2}\left[\dfrac{1}{3} - \dfrac{2}{4} + \dfrac{1}{5}\right]$

$T_3 = \dfrac{1}{2}\left[\dfrac{1}{5} - \dfrac{2}{6} + \dfrac{1}{7}\right]$

$\therefore$ Required sum,

$S = \dfrac{1}{2}\left[\left(\dfrac{1}{1} - \dfrac{2}{2} + \dfrac{1}{3}\right) + \left(\dfrac{1}{3} - \dfrac{2}{4} + \dfrac{1}{5}\right) + \left(\dfrac{1}{5} - \dfrac{2}{6} + \dfrac{1}{7}\right) + \ldots\right]$

$\Rightarrow 2S = \left(\dfrac{1}{1} - \dfrac{2}{2} + \dfrac{1}{3}\right) + \left(\dfrac{1}{3} - \dfrac{2}{4} + \dfrac{1}{5}\right) + \left(\dfrac{1}{5} - \dfrac{2}{6} + \dfrac{1}{7}\right) + \ldots$

$= \dfrac{2}{3} - \dfrac{2}{4} + \dfrac{2}{5} - \dfrac{2}{6} + \dfrac{2}{7} - \dfrac{2}{8} + \ldots$

$= 2\left[\dfrac{1}{3} - \dfrac{1}{4} + \dfrac{1}{5} - \dfrac{1}{6} + \dfrac{1}{7} - \dfrac{1}{8} + \ldots\right]$

$\Rightarrow 1 + 2S = 2\left[1 - \dfrac{1}{2} + \dfrac{1}{3} - \dfrac{1}{4} + \dfrac{1}{5} - \dfrac{1}{6} + \dfrac{1}{7} - \dfrac{1}{8} + \ldots\right]$

$= 2\log_e(1 + 1) = 2\log_e 2$

$\left[\because \text{Here } x = 1 \text{ and } \log_{(1+x)} = \dfrac{x - x^2}{2} + \dfrac{x^3}{3} - \dfrac{x^4}{4} + \ldots\right]$

$\therefore S = \dfrac{2\log_e 2 - 1}{2} = \left(\log_e 2 - \dfrac{1}{2}\right)$

Hence, option (d) is the correct choice.

54. Total distance traveled by the ball

$= 45 + 2\left[(45)\dfrac{3}{5} + 45\left(\dfrac{3}{5}\right)^2 + 45\left(\dfrac{3}{5}\right)^3 + \ldots\right]$

$= 45 + 2 \times 45\left(\dfrac{\dfrac{3}{5}}{1 - \dfrac{3}{5}}\right) = 45 + 45 \times 3 = 180 \text{ m}$

55. $\left[\sqrt{1}\right] + \left[\sqrt{2}\right] + \left[\sqrt{3}\right] = 1 \times 3$.

$\left[\sqrt{4}\right] + \left[\sqrt{5}\right] + \left[\sqrt{6}\right] + \left[\sqrt{7}\right] + \left[\sqrt{8}\right] = 2 \times 5$

$\left[\sqrt{9}\right] + \left[\sqrt{10}\right] + \cdots \left[\sqrt{15}\right] = 3 \times 7$

n^{th} term is $n \times (2n + 1) = 2n^2 + n$

and $S_n = 2\Sigma n^2 + \Sigma n = \dfrac{n(n + 1)(4n + 5)}{6}$

Put n = 18

$S_{18} = 4389$

$\left[\sqrt{361}\right] = 19$

Total sum = 4389 + 19 = 4408.

56. Let 'd' be the common difference.

Therefore, 2 + 7d = 65 or d = 9.

Now, e = 2 + 5d = 47.

57. The ball travels a distance of 180 m in the first fall and then the height to which it reaches after subsequent falls follow a geometric progression, with common ratio (r) < 1.

Sum of the series = $\dfrac{a}{1-r} = \dfrac{108}{1-\dfrac{3}{5}} = 270$

Hence, the total distance traveled by the ball = 2(270) + 180 = 720 m.

58. The required distance = 32 + 2 (16 + 8 + 4 + 2 +... + 10 terms)

$= 32 + 2 \times \dfrac{16\left(1-\dfrac{1}{2^{10}}\right)}{1-\dfrac{1}{2}} \approx 96.$

59. Radius of P1 = r

Side of Q1 = $\sqrt{2}r$

Radius of P2 = $\dfrac{r}{\sqrt{2}}$

Side of Q2 = r

$S1 = Q1 - P2 = (\sqrt{2}r)^2 - \pi\left(\dfrac{r}{\sqrt{2}}\right)^2 = \dfrac{1}{2}r^2(4-\pi)$

$S2 = Q2 - P3 = \dfrac{1}{4}r^2(4-\pi)$

$S3 = \dfrac{1}{8}r^2(4-\pi)$

Required ratio

$= \dfrac{\dfrac{1}{2}r^2(4-\pi)+\dfrac{1}{4}r^2(4-\pi)+\dfrac{1}{8}r^2(4-\pi)+...}{2r^2} = \dfrac{(4-\pi)}{2}.$

60. 4 + 44 + 444 + ... n terms

$= 4 (1 + 11 + 111 + ... $ n terms

$= \dfrac{4}{9} (9 + 99 + 999 + ... $ n terms)

$= \dfrac{4}{9} [(10-1) + (100-1) + (1000-1) + ... + n\ terms]$

$= \dfrac{4}{9} [10 + 100 + 1000 + ... -n]$

$= \dfrac{4}{9}\left[\dfrac{10\left(10^n-1\right)}{9} - n\right] = \dfrac{40}{81}(10^n-1) - \dfrac{4n}{9}.$

61.

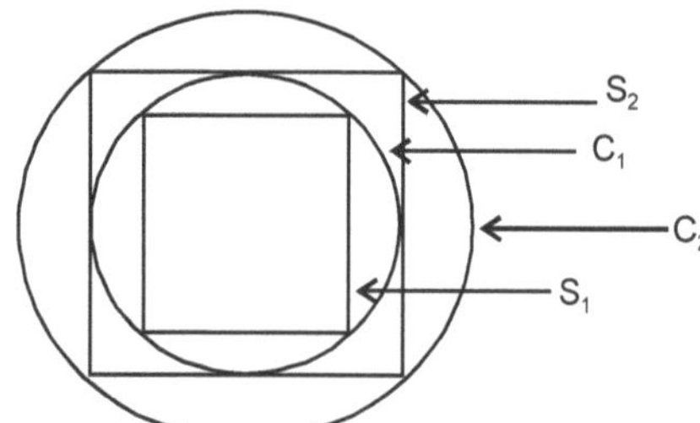

A_1 = Area of C_1 − Area of S_1

A_1 = $8\pi - 16$

A_2 = Area of C_2 − Area of S_2

A_2 = $16\pi - 32$

Now we can observe that A_3 will be greater than A_2 and the value keeps on increasing with increasing value of n.

$$\dfrac{A_1 + A_2 + A_3 .... A_n}{A_1}$$

As numerator will change and denominator remains the same, the value keeps on changing. So, cannot be determined.

62. The complex number $\omega = -\dfrac{1}{2}+\dfrac{\sqrt{3}}{2}i$ is a cube root of 1 i.e. $\omega^3=1$. Using this, we can expand and then simplify the determinant as following:

$$\begin{vmatrix} 1 & 1 & 1 \\ 1 & -1-\omega^2 & \omega^2 \\ 1 & \omega^2 & \omega^4 \end{vmatrix}$$

$= 1\times\left[\omega^4\left(-1-\omega^2\right)-\omega^2\times\omega^2\right] - 1\times\left[\omega^4-\omega^2\right]+1\times\left[\omega^2+1+\omega^2\right]$

$= -\omega^4 - \omega^6 - \omega^4 - \omega^4 + \omega^2 + \omega^2 + 1 + \omega^2$

$= 1 + 3\omega^2 - 3\omega^4 - 1$

$= 3\omega^2 - 3\omega \qquad\qquad (\because \omega^3 = 1)$

$= 3\omega(\omega-1)$

63. The recommended calorie requirement for men, women and children are 2400, 1900 and 1800 respectively and the recommended protein requirement for men, women and children are 55 gm, 45 gm and 33 gm respectively.

<u>For Pradeep's family:</u>

Calorie requirement = 2 × 2400 + 3 × 1900 + 1 × 1800 = 12300

Protein requirement = 2 × 55 + 3 × 45 + 1 × 33 = 278 gm

<u>For Prabhat's family:</u>

Calorie requirement = 1 × 2400 + 1 × 1900 + 2 × 1800 = 7900

Protein requirement = 1 × 55 + 1 × 45 + 2 × 33 = 166 gm

Hence, (a) is the correct option.

64. The angle between $\vec{a}$ and $\vec{b}$ is θ.

$(\vec{a}+3\vec{b}).(7\vec{a}-5\vec{b})=0$

$\qquad\qquad\qquad\qquad ...(i)$

and $(\vec{a}-4\vec{b}).(7\vec{a}-2\vec{b})=0$

$\qquad\qquad\qquad\qquad ...(ii)$

From (i), $(\vec{a}).(7\vec{a})+(\vec{a}).(-5\vec{b})+(3\vec{b}).(7\vec{a})+(3\vec{b})(-5\vec{b})=0$

$\Rightarrow 7|\vec{a}|^2\cos 0° - 5|\vec{a}||\vec{b}|\cos\theta + 21|\vec{a}||\vec{b}|\cos\theta - 15|\vec{b}|^2\cos 0° = 0$

$\Rightarrow \quad 7a^2 - 5ab\cos\theta + 21ab\cos\theta - 15b^2 = 0$

$\Rightarrow \quad 7a^2 - 15b^2 + 16ab\cos\theta = 0 \qquad \ldots(iii)$

Similarly, solving the dot product in (2), we get

$7a^2 + 8b^2 - 30ab\cos\theta = 0 \qquad \ldots(iv)$

Subtracting (iii) from (iv),

$23b^2 = 46ab\cos\theta$

$\Rightarrow \dfrac{b}{2a} = \cos\theta \Rightarrow \cos^2\theta = \dfrac{b^2}{4a^2}$

$\Rightarrow \sin^2\theta = 1 - \dfrac{b^2}{4a^2} \Rightarrow \tan^2\theta = 4\left(\dfrac{a^2}{b^2}\right) - 1$

From equation (iii) and (iv), $7a^2 - 15b^2 = -16ab\cos\theta$ and

$7a^2 + 8b^2 = 30ab\cos\theta$

$\Rightarrow \dfrac{7a^2 - 15b^2}{7a^2 + 8b^2} = \dfrac{-16}{30} \quad \Rightarrow \dfrac{7\left(\dfrac{a^2}{b^2}\right) - 15}{7\left(\dfrac{a^2}{b^2}\right) + 8} = \dfrac{-8}{15} \quad \Rightarrow \dfrac{a^2}{b^2} = 1$

$\therefore \tan^2\theta = 3 \Rightarrow \tan\theta = \pm\sqrt{3}$

Option (a) has one of the two possible values i.e., $\sqrt{3}$. Hence, option (a) is correct.

65. 5 students out of 4 boys and y girls can be chosen in 2 ways:

(i) 3 Boys & 2 Girls $= {}^4C_3 \times {}^yC_2$

(ii) 4 Boys & 1 Girl $= {}^4C_4 \times {}^yC_1$

Since only boys are given a ball

Thus, total balls given to 3 boys each in 1st case + Total balls given to 4 boys each in 2nd case = 368.

$\Rightarrow 3 \times {}^4C_3 \times {}^yC_2 + 4 \times {}^4C_4 \times {}^yC_1 = 368$

$\Rightarrow 3 \times 4 \times \dfrac{y(y-1)}{2} + 4 \times 1 \times y = 368$

$\Rightarrow 6y\,(y-1) + 4y = 368$

$\Rightarrow 6y^2 - 6y + 4y = 368$

$\Rightarrow 3y^2 - y = 184 \Rightarrow y(3y-1) = 184$

Using options, we can check that only option (d) satisfies the above equation.

66. The two sides of the square are

$6x - 8y = 15$ and $4y - 3x = 2$

or $\qquad 6x - 8y = 15 \qquad\qquad \ldots(1)$

and $\qquad 6x - 8y = -4 \qquad\qquad \ldots(2)$

These two lines are parallel. So the distance between these lines is the side of the square.

$\therefore \quad$ Side of square $= \dfrac{|15 - (-4)|}{\sqrt{6^2 + 8^2}} = \dfrac{19}{10}$

$\therefore \quad$ Area of square $= \left(\dfrac{19}{10}\right)^2 = \dfrac{361}{100} = 3.61 \text{ sq. unit}.$

Logical Reasoning &
Data Interpretation

1. Analytical Reasoning

2007-09

Directions for Questions 1 to 6: Study the 10 statements given below and answer the questions.

1. Six businessmen from six different nations are staying in different rooms in succession in the same row in a hotel.

2. Each of them owns a different number of cars and has donated to different number of institutions during the last year.

3. The businessman in Room no. 102 owns twice as many as the number of cars owned by the businessmen who has donated to 8 institutions in the last year.

4. The businessman from Uruguay and the businessman in Room no. 106 together own 40 cars in total.

5. The businessman from Argentina owns 8 cars less than the businessman from England but donated to 10 more institutions in the last year.

6. Four times the number of cars owned by the businessman in Room no. 104 is lesser than the number of institutions to which he has donated in the last year.

7. The businessman in Room No. 103 owns 12 cars and donated to 8 institutions in the last year.

8. The businessman who owns 16 cars donated to 24 institutions in the last year.

9. The businessman in Room no. 105 owns 8 cars and donated to 2 institutions less than those donated to by the businessman from Canada in the last year.

10. The Brazilian businessman is staying two rooms ahead of the English businessman who is staying two rooms ahead of the Canadian businessman.

1. In which room is the Brazilian businessman staying?
   - (a) Room no. 102
   - (b) Room no. 103
   - (c) Room no. 104
   - (d) Room no. 105

2. What is the number of institutions to which the Argentinean businessman donated in the last year?
   - (a) 8
   - (b) 3
   - (c) 18
   - (d) 24

3. The businessman of which country is staying in Room no. 106?
   - (a) Argentina
   - (b) Canada
   - (c) Uruguay
   - (d) Germany

4. The businessman of which country has donated to 24 institutions in the last year?
   - (a) Argentina
   - (b) Uruguay
   - (c) Canada
   - (d) Germany

5. The businessman of which country owns the highest number of cars?
   - (a) Argentina
   - (b) Uruguay
   - (c) Germany
   - (d) Brazil

6. How many cars are owned by the English businessman?
   - (a) 8
   - (b) 12
   - (c) 4
   - (d) 20

Direction for Question 7: Read the information given below and answer the question.

A school in Bhopal decided to stage a historical drama, involving a battle between two ancient kingdoms. As a part of the battle, four students, namely - Aslam, Bimal, Chris and Dilip dressed as soldiers, marched through the stage at one point. When the make-up man dressed these four students, he put a helmet on each one's head, without any one realizing the colour of their respective helmets. The make-up man selected the helmets for these four students from 3 gold-plated helmets, 2 silver-plated helmets and one copper-plated helmet at the make-up room. Now, when Aslam, Bimal, Chris and Dilip marched in that order, Aslam being the first person in the queue could not see the helmet on the heads of the other three. Bimal saw the colour of helmet on Aslam's head; Chris saw the same on Aslam's head and Bimal's head and Dilip saw the helmets on the heads of all others. After the drama, a classmate of them asked whether they were aware of the colour of the helmet on their own head, starting from Dilip. No one could answer the question.

7. Mark all the incorrect statements
   - (a) Dilip did not observe the helmets on the heads of the other three actors, two of which were silver-plated and one copper-plated.
   - (b) Bimal did not observe Aslam wearing either silver-plated or copper-plated helmet.
   - (c) Chris did not observe the helmets worn by Aslam and Bimal, one of which could be silver-plated and the other copper-plated or both could be silver-plated helmets.
   - (d) None of the above.

Direction for Question 8: Read the information given below and answer the question.

My father had given Rs. 50 lakh worth of property to me in his will but with a strange condition. To own the property, I need to spend Rs. 2,000 on a commodity bundle which consists of 5 products. Every unit of product 1 costs Rs. 115, of product 2 costs Rs. 90, of product 3 costs Rs. 70, of product 4 costs Rs. 40 and product 5 cost Rs. 45. For every unit of product 4 that I purchase, I must also buy only two units of product 2. For every unit of product 1, I must buy one unit of product 3. For every unit of product 5, I must also buy two units of product 4 and one unit of product 2. For every unit of any product purchased, I earn 1000 points and for every rupee not spent, I face a penalty of 500 points. I will get the property only if my points are positive, otherwise the money in the will goes to charity.

8. Mark all the correct statements.

   (a) I can claim the property with current conditions.

   (b) I can claim the property if every unit of product 3 costs Rs. 60, other prices remaining unchanged.

   (c) I can claim the property if unit price of product 4 increases by Rs. 5, other prices remaining unchanged.

   (d) I can claim the property if unit price of product 4 decreases by Rs. 5, other prices remaining unchanged.

2008-10

Directions for Questions 9 to 11:

   i) Five girls - Seema, Reema, Neeta, Mona and Veena have total five tickets of movie theaters - Priya, Chanakya, M2K, PVR Saket, Satyam where movies- Gangster, Khiladi, Hero, Salaam Namaste and Iqbal are currently playing. Each girl has one movie ticket of one of the five theaters.

   ii) Movie Gangster is running in Priya theater whose ticket is not with Veena and Seema.

   iii) Mona has ticket of Iqbal movie.

   iv) Neeta has ticket for the M2K theater. Veena has the ticket of Satyam theatre where Khiladi is not running.

   v) In PVR Saket theater, Salaam Namaste is running.

9. Which is the correct combination of the Theater - Girl - Movie?

   (a) M2K - Neeta - Hero

   (b) Priya - Mona - Gangster

   (c) Satyam - Veena - Iqbal

   (d) PVR Saket - Seema - Salaam Namaste

10. Which movie is running in Chanakya?

   (a) Gangster   (b) Iqbal

   (c) Hero   (d) Data inadequate

11. Who is having the ticket of the movie Hero?

   (a) Reema   (b) Veena

   (c) Seema   (d) Mona

Direction for Questions 12 to 14: Director of a drama group has to assign different roles to two artists - Paramjeet and Kamaljeet to play in a drama depending on four different symbols - @ for father, $ for wife, # for brother and * for daughter. There were four combinations decided by the director showing following result.

Answer the following questions on the basis of results I, II, III, IV

   I. Paramjeet @ Kamaljeet stands for Paramjeet is father of Kamaljeet

   II. Paramjeet $ Kamaljeet implies Paramjeet is the wife of Kamaljeet

   III. Paramjeet # Kamaljeet stands for Paramjeet is brother of Kamaljeet

   IV. Paramjeet * Kamaljeet stands for Paramjeet is daughter of Kamaljeet

12. If Daljeet # Chiranjeet $ Baljeet which of the following is **true**?

   (a) Daljeet is the brother of Baljeet

   (b) Daljeet is the father in-law of Baljeet

   (c) Daljeet is the father of Baljeet

   (d) Daljeet is the brother in-law of Baljeet

13. If Manjeet * Chiranjeet @ Daljeet @ Baljeet, which of the following is **not true**?

   (a) Manjeet is the mother of Baljeet

   (b) Chiranjeet is the grandfather of Baljeet

   (c) Manjeet and Daljeet are siblings

   (d) Manjeet is the aunt of Baljeet

14. If Abhijeet # Chiranjeet * Baljeet, which of the following is **not true**?

   (a) Baljeet is the parent of Abhijeet

   (b) Abhijeet and Chiranjeet are siblings

   (c) Abhijeet is the son of Baljeet

   (d) Baljeet is the mother in-law of Chiranjeet

Directions for Questions 15 to 18: Answer the questions based on following information

Four persons (1) Mohit, (2) Manohar, (3) Prasant and (4) Dinesh each had some initial money with them. They all were playing bridge in a way that the loser doubles the money of each of the other three persons from his share. They played four rounds and each person lost one round in the order 1, 2, 3 and 4 as mentioned above. At the end of fourth round each person had Rs. 32000/-

15. What was the amount with Mohit to start with?

   (a) Rs. 60000   (b) Rs. 34000

   (c) Rs. 66000   (d) Rs. 80000

16. What was the amount with Manohar at the end of first round?

   (a) 68000   (b) 72000

   (c) 64000   (d) 80000

17. Who had the lowest amount at any round of play throughout the tournament?

(a) Mohit

(b) Manohar

(c) Prasant

(d) Dinesh

18. What was the amount with Prasant at the end of the second round?

(a) 36000

(b) 72000

(c) 16000

(d) 68000

19. The VC (Vice-Chancellor) of a university has to select four professors, out of eight professors for a committee. The VC decided to select these four professors in such a manner that each selected professor has a habit common with at least one of the other three professors selected. The selected professors must also share at least one of the non-common habits of any of the other three professors selected.

Professor Arora likes surfing and smoking but hates gambling

Professor Bhalla likes smoking and drinking but hates surfing

Professor Chadha likes gambling but hates smoking

Professor Dhyani likes movie but hates drinking

Professor Eswar likes drinking but hates smoking and movie

Professor Fazil likes surfing but hates smoking and movie

Professor Goyal likes gambling and movie but hates surfing

Professor Hooda likes smoking and gambling but hates movie

Who are the four professors selected by the VC for the committee?

(a) Prof. Chadha, Prof. Dhyani, Prof. Eswar, Prof. Goyal

(b) Prof. Arora, Prof. Bhalla, Prof. Eswar, Prof. Fazil

(c) Prof. Bhalla, Prof. Chadha, Prof. Goyal, Prof. Hooda

(d) Prof. Dhyani, Prof. Eswar, Prof. Fazil, Prof. Hooda

Directions for Questions 20 to 23: While selecting candidates for positions of engineering, a software firm followed criteria as given below. A candidate must

i. be an engineering graduate with at least 60% marks at degree and 80% marks at higher secondary level.

ii. have at least one year's experience of working

iii. be ready to sign a bond of three years

iv. must not be more than 28 years of age on 1.2.2007

However, if a candidate fulfills all the criteria except-

a. at (i) above has obtained 50% marks at degree and 70% at higher secondary respectively and has at least three years experience of working, the case may be referred to the director of the firm.

b. at (ii) above, but is willing to pay an amount of 1 lakh if required to leave, the case may be referred to the president of the firm

c. at (ii) above but is a computer engineer, the case may be referred of DGM.

Based on the above criteria and the information given in each of the following cases, you have to take the decision on employing a candidate. You are not to assume anything and in the absence of adequate information, your answer will be not to be selected. The case is given to you as on 1.2.2007. The options available for you are provided in A, B, C and D.

20. Amar is a mechanical engineer with 65% marks at degree and 88% marks at HSC. He completed his engineering degree in 2003 at the age of 22 years and immediately started working in an engineering firm. He is keenly interested in going to USA and is not ready to sign a bond. However, he does not mind paying an amount of Rs. 1 lakh

(a) if the case is to be selected

(b) if the case is not to be selected

(c) if the case is to be referred to Director

(d) if the case is to be referred to President

21. Rajkishore, a computer engineer, has just completed graduation in July 2006, at the age of 23 years obtaining 72% marks. He had obtained 92% marks in HSC. He is willing to sign a bond with the company. He was joined a software company as trainee in August 2006 and working there till date

(a) if the case is to be selected

(b) if the case is not to be selected

(c) if the case is to be referred to Director

(d) if the case is to be referred to President

22. Madhuri is an electrical engineer and working as an assistant engineer for past two years. She had secured 85% and 69% marks at HSC and degree receptively. She has just completed 25 years of age.

(a) if the case is to the selected

(b) if the case is not to be selected

(c) if the case is to be referred to Director

(d) if the case is to be referred to President

23. Kamla is an engineering graduate wit 66% marks at degree and 90% at HSC. She has joined engineering firm 2 years ago at the age of 24 years. She is ready to sign the bond.

    (a) if the case is to be selected

    (b) if the case is not to be selected

    (c) if the case is to be referred to director

    (d) if the case is to be referred to President

Directions for Questions 24 to 26:

Answer the questions on the basis of the information given below:

There was an effort to study the relative importance that beneficiaries of five states assigned to five different development programme implemented by their governments. The programmes were Jawahar Rozgar Yojna (JRY), Indira Awas Yojna (IAY), Mid Day Mal (MDM), Rural Health Mission (RHM), National Rural Employment Guarantee Scheme (NREG). The level of dissimilarity between two states is the maximum difference in the rank allotted by the two states to any five programmes. The following table indicates the rank order of the five programmes of each state.

Rank	Orissa	Bihar	Rajasthan	Kerala	Karnataka
1	JRY	MDM	IAY	NREG	NREG
2	RHM	JRY	MDM	IAY	JRY
3	MDM	RHM	JRY	RHM	MDM
4	NREG	IAY	NREG	JRY	RHM
5	IAY	NREG	RHM	MDM	IAY

24. Which of the following states is least dissimilar to Orissa?

    (a) Bihar

    (b) Rajasthan

    (c) Kerala

    (d) Karnataka

25. Which of the following states is most dissimilar to Orissa?

    (a) Bihar

    (b) Rajasthan

    (c) Kerala

    (d) Karnataka

26. Three of the following four pairs of states have identical levels of dissimilarity. Which is the odd one out?

    (a) Kerala & Bihar

    (b) Bihar and Karnataka

    (c) Rajasthan & Kerala

    (d) Karnataka & Rajasthan

2009-11

Direction for the questions 27 – 28: Answer the questions based on the following information.

To get admission in a management course at Dadhichi Institute of Management (DIM) following criteria are given. A candidate must:

1. be a graduate from a recognized university with minimum 54 percent marks.

2. not be more than 33 years of age as on 1.4.2008

3. have secured 60 percent or more marks in the entrance test.

4. pay one-time deposit fee of Rs. 2,00,000 at time of admission.

5. pay tuition fee of Rs. 4,000 per month.

    – Any candidate who fails to fulfill the condition (4) at above, he/she may be referred to the chairman-admission.

    – Any candidate who has scored 80 percent mark in the entrance test but does not fulfill the condition (1) at above, he/she may be referred to the director.

    – Any candidate having work experience of at least 10 years in supervisory cadre and does not satisfy the condition (2) at above, he/she may be admitted under sponsored quota.

Given the above information and condition in each of the following questions, you have to decide which of the following course of action should be taken. You should not assume anything in case of any of the candidates. Mark answer

I.   if the candidate is admitted

II.   if the candidate is not admitted

III.   if the candidate is referred to the director

IV. if the candidate is referred to the chairman-admission

V.   if the candidate is admitted under sponsor quota

27. Kamaljeet secured 60 percent marks in graduation and was born on 15th April 1976. He scored 56 percent marks in the entrance test. He can pay one-time deposit of Rs. 2,00,000 and monthly tuition fee of Rs. 4,000.

    (a) I   (b) II

    (c) III   (d) IV

28. Gourav is a first-class science graduate who obtained 81 percent marks in entrance test. He has 12 years of work experience in supervisory cadre. He can pay the stipulated one-time deposit and monthly tuition fees. His date of birth is 20th October, 1970.

    (a) I   (b) IV

    (c) III   (d) V

29. Three children won prizes in the 'Tech India Quiz' contest. They are from three schools: Lancer, Columbus and Leelavati, which are located in different states. One of the children is named Binod. Lancer school's contestant did not come first. Leelavati school's contestant's name is Rahman. Columbus school is not located in Andhra Pradesh. The contestant from Maharashtra got third place and is not from Leelavati School. The contestant from Karnataka did not secure first position. Columbus school's contestant's name is not Badal.

    Which of the following statements is TRUE?

    (a) 1ˢᵗ prize: Rahman (Leelavati), 2ⁿᵈ prize: Binod (Columbus), 3ʳᵈ prize: Badal (Lancer)

    (b) 1st prize: Binod (Columbus), 2nd prize: Rahman (Leelavati), 3rd prize: Badal (Lancer)

    (c) 1st prize: Rahman (Leelavati), 2nd prize: Badal (Lancer), 3rd prize: Binod (Columbus)

    (d) 1st prize: Binod (Columbus), 2nd prize: Badal (Lancer), 3rd prize: Rahman (Leelavati)

30. Mother Dairy sells milk packets in boxes of different sizes to its vendors. The vendors are charged Rs. 20 per packet up to 2000 packets in a box. Additions can be made only in a lot size of 200 packets. Each addition of one lot to the box results in a discount of one rupee on all the packets in the box. What should be the maximum size of the box that would maximize the revenue per box for Mother Dairy?

    (a) 2400 packets   (b) 3000 packets

    (c) 4000 packets   (d) none of above

31. All employees have to pass through three consecutive entrance doors to enter into the office and one security guard is deployed at each door. These security guards report to the manager about those who come to office after 10 AM. Ms. Rani is an employee of this office and came late on the annual day. In order to avoid report to the manager she had to pay each security guard half of the money she had in her purse and 2 rupees more besides. She found only one rupee with her at the end. How much money Ms. Rani had before entering the office on the annual day?

    (a) Rs. 40   (b) Rs. 36

    (c) Rs. 25   (d) Rs. 42

Direction for questions 32 – 33: Answer the questions based on the following information.

Director of an institute wants to distribute teaching assignments of HRM, Psychology, Development Studies, Trade policy and Finance to five of six newly appointed faculty members. Prof. Fotedar does not want any assignment if Prof. Das gets one of the five. Prof. Chaudhury desires either HRM or Finance or no assignment. Prof. Banik opines that if Prof. Das gets either Psychology or Trade Policy then she must get the other one. Prof. Eswar insists on an assignment if Prof. Acharya gets one.

32. Which of the following is a valid faculty-assignment combination if all the faculty preferences are considered?

    (a) Prof. Acharya-HRM, Prof. Banik-Psychology, Prof. Chaudhury-Development studies, Prof. Das-Trade policy, Prof. Eswar-Finance

    (b) Prof. Chaudhury-HRM, Prof. Das-Psychology, Prof. Acharya-Development studies, Prof. Banik-Trade policy, Prof. Eswar-Finance

    (c) Prof. Acharya-HRM, Prof. Banik-Psychology, Prof. Eswar-Development studies, Prof. Das-Trade policy, Prof. Fodetar-Finance

    (d) Prof. Banik-HRM, Prof. Fotedar-Psychology, Prof. Eswar-Development studies, Prof. Chaudhury-Trade Policy, Prof. Acharya-Finance

33. If Prof. Acharya gets HRM and Prof. Chaudhury gets Finance, then which of the following is not a correct faculty-assignment combination assuming all faculty preferences are considered?

    (a) Prof. Das-Development Studies, Prof. Banik-Trade Policy

    (b) Prof. Fotedar-Development studies, Prof. Banik-Trade Policy

    (c) Prof. Banik-Development Studies, Prof. Eswar-Trade Policy

    (d) Prof. Banik-Development Studies, Prof. Das-Trade Policy

Direction for questions 34 – 36: Answer the questions based on the following information.

Five women decided to go for shopping to South Extension, New Delhi. They arrived at the designated meeting place in the following order: 1. Aradhana, 2. Chandrima, 3. Deepika, 4. Heena, and 5. Sumitra. Each of them spent at least Rs. 1000. The woman who spent Rs. 2234 arrived before the woman who spent Rs. 1193. One of them spent Rs. 1340 and she was not Deepika. One woman spent Rs. 1378 more than Chandrima. One of them spent Rs. 2517 and she was not Aradhana. Heena spent more than Deepika. Sumitra spent the largest amount and Chandrima the smallest.

34. What was the amount spent by Heena?

    (a) Rs. 1193   (b) Rs. 1340

    (c) Rs. 2234   (d) Rs. 2517

35. Which of the following amount is spent by one of the women?

    (a) Rs. 1139   (b) Rs. 1378

    (c) Rs. 2571   (d) Rs. 2518

36. The lady who spent Rs. 1193 is:
    (a) Aradhana
    (b) Chandrima
    (c) Deepika
    (d) Heena

Direction for questions 37 – 39: Answer the questions based on the following information.

In a motor race competition certain rules are given for the participants to follow. To control direction and speed of the motorists, guards are placed at different signal points with caps of different colour. Guard with red cap indicates the direction of participant's movement and guards with green cap indicates speed of the participant's movement. At any signal point presence of three guards, two guards and one guard with red cap means the participants must stop, turn left and turn right respectively. Signal points with three guards, two guards and one guard with green cap means the participants must move at 10, 4 and 2 km/hour respectively.

Kartikay, one of the participants, starts at a point where his car was heading towards north and he encountered signals as follows: at starting point one guard with green cap; after half an hour two guards with red cap and two guards with green cap at first signal; after fifteen minutes one guard with red cap at second signal; after half an hour one guard with red cap and three guards with green caps at third signal; after 24 minutes two guard with red cap and two guards with green cap at fourth signal; after 15 minutes three guards with red cap at fifth signal. (Time mentioned in each case is applicable after crossing the previous signal).

37. Total distance traveled by Kartikay from starting point till last signal is:
    (a) 9 km.   (b) 10 km.
    (c) 8 km.   (d) 12 km.

38. What would be the final position of Kartikay if one guard with red cap and two guards with green caps were placed at the first signal point after the starting point?
    (a) 3.0 km to the west and 2.0 km to the south
    (b) 3.0 km to the west and 4.0 km to the north
    (c) 5.0 km to the east and 4.0 km to the north
    (d) 2.0 km to the west and 4.0 km to the south

39. If at the starting point Kartikay was heading towards south what would be his final position?
    (a) 3.0 km to the east and 4.0 km to the south
    (b) 5.0 km to the east and 4.0 km to the south
    (c) 3.0 km to the west and 4.0 km to the south
    (d) 5.0 km to the west and 2.0 km to the north

Direction for questions 40 – 43: Answer the questions based on the following information.

Mr. Mansingh has five sons – Arun, Mahi, Rohit, Nilesh and Sourav, and three daughters – Tamanna, Kuntala and Janaki. Three sons of Mr. Mansingh were born first followed by two daughters. Sourav is the eldest child and Janaki is the youngest. Three of the children are studying at Trinity School and three are studying at St Stefan. Tamanna and Rohit study at St Stefan school. Kuntala, the eldest daughter, plays chess. Mansorover school offers cricket only, while Trinity school offers chess. Beside, these schools offer no other games. The children who are at Mansorover school have been born in succession. Mahi and Nilesh are cricketers while Arun plays football. Rohit who was born just before Janaki, plays hockey.

40. Arun is the ______________ child of Mr. Mansingh.
    (a) 2nd   (b) 3rd
    (c) 6th   (d) 5th

41. Sourav is a student of which school?
    (a) Trinity   (b) St. Stefan
    (c) Mansorover   (d) Cannot be determined

42. What game does Tamanna play?
    (a) Cricket   (b) Hockey
    (c) Football   (d) Cannot be determined

43. Which of the following pairs was not born in succession (ignore the order)?
    (a) Mahi and Nilesh   (b) Kuntala and Arun
    (c) Rohit and Janaki   (d) Arun and Rohit

44. Pointing to Priya, father of Pritu says, "She is the daughter of the daughter of the wife of the only son of the grandfather of my sister." How is Sushma related to Priya if Sushma is the sister of Pritu?
    (a) Mother   (b) Aunt
    (c) Niece   (d) None of the above

Direction for the question 45 – 47: Read the following information and answer the questions given below it.

For selection of films produced before December 2007 for the national film festival of India, following criteria are given.

1. The film must be submitted to the National Film Development Corporation (NFDC) by 31.10.2007.

2. The production cost of the film should not exceed Rupees Five crores.

3. The director of the film should have passed a three year course either from the Film and Television Institute of India (FTII) or from Satyajit Ray Film & Television Institute.

4. The length of the film should not exceed 150 minutes.

5. The film must have been approved by the film censor board of India.

6. However, if the film fulfils all the above criteria except

(a) criteria 2 above, it must be sent to the finance secretary.

(b) criteria 3 above, the director has done at least a one year course from FTII or Satyajit Ray Film & Television Institute, the film is kept as a stand-bye.

On the basis of above information and information provided below, decide the course of action in each case. No further information is available. You are not to assume anything. Mark answer

I.   if the film is to be selected

II. if the film is not be selected

III. if the film should be sent to the finance secretary

IV. if the film should be kept as a stand-bye

V.   if the data given about the film are not adequate to make a decision.

45. Film *Dainandini* was produced at the cost of Rupees 2.5 crore. It was submitted to the NFDC on 29th September 2007. The director of the film Govind Chadha passed a 3-year course from FTII. Length of film was 120 minutes and has been approved by the censor board of India.

(a) I   (b) II

(c) IV   (d) V

46. *Bhadrasalam* is a 135-minute film directed by Katyani, who was a student of Satyajit Ray Film & Television Institute from 1996 to 1999. The cost of producing the film was Rupees 2.3 crore and it was submitted to NFDC on 24th July 2007. The film has been approved by the censor board of India.

(a) I   (b) V

(c) III   (d) IV

47. Rakesh Mohan, the director of film *Ek Bar Achanak,* has successfully completed a 2-years course at Stayjit Ray Film & Television Institute. The 150-minute film was produced at Rupees 4.85 crore. It has been approved by the censor board of India and submitted to NFDC on 30th Nov. 2007.

(a) I   (b) III

(c) IV   (d) II

48. Among Anil, Bibek, Charu, Debu, and Eswar, Eswar is taller than Debu but not as fat as Debu. Charu is taller than Anil but shorter than Bibek. Anil is fatter than Debu but not as fat as Bibek. Eswar is thinner than Charu, who is thinner than Debu. Eswar is shorter than Anil. Who is the thinnest person?

(a) Bibek

(b) Charu

(c) Debu

(d) Eswar

49. Pointing to a photograph Yuvraj says, "He is the only brother of the only daughter of my sister's maternal grandmother." Pointing to another photograph Sourav says, 'he is the only brother of the only daughter of my sister's maternal grandmother." If among the two photographs, one was either of Sourav or Yuvraj, and the photograph, towards which Yuvraj was pointing, was not of Sourav, then how is Yuvraj related to Sourav?

(a) Paternal uncle   (b) Maternal uncle

(c) Grandfather   (d) None of the above

2010-12

Directions for questions 50 – 52: Study the following information carefully and answer the questions.

Four houses Blue, Green, Red, and Yellow are located in a row in the given order. Each of the houses is occupied by a person earning a fixed amount of a salary. The four persons are Paul, Krishna, Laxman, and Som.

Read the following instructions carefully:

I.   Paul lives between Som and Krishna

II   Laxman does not stay in Blue house

III. The person living in Red house earns more than that of person living in Blue

IV. Salary of Som Is more than that of Paul but lesser than that of Krishna

V.   One of the person earns Rs.80,000

VI. The person earning Rs.1,10,000 is not Laxman

VII. The salary difference between Laxman and Som is Rs. 30,000

VIII. The house in which Krishna lives is located between houses with persons earning salaries of Rs. 30,000 and Rs.50,000

IX. Krishna does not live in Yellow house, and the person living in yellow house is not earning lowest salary among the four persons.

50. Who lives in Red house?

(a) Paul   (b) Krishna

(c) Laxman   (d) Som

51. Which house is occupied by person earning highest salary?

(a) Blue   (b) Green

(c) Red   (d) Yellow

52. What is the salary earned by person living in Green house?

(a) Rs. 30,000

(b) Rs. 50,000

(c) Rs. 80,000

(d) Rs. 110,000

53. Mr Raghav went in his car to meet his friend John. He drove 30 kms towards north and then 40 kms towards west. He then turned to south and covered 8 kms. Further he turned to east and moved 26 kms. Finally he turned right and drove 10 kms and then turned left to travel 19 kms. How far and in which direction is he from the starting point?

(a) East of starting point, 5 kms

(b) East of starting point, 13 kms

(c) North East of starting point, 13 kms

(d) North East of starting point, 5 kms

54. Mr. Raju took the members of his family for a picnic. His father's mother and mother's father including their two children were in one car. His father's son and sister's husband, brother's wife were in second car. He along with his wife, wife's sister, wife's brother and son's wife with a kid was in the third car. How many members of Mr. Raju's family were there in the picnic along with Mr. Raju and how many were left behind (assuming all members of the third generation are married)?

(a) 13 and 4   (b) 14 and 5

(c) 12 and 5   (d) 13 and 6

55. ABCDE play a game of cards. 'A' tells 'B' that if 'B' gives him five cards, 'A' will have as many cards as 'E' has. However if 'A' gives five cards to 'B' then 'B' will have as many cards as 'D'. A and B together has 20 cards more than what D and E have together. B has four cards more than what C has and total number of cards are 201. How many cards B have?

(a) 185

(b) 37

(c) 175

(d) 27

56. Ganesh Cultural Centre for promoting arts has appointed 3 instructors for music, dance, and painting. Music instructor takes session from 12 noon to 4:00 pm on Monday, Thursday and Sunday. The sessions of dance instructor are scheduled on Tuesday, Thursday, Wednesday and Sunday between 10:00 am to 2:00 pm. The 9:00 am to 12:00 noon slot on Tuesday, Friday and Thursday and also 2:00 pm to 4:00 pm slot on Wednesday, Saturday and Sunday is filled up by Painting Instructor. On which day(s) of a week the dance and painting sessions are simultaneously held?

(a) Sunday and Wednesday

(b) Tuesday and Friday

(c) Tuesday and Thursday

(d) Only on Tuesday

Directions for question 57: Study the information given below and answer the question.

A Prime Minister is contemplating the expansion of his cabinet. There are four ministerial berths and there are eight probable candidates (C1-C8) to choose from. The selection should be in a manner that each selected person shares a liking with at least one of the other three selected members. Also, the selected must also hate at least one of the likings of any of the other three persons selected.

   I. C1 likes travelling and sightseeing, but hates river rafting

   II. C2 likes sightseeing and squash, but hates travelling

   III. C3 likes river rafting, but hates sightseeing

   IV. C4 likes trekking, but hates squash

   V. C5 likes squash, but hates sightseeing and trekking

   VI. C6 likes travelling, but hates sightseeing and trekking

   VII. C7 likes river rafting and trekking, but hates travelling, and

   VIII. C8 likes sightseeing and river rafting, but hates trekking

57. Who are the four people selected by the Prime Minister?

(a) C1, C2, C5, C6   (b) C3, C4, C5, C6

(c) C1, C2, C4, C7   (d) None of the above

2011-13

Directions for questions 58 to 62: Read the following information and choose the right alternative in the questions that follow.

During the cultural week of an institute six competitions were conducted. The cultural week was inaugurated in the morning of 19th October, Wednesday and continued till 26th October. In the span of 8 days six competitions namely debate, folk dance, fash-p, street play, rock band, and group song, were organized along with various other cultural programs. The information available from the institute is:

   i. Only one competition was held in a day

   ii. Rock band competition was not conducted on the closing day.

   iii. Fash-p was conducted on the day prior to debate competition.

   iv. Group song competition was conducted neither on Wednesday nor on Saturday

   v. None of the competition was conducted on Thursday and Sunday

   vi. Street play competition was held on Monday

   vii. There was gap of two days between debate competition and group song competition

58. The cultural week started with which competition?

(a) Fash-p competition

(b) Debate competition

(c) Street play competition

(d) Rock band competition

59. How many days gap is there between rock band competition and group song competition?

(a) Two   (b) Three

(c) Four   (d) Five

60. Which pair of competition was conducted on Wednesday?

(a) Rock band competition and debate competition

(b) Debate competition and fash-p competition

(c) Rock band competition and folk dance competition

(d) None of these

61. Which competition exactly precedes the street play competition?

(a) Rock band competition

(b) Group song competition

(c) Debate competition

(d) Fash-p competition

62. Fash-p competition follows which competition?

(a) Debate competition

(b) Street play competition

(c) Rock band competition

(d) None of these

Directions for questions 63 to 65: Read the information given below and answer the questions that follow the information.

A parking lot can accommodate only six cars. The six cars are parked in two rows in such a way that the front of the three cars parked in one row is facing the other three cars in the other row.

i. Alto is not parked in the beginning of any row

ii. Esteem is second to the right of i10

iii. Punto, who is the neighbor of Alto is parked diagonally opposite to i10

iv. Swift is parked in front of Alto

v. SX4 is parked to the immediate right of Alto

63. If SX4 and Esteem exchange their positions mutually then car (s) adjacent to Esteem is (are)?

(a) i10 and Swift

(b) Only Swift

(c) Only Alto

(d) Alto and Punto

64. If Alto changes position with i10 and Punto changes position with SX4 and Swift shifts one position to the right to accommodate Beatle then the car (s) parked adjacent to Beatle is (are)?

(a) Punto only   (b) i10 and SX4

(c) Punto and Alto   (d) Alto and Swift

65. In the original parking scheme four new cars enter the parking lot such that Wagon-R is second to the right of i10 and Zen is second to the left of SX4. Jazz is parked second to the left to Wagon-R and Beat is parked to the right of Alto then the cars that moved out are?

(a) Esteem and Swift   (b) Punto and Alto

(c) i10 and Alto   (d) Punto and SX4

Directions 66 to 70: Read the information given below and answer the next five question that follow:

i. Six friends Rahul, Kabeer, Anup, Raghu, Amit and Alok were engineering graduates. All six of them were placed in six different companies and were posted in six different locations, namely Tisco-Jamshedpur, Telco-Pune, Wipro-Bangalore, HCL-Noida, Mecon-Ranchi and Usha Martin-Kolkata. Each of them has their personal e-mail id's with different email providers i.e., Gmail, Indiatimes, Radiffmail, Yahoo, Hotmail, Sancharnet, though not necessarily in the same order.

ii. The one having e-mail account with Sancharnet works in Noida and the one having an e-mail account with Indiatimes works for Tisco.

iii. Amit does not stay in Bangalore and does not work for Mecon, the one who works for Mecon has an e-mail id with Gmail.

iv. Rahul has an e-mail id with Rediffmail and works at Pune.

v. Alok does not work for Mecon and the one who works for Wipro does not have an e-mail account with Yahoo.

vi. Kabeer is posted in Kolkata, and does not have an account with Hotmail.

vii. Neither Alok nor Raghu work in Noida.

viii. The one who is posted in Ranchi has an e-mail id which is not an account of Rediffmail or Hotmail.

ix. Anup is posted in Jamshedpur.

66. The man who works in Wipro has a e-mail account with?

(a) Sancharnet   (b) Yahoo

(c) Rediffmail   (d) None of these

67. Which of the following e-mail-place of posting-person combination is correct?

(a) Kabeer-Kolkata-Rediffmail

(b) Alok-Bangalore-Indiatimes

(c) Amit-Noida-Yahoo

(d) Raghu-Ranchi-Gmail

68. Which of the following is true?

   (a) Amit is posted at Ranchi

   (b) Raghu is posted at Jamshedpur

   (c) Kabeer has an e-mail id with Yahoo

   (d) Rahul has an e-mail id with Indiatimes

69. Which of the following sequences of location represents Alok, Kabeer, Anup, Rahul, Raghu and Amit in the same order?

   (a) Bangalore, Noida, Pune, Jamshedpur, Ranchi, Kolkata

   (b) Bangalore, Kolkata, Jamshedpur, Pune, Noida, Ranchi

   (c) Kolkata, Bangalore, Jamshedpur, Pune, Noida, Ranchi

   (d) None of these

70. People who have e-mail account with Indiatimes, Sancharnet and Yahoo work for which companies, in the same sequence as the e-mail accounts mentioned?

   (a) Usha Martin, HCL, Wipro

   (b) Tisco, Wipro, Usha Martin

   (c) HCL, Tisco, Wipro

   (d) Tisco, HCL, Usha Martin

71. How many 'zeroes' are there in the following sequence which are immediately preceded by a nine but not immediately followed by seven?

709007089070203004 5703907

   (a) One   (b) Two

   (c) Three   (d) Four

72. A Retail chain has seven branches in a city namely R1, R2, R3, R4, R5, R6, R7 and a central distribution center (DC). The nearest branch to the DC is R6 which is in the south of DC and is 9 km away from DC. R2 is 17 km away from DC in the west. The branch R1 is 11 km away from R2 further in the west. The branch R3 is 11 km in the north east of R1. R4 is 13 km away from R3 in the east. R5 is 11 km in the north east of the distribution center. In the north east of R6 is R7 and distance between them is 15 km. The distance between R1 and R6, R2 and R6, R6 and R5 is 23 km, 19 km, 13 km respectively. R3 is 14 km away from the DC in the north west direction, while R2 is also 14 km away from R4 in the north east direction of R2. A truck carrying some goods starts from the distribution center and has to cover at least four stores in a single trip. There is an essential good that has to be delivered in the store R7, but the delivery at R7 has to be done in the end, so what is the shortest distance the truck would travel?

   (a) 55   (b) 56

   (c) 63   (d) 66

Directions for questions 73 – 75: Read the following instructions and answer the questions.

After the discussion at a high level meeting of government officers, the criteria for issuing of import / export licence to eligible business firms for the year 2011-12 were finalized as follows. The firms must –

   I.   have a Grade – 'A' certified unit for any products.

   II. not have any legal dispute case against it.

   III. possess minimum asset worth Rs. 40 lakhs.

   IV submit an environmental clearance certificate issued by the Pollution Control Board (PCB) of the state where the firm is located.

   V.   deposit the margin money of Rs. 1 lakh.

   VI. arrange for three guarantors with their personal identity cards (IDs).

However, if the firm satisfies all the above mentioned criteria except:

   a) criteria (I), but is a traditional handloom production unit, then the case may be referred to Development Commissioner, Handloom (DCH) of the state.

   b) criteria (IV), but is a local employment provider / thread (input) supplier / cloth supplier, the case may be referred to the Director, Department of Industry of the state.

   c) criteria (V) but can deposit at least Rs. 50000, the firm will be given import licence only and the case may be referred to the Deputy Director, Department of Industry of the state.

Based on the above criteria and information provided on each of the firms in the questions below, you have to decide which course of action should be taken against each firm. Without assuming anything regarding any applicant firm, the decision should be based on the information provided.

73. Mahalaxmi Weaving Centre is a traditional handloom production unit. It has property worth more than Rs. 1 crore. It managed to get three guarantors with their personal IDs. No legal case is there against it. There is no problem submitting an environmental clearance, as the same is already issued to it by the State Pollution Control Board. It is also ready to deposit Rs. 1 lakh.

   (a) Licence can be issued

   (b) Licence not to be issued

   (c) May be referred to the Development Commissioner, Handloom

   (d) May be referred to the Director of Industry

74. Ramayan Enterprise is a textiles firm which possesses assets worth Rs. 50 lakhs and is located in Surat where no firm having any legal dispute is permitted to operate. The firm agreed to deposit Rs. 1 lakh and give details of three guarantors with their personal details as required. It has got grade-A certificate and can submit an environment clearance certificate issued by the Pollution Control Board of the state.

    (a) Licence can be issued

    (b) Licence not to be issued

    (c) May be referred to the Development Commissioner, Handloom

    (d) May be referred to Deputy Director of Industry

75. Hirabhai Handlooms is a Vadodara based traditional Gujarati handloom firm keen to get an export licence. It is ready to pay the required security amount and possesses assets of Rs. 55 lakhs. Hirabhai Chamanlal is the owner of the firm as well as the President of State Handloom Association. Hence getting more than three guarantors with their IDs is not a problem. The firm possesses the environmental clearance certificate from the State Pollution Control Board after it was made mandatory for all handloom firms in the state.

    (a) Licence to be issued

    (b) Licence not to be issued

    (c) May be referred to the Development Commissioner, Handloom

    (d) May be referred to the Director of Industry

Directions for questions 76 – 77: Read the following information carefully to answer the questions given below it.

Mr. Malhotra's family is a traditional joint family from Jalandhar having six persons from three generations. Each member of the family has different food preference and they support different sports / games. Only two couples are there in the family. Rakesh likes continental food and his wife neither likes dry fruits nor supports gymnastics. The person who likes egg supports Rugby and his wife likes traditional food. Mona is mother-in-law of Sonalika and she supports Athletics. Varun is grandfather of Tarun and Tarun, who likes Punjabi food, supports Basketball. Nuri is granddaughter of Mona and she supports Badminton. Nuri's mother supports horse riding.

76. Identify the *correct* pair of two couples from the following:

    (a) Mona-Varun and Rakesh-Sonalika

    (b) Varun-Mona and Rakesh-Nuri

    (c) Rakesh-Sonalika and Tarun-Nuri

    (d) Cannot be determined

77. Who likes Punjabi food, and what sport / game does he / she support?

    (a) Nuri and Badminton

    (b) Sonalika and horse riding

    (c) Tarun and Basketball

    (d) None of the above

Directions for questions 78 – 79: Read the following paragraph and following conditions to answer the questions.

The Vice Chancellor of a University wants to select a team of five member organizing committee for the next convocation of the University to be held in March 2012. The committee members are to be selected from five shortlisted professors (Prof. Ahuja, Prof. Banerjee, Prof. Chakravarty, Prof. Das and Prof. Equbal) and four short listed students (Prakash, Queen, Ravi and Sushil). Some conditions for selection of the committee members are given below:

    1. Prof. Ahuja and Sushil have to be together

    2. Prakash cannot be put with Ravi

    3. Prof. Das and Queen cannot go together

    4. Prof. Chakravarty and Prof. Equbal have to be selected

    5. Ravi cannot be selected with Prof. Banerjee.

78. If two members of the committee are students and Prof. Das is one of the members of the committee, who are the other committee members?

    (a) Prof. Banerjee, Prof. Chakravarty, Prakash and Queen

    (b) Prof. Ahuja, Prof. Banerjee, Sushil and Prakash

    (c) Prof. Chakravarty, Prof. Equbal, Prakash and Sushil

    (d) None of the above

79. In case Prof. Ahuja and Prof. Chakravarty are members, who are the other members who *cannot* be selected for the committee?

    (a) Prof. Banerjee, Prof. Equbal and Sushil

    (b) Prof. Equbal, Sushil and Prakash

    (c) Prof. Equbal, Prakash and Queen

    (d) None of the above

Directions for questions 80 – 81: Read the following information carefully and mark the correct answer to the questions given below.

Sampada Apartment is a housing society formed by a group of professors of a University. It has six flats on a floor in two rows facing North and South which are allotted to Prof. Purohit, Prof. Qureshi, Prof. Rathor, Prof. Sawant, Prof. Tripathy and Prof. Usman. Prof. Qureshi gets a North facing flat and it is not next to Prof. Sawant's flat. Prof. Sawant and Prof. Usman get their flats which are diagonally opposite to each other. Prof. Rathor gets a south facing flat which is next to Prof. Usman's flat. Prof. Tripathy's flat is North facing.

80. Which of the following professors get South facing flats?

   (a) Prof. Qureshi, Prof. Tripathy and Prof. Sawant

   (b) Prof. Usman, Prof. Tripathy and Prof. Purohit

   (c) Prof. Usman, Prof. Rathor and Prof. Purohit

   (d) None of the above

81. If the flats of Prof. Tripathy and Prof. Purohit are interchanged, whose flat will be next to that of Prof. Usman?

   (a) Prof. Rathor   (b) Prof. Tripathy

   (c) Prof. Usman   (d) None of the above

2013-15

Direction for Questions 82 - 83: Some information is provided in the paragraph below. Answer the questions based on this information.

A weekly television show routinely stars six actors, J, K, L, M, N, and O. Since the show has been on the air for a long time, some of the actors are good friends and some do not get along at all. In an effort to keep peace, the director sees to it that friends work together and enemies do not. Also, as the actors have become more popular, some of them need time off to do other projects. To keep the schedule working, the director has a few things she must be aware of :

- J will only work on episodes on which M is working.

- N will not work with K under any circumstances.

- M can only work every other week, in order to be free to film a movie.

- At least three of the actors must appear in every weekly episode.

82. In a show about L getting a job at the same company J already works for and K used to work for, all three actors will appear. Which of the following is true about the other actors who may appear?

   (a) M, N, and O must all appear.

   (b) M may appear and N must appear.

   (c) M must appear and O may appear.

   (d) O may appear and N may appear.

83. Next week, the show involves N's new car and O's new refrigerator. Which of the following is true about the other actors who may appear?

   (a) M, J, L, and K all may appear.

   (b) J, L, and K must appear.

   (c) L and K must appear.

   (d) Only L may appear.

Direction for Questions 84 - 85: Some information is provided in the paragraph below. Answer the questions based on this information.

Era is in charge of seating the speakers at a table. In addition to the moderator, there will be a pilot, a writer, an attorney, and an explorer. The speakers' names are Gaj, Hema, Jaya, Kumar, and Lalit.

- The moderator must sit it in the middle, in seat #3.

- The attorney cannot sit next to the explorer.

- Lalit is the pilot.

- The writer and the attorney sit on either side of the moderator.

- Hema, who is not the moderator, sits between Kumar and Jaya.

- The moderator does not sit next to Jaya or Lalit.

- Gaj, who is the attorney, sits in seat #4.

84. Who is the moderator?

   (a) Lalit   (b) Gaj

   (c) Hema   (d) Kumar

85. Where does Jaya sit?

   (a) seat #1   (b) seat #2

   (c) seat #3   (d) seat #4

2014-16

Directions for questions 86 to 91: Read the following passage and solve the questions based on it.

a. Six Indian professors from six different institutions (Jupiter, Mars, Mercury, Neptune, Pluto, Uranus) went to China to attend an international conference on "Sustainability and Innovation in Management: A Global Scenario" and they stayed in six successive rooms on the second floor of a hotel (201-206).

b. Each of them has published papers in a number of journals and has donated to a number of institutions last year.

c. The professor in room no. 202 has published in twice as many journals as the professor who donated to 8 institutions last year.

d. The professor from Uranus and the professor in room number 206 together published in a total of 40 journals.

e. The professor from Jupiter published in 8 journals less than the professor from Pluto but donated to 10 more institutions last year.

f. Four times the number of 4 journal publications by the professor in room number 204 is lesser than the number of institutions to which he donated last year.

g. The professor in room number 203 published in 12 journals and donated to 8 institutions last year.

h. The professor who published in 16 journals donated to 24 institutions last year.

i. The professor in room number 205 published in 8 journals and donated to 2 institutions less than the professor from Mercury last year. The Mercury professor is staying in an odd numbered room.

j. The Mars professor is staying two rooms ahead of the Pluto professor who is staying two rooms ahead of the Mercury professor in ascending order of room numbers.

k. The professors from Mercury and Jupiter do not stay in room number 206.

86. In which room is the Mars professor staying?

(a) Room number 201   (b) Room number 203

(c) Room number 205   (d) None of the above

87. How many institutions did the Jupiter professor donate to last year?

(a) 8   (b) 3

(c) 18   (d) 24

88. The professor of which institute is staying in room number 206?

(a) Jupiter

(b) Uranus

(c) Mercury

(d) Neptune

89. The professor of which institute donated to 24 institutions last year?

(a) Jupiter

(b) Uranus

(c) Mercury

(d) Neptune

90. The professor of which institute published in the maximum number of journals?

(a) Jupiter

(b) Uranus

(c) Neptune

(d) Mars

91. In how many journals did the Jupiter professor publish?

(a) 8   (b) 4

(c) 12   (d) 20

Directions for questions 92 to 94: Study the information below and answer the questions based on it:

i. There are 5 persons in a group - P, Q, R, S and T.

ii. In this group, there is one badminton player, one chess player and one tennis player.

iii. P and S are unmarried ladies who do not play any games.

iv. No lady is either a chess player or a badminton player.

v. There is one married couple in this group of which T is the husband.

vi. Q is the brother of R and is neither a chess player nor a tennis player.

92. Which of the following groups has only ladies?

(a) PQR

(b) QRS

(c) RST

(d) None of the above

93. Who is the tennis player?

(a) Q

(b) R

(c) S

(d) T

94. Who is the wife of T?

(a) P

(b) S

(c) Q

(d) R

2015-17

Directions for questions 95 to 98 : Read the given information carefully and answer the questions below.

The management of the national daily newspaper *Tomorrow Digest* decides to enhance its subscriber base through major changes in the style, layout, design and content of the paper. In order to make the content more amenable to the mindset of the growing younger population of the country, the paper decides to appoint a number of young and promising Associate Editors. For facilitating the appointment process, several selection criteria were finalized and provided to the selection panel, which are noted in the following. It was noted that in order to get selected, the candidates are required to fulfill, in addition to I, least three of the following conditions.

I. The age of the candidates must not be lower than 25 years, but should not cross 30 year.

II. The candidates has secured 60 percent and above at her / his Graduation level.

III. The candidate has obtained a Post Graduate Diploma in journalism with at least 55 percent marks

IV. The candidate has gained working experience of a minimum period of 2 years in a daily newspaper with responsibility of regular writing assignments.

V. The candidate has been awarded at stat-level for her / his articles published in state level English daily.

If, however, it is observed that some candidates fulfill only two conditions from II-V, but does *not* fulfill:

(a) V above, but he/she has already gathered an experience of 5 years in a news agency, the case of the candidate will be referred to the Managing Editor of *Tomorrow Digest*.

(b) II above, but he / she holds a post Graduate Diploma in Journalism with 80 percent marks, the case of the candidate will be referred to the Chairman of *Tomorrow Digest*.

(c) III above, but he/she has completed Graduation with 70 percent marks, the case of the candidate will be referred to the Editor of *Tomorrow Digest.*

All the information above a few candidates applying for the Associate Editor position provided in the following are dated on August 31, 2014. Based on the information furnished, decide in each case, which of the following course of action the selection panel should adopt, from the available options. You are not to assume any information.

95. Sarangsh Malhotra has graduated from Agra University with 66 percent marks and later has completed PG Diploma in Journalism from Indian Institute of Mass Communication, New Delhi with 71 percent. After completion of the PG Diploma programme, she joined Galaxy News at Jaipur on Christmas Eve in 2006. She received an award from the hands of the Governor of Rajasthan for her series of investigative articles on January 26, 2008, a day which coincided with her twenty-fifth birthday. During June next year, she joined in a corporate house and is working there since then.

(a) The candidate is to be selected

(b) The candidate is not to be selected

(c) The case of the candidate is to be referred to the Managing Editor

(d) The case of the candidate is to be referred to the Chairman

96. Nalin Saxena graduated in Sociology Honours from Bangalore University with 61 percent marks, after which he joined an NGO for social work. After two years, he took migration and joined Mumbai University for the PG Diploma in Journalism Programme, and he secured 59 percent in the exam. He subsequently joined *Ahmadabad Weekly* magazine, which is published in English, in July 18, 2011, to write regular features on city life. He was born in June 1986, in the midst of the FIFA World Cup.

(a) The candidate is to be selected

(b) The candidate is not to be selected

(c) The case of the candidate is to be referred to the Chairman

(d) The case of the candidate is to be referred to the Editor

97. Geetika Arora is working as a reporter on issues pertaining to international news events in the Indore-base English news daily *The New Dawn* since September 20, 2012. She was awarded by the Madhya Pradesh Newspapers Guild in 2013 for her series of articles on global climate change concerns. Geetika had graduated in Political Science from Udaipur University in 2010 with 58 percent marks. After graduation, she immediately joined Allahabad University and earned her Gold Medal in PG Diploma in Journalism by securing 82 percent marks two years later. While studying at Allahabad, she celebrated her twenty-fourth birthday.

(a) The candidate is to be selected

(b) The candidate is not to the selected

(c) The case of the candidate is to be referred to the Chairman

(d) The case of the candidate is to be referred to the Editor

98. Manjeet Tyagi was born on September 5, 1988 and completed his graduation in Economics from Garwal University with 68 percent marks in 2009. He subsequently completed his PG Diploma in Journalism from Punjab University in July 2010, but his marks dropped by ten percentage points vis-à-vis his graduation results. After completing PG degree, Manjeet immediately joined in a data analytics firm and worked there for one and half years as business analyst, after which he joined the Delhi-based English daily *Financial Standard* as a trade and industry expert for writing regular columns on these areas.

(a) The candidate is to be selected

(b) The candidate is not to the selected

(c) The case of the candidate is to be referred to the Managing Editor

(d) The case of the candidate is to be referred to the Editor

Directions for questions 99 to 102: Read the following passage and solve the questions based on it.

In an Engineering College, five students from five different cities were elected as Secretaries by the students to perform different student activities. Each student studies in a different branch of engineering. Additionally, the following information is provided:

 (i) Abhishek does not stay in the Aravalli hostel where the student from Nagpur stays.

 (ii) The student, whose name is not Abhishek and does not study in Metallurgy, stays in Satpura hostel. He is the only student among the five to stay at Satpura hostel.

 (iii) Hardeep neither belongs to Jodhpur, nor does he study Mechanical Engineering.

 (iv) The student-in-charge of Cultural activity stays in the Aravalli hostel where Civil Engineering student does not stay.

 (v) Sanjoy and the student, who studies Metallurgy, bath stay in the same hostel.

 (vi) The student who belongs to Allahabad does not stay with the student-in-charge of the Sports activity staying at Aravalli hostel.

 (vii) Sanjoy is not the student-in-charge of the Cultural activity.

 (viii) Ravi, the student-in-charge of Mess activity, stays at Satpura hostel.

 (ix) The student from Patna and the student, who studies Mechanical Engineering, both stay at Aravalli hostel. They are the only two among the five students to stay at this hostel.

 (x) The student, who stays at Satpura hostel, studies Computer Science.

 (xi) Hemant, who does not belong to Kochi, studies Chemical Engineering. He is not General Secretary of the Student Body.

 (xii) Sanjoy does not belong to Allahabad.

 (xiii) The student from Kochi and the student-in-charge of Placement activity, both stay the Vindhya hostel.

99. Which of the following statement(s) is (are) <u>incorrect</u>?

 I. The Chemical Engineering student and the student-in-charge of Cultural activity, both stay in the same hostel.

 II. The student-in-charge of Placement activity is studying Metallurgy.

 III. The student who belongs to Nagpur is the student-in-charge of Sports activity.

 IV. Ravi belongs to Jodhpur.

 (a) Only I
 (b) Both I and II
 (c) All of I, II and III
 (d) None of the statements is incorrect

100. Which of the following statements is <u>correct</u>?

 I. Sanjoy and Abhishek stay at the same hostel.

 II. The General Secretary of the Student Body studies Mechanical Engineering.

 III. The student who belongs to Patna is studying Metallurgy.

 IV. The student who belongs to Kochi is studying Computer Science.

 (a) Only I
 (b) Only II
 (c) Only III
 (d) None of the statements is correct

101. The student who belongs to Allahabad is studying in

———.

 (a) Metallurgy
 (b) Mechanical Engineering
 (c) Civil Engineering
 (d) None of the above

102. The General Secretary of the Student Body belongs to:

 (a) Patna
 (b) Nagpur
 (c) Kochi
 (d) Jodhpur

Directions for questions 103 to 105: Read the following passage and solve the questions based on it.

Taking note of the day-long heavy queue in front of the Tarangabad Transport Department office everyday for obtaining transport permits, the City Administration comes out with a 'Single Office-Five Windows' system for facilitating the process. For simplicity, the windows are named as W1, W2, W3, W4 and W5 respectively. Office hours are from 8:00 AM to 5:30 PM, barring Saturday, when the office closes by 2.30 PM. To streamline the rush and reduce pressure on the employees, the working hour of the aforesaid windows are defined in the following manner:

 • W1 is open between 9.30 AM and 2.30 PM on Monday and Wednesday, between 8.00 AM and 11.30 AM on Tuesday and Thursday and between 3.00 PM and 5.00 PM on Friday.

 • W2 is open between 8.30 AM and 11.30 AM on Wednesday and Thursday, between 8.00 AM and 10.00 AM on Friday, and between 12.30 PM and 2.30 PM on Monday and Saturday.

 • W3 is open between 10.00 AM and 12.30 PM on Wednesday and Saturday, between 10.00 AM and 12.00 Noon on Friday and between 3.30 PM to 5.30 PM on Monday and Thursday.

- W4 is open between 11.30 AM and 3.00 PM on Tuesday, between 12.30 PM and 3.00 PM on Thursday and Friday, between 8 AM and 10 AM on Saturday and Monday and between 3.30 PM to 5.30 PM on Wednesday,

- W5 is open between 2.00 PM and 4.00 PM on Monday, 3.30 PM and 5.30 PM on Tuesday and Friday, between 8 AM and 10 AM on Wednesday and between 10.30 AM to 12.30 PM on Thursday.

103. On which of the following days, maximum number of windows is simultaneously on at 9.45 AM?

    (a) Monday   (b) Wednesday

    (c) Thursday   (d) Friday

104. On which of the following days, not more than one window is on simultaneously at any given time during office hours?

    (a) Monday   (b) Wednesday

    (c) Friday   (d) Saturday

105. All windows of the transport permit office are closed for 1 hour during the office hours on which of the following days?

    (a) Wednesday   (b) Monday

    (c) Tuesday   (d) Thursday

Directions for questions 106 and 107: Read the following passage and solve the questions based on it.

Federation of Indian Chamber of Commerce and Industries organized a business conclave on India's emerging electronic goods sector. CFOs and Managing Directors of four leading companies, namely, *Klentech Industries, Andromeda Infotech, Zoomerng, Technologies, and Spearhead Unlimited* were invited to deliver lectures on this occasion. The CEOs of the four companies were Mr. Sethi, Mr. D'Souza, Mr. Puri and Mr. Bisht respectively, while the Managing Directors were Mr. Tandon, Mr. Arora, Mr. Karare and Mr. Reddy in that order. The speeches were delivered subject to the condition that each of the Managing Directors delivered their speeches immediately alter that of the CEOs of their company.

106. The first CEO to speak was Mr. D'Souza and the next CEO to deliver his address was Mr. Puri. If Mr. Tandon is the third Managing Director to deliver his address, which of the fallowing statements must be true?

    (a) Mr. Bisht delivered his address sometime before Mr. Sethi.

    (b) Mr. Reddy delivered his address sometime before Mr. Tandon.

    (c) Mr. Puri delivered his address sometime before Mr. Reddy.

    (d) Mr. Karare delivered his address sometime before Mr. Arora.

107. If Mr. Bisht was the second CEO to speak after Mr. D'Souza, and two more Managing Directors speak after the address of the Managing Director of *Spearhead Unlimited*, then who is the last CEO to speak?

    (a) Mr. Sethi

    (b) Mr. Puri

    (c) Mr. Tandon

    (d) Cannot be determined.

2016-18

Directions (Q. 108-112) : *Solve the questions based on the information provided in the passage below :*

Six engineers Anthony, Brad, Carla, Dinesh, Evan and Frank are offered jobs at six different locations - England, Germany, India, Australia, Singapore and UAE. The jobs offered are in six different branches, and are based on their competence as well as preference. The branches are IT, Mechanical, Chemical, Electronics, Metallurgy and Electrical, though not necessarily in the same order. Their placements are subject to the following conditions:

    i. The engineer in the Electrical Department is not placed in Germany.

    ii. Anthony is placed in Singapore while Dinesh in UAE.

    iii. Frank is not in the Metallurgy Department but Brad is in the Chemical Department.

    iv. Evan is placed in the Mechanical Department while Frank is offered a job in Australia.

    v. The only department offering jobs in India is the Chemical Department while there are no vacancies for IT in Singapore.

    vi. Anthony is interested in IT and Electrical Department while Frank is interested in IT and Mechanical Department. Both of them settle for the options available based on their interests in the locations allotted to them.

    vii. In recent years, UAE has emerged as a hub for metallurgy exports and thus recruitment is done for the same while all mechanical posts are in England.

108. Who joined the Electronics Department?

    (a) Dinesh   (b) Anthony

    (c) Carla   (d) Brad

109. The person placed in UAE is in the _________ Department

(a) Electronics   (b) Mechanical

(c) Metallurgy   (d) Chemical

110. Out of the following, which is the correct combination?

(a) Anthony-Germany-Electrical

(b) Brad-India-Chemical

(c) Evan-England-Electronics

(d) Frank-Australia-Metallurgy

111. Who joined the IT Department in Australia?

(a) Frank   (b) Carla

(c) Evan   (d) Brad

112. Which combination is true for Dinesh?

(a) India-Electrical

(b) UAE-Electronics

(c) England-Metallurgy

(d) UAE-Metallurgy

Directions (Q. 113-116) : *Read the details below and answer the questions that follow.*

Due to astrological reasons, a mother named all her daughters with the alphabet 'K' as Kamla, Kamlesh, Kriti, Kripa, Kranti and Kalpana.

  i. Kamla is not the tallest while Kripa is not the most qualified.

  ii. The shortest is the most qualified amongst them all.

  iii. Kalpana is more qualified than Kamlesh who is more qualified than Kriti.

  iv. Kamla is less qualified than Kamlesh but is taller than Kamlesh.

  v. Kalpana is shorter than Kriti but taller than Kranti.

  vi. Kriti is more qualified than Kamla while Kamlesh is taller than Kriti.

  vii. Kripa is the least qualified amongst the daughters.

113. Who is the third tallest starting in decreasing order of height?

(a) Kamla   (b) Kamlesh

(c) Kriti   (d) Kranti

114. Who is the most qualified?

(a) Kamlesh   (b) Kriti

(c) Kripa   (d) Kranti

115. What is the rank of Kriti in increasing order of qualification?

(a) 2   (b) 3

(c) 5   (d) 4

116. What is the rank of Kamla in increasing order of height?

(a) 3   (b) 5

(c) 4   (d) 2

Directions (Q. 117-119) : *Based on the conditions stated in the passage below, answer the questions that follow.*

There are three countries, USA, UAE and UK. An exporter can select one country or two countries or all the three countries subject to the conditions below:

Condition 1 : Both USA and UAE have to be selected.

Condition 2 : Either USA or UK, but not both have to be selected.

Condition 3 : UAE can be selected only if UK has been selected.

Condition 4 : USA can be selected only if UK is selected.

117. How many countries can be selected if no condition is imposed?

(a) 6   (b) 4

(c) 7   (d) 8

118. How many countries can be selected to meet only condition 1?

(a) 0   (b) 2

(c) 1   (d) 3

119. How many countries can be selected to meet only conditions 2 and 3?

(a) 0   (b) 2 or 1

(c) O or 1   (d) None of these

Directions (Q. 120-122) : *Read the passage below and answer the questions that follow.*

Export cargo of a trader can go through seven cities P, Q, R, S, T, U and V. The following cities have a two way connection i.e., Cargo can move in both directions between them; S and U, P and Q, Q and R, V and T, R and T, V and U. Cargo can move only in one direction from U to Q.

120. If the trader wants the cargo to move from City S to City T then excluding cities S and T, what is the minimum number of cities that the cargo has to cross in transit?

(a) 4   (b) 3

(c) 2   (d) 5

121. If the trader wants the cargo to go to City U from City P through the longest route, how many cities will he be-required to cross (excluding cities P and U)?

(a) 2

(b) 4

(c) 3

(d) 5

122. To move cargo from City P to City U, which of the following statements will minimise the number of cities to be crossed in transit?

(a) Connect cities U to R with a two way connection

(b) Connect cities P to S with a one way connection from cities S to P

(c) Connect cities U to Q with a two way connection

(d) Connect cities R to V with a two way connection

2017-19

Direction (Q.123-125): *Read the information provided and answer the questions which follows.*

In one of the islands of Neverland, people from two tribes exist namely A and B. On the island there is no other tribe except these two. The activities of these tribes are governed by rigid norms and are strictly obeyed for marriages. The norms are:

- The people of one tribe cannot marry any other member of their own tribe though they can marry people from other tribe.

- After being married, each male member ceases to be a member of that tribe in which he was born and becomes the member of the tribe to which his wife belongs.

- The females continue to remain members of the tribe in which they were born even after marriage.

- On birth, the child becomes the member of the mother's tribe.

- The males become members of the tribe in which they were born when they become divorcee or widower.

- As per norms, nobody can have more than one spouse at a given point of time.

123. A female in tribe B can have

A. Maternal Grandmother born in tribe A

B. Paternal Grandmother born in tribe A

(a) Only A can be true

(b) Only B can be true

(c) Both A and B are true

(d) Neither A nor B can be true

124. A boy born in tribe B

(a) Can have daughter in tribe B

(b) Can have his daughter in law in tribe A

(c) Can have uncle from any tribe

(d) Can have a divorced son in tribe B

125. Which of the following marriages are not permissible as per norms

(a) Any widower marries his wife's sister

(b) Any widow marries the former divorced husband of her daughter

(c) Any girl of tribe B marries her mother's brother

(d) Any widower born in tribe A marries his brother's widow

Direction (Q. 126-129): *On the basis of the information provided, answer the questions below.*

Six friends Ana, Belle, Cinderella, Diana, Elsa and Ferida are sitting on the ground in a hexagonal shape discussing their trades i.e. cook, hairdresser, washerwoman, tailor, carpenter and plumber. All the sides of the hexagon are of the same length. The seating arrangement is subject to following conditions.

- An is not adjacent to the hairdresser or Cinderella

- The tailor is not adjacent to Cinderella or Elsa but adjacent to Ana

- Hairdresser and Cinderella are adjacent to each other.

- Plumber is in the middle of tailor and Cinderella in a clockwise direction.

- Cook is adjacent to the carpenter who is adjacent to belle in an anti-clockwise direction.

- Ferida is a plumber and Elsa is adjacent the cook.

- In a clockwise direction, the washerwoman is followed by the hairdresser

126. Who is at the same distance from Diana as carpenter is from Diana?

(a) Belle   (b) Cinderella

(c) Tailor   (d) Plumber

127. If one neighbor of cook is Elisa, who is the other?

(a) Cinderella   (b) Diana

(c) Belle   (d) Ferida

128. What are the trades of Diana and Elisa?

    (a) Tailor and Carpenter

    (b) Cook and Carpenter

    (c) Tailor and Washerwoman

    (d) Tailor and Plumber

129. Who is sitting opposite to the plumber?

    (a) Ana   (b) Elsa

    (c) Diana   (d) Cinderella

Direction (Q.130-132): *On the basis of the information provided, answer the questions below.*

A, B, C, E, F, G and H are 7 employees in an organisation working in different departments of Administration, Finance and Logistics. There are at least two employees gets a different salary. F works in Administration and his only other colleague G earns the maximum. C, the least earner works in Finance. B and E are brothers and are not in the same department. A, husband of H, works in Finance and earns more than F, B and E. The wife in the couple earns more than the husband.

130. In which of the departments, does a group of 3 work?

    (a) Logistics

    (b) Logistics or Administration

    (c) Administration or Finance

    (d) Finance or Logistics

131. Which of the following statement is true?

    (a) B earns less than A and H

    (b) B earns less than F and H

    (c) F earns more than B and E

    (d) B earns more than E and C

132. In the descending order of income, H is at which position?

    (a) 2   (b) 3

    (c) 5   (d) 1

Directions(Q 133–135): *On the basis of the information provided, answer questions below.*

Eight doctors P, Q, R, S, T, U, V, and W of the same family i.e. father, mother, father's sister, mother's brother, 2 daughters and 2 sons visit a clinic every day for one hour each except on Monday which is a holiday. The tunings are 9 am to 1 pm and 2 pm to 6 pm, with lunch tune from 1 pm to 2 pm. Each has a different specialisation namely Cardiologist, Orthodontist, Neurologist, Paediatrician, Gynaecologist, Urologist, Radiologist and General Physician.

  • No doctor visits the clinic before doctor Q and after doctor U.

  • The Orthodontist visits right after lunch and is followed by R who is a female.

  • The mother comes in at the same place before lunch as the younger son P after lunch.

  • The General Physician is the sister of Urologist's father and is last to visit before lunch.

  • The Cardiologist is the first while the elder daughter is the last to visit.

  • T is the mother's brother of U and visits between the father and mother.

  • Before 1 pm, V comes after the Radiologist, who is second to visit during the day

  • S, the mother comes at 11 am after the father.

  • The Neurologist is at the same place after lunch as the Gynaecologist before lunch and comes right after Urologist.

133. The General Physician is a________and comes at___

    (a) Female, 11am   (b) Female, 12 noon

    (c) Male, 11am   (d) Male, 12 noon

134. R is a________by specialisation and is Cardiologist's

    (a) Orthodontist, Sister (b) Pediatrician, Daughter .

    (c) Urologist, Mother   (d) Urologist, Daughter

135. If lunch break and subsequent working hours are reduced by 15 minutes on Wednesday, then Doctor U who is_____ and Cardiologist's_____will reach the clinic at -

    (a) Radiologist, Sister, 3 : 15 pm

    (b) Urologist, Daughter, 4 : 15 pm

    (c) Paediatrician, Daughter, 5 : 45 pm

    (d) Paediatrician, Daughter, 4 : 15 pm

2018-20

Directions for Questions 136-140: *Read the information provided and answer the questions which follow.*

Five MBA students - Aman, Manish, Rohit, Sandeep and Vinay, specializing in sales and marketing got final campus placement in five different companies - Asian Paints, Dabur, Hindustan Unilever, ITC and L'Oreal. (though not necessarily in the same order). Their initial job assignment has been fixed in five different cities - Bhopal, Chennai, Delhi, Mumbai and Patna (in any order). They are avid book readers, but like different themes - business and management, classic fiction, historical fiction, mystery fiction and non-fiction (again in any order). Further the following additional information are provided:

    (a) Vinay got placed in Asian Paints.

    (b) Aman is not placed in Hindustan Unilever.

    (c) Manish's job location is not in Chennai and he does not like books on mystery fiction.

    (d) Sandeep got placed at Delhi, while Vinay is not placed at Mumbai.

(e) Aman likes reading books on historical fiction and is placed either at Chennai or Patna and the student who got placed in ITC does not like mystery fiction and his job posting is in the other city amongst Chennai or Patna.

(f) The student who got placed in L'Oreal likes reading non-fiction books and is not posted at Mumbai.

(g) The student who likes reading classic fiction, is posted at Bhopal.

136. In which company has Aman got placed?

   (a) Dabur   (b) Hindustan Unilever

   (c) ITC   (d) L'Oreal

137. Name the person who likes reading books on business and management.

   (a) Manish   (b) Rohit

   (c) Sandeep   (d) Vinay

138. Name the type of books the student who is placed in Mumbai likes reading.

   (a) Business and management

   (b) Historical fiction

   (c) Mystery fiction

   (d) Non-fiction

139. If Sandeep is transferred to Rohit's city and Rohit is transferred to Sandeep's city, then in which city the student who likes reading mystery fictions will work?

   (a) Chennai   (b) Delhi

   (c) Mumbai   (d) Patna

140. Who among the following is posted in Patna?

   (a) Manish   (b) Rohit

   (c) Aman   (d) Cannot be determined

Directions for Questions 141-142: *Read the information provided and answer the questions which follow.*

In ISL football competition, eight football teams - Atletico De Kolkata, Chennaiyan FC, Delhi Dynamos, FC Goa, FC Pune City, Kerala Blasters, Mumbai City FC and North-East United FC - participated where each team played against every other team exactly once. Every win earned three points for the teams and a loss earned 0. If there was a draw, each team was rewarded one point. Now, as per the fixtures, following are some of the observations:

(a) Out of the seven matches played by Chennaiyan FC, it won five and the other two matches were drawn.

(b) FC Pune City won the match against FC Goa and Kerala Blasters but lost the match against Delhi Dynamos and Chennaiyan FC.

(c) Atletico De Kolkata drew a match against FC Goa, Chennaiyan FC and FC Pune City.

(d) None of the teams lost all the matches.

141. If Chennaiyan FC won the match against FC Goa, what could have been the maximum score of FC Goa?

   (a) 11   (b) 12

   (c) 13   (d) 14

142. What could be the minimum absolute difference between the scores of FC Pune-City and Chennaiyan FC?

   (a) 0   (b) b

   (c) 3   (d) 4

Directions for Questions 143-144: *Read the information provided below and answer the questions which follow.*

Seven friends - A, B, C, D, E, F and G - are traveling from Delhi to Amritsar in Swarna Shatabdi train. They are seated in three different coaches - A1, A2 and A3. Further the following additional information are provided:

(a) There are two married couples among them.

(b) Three friends love playing tennis, two love playing cricket and two love playing volleyball amongst them.

(c) There are at least two of them in each coach and each of them loves playing different games.

(d) No husband-wife couple loves playing the same game.

(e) C is seated in coach A1 and is married to A, who loves playing tennis.

(f) G loves playing volleyball and is married to D who is seated in coach A2 with F, a cricket enthusiast.

(g) B and G are not seated with C.

(h) E, who loves playing tennis, is seated in Coach A3.

143. Which game does C like to play?

   (a) cricket or tennis   (b) volleyball

   (c) tennis or volleyball   (d) cricket or volleyball

144. How many friends are seated in coach A1?

   (a) 2   (b) 3

   (c) 2 or 3   (d) Data inadequate

Directions for Questions 145-146: Read the information provided below and answer the questions which follow.

Last week, Rajeev watched four sports of different types: tennis, cricket, football and kabaddi. The sports were shown by four different channels - Star Sports 1, Ten Sports 2, Sony Six and Neo Sports (not necessarily in the same order). These sports were telecasted on different days - Monday, Tuesday, Thursday and Friday (not necessarily in the same order). Further the following additional information are provided:

(a) The sports by Star Sports 1 was shown on Friday.

(b) Tennis was shown on Monday.

(c) Kabaddi was shown by Sony Six and not telecasted on Thursday. .

(d) Football was shown by Neo Sports

145. Which of the following combination is true?

    (*a*) Star Sports 1 - Tennis

    (*b*) Neo Sports - Thursday

    (*c*) Kabaddi - Thursday

    (*d*) Data inadequate

146. Which sports was telecasted in Ten Sports 2 and on which day of the week?

    (*a*) Football on Friday   (*b*) Kabaddi on Thursday

    (*c*) Cricket on Monday   (*d*) Tennis on Monday

2019-21

Directions (147-150): Based on the information below, answer the questions which follow.

Six friends Albert, Betty, Claire, Daisy, Evan and Fred who are working in different organisations, are looking for a switch in their jobs. They came across an advertisement in the newspaper regarding a job fair being organised in New Delhi. After enrolling for the fair, different days are allotted to each one of them from Monday to Saturday not necessarily in the same order, starting from Monday. They also had to arrange for their stay in different hotels to concentrate well while preparing for the upcoming interviews namely Taj, Hilton, Crowne Plaza, Radisson, Hyatt and Marriott. Additional information provided is as follows:

    i. Albert prefers to stay in Taj but not in Hilton. Albert does not work in Whirlpool and participates in the Job fair on Monday. The person who works in Whirlpool participates in the Job fair on Saturday.

    ii. Fred does not stay in Hyatt but works in Himalaya.

    iii. Betty and Daisy participate in the Job fair on consecutive days.

    iv. Claire participates in the Job fair on the day before the person staying in Crowne Plaza but on the next day of Pepsi employee.

    v. The person working with Oppo participates in the Job fair on Friday and does not stay in Hilton.

    vi. Claire who is working with Nestle participates in the Job fair at a gap of one day prior to Evan.

    vii. Daisy stays in Marriott and attends the conference on the last day of the week.

    viii. The person working with Apple stays in Radisson.

147. Which of the following friend is working with Apple?

    (a) Albert   B. Daisy

    (c) Evan   D. Fred

148. Who participated in the job fair on Wednesday?

    (a) Claire   B. Daisy

    (c) Fred   D. Albert

149. If the current salary packages of the friends working in Whirlpool, Nestle, Himalaya, Pepsi, Oppo and Apple are 20, 30, 40, 50, 60 and 70 lakhs per annum in the same order, then at the time of participating in job fair find the average annual package of Albert, Betty and Fred?

    (a) 30 lakhs per annum

    (b) 90 lakhs per annum

    (c) 20 lakhs per annum

    (d) 50 lakhs per annum

150. Which of the following friend is staying in Hilton?

    (a) Daisy   B. Claire

    (c) Albert   D. Betty

Directions (151-153): Based on the information below, answer the questions which follow.

Richie invites three of his friends Sunny, Pinky and Nancy for his birthday party organised at his home. As the party goes on till late in the night, Sunny, Pinky and Nancy choose to stay at Richie's house. Being good friends they usually stay back at each other's house. Each one of them including Richie stay either in the room painted blue or in the room painted purple. They have adequate number of rooms of both colours. The preferences which need to be fulfilled are:

    i. If Sunny stays in the room painted purple, then Pinky and Richie stay in the same room as Nancy.

    ii. If Pinky stays in the room painted purple, then Sunny stays in the room in which Nancy and Richie don't stay.

    iii. If Nancy stays in the room painted blue, then Sunny and Richie stay in the room which Pinky has chosen.

    iv. If Richie stays in the room painted Blue then Sunny and Pinky do not stay in the same room as Nancy.

151. Under all possible combinations which of the two friends will always have their room colours unchanged.

    (a) Richie & Sunny   (b) Pinky & Richie

    (c) Nancy & Sunny   (d) Nancy & Pinky

152. If Richie chose to stay in the room painted blue, then in which room does Pinky stay?

    (a) Purple   (b) Blue

    (c) Data Inadequate   (d) None of the above

153. If Pinky does not like to stay in the blue painted room, then where will Sunny stay?

    (a) Blue

    (b) Purple

    (c) Data Inadequate

    (d) None of the above

Directions (154-157): Based on the information answer the questions which follow.

An agent has to send a secret message to CBI office in Delhi. He needs to compile his message using following 12 code words- Scare, Logical, Mouse, Beauty, Helping, Roses, Cats, Doctor, Arguments, Crude, Ferry and Mineral. The agent compiles the coded message and delivers it to CBI office in form of a 4 × 3 matrix. Each coded word has been allocated a position in the matrix (1 × 2 position represents row 1 and column 2). The clues to compile the secret message are:

i. The words in 2 × 1 and 3 × 1 have the same number of letters.

ii. Roses is to the immediate left of Beauty and Mineral is immediately above Roses.

iii. The word in 4 × 3 is shorter than the word in 1 × 2.

iv. Ferry is separated from Helping horizontally by only one word Logical.

v. Arguments is at position 2 × 3 in the matrix and the word immediately below it has odd number of letters.

vi. Crude and Doctor are in the same horizontal row and Crude is to the right of Doctor.

vii. Cats is not in the same row or column as Mouse.

154. The product of the position of a coded word is 8. Identify the word.

    (a) Crude   (b) Helping

    (c) Beauty   (d) Scare

155. The sum of letters of which row is 19?

    (a) 1   (b) 2

    (c) 3   (d) 4

156. Which word is represented in 4 × 3?

    (a) Scare   (b) Crude

    (c) Cats   (d) Data Inadequate

157. Which of the following are placed diagonally in the matrix?

    (a) Ferry-Mineral   (b) Mineral-Mouse

    (c) Beauty-Scare   (d) Arguments-Roses

Directions (158-161): Based on the information answer the questions which follow.

Eight officers of Indian Trade Service meet for a cup of coffee at Coffee Point. The officers P, Q, R, S, T, U, V and W are seated in a circle and discuss issues related to Trade in Services, Trade in Intellectual Property Rights, Investments, Tariffs, Remedies, Standards Trade Facilitation and Subsides not necessarily in the same order. An MBA student sitting on the next table overhears the discussion and ranks the issues as per their importance from 1 to 8. No two issues can have the same rank and no two officers can have the same position. Additional information available is:

i. P is sitting to the immediate left of S and the officer opposite to S discusses issues pertaining to Remedies.

ii. U's issue is ranked 7th and there is one officer between U and the officer whose issue is ranked 2nd.

iii. The officer whose issue is ranked 1 is not opposite to the officer whose issue is ranked 8 who represents issues related to Investments.

iv. The ranks of the issues raised by the officers sitting opposite to each other cannot be both even or both odd.

v. The officer discussing issues related to Trade in Services is sitting opposite to T. T is sitting at a gap of one place from P.

vi. R is sitting opposite to Q and represent issues related to Standards and Trade in Intellectual Property Rights not necessarily in the same order.

vii. P's issue was ranked 4th and he was discussing issues related to Tariffs and sits opposite to the officer ranked 5th who represents issues related to Subsidies.

viii. The officers representing issues related to Trade in Services and Trade Facilitation are sitting adjacent to each other.

158. Which officer discusses Remedies and what is its rank?

    (a) P-4   (b) S-1

    (c) U-7   (d) V-5

159. If the officer V is to the immediate right of the officer representing Trade Facilitation, then the officer 4th to the right of V discusses which issue?

    (a) Tariffs

    (b) Remedies

    (c) Subsidies

    (d) Investments

160. Which possible issues can be represented by W?

    (a) Standards-Trade in Intellectual Property Rights

    (b) Subsidies-Standards

    (c) Trade in Services-Subsidies

    (d) Trade in Services-Trade in Intellectual Property Rights-Subsidies

161. The officer to the 4th right to the officer discussing the issues related to Remedies, is discussing which issue?

    (a) Trade in Intellectual Property Rights

    (b) Trade Facilitation

    (c) Investments

    (d) Subsidies

Directions (162-163): Based on the information answer the questions which follow.

A consultant to Department of Commerce, Government of Bianca has suggested 30 products which have high export potential. Dora an entrepreneur and prospective exporter notices that these products can be grouped in three ways- Machine made goods, Handmade goods and Intermediate goods. Among these 30 products some products are both machine made and intermediate goods but not handmade goods. Few products have a combination of handmade and machine made goods but not intermediate goods. Some products are handmade and intermediate goods but not machine made goods. Further it is seen that handmade-machine made goods are 1 less than machine made-intermediate goods. Similarly the total number of handmade-intermediate goods is 1 less than machine made-intermediate goods. There are just 4 products common across all product groups i.e. machine made-handmade-intermediate goods. Apart from this the number of only handmade goods is same as only machine made goods but less than only intermediate goods. Each product group/combination has at least one product.

Dora prefers to export machine made goods and avoid hand made goods. She finds out that- only handmade goods are twice the machine made-intermediate goods and the number of only intermediate goods is an even number. Whereas her close friend Sara prefers to export intermediate goods followed by only handmade goods.

162. Sara and Dora prefer to export as many common products as possible in order to understand the regulatory conditions. Keeping their preferences intact, what is the maximum number of common products which can be exported by both of them?

(a) 2
(b) 4
(c) 14
(d) Data Inadequate

163. If another exporter Abeer prefers to export only intermediate goods, then the total number of products which both Abeer and Dora export are

(a) 24
(b) 20
(c) 22
(d) 21

Directions (164-165): Based on the information answer the questions which follow.

Nautanki a famous play group from Eastern India is playing different shows every hour starting from 10am with a two hour lunch break from 1 pm to 3 pm after which the show resumes at 3 pm. Entry tickets for different shows are coded with 7 words each day. The same words are rearranged for different shows following a definite rule. For example:

Show 1: Banana   is   the favourite   fruit   of   Bina

Show 2: the   is   of   favourite   Bina   fruit   Banana

Show 3: of   is   fruit   favourite   Banana   Bina   the

And so on till the last show at 9 pm.

164. If on some other day, for the fourth show the code is 'All of Delhi welcome to the show' Then the code for entry ticket for the first show on that day is

(a) The of all welcome to show Delhi

(b) The of Delhi welcome all show to

(c) The of to welcome all show Delhi

(d) The of show welcome all to Delhi

165. If the entry code for the show at 7 pm is

'Do things to help others in difficulty'

Then the code for entry ticket for the show at 12 noon of that day was

(a) Do things others help to in difficulty

(b) Do things to help others in difficulty

(c) Do things to help in difficulty others

(d) Do things difficulty help to others in

2. Data Sufficiency

`2018-20`

Directions for Questions 166-167: In each of the following problems, there is one question and three statements I, II and III given below the question. You have to decide whether the data given in the statements is sufficient to answer the question. Read all the statements carefully and find which of the statement(s) is/are sufficient to answer the given question.

166. What is Mohit's rank from the top in an annual appraisal of a FMCG Company comprising of 70 sales executives?

I.   Mohit is 5 ranks below Rashmi from the top

II.   Rashmi's rank from the bottom is 44

III.   Mohit is 5 ranks above Rashmi from the bottom

(a) Any two of the three

(b) Only II and III

(c) Only I and either II or III

(d) Only II and either I or III

167. What does 'orange' represent in a code language?

I.   'rim pa xab' means 'orange and apple' in that code language

II.   'na pie tac' means 'I dislike sweet' in that code language

III.   'na tsi pa' means 'orange is sweet.' in that code language

(a) All I, II and III   *(b)* Only II and III

(c) Only I and III   *(d)* Only I and either II or III

3. Input and Output

2007-09

Directions for Questions 168 to 171: Study the information given below and answer the questions.

A word arrangement machine, when given a particular input, rearranges it using a particular rule. The following is the illustration and the steps of the arrangement.

INPUT :	lemon	apple	choco	college	girl	dream	room	book	calf
STEP 1:	choco	apple	lemon	college	girl	dream	calf	book	room
STEP 2:	lemon	apple	choco	dream	girl	college	room	book	calf
STEP 3:	calf	lemon	apple	book	choco	college	room	girl	dream
STEP 4:	apple	calf	lemon	book	choco	college	dream	room	girl
STEP 5:	lemon	calf	apple	college	choco	book	girl	room	dream
STEP 6:	dream	lemon	calf	room	apple	book	girl	choco	college

168. Which of the following will not be Step 10 for the given input

(a) calf	lemon	dream	room	apple	book	college	choco	girl
(b) apple	calf	lemon	book	choco	college	dream	room	girl
(c) lemon	college	dream	choco	calf	room	book	girl	apple
(d) dream	college	lemon	room	calf	choco	apple	girl	book

169. Indicate all the step numbers for which the following will not be an output

dream lemon calf book apple room girl choco college

(a) Step 7　　　(b) Step 8　　　(c) Step 9　　　(d) Step 12

170. Mark all the arrangements that do not fall between step numbers 11 and 15

(a) choco	book	dream	calf	college	lemon	apple	girl	room
(b) book	dream	college	girl	lemon	calf	apple	room	choco
(c) book	dream	college	room	lemon	girl	apple	calf	choco
(d) college	dream	book	girl	lemon	calf	choco	room	apple

171. Mark two arrangement which will fall as consecutive steps at any time.

(a) calf	lemon	dream	room	apple	book	college	choco	girl
(b) choco	book	dream	calf	college	lemon	apple	girl	room
(c) book	dream	college	girl	lemon	room	apple	calf	choco
(d) college	dream	book	girl	lemon	room	choco	calf	apple

2009-11

Direction for the questions 172 – 175: Answer the questions based on the following information.

A number arrangement machine, when given a particular input, rearranges it following a particular rule. Illustration of the input and the steps of arrangement is given below.

Input: 245, 316, 436, 519, 868, 710, 689

Step 1: 710, 316, 436, 519, 868, 245, 689

Step 2: 710, 316, 245, 519, 868, 436, 689

Step 3: 710, 316, 245, 436, 868, 519, 689

Step 4: 710, 316, 245, 436, 519, 868, 689

Step 4 is the last step for the given input

172. If the input is given as "655, 436, 764, 799, 977, 572, 333", which of the following step will be "333, 436, 572, 655, 977, 764, 799"?

(a) Step Third　　　(b) Step Second

(c) Step Fourth　　　(d) None of the above

173. How many steps will be required to get the final output from the following input?

Input: 544, 653, 325, 688, 461, 231, 857

(a) 6

(b) 5

(c) 4

(d) None of the above

174. Step third for an input is "432, 433, 542, 666, 734, 355, 574". What will be the first step for the input?

(a) 666, 542, 432, 734, 433, 574, 355

(b) 542, 666, 734, 432, 433, 574, 355

(c) 355, 574, 433, 432, 734, 666, 542

(d) Cannot be determined

175. What will be the third step for the following input?

Input: 653, 963, 754, 345, 364, 861, 541

(a) 541, 345, 754, 963, 364, 861, 653

(b) 541, 345, 364, 653, 963, 754, 861

(c) 541, 345, 364, 963, 754, 861, 653

(d) 541, 345, 364, 653, 861, 754, 963

Direction for the questions 176 – 178: Answer the questions based on the following information.

A word arrangement machine, when given a particular input, rearranges it following a particular rule. Following is the illustration of the input the steps of arrangement:

Input: She was interested in doing art film

Step 1: art she was interested in doing film

Step 2: art was she interested in doing film

Step 3: art was in she interested doing film

Step 4: art was in film she interested doing

Step 5: art was in film doing she interested

Step 5 is the last step of the given input. Now study the logic and rules followed in the above steps, find out appropriate step for the question given below for the given input.

176. Which of the following will be last step for the input given below?

Input: He is going out to search air

(a) out is air to going search he

(b) out is air to search going he

(c) search he out is air to going

(d) None of the above

177. If step 2 of an input is not "not is the casino considering legal action", which step is: "not is casino action legal the considering"?

(a) Step: 3   (b) Step: 6

(c) Step: 4   (d) None of the above

178. How many steps will be required to get the final output from the following input?

Input: Father needs to check on the boy

(a) Four   (b) Five

(c) Six   (d) None of the above

`2010-12`

Directions for questions 179 – 181: Study the information given below and answer the questions.
A word arrangement machine, when given a particular input, rearranges it using a particular rule. The following is the illustration and the steps of the arrangement.

INPUT: Smile	Nile	Style	Mile	Shine	Wine	Mine	Swine	Bovine	Feline
STEP 1:Smile	Nile	Style	Mile	Shine	Wine	Bovine	Feline	Mine	Swine
STEP 2:Style	Mile	Smile	Nile	Shine	Wine	Bovine	Feline	Mine	Swine
STEP 3:Style	Mile	Smile	Nile	Wine	Shine	Bovine	Feline	Mine	Swine
STEP 4:Mile	Style	Nile	Smile	Wine	Shine	Feline	Bovine	Swine	Mine
STEP 5:Nile	Smile	Mile	Style	Wine	Shine	Swine	Mine	Feline	Bovine
STEP 6:Nile	Smile	Mile	Style	Wine	Shine	Feline	Bovine	Swine	Mine
STEP 7:Mile	Style	Nile	Smile	Wine	Shine	Feline	Bovine	Swine	Mine

179. Which of the following will be step 14 for the given input:

(a) Style	Mile	Smile	Nile	Wine	Shine	Bovine	Feline	Mine	Swine
(b) Smile	Nile	Style	Mile	Shine	Wine	Mine	Swine	Bovine	Feline
(c) Mile	Style	Nile	Smile	Shine	Wine	Feline	Bovine	Swine	Mine
(d) Style	Mile	Smile	Nile	Shine	Wine	Bovine	Feline	Mine	Swine

180. Mark the arrangement that does not fall between step numbers 12 and 14.

(a) Style	Mile	Smile	Nile	Wine	Shine	Bovine	Feline	Mine	Swine
(b) Mile	Style	Nile	Smile	Wine	Shine	Feline	Bovine	Swine	Mine
(c) Style	Mile	Smile	Nile	Shine	Wine	Bovine	Feline	Mine	Swine
(d) Smile	Nile	Style	Mile	Shine	Wine	Bovine	Feline	Mine	Swine

181. If the arrangement is repeated which of the steps given below is same as the INPUT row?

(a) Step 9

(b) Step 11

(c) Step 20

(d) Step 14

2013-15

Directions for Questions 182 - 183: Some information is provided below. Study the information and answer the questions based on this information.

A word arrangement machine, when given a particular input, rearranges it using a particular rule. The following is the illustration and the steps of the arrangement.

Input   105 241 67 347 150 742 292 589

Step I   67   105 241 347 150 742 292 589

Step II 67   742 105 241 347 150 292 589

Step III 67   742 105 589 241 347 150 292

Step IV 67   742 105 589 150 241 347 292

Step V 67   742 105 589 150 347 241 292

Arrangement at Step V is the last for the given input

182. What should be the fourth step of the following input?

        64   326 187 87   118 432 219 348

(a)   64   432 87   326 118 187 219 348

(b)   64   432 87   348 326 187 118 219

(c)   64   432 87   348 118 326 187 219

(d)   None of the above

183. How many steps will be required to get the final output from the following input?

319 318 746 123 15   320 78   426

(a) Four

(b) Five

(c) Six

(d) Seven

2015-17

Directions for questions 184-188: A word arrangement machine, when given a particular input, rearranges it following a particular rule upto step 4. The following is the illustration of the input and the steps of the arrangement. Study the inherent logic and the answer the following question.

Input	be	the	change	you	wish	to	see	in	this	world
Step 1	the	be	you	change	to	wish	in	see	world	this
Step 2	you	be	the	change	to	world	in	see	wish	this
Step 3	you	see	the	this	to	world	in	be	wish	change
Step 4	see	you	this	the	world	to	be	in	change	wish

184. If the input is, 'don't cry because it's over smile since it actually happened', then Step 4 will be:

(a) it's since actually happened cry smile don't it over because

(b) since cry it's happened actually smile it don't because over

(c) since it's actually cry happened smile don't it because over

(d) since its cry actually happened don't smile it over because

185. If Step 4 generates, 'dog sea school star ice moon flower home rock ball', then the input was:

(a) flower star rock sea ball moon dog home school ice

(b) rock flower sea ball dog star moon school home ice

(c) flower ball star sea rock dog moon ice home school

(d) star moon rock sea home flower ice ball dog school

2018-20

Directions for Questions 186-189: *Read the information provided and answer the questions which follow.*

Given an input, a coding machine generates pass codes everyday as follows:

Input : my bag carries no more than ten books

Pass codes :

Batch I   : more my than bag ten carries books no

Batch II : bag ten than carries my books more no

Batch III : my bag books ten more than no carries

Batch IV: ten more books than bag no my carries and so on.

The first batch timing is 9.30 AM and each batch is of one hour's duration. There is a rest period of one hour after the work for the fourth batch is over.

186. If the pass code on a particular day for the second batch is 'if winter comes can spring be far behind', what will be the pass code for the batch at 2.30 PM on that day?

(*a*) if winter behind far comes can spring be

(*b*) behind winter if spring comes can far be

(*c*) behind winter if spring comes far be can

(*d*) if winter behind far spring be can comes

187. On a particular day, Rahul was to begin the work in the batch at 10.30 AM with a pass code 'I like tea and biscuit but not together'. However, he came late on that day and hence joined the next batch. What was his new pass code?

(*a*) together but like not biscuit I tea and

(*b*) together but like I tea and biscuit not

(*c*) biscuit I but like not tea together and

(*d*) biscuit I but tea together like and not

188. On a particular day, the pass code for the batch immediately before the rest hour was 'bah bah black sheep have you any wool'. What was the input for the pass code on that day?

  (a) any have wool bah sheep you black bah

  (b) any have wool you bah sheep bah black

  (c) any have wool you bah black bah sheep

  (d) None of the above

189. On a particular day, the pass code for the second batch was 'India's core strength lies in unity in diversity'. What was the input on that day in the reverse order of its words?

  (a) in in India's lies diversity strength core unity

  (b) unity core strength in diversity lies India's in

  (c) in in strength India's core diversity unity lies

  (d) None of the above

4. Coding and Decoding

2012-14

Directions for questions 190 – 191: Study the information given below carefully to answer the following questions.

In a certain code language, the following lines written as

'lop eop aop fop' means 'Traders are above laws'

'fop cop bop gop' means 'Developers were above profitable'

'aop bop uop qop' means 'Developers stopped following traders'

'cop jop eop uop' means 'Following maps were laws'

190. 'Developers are following laws' would be correctly written as

  (a) 'bop cop uop eop' (b) 'lop bop eop uop'

  (c) 'oup cop lop aop' (d) None of the above

191. 'qop gop cop eop' would correctly mean:

  (a) Profitable laws were stopped

  (b) Developers stopped following laws

  (c) Traders were above profitable

  (d) None of the above

192. If the word 'EXAMINATION' is coded as 56149512965, then the word 'GOVERNMENT' is coded as:

  (a) 7645954552 (b) 7654694562

  (c) 7645965426 (d) 7654964526

193. In a certain code language 'HORSE' is written as 71417184, then the word 'MONKEY'is coded as:

  (a) 11141216425

  (b) 12141310424

  (c) 12151411325

  (d) 12151210424

2014-16

Directions for questions 194 to 195:

LETTER	E	R	C	F	L	N	H	K	P	T	A	S	G
CODE	%	3	2	5	@	7	#	6	1	8	4	%	9

  i. If the first letter is a vowel and the last letter is a consonant, both are to be coded as ©

  ii. If the first letter is a consonant and the last letter is a vowel, both are to be coded as 0

  iii. If the first letter as well as the last letter are vowels, both are to be coded as the code of the last letter.

194. N F R S C A

  (a) 753%20 (b) 053%24

  (c) 0232%0 (d) 053%20

195. A R F T H E

  (a) %358#% (b) 4358#%

  (c) 4358#4 (d) %385#%

196. Given below are some words from an artificial language.

  agnoscrenia means poisonous spider

  delanocrenia means poisonous snake

  agnosdeery means brown spider

  Which of the following is most likely to mean "black widow spider"?

  (a) aeeryclostangus (b) agnosvitriblunin

  (c) agnosdelano (d) trymuttiangus

5. General Mental Ability

2012-14

Direction for questions 197–198: In each of the following letter series, some of the letters are missing, which are given below it. Choose the *correct* alternative.

197. D _ F _ DEE _ D _ EF _ DE _ F

  (a) EFFDED (b) EFFDDF

  (c) EFFDFE (d) None of the above

198. _ OPO _ QOPQ _ RQPO _ POR _ O

  (a) APRQO (b) QPORO

  (c) QPROO (d) None of the above

Directions for questions 199 – 200: In each of the following questions, find the relationship that can definitely be deduced on the basis of the relations given. The symbols used to define the relationship are as follows:

  @ means 'greater than'

  # means 'less than'

  $ means 'not equal to'

  % means 'equal to'

199. If it is given that, 3 M % 2 N and N % 3 O, then:

    (a) O @ M   (b) M # O

    (c) 2 O % M   (d) None of the above

200. If it is given that, N @ P, P # O, O @ M and N % M, then:

    (a) O @ N   (b) O # N

    (c) O $ N   (d) None of the above

2013-15

201. In the word HEIRARCHICAL, if the first and second, third and fourth, fourth and fifth, fifth and sixth words are interchanged up to the last letter, which are the two positions from the left on which R would appear and on which position would C appear twice?

    (a) R-3 and 5; C-8 and 9

    (b) R-9 and 10; C-4 and 5

    (c) R-4 and 5; C-7 and 8

    (d) 4 and 5; C-7 and 8

202. In the following series what numbers should replace the question marks?

    –1, 0, 1, 0, 2, 4, 1, 6, 9, 2, 12, 16, ? ? ?

    (a) 11, 18, 27   (b) –1, 0, 3

    (c) 3, 20, 25   (d) Cannot be ascertained

203. Here are some words translated from an artificial language.

    dionot means oak tree

    blyonot means oak leaf

    blycrin mean maple leaf

    Which word could mean "maple syrup"

    (a) blymuth   (b) hupponot

    (c) patricrin   (d) crinweel

204. Gita is older than her cousin Mita. Mita's brother Bhanu is older than Gita. When Mita and Bhanu are visiting Gita, all three like to play a game of Monopoly. Mita wins more often than Gita does.

    Which of the following can be concluded from the above?

    (a) When he plays Monopoly with Mita and Gita, Bhanu often loses.

    (b) Of the three, Gita is the oldest.

    (c) Gita hates to lose at Monopoly.

    (d) Of the three, Mita is the youngest.

205. Priya is taller than Tiya and shorter than Siya.

    Riya is shorter than Siya and taller than Priya.

    Riya is taller than Diya, who is shorter than Tiya. Arrange them in order of ascending heights.

    (a) Priya- Siya- Riya-Tiya- Diya

    (b) Riya- Siya- Priya- Diya- Tiya

    (c) Siya- Riya- Priya- Tiya- Diya

    (d) Siya- Priya- Riya- Diya- Tiya

206. If IQS: LNV, then JRM: ?

    (a) OKS   (b) MOP

    (c) NIP   (d) MOQ

207. P ≠ Q implies that Q is standing 2 kms to the right of P

    P*Q implies that Q is 2 kms to the left of P

    P@Q implies that Q is 2 kms below P

    P$Q implies that Q is standing 2 kms above P

    If F ≠ S $ B *V, in which direction is F with respect to V?

    (a) North   (b) South

    (c) East   (d) West

208. Immediately after leaving his house, Ritvik turned right and walked for 40 m. Then he turned left and walked for 20 m. Then he again took a left turn and walked for 30 m. There he met a friend and turned right to go to the coffee shop 20 m away. After having coffee, he walked back straight for 40 m in the direction he had come from. How far is he from his house?

    (a) 20 m   (b) 0 m

    (c) 10 m   (d) 40 m

209. Find the missing alphabet

H	C	?
B	F	E
P	R	T

    (a) Y   (b) O

    (c) D   (d) G

210. In a four-day period—Monday through Thursday—each of the following temporary office workers worked only one day, each a different day. Jai was scheduled to work on Monday, but he traded with Raj, who was originally scheduled to work on Wednesday. Farid traded with Kajal, who was originally scheduled to work on Thursday. Finally, Jai traded with Kajal. After all the switching was done, who worked on Tuesday?

    (a) Jai   (b) Farid

    (c) Raj   (d) Kajal

211. Which four bits can be joined together to form two words that have opposite meanings?

ERT,	UCE,	DES,	END,	EXP,	EAR,	AND,
SIP,	RED,	GOS				
1	2	3	4	5	6	7
8	9	10				

    (a) 2, 5, 7, 9   (b) 1, 3, 8, 10

    (c) 1, 5, 8, 10   (d) 2, 4, 7, 8

212. If a clock is kept on the table in such a way that at 3:10 pm the hour hand points south, after how much time will the minute hand point east?

    (a) 20 minutes   (b) 35 minutes

    (c) 50 minutes   (d) 90 minutes

2014-16

213. Read the following information to answer the question that follows.

P–Q means Q is father of P

P*Q means Q is brother of P

P ÷ Q means Q is wife of P

P + Q means Q is sister of P

Which of the following means M is the grandfather of T?

(a) T– C ÷ L+N*M   (b) T–R ÷ Z+L*M

(c) T÷Z*L+F–M   (d) None of these

214. There are five houses P, Q, R, S and T. P is right of Q and T is left of R and right of P. Q is right of S. Which house is in the middle?

(a) P   (b) Q

(c) T   (d) R

215. Find the statement which is necessarily true according to the given information:

The Asatra Vriksh is an evergreen tree that grows in the Nilgiris. The Asatra Vriksh has a fleshy, poisonous fruit. Recently, Purol, a substance found in the bark of the Asatra Vriksh, was discovered to be a promising new antidepressant drug.

(a) Purol is poisonous when taken by healthy people.

(b) Purol has cured people from various diseases.

(c) People should not eat the fruit of the Asatra Vriksh.

(d) No treatment for depression was known till Purol was discovered.

216. A research study recorded that the number of unemployed educated youth was equal to the number of unemployed Uneducated youth. It was concluded by the researchers that being educated does not enhance the probability of being employed. Which of the following information would be required to validate the above conclusion?

(a) The number of unemployed educated and uneducated people in other age groups

(b) The number of organisations employing youth

(c) The percentage of unemployment in educated youth versus percentage of unemployment in uneducated youth.

(d) The percentage increase in number of educated youth versus last year

217. The time in a clock is 20 minutes past 2. Find the angle between the hands of the clock.

(a) 45 degrees   (b) 50 degrees

(c) 60 degrees   (d) 120 degrees

Directions for questions 218 to 220: Select the correct option to fill in the blank space/s

218. c_bba_cab_ac_ab_ac

(a) b,c,b,a,c   (b) c,a,b,c,b

(c) a,c,c,b,c   (d) a,c,b,c,b

219. B_2CD, ____ , BCD_4, ____ , BC_6D

(a) BC_3D; B_5CD (b) BC_2D; BC_3D

(c) BC_3D; B_3CD (d) BC_3D; BC_5D

220. P3, M8, ____ , G24, D35

(a) K15   (b) J13

(c) 113   (d) J15

2015-17

221. Complete the series:

EPFS, GPHS, IPJS, __________ , MPNS

(a) OPLS   (b) KPMS

(c) LMPS   (d) KPLS

2016-18

222. Based on the number series given, fill in the missing number.

18, 37, 76, 155, ____ , 633, 1272

(a) 322   (b) 314

(c) 341   (d) 250

223. Based on the following relations, which of the given options indicate that W is the niece of X?

A + B means that A is the brother of B.

A * B means that A is the father of B.

A – B means that A is the sister of B.

(a) X + Y + Z – W   (b) Z – W * Y + X

(c) X + Y * W – Z   (d) X * Y + W – Z

224. Alex walks 1 mile towards East and then he turns towards South and walks further 5 miles. After that he turns East and walks 2 miles further. Finally he turns to his North and walks 9 miles. How far is he from the starting point?

(a) 25 miles   (b) 2 miles

(c) 5 miles   (d) 4 miles

2017-19

225. Insert the missing number

15		2		9		7		13		16
	80				65				?	
5		6		4		6		11		8

(a) 35   (b) 48

(c) 72   (d) 120

226. In the following question, one term in the number series is wrong. Find out the wrong term.

10, 26, 74, 218, 654, 1946, 5834

(a) 654   (b) 26

(c) 1946   (d) 218

227. In the question below, three incomplete rows of letters/numericals are given which correspond to each other in some way. Find the letters/numerals which come in the vacant places marked by "?"

(a) a, c, d, d

(b) d, a, c, c

(c) c, a, d, d

(d) d, c, a, a

Direction (228-231) : *Based on the figure given below, the relationship of the terms of the right of :: is same as that on the left. Find the missing terms.*

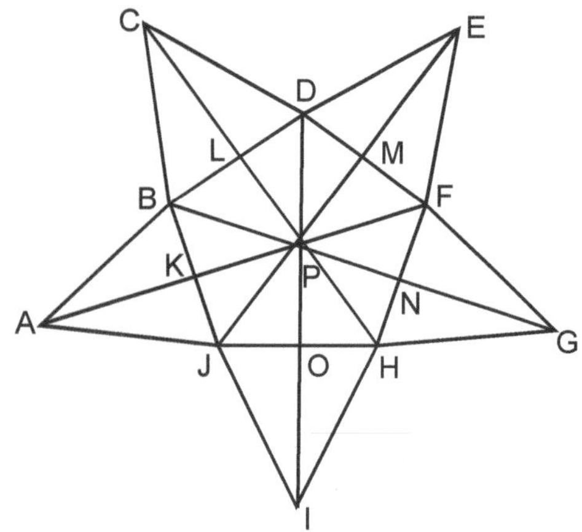

228. GHF : CDB :: EFD : ?

(a) ABJ

(b) CBD

(c) IJH

(d) AJB

229. HNP : PDA :: DLP : ?

(a) CDP

(b) PJG

(c) PHE

(d) PME

230. AKJO : IOHN :: ? : CLBK

(a) LDME

(b) EMGH

(c) EMDL

(d) CLDM

231. BPM : GNJ :: ? : AKD

(a) FPO

(b) KPD

(c) HPB

(d) FPM

Directions for Questions 232-233: *Read the information provided and answer the questions which follow.*

On a cricket ground, five players - A, B, C, D and E are standing as described below facing the North

(a) B is 75 metres to the right of D

(b) A is 95 metres to the south of B

(c) C is 45 metres to the west of D

(d) E is 110 metres to the north of A

232. Who is to the north-east of the player who is to the left of B?

(*a*) A

(*b*) C

(*c*) Either A or C

(*d*) None of the above

233. If a player walks from C, meets D followed by B, then A and finally E, how many metres has the player walked if he has travelled the straight distance all through?

(*a*) 185

(*b*) 135

(*c*) 230

(*d*) 325

234. Find the value of X.

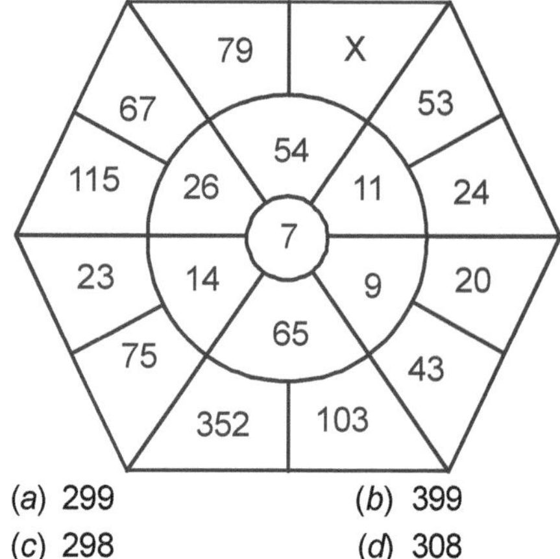

(*a*) 299

(*b*) 399

(*c*) 298

(*d*) 308

ANSWERS

1. (d)	**2.** (c)	**3.** (d)	**4.** (d)	**5.** (b)	**6.** (b)	**7.** (d)	**8.** (a,b,c,d)
9. (d)	**10.** (b)	**11.** (b)	**12.** (d)	**13.** (a)	**14.** (d)	**15.** (c)	**16.** (a)
17. (a)	**18.** (b)	**19.** (b)	**20.** (b)	**21.** (*)	**22.** (b)	**23.** (a)	**24.** (a)
25. (b)	**26.** (c)	**27.** (b)	**28.** (d)	**29.** (*a,c)	**30.** (b)	**31.** (b)	**32.** (b)
33. (d)	**34.** (b)	**35.** (a)	**36.** (c)	**37.** (a)	**38.** (a)	**39.** (c)	**40.** (c)
41. (a)	**42.** (d)	**43.** (b)	**44.** (d)	**45.** (a)	**46.** (b)	**47.** (d)	**48.** (d)
49. (b)	**50.** (b)	**51.** (c)	**52.** (a)	**53.** (c)	**54.** (a)	**55.** (*)	**56.** (c)
57. (c)	**58.** (d)	**59.** (d)	**60.** (c)	**61.** (c)	**62.** (c)	**63.** (c)	**64.** (d)
65. (d)	**66.** (d)	**67.** (d)	**68.** (c)	**69.** (d)	**70.** (d)	**71.** (a)	**72.** (c)
73. (c)	**74.** (a)	**75.** (b)	**76.** (a)	**77.** (c)	**78.** (d)	**79.** (d)	**80.** (c)
81. (a)	**82.** (c)	**83.** (d)	**84.** (d)	**85.** (a)	**86.** (c)	**87.** (c)	**88.** (d)
89. (d)	**90.** (b)	**91.** (b)	**92.** (d)	**93.** (b)	**94.** (d)	**95.** (b)	**96.** (b)
97. (c)	**98.** (a)	**99.** (b)	**100.** (c)	**101.** (d)	**102.** (c)	**103.** (b)	**104.** (d)
105. (a)	**106.** (c)	**107.** (d)	**108.** (c)	**109.** (c)	**110.** (b)	**111.** (a)	**112.** (d)
113. (b)	**114.** (d)	**115.** (b)	**116.** (b)	**117.** (c)	**118.** (b)	**119.** (b)	**120.** (c)
121. (b)	**122.** (c)	**123.** (b)	**124.** (c)	**125.** (c)	**126.** (b)	**127.** (b)	**128.** (a)
129. (b)	**130.** (*)	**131.** (a)	**132.** (a)	**133.** (b)	**134.** (d)	**135.** (d)	**136.** (a)
137. (a)	**138.** (c)	**139.** (b)	**140.** (a)	**141.** (c)	**142.** (d)	**143.** (d)	**144.** (a)
145. (b)	**146.** (d)	**147.** (c)	**148.** (c)	**149.** (d)	**150.** (b)	**151.** (c)	**152.** (b)
153. (a)	**154.** (a)	**155.** (c)	**156.** (c)	**157.** (c)	**158.** (c)	**159.** (d)	**160.** (c)
161. (b)	**162.** (a)	**163.** (b)	**164.** (c)	**165.** (b)	**166.** (d)	**167.** (c)	**168.** (a,b,d)
169. (a,c,d)	**170.** (a,b,c, d)	**171.** (c,d)	**172.** (a)	**173.** (b)	**174.** (d)	**175.** (c)	**176.** (b)
177. (c)	**178.** (d)	**179.** *	**180.** (d)	**181.** (c)	**182.** (c)	**183.** (d)	**184.** (c)
185. (a)	**186.** (d)	**187.** (c)	**188.** (b)	**189.** (b)	**190.** (b)	**191.** (a)	**192.** (a)
193. (b)	**194.** (d)	**195.** (a)	**196.** (b)	**197.** (c)	**198.** (d)	**199.** (c)	**200.** (a)
201. *(a)	**202.** (c)	**203.** (c)	**204.** (d)	**205.** *(c)	**206.** (b)	**207.** (b)	**208.** (c)
209. (c)	**210.** (a)	**211.** (a)	**212.** (c)	**213.** (d)	**214.** (a)	**215.** (c)	**216.** (c)
217. (b)	**218.** (d)	**219.** (a)	**220.** (d)	**221.** (d)	**222.** (b)	**223.** (c)	**224.** (c)
225. (b)	**226.** (a)	**227.** (d)	**228.** (a)	**229.** (b)	**230.** (c)	**231.** (a)	**232.** (d)
233. (d)	**234.** (a)						

EXPLANATIONS

For questions 1 to 6:

The information given in the question is vague and insufficient to solve the question. However, in exams, it is advisable to look through the questions and its options to chalk out some additional information which might be helpful in solving problems. We have attempted the same in the following solution:

From information 7, the occupant of room number 103 owns 12 cars and he donated to 8 institutions. Then from information 3, the occupant of room number 102 must be having 24 cars. From information 6, the occupant of room number 104 must be having 'z' number of cars and donated to y number of institutions, where $4z < y$. From information 9, the occupant of room number 105 owns 8 cars and if the businessman from Canada donated to 'x' number of institutions, then the occupant of room number 105 must have donated to $(x - 2)$ number of institutions.

From information 10, the residents of Canada, England and Brazil are staying in alternate rooms in that order, starting from left. Though room numbers of residents of Canada, England and Brazil can also be 102, 104 and 106 respectively. But from question 80 we can conclude that room numbers are 101, 103, and 105 respectively as room number 106 is not given to Brazilian businessman. Although the nationality of the occupant of room number 106 is not known from the information given, it can be found out to be Germany from the options of the 3rd question in the set.

We can compile the following table now and answer all questions.

Room No	101	102	103	104	105	106
Nationality	Canada	Uruguay	England	Argentina	Brazil	(Germany)
Number of Cars		24	12	4	8	16
Number of Institutions in which they have donated	x		8	18	x-2	24

1. Room number 105
2. 18
3. Germany
4. Germany
5. Uruguay
6. 12
7. By checking the options.

   Option(A): If Dilip observed the other three actors' helmets were 2 silver-plated and 1 copper-plated, then he could tell his helmet colour i.e., Gold. But he did not give the right answer. So option (a) is the correct statement.

   Option (b): Bimal knows that Chris and Dilip cannot tell their helmets' colour. If Bimal observed the helmet colour of Aslam, then he could tell his helmet colour i.e., Gold. But he did not give the right answer. So option (b) is the correct statement.

   Option (c): Chris knows that Dilip cannot tell his helmet colour. If Chris observed the other two actors' helmets which were of 1 silver plated and one copper or both silver plated, then he can identify his helmet colour as Gold. But he did not give right answer.

   So option (c) is the correct statement.

   Option (d): None of the statements is wrong. So option (d) is answer.
8. By checking the options, the following table can be made.

	Option -A	Option -B	Option -C	Option -D
No. of Units of Product-1	2	2	2	2
No. of Units of Product-2	14	14	10	14
No. of Units of Product-3	2	4	8	4
No. of Units of Product-4	6	4	4	4
No. of Units of Product-5	2	2	2	2
Cost	1960	1980	1960	1980
No. of points	26000	26000	26000	26000
No. of Penalty points	20000	10000	20000	10000

   Hence, (a), (b), (c) and (d) are the right options.

For questions 9 to 11: Following table can be prepared according to the statements mentioned in the question:

	Movie	Theatre
Veena	Hero	Satyam
Seema	Salaam Namaste	PVR Saket
Mona	Iqbal	Chanakya
Neeta	Khiladi	M2K
Reema	Gangster	Priya

12. Daljeet is brother of Chiranjeet & Chiranjeet is wife of Baljeet. Therefore, Daljeet must be brother in-law of Baljeet. Hence, (d) is the correct option.

13. Manjeet is daughter of Chiranjeet & Chiranjeet is father of Daljeet. Therefore, Manjeet and Daljeet are siblings. Hence, Manjeet can't be Baljeet's mother.

14. Abhijeet is brother of Chiranjeet & Chiranjeet is daughter of Baljeet. Therefore, Baljeet can't be mother- in-law of Chiranjeet.

For questions 15 to 18:

Let us consider the rounds in a reverse order, beginning with the last one wherein each person had Rs.32,000 in the end. We can draw the following table.

(The figures are in Rs.'000)

	Mohit	Manohar	Prasant	Dinesh
Initially	66	34	18	10
Round – 1	4	68	36	20
Round – 2	8	8	72	40
Round – 3	16	16	16	80
Round – 4	32	32	32	32

19. Option (b) is the correct choice.

For questions 20 to 23: Please make the following correction in this problem set. In exception b, replace "*at (ii)*" by "*at (iii)*"

20. Amar satisfies the conditions in (i) and (iv). He does not meet the condition in (iii) but as he is willing to pay an amount of Rs.1 lakh, if required to leave the software firm, his case could have been referred to the "President" of the firm. We are given that in 2003, he had started working for an engineering firm but we have no information about the duration of his employment in that firm, hence, we cannot conclude that he satisfies the condition of having at least one year's experience which is required as per condition (ii). Due to lack of this information, he should not be selected. Hence, (d) is the correct answer.

21. Rajkishore satisfies the conditions in (i), (iii) and (iv). He does not satisfy the condition in (ii) but as he is a computer engineer, his case may be referred to DGM. As none of the answer options mention this, none of them is correct.

***Correct answer is not available.**

22. Madhuri satisfies the conditions in (i), (ii) and (iv). However, there is no information on either her acceptance or her non-acceptance of the condition of bond in (iii). Thus, due to lack of information, she should not be selected. Hence, (b) is the correct answer.

23. Kamla satisfies the conditions in (i),(ii), (iii) and (iv). Hence, (a) is the correct option.

For questions 24 to 26:

24. Bihar has a level of dissimilarity of 2 with Orissa. Others have a level of dissimilarity higher than 2.

25. Rajasthan has a level of dissimilarity of 4 with Orissa and it is the highest.

26. In all the options except option (c), the level of dissimilarity is 4. However, in option (c), Rajasthan and Kerala have a level of dissimilarity of 3.

27. He does not have the required marks in the entrance test, so he is not admitted.

28. He is more than 33 years old but has 12 years of work experience. So he should be admitted under sponsored quota.

29. From the given information, it can be drawn that the child-school combinations are:

Rahman - Leelavati , Binod - Colombus , Badal - Lancer.

Also, the child from Andhra Pradesh won the 1st prize, that from Karnataka won the 2nd and that from Maharashtra won the 3rd prize.

Since the school in Andhra Pradesh cannot be Columbus and Lancer school did not secure 1st prize, so Leelavati is in Andhra Pradesh. Hence, Rehman won the 1st prize. This negates options (b) and (d).

Since the states and the positions of Badal and Binod cannot be determined from the given information, both options (a) and (c) hold true.

30. Number of milk packet = 2000 + 200n,

where n is a natural number.

Price per packet = Rs. (20 – n)

Revenue = (2000 + 200n)(20 – n) = 40000 + 2000n $- 200n^2$

Differentiating the above polynomial, we get

$$200 - 400 n \qquad \qquad ...(i)$$

For maxima, equating (i) to zero, we get

200 – 400n = 0

$\Rightarrow$ n = 5

$\therefore$ Maximum revenue will be at (2000 + 200 × 5)

= 3000 milk packets.

31. Rani found only 1 rupee with her at the end.

Before 3rd security guard, she had $(1 + 2) \times 2$

$= Rs.6$

Before 2nd security guard, she had $(6 + 2) \times 2$

$= Rs.16$

Before 1st security guard, she had $(16 + 2) \times 2$

$= Rs.36$.

For questions 32 and 33:

Let Professor Fotedar, Professor Das, Professor Chaudhury, Professor Banik, Professor Eswar and Professor Acharya be represented by F, D, C, B, E and A respectively.

If D gets assignment, F does not or vice-versa.

C wants only HRM or Finance or none.

If D gets Psychology, B must get Trade policy; if D gets Trade policy then B must get Psychology.

If A gets assignment, E should get one too.

32. Option (a) gets eliminated because C can have either HRM or Finance.

Option (c) gets eliminated because F and D cannot be in the same team.

Option (d) gets eliminated because C cannot have Trade policy.

Hence, (b) is the correct option.

33. B-Development Studies, D – Trade policy because if D gets Trade policy, then B must get Psychology.

For questions 34 to 36:

Four of the amounts spent by the five women are Rs.2234, Rs.1193, Rs.1340 ad Rs.2517.

Two cases arise:

(i) <u>The lowest amount spent is Rs.1193</u> (by Chandrima):

Then, the fifth amount will be Rs.(1193 + 1378) = Rs.2571, which will then be the highest amount and is spent by Sumitra. As Aradhana arrived before Chandrima, so she must have spent Rs.2234. This implies Heena spent Rs.2517 and Deepika spent Rs.1340, which is a contradiction.

Hence, this case is not possible.

(ii) <u>The highest amount spent is Rs.2517</u> (by Sumitra):

Then the fifth amount will be Rs.(2517 – 1378) = Rs.1139. Since it is the lowest amount, it will be spent by Chandrima.

Further analysis leads to the following table:

Order of arrival	1	2	3	4	5
Name	Aradhana	Chandrima	Deepika	Heena	Sumitra
Amount spent	Rs.2234	Rs.1139	Rs.1193	Rs.1340	Rs.2517

37.

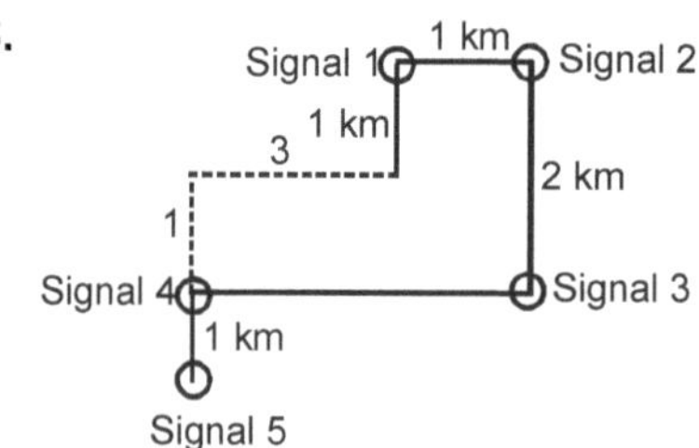

Note: s = Distance covered; v = Velocity (km/hr)

t = Time taken; s = v × t

The total distance travelled by the motorist from the starting point till last signal is $1 + 1 + 2 + 4 + 1$

$= 9 \text{ km}$

38.

39. When heading towards North direction, the final position of Kartikey is 3.0 km to East and 4.0 km to the North (Refer to the figure in question 76). Therefore, when heading towards South, his final position will be the mirror image of his final position when driving to North, i.e., 3.0 km to West and 5.0 km to the South.

For questions 40 to 43:

Sons – Arun (A), Mahi (M), Rohit (R), Nitesh (N), Sourav (S)

Daughters – Tamanna (T), Kuntala (K), Janaki (J)

From the given information, we can arrange the sons & daughters in descending order of their age.

Son/Daughter	Son	Son	Son	Daughter	Daughter	Son	Son	Daughter
Name	S	M/N	N/M	K	T	A	R	J
School	Trinity	Mansrover	Mansrover	Trinity	St. Stefan	St. Stefan	St. Stefan	Trinity
Game		Cricketer	Cricketer	Chess		Football	Hockey	

44. Pritu's father's sister's grandfather is Pritu's father's grandfather. His grandfather's only son is Pritu's father's father. His father's wife is Pritu's father's mother. His mother's daughter's daughter is Pritu's father's niece. Sushma is Pritu's sister. Hence, Sushma is Priya's Cousin.

45. It satisfies all the conditions.

46. The given information is not adequate as the director has passed the three years course or not, is not given.

47. It was submitted to NFDC after 31/10/07.

48. From the data given in the question, we arrive at the final sequence in the order of fattest to thinnest as Bibek, Anil, Debu, Charu and Eswar.

Hence, Eswar is the thinnest of all.

49. According to Yuvraj,

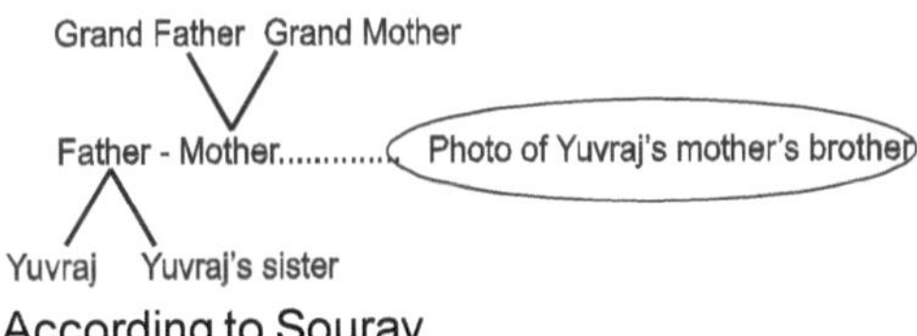

According to Sourav

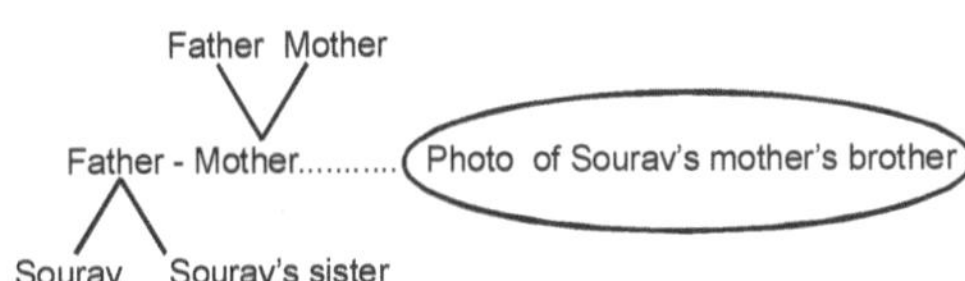

After adding the third information we get.

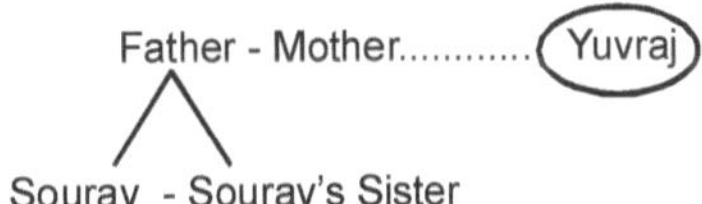

So Yuvraj is maternal uncle of Sourav.

For question 50 to 52:

Following is the table relating the persons with their corresponding salary and colour of their houses.

Houses	Blue	Green	Red	Yellow
Persons	Som	Paul	Krishna	Laxman
Salary	80K	30K	110K	50K

50. Krishna

51. Red

52. Rs.30,000

53.

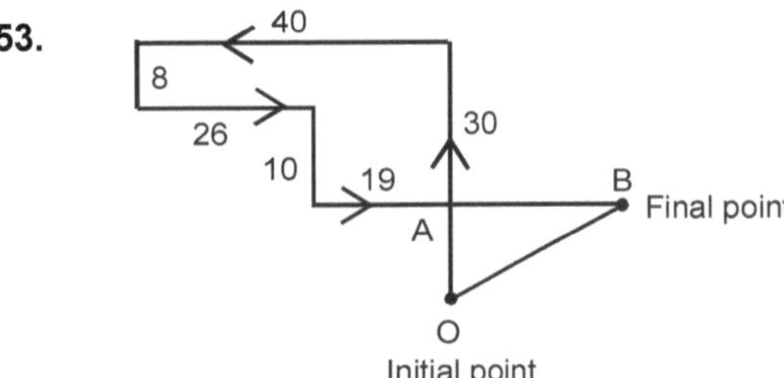

Hence, AB = (26 + 19) – 40 = 5

AO = 30 – (8 + 10) = 12

Hence, $OB = \sqrt{5^2 + 12^2} = 13$ kms, **North-east of starting point.**

54. The number of members going for the picnic along with Mr. Raju are:

Car 1: His father's mother, his mother's father, their two children i.e. his father and mother

Car 2: His father's son (his brother), his sister's husband, his brother's wife

Car 3: Raju, his wife, wife's sister, wife's brother, son's wife + kid

Therefore, total of 13 members are going for the picnic.

The members who are left behind:

Raju's sister, his wife's sister's husband, his wife's brother's wife and Raju's son.

Therefore, a total of 4 members are left behind.

55. Let a, b, c, d and e be the number of cards A, B, C, D and E respectively. According to the information provided in the question;

a + 5 = e; b + 5 = d.

So a + b + 10 = d + e, which means that A and B has less number of cards than D and E put together.

But, it is given that the number of cards with A and B put together is 20 more than the number of cards with D and E put together.

*** So the data provided in the question is inconsistent.**

56.

	Dance	Music	Painting
Monday		12 – 4	
Tuesday	10 – 2		9 – 12
Wednesday	10 – 2		2 – 4
Thursday	10 – 2	12 – 4	9 – 12
Friday			9 – 12
Saturday			2 – 4
Sunday	10 – 2	12 – 4	2 – 4

It is clear from the above table that the dance and painting sessions were simultaneously held on Tuesday and Thursday.

Hence, option (c) is the correct answer.

57.

Person	Likes	Dislikes
C_1	Travelling , Sightseeing	River rafting
C_2	Sightseeing , Squash	Travelling
C_3	River rafting	Sightseeing
C_4	Trekking	Squash
C_5	Squash	Sightseeing, Trekking
C_6	Travelling	Sightseeing, Trekking
C_7	River rafting, Trekking	Travelling
C_8	Sightseeing, River rafting	Trekking

Of the given combinations, the feasible team of 4 persons is: C_1, C_2, C_4 and C_7.

Option (c) matches with the conditions given in the question.

For questions 58 to 62: The competitions will be held as follows.

DATE	DAY	COMPETITION
19th October	Wednesday	Rock Band
20th October	Thursday	No Competition
21st October	Friday	Fash-P
22nd October	Saturday	Debate
23rd October	Sunday	No Competition
24th October	Monday	Street Play
25th October	Tuesday	Group Song
26th October	Wednesday	Folk Dance

58. The cultural week started with Rock Band Competition.

59. Rock Band competition was held on 19th October whereas the Group Song competition was held on 25th October. Therefore, there is a gap of 5 days between the two competitions.

60. Both Rock Band competition and Folk Dance competition were held on a Wednesday. While Rock Band competition was held on 19th October, the Folk Dance competition was held exactly after one week on 26th October.

61. Street Play was preceded by the Debate competition.

62. Fash-P follows Rock Band competition.

For questions 63 to 65: The arrangement according to the given conditions is as follows.

Esteem	Swift	i10
Punto	Alto	SX4

63. If SX4 and Esteem exchange their positions mutually then following will be the arrangement of cars:

SX4	Swift	i10
Punto	Alto	Esteem

Therefore only Alto will be adjacent to Esteem.

64. After the changes mentioned in the question the arrangement will be as follows

Swift	Beatle	Alto
SX4	i10	Punto

Therefore the cars parked adjacent to Beatle are Alto and Swift.

65. Under the given conditions, the arrangement is:

WagonR	Swift	Jazz
Zen	Alto	Beat

The cars that moved out are Esteem, Punto, i10 and SX4.

For questions 66 to 70: The arrangement according to the given conditions is as follows.

PERSON	COMPANY	PLACE OF WORK	E-MAIL ACCOUNT
Rahul	Telco	Pune	Rediffmail
Kabeer	Usha Martin	Kolkata	Yahoo
Anup	Tisco	Jamshedpur	Indiatimes
Raghu	Mecon	Ranchi	Gmail
Amit	HCL	Noida	Sancharnet
Alok	Wipro	Bangalore	Hotmail

66. Alok works in Wipro and he has an e-mail account with Hotmail.

67. Among the given options only Raghu-Ranchi-Gmail is the correct combination.

68. Among the given statements the only true statement is that Kabeer has an e-mail id with Yahoo.

69. As evident from the table above none of the given sequences of locations is correct.

70. As shown in the table above the correct match of e-mail account and Company is:

Tisco	Indiatimes
HCL	Sancharnet
Usha Martin	Yahoo

71. 70**900**070890702030045703907

There is only one such zero.

72.

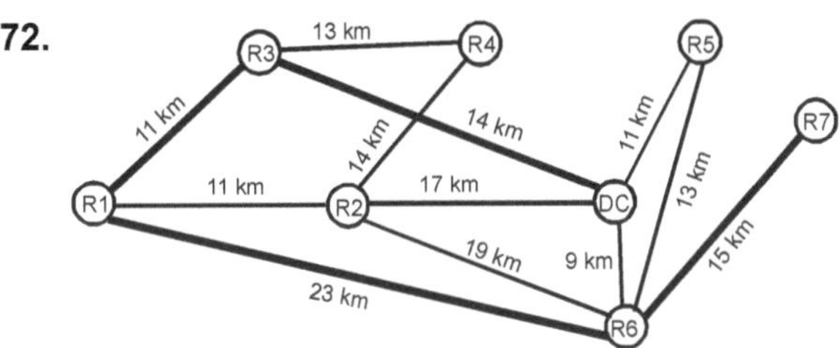

The shortest path is

DC → R3 → R1 → R6 → R7

and the shortest distance = 14 + 11 + 23 + 15

= 63 km.

73. Only condition I is not satisfied but is a traditional handloom production unit, therefore, the case may be referred to Development Commissioner, handloom.

74. As the firm satisfies all the criteria, therefore, license can be issued.

75. Both criteria I and II are not satisfied. Hence the license is not to be issued.

For questions 76 and 77:

The six persons in the family are Mona, Varun, Sonalika, Rakesh, Nuri and Tarun.

The given information can be shown with the help of the family tree as given below:

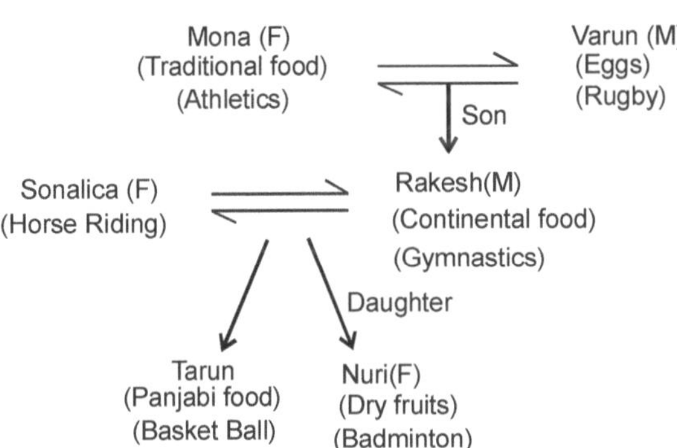

76. Mona – Varun and Sonalika – Rakesh are the two couples.

77. Tarun likes Punjabi food and he supports Basketball

For questions 78 and 79:

78. From condition (iv), Prof. Chakravarty and Prof. Equbal must be there in the committee, therefore, the third professor selected is Prof. Das.

From condition (iii), Queen cannot be selected and from condition (i), Sushil cannot be selected.

The other member selected must be Prof. Chakravarty, Prof. Equbal, Prakash and Ravi.

79. It is given in the question that Prof. Ahuja and Prof. Chakravarty are selected. From condition (iv), Prof. Equbal must be selected. In all the first three options, Prof Equbal is given as the member, who is not selected; therefore, option (d) is correct.

For questions 80 and 81:

The given information can be shown with the help of the table below:

South	Prof. Tripathi	Prof. Qureshi	Prof. Sawant
North	Prof. Usman	Prof. Rathor	Prof. Purohit

Or

South	Prof. Sawant	Prof. Qureshi	Prof. Tripathi
North	Prof. Purohit	Prof. Rathor	Prof. Usman

For questions 82 and 83:

82. In the week J, K, L are three actors who will appear. This implies N will not appear that week. Also, since J is working, it implies M must appear. These conditions are satisfied in option (c) only.

83. Since M works every other week, so M will not appear in the next week. Also, K will not appear as N is to appear next week. J will not appear as M cannot appear next week. Therefore, only L may appear other than N and O.

For questions 84 and 85:

The given information can be shown as:

Seat No.	1	2	3	4	5
Speaker	Jaya	Hema	Kumar	Gaj	Lalit
	Explorer	Writer	Moderator	Attorney	Pilot

For questions 86 to 91: The given information can be tabulated as:

Institution	Jupiter	Mars	Mercury	Neptune	Pluto	Uranus
Room no	204	205	201	206	203	202
No. of Journals	4	8		16	12	24
No. of Institutions donated to	18			24	8	

86. The professor from Mars is staying in room no. 205.

87. The professor from Jupiter has donated to 18 institutions.

88. The professor from Neptune is staying in room no. 206.

89. The professor from Neptune donated to 24 institutions last year.

90. The professor from Uranus published in the maximum number of journals.

91. The professor from Jupiter published 4 journals.

For questions 92 to 94: The given information can be tabulated as:

Person	Sex	Sport	Martial Status
P	F		Unmarried
Q	M	Badminton	
R	F	Tannis	Married (Wife)
S	F		Unmarried
T	M	Chess	Married (Husband)

92. The group "PRS" has only ladies.

93. R is the tennis player.

94. R is the wife of T.

95. Sarangsh Malhotra in the year 2014 will be more than 31 years old if his 25th birthday was in the year 2008. According to the enlisted conditions, the candidate must be between 25-30 years of age, which this candidate does not fulfill. Therefore, he will not be selected. This renders option B as the answer.

96. Nalin Saxena fulfills conditions I, II and III but is not able to fulfil one more condition to be an eligible candidate for the post. Also, his experience cannot be considered valid as per the condition as he does not work in a daily newspaper (according to condition number IV) but in a weekly magazine. So, he will be rejected. Hence, option (b) is the answer

97. Geetika Arora fulfills mandatory condition I and with it conditions III and V. She does not fulfill condition II but instead secures 80% above marks during her Post Graduation degree in Journalism. This fulfills the flexible condition (b). So, as per the condition, Geetika will be referred to the chairman of Tomorrow Digest. Hence, option (c) is the answer.

98. Manjeet Tyagi fulfills conditions I, II and III. Since Manjeet completed his PG in July 2010, he left Data Analytics firm by January 2011 and then joined Financial Standard. We will have to assume that he joined Financial Standard immediately after he left Data Analytics and also that he worked in the newspaper till August 2014. It is so because otherwise it is not possible to determine his selection or rejection in this case and 'cannot be determined' is not an option in this question. Accordingly, this fulfills condition IV also. So, we can say that Manjeet will be selected, rendering option A correct.

For question 99 to 102: The given information can be tabulated as follows:

Name	Activity	Hostel	Discipline	City
Ravi	Mess	Satpura	Computer Science	Jodhpur
Sanjay	Sports	Aravalli	Mech. Engineering	Nagpur
Hardeep	Cultural	Aravalli	Metallurgy	Patna
Abhishek	Student Body	Vindhya	Civil Engineering	Kochi
Hemant	Placement	Vindhya	Chemical Engineering	Allahabad

99. From the above table, the student belonging to Chemical Engineering branch stays in Vindhya Hostel, whereas Cultural activity student stays in Aravalli Hostel. So statement I is incorrect. Also the student incharge of placement activity is studying chemical Engineering. So, second statement is also incorrect. Also, the student who belongs to Nagpur is student in charge of sports activity and Ravi belongs to Jodhpur.

Hence, option (b) is the correct answer.

100. From the above table, it is clear that the student from Patna studies metallurgy.

101. The student from Allahabad is studying in Chemical Engineering.

102. The general secretary of the student body belongs to Kochi.

For questions 103 to 105: The given information is tabulated below:

	W1	W2	W3	W4	W5
Mon	9:30 AM to 2:30 AM	12:30 PM to 2:30 PM	3:30 PM to 5:30 PM	8:00 AM to 10:00 AM	2:00 PM to 4:00 PM
Tues	8:00 AM to 11:30 AM	...	...	11:30 AM to 3:00 PM	3:30 PM to 5:30 PM
Wed	9:30 AM to 2:30 PM	8:30 AM to 11:30 AM	10:00 AM to 12:30 PM	3:30 PM to 5:30 PM	8:00 AM to 10:00 AM
Thur	8:00 AM to 11:30 PM	8:30 AM to 11:30 AM	3:30 PM to 5:30 PM	12:30 PM to 3:00 PM	10:30 AM to 12:30 PM
Fri	3:00 PM to 5:00 PM	8:00 AM to 10:00 AM	10:00 AM to 12:00 PM	12:30 PM to 3:00 PM	3:30 PM to 5:30 PM
Sat	...	12:30 PM to 2:30 PM	10:00 AM to 12:30 PM	8:00 AM to 10:00 AM	...

103. The maximum is on Wednesday.

104. Only on Saturday not more that one window is open simultananeously at any given time.

105. All windows are closed for one hour between 2:30 PM to 3:30 PM only on Wednesday.

106. From the given information, the order in which they deliver the speeches is Mr. D'souza , Mr. Arora, Mr.Puri, Mr. Kaare, Mr. Sethi, Mr. Tondon, Mr. Bisht , Mr. Reddy. So, Mr. puri delivered his address before Mr. Reddy

107. From the given information, the order in which they delivered the speeches is Mr. D'souza , MrArora, Mr. Bisht , Mr. Reddy. Since Mr. Reddy is managing director of spearhead unlimited and there are two MD's who will speak after Mr. Reddy, we cannot definitely say who will be the last CEO to speak between Mr. Sethi and Mr. puri.

For questions 108 to 112:

From statement (iv) and (vi), it is clear that Frank is offered a job in IT department.

From statement (iii) and (v), it is clear that Brad is offered a job in India.

Now, further analysis leads to the following table:-

Name	Location	Branch
Anthony	Singapore	Electrical
Brad	India	Chemical
Carla	Germany	Electronics
Dinesh	UAE	Metallurgy
Evan	England	Mechanical
Frank	Australia	IT

108. Carla Joined the Electronics department.

109. The Person Placed in UAE is in the Metallurgy Department.

110. Brad – India – chemical is the correct combination.

111. Frank joined the IT Department in Australia.

112. UAE-Metallurgy is true Combination for Dinesh.

For questions 113 to 116 :

From statement III and VI; The order of qualification will be as followed:

Kalpana > Kamalesh > Kriti > Kamla > Kripa.

From Statement IV, V and VI,

The order of height will be as followed:

Kamla > Kamlesh > Kriti > Kalpana > Kranti

From Statement I; Kamla can't be the tallest. So, It is clear that kripa will be the tallest among them:

Hence, final arrangement will be as following:

Kripa > Kamla > Kamlesh > Kriti > Kalpana > Kranti

From Statement II, It is clear that Kranti is the most qualified.

On the basis of qualification, they can be arranged as following:

Kranti > Kalpana > Kamlesh > Kriti > Kamla > Kripa

113. Kamlesh is the third tallest Starting in decreasing order of height.

114. Kranti is the most qualified.

115. The rank of kriti in decreasing order of qualification is 3.

116. The rank of Kamla in increasing order of height is 5.

117. The correct question should be, 'In how many ways can contries be selected if no condition is imposed:

$$3_{C_1} + 3_{C_2} + 3_{C_3} = 2^3 - 1 = 7$$

118. The Correct question should be, 'In how many ways can countries be selected to meet only condition 1.'

There are 2 ways.

I : USA, UAE

II : USA, UAE UK

119. Case I : UAE, UK

Case II : USA

Case III : UK

Hence, 2 or 1 countires can be selected to meet only conditions 2 and 3.

For questions 120 to 122 :

Information given in the question may be Summarized as following:-

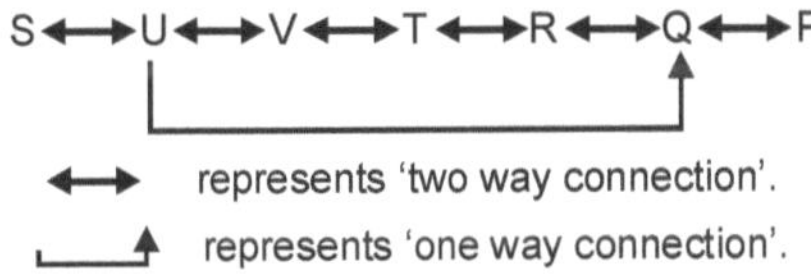

120. From the above diagram, it is clear that If the trader wants the cargo to move from city S to city T, excluding cities S and T, The minimum number of cities that the Cargo has to cross in transit is 2.

121. If the trader wants the cargo to go to city U from city P through the longest route then he will be required to cross four cities (excluding cities P and U).

122. To move Cargo from City P to city U, Statement 'C' will minimise the number of cities to be crossed in transit.

123. (a) If the Maternal grandmother is from tribe A, then mother will be from tribe A and the female is from tribe A. As given that the female is from tribe B, so statement a is false.

   (b) If paternal grandmother is from A, then father is from tribe A and after marriage, he will become member of tribe B. His daughter, the female will be of tribe B. Hence statement b is true.

124. We will check the options one by one.

   (a) If the boy is born in tribe B then he will marry in tribe A and his daughter will be in tribe A. Hence it is incorrect.

   (b) If the boy is born in tribe B, then he will marry in tribe A. His son will be in tribe A. So his daughter in law will be from tribe B. Hence it is incorrect.

   (c) If the boy is born in tribe B, then his mother's brother can be from tribe B and his father's brother can be from tribe A. Hence it is correct.

   (d) If the boy is born in tribe B, then he will marry in tribe A and his divorced son will be in tribe A. Hence option (d) is incorrect.

125. (a) Any widower will return to his tribe. So he can marry his wife's sister which is from other tribe. Hence this marriage is permissible.

   (b) This marriage is also permissible as the divorced husband will return to his tribe. Hence the mother can marry the divorced husband of her daughter.

   (c) The mother's brother will be of same tribe as that of girl. Hence the girl cannot marry him. Hence this marriage cannot take place.

   (d) Any widower will return to his own tribe A. His brother's widow will be of tribe B. So he can marry his brother's widow.

For questions 126 to 129: The arrangement is given below.

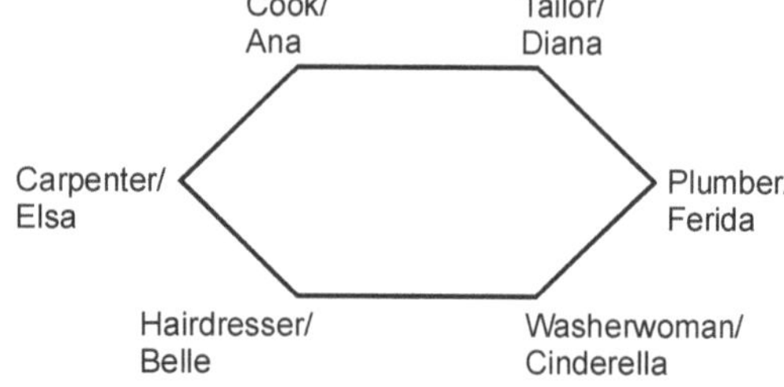

For questions 130 to 132:

From the given information

We can infer that

   Admin → E & G (female)

Finance → C, A and one of B & E

Logistics → H and one of B & E.

Order of income → G > H > A > F, B, E > C

130. * Finance department will have 3 people and in official answer key, the question is deleted.

131. B earns less than A and H.

132. H is at 2nd in descending order of income.

For questions 133 to 135: The information is summarised below.

Time slot	Person	Relation	Profession
9 am – 10 am	Q (male)	Father	Cardiologist
10 am – 11 am	T (male)	Mother's Brother	Radiologist
11 am – 12 pm	S (female)	Mother	Gynaecologist
12 pm – 1 pm	V (female)	Father's sister	General Physician
1 pm – 2 pm		LUNCH	
2 pm – 3 pm	W (male)	Elder son	Orthodontist
3 pm – 4 pm	R (female)	Younger daughter	Urologist
4 pm – 5 pm	P (male)	Younger son	Neurologist
5 pm – 6 pm	U (female)	Elder daughter	Pediatrician

135. If lunch break and subsequent working are reduced by 15 min. then the new timings in order will be 1 : 00 pm – 1 : 45 pm (lunch), 1 : 45 pm – 2 : 30 pm, 2 : 30 pm – 3 : 15 pm, 3 : 15 pm – 4 : 00 pm & 4 : 00 pm – 4 : 45 pm.

Since U is the last doctor and she is Pediatrician, daughter of Cardiologist will reach the clinic at 4 : 00 pm.

For questions 136 to 140: *From the given information we can make the following arrangement.*

Name	Company	City	Book
Vinay	Asian Paints	Bhopal	Classic fiction
Aman	Dabur	Chennai	Historical fiction
Manish	ITC	Patna	Business and management
Rohit	HUL	Mumbai	Mystery fiction
Sandeep	L'Oreal	Delhi	Non fiction

136. Aman got placed in Dabur

137. Manish reads books on business and management

138. Rohit lives in Mumbai and he reads mystery fiction

139. Rohit reads mystery fiction and he will go to Delhi.

140. Manish is posted in Patna.

141. Every team played seven matches

   Chennai score = 5 wins a 2 draws

   $\Rightarrow 5 \times 3 + 2 \times 1 = 17$

   Goa lost against Pune and Chennai played a draw against Kolkata.

For maximum score of Goa. It should win the remaining four matches.

So Goa score = 4 × 3 + 1 = 13

Answer is option (c).

142. Chennai score = 5 × 3 + 2 = 17

From (b) and (c) Pune loses to Delhi & Chennai and 2 wins and 1 draw

For minimum difference Pune should win the remaining 2 matches.

Pune score = 4 × 3 + 1 = 13

Difference = 17 – 13 = 4

Answer is option (d).

For questions 143 and 144:

From the given information we can draw the following table.

	Coach	Game
A	A_1	
B		
C	A_1	Cricket / Volleyball
D	A_2	
E	A_3	Tennis
F	A_2	Cricket
G		Volleyball

143. Cannot play tennis because her wife 'A' play tennis

So Answer is option (d).

144. and G cannot sit with C. So A will sit with C because minimum two persons should be in a coach. So Answer is option (a).

For questions 145 and 146: *From the given information, we can make the following arrangement*

Sport	Channel	Day
Cricket	Star Sports 1	Friday
Tennis	Ten Sports 2	Monday
Kabaddi	Sony Six	Tuesday
Football	Neo Sports	Thursday

145. Hence Neo sports telecasted Fotoball on Thursday.

146. Ten Spots 2 telecasted Tennis on Monday.

For questions 147 to 148:

Using the information given in the question, we can form the following table:

DAY	NAME	Organisation	Hotel
Monday	Albert	Pepsi	Taj
Tuesday	Claire	Nestle	Hilton
Wednesday	Fred	Himalaya	Crowne Plaza
Thursday	Evan	Apple	Radisson
Friday	Betty	Oppo	Hayat
Saturday	Daisy	Whirlpool	Marriott

147. Evan is working in Apple.

148. Fred participated on Wednesday.

149. As Albert, Betty and Fred work in Pepsi, Oppo and Himalaya, then their average salary

$$= \frac{50 + 40 + 60}{3} = 50 \text{ lakh per annum.}$$

150. Claire is staying in Hilton.

For question 151 to 153:

Using the given four conditions lets make all the possible cases first for every condition.

	Sunny	Pinky	Nancy	Richie
I	Purple	Purple	Purple	Purple
II	Purple	Blue	Blue	Blue
III	Blue	Purple	Purple	Purple
IV	Purple	Purple	Blue	Blue
V	Purple	Purple	Blue	Purple
VI	Blue	Blue	Blue	Blue
VII	Purple	Purple	Blue	Blue
VIII	Blue	Blue	Purple	Blue

Now if we apply the other three conditions once again on every case, we are left with the only two cases i.e I and VIII.

	Sunny	Pinky	Nancy	Richie
I	Purple	Purple	Purple	Purple
II	Blue	Blue	Purple	Blue

151. The room colours of Sunny and Nancy remain unchanged in both the possible cases.

152. If Richie stays in blue painted room, then Pinky also stays in blue painted room.

153. If Pinky does not like to stay in blue room, then she must stay in purple room.

Hence, Sunny will stay in blue room in that case.

For question 154 to 157:

From the given information we can make the following arrangement for the given 4 × 3 matrix:

Mineral	Mouse	Scare
Roses	Beauty	Arguments
Ferry	Logical	Helping
Doctor	Crude	Cats

154. For product to be 8, only possibility is 4 × 2, so the word at the position 4 × 2 is Crude.

155. Words present in the 3rd row are Ferry, Logical and Helping, total of which is 19.

156. The word at position 4 × 3 is Cats.

157. Out of the given options, only Beauty-Scare are placed diagonally in the matrix.

For question 158 to 161:

Sitting arrangement of the eight officers is as follows:

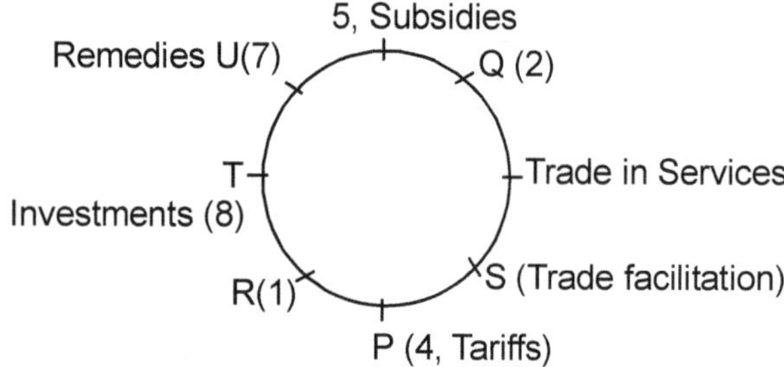

158. Remedies is discussed by U having rank 7.

159. If V is on right of Trade facilitation, then fourth to the right will be T serving investments.

160. W can represent both Trade in services and Subsidies.

161. Fourth to right of U is S discussing Trade facilitation.

For question 162 to 163:

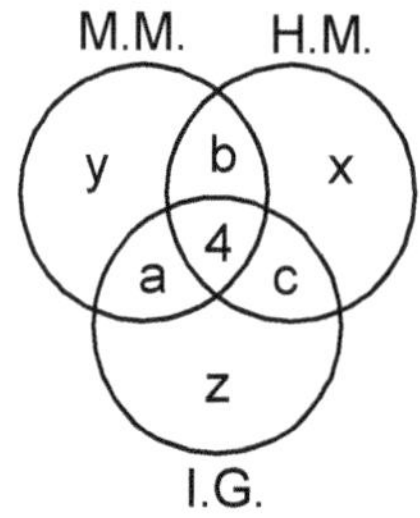

Given,

$b + 4 = (a + 4) - 1 = a + 3$

and $c + 4 = (a + 4) - = a + 3$

$\Rightarrow b + 4 = c + 4 \Rightarrow b = c$

Also $b = a - 1 = c$

and $x = y < z$ and z is even and $x = y = 2a$.

Now $x + y + z + a + b + c + 4 = 30$

$\Rightarrow 2a + 2a + z + a + a - 1 + a - 1 + 4 = 30$

$\Rightarrow 7a + z = 28$ -------(1)

Since z is even and $x = y < z$ so only $a = 2$ and $z = 14$ satisfy (1)

$\therefore$ $b = c = 1$, $x = y = 4$, $z = 14$, $a = 2$.

Hence the final Venn-diagram is

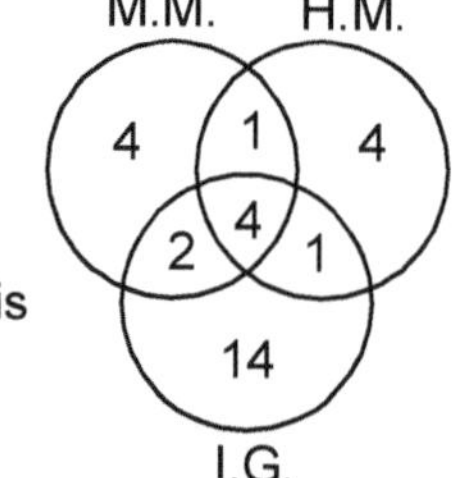

162. Dora will export machine made goods and will avoid hand made goods.

So Dora will export $y + a$.

Similarly, Sara will export $a + c + z + 4 + x$.

So, the common value to them is $a = 2$.

163. The total number of products exported by Abeer and Dora = $y + a + z = 20$.

For question 164 to 165:

We have

	1	2	3	4	5	6	7
10:00 AM	Banana	is	the	favourite	fruit	of	Bina
	3	2	6	4	7	5	1
11:00 AM	the	is	the	favourite	Bina	fruit	Banana
	6	2	5	4	1	7	3
12 noon	of	is	fruit	favourite	Banana	Bina	The

So if we look at the pattern, we get

10:00 AM	1	2	3	4	5	6	7
11:00 AM	3	2	6	4	7	5	1
12 noon	6	2	5	4	1	7	3
3:00 PM	5	2	7	4	3	1	6
4:00 PM	7	2	1	4	6	3	5
5 pm (10am)	1	2	3	4	5	6	7
6 pm (11am)	3	2	6	4	7	5	1

So at 5pm, the pattern is same as that of 10am. Hence after that the patterns will star repeating.

164. The order of the fourth show is

5	2	7	4	3	1	6
All	of	Delhi	welcome	to	the	Show

Hence the entry ticket will be

1	2	3	4	5	6	7
The	of	to	welcome	all	show	Delhi

165. The code of 12 noon will be same as the code at 7pm.

So the code is "Do things to help others in difficulty".

166. From statement II we know the rank of Rashmi from bottom. From statement I Mohit is 5 ranks below Rashmi from top and from statement III. Mohit is 5 ranks above Rashmi from bottom. S(by combining II statement with either I or III we will get the rank of Mohit. The answer is option (d).

167. Combining statement I and III we come to know that code of Orange is common and remaing two words in each statements are different.

So code of Orange.

'Pa' Answer is option (c).

For questions 168 to 171:

The following table can be made after observing the rules:

INPUT	lemon	apple	choco	college	girl	dream	room	book	calf	
	1	2	3	4	5	6	7	8	9	
STEP-1	3	2	1	4	5	6	9	8	7	Rule-1
STEP-2	1	2	3	6	5	4	7	8	9	Rule-2
STEP-3	9	1	2	8	3	4	7	5	6	Rule-3
STEP-4	2	9	1	8	3	4	6	7	5	Rule-4
STEP-5	1	9	2	4	3	8	5	7	6	Rule-2
STEP-6	6	1	9	7	2	8	5	3	4	Rule-3
STEP-7	9	1	6	7	2	8	4	3	5	Rule-1
STEP-8	6	1	9	8	2	7	5	3	4	Rule-2
STEP-9	4	6	1	3	9	7	5	2	8	Rule-3
STEP-10	1	4	6	3	9	7	8	5	2	Rule-4
STEP-11	6	4	1	7	9	3	2	5	8	Rule-2
STEP-12	8	6	4	5	1	3	2	9	7	Rule-3
STEP-13	4	6	8	5	1	3	7	9	2	Rule-1
STEP-14	8	6	4	3	1	5	2	9	7	Rule-2
STEP-15	7	8	6	9	4	5	2	1	3	Rule-3

168. From the table, STEP 10 is:

STEP-10	1	4	6	3	9	7	8	5	2
	lemon	college	dream	choco	calf	room	book	girl	apple

So Step 10 is option (c).

Hence, the right options are (a), (b) and (d).

169. From the table, STEP 8 is:

STEP-8	6	1	9	8	2	7	5	3	4
	dream	lemon	calf	book	apple	room	girl	choco	college

So option (b) can be the output. Hence, the right options are (a), (c) and (d).

170. By observing the table, none of the arrangement in the options will fall between STEP 11 to 15.

171. By checking the options, Rule-1 is applied in options (c) and (d).

For questions 172 to 175: In the given arrangement, the numbers have been arranged in the ascending order of sum of digits in a sequence and the moving out number is replaced by that number in whose place it sits in each

172. Input: 655, 436, 764, 799, 977, 572, 333

Step 1: 333, 436, 764, 799, 977, 572, 655

Step 2: 333, 436, 572, 799, 977, 764, 655

Step 3: 333, 436, 572, 655, 977, 764, 799

173. Input: 544, 653, 325, 688, 461, 231, 857,

Step 1: 231, 653, 325, 688, 461, 544, 857

Step 2: 231, 325, 653, 688, 461, 544, 857

Step 3: 231, 325, 461, 688, 653, 544, 857

Step 4: 231, 325, 461, 544, 653, 688, 857

Step 5: 231, 325, 461, 544, 653, 857, 688(Last step)

174. Case 1:

Input: 666, 734, 355, 432, 433, 542, 574

Step 1: 432, 734, 355, 666, 433, 542, 574

Step 2: 432, 433, 355, 666, 734, 542, 574

Step 3: 432, 433, 542, 666, 734, 355, 574

Case 2:

Input: 666, 734, 574, 432, 433, 355, 542

Step 1: 432, 734, 574, 666, 433, 355, 542

Step 2: 432, 433, 574, 666, 734, 355, 542

Step 3: 432, 433, 542, 666, 734, 355, 574

175. Input: 653, 963, 754, 345, 364, 861, 541

Step 1: 541, 963, 754, 345, 364, 861, 653

Step 2: 541, 345, 754, 963, 364, 861, 653

Step 3: 541, 345, 364, 963, 754, 861, 653

For questions 176 to 178: In this input output solution, the ultimate aim is to arrange the last letter of each word in alphabetically reverse order.

176. When we arrange the words of the sentence "He is going out to search air" in a similar fashion we get the sequence as "out is air to search going he".

177. In the sentence "not is the casino considering legal action" we see that only the starting two words are in order so it has to be either 1st step or the 2nd step.

Since it is given that it is not the second step, we can conclude that it is the first step.

1st step	not	is	the	casino	considering	legal	action
2nd step	not	is	casino	the	considering	legal	action
3rd step	not	is	casino	action	the	considering	legal
4th step	not	is	casino	action	legal	the	considering

178.

Input	Father	needs	to	check	on	the	boy
1st step	boy	Father	needs	to	check	on	the
2nd step	boy	needs	Father	to	check	on	the
3rd step	boy	needs	Father	to	on	check	the

Hence, three steps are required to reach the final output.

For questions 179 to 181

The whole arrangement upto step 14 is depicted in the table given below.

Input	Smile	Nile	Style	Mile	Shine	Wine	Mine	Swine	Bovine	Feline
Step 1	Smile	Nile	Style	Mile	Shine	Wine	Bovine	Feline	Mine	Swine
Step 2	Style	Mile	Smile	Nile	Shine	Wine	Bovine	Feline	Mine	Swine
Step 3	Style	Mile	Smile	Nile	Wine	Shine	Bovine	Feline	Mine	Swine
Step 4	Mile	Style	Nile	Smile	Wine	Shine	Feline	Bovine	Swine	Mine
Step 5	Nile	Smile	Mile	Style	Wine	Shine	Swine	Mine	Feline	Bovine
Step 6	Nile	Smile	Mile	Style	Wine	Shine	Feline	Bovine	Swine	Mine
Step 7	Mile	Style	Nile	Smile	Wine	Shine	Feline	Bovine	Swine	Mine
Step 8	Mile	Style	Nile	Smile	Shine	Wine	Feline	Bovine	Swine	Mine
Step 9	Style	Mile	Smile	Nile	Shine	Wine	Bovine	Feline	Mine	Swine
Step 10	Smile	Nile	Style	Mile	Shine	Wine	Mine	Swine	Bovine	Feline
Step 11	Smile	Nile	Style	Mile	Shine	Wine	Bovine	Feline	Mine	Swine
Step 12	Style	Mile	Smile	Nile	Shine	Wine	Bovine	Feline	Mine	Swine
Step 13	Style	Mile	Smile	Nile	Wine	Shine	Bovine	Feline	Mine	Swine
Step 14	Mile	Style	Nile	Smile	Wine	Shine	Feline	Bovine	Swine	Mine

179. All the options provided in the question is wrong. It can easily be seen that the final series comes out to be as follows:

Mile Style Nile Smile Wine Shine Feline Bovine Swine Mine

Hence, none of the options is correct.

180. Option (d) does not fall between step number 12 and 14.

181. It can be seen from the above table that the input repeats itself in the 10th step. So, it will continue to repeat its original self after steps that are multiples of 10. Hence, option (c) is the correct choice.

182.

Input:	64	326	187	87	118	432	219	348
Step I:	64	432	326	187	87	118	219	348
Step II:	64	432	87	326	187	118	219	348
Step III:	64	432	87	348	326	187	118	219
Step IV:	64	432	87	348	118	326	187	219

183.

Input:	319	318	746	123	15	320	78	426
Step I:	15	319	318	746	123	320	78	426
Step II:	15	746	319	318	123	320	78	426
Step III:	15	746	78	319	318	123	320	426
Step IV:	15	746	78	426	319	318	123	320
Step V:	15	748	78	426	123	319	318	320
Step VI:	15	748	78	426	123	320	319	318
Step VII:	15	748	78	426	123	320	318	319

For questions 184 and 185: There is no as such logic followed in this arrangement, instead it is a random arrangement and we can just compare as shown below:

Input	STEP 1	STEP 2	STEP 3	STEP 4
Be	the	You	You	see
the	Be	Be	See	You
change	You	The	The	This
you	Change	Change	This	The
wish	To	To	To	World
to	Wish	World	World	To
see	In	In	In	Be
in	See	See	Be	In
this	World	Wish	Wish	Change
world	This	This	Change	wish

184. Given input: ' Don't cry because it's over smile since it's actually happened'.

And we are asked to find step 4 of this input, now instead of solving we can simply compare that first word of step 4 is the 7th word of input and the last word is 5th word of the input. Based upon this, we can judge that first word is 'since' and the last word will be 'over'. So option 1st and 4th options are eliminated Now the second word of step 4 is the 4th word of input. Therefore, word of step 4 should be 'it' and from here we can conclude that (c) is the correct choice.

185. We are given the 4th step as 'dog sea school star ice moon flower home rock ball' and we are asked to find the input of this. Now, instead of solving, we can simply compare that first word of step 4 is 7th word of input and the the last word is 5th word of the input. Based

upon this we can judge that the 7th word of input should be dog. Only option (a) has 7th word as dog and hence is the required input. Further to ensure the last word should be ice and is also true for option (a).

For questions 186 to 189: *To understand the logic, first number the words in the input*

	1	2	3	4	5	6	7	8
Input	My	Bag	Carries	No	More	Than	Ten	books

To write the Batch I, write the second half numbers 5, 6, 7, 8 in front to the 1st half as follows.

	5	1	6	2	7	3	8	4
Batch I:	More	My	Than	Bag	Ten	Carries	Books	no

Now to go from Batch I to Batch II, start from the middle and more towards outside as follows.

Batch I:

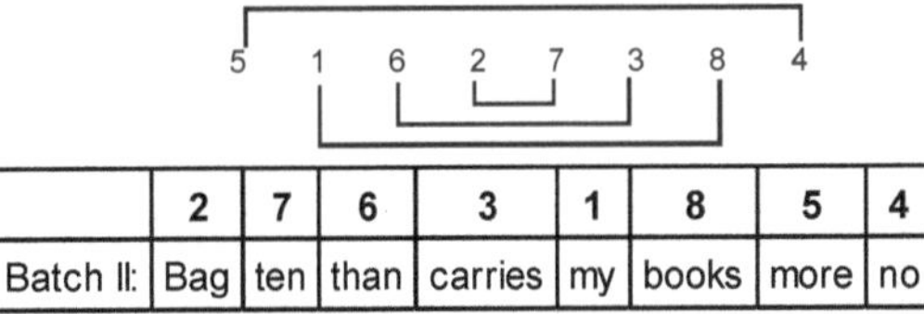

	2	7	6	3	1	8	5	4
Batch II:	Bag	ten	than	carries	my	books	more	no

To write batch III: repeat the process done to write batch I i.e, put the

2nd half numbers before the 1st half

	1	2	8	7	5	6	4	3
Batch III:	My	bag	books	ten	more	than	no	carries

To write the batch IV: repeat the process done to write Batch II i.e. start from the middle and more towards outside

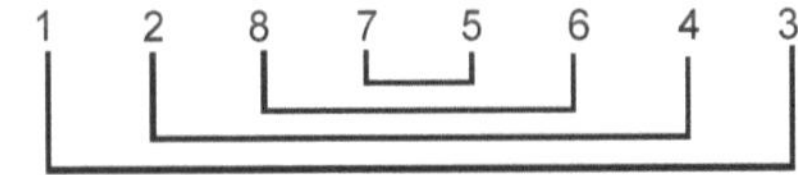

	7	5	8	6	2	4	1	3
Batch IV:	Ten	More	Books	Than	Bag	No	My	carries

This process will go on.

186.

	Input	1 my	2 bag	3 carries	4 no	5 more	6 than	7 ten	8 books
9:30 - 10:30	Batch I:	5	1	6	2	7	3	8	4
10:30 - 11:30	Batch II:	2	7	6	3	1	8	5	4
11:30 - 12:30	Batch III:	1	2	8	7	5	6	4	3
12:30 - 1:30	Batch IV:	7	5	8	6	2	4	1	3
1:30 - 2:30	Break								
2:30 - 3:30		2	7	4	5	1	8	3	6

Now there the code of second batch is given and compare it with the above arrangement for second batch.

	2	7	6	3	1	8	5	4
Batch II:	if	winter	comes	can	spring	be	for	behind

The order of pass code batch at 2:30 pm is

2	7	4	5	1	8	3	6
If	winter	behind	for	spring	be	can	comes

187.

		1	2	3	4	5	6	7	8
	Input	my	bag	carries	no	more	than	ten	books
9:30 - 10:30	Batch I:	5	1	6	2	7	3	8	4
10:30 - 11:30	Batch II:	2	7	6	3	1	8	5	4
11:30 - 12:30	Batch III:	1	2	8	7	5	6	4	3
12:30 - 1:30	Batch IV:	7	5	8	6	2	4	1	3
1:30 - 2:30	Break								
2:30 - 3:30		2	7	4	5	1	8	3	6

Now the 10:30 am pairs code is

2	7	6	3	1	8	5	4
I	like	tea	and	biscuit	but	not	together

The code for the next batch has the order

1	2	8	7	5	6	4	3
Biscuit	I	But	Like	Not	Tea	Together	and

188.

		1	2	3	4	5	6	7	8
	Input	my	bag	carries	no	more	than	ten	books
9:30 - 10:30	Batch I:	5	1	6	2	7	3	8	4
10:30 - 11:30	Batch II:	2	7	6	3	1	8	5	4
11:30 - 12:30	Batch III:	1	2	8	7	5	6	4	3
12:30 - 1:30	Batch IV:	7	5	8	6	2	4	1	3
1:30 - 2:30	Break								
2:30 - 3:30		2	7	4	5	1	8	3	6

Now the batch immediately before rest hour was

7	5	8	6	2	4	1	3
bah	bah	black	sheep	have	you	any	wool

Hence the input is

1	2	3	4	5	6	7	8
any	have	wool	you	bah	sheep	bah	black

189.

		1	2	3	4	5	6	7	8
	Input	my	bag	carries	no	more	than	ten	books
9:30 - 10:30	Batch I:	5	1	6	2	7	3	8	4
10:30 - 11:30	Batch II:	2	7	6	3	1	8	5	4
11:30 - 12:30	Batch III:	1	2	8	7	5	6	4	3
12:30 - 1:30	Batch IV:	7	5	8	6	2	4	1	3
1:30 - 2:30	Break								
2:30 - 3:30		2	7	4	5	1	8	3	6

The second batch is

2	7	6	3	1	8	5	4
India's	core	strength	lies	in	unity	in	diversity

The reverse of the input is

8	7	6	5	4	3	2	1
Unity	core	strength	in	diversity	lies	India's	in

For questions 190 and 191:

From statements (i) and (ii), code for 'above' is 'fop'.

From statements (i) and (iii), code for 'traders' is 'aop'.

From statements (i) and (iv), code for 'laws' is 'eop'.

From statements (ii) and (iii), code for 'developers' is 'bop'.

From statements (ii) and (iv), code for 'were' is 'cop'.

From statements (iii) and (iv), code for 'following' is 'uop'.

Therefore, we can conclude that:

Code for 'are' is 'lop'

Code for 'profitable' is 'gop'

Code for 'stopped' is 'qop'

Code for 'maps' is 'jop'

192. It can be concluded that code for each letter is the sum of the digits of its position number in the alphabetical series.

Code for word GOVERNMENT is:

G (7) ⇒ 7

O (15) ⇒ 1 + 5 ⇒ 6

V (22) ⇒ 2 + 2 ⇒ 4

E (5) ⇒ 5

R (18) ⇒ 1 + 8 ⇒ 9

N (14) ⇒ 1 + 4 ⇒ 5

M (13) ⇒ 1 + 3 ⇒ 4

E (5) ⇒ 5

N (14) ⇒ 1 + 4 ⇒ 5

T (20) ⇒ 2 + 0 ⇒ 2

193. It can be concluded that code for each letter is one less than its position number in the alphabetical series.

Code for word MONKEY is:

M (13 − 1) ⇒ 12

O (15 − 1) ⇒ 14

N (14 − 1) ⇒ 13

K (11 − 1) ⇒ 10

E (5 − 1) ⇒ 4

Y (25 − 1) ⇒ 24

194. Since the first letter is a consonant and the last letter is a vowel, both of these letters will be coded as 0. According to the table. Hence, the code for NFRSCA is 053%20.

195. Since the first and last letters are vowels, both of these letters will be coded as %. Hence, to the table the code for ARFTHE is 0358#%.

196. The word "agnosvitriblunin" is most likely to mean "black widow spider" in the artificial language.

197. The question can easily be solved using options.

Using option (c), we get

DEFFDEEFDDEFFDEEF

The sequence is:

DEF, FDE, EFD, ...

The third letter of a term takes first position in each subsequent term of the series.

For questions 199 and 200:

199. 3M % 2N means 3M = 2N   ...(i)

N % 3O means N = 3O   ...(ii)

From equations (i) and (ii), we get

$$\frac{3M}{2} = 3O \text{ or } M = 2O$$

Therefore, option (c) is correct.

200. N @ P means N > P   ...(i)

P # O means P < O   ...(ii)

O @ M means O > M   ...(iii)

N % M means N = M   ...(iv)

From equations (iii) and (iv), we get O > N

Therefore, both options (a) and (c) are correct, but option (a) is more appropriate here.

201. Assuming that the pattern from 7 to 12 is similar to the pattern followed from 1 to 6, we can arrive at the following output.

Input: H E I R A R C H I C A L
      1 2 3 4 5 6 7 8 9 10 11 12

Interchange	Output
1 and 2	EHIRARCHICAL
3 and 4	EHRIARCHICAL
4 and 5	EHRAIRCHICAL
5 and 6	EHRARICHICAL
7 and 8	EHRARIHCICAL
9 and 10	EHRARIHCCIAL
10 and 11	EHRARIHCCAIL
11 and 12	EHRARIHCCALI

Hence, R appears at 3rd and 5th positions, while C appears at 8th and 9th positions.

202. The given series consists of three different series:

−1, 0, 1, 0, 2, 4, 1, 6, 9, 2, 12, 16 ...

Series I : −1, 0, 1, 2, ...   or −1, −1 + 1, 0 + 1, 1 + 1,
...

Series II: 0, 2, 6, 12, ...   or 0, 0 + 2, 2 + 4, 6 + 6, ...

Series III: 1, 4, 9, 16, ... or   12, 22, 32, 42, ...

The next terms of

Series I: 2 + 1 = 3;   Series II : 12 + 8 = 20;

Series III: 52 = 25.

Hence, the missing terms are 3, 20, 25.

203. *di onot* means oak tree

bly onot means oak leaf

bly crin means maple leaf

From the three statements, we get

onot means oak; *bly* means leaf; *crin* means maple; *di* means tree.

Also, the code consists of two codes such that the first code corresponds to the second word and the second code corresponds to the first word.

Hence, a possible code for 'maple syrup' is *patricrin*.

204. From the given information, the three persons can be arranged in descending order of their ages as

Bhanu > Gita > Mita

Hence, of the three, Mita is the youngest, which is option (d).

205. From statement I, we get

Siya > Priya > Tiya   ... (i)

From statement II, we get

Siya > Riya > Priya   ... (ii)

From statement III, we get

Riya > Diya < Tiya   ... (iii)

Combining (i), (ii) and (iii), we get

Siya > Riya > Priya > Tiya > Diya.

* Note: The question asks for the correct ascending order of ages which is

Diya - Tiya - Priya - Riya - Siya, which matches none of the given options.

Option (c) states the descending order correctly and hence, should be the correct option.

206. The pattern followed in the given pair is:

I(9) + 3 = L(12)

Q(17) − 3 = N(14)

S(19) + 3 = V(22)

Similarly,

J(10) + 3 = M(13)

R(18) − 3 = O(15)

M(13) + 3 = P(16)

Hence, required term is MOP.

207. F # S $ B * V

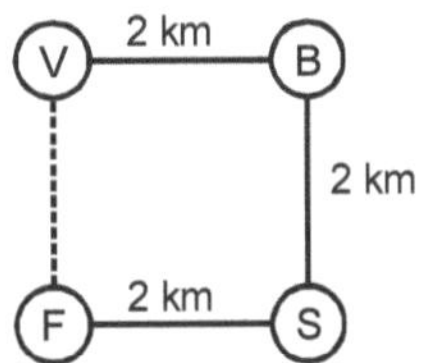

Hence, F is to the South of V.

208. The route followed by Ritvik is as below:

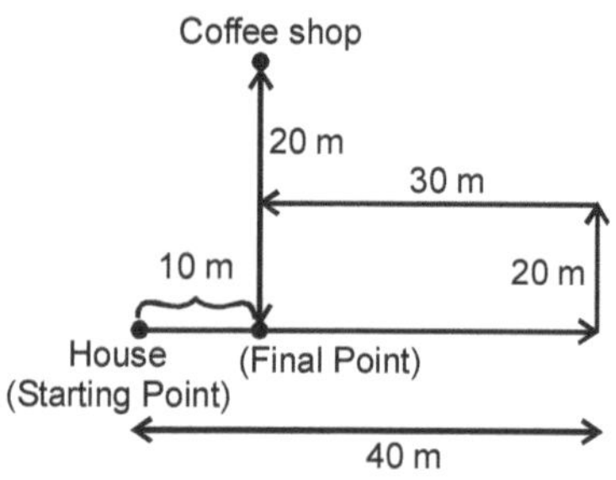

Hence, Ritvik is 10 m from his house finally.

209. The pattern followed columnarise is :

H(8) × B(2) $\longrightarrow$ P(16)

C(3) × F(6) $\longrightarrow$ R(18)

Hence, the missing alphabet will be

?(4) × E(5) $\longrightarrow$ T(20)

? = D

210. The arrangement of the periods is as follows.

Day	Original	1st Interchange	2nd Interchange
Monday	Jai	Raj	Raj
Tuesday	Farid	Kajal	Jai
Wednesday	Raj	Jai	Kajal
Thursday	Kajal	Farid	Farid

Hence, Jai worked on Tuesday.

211. The question can be best solved by picking the options one by one. Option (a) gives the two words REDUCE and EXPAND, that have opposite meanings.

No other options give any two such words.

212. In the dial, if 3 is to the South, then 12 is to the East.

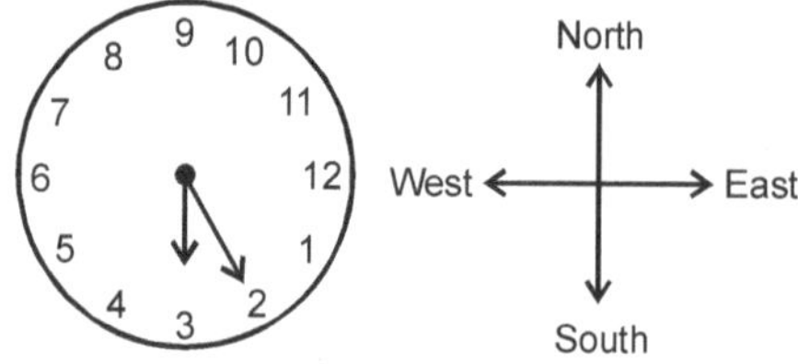

So after 50 minutes the minute hand will point East.

213. None of the options satisfies the given relation. Going through the first three options, is can be seen that none of the options represents the required relationship. Hence, option (d) is the correct answer.

214. The order of the houses is S – Q – P – T – R. Hence, the house which is in the middle is P.

215. The passage mentions two important points about the Asatra Vriksh. The first point is the presence of a fleshy, poisonous fruit. Therefore, option (c) is correct. The second point refers to the discovery of Purol, a promising new antidepressant drug. Option

(a) is incorrect because the passage makes no reference to healthy people. Also, Purol is a new drug and no successes for it have been mentioned as of yet, making option (b) incorrect. Nothing about the treatment for depresssion prior to Purol's discovery is mentioned. Hence, option (d) is incorrect.

216. The passage draws a conclusion regarding the probability of being employed based upon the number of unemployed educated youth and employed educated youth. The passage states that since these numbers are equal, education doesn't enhance the probability of being employed. Such a conclusion can be correctly drawn only if one is aware of the total numbers of educated youth and of uneducated youth. In other words, the percentages of unemployment in educated youth and unemployment in uneducated youth would give the correct basis for a logical comparison between the two. Option (c) provides this data and hence would help in validating the given conclusion. Option (a) is incorrect as, even though the passage tends to draw a general conclusion (probability of employment) based on a specific piece of information (employment in youth), the information in option (a) gives only absolute numbers and not percentages and hence cannot help validate the conclusion. Options (b) and (d) are incorrect as they provide information that has no bearing on the conclusion being drawn.

217. Angle between the hands of a clock is given by,

$$\left|\frac{11}{2}m - 30h\right|$$

$$= \left|\frac{11}{2} \times 20 - 30 \times 2\right|$$

$$= |110 - 60| = 50°.$$

218. The term cabbac is getting repeated and the sequence formed is cabbac, cabbac, cabbac. Hence, the correct answer is option (d) i.e. a, c, b, c, b.

219. The subscript moves in cyclic order and increases by 1.

220. In each term, the alphabetic position of the first letter decreases by three. The differences between the numbers in consecutive terms are in A.P. Hence, the correct answer is option (d) i.e. J15.

221. The alphabetic position of the first letter of each term, starting from the second term, of the of the sequence is two more than that of the previous term. The second letter in all the terms is the same i.e. P. The third letters follow the same pattern as that of the first letters. The last letter remains the same in all the terms i.e. S. So the answer is KPLS.

222. $18 \times 2 + 1 = 37$

$37 \times 2 + 2 = 76$

$76 \times 2 + 3 = 155$

$155 \times 2 + 4 = \boxed{314}$

$314 \times 2 + 5 = 633$

$633 \times 2 + 6 = 1272$

223. 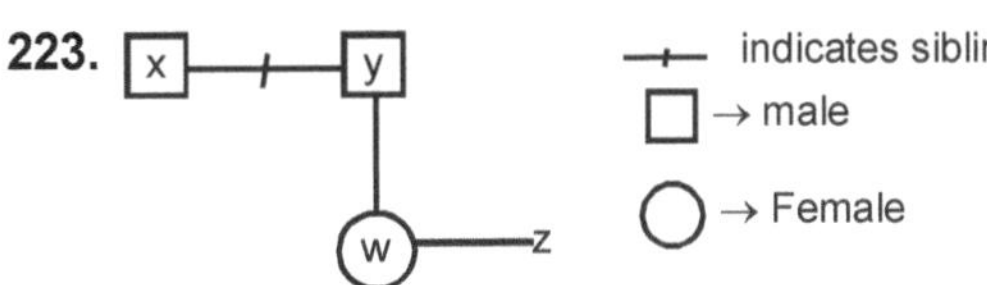

Hence, It is clear that W is the niece of x.

224. 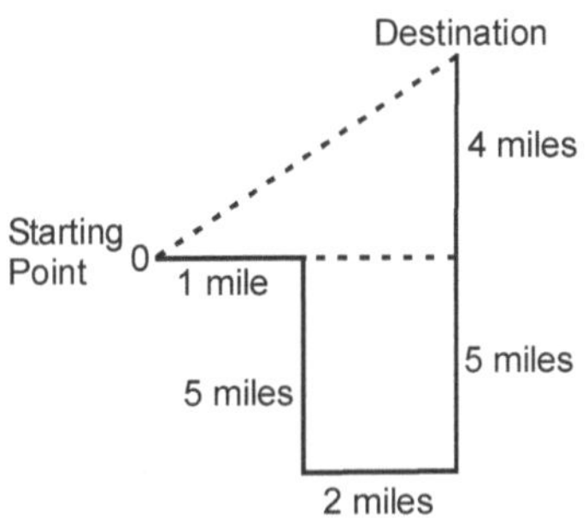

Required Distance = $\sqrt{(1+2)^2 + (4)^2}$

$= \sqrt{3^2 + 4^2} = 5$ miles.

225. $(2 + 6) \times (15 - 5) = 80$

$(7 + 6) \times (9 - 4) = 65$

Similarly, $(16 + 8) \times (13 - 11) = 24 \times 2 = 48$.

226. 10, 26, 74, 218, 654

$10 \times 3 - 4 = 26$

$26 \times 3 - 4 = 74$

$74 \times 3 - 4 = 218$

$218 \times 3 - 74 = 650$

Hence 654 is wrong and should be replaced by 650.

227. Sum of alphabetic position in 1st row

$= 1 + 4 + 1 + 3 + 2 + 2 + 4 + 3 + 3 = 23$

Similarly, sum of digits in 2nd row

$= 1 + 3 + 1 + 2 + 4 + 2 = 13$

Since these are prime numbers, sum of all given and unknown alphabets in 3rd row should also be a prime number.

Thus, 3rd row $= 1 + 2 + 3 + 4 + 4 + 3 + 1 + 1 = 19$ (taking D option as correct).

No other option gives a prime value in such manner, hence correct answer is (d).

228. CDB is 2 triangles ahead of GHF in the CW direction and both GHF, CDB have alphabets in the same order in their respective triangles.

229. HNP & DLP are vertices of 2 different triangles. We are moving anticlockwise from HNP to DLP. This means we have to move ACW from PDA. While in option PHE we are moving clockwise from PDA. So PHE is not possible. Also answer has to start from P. Answer can't be PME because it's a straight line. Hence answer is PJG.

230. Line IO comes after AK in ACW direction. Thus CL must be after EM in ACW direction. By observing closely the 2 options starting with EM, we get the answer as EMDL.

231. BPM is not a triangle. BPM is almost opposite to GN. So FP is almost opposite to AK. Hence answer is FPO.

For questions 232 and 233: *From the given information, we have the following diagram*

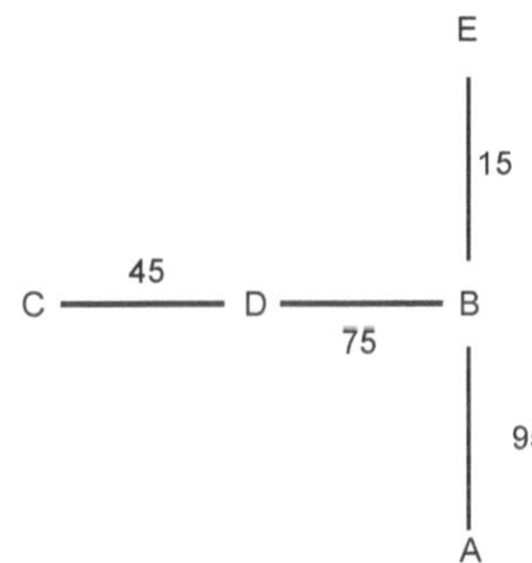

232. D is to the left of B and the person to the north - east of D is E.

233. The total distance travelled is 45 + 75 + 95 + 110

$= 325$ m

234. Inside each side of hexagon, sum of two outer elements is equals to the 7 times of the elements written inside the circle.

i.e., $11 \times 7 = 77 = 53 + 24$

$9 \times 7 = 63 = 43 + 20$

and so on.

Therefore, $54 \times 7 = 378 = 79 + x$

Hence, $x = 299$

Data Interpretation

1. Logic Based DI

2008-10

Directions for Question 1 and 2:

TT School of Management is a management institute involved in teaching, training and research. Currently it has 37 faculty members. They are involved in three jobs: teaching, training and research. Each faculty member working with TT School of Management has to be involved in at least one of the three jobs mentioned above:

- A maximum number of faculty members are involved in training. Among them, a number of faculty members are having additional involvement in the research.

- The number of faculty members in research alone is double the number of faculty members involved in all the three jobs.

- 17 faculty members are involved in teaching.

- The number of faculty members involved in teaching alone is less than the number of faculty members involved in research alone.

- Ten faculty members involved in the teaching are also involved in at least one more job.

1. After some time, the faculty members who were involved in all the three tasks were asked to withdraw from one task. As a result, one of the faculty members each opted out of teaching and research, while remaining ones involved in all the three tasks opted out of training. Which one of the following statements, then necessarily follows:

   (a) The least number of faculty members is now involved in teaching.

   (b) More faculty members are now associated with training as compared to research.

   (c) More faculty members are now involved in teaching as compared to research.

   (d) None of the above.

2. Based on the information given above, the minimum number of faculty members involved in both training and teaching, but not in research is:

   (a) 1   (b) 3

   (c) 4   (d) 5

3. Gujarat Fisheries processes two kinds of prawns, P1 and P2, before exporting. The profit margin is Rs. 20/kg on the P1 variety and Rs. 30/kg on the P2 variety. The prawns must be processed and dried on dried on dryer and on dryer B. The processing time per kg of prawn on the two dryers is as follows:

Type of Prawn	Time Requierd (hours/prawn per kg)	
	Dryer A	**Dryer B**
P1	4	6
P2	5	10

The total time available for using Dryer A is 700 hours and on Dryer B is 1250 hours. Among the following production plans, which of the following combination meets the machine availability constraints and maximizes the profit?

(a) P1 75 kg, P2 80 kg   (b) P1 100 kg, P2 60 kg

(c) P1 50 kg, P2 100 kg   (d) P1 60 kg, P2 90 kg

2009-11

Direction for questions 4 – 6: Answer the question based on the following information.

Rajat is sales manager of Dubin Computers Ltd. and looks after Delhi market. The company sells laptops in India. He is currently trying to select a distributor for coming five years. The distributor ensures that the products are accessible to the customers in the market. Market share of a company depends on the coverage by the distributor.

The total profit potential of the entire laptop market in Delhi is Rs. 5 crores in the current year and present value of next four years' cumulative profit potential is Rs. 15 crores.

The first choice for Rajat is to enter into a long-term contract with a distributor M/s Jagan with whom Dubin has done business in the past, and whose distribution system reaches 55 percent of all potential customers. At the last moment, however, a colleague suggests Rajat to consider signing a one-year contract with other distributors. Distributors M/s Bola and M/s James are willing to be partner with Dubin. Although a year ago M/s Bola's and M/s James's coverage reached only 40 and 25 percent of customers respectively, they claim to have invested heavily in distribution resources and now expect to be able to reach 60 percent and 75 percent of customers respectively. The probability of M/s Bola's claim and M/s James's claim to be true is 0.60 and 0.20 respectively. The knowledge about distributors' coverage will evolve over time. The assumption is that the true level of coverage offered by the new distributors could be discovered, with certainty, through a one-year trial, and this trial will reveal exactly one of the two levels of coverage: for example in case of

M/s Bola - 40 per cent (as it was last year) or 60 percent (as claimed). In addition, it is also assumed that whatever the coverage is for both distributors, it will not change over time. Rajat narrows down on three choices, which are as follows:

Choice 1. Give a five year contract to the familiar distributor M/s Jagan.

Choice 2. Give a one year contract to the new distributor M/s Bola, and base next year's decision to renew contract with M/s Bola on observed coverage for next four years or enter into a four years' contract with M/s Jagan.

Choice 3. Give a one-year contract to the new distributor M/s James, and base next year's decision to renew contract with M/s James on observed coverage for next four years or enter in to a four years contract with M/s Jagan.

4. The expected present value of the five years cumulative profit with choice 3 is:
   (a) Rs. 12.7 crores
   (b) Rs. 10.6 crores
   (c) Rs. 11.7 crores
   (d) None of the above

5. Which of the following statement is TRUE?
   (a) Choice 1 is more profitable than Choice 2
   (b) Choice 3 is more profitable than Choice 2
   (c) Choice 3 is more profitable than Choice 1
   (d) None of the above

6. If the Distributor M/s James claims a coverage of 55% instead of 75% and probability of this claim to be true is 0.70 instead of 0.20 then which of the following statement is true?
   (a) Choice 1 is more profitable than Choice 2
   (b) Choice 2 is more profitable than Choice 3
   (c) Choice 3 is more profitable than Choice 1
   (d) None of the above

2015-17

Directions for questions 7 to 11: Read the following information and Tables and answer the questions.

Bhubaneswar, Chennai, Kanyakumari, Kochi, Mumbai and Vizag are 6 major Indian cities. For some reason people use only a certain mode of transport between a pair of cities. The modes of transport are provided in Table 1, while in Table 2 the distances between different pairs of cities are given. Table 3 provides the speed of the mode of transport and the cost associated with each of them.

Table 1 : Mode of Transport between Cities

Origin	Destination					
	Bhubaneswar	Chennai	Kanyakumar	Kochi	Mumbai	Vizag
Bhubaneswar	-	Ship	Train	Airplane	Bus	Train
Chennai	Ship	-	Train	Ship	Ship	Train
Kanyakumar	Train	Train	-	Train	Bus	Ship
Kochi	Airplane	Ship	Train	-	Train	Airplane
Mumbai	Bus	Ship	Bus	Train	-	Airplane
Vizag	Train	Train	Ship	Airplane	Airplane	-

Table 2 : Distance between Cities (KM)

Origin	Destination					
	Bhubaneswar	Chennai	Kanyakumar	Kochi	Mumbai	Vizag
Bhubaneswar	-	950	700	798	701	1002
Chennai	950	-	999	901	1000	300
Kanyakumar	700	999	-	1100	950	250
Kochi	798	901	1100	-	300	600
Mumbai	701	1000	950	300	-	500
Vizag	1002	300	250	600	500	-

Table 3 : Mode of Transport and Cost

Mode of Transport	KMPH	Cost per KM (in Rupees)
Airplane	60	5
Bus	40	2
Ship	30	1.5
Train	25	2.5

7. For which of the following options, travel time is the least?
   (a) Mumbai - Kanyakumari
   (b) Bhubaneswar-Chennai
   (c) Chennai-Kochi
   (d) Mumbai-Chennai

8. Mr. Ranjith lives in Mumbai and wants to travel to Kochi. However, the train services are on halt due to laying of track for bullet trains across the country. In this scenario, which of the following is the least cost route to reach Kochi?
   (a) Mumbai - Bhubaneswar - Kochi
   (b) Mumbai - Chennai - Kochi
   (c) Mumbai - Kanyakumari - Kochi
   (d) Mumbai - Viza - Kochi

9. A school in Chennai is planning for an excursion tour for its students. They want to show them Kanyakumari, Vizag, and Bhubaneswar, not necessarily in the same order. What is the minimum travel cost (in Rs.) the school should charge from each of the student for the entire tour?
   (a) Rs. 4300
   (b) Rs. 5000
   (c) Rs. 7500
   (d) Rs. 6800

10. Which of the following cities can be reached from Bhubaneswar in least tune?
    (a) Chennai
    (b) Kanyakumari
    (c) Mumbai
    (d) Vizag

11. What is the least cost way to reach to Vizag from Kochi?
    (a) Take a flight from Kochi to Vizag
    (b) Take a ship from Kochi to chennai and then take a train to Vizag
    (c) Take a train from Kochi to Kanyakumari and then take a ship to Vizag
    (d) Take a train from Kochi to Mumbai and then take a flight to Vizag

2016-18

Directions (Q. 12-16) : *Read the following information, graph and table and answer the questions that follow.*

Ellen Inc. is a Mumbai based company which sells five products branded as A, B, C, D and E in India. Anita looks after entire sales of North India working from regional office in Delhi. She was preparing for annual review meeting scheduled next day in Mumbai. She was attempting to analyse sales in Norlh India for the seven year period from 2009 to 2015. She first calculated average sales in rupees of all the five brands and constructed a table exhibiting the difference between average sales of each pair of brands as shown in the following table:

Difference Between Average Sales of Products for the 7 year period 2009-15 in Rs Crores					
	Product A	Product B	Product C	Product D	Product E
Product A	0	214.29	−128.57	142.86	42.86
Product B		0	−342.86	−71.43	−171.43
Product C			0	271.43	171.43
Product D				0	−100
Product E					0

Average Sales of Product A minus Average Sales of Product B

After taking a prirft out of the above table, she attempted to look at the trend of sales and plotted a graph in MS Excel. Later she took a print out of the graph and left for a meeting. While on her way she figured out that due to some printer cartridge problem sales of Product A in 2013, Product C in 2010, and Product D in 2012 were not visible in the graph as reproduced below. Anita had to make some quick calculations to arrive at the information outlined in the following questions:

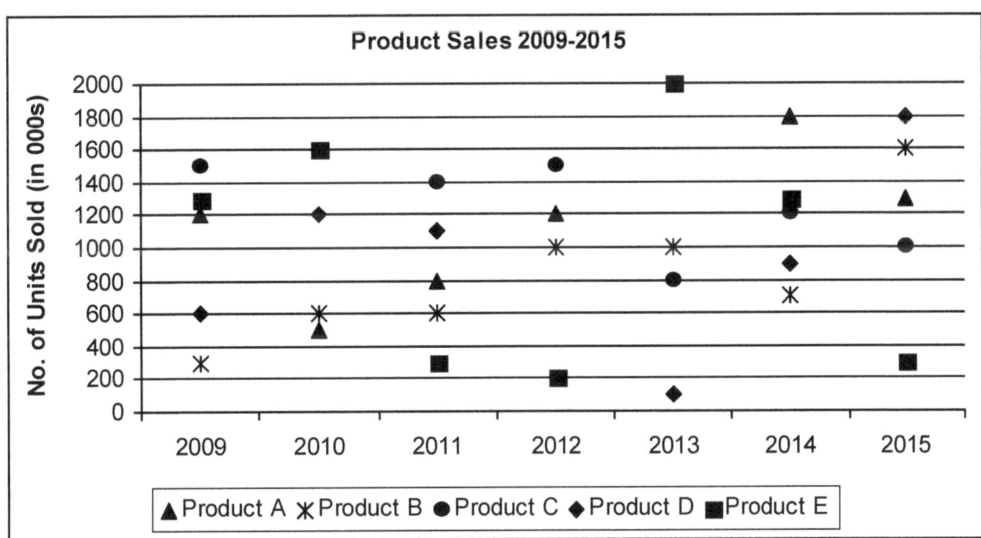

12. What are the sales of Product A in 2013, Product C in 2010 and Product D in 2012?

(a) ₹ 550 Crores, ₹ 800 Crores and ₹ 500 Crores

(b) ₹ 500 Crores, ₹ 700 Crores and ₹ 600 Crores

(c) ₹ 500 Crores, ₹ 800 Crores and ₹ 600 Crores

(d) ₹ 400 Crores, ₹ 800 Crores and ₹ 600 Crores

13. Annual sales average of all products is the least in which year?

(a) 2010   (b) 2011

(c) 2012   (d) 2013

14. Which product has the least average sales for the seven year period 2009-15?

(a) Product A   (b) Product B

(c) Product D   (d) Product E

15. The difference between average sales of products for the period 2009-15 is the least for which pair of products?

(a) Product A and Product B

(b) Product B and Product C

(c) Product C and Product D.

(d) Product D and Product E

16. If Year on Year (YoY) Growth is

$$\left\{\frac{\text{Current Year Sales} - \text{Previous Year Sales}}{\text{Previous Year Sales}}\right\}$$

then the YoY growth of combined sales of all products has suffered maximum decline in which year?

(a) 2010   (b) 2011

(c) 2013   (d) 2015

2017-19

Directions (Q. 17-21) : *After receiving the disturbing news of falling standards the Supreme Council of Confederation of five kingdoms is considering to conduct joint entrance examination for all students in these kingdoms for Vaidya Ratna course. As a first step, it has been decided to review the past five year data about the individual entrance examination of the kingdoms so that an appropriate action can be taken. Study the table given below and answer the questions.*

		Anga	Banga	Chedi	Dwarka	Gandhar
2012	Appeared	5000	4000	2600	6000	4500
	Passed	850	640	468	780	765
2013	Appeared	5500	4500	2500	8000	3500
	Passed	770	810	275	1120	595
2014	Appeared	6000	6500	1900	6500	4500
	Passed	1200	1235	266	715	810
2015	Appeared	5000	5500	2500	5500	4000
	Passed	750	880	275	935	520
2016	Appeared	7000	6000	2000	7000	6000
	Passed	1190	660	400	1330	1200

17. What is the overall pass percentage from Anga kingdom for all the years together?

(a) 16.7   (b) 17.5

(c) 18.7   (d) 15.5

18. In which of the following years, total number of candidates passed from all the kingdoms is lowest?

(a) 2012   (b) 2013

(c) 2014   (d) 2015

19. In which of the following years, Banga kingdom recorded highest pass percentage?

(a) 2012   (b) 2013

(c) 2014   (d) 2016

20. What is the overall pass percentage of all the kingdoms together in the year 2013?

(a) 13.88   (b) 14.88

(c) 15.88   (d) 16.88

21. Highest number of candidates passed are from which of the following kingdoms for all the years together?

(a) Anga   (b) Banga

(c) Gandhar   (d) Dwarka

Directions (Q.22-26): *Given below is the data about Domestic Investment (DI) and Foreign Investment (FI) in 9 different sectors over 5 year period. (In Rs. Crores)*

Sectors	2009		2010		2011		2012		2013	
	DI	FI	DI	FI	DI	FI	DI	FI	DI	FI
Basic Materials	1500	800	1500	1300	2500	1400	2000	900	2500	800
Communication Services	2000	1400	1200	1000	1600	1100	1000	300	500	1200
Consumer Cyclical	1000	1500	1200	1500	1100	3000	500	700	900	1900
Consumer Defensive	1300	1000	700	1600	1500	800	2000	500	1800	1600
Energy	800	1200	500	1400	700	2500	600	1000	1100	500
Financial Services	1800	500	400	2000	1200	1600	'1000	1500	700	1400
Healthcare	2000	3000	600	3000	400	6000	1000	1500	3500	600
Real Estate	500	2000	1000	1500	4000	3000	6000	1500	2000	2100
Technolog	1500	2500	1000	2800	1500	5000	1200	2000	3000	4000

Note: DI = Domestic Investment; FI = Foreign Investment

22. What is the approximate ratio of the total investment in Energy sector to that of Financial services sector?

(a) 1 : 1.2   (b) 3 : 4.5

(c) 1 : 0.5   (d) 2:3.8

23. Absolute difference between the Total DI and Total FI is highest for which sector?

(a) Technology   (b) Healthcare

(c) Basic Material   (d) None of the above

24. In which year the average DI is the highest?

(a) 2013   (b) 2011

(c) 2010   (d) 2009

25. Which Sector has received the 2nd lowest investment from DI for the total period?

(a) Consumer cyclical   (b) Consumer durable

(c) Energy   (d) None of the above

26. What is the approximate ratio of total DI to total FI?

(a) 1 :1.10   (b) 2 : 2.36

(c) 0.75 : 1   (d) 0.75 : 1.5

2019-21

Directions (Q. 27-30): Based on the information given below, answer the questions which follow.

The data on select economic indicators for entire world comprising of 7 regions namely East Asia & Pacific, Europe & Central Asia, Latin America & Caribbean, Middle East & North Africa, North America, South Asia and Sub-Saharan Africa is presented in Table-1 for the year 2017. Further, Table-2 represents the economic indicators for select countries.

GNI refers to Gross National Income (USD Billions), PPP refers to Purchasing Power Parity (USD Billions), POP refers to Population (Millions) and SA refers to Surface Area (Thousands sq. km)

Table-1 : Economic Indicators for Different Regions of World

Regions /Indicators	POP	SA	GNI	PPP
East Asia & Pacific	2,314	24,825	23,538	42,085
Europe & Central Asia	915.5	28,461	20,738	29,793
Latin America & Caribbean	644	20,426	5,282	9,838
Middle East & North Africa	444	11,371	3,220	8,890
North America	363	19,816	20,561	21,291
South Asia	1,788	5,135	3,118	11,693
Sub-Saharan Africa	1,061	24,291	1,543	3,908

Table-2 : Economic Indicators for Select Countries

Countries /Indicators	POP	SA	GNI	PPP
India	1,339	3,287	2,430	9,449
Estonia	1.3	45	24	41
Kyrgyz Republic	6.5	200	7	22
Lao PDR	7	237	16	46
Latvia	2	65	29	53
United States	326	9,832	18,980	19,608

27. Arrange the countries in order of increasing population density (number of people per sq. kms).
    (a) Estonia, Kyrgyz Republic, Lao PDR and Latvia
    (b) Estonia, Latvia, Kyrgyz Republic and Lao PDR
    (c) Estonia, Lao PDR, Kyrgyz Republic and Latvia
    (d) Estonia, Lao PDR, Latvia and Kyrgyz Republic

28. For which of the region, the 'GNI per capita' is closest to that of 'GNI per capita' of world?
    (a) East Asia & Pacific
    (b) Europe & Central Asia
    (c) Latin America & Caribbean
    (d) North America

29. What percentage of world's GNI is represented by combined GNI of India and US?
    (a) 28.98
    (b) 28.42
    (c) 27.45
    (d) 30.19

30. Which region has third lowest difference between 'PPP per capita' and 'GNI per capita'?
    (a) Latin America & Caribbean
    (b) South Asia
    (c) Middle East & North Africa
    (d) East Asia & Pacific

2. Calculation Based DI

2007-09

Directions for Questions 31 to 35: Questions are based on the table below. Unless otherwise stated, all changes (increases, decreases) indicated in the questions must be calculated over the immediately preceding year.

(Rs. Crore)

Sector / Companies	Sales			Salaries & wages			R & D			Profit / Loss		
	2001	2002	2003	2001	2002	2003	2001	2002	2003	2001	2002	2003
Textile (Total)	53145	50184	52616	4296	4360	4315	26	36	39	– 3770	– 3437	– 2441
Indo Rama Synthetics Ltd.	2000	1953	2224	48	50	33	0	0	0	19	41	138
Arvind Mills Ltd.	1970	740	1552	136	46	102	0	0	0	– 499	20	129
Raymond Ltd.	1477	992	1035	160	167	168	0	0	1	332	88	90
Century Enka Ltd.	960	892	946	32	34	35	0	0	1	70	35	58
Pharmaceuticals (Total)	25245	30273	34731	2009	2291	2716	538	820	993	1758	2586	3069
Ranbaxy Laboratories Ltd.	2363	3461	4243	167	197	255	77	192	276	262	478	795
Dr. Reddy's Laboratories Ltd	991	1712	1705	83	121	137	42	102	163	144	460	392
Cipla Ltd.	1064	1401	1573	50	63	73	41	47	0	179	208	248
Glaxosmithkline Ltd.	1143	1197	1242	139	139	139	4	4	4	49	98	172
Electronics (Total)	26944	29323	30022	2164	2218	2323	200	263	247	830	692	– 287
Wipro Ltd.	3137	3487	4048	422	508	642	0	15	28	657	866	813
Infosys Technologies Ltd.	1901	2604	3623	718	1119	1678	17	15	14	629	808	958
Videocon International Ltd.	3244	4974	3602	43	63	53	0	0	0	155	156	– 100
Bharat Electronics Ltd.	1722	1947	2517	394	364	368	89	90	109	155	200	261
Iron and Steel (Total)	54396	55582	70341	5367	5643	6377	73	64	74	– 2983	– 4604	310
Steel Authority of India Ltd.	17320	16624	20665	3135	3255	3728	52	50	55	– 729	– 1707	– 304
Tata Steel Ltd.	8491	8277	10517	922	1098	1218	10	8	16	553	205	1012
Rashtriya Ispat Nigam Ltd.	3585	4200	5185	408	375	406	0	3	0	– 291	– 75	521
Ispat Industries Ltd.	3217	2812	4658	45	40	55	9	0	0	– 312	– 443	83

31. Mark all the correct statements

(a) Wipro's share in total sales of the electronics sector was lower than the share of Tata Steel in total sales of the iron & steel sector in each given year.

(b) From the group consisting of the textiles and the iron & steel sector, there were 5 companies whose salaries & wages as percent of total salaries & wages of their respective sectors increased in 2003 as compared to 2001.

(c) Tata Steel's R & D expenditure in each given year as percent of sales was lower than that of the iron and steel sector as a whole.

(d) From the group consisting of the pharmaceuticals and the electronics sectors, there were 5 companies which experienced a decline in the growth rate of sales in 2003.

32. Mark all the correct statements

(a) Total salaries & wages over 2001-2003 as percent of total sales of the same period had been the highest for the iron & steel sector.

(b) In the year 2003, if all the companies were ranked in descending order in terms of salaries & wages as percent of sales, Videocon International would have been ranked the lowest.

(c) In the year 2002, if all companies were ranked in descending order in terms of R & D as percent of sales, Bharat Electronics Limited would have been ranked third.

(d) Of all companies that made profits in each year during 2001-2003, Wipro registered the highest growth in profits for the period.

33. Mark all the incorrect statements

(a) Salaries & wages of each company in the iron & steel sector were up to 13 times its losses reported in each of the loss-marking years.

(b) Total salaries & wages over 2001-2003 as percent of total sales of the same period for the pharmaceuticals sector had been the minimum.

(c) Total salaries & wages over 2001-2003 as percent of total sales of the same period for only two companies exceeded 20 percent.

(d) Total profits / Total Sales for all the four sectors taken together was higher in 2002 than in 2001.

34. Mark all the correct statements

(a) Tata Steel experienced the highest percent decline in R & D expenditure in any single year during the given period.

(b) Of all companies which incurred R & D expenditure every year during 2001-2003, total R & D expenditure / total sales was the highest for Dr. Reddy's Laboratories Ltd.

(c) During 2001-2003, in terms of sales growth, the best performer in the pharmaceuticals sector fared better than the best performer in the iron & steel sector.

(d) Videocon International Ltd experienced the second largest percent decline in salaries & wages in any single year during the given period.

35. Mark all the situations described in the options below, which when plotted, closely resemble the figure

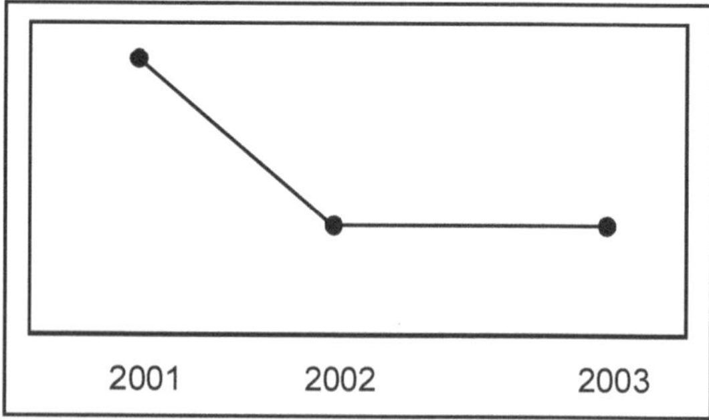

(a) Raymond Limited's share in the total sales of the textiles sector.

(b) Tata Steel's share in the total sales of the iron & steel sector.

(c) Glaxosmithkline Ltd's salaries & wages as percent of sales.

(d) Raymond Limited's profit as percent of sales.

Directions for Questions 36 to 39: The graphs below give vote share and distribution of seats of different parties in election years during the period 1996-2002. Study the graphs and answer the questions, taking into account the following:

i. Independents may be considered as a separate party

ii. Unless otherwise stated, all changes, jumps, gains or losses should be calculated over the immediately preceding election year

iii. For forming government, the party / alliance should obtain majority seats (more than 50%)

Vote Share - 1996

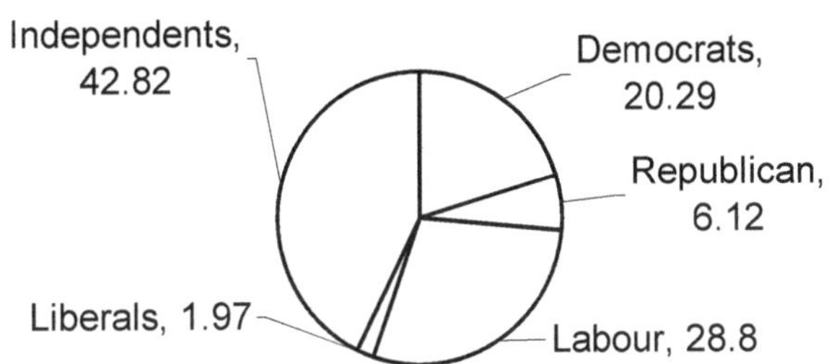

Vote Share - 1998

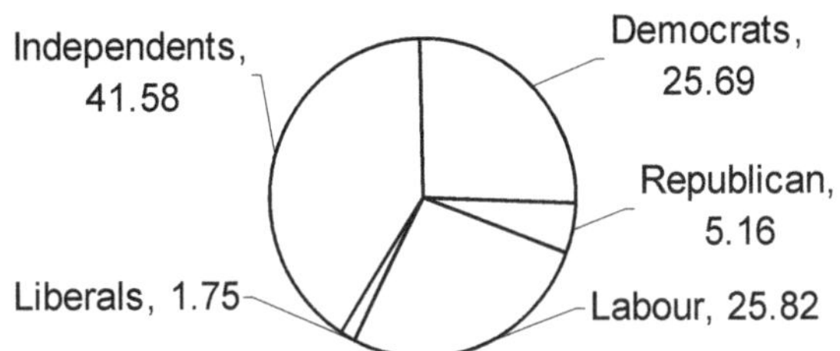

Vote Share - 2000

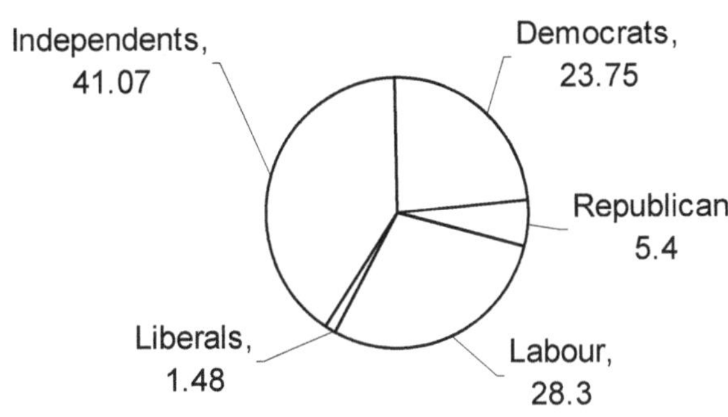

Vote Share - 2002

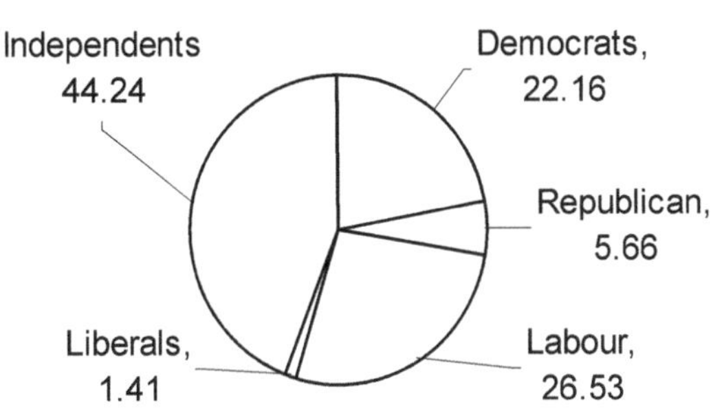

Distribution of Seats - 1996
Total No. of Seats = 510

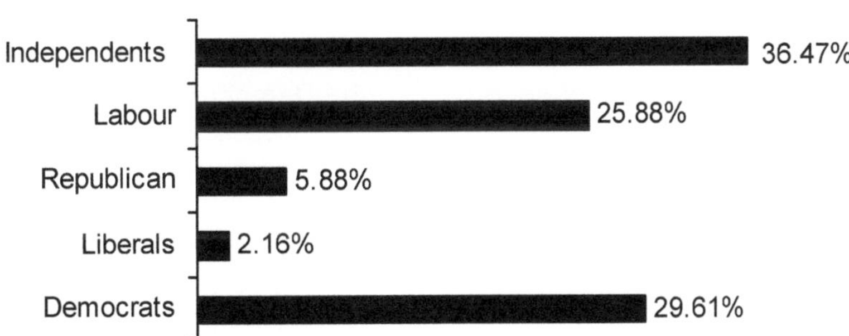

Distribution of Seats - 1998
Total No. of Seats = 570

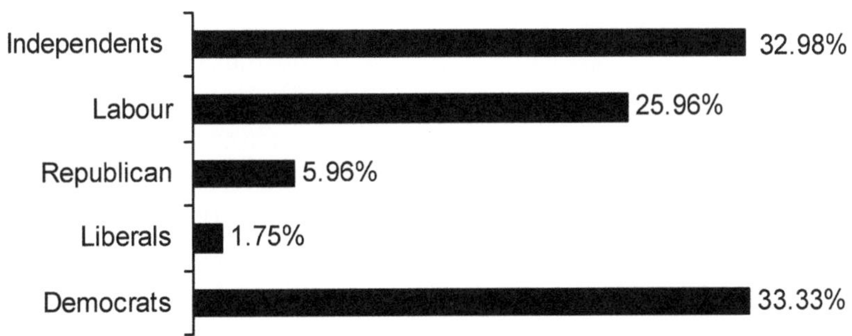

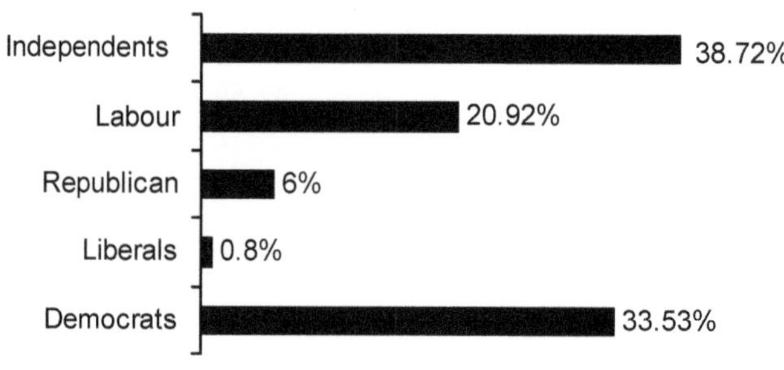

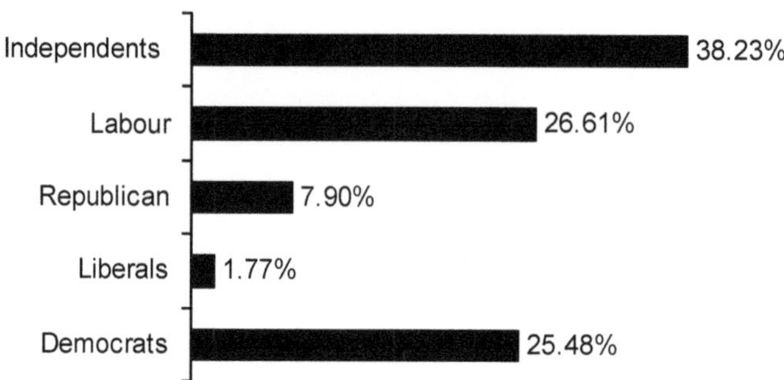

36. Mark all the correct statements

(a) Democrats and Labour together improved their vote share by a larger margin in 1998 over 1996 as compared to the one in 2002 over 1996.

(b) The number of seats lost by Democrats in 2002 elections was less than the number of seats gained by Republicans in the same year.

(c) In 2002, the Independents gained the most both in terms of vote share and number of seats obtained.

(d) If 70% of Independents had joined Labour, they could have formed government in 2002 but not in 1996.

37. Mark all the incorrect statements

(a) In 2002, the percent increase in the number of seats of Liberals and Labour together over 1998 was more than 5 times the increase in the vote share obtained by these parties during the same period.

(b) In the 2000 elections, in terms of vote share, Labour was the major beneficiary of Democrat's loss.

(c) In terms of vote share, it was in the 2000 elections that most number of parties faced a decline in their individual vote shares.

(d) The highest jump in the percentage of seats obtained by any party in any election year over the immediately preceding election year has been smaller than the highest jump in the vote share of any party in any election year.

38. Mark all the correct statements

(a) In terms of vote share, Labour and Liberal parties taken together lost 3.2 percent in 1998 but gained a total of 16 seats in the same period.

(b) Democrats, Republicans and 35% of the Independents could have formed the government only in two election years.

(c) No party increased its vote share in every succeeding election.

(d) In the 2000 elections, as compared to the 1996 elections, Republicans and Democrats taken together, gained more in terms of vote share than in terms of percentage of seats.

39. Mark all the incorrect statements

(a) In the year 2002, in terms of percentage of seats obtained, Democrats and Labour together lost the maximum.

(b) Liberals and Republicans taken together lost both in terms of vote share and the number of seats obtained in the year 2000.

(c) In the 2000 elections, all parties lost in terms of number of seats.

(d) The highest gain in the number of seats for Labour was in the year 2002.

Directions for Questions 40 and 41: The graphs below relate to export and import rates for six regions for the period 1997-2003. Study the graphs and answer the questions.

Annual percentage change in world merchandise trade by region, 1996-03

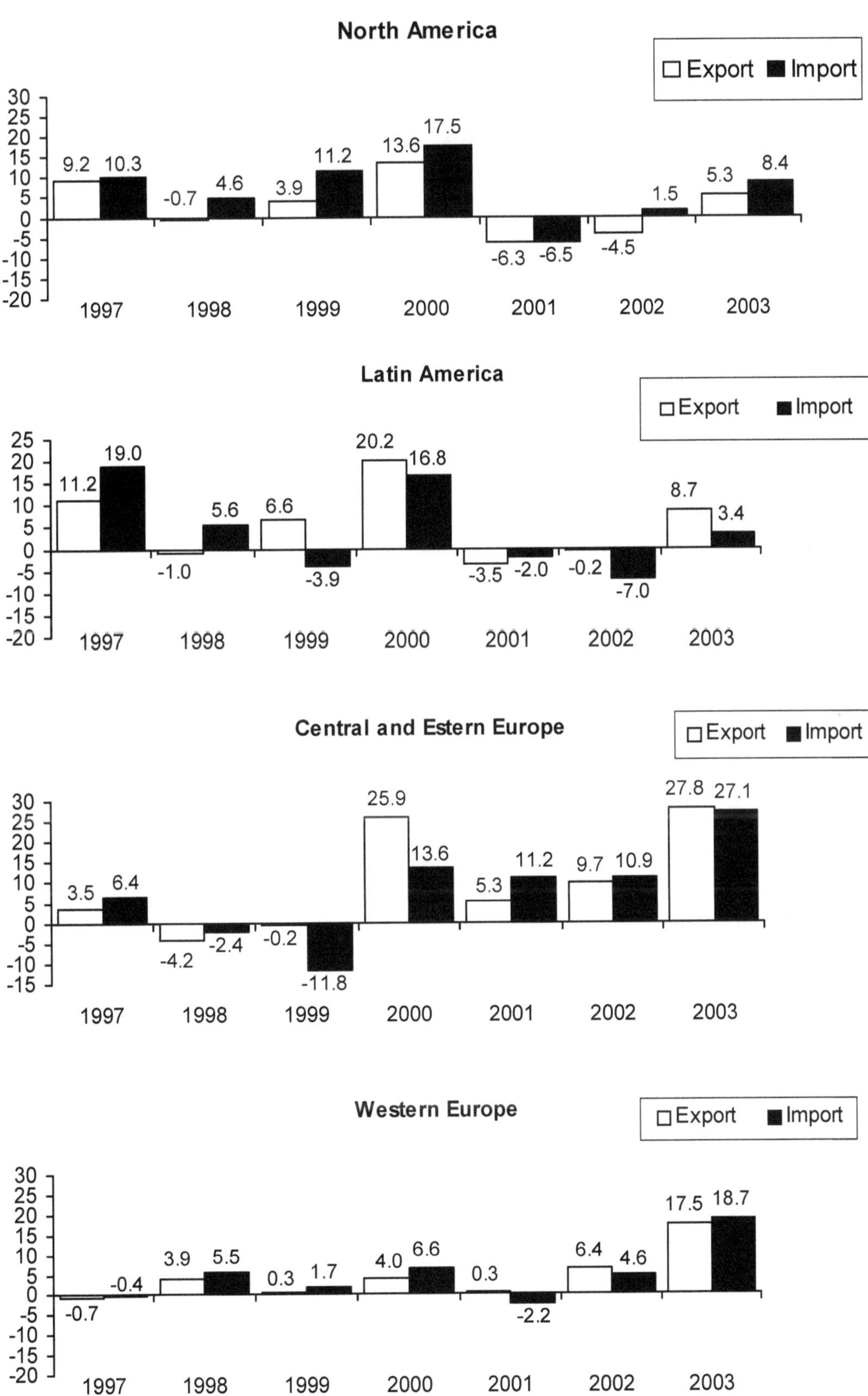

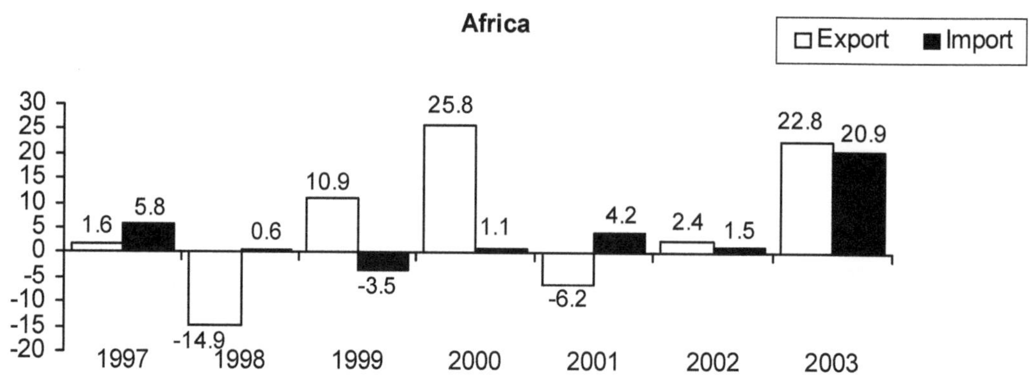

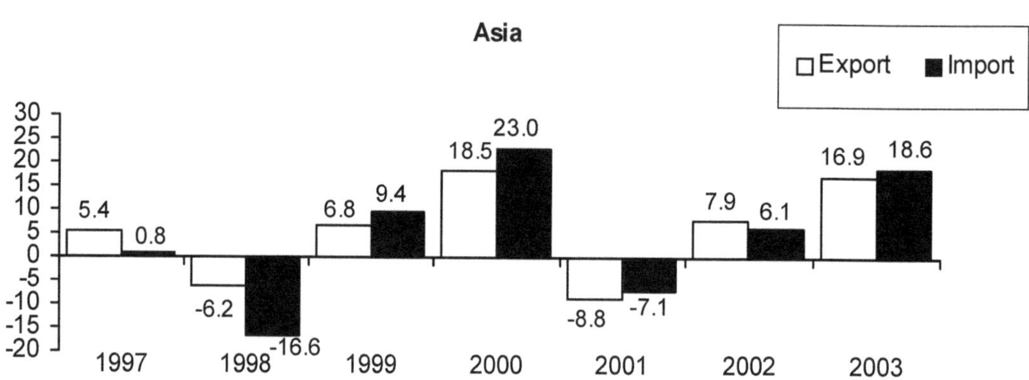

40. Mark all the correct statements

(a) In 1999, if the regions were ranked in descending order based on the gap between the annual percentage change in exports and imports, Central and Eastern Europe would be ranked second.

(b) The unweighted average annual percentage change in exports of the six regions was the highest during 2003.

(c) In 2001, if the regions were ranked in ascending order based on the gap between the annual percentage change in exports and imports, Asia would be ranked second.

(d) The unweighted average annual percentage change in imports of the six regions was the lowest during 1998.

41. Mark all the correct statements

(a) During 2000-2003, North American region experienced the highest average annual percentage change in exports as compared to other regions.

(b) During 1997-2000, Western European region experienced the lowest average annual percentage change in imports as compared to other regions.

(c) Central and Eastern European region experienced the highest jump in percentage change in exports in any year during the sample period.

(d) Asian region experienced the largest slump in imports in any single year during the sample period.

Directions for Questions 42 to 45: Study the graph below and answer the questions.

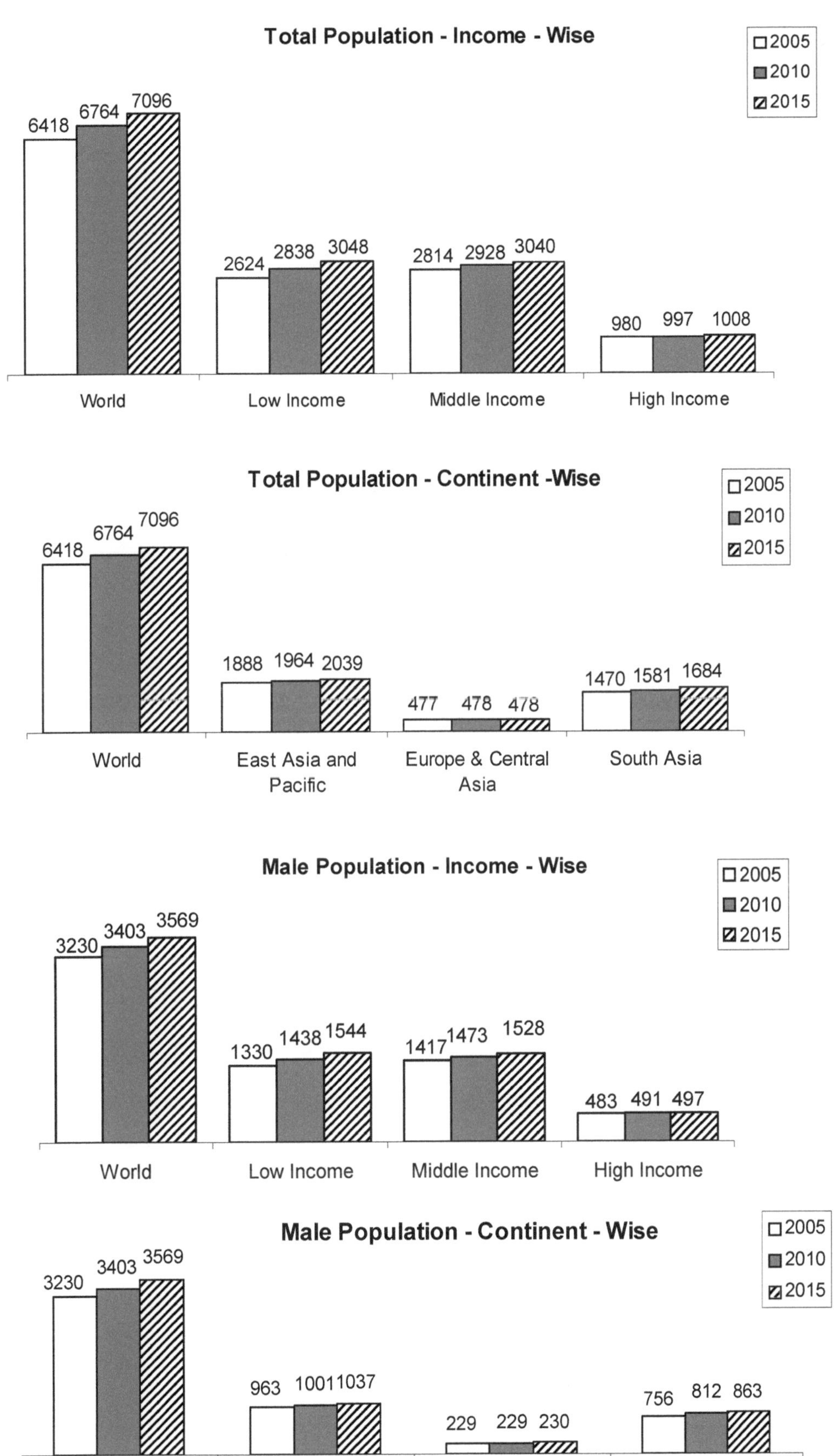

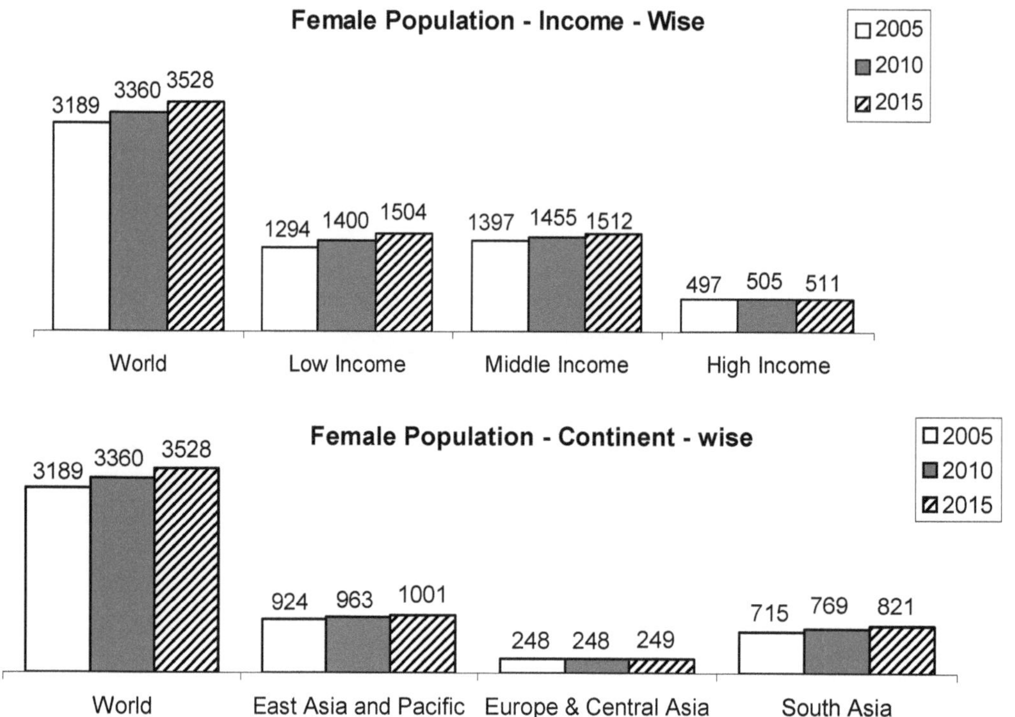

42. Mark <u>all</u> correct statements

(a) The growth rate of female population in the world during the period 2005-2010 is expected to be greater than the growth rate in male population in the world during 2010-2015.

(b) The growth rate of total population in high income countries during 2005-2010 is expected to be greater than the growth rate of male population in East Asia and Pacific during 2010-2015.

(c) During 2005-2010, the growth rate of male population in low income countries is expected to be lower than the growth rate of female population in low income countries.

(d) The growth rate of total world population during 2005-2010 and 2010-2015 is expected to greater than 5 percent.

43. Mark <u>all</u> incorrect statements

(a) The share of high income countries in total world population in 2005 is expected to be not lower than the share of high income countries in total female population during 2005.

(b) The share of Europe and Central Asia in the total male population in all three periods given is likely to be greater than seven percent.

(c) The share of middle income countries in total female population in 2015 is not expected to be lower than the share of low income countries in total world population in 2010.

(d) The share of South Asia in total female population in 2015 is not expected to be lower than the share of South Asia in total world population in 2010.

44. Mark <u>all</u> the correct statements

(a) The share of high income countries in total female population is expected to be larger than the share of these countries in total male population in each year.

(b) Population in high income countries is expected to grow at a faster rate than total world population between 2010 and 2015.

(c) The share of South Asia's female population in total world population is expected to grow at a higher rate than the rate at which the region's female population in total female population will grow between 2005 and 2015.

(d) The growth rate in population of middle income countries is expected to be higher during 2010-2015 as compared to that during 2005-2010, while that of the high income countries is expected to be lower taking the same periods into account.

45. Mark <u>all</u> the incorrect statements
    (a) The share of South Asia in total world population is expected to rise by a larger margin than the share of low income countries in total world population between 2005 and 2015.
    (b) The share of high income countries in total female population is expected to be larger than the share of high income countries in total world population in both 2010 and 2015.
    (c) The average annual growth rate of female population in the East Asia & Pacific region between 2010 and 2015 is expected to be higher than the average annual growth rate of female population in South Asia during the same period.
    (d) As compared to female population, male population in Europe & Central Asia is expected to grow at a higher rate between 2005 and 2015.

2008-10

Directions for Questions 46 and 47:

Space Institute which is involved in training and helping students prepare for Management Institute Entrance Exams, was established on January 1, 2004 with 3, 4, 5 and 6 faculty members in the Logical Reasoning (LR), Data Interpretation (DI), English Language and Quantitative Analysis (QA) areas respectively, to start with. No faculty member retired or joined the institute in the first three months, of the year 2004. In the next four years, the institute recruited faculty members in each of the four areas. All these new faculty members who joined the institute subsequently over the years were 25 years old at the time of their joining the institute. All of them joined the institute on April 1. During these four years, one of the faculty members retired at the age of 60. The following table gives the area-wise average age (in terms of number of completed years) of faculty members as on April 1 of 2004, 2005, 2006 and 2007.

Faculty	2004	2005	2006	2007
LR	49.33	44	45	46
DI	50.5	51.5	52.5	47.8
Englsih	50.2	49	45	46
Quants	45	43	44	45

46. In which year did the new faculty member join as the faculty of English?
    (a) 2004   (b) 2005
    (c) 2006   (d) 2007

47. Professor Sharma and Professor Verma, two faculty members in the LR area, who have been with the Institute since its inception, share a birthday, which falls on 30th November. One was born in 1951 and the other one in 1954. On April 1, 2009 what would be the age of the third faculty member, who has been in the same area since inception?
    (a) 47   (b) 50
    (c) 51   (d) 52

Study the tables below and answer the questions that follow each table:

Table 1: World merchandise exports by Select Countries

Countries	1999	2000	2001	2002	2003	2004	2005
							(Million Dollars)
Cambodia	1129	1389	1500	1923	2118	2798	3100
China	194931	249203	266098	325596	438228	593326	761654
India	35667	42379	43361	49250	57085	75562	95096
Japan	417610	479249	403496	416726	471817	565675	594905
South Korea	143686	172267	150439	162471	193817	253845	284419
Myanmar	1136	1646	2381	3046	2483	2380	2925
Singapore	114680	137804	121751	125177	159902	198637	229649
Thailand	58440	69057	64968	68108	80324	96248	110110
Viet Nam	11540	14449	15029	16530	20176	25625	31625

48. The third highest average annual export growth over the entire period (1999-2005) has been experienced by
    (a) Cambodia   (b) India
    (c) Myanmar   (d) Vietnam

49. Which of the following statement is **not true**?
    (a) During 1999-2000, Myanmar registered the highest annual export growth rate.
    (b) India witnessed second highest annual export growth rate during 2003-2004.
    (c) Cambodia registered third highest annual export growth rate during 2001-2002.
    (d) The change in Thailand's export growth rate from 2000-2001 to 2001-2002 was more than 10 percent.

50. Which of the following statements is **not false**?
    (a) South Korea registered the third lowest export growth rate during the year 2000-2001.
    (b) The sum of the export growth rate of India and Vietnam during 2001-2002 is lower than the export growth rate of China during that particular year.
    (c) Myanmar witnessed maximum number of years of positive export growth rate during the entire period.
    (d) The difference between the export growth rate of China and Japan during 2004-2005 was lower than the export growth rate of Vietnam during that particular year.

51. If we calculate the difference between the highest and the lowest average annual export growth rate experienced by the countries between 1999-2000 and 2004-2005, _____ would get the second rank among all countries.
    (a) South Korea   (b) India
    (c) China   (d) Japan

52. If we calculate the difference between the highest and the lowest average annual export growth rate experienced by the countries year-wise, the difference would be minimum during
    (a) 1999-2000   (b) 2001-2002
    (c) 2004-2005   (d) 2003-2004

Table 2: Industrial Emission Level of SO_2 in Select City Points (1997-2003)

Annual Mean Concentration Range ($\mu g/m^3$)

City	1997	1998	1999	2000	2001	2002	2003
Anpara	54.1	57.9	59.3	64.6	53	30.1	18.7
Bangalore	28.1	37.2	37.9	19.1	19.3	12.1	7.6
Bombay	36	21.7	22.3	11.8	12	9.7	7.4
Calcutta	33.2	40.8	66.9	25.3	21.9	13.3	18.1
Cochin	7.4	4.9	10.5	41.6	24.6	31.5	23.4
Faridabad	37.8	35.7	31.3	37.3	23.1	13.1	9.5
Gajroula	25.8	19.7	25.7	26.6	35.5	41.1	39.3
Madras	26.3	14.2	11.7	20.1	26.1	40.9	26.3
Mysore	32.4	32.1	31	30.7	24.1	20.6	11.2
Nagda	81.8	55.2	26.9	52.6	46.5	36.5	36.5
Pondichery	112.3	114.9	93.3	37.6	17.5	19.8	25.3
Solapur	19.4	17.2	18	18.9	19.4	20.1	19.9
Yamuna Nagar	27.8	32.2	9.8	18.9	22.1	28.6	28.2

53. Which of the following statement is **false**?
    (a) Average annual levels of SO_2 emission for Pondichery over 1998-2003 is approximately 51.40 $\mu g/m^3$.
    (b) Average annual levels is SO_2 emission for Anpara over 1997-2003 is approximately 48.24 mg/μ^3.
    (c) Average annual levels of SO_2 emission for Madras over 1999-2003 is approximately 25.02 $\mu g/m^3$.
    (d) Average annual levels of SO_2 emission for Yamuna Nagar during 1997-2003 is approximately 23.47 $\mu g/m^3$.

54. If the highest average annual level of SO_2 emission among the given cities is noted year-wise, then their difference would be maximum for the following pair of years:
    (a) 1998 and 2003   (b) 1997 and 2001
    (c) 1997 and 2003   (d) 1998 and 2002

55. Which of the following statement is **true**?
    (a) Bangalore in 2003 registered the lowest level of SO_2 emission in relation to the given dataset.
    (b) The difference between the average annual level of SO_2 emission during 1997-2003 for Pondichery and Gajroula is lower than the corresponding average annual level for Mysore.
    (c) The average annual level of SO_2 emission during 1997-2000 for Faridabad is higher than the average annual level for the city for the entire period (1997-2003).

    (d) The sum of the average annual level of SO_2 emission during 1997-2003 for Bombay and Calcutta is lower than the corresponding average annual level for Anpara.

56. If the SO_2 emission level change for the given cities is noted year-wise, the difference would be maximum for which of the following option?
    (a) Cochin and Pondichery during 1999-2000.
    (b) Calcutta and Nagda during 1998-1999.
    (c) Madras and Anpara during 2001-2002.
    (d) Nagda and Pondichery during 1997-1998

57. Which of the following statement is **true**?
    (a) While for Anpara, the SO_2 annual emission level declined consistently during 2000-2001 and 2002-2003, the same increased consistently for Yamuna Nagar between 1998-1999 and 2001-2002.
    (b) During 2002-2003, the SO_2 annual emission level declined for maximum number of cities.
    (c) The absolute declined in annual SO_2 emission level for Bombay during 1997-1998 was lower than the corresponding figure for Faridabad during 2000-2001.
    (d) The number of cities which experienced a decline in their annual SO_2 emission level during 1999-2000 was more than the corresponding figure during 1998-1999.

Table 3: Estimate of some Important Characteristics of Select Industries

Chracteristics	Industry Groups and Year									
	2003-2004					2004-2005				
	A	B	C	D	E	A	B	C	D	E
Number of Factories	1085	916	652	239	403	5252	567	12656	3513	1152
Working Capital (Rs. Lakh)	281895	149780	29662	28921	17729	401385	101370	600909	1884332	480972
Invested Capital (Rs. Lakh)	464446	217230	421005	156983	121030	1862522	557576	4055974	9832961	2438776
Number of Workers	43977	34972	24259	13394	16169	139918	41274	381337	294973	57424
Wages to Workers (Rs. Lakh)	42082	24245	13858	9691	8192	55829	20584	140109	293126	56924
Total Inputs (Rs. Lakh)	1060692	474480	682340	197711	161375	2862201	425601	3209790	14046464	3729397
Depreciation (Rs. Lakh)	23095	14544	27412	12619	12476	145745	43264	277640	636351	140743
Net Value Added (Rs. Lakh)	303706	145547	53441	65180	42672	382864	128489	1062762	3944815	820172
Net Fixed Capital Formation (Rs. Lakh)	4789	604	−12531	−250	464	168539	52500	100152	374612	220840
Profits (Rs. Lakh)	131337	55952	−41744	35223	11756	142098	67338	563800	2735760	615832

58. Which of the following statement is **not false**?

(a) Between 2003-2004 and 2004-2005, the average no. of workers per factory increased for industries B and C, but decreased for A.

(b) The percentage change in no. of workers between 2003-2004 and 2004-2005 is higher in industry A than industry E.

(c) The average no. of workers per factory between industries D and E jointly increased by more than corresponding figure for B.

(d) The average no. of workers per factory C decreased between 2003-2004 and 2004-2005 by 6.

59. Which of the following statement is **true**?

(a) The increase in invested capital per worker for industries B and D over the period is jointly higher than the same for E.

(b) The invested capital per worker has remained second highest for industry D both between 2003-2004 and 2004-2005.

(c) The working capital per worker has been highest for industry B during 2003-2004 but not the lowest during 2004-2005.

(d) The working capital to worker ratio has declined by more than 50 percent in case of industry A over the period, but by less than 50 percent for industry B.

60. Which of the following statement is **false**?

(a) Working capital to invested capital ratio has been second highest for industry E during 2004-2005.

(b) Industry C is the only industry for which the net value added to total input ratio has increased between 2003-2004 and 2004-2005.

(c) If average wage rate is defined by total wage bill divided by number of workers, then for a total number of three industries, average wage rate declined between 2003-2004 and 2004-2005.

(d) Net value added to total input ratio has been highest for industry B during 2004-2005.

61. If gross fixed capital formation is defined as net fixed capital formation plus depreciation, then which of the following statement is **true**?

(a) Gross fixed capital formation has been third highest for industry C during 2004-2005.

(b) Gross fixed capital formation is the lowest for industry E during 2003-2004

(c) The increase in gross fixed capital formation between 2003-2004 and 2004-2005 for industry D is higher than the sum total of the same for industries C and E.

(d) The increase in average depreciations per factory between 2003-2004 and 2004-2005 has been second highest for industry D.

62. Which of the following statement is **false**?

(a) Average profit per factory is second highest for industry A during 2003-2004 but lowest during 2004-2005.

(b) Average profit earned per unit of input cost incurred is second highest for industry A and C both between 2003-2004 and 2004-2005 respectively.

(c) The average profit to the number of workers ratio is second highest for industry D both between 2003-2004 ad 2004-2005.

(d) The increase in average expenditure on input per factory between 2003-2004 and 2004-2005 has been highest for industry D.

Table 4: Major Regional Trade Flows in World Exports (Annual Percentage change)

									(in percentage)
Region	Chemicals			Iron and Steel			Automotive Parts		
	2003	2004	2005	2003	2004	2005	2003	2004	2005
Intra-Europe	22	21	11	27	45	10	24	20	1
Intra-Asia	23	33	19	31	42	22	39	23	12
Europe to North America	19	11	6	-9	81	21	14	8	6
Intra-North America	11	18	14	4	41	23	0	9	6
Europe to Asia	18	24	8	0	16	39	0	9	-1

63. If the region-wise increase in the export growth rate of the three industries during 2003-2004 is noted, ________ would be ranked second.

(a) Intra-North America iron and steel export.

(b) Intra- Europe iron and steel export.

(c) Intra- Asia chemicals export.

(d) None of the above.

64. If the region-wise decline in the export growth rate of the three industries during 2004- 2005 is noted, ________ would be ranked second.

(a) Intra-Europe authomotive parts export.

(b) Intra-Europe iron and steel export.

(c) Intra-Asia chemicals export.

(d) Europe to Asia chemicals export.

65. The difference between the highest and the lowest average export growth rate during 2005 among all three industries and regions is:

(a) 40 percent.

(b) 33 percent.

(c) 29 percent.

(d) None of the above.

66. If the region-wise average export growth rates of the three industries are analyzed, ________ would be ranked second.

(a) Intra-Asia average export of chemicals during 2003-05.

(b) Intra-Europe average export of iron and steel during 2004-05.

(c) Intra-Asia average export of automotive part during 2003-05.

(d) Intra-North America average export of iron and steel during 2003-05.

Table 5: FDI Projects, by Investor/Destination Region

Note: FDI projects 'by source' is defined as 'outflow', while the same 'by destination' is defined as 'inflow'.

(in Number)

Country	World as Destination				World as Source			
	2002	2003	2004	2005	2002	2003	2004	2005
	By Source				By Destination			
Total World	5685	9348	9927	9488	5685	9348	9927	9488
Developed Countries	4903	7735	8443	8057	2746	3867	4144	3981
France	322	475	525	502	140	159	229	385
Germany	473	833	862	919	131	272	251	212
UK	438	709	746	752	326	414	490	541
US	1604	2397	2507	2479	417	589	584	527
Japan	472	878	1025	744	106	133	155	118
Developing Countries	707	1440	1294	1243	2362	4467	4806	4296
China	35	107	96	128	586	1303	1547	1196
South Korea	117	179	169	173	60	110	104	115
India	89	175	199	182	249	452	688	564
Singapore	57	90	103	79	108	154	174	154
Russian Federation	51	119	108	126	199	429	380	479

67. During 2003-04, which pair of developed and developing countries registered the highest growth rate in their number of FDI outflow projects?

(a) France, India

(b) France, Singapore

(c) Japan,Singapore

(d) UK, India

68. An analysis of the annual FDI projects inflow growth rate reveals that the second largest decline has occurred for __________ during __________ .

(a) India, 2004-05

(b) Russian Federation, 2003-04.

(c) China, 2004-05.

(d) Germany, 2004-05.

69. The absolute difference between Singapore's highest growth rate in number of FDI projects inflow in a single year during 2002-05 and UK's highest growth rate in FDI projects outflow in a single year during the same period is:

(a) 19.28 percent.

(b) 15.28 percent.

(c) 21.26 percent.

(d) None of the above.

70. Which of the following statement is **_true_**?

(a) The growth rate of FDI projects inflow in UK was lower than the same in Japan during 2002-03.

(b) The average FDI projects inflow growth rate in Germany between 2002-03 and 2004-05 has been higher than its average FDI projects outflow growth rate over the same period.

(c) The growth rate in FDI projects outflow from the US during 2002-03 has been higher than the corresponding figure for France.

(d) The growth rate in FDI projects inflow to UK during 2003-04 has been lower than the corresponding figure for Japan.

71. Which of the following statement is **_false_**?

(a) The growth rate of FDI projects outflow from the developed countries during 2004-05 has been lower than the same for the world as a whole.

(b) The growth rate of FDI projects inflow to Singapore during 2003-04 has been higher than the same for South Korea during 2004-05.

(c) The average growth rate of FDI projects inflow from developing countries between 2002-03 and 2004-05 has been higher than their corresponding figure for FDI projects outflow.

(d) The growth rate of FDI projects inflow to Singapore during 2004-05 has been more negative as compared to the corresponding figure for Russian Federation during 2003-04.

72. Which of the following statement is **_true_**?

(a) The average growth rate of FDI projects outflow from India between 2002-03 and 2004-05 has been higher than it's corresponding figure for FDI project inflow.

(b) The average growth rate of FDI project outflow from Germany between 2002-03 and 2004-05 has been lower than the average growth rate of FDI project inflow to South Korea over the same period.

(c) The average absolute FDI project outflow from the UK during 2002-05 has been higher than the average absolute FDI project inflow to India over the same period.

(d) Germany is the only country which did not experience a decline in FDI project outflow during 2002-05.

73. Which of the following statement is **_false_**?

(a) The average FDI project outflow from South Korea expressed as a percentage of the total FDI project from the developing countries during 2002-05 was higher than the average FDI project inflow to the UK expressed as a percentage of the FDI project inflow to the developed countries during the same period.

(b) The FDI project outflow from the US expressed as a percentage of the total FDI project outflow from the developed countries in 2002 was higher than the FDI project inflow to China expressed as a percentage of the FDI project inflow to the developing countries in 2004.

(c) The average FDI project outflow from Germany expressed as a percentage of the total FDI project outflow from the developed countries during 2002-05 is higher than the average FDI project inflow to Russian Federation expressed as a percentage of the FDI project inflow to the developing countries during the same period.

(d) The FDI project outflow from India expressed as a percentage of the total FDI project outflow from the developing countries in 2004 is lower than the FDI project inflow to the US expressed as a percentage of the FDI project inflow to the developed countries in 2003.

2009-11

Direction for questions 74 – 79: Answer the questions based on the following table.

Growth Trend in Rail Wagons								
Year	Total wagons	Covered wagons	Open High sided wagons	Open Low sided wagons	Departmental wagons	Special type wagons	Total wagons capacity	Average wagon capacity
	Number	Number	Number	Number	Number	Number	(Million Tonnes)	(Tonnes)
1993	337562	157581	105469	12221	12009	50282	11.79	34.9
1994	312405	138642	101160	11922	11473	49208	11.32	36.2
1995	291360	121946	98795	11507	11185	47927	10.76	36.9
1996	280791	114065	98297	11196	11008	46225	10.62	37.8
1997	272127	106634	98906	10601	10645	45341	10.64	39.1
1998	263981	102217	97616	9726	10569	43853	10.69	40.5
1999	252944	96371	95613	9106	9612	42242	10.7	42.3
2000	234397	86024	91415	7735	8907	40316	10.26	43.8
2001	222193	75768	91099	7999	8443	38884	10.19	45.9
2002	216717	71950	90371	7585	9536	37275	10.09	46.6
2003	214760	68467	90765	7160	10718	37650	9.98	46.5
2004	227752	67870	100211	8882	11388	39401	10.66	46.8
2005	222379	64417	101757	8787	10964	36454	10.6	47.7

74. Find out the TRUE Statement:

    (a) The number of covered wagons expressed as a percentages of total wagons declined consistently from 1993 to 2002, but increased marginally in 2003 as compared to the pervious year level.

    (b) The special type wagons expressed as a percentage of total wagons is maximum during 2003.

    (c) The open high sided wagons expressed as a percentage to total wagons increased during 1994 to 2001, but declined from the 2001 level in 2002.

    (d) None of the above.

75. The special type wagons expressed as a percentage of total wagons were at almost same level during the following pair of years:

    (a) 1995 and 2001

    (b) 1998 and 2004

    (c) 2000 and 2002

    (d) 1993 and 1994

76. The Departmental wagons expressed as a percentage of total wagons was maximum during:

    (a) 2002
    (b) 2005
    (c) 2004
    (d) 2003

77. Find out the LOWEST annual growth rate among the following:

    (a) Annual growth rate of total wagons in 1999

    (b) Annual growth rate of covered wagons in 1998

    (c) Annual growth rate of special type wagons in 2002

    (d) Annual growth rate of total wagons capacity in 2000

78. Find out the FALSE statement:

    (a) The annual growth rate of covered wagons in 1996 was higher than the same in 2000.

    (b) The annual growth rate of open high sided wagons in 1997 was higher than the same in 2003.

    (c) The annual percentage growth rate of average wagon capacity has been maximum in 1999.

    (d) None of the above.

79. Find out the HIGHEST annual growth rate among the following:

    (a) Annual growth rate of total wagons in 1995.

    (b) Annual growth rate of covered wagons in 2002.

    (c) Annual growth rate of open Low sided wagons in 1998.

    (d) Annual growth rate of departmental wagons in 2000.

Direction for questions 80 – 84: Answer the questions based on the following graph.

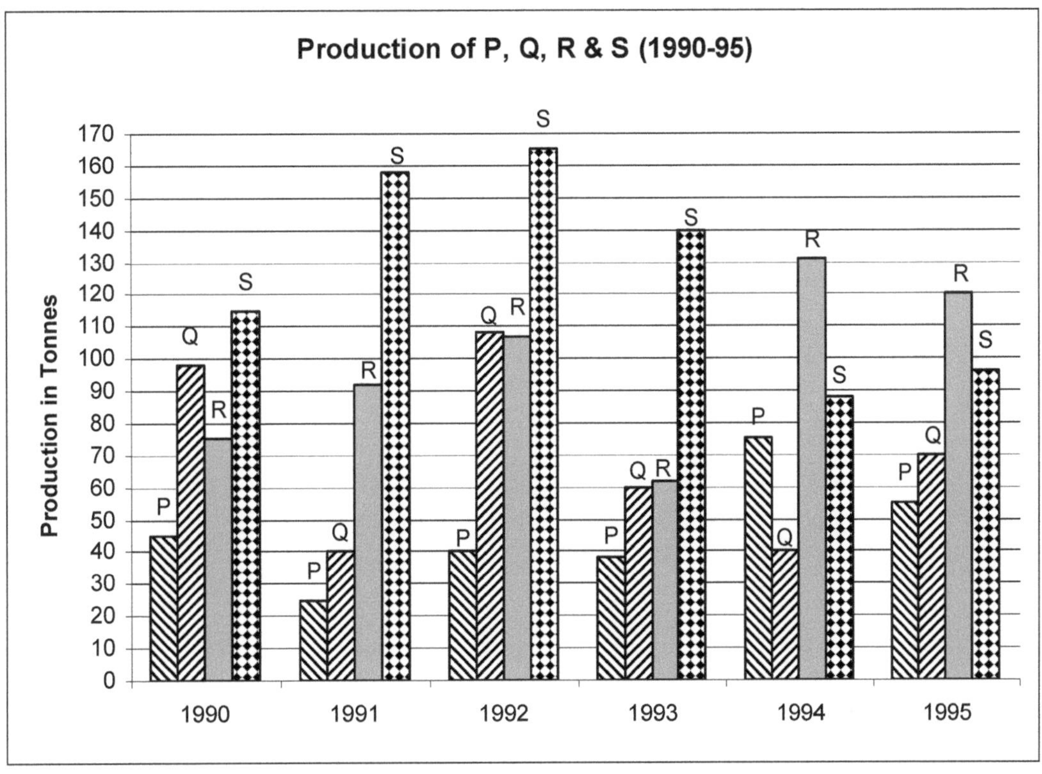

80. In which year the annual growth rate of total production (of all products) is highest?
    (a) 1991   (b) 1992
    (c) 1993   (d) 1995

81. If the stability of the production during 1990 to 1995 is defined as,

$$\frac{\text{Average Production}}{\text{Maximum Production} - \text{Minimum Production}}$$

then which product is most stable?
    (a) Product P
    (b) Product Q
    (c) Product R
    (d) Product S

82. If four products P, Q, R and S shown in the graph are sold at price of Rs.9, Rs.4, Rs.13 and Rs.3 respectively during 1990-1995, then the total revenue of the all the products is lowest in which year?
    (a) 1991
    (b) 1992
    (c) 1993
    (d) None of the above

83. Individual revenue of P, Q, R and S for the entire period (1990-1995) is calculated based on the price of Rs.9, Rs.4, Rs.13 and Rs.3 respectively. Which product fetches the lowest revenue?
    (a) Product P
    (b) Product Q
    (c) Product R
    (d) Product S

84. Four products P, Q, R and S shown in the graph are sold at price of Rs.9, Rs.4, Rs.13 and Rs.3 respectively during 1990-1995. Which of the following statements is TURE?
    (a) Product R fetches second highest revenue across products in 1991.
    (b) Sum of revenue of P, Q and S is more than the revenue of R in 1994.
    (c) Cumulative revenue of P and Q is more than the revenue of S in 1993.
    (d) None of the above

Direction for questions 85 – 89: Answer the questions based on the following table:

State-wise FDI Inflow								
State	**2000**	**2001**	**2002**	**2003**	**2004**	**2005**	**2006**	**2007**
Andhra Pradesh	3707	34522	14566	8708	16256	15819	17311	47828
Bihar	659	5586	52	346	1878	10849	58002	40107
Gujarat	14193	10889	10781	10020	32043	29648	82793	72093
Haryana	3414	1201	800	834	8345	2685	5577	16095
Karnataka	3299	3553	4101	2164	14071	10904	15066	71844
Kerala	376	535	197	70	199	290	600	1141
Madhya Pradesh	7099	2726	2472	13891	17761	56138	58679	131267
Maharashtra	37275	14442	9780	21440	6909	10675	24480	60864
Orissa	6144	2342	897	3477	17718	45565	38255	97185
Punjab	13657	2184	11274	627	1747	3894	6340	9228
Rajasthan	4204	3236	2823	710	1096	2162	5077	10034
Tamil Nadu	5906	4066	2867	1424	2622	54107	11365	19850
Uttar Pradesh	5160	1936	2899	2419	3483	24058	37405	48622
West Bengal	6706	2111	1933	8584	7569	13994	12028	51830

85. Mark the HIGHEST FDI inflow growth rate among the following:

   (a) Annual FDI inflow growth rate in Gujarat in 2006.

   (b) Annual FDI inflow growth rate in Kerala in 2004.

   (c) Annual FDI inflow growth rate in Haryana in 2007.

   (d) Annual FDI inflow growth rate in Punjab in 2004.

86. Mark the LOWEST FDI inflow growth rate among the following:

   (a) Annual FDI inflow growth rate in West Bengal in 2001.

   (b) Annual FDI inflow growth rate in Kerala in 2002.

   (c) Annual FDI inflow growth rate in Maharashtra in 2004.

   (d) Annual FDI inflow growth rate in Haryana in 2005.

87. Mark the TRUE statement:

   (a) The decline in annual FDI growth rate for Gujarat in 2001 was smaller than the corresponding figure for Karnataka in 2005.

   (b) The annual growth rate of FDI in Kerala in 2001 was greater than the corresponding figure for Uttar Pradesh in 2004.

   (c) The annual growth rate of FDI in Kerala in 2005 was greater than the corresponding figure for Punjab in 2007.

   (d) None of the above.

88. Mark the FALSE statement:

   (a) The absolute annual increase in FDI inflow in Bihar in 2001 is lower than the corresponding figure for Rajasthan in 2007.

   (b) The annual FDI growth rate in West Bengal in 2006 was higher than the corresponding figure for Uttar Pradesh in 2003.

   (c) The absolute annual increase in FDI inflow in Madhya Pradesh in 2004 is lower than the corresponding figure for Maharashtra in 2005.

   (d) None of the above

89. Mark the TRUE statement:

   (a) The absolute annual increase in FDI inflow in Haryana in 2006 is lower than the corresponding figure for Punjab in 2007.

   (b) Among all States, in 2003 the absolute annual increase in FDI inflow was maximum for Madhya Pradesh.

   (c) The absolute annual increase in FDI inflow in Bihar in 2003 is higher than the corresponding figure for Karnataka in 2001.

   (d) The FDI inflow in Kerala over 2002 to 2007 was consistently the lowest across all the states.

Direction for questions 90 – 94: Answer the questions based on the following table.

World Merchandise Exports by Regions and Selected Economics							
Region / Country	**2000**	**2001**	**2002**	**2003**	**2004**	**2005**	**2006**
World	6454000	6187000	6487000	7580000	9210000	10472000	12083000
North America	1224975	1147545	1106240	1162965	1324235	1479330	1678315
Canada	276635	259858	252394	272739	316548	359399	389538
US	781918	729100	693103	724771	818520	905978	1038278
Latin America	195800	188600	190700	219100	284700	355000	429900
Argentina	26341	26543	25650	29566	34576	40351	46569
Brazil	55086	58223	60362	73084	96475	118308	137470
Europe	2633930	26545555	2839440	3386490	4051000	4396895	4962980
Germany	551818	571645	615831	751560	909887	970915	1111969
UK	285429	272715	280195	305627	347493	384477	448291
Africa	147800	137400	141100	176400	229900	299500	363300
Nigeria	20975	17261	15107	22605	31148	42277	52000
South Africa	29983	29258	29723	36482	46146	51626	58412
Asia	1837300	1674400	1807800	2138300	2653100	3059000	3577700
China	249203	266098	325596	438228	593326	761953	968936
India	42379	43361	49250	58963	76427	99376	120254
Japan	479249	403496	416726	471817	565675	594905	649931

90. Mark the LOWEST percentage among the following:

(a) Export from Canada expressed as a proportion of export from North America in 2000.

(b) Export from Germany expressed as a proportion of export from Europe in 2004.

(c) Export from China expressed as a proportion of export from Asia in 2004.

(d) Export from Japan expressed as a proportion of export from Asia in 2003.

91. Identify the TRUE statement:

(a) The annual export growth rate of Argentina in 2003 was lower than the corresponding figure for US in 2006.

(b) The annual export growth rate of Africa in 2004 was lower than the corresponding figure for Latin America during the same period.

(c) The annual export growth rate of US in 2004 was lower than the corresponding figure for Canada in 2005.

(d) None of the above.

92. Mark the HIGHEST annual growth rate among the following:

(a) Annual growth rate of World export in 2005.

(b) Annual growth rate of North American export in 2004.

(c) Annual growth rate of India's export in 2002.

(d) Annual growth rate of Japan's export in 2003.

93. Mark the FALSE statement:

(a) The exports from Argentina expressed as a proportion of export from Latin America in 2001 was greater than the exports from Nigeria expressed as a proportion of exports from Africa in 2004.

(b) The exports from UK expressed as a proportion of exports from Europe in 2000 is lower than the exports Argentina expressed as a proportion of export from Latin America in 2005.

(c) The annual export growth rate of Argentina in 2004 was higher than the corresponding figure for Asia in 2005.

(d) The exports from South Africa in 2001 expressed as a proportion of exports from Africa is lower than the exports from China expressed as a proportion of expressed from Asia in 2003.

94. Mark the FALSE statement:

(a) The absolute annual increase in exports from Asia in 2003 was less than the corresponding figure in 2006.

(b) The absolute annual increase in exports from Germany in 2001 was higher than the corresponding figure for US in 2003.

(c) The absolute annual increase in exports from Brazil in 2005 was higher than the corresponding figure for Japan in 2002.

(d) None of the above.

Direction for the questions 95 – 99: Answer the questions based on the following two graphs, assuming that there is no fixed cost component and all the units produced are sold in the same year.

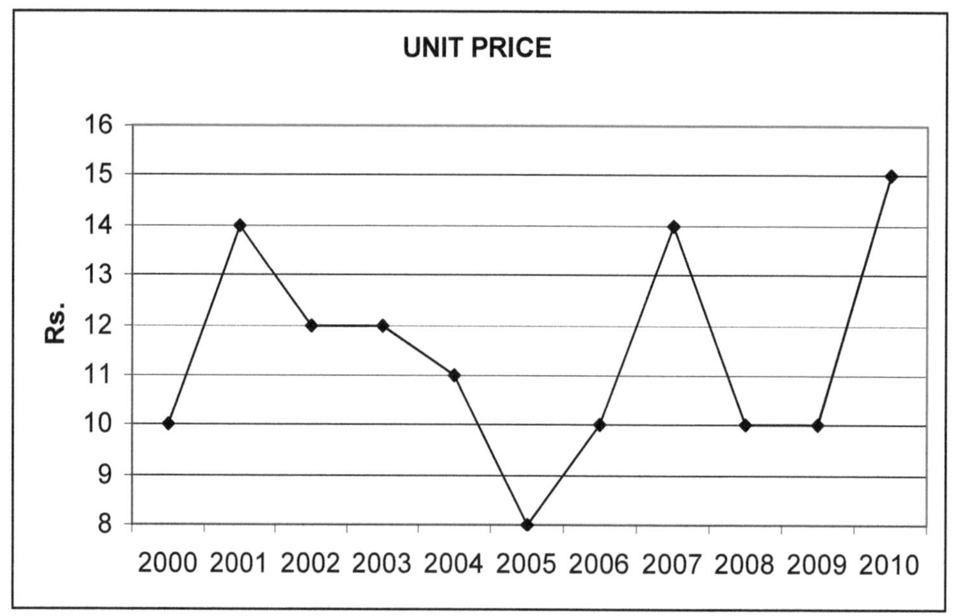

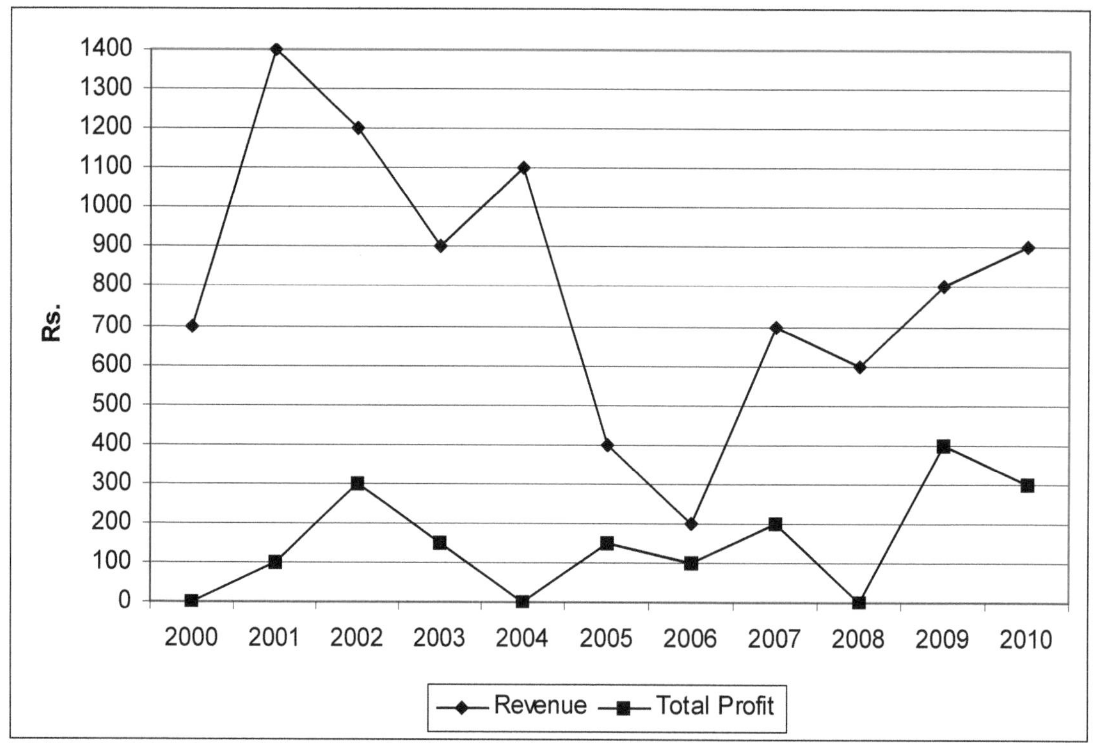

95. In which year per unit cost is HIGHEST?

   (a) 2002   (b) 2001

   (c) 2005   (d) 2007

96. What is the approximate average quantity sold during the period 2000-2010?

   (a) 64 units   (b) 70 units

   (c) 77 units   (d) 81 units

97. If volatility of a variable during 2000-2010 is defined as $\dfrac{\text{Maximum Value} - \text{Minimum Value}}{\text{Average Value}}$, then which of the following is TRUE?

   (a) Price per unit has highest volatility

   (b) Cost per unit has highest volatility

   (c) Total profit has highest volatility

   (d) Revenue has highest volatility

98. If the price per unit decreases by 20% during 2000-2004 and cost per unit increases by 20% during 2005-2010, then during how many number of years there is a loss?

(a) 3 years   (b) 4 years

(c) 5 years   (d) 7 years

99. If the price per unit decreases by 20% during 2000-2004 and cost per unit increases by 20% during 2005-2010, then the cumulative profit for the entire period 2000-2010 decreases by:

(a) Rs.1650   (b) Rs.1550

(c) Rs.1300   (d) Rs.1250

2010-12

Directions for questions 100 – 105: Answer the questions based on the following graphs

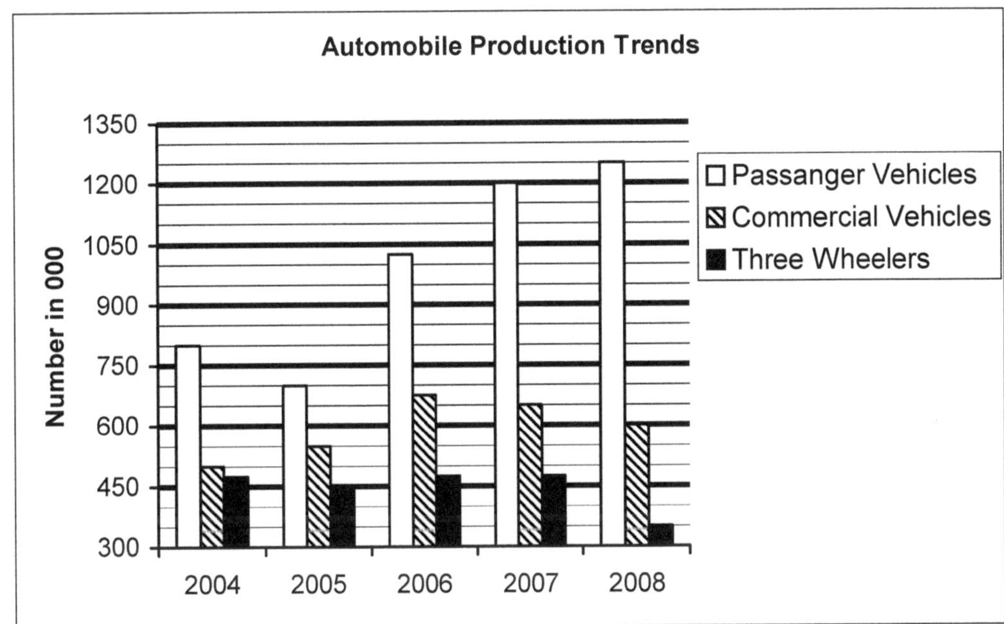

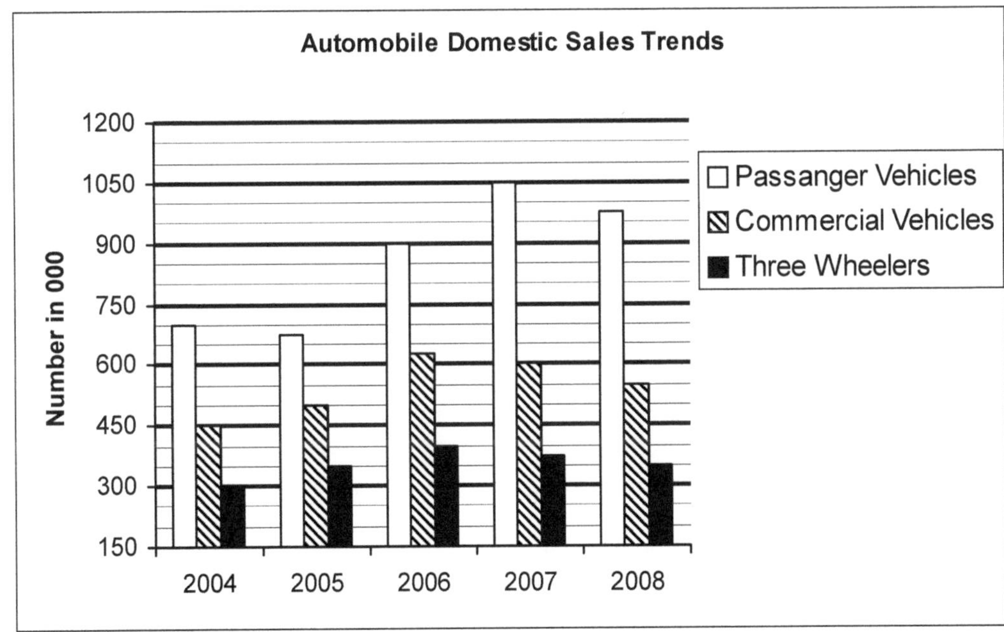

100. Which of the following year exhibited highest percentage decrease over the preceding year in the automobile production?

(a) 2005   (b) 2006

(c) 2007   (d) 2008

101. Assuming whatever that is not sold domestically was exported, then which year has registered highest growth in exports of automobiles?

(a) 2005   (b) 2006

(c) 2007   (d) 2008

102. If the ratio of the domestic sale price of a commercial vehicle, a passenger vehicle, and a three wheeler is 5:3:2 then what percent of earnings (approximately) is contributed by commercial vehicle segment to the overall earnings from domestic sales during the period 2004-2008?

(a) 45%   (b) 43%

(c) 11%   (d) 27%

103. For which year were the domestic sales of automobiles closest to the average (2004-2008) domestic sales of automobiles?

(a) 2005   (b) 2006

(c) 2007   (d) 2008

104. Which of the following years exhibited highest percentage increase over the preceding year in the automobile sales?

(a) 2005   (b) 2006

(c) 2007   (d) 2008

105. The ratio between absolute increase in domestic sales over preceding year and absolute increase in production over the preceding year is highest during which year?

(a) 2005

(b) 2006

(c) 2007

(d) 2008

Directions for questions 106– 108: Answer the questions based on the following information.

The table below gives the details of money allocation by three Mutual funds namely, Alpha Beta and Gama. The return for each fund depends on the money they allocate to different sectors and the returns generated by the sectors. The last column of the table gives return for each of the sectors for a one year period.

Sl. No	Sectors	Money Allocation			Sectoral Return
		Alpha	Beta	Gama	
1	Automobile	1.49	5.98	0.00	5%
2	Chemicals	3.01	2.01	5.00	12%
3	Communication	7.01	5.00	4.00	-5%
4	Construction	1.51	0.00	6.01	15%
5	Diversified	7.48	6.99	9.50	11%
6	Energy	9.99	17.5	20.50	21%
7	Engineering	9.01	10.99	15.50	8%
8	Financial	25.98	24.00	17.01	6%
9	FMCG	14.50	2.00	2.00	25%
10	Health Care	5.98	0.00	3.00	18%
11	Metals	0.00	10.99	9.98	-8%
12	Services	4.50	7.04	4.00	10%
13	Technology	5.51	7.50	3.50	-2%
14	Textiles	4.03	0.00	0.00	17%
		100.00	100.00	100.00	

106. Which fund has received more return per rupee of investment for one year period?

(a) Alpha

(b) Beta

(c) Gama

(d) Both Beta and Gama gives same return

107. If the allocation of money by the fund managers to different sectors is based on the internal ranking (i.e. Sector with 1st rank gets highest allocation). Sectors with 0 allocation of money should be considered as 14th rank irrespective of the number of sectors in that category. In the light of these examine the following statements:

I.   Automobile is ranked by both Alpha and Beta as same

II. Financial is most favoured by all three Mutual Funds

III. Services is ranked by all three Mutual Funds within top 9 ranks

Select the best option:

(a) Statement I and II are correct

(b) Statement I and III are correct

(c) Statement I alone is correct

(d) Statement III alone is correct

108. Ms. Hema invested Rs.10.00 lakhs in fund Gama in the beginning of the period. What will be the value of the investment at the end of 1 year period?

(a) Approximately Rs.10.40 lakhs

(b) Approximately Rs.10.95 lakhs

(c) Approximately Rs.11.24 lakhs

(d) Approximately Rs.11.38 lakhs

Directions for questions 109 – 113: Answer the questions based on the following Table

Crops	Area under production ('000 Hectare)			Quantity of Production ('000 Tonne)		
	2006	**2007**	**2008**	**2006**	**2007**	**2008**
Cereals						
Rice	107	108	110	153	170	190
Jowar	598	673	720	173	368	380
Bajra	4992	4890	4800	2172	3421	3350
Maize	1004	1020	1101	1102	1116	1182
Millets	16	16	15	5	4	4
Pulses						
Moong	799	751	725	130	270	260
Urd	124	101	102	31	30	35
Moth	1228	1151	1199	149	191	250
Arhar (Tur)	20	19	19	13	9	9
Chaula	126	110	101	26	45	30
Other Pulses	5	5	5	2	3	2
Oil Seeds						
Sesamum	422	273	280	63	89	70
Groundnut	317	302	298	491	396	374
Soyabean	744	641	650	856	771	799
Sunflower	472	350	325	880	751	699
Castor Seed	106	79	80	135	104	106

Note: Yield (or Productivity) is defined as quantity produced per hectare.

109. What is the ratio between Jowar yield (2007) and Soyabean yield (2008)?

(a) 1.00 : 2.10

(b) 1.21 : 1.89

(c) 0.89 : 2.09

(d) 0.78 : 1.61

110. Top 3 crops by yield in the year 2006 are:

(a) Castor Seed, Groundnut, Maize

(b) Sunflower, Groundnut, Rice

(c) Castor Seed, Sunflower, Rice

(d) Bajra, Maize, Caster Seed

111. Bottom 3 crops by yield in the year 2008 are:

(a) Moth, Sesamum, Millets

(b) Moong, Moth, Millets

(c) Arhar, Urd, Moong

(d) Moong, Sesamum, Chaula

112. Examine the following statements:

I. Total productivity of pulses has gone down over the years

II. Maize is the most stable cereal in terms of productivity over the years

III. Percentage growth in area and quantity of production is highest in the case of Jowar during the entire period.

Select the best option:

(a) Statement I and II are correct

(b) Statement I and III are correct

(c) Statement II and III are correct

(d) Statement III alone is correct

113. Examine the following statements:

I. Over the period total cereal productivity has gone up

II. Area, Production and yield of the total oil seeds is on decline

III. Though there is a decline in the area under Urd production but the quantity of production and yield has gone up over the years.

Select the best option:

(a) Statement I and III are correct

(b) Statement I and II are correct

(c) Statement I alone is correct

(d) Statement III alone is correct

Directions for questions 114 – 118: Study the following table carefully and answer the questions

Oil Sales by Type of Use and Production Loss					(MT)
	Oil Used				
	Metro City				Oil Production Loss
Year	House Hold	Transport	Industrial	Suburban	
1996	10	700	1794	104	650
1997	16	920	1864	114	732
1998	22	1012	1732	104	834
1999	22	1054	1668	90	1102
2000	20	1092	1700	108	702
2001	22	1320	1752	168	492
2002	14	1854	1618	172	386
2003	6	2046	1270	178	444
2004	16	2118	1480	208	506
2005	4	2252	1132	230	1032
2006	4	2384	1228	210	1142
2007	8	2096	1672	254	1454
2008	0.2	2240	1646	266	1428

Note: Whatever is produced in a year is either used or lost in the production in the same year.

114. During which year the Oil used for House Hold as a percentage of Total Oil Used is highest?

(a) 1998

(b) 1999

(c) 2000

(d) 2001

115. During which year the 'Oil Production Loss' as a proportion of 'Total Oil Produced' is the lowest?

(a) 2002

(b) 2003

(c) 2004

(d) 2006

116. During which year use of oil by 'Suburban' as a proportion of Total Oil Used' was the highest?

(a) 2005

(b) 2006

(c) 2007

(d) 2008

117. For how many number of years the growth rate in 'Production of Oil' is more than the growth rate in 'Total Oil Used'?

(a) 3 years

(b) 4 years

(c) 5 years

(d) 6 years

118. Which of the below statements are true, based on the data in the above table?

(a) Oil used for 'Transport' purpose by Metro City is increasing every year since 1996.

(b) Oil used for 'Industrial' purpose by Metro City increasing every year since 1996.

(c) Oil used by 'Suburban' is increasing every year since 2000.

(d) 'Total Oil Produced' is increasing every year since 2003.

Directions for questions 119 – 122: Study the information below and answer the questions.

The following table contains the pre and post revision pay structure of a Government department:

Components	Pre-revised			Revised		
	Minimum	Maximum	Annual Increment	Minimum	Maximum	Grade Pay
Pay Scale						
	Rs. 8000	Rs. 13500	Rs. 275	Rs. 15600	Rs. 39100	Rs. 5400
	Rs. 12000	Rs. 16500	Rs. 375	Rs. 15600	Rs. 39100	Rs. 7600
	Rs. 16400	Rs. 20000	Rs. 450	Rs. 37400	Rs. 67000	Rs. 8900
	Rs. 18400	Rs. 22400	Rs. 500	Rs. 37400	Rs. 67000	Rs. 10000
Dearness Allowance (DA)	78%			28%		
House Rent Allowance (HRA)	30% of Basic pay			30% of Basic pay		
Transport Allowance (TA)	Rs. 800			Rs. 3200 + Rs. 3200* DA		

The revision has been done based on the following terms:

- In pre-revised pay scale, the basic pay is the sum of the minimum pay in the appropriate pay scale and the admissible increment. After revision, the basic pay is the sum of minimum pay in the appropriate pay scale and the respective grade pay and the admissible increments.

- Annual increment of 3% of the basic pay (on a compounded basis) is paid under the revised pay rules.

- Monthly Dearness Allowance (DA) is calculated as percentage of basic pay.

- In pre-revised pay scales, the increment was given after the completion of each year of service, but, after revision annual increments are given only in the month of July every year and there should be a gap of six months between the increments. The employees who had joined the department in the month of September, October, November and December are given an increment at the time of revised pay fixation in September, 2008.

- The revised pay is applicable from 1st September, 2008.

119. Abhijit joins the department on November 10, 2006 in the pay scale of Rs. 18400-500-22400 with the pay of Rs. 18400 plus 2 increments. What is his basic salary, after revision, on August 1, 2009?

  (a) Rs. 53010

  (b) Rs. 53349

  (c) Rs. 54950

  (d) Rs. 54903

120. Nitin joined the department on November 24, 2004 in the pay scale of Rs. 8000-275-13500, at the minimum pay. At the time of pay revision, due to some error, his pay was fixed at the base (minimum) of the corresponding revised pay scale. The loss in his total emoluments for September 2008, due to this error, will be:

  (a) Rs. 3915

  (b) Rs. 3982

  (c) Rs. 4164

  (d) No loss.

121. Sunitha joined the department at the basic pay of Rs. 13500 in the pay scale of Rs. 12000-16500. On completion of her four years of service in December, 2008, she was promoted to the next higher pay scale, the percentage increase in her gross salary is:

  (a) 53%

  (b) 43%

  (c) 50%

  (d) 60%

122. Dinesh joined on July 1, 2008 in the pay scale of Rs. 16400-20,000 at the basic pay of Rs. 16850. On August 10, 2009, the department revised the rates of DA to 31% with effect from January, 2009 and further to 36% effective from July 2009. How much arrear will Dinesh get in August, 2009 because of these revisions?

  (a) Rs. 12981

  (b) Rs. 10395

  (c) Rs. 17052

  (d) Rs. 13302

2011-13

Directions for question 123 to 125: Following graph represents the cost per square feet of four retailers from the financial year 2004 to 2012. The expected cost per square feet for year 2010, 2011 and 2012 are forecasted figures.

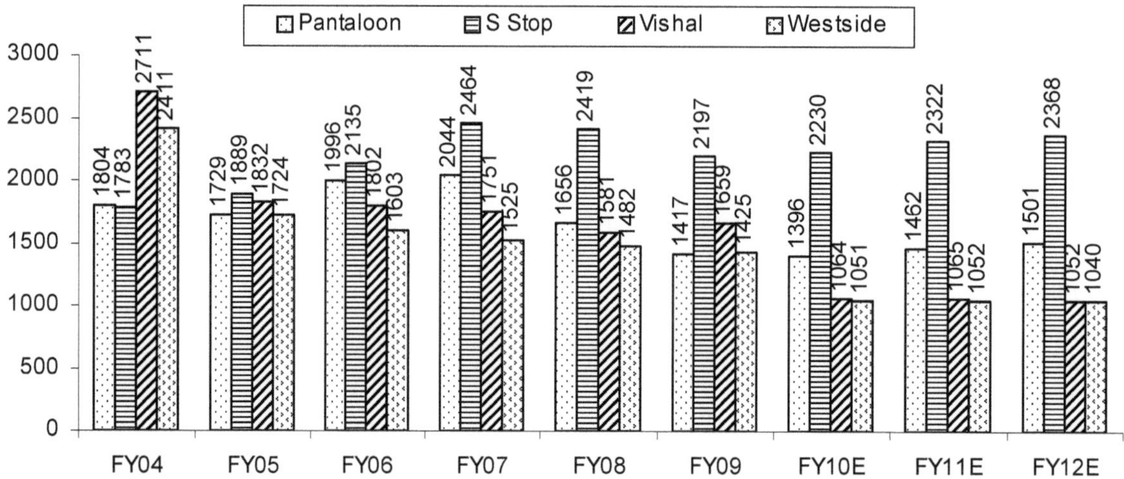

123. Which retailer shows the sharpest decline in cost per square feet and in which year?

(a) Westside, 2005   (b) Pantaloon, 2008

(c) S.Stop, 2009   (d) Vishal, 2010

124. Which retailer has shown the maximum increase in its cost per square feet and in which year?

(a) S.Stop, 2006   (b) S.Stop, 2007

(c) Pantaloon, 2006   (d) Vishal, 2006

125. What is the average rate of change in the cost per square feet of the retail sector, if the sector is represented by the above four retailers in the period FY07 to FY10E?

(a) -8.12

(b) -10.86

(c) -6.73

(d) None of these

Directions 126 to 129: The table below represents the information collected by TRAI about the Service Area wise Access of (Wireless + Wire line) subscribers in India. On the basis of the information provided in the table answer the questions that follow.

Service Area	Subscribers (in Millions)		Service Area	Subscribers (in Millions)	
	Dec 2009	March 2010		Dec 2009	March 2010
U.P. (E)	39.68	45.53	Orissa	13.57	15.89
Bihar	33.17	38.36	Mumbai	27.21	29.43
Karnataka	35.5	39.91	Kerala	25.69	27.65
Andhra Pradesh	43.89	48.09	Punjab	20.03	21.7
TN (Chennai Included)	53.17	57.26	Delhi	29.38	31.01
Madhya Pradesh	29.89	33.55	Haryana	13.59	14.96
Maharashtra	43.02	46.53	Kolkata	16.55	17.87
U.P (W)	28.47	31.97	Assam	8.11	9.06
West Bengal	22.68	26.07	North East	4.94	5.64
Gujarat	31.37	34.43	Jammu and Kashmir	5.22	5.78
Rajasthan	32.22	35.27	Himachal Pradesh	4.83	5.34

126. Which service area has observed maximum rate of change from Dec 2009 to March 2010 (in percentage)?

(a) U.P. (E)

(b) Bihar

(c) Orissa

(d) Haryana

127. As a result of a decision to allow only two or three telecom operators in a particular service area, TRAI allocates R-Com and Vodafone to operate only in the east of India and Idea and Airtel operate only in south. R-Com has got 28% subscribers in east while Vodafone has 72% subscribers; similarly Idea has 48% subscribers in the south while Airtel has 52% subscribers. How many subscribers do these four players have in 2010?

(a) R-Com-28.03, Vodafone-73.22, Idea-86.22, Airtel-89.5

(b) R-Com-30.03, Vodafone-72.82, Idea-85.02, Airtel-80.04

(c) R-Com-28.03, Vodafone-76.24, Idea-84.01, Airtel-85.67

(d) R-Com-30.03, Vodafone-77.22, Idea-82.99, Airtel-89.91

128. Due to operability issues early in 2010 Madhya Pradesh and entire UP was added to the eastern telecom circle. The telecom operators in Madhya Pradesh and entire UP namely R-Com, Vodafone and Idea had 28%, 40% and 32% subscribers respectively. What is the percentage of subscribers that each player has in the newly formed eastern circle in March 2010?

(a) R-Com-30.01%, Vodafone-55.72%, Idea-14.27%

(b) R-Com-32.01%, Vodafone-53.72%, Idea-14.27%

(c) R-Com-28%, Vodafone-55.72%, Idea-16.27%

(d) None of these

129. The all India rate of change in number of subscribers from December 2009 to March 2010 is?

(a) 10.7%   (b) 10.5%

(c) 11.8%   (d) 12.4%

Directions for questions 130 to 134: In order to quantify the intangibles and give incentives to the multi brand dealers (dealers who stock multiple goods as well as competing brands) and the associated channel members, a **Company(X)** formulates a point score card, which is called as brand building points. This brand building point is added to the sales garget achieved points for redemption. The sales target achieved point is allotted as per the table 3 of this question. The sum of brand building point and sales achieved points is the total point that can be redeemed by the dealer against certain goods, as shown in the second table.

The detail of the system is shown in the tables below:

Table1: Brand Building Score Card						
Brand Building Criteria	Points that is allotted if any of the each is achieved					
Company(X) Signage	Only Company X signage on main entrance on the store	Company X signage on the main entrance along with other brands	Company X signage in the corner of the counter	Company X signage outside the counter	No signage of Company X	Other brands signage only
Points	20	10	5	5	0	-20
Company(X) Wall painting in the exterior of the sotre	Only Company X painting in the walls of the store	Company X painting on main entrance with other brands	Company X painting On the side wall of the store	Company X painting Outside the store on some other structure	No painting of Company X	Other brands painting only
Points	20	5	2.5	2.5	0	-10
Company(X) painting in the interior of the store	The interior of the store has only Company X painting	Company X painting in the Back side of the counter	Company X painting On the side wall in the interior	Not painted	Others' painting only	
Points	10	5	2.5	2.5	-10	
POP (points of purchase) display of Company (X)	All POP display is of Company X	The POP display of company X is at the eye level with other brands	Above the eye level with other	Below the eye level with other brands	Store does not have any POP material	Store has only Other brands POP material
Points	25	10	5	5	0	-20
Stacking of Company (X) goods in the shelves	Goods of Company X only in the front row	Goods of Company X share front row with other brands	Company X goods are only in the back row	Goods of Other brands in the frong row only		
Points	25	10	0	-20		

Table 2: Point Redemption Options

Sl. No	Goods in offer	Total Points required for Redemption
1	Umbrella	40
2	Nike Cap	100
3	T-Shirt	200
4	Tupperware Set	600
5	Ray Ban Glasses	800
6	Banarasi Silk Saree	2000
7	Kanjivaram Saree	4000

Table 3: The point calculation on sales target achieved is

Sales Target	Points Assigned
<50% of the Sales Target	0
50%-75%	10
75%-99%	12
100%	15
Each extra unit sold above the sales target	0.25

There are 10 multi brand dealers in Nasik and the sales that they have achieved in the end of a quarter are:

Dealers	Sales (Target (July-Sep) in units	Actual Sales
Bhoumik Brothers	25,000	24,378
Subhajit Traders	28,000	29,241
Srikrishna Traders	40,000	42,000
Nikil Choudhary & Co	43,000	42,000
M/s Dinesh Kumar	25,000	25,000
Variety Stores	22,000	23,000
Rajib & Co	22,000	22,000
Malling Enterprise	23,000	24,000
Saha H/W	24,000	24,512
Maheshwari & Co	50,000	56,241

130. Maheshwari & Co has Company X signage along with other brand signage in the main entrance of the store, the exterior walls of the store have the painting of only company X, the side wall in the interior has the painting of Company X. The POP display of Company X is above the eye level with other brands while the stacking of goods of Company X is in the back row of the shelves. The brand building points when combined with the sales achieved points amounts to the total points that a dealer can accumulate in a quarter. The number of Tupperware Sets that Maheshwari & Co can redeem after the quarter (July to September) is?
    (a) 2 (b) 3
    (c) 4 (d) 5

131. Bhowmik Brothers has only other brands signage in the front of the store, and company X painting on the side wall in the exterior of the store, Company X painting on the side wall in the interior of the store, no POP display of any Company and the goods of Company X is stacked in the front row with other brands. What is the total point Bhowmik Brothers need to accumulate to make them eligible for minimum redemption?
    (a) 27 (b) 37
    (c) 38 (d) 33

132. The Brand building points of Saha H/W is 85, and Mr. Saha the proprietor of the store wants to redeem a Kanjivaram Saree the next quarter by carrying forward the points accumulated this quarter to the next quarter. The sales target of Saha H/W is 25,000 units in the next quarter. It is assumed the brand building points for the next quarter is also going to be 85. How many extra units Saha H/W has to sell in order to get the Kanjivaram Saree?
    (a) 14688 (b) 12569
    (c) 13658 (d) 15698

133. Malling Enterprise exhausted all its points while redeeming three Nike Caps and an Umbrella, what is its brand building points?
    (a) 75 (b) 85
    (c) 95 (d) 90

134. If Srikrishna Trader has 80 brand building points then the good that it can redeem are _______?
    (a) Tupperware set, Kanjivaram
    (b) Umbrella and Tupperware set
    (c) Tupperware Set, Nike Cap
    (d) Nike Cap and T-Shirt

Directions for questions 135 to 138: Study the following graph and answer the question that follow

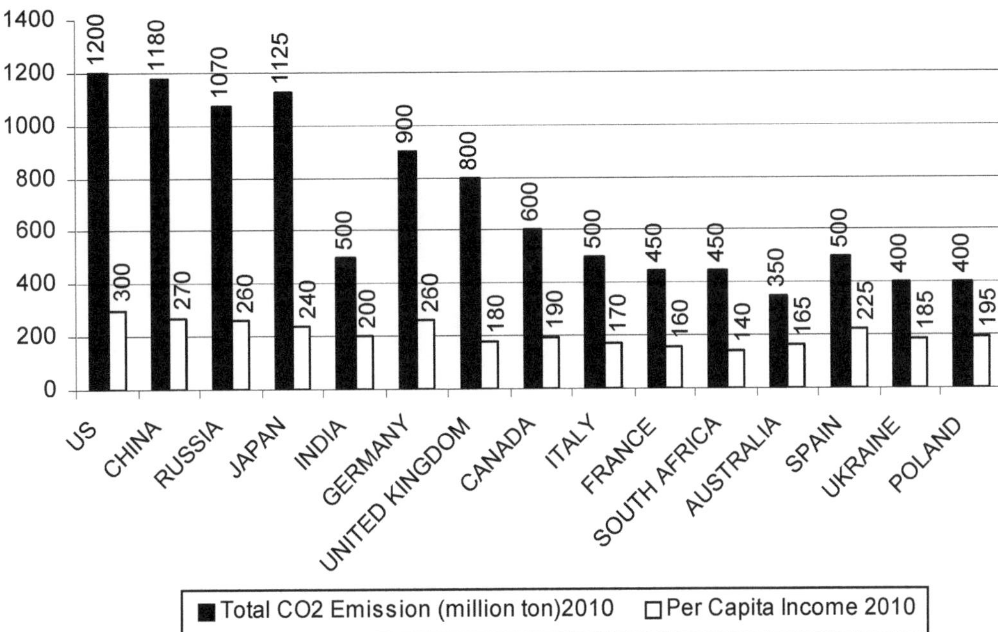

135. If the world energy council formulates a norm for high emission countries to reduce their emission each year by 12.5% for the next two years then what would be the ratio of CO_2 *emission to per capita income* of US, China and Japan after two years. The per capita income of China, Japan and US is expected to increase every year by 4%, 3% and 2% respectively.

(a) 3.5, 3.8, 4.1   (b) 3.4, 3.5, 3.

(c) 2.9, 3.1, 3.4   (d) None

136. If US and China decide to buy carbon credits, from Spain and Ukraine to make up for their high emissions, then in how many years US and China would be able to bring down its ratio of CO_2 *emission (million ton) to per capita income* to world standard benchmark of 0.75. (per capita income of the given countries remain same, 0.5 CO_2 emissions [million ton] is compensated by purchase of 1.25 units of carbon credit, and a country can buy carbon credit units in three lots of 15, 20 and 30 units in a single year.)

(a) 3.8 years   (b) 38 years

(c) 30 years   (d) None

137. France, South Africa, Australia, Ukraine and Poland form an energy consortium which declares CO_2 emission of 350 million ton per annum as standard benchmark. The energy consortium decides to sell their carbon emission savings against the standard benchmark to high carbon emission countries. It is expected that the per capita income of each country of the energy consortium increases by 2%, 2.5%

and 3.5% p.a. for the next three years respectively. The *ratio of CO_2 emission to per capita income* of each energy consortium country reduces by 50% and remains constant for the next three years. By selling 0.5 CO_2 emissions [million ton] the energy consortium earns 1.25 carbon credits, then determine the total credits earned by energy consortium in three years.

(a) 3560   (b) 4506

(c) 5060   (d) None

138. Select the wrong statement in reference to the position of India vis-à-vis other countries in the graph in terms of the ratio of CO_2 emission to per capita income (increasing order)

(a) India stands at 5th position if 50 is added to the given per capita income figures of each country.

(b) India stands at 5th position at the given CO_2 emission level and per capita income of each country.

(c) India stands at 5th position if 200 million ton CO_2 emission is deducted from the given CO_2 emission figures of each country.

(d) India stands at 5th position if 200 million ton CO_2 emission is deducted from the given CO_2 emission figures of each country and 50 is added to the given per capita income of each country.

Direction for question 139: Refer to the following pie chart and answer the question that follows. The chart shows the no. of units produced in degrees, by Company X in different States of India for the quarter July-Sep 2010.

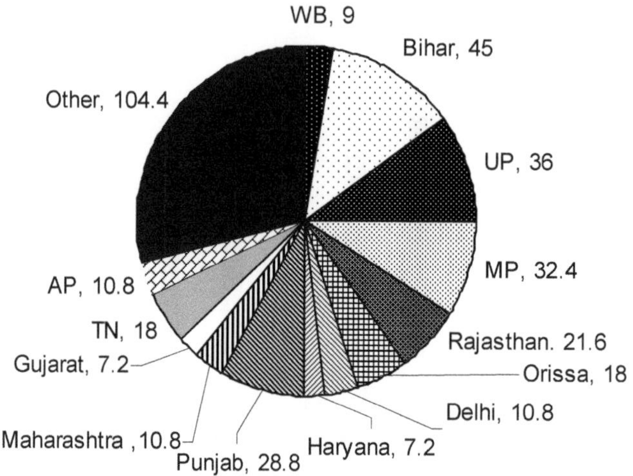

139. By how many units does the number of units produced in Bihar exceed the number of units produced in Madhya Pradesh, if the total production in the quarter is 72,000 units?

(a) 2300 units   (b) 2520 units   (c) 3516 units   (d) 2860 units

Directions for questions 140 to 142: The following graph shows population data (males and females), educated people data(males and females) and number of male in the population for a given period of 1995 to 2010. All data is in million. From the information given in the graph answer the questions that follow.

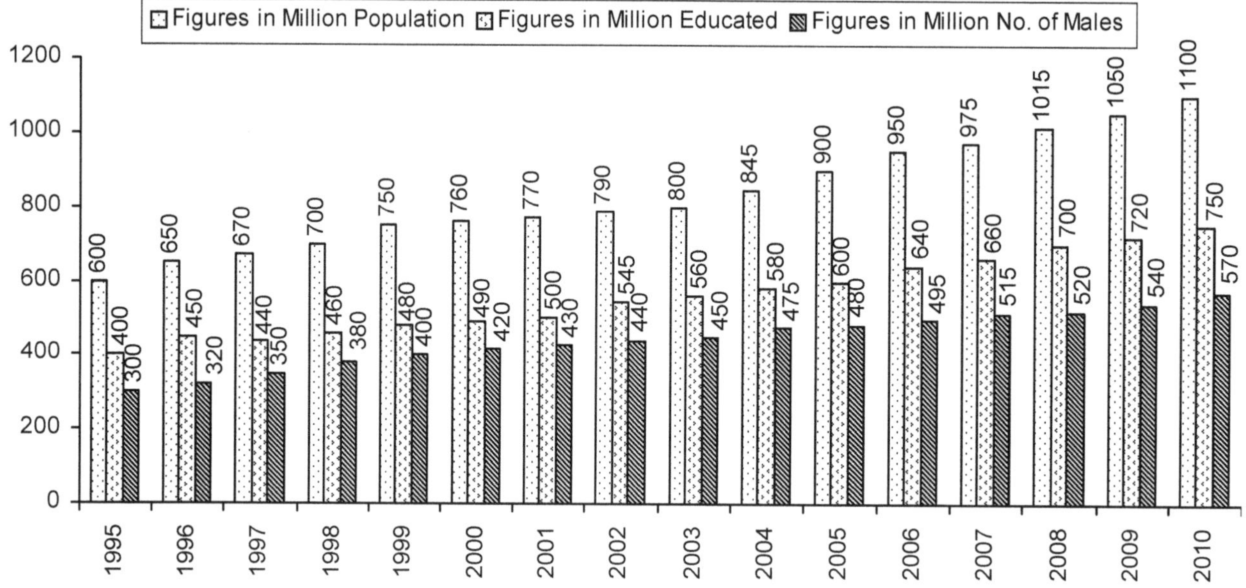

140. In which year the percentage increase in the number of females over the previous year is highest?

(a) 1996   (b) 1999

(c) 2004   (d) 2005

141. In 2002 if the ratio of number of educated male to professionally educated female was 5:4. If the number of educated males increased by 25% in 2003, what is the percentage change in number of uneducated females in 2003?

(a) +25%   (b) +30%

(c) +34%   (d) +56%

142. In year 2005 total production living in urban area is equal to sixty eight percent of educated population. The ratio of number of people living in urban area to people living in rural area is 43:12 in 2010. What is the ratio of the rural population in 2005 to that in 2010?

(a) 0.8   (b) 0.47

(c) 2.05   (d) None

2012-14

Directions for questions 143 to 147: Answer the following questions based on the Diagram below, which reports Country XX's monthly Outward Investment flows to various countries and the World. The FDI figures are reported in US$ Million.

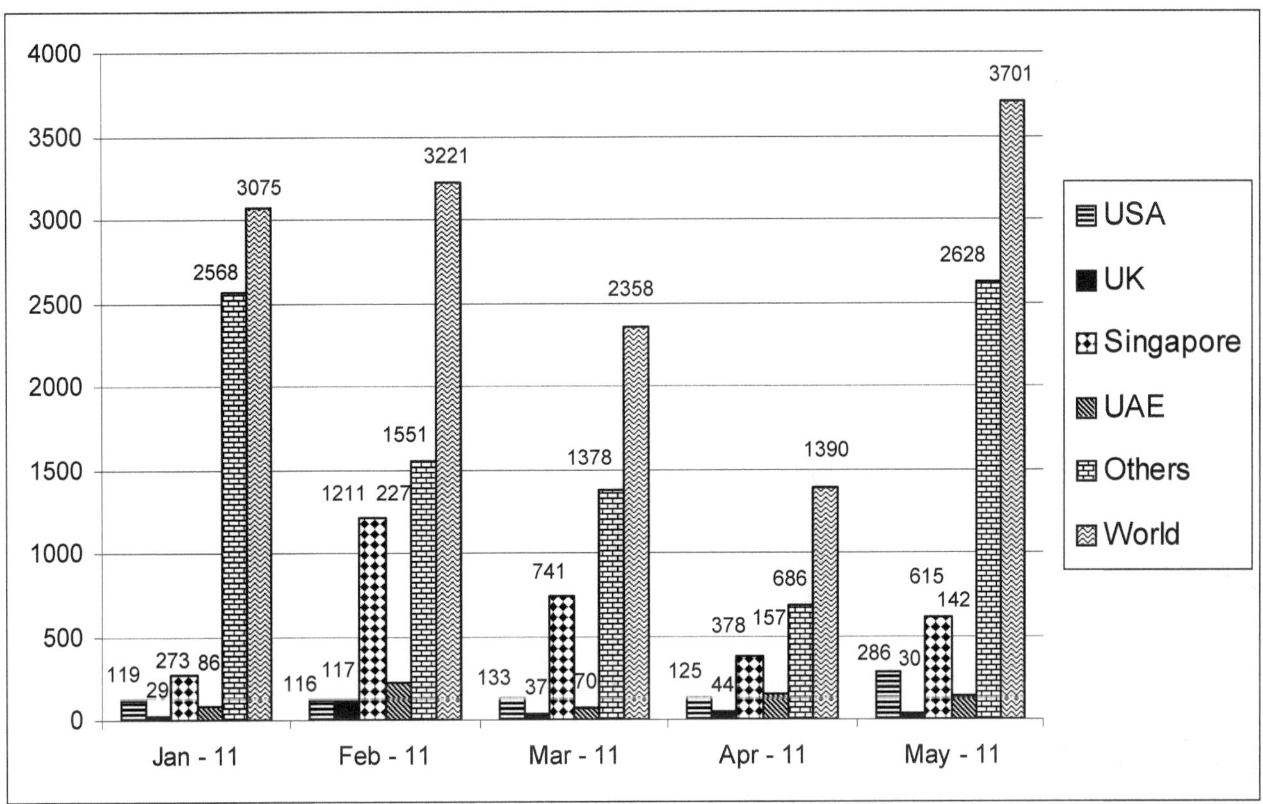

143. What is the compound average growth rate of Country XX's overall Outward Investment during the period January 2011 and May 2011?

  (a) Approximately 6 percent

  (b) Approximately 3.5 percent

  (c) Approximately 5.75 percent

  (d) None of the above

144. In which month Country XX's Outward Investment to Singapore dropped most and what is the 'month on month' growth in that period?

  (a) April, Approximately negative growth of 39 percent

  (b) March, Approximately negative growth of 49 percent

  (c) April, Approximately negative growth of 49 percent

  (d) None of the above

145. What is the share of Country XX's Outward Investment together in USA and UK in February 2011 of its total investment in the world?

  (a) 7.24 percent   (b) 8.30 percent

  (c) 6.79 percent   (d) None of the above

146. In which month the share of Country XX's total Outward Investment together in Singapore and UAE achieved the highest level and what is the value?

  (a) April, 40 percent

  (b) February, 45 percent

  (c) March, 45 percent

  (d) None of the above

147. Between February 2011 and April 2011, to which country did Outward Investment from XX witness the highest decline?

  (a) Singapore   (b) UK

  (c) UAE   (d) Others

Directions for questions 148 – 152: Answer the following questions based on the table below, which reports certain data series from National Accounts Statistics of India at Current Prices.

Year	Value of GDP From Primary Sector (at Factor Cost)	Value of GDP From Secondary (Manufacturing) Sector (at Factor Cost)	Value of GDP (at Factor Cost)	Value of GDP (at Market Prices)	Value of GNP (at Factor Cost)	Gross Domestic Savings	Gross Domestic Capital Formation
	Rs. Crore	Rs. Crore	Rs. Crore	Rs. Crore	Rs. Crore	Rs. Crore	Rs. Crore
A	B	C	D	E	F	G	H
2004-05	650454	744755	2971464	3242209	2949089	1050703	1052232
2005-06	732234	859410	3389621	3692485	3363505	1235288	1266245
2006-07	829771	1033410	3952241	4293672	3919007	1486044	1540749
2007-08	961330	1205464	4581422	4986426	4560910	1837498	1896563
2008-09	1067592	1351795	5282086	5582623	5249163	1798347	1973535
2009-10	1243566	1499601	6133230	6550271	6095230	2207423	2344179

148. The GDP is sum total of the contributions from primary sector, secondary sector and the tertiary sector. If that be the case, then over 2004-05 to 2009-10, the share of tertiary sector at factor cost in GDP has increased from:

(a) 53.05 percent to 55.27 percent

(b) 52.86 percent to 54.20 percent

(c) 53.04 percent to 55.83 percent

(d) 52.70 percent to 56.14 percent

149. The annual growth rate in the GNP series at factor cost was *highest* between;

(a) 2008-09 and 2009-10

(b) 2006-07 and 2007-08

(c) 2007-08 and 2008-09

(d) 2005-06 and 2006-07

150. Had Gross Domestic Savings (GDS) between 2008-09 and 2009-10 increased by 30 percent, then during 2009-10 GDS expressed as a percentage of GDP at market prices would have been:

(a) 33.70 percent

(b) 36.85 percent

(c) 35.69 percent

(d) None of the above

151. Mark the *highest* figure from the following:

(a) Percentage change in GDP from Secondary sector (at Factor Cost) between 2006-07 and 2007-08.

(b) Percentage change in GDP at Market Prices between 2008-09 and 2009-10.

(c) Percentage change in Gross Domestic Savings between 2004-05 and 2005-06.

(d) Percentage change in Gross Domestic Capital Formation between 2008-09 and 2009-10.

152. Identify the *correct* Statement:

(a) GDP (at Factor Cost) expressed as a percentage of GNP (at Factor Cost) has increased consistently between 2004-05 and 2009-10.

(b) GDP (at Factor Cost) expressed as a percentage of GDP (at Market Prices) has increased consistently between 2004-05 and 2008-09.

(c) Gross Domestic Capital Formation expressed as a percentage of GDP (at Market Prices) has increased consistently between 2004-05 and 2007-08.

(d) Contribution to GDP from Primary Sector (at Factor Cost) expressed as a percentage of GDP (at Factor Cost) has decreased consistently between 2004-05 and 2009-10.

Directions for questions 153 – 158: Answer the following questions based on the table below, which reports global market share of Leading Exporting and Importing countries for Select Product groups.

Percentage Shares of selected countries in Global Exports										
	Sectors									
Exporting Countries	Clothing Products		Chemical Products		Automotive Products		Office and Telecom Equipment		Integrated Circuits and Electronic Components	
	2000	2009	2000	2009	2000	2009	2000	2009	2000	2009
EU (27)	28.5	30.7	53.9	54.1	49.7	53.8	29.2	24.8	19.1	13.5
USA	4.4	1.3	14.1	11.0	11.6	8.6	15.8	8.5	20.4	10.7
Canada	1.1	0.3	2.5	1.9	10.5	4.0	2.1	0.8	1.1	0.6
China	18.3	34.0	2.1	4.3	0.3	2.3	4.5	26.2	1.7	11.4
Thailand	1.9	1.2	0.7	0.9	0.4	1.4	1.9	2.2	1.9	2.1
Malaysia	1.1	1.0	0.4	0.7	0.1	0.1	5.4	4.3	6.1	7.5
India	3.0	3.6	0.7	1.3	0.1	0.6	0.1	0.3	0.1	0.1
Mexico	4.4	1.3	0.2	0.3	5.3	4.3	3.5	3.8	1.0	0.5
Japan	0.3	0.2	6.0	4.2	15.2	12.2	11.2	5.9	13.8	10.3
South Korea	0.1	0.1	2.4	2.6	2.6	4.4	6.1	5.8	8.0	7.6

Percentage Shares of selected countries in Global Imports										
Importing Countries	Clothing Products		Chemical Products		Automotive Products		Office and Telecom Equipment		Integrated Circuits and Electronic Components	
	2000	2009	2000	2009	2000	2009	2000	2009	2000	2009
EU (27)	41.0	48.5	43.8	44.9	42.3	45.0	33.8	30.7	22.6	15.2
USA	33.1	21.8	12.2	10.4	29.4	15.5	21.2	16.6	14.9	5.2
Canada	1.8	2.3	3.2	2.5	8.0	5.1	3.0	1.9	2.5	0.9
China	0.6	0.6	4.9	7.5	0.7	3.6	4.4	15.1	6.3	32.8
Thailand	0.1	0.1	0.9	1.4	0.4	0.6	1.4	1.4	2.5	2.2
Malaysia	0.3	0.6	1.2	1.6	0.3	0.5	3.2	2.6	7.4	5.3
India	0.4	0.9	0.8	1.8	0.1	0.4	0.3	1.2	0.2	0.5
Mexico	1.8	0.6	2.4	1.9	3.5	2.5	2.9	3.1	4.2	2.3
Japan	9.7	7.7	4.2	3.3	1.7	1.2	6.0	4.4	6.0	4.5
South Korea	0.6	1.0	2.2	2.1	0.3	0.7	3.3	2.9	6.1	6.1

153. Identify the *highest* number:

(a) Increase in Malaysia's share in global Chemical Products export between 2000 and 2009

(b) Increase in India's share in global Office and Telecom Equipment export between 2000 and 2009

(c) Increase in Mexico's share in global Chemical Products export between 2000 and 2009

(d) Increase in Thailand's share in global Integrated Circuits and Electronic Components export between 2000 and 2009

154. Mark the *correct* statement:

(a) Barring the exception of Integrated Circuits and Electronic Components, the share of the EU has increased in global import for all other product groups.

(b) Between 2000 and 2009, global export share has remained unchanged only for two countries.

(c) Between 2000 and 2009, global import share has remained unchanged only for five countries.

(d) Among all reported product groups, between 2000 and 2009, the increase in global import share in case of India has been highest for Chemical Products.

155. Mark the *false* statement:

(a) India's global export share for Clothing Products between 2000 and 2009 has increased by 20 percent.

(b) Japan's global export share for Chemical Products between 2000 and 2009 has decreased by 30 percent.

(c) South Korea's global export share for Integrated Circuits and Electronic Components between 2000 and 2009 has decreased by 6 percent.

(d) Malaysia's global import share for Clothing Products between 2000 and 2009 has increased by 100 percent.

156. If between 2000 and 2009, India's export market share in Integrated Circuits and Electronic Components had increased by 600 percent, the rank of the country in terms of market share in 2009 would have been:

(a) Sixth

(b) Eighth

(c) Seventh

(d) None of the above

157. Considering both global export and import market dynamics, China has witnessed highest percentage change in its market share between 2000 and 2009 in the following product groups:

(a) Integrated Circuits and Electronic Components imports

(b) Office and Telecom Equipment exports

(c) Integrated Circuits and Electronic Components exports

(d) Automotive Products imports

158. Suppose the ten countries reported in the above table are arranged according to their continent: North America, EU and Asia. Then in terms of *export* market share for (i) Chemical Products, (ii) Automotive Products, (iii) Office and Telecom Equipment Products and (iv) Integrated Circuits and Electronic Components respectively, the continent-wise ranking in 2009 would be:

(a) (i)   EU, Asia, North America;

(ii) EU, Asia, North America;

(iii) Asia, EU, North America;

(iv) Asia, EU, North America.

(b) (i)   Asia, EU, North America;

(ii) EU, Asia, North America;

(iii) Asia, EU, North America

(iv) Asia, North America, EU.

(c) (i)   EU, Asia, North America;

(ii) EU, North America, Asia;

(iii) Asia, EU, North America;

(iv) Asia EU, North America.

(d) (i)   EU, Asia, North America;

(ii) EU, North America, Asia;

(iii) Asia, EU, North America;

(iv) Asia, North America, EU

2013-15

Direction for question 159 - 163: Analyse the following chart showing the exports and imports of Sono Ltd. and answer the questions based on this chart.

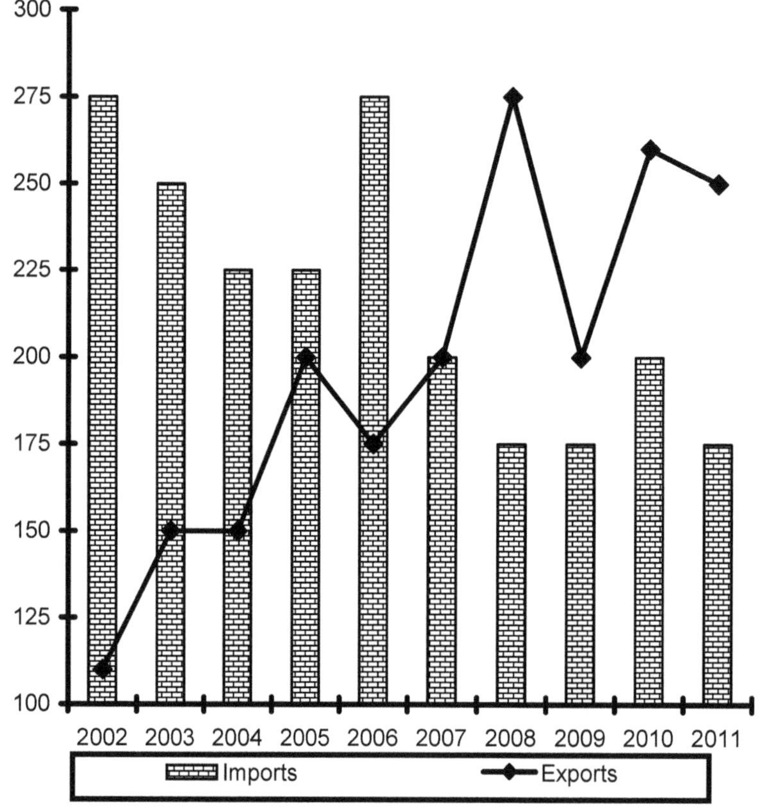

159. Approximately by what percentage are the total Exports greater/smaller than the total imports for the given period?

(a) Greater by 9 percent (b) Smaller by 10 percent

(c) Smaller by 9 percent (d) Greater by 10 percent

160. If the absolute difference between imports and exports are ranked in ascending order, which year gets 4th rank?

(a) 2010 (b) 2008

(c) 2009 (d) None of the above

161. In which year was the fifth largest annual percentage increase in exports recorded?

(a) 2007 (b) 2005

(c) 2009 (d) None of the above

162. Which year was the second largest annual percentage increase in imports?

(a) 2010 (b) 2005

(c) 2006 (d) None of the above

163. What is the approximate percentage point difference in the maximum annual percentage increase in exports and the minimum annual percentage decrease in Imports?

(a) 28 (b) 48

(c) 64 (d) 12

Direction for Questions 164- 169: Answer the questions on the basis of the table given below:

Table: Production of Major Minerals and Metals

(Million Tonnes)

Year	Aluminium	Coal	Copper	Gold	Iron Ore
2005	69	91	71	15	100
2006	75	88	75	18	120
2007	81	97	79	21	102
2008	98	107	88	25	131
2009	93	110	92	24	143
2010	99	116	97	20	154
2011	105	122	103	25	163

164. Which mineral/metal witnessed highest growth rate in production from 2005 to 2011?

(a) Iron Ore (b) Aluminium

(c) Gold (d) Copper

165. Which year has witnessed highest absolute increase in total production of minerals and metals?

(a) 2006 (b) 2008

(c) 2011 (d) None of these

166. Highest annual growth rate in production is recorded in

(a) Iron Ore in 2008 (b) Gold in 2011

(c) Aluminium in 2008 (d) Gold in 2006

167. If annual average growth rate in production exhibited during 2006 to 2011 continues for next 4 years, then what will be the approximate production of aluminium in the year 2015?

(a) 125 million tonnes (b) 140 million tonnes

(c) 155 million tonnes (d) 160 million tonnes

168. In which year is the proportion of copper production in the total mineral and metal production the highest?

(a) 2010 (b) 2008

(c) 2009 (d) 2007

169. Which mineral/metal witnessed the minimum growth rate in production from 2006 to 2010?

(a) Aluminium (b) Coal

(c) Copper (d) Gold

Direction for Questions 170 - 172: Answer the questions on the basis of the following table

Table: Region Wise Origin of Foreign Tourists Arriving Into India

	Region	Number of Arrivals			
		2007	2008	2009	2010
1	North America	1,007,276	1,027,297	1,051,209	1,173,664
2	Central & South America	42,319	43,505	46,604	54,728
3	Western Europe	1,686,083	1,709,525	1,634,042	1,750,342
4	Eastern Europe	152,764	185,110	183,475	227,650
5	Africa	157,485	141,750	164,474	204,525
6	West Asia	171,661	210,542	204,843	235,317
7	South Asia	982,428	1,051,846	1,001,401	1,047,444
8	South East Asia	303,475	332,925	360,191	409,043
9	East Asia	352,037	355,230	322,797	411,947
10	Australasia	167,063	178,308	182,451	210,275
11	Others	58,913	35,565	16,212	12,757

170. Which region witnessed the highest compound annual growth rate (CAGR) of tourists arriving into India?

(a) Eastern Europe (b) Central & South America

(c) West Asia (d) South East Asia

171. Tourists arriving into India from how many regions experienced CAGR of more than 10%?

(a) Three (b) Four

(c) Five (d) Two

172. The highest annual growth rate recorded in tourists arriving from any region in any year is

(a) Africa (b) Eastern Europe

(c) West Asia (d) East Asia

Direction for Questions 173 - 175: Read the information given below, analyse the following chart of Domestic Sales and Production of a country and answer the questions

Following charts present data about the domestic sales and production of LCD, LED and Plasma TVs produced and sold in a country (in number of units). Differences in production and sales will be bridged through external trade (i.e. export and imports) of the TV category during a given year

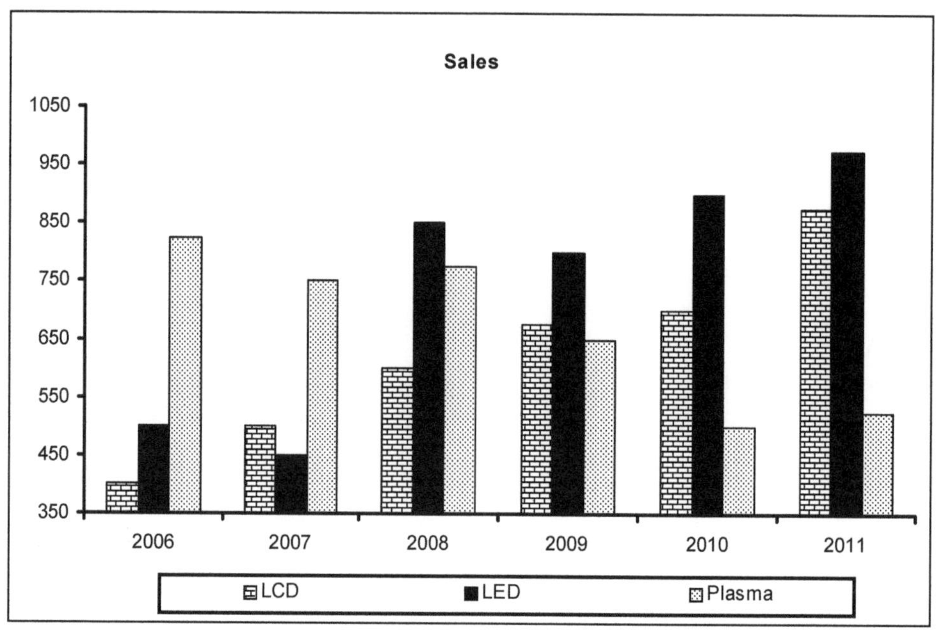

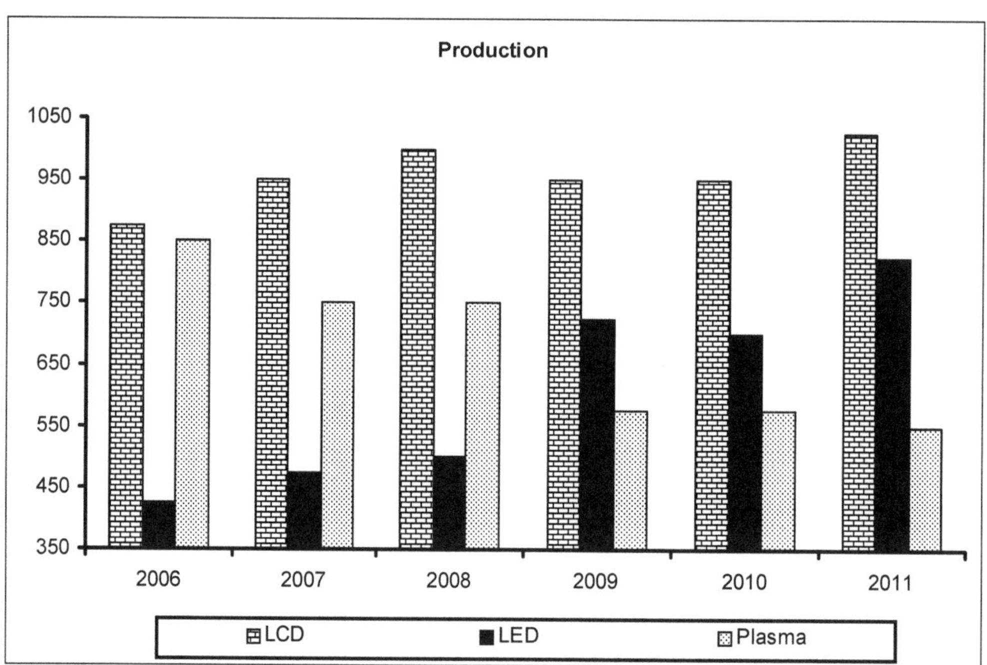

173. What year has registered the highest external trade in total number of TV units?

    (a) 2006

    (b) 2007

    (c) 2008

    (d) 2010

174. In which year are the net exports (exports - imports) of all the categories taken together the highest?

    (a) 2006

    (b) 2007

    (c) 2009

    (d) 2010

175. Examine the following statements

I.   LCD TVs were always exported

II. Net exports of all the categories of TVs for all the years is 1275

III. In only one year the production of plasma TVs fell short of sales

Select the best option

(a) Statement I alone is correct

(b) Statement I and II are correct

(c) Statement I and III are correct

(d) All three statements are correct

Direction for Questions 176 - 177: Study the following pie charts relating to sales of 5 models of cars for the years 2010 and 2011, and answer the questions

2010

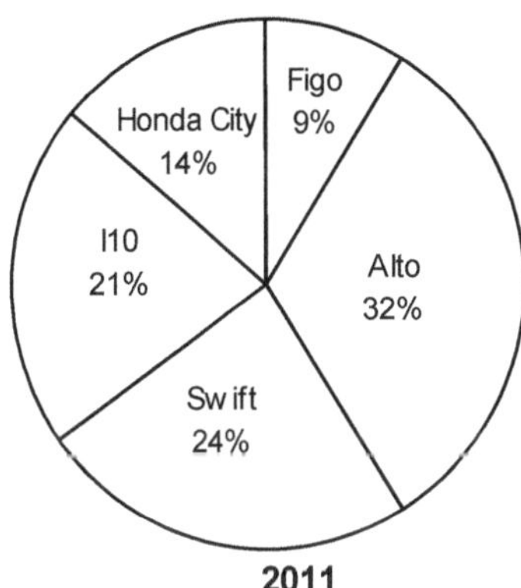

2011

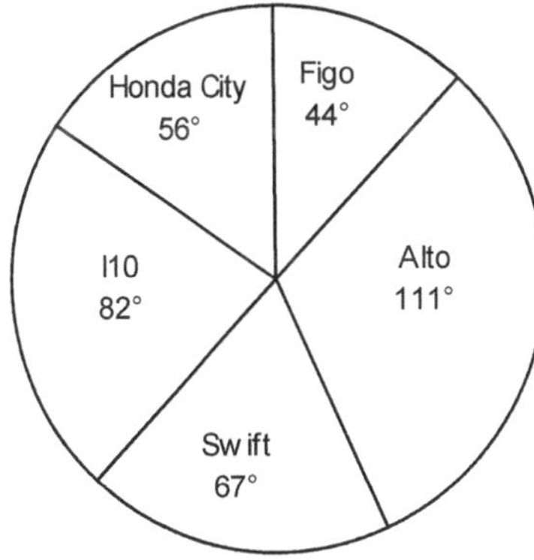

176. If the 2010 sales for all car models is 80,000 and these have grown by 25% in 2011, then what is the approximate increase in the number of Figo cars sold in 2011 over 2010?

(a) 4,860 (b) 12,200

(c) 4,500 (d) 2,200

177. If the 2010 sales for all car models is 80,000 and these have grown by 25% in 2011, then how many models have grown more than the average growth rate for all the models taken togethers?

(a) 2 (b) 3

(c) 4 (d) None of these

Directions for questions 178 to 182: Given below are the shares of sectoral FDI inflow to India in different years (figures in percentage). Answer the questions on the basis of the following data.

Sector	2007	2008	2009	2010	2011	2012
Services Sector	18.2	24.3	20.8	16.8	14.9	20.8
Construction Development	7.6	8.1	12.2	11.7	5.9	10.5
Telecommunications	5.5	8.3	9.4	7.2	6.6	0.4
Drugs and Pharmaceuticals	1.4	0.8	0.7	1.0	9.1	2.7
Computer Software and Hardware	12.8	5.6	2.5	4.7	2.0	2.8
Chemical (other than Fertilizers)	1.3	1.9	1.7	2.1	16.6	1.5
Automobile Industry	1.9	3.4	5.1	5.9	2.5	4.9
Power	1.3	3.9	5.8	5.1	4.9	3.2
Metallurgical Industries	2.5	4.5	1.8	4.9	4.7	6.9
Hotel and Tourism	1.3	1.6	2.2	2.4	2.6	14.9

178. Among the four sectors mentioned below, the increase in share of FDI inflows between the terminal years 2007 and 2012 has been HIGHEST for

(a) Services Sector

(b) Construction Development

(c) Automobile Industry

(d) Power

179. Over 2007 to 2012, the simple average share of FDI inflows has been SECOND LOWEST for

(a) Chemicals (other than Fertilizers)

(b) Automobile Industry

(c) Metallurgical Industries

(d) Hotel and Tourism

180. Identify the FALSE Statement from the following sentences

(a) During 2009 to 2012 the percentage share of FDI inflow in power sector has witnessed a continuous decline.

(b) During 2007 to 2009 the percentage share of FDI inflow in drugs and pharmaceuticals sector has witnessed a continuous decline.

(c) During 2009 to 2011 the percentage share of FDI inflow in Hotel and Tourism sector has witnessed a continuous increase.

(d) During 2007 to 2010 the percentage share of FDI inflow in Chemicals (other than Fertilizers) sector has witnessed a continuous increase.

181. Identify the TRUE alternative from the given options based on the following statements

   i.   In 2011, the construction development sector was ranked fifth in terms of percentage share of FDI inflow in the country

   ii.   In 2009, the Computer Software and Hardware sector was ranked sixth in terms of percentage share of FDI inflow in the country

   iii.   In 2012, the drugs and pharmaceuticals sector was ranked fourth lowest from the bottom in terms of percentage share of FDI inflow in the country

  (a) Statement ii only   (b) Both statements i and ii

  (c) Statement iii only   (d) All three statements

182. Mark the HIGHEST figure among the following options

  (a) Increase in FDI inflow percentage share for Telecommunications sector between 2007 and 2008

  (b) Increase in FDI inflow percentage share for Computer Software and Hardware sector between 2009 and 2010

  (c) Increase in FDI inflow percentage share for Automobile sector between 2011 and 2012

  (d) Increase in FDI inflow percentage share for Power sector between 2007 and 2008

Directions for questions 183 to 187: Given below are the shares of India's export basket to different regions (figures in percentage). Answer the questions on the basis of the following data.

Region	2002-2003	2003-2004	2004-2005	2005-2006	2006-2007	2007-2008	2008-2009	2009-2010	2010-2011	2011-2012
EU Countries	22.55	22.74	21.85	22.53	21.21	21.17	21.32	20.16	18.33	17.17
West Africa	2.02	1.99	1.98	1.80	1.93	2.13	1.84	1.76	1.71	2.12
East Africa	1.20	1.35	1.37	1.39	2.33	2.58	2.40	1.97	2.13	2.17
North Africa	1.28	1.21	1.62	1.55	1.47	1.63	1.84	1.75	1.59	1.54
North America	22.49	19.61	17.96	18.25	16.23	13.85	12.57	11.89	10.98	12.48
Latin America	2.06	1.40	2.15	2.47	2.95	3.11	2.96	3.13	3.72	4.00
ASEAN	8.76	9.12	10.09	10.10	9.98	10.05	10.29	10.16	10.21	12.00
West Asia -Gulf Cooperation Council (GCC)	9.32	11.07	11.75	11.42	12.96	13.35	17.21	17.06	16.90	14.85
West Asia (Other than GCC)	3.68	3.68	3.67	3.26	3.81	3.66	3.32	3.22	3.09	3.12
North East Asia	14.92	14.70	15.83	15.74	15.33	16.23	13.80	16.12	14.83	14.86
South Asia	5.28	6.73	5.51	5.38	5.12	5.90	4.62	4.69	4.64	4.37

183. Among the four options mentioned below, export share of India witnessed HIGHEST year-to-year decline in absolute terms in which of the region-period combinations?

  (a) In ASEAN region from 2005-06 to 2006-07

  (b) In South Asian region from 2004-05 to 2005-06

  (c) In West Asia (GCC) region from 2008-09 to 2009-10

  (d) In North African region from 2009-10 to 2010-11

184. Among the four options mentioned below, for which region have the export shares declined maximum number of times in a year-on-year basis?

  (a) South Asia   (b) North Africa

  (c) North America   (d) West Africa

185. Between 2009-10 and 2010-11, the annual growth rate in India's (percentage) export share has been LOWEST for

  (a) North Africa   (b) North East Asia

  (c) North America   (d) EU Countries

186. Mark the HIGHEST figure from the following options

   (a) India's simple average export share to North Africa during 2008-09 and 2009-10

   (b) India's simple average export share to East Africa during 2004-05 and 2007-08

   (c) India's simple average export share to Latin America during 2002- 03 and 2004-05

   (d) India's simple average export share to West Africa during 2007-08 and 2010-11

187. Identify the FALSE statement

   (a) In 2011 -12, South Asia was ranked sixth in India's export basket

   (b) The export share of North Africa in India's export basket has been the lowest for maximum number of years

   (c) In 2004-05, Latin America was ranked fourth from the bottom in India's export basket

   (d) Between 2002-03 and 2003-04, the annual growth rate in India's (percentage) export share has been highest for West Asia (GCC) market.

Directions for questions 188 to 192: Given below are the detailed characteristics of select Indian industries. Answer the questions on the basis of the following data.

	Industry 1	Industry 2	Industry 3	Industry 4	Industry 5	Industry 6	Industry 7
Number of Factories	65	110	32	30	78	39	300
Number of Workers	9066	877	5656	1099	7508	3333	15670
Total Number of Persons Engages	9466	1255	6830	1330	9088	4271	19159
Wage to Workers (Rs. Lakh)	1875	420	3706	596	5800	3117	6966
Total Emoluments (Rs. Lakh)	2059	747	6479	1024	9284	6084	15053
Fuels Consumed (Rs. Lakh)	88	762	10817	1384	14790	6461	32178
Materials Consumed (Rs. Lakh)	2519	4135	57275	34027	327400	123275	106233
Total Inputs (Rs. Lakh)	3256	5990	80238	41037	371605	138780	171246
Depreciation (Rs. Lakh)	41	149	6667	1044	25674	3515	11246
Net Value Added (Rs. Lakh)	3178	2284	23640	5831	71739	42434	72290
Profit (Rs. Lakh)	816	913	9356	3990	34943	31219	45392

188. If total managerial wage bill is defined as the difference between total emoluments and total wage to workers, and total managerial staff is defined as the difference between total persons engaged and total number of workers, then average managerial wage would be HIGHEST for:

   (a) Industry 5

   (b) Industry 6

   (c) Industry 3

   (d) Industry 7

189. Profit expressed as a ratio of net value added is HIGHEST for

   (a) Industry 6

   (b) Industry 7

   (c) Industry 4

   (d) Industry 5

190. If gross value added is defined as the sum of net value added and depreciation, then the difference in gross value added per worker is maximum between which of the following pairs?

   (a) Industry 6 and Industry 3

   (b) Industry 7 and Industry 1

   (c) Industry 5 and Industry 2

   (d) Industry 6 and Industry 4

191. Expense on Fuel consumption as a percentage of input cost has been HIGHEST for

   (a) Industry 3

   (b) Industry 7

   (c) Industry 2

   (d) Industry 6

192. Identify the TRUE statement

   (a) Number of workers per factory is third highest for Industry 6

   (b) Expense on Materials consumption expressed as a percentage of input cost is second highest for Industry 4

   (c) Profit earned expressed as a percentage of emolument is second highest for Industry 7

   (d) Emoluments expressed as a percentage of net value added is lowest for Industry 5

Directions for questions 193 to 196: Given below is information relating to cost of starting a business and number of days required for specific business activities in select countries. Answer the questions on the basis of the data in the following figure.

The data labels for the bars are placed above them, while the same for the line graph are placed in boxes. Legend for the bars is given in the order of left bar to right bar.

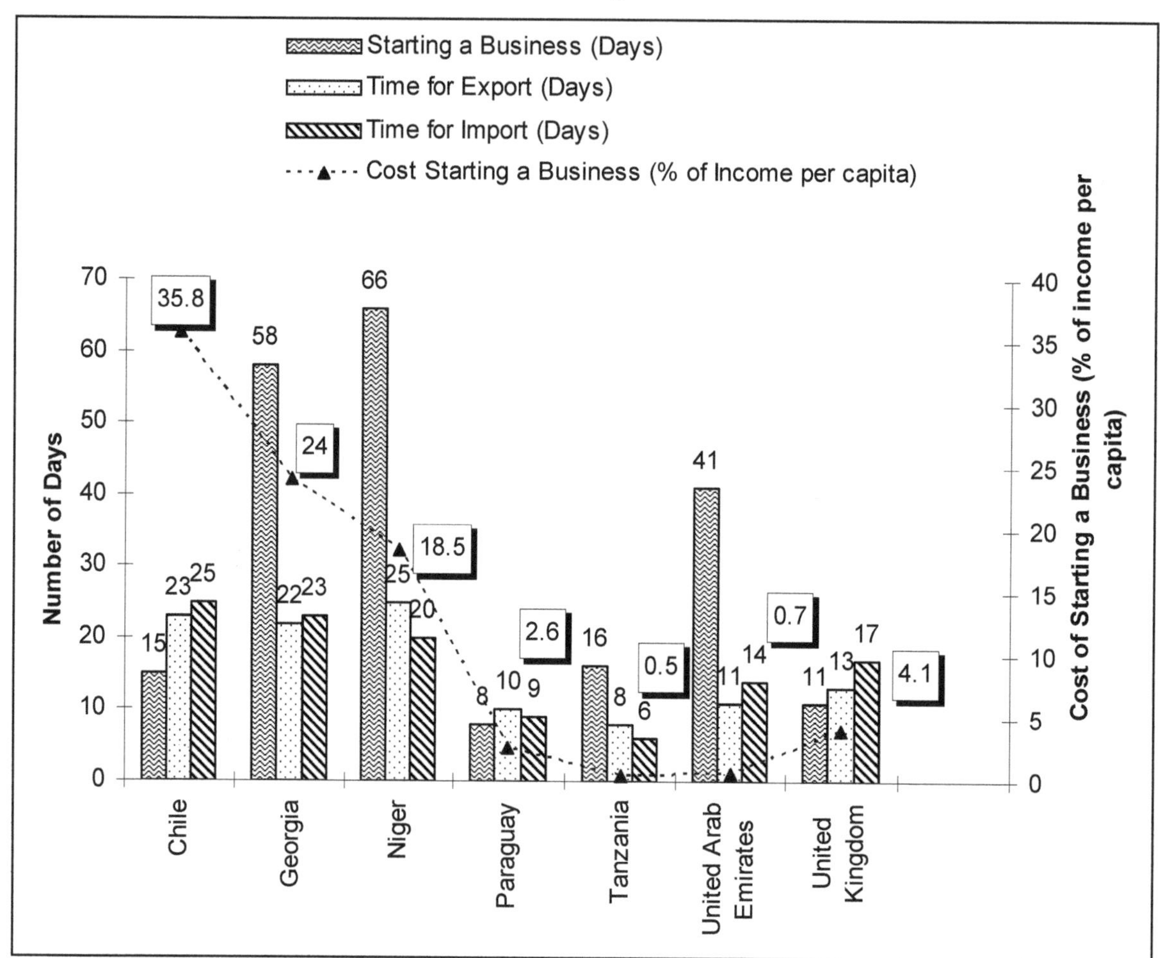

193. If countries were ranked according to the number of days required to start a business, (with the country requiring least number of days being rank highest), which of the top three countries would have the least cost to per capita income ratio?

(a) Chile   (b) Tanzania

(c) Paraguay   (d) None of the above

194. Ratio of number of days required for export to import is the least for which country?

(a) UK   (b) UAE

(c) Chile   (d) Georgia

195. Identify the TRUE Statement

(a) In Tanzania, the number of days required for exporting is lower than the number of days required for importing.

(b) The sum of number of days required for exporting and the number of days required for importing is the third lowest for UK.

(c) In Paraguay, the number of days required for starting a business is higher than the number of days required for importing.

(d) In Georgia, the number of days required for exporting is lower than the number of days required for importing.

196. Identify the FALSE Statement

(a) The number of days required for starting a business in Chile is lower than the corresponding figure in Tanzania.

(b) The number of days required for starting a business in UK is equal to the number of days required for exporting in UAE.

(c) The number of days required for importing in Georgia is higher than the number of days required for exporting in Niger.

(d) The cost of starting a business as percentage of per capita income in Tanzania is lower than the corresponding figure in UAE.

2015-17

Directions for questions 197 to 201: Read the following information on 'Sectoral Trends in Mergers & Acquisitions in India (2001 - 02 to 2006 - 07)' given in Tables below and answer the questions.

Table 1: Sector wise Number of 'Mergers & Acquisitions'

Sectors	2001-02	2002-03	2003-04	2004-05	2005-06	2006-07
Food & Beverage	113	77	77	74	63	61
Textile	57	59	59	64	77	55
Chemicals	134	98	112	99	79	62
Drugs & Pharma	64	60	44	50	60	72
Cement	11	7	8	22	0	0
IT & Telecom	153	114	84	80	109	103
Diversified	15	8	13	4	7	5
Financial Services	194	201	160	116	193	177
Other Services	297	280	287	281	271	293
Misc Manufacturing	31	36	31	35	35	24
Non Metallic Mineral Products	32	24	27	27	47	34

Table 2: Sector wise Number of 'Mergers'

Sectors	2001-02	2002-03	2003-04	2004-05	2005-06	2006-07
Food & Beverage	17	23	10	19	20	8
Textile	7	7	8	11	21	23
Chemicals	27	15	12	23	24	15
Drugs & Pharma	6	17	14	10	15	12
Cement	0	2	1	3	0	0
IT & Telecom	19	19	13	16	17	12
Diversified	1	0	1	0	0	0
Financial Services	91	107	87	41	75	51
Other Services	90	92	105	81	61	83
Misc Manufacturing	3	13	0	4	11	3
Non Metallic Mineral Products	3	5	1	5	8	11

197. What is the approximate proportion of 'merges' to 'acquisitions' for the entire period (2001 - 02 to 2006 - 07)?

(a) 26%   (b) 36%

(c) 30%   (d) 20%

198. For how many sectors is the proportion of 'mergers' to 'mergers & acquisitions' greater then 20% for the entire period (2001 - 02 to 2006 - 07)?

(a) 2   (b) 3

(c) 4   (d) 5

199. For how many sectors merger activity (measured by number of mergers) is more in the first 3 years as compared to the last 3 years?

(a) 7   (b) 3

(c) 6   (d) 5

200. If the turbulence over a period is defined by the sum of each of the differences (in absolute terms) in number of mergers & acquisitions on a year-on-year basis, then which sector is considered most turbulent for the entire period (2001-02 to 2006-07)?

(a) Financial services   (b) IT & Telecom

(c) Food and beverage   (d) Other services

201. In which year maximum sectors have exhibited higher number of acquisitions compared to previous year?

(a) 2003 - 04

(b) 2004 - 05

(c) 2005 - 06

(d) 2006 - 07

Directions for questions 202 to 206: Charts given below describe the energy scenario of a country. Assume that the country does not export any form of energy and whatever is produced and imported is consumed in the same year. Go through the Charts and answer the questions.

Chart 1: Proportion of energy consumption in 2009

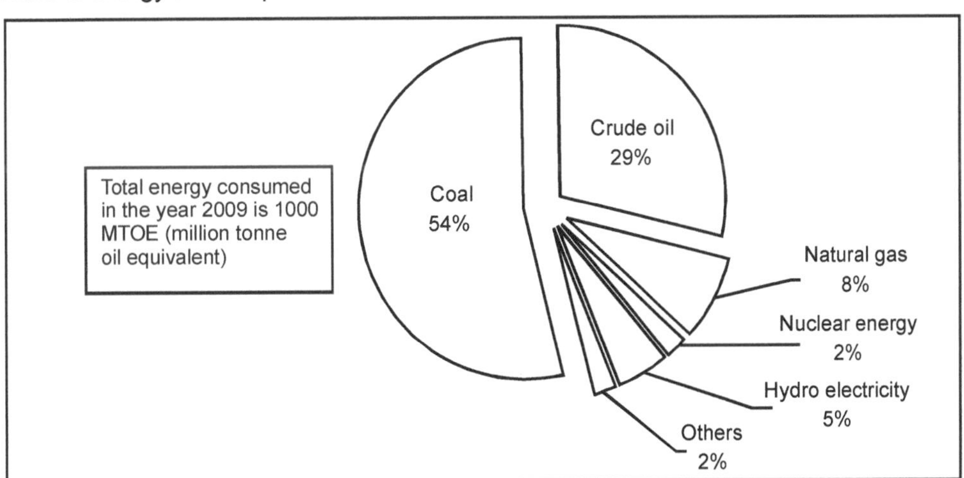

Chart 2: Annual (year-on-year) growth rate in consumption of different sources of energy for 2010 to 2012

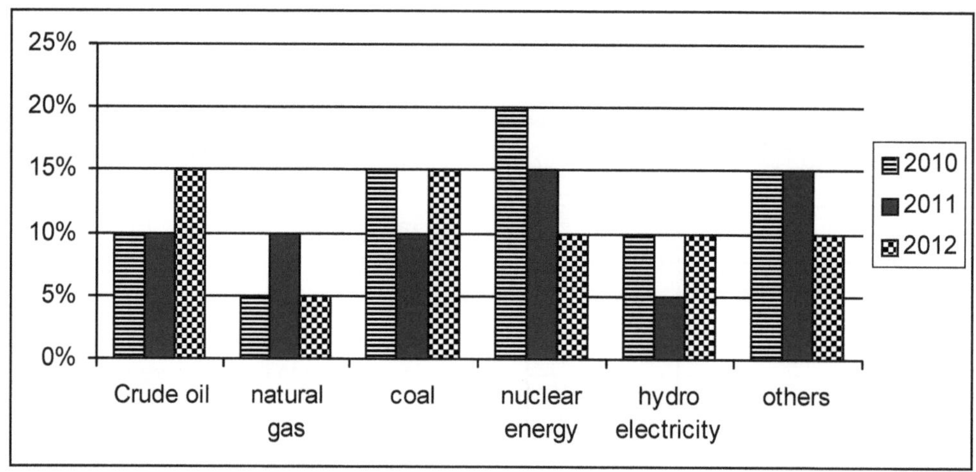

Chart 3: percentage of imports to consumption of different sources of energy during 2010 to 2012

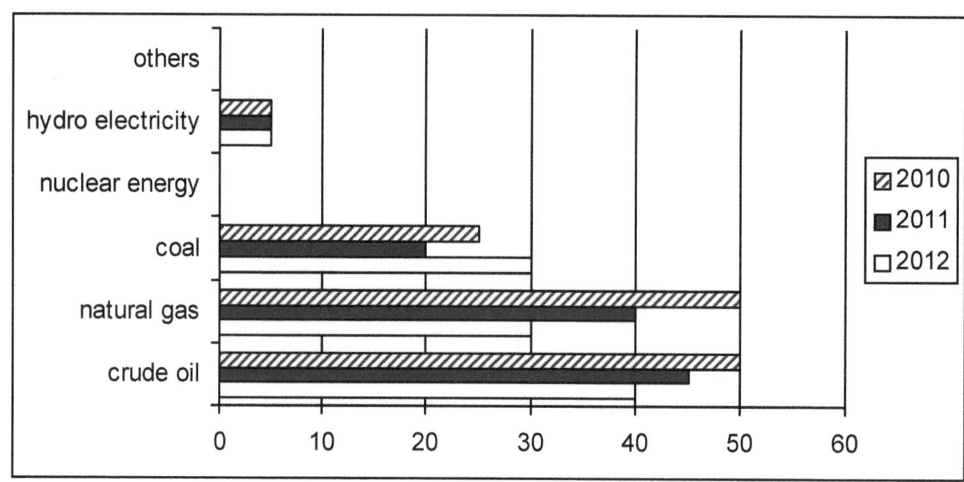

202. What was the approximate total import of energy in 2010?

(a) 400 MTOE (b) 300 MTOE

(c) 360 MTOE (d) 430 MTOE

203. The import of natural gas in 2012, when compared to 2010, is approximately:

(a) Reduced by 10 MTOE

(b) Reduced by 13 MTOE

(c) Increased by 10 MTOE

(d) Increased by 5 MTOE

204. What is the approximate domestic production of crude oil in 2011?

(a) 220 MTOE (b) 190 MTOE

(c) 160 MTOE (d) 280 MTOE

205. What is the approximate proportion of coal in the domestic consumption of energy in 2012?

(a) 52

(b) 54

(c) 58

(d) 56

206. What is the sum of the approximate domestic production of nuclear energy and hydro electricity in 2011?

(a) 75 MTOE

(b) 80 MTOE

(c) 90 MTOE

(d) 100 MTOE

2016-18

Directions (Q. 207-211): *Read the following information and tables and answer the questions that follow.*

Torrent Enterprises sells air conditioners of Eagle Brand in the retail market of Delhi. The month-wise total number of Window Air Conditioner (WAC) units sold by Torrent during April 2014 to March 2015 are shown below in Table A. Table B shows the share of different types of WACs in total monthly sales for the said period.

Number of Units Sold by Torrent Enterprises During the Period April 14 to March 15

Table A

Month	Units Sold	Month	Units Sold	Month	Units Sold
Apr-14	1266	Aug-14	1296	Dec-14	1300
May-14	1268	Sep-14	1296	Jan-15	1330
Jun-14	1272	Oct-14	1298	Feb-15	1340
Jul-14	1292	Nov-14	1300	Mar-15	1350

Table B

WAC Type (Tonnage)	April, May & Sep	Jun, Jul & Dec	Aug, Feb & Mar	Oct, Nov & Jan
18	20.00%	25.00%	31.00%	25.00%
One & Half Ton	19.00%	33.00%	19.00%	33.00%
One Ton	14.00%	12.00%	34.00%	26.00%
Half Ton	47.00%	30.00%	16.00%	16.00%

Performance measures are as follows:

Half Yearly Sales Performance :
$$\frac{\text{Oct 14 to Mar 15 Average Sales} - \text{April 14 to Sep 14 Average Sales}}{\text{April 14 to Sep 14 Average Sales}}$$

Monthly Sales Performance:
$$\frac{\text{Current Month Sales} - \text{Previous Month Sales}}{\text{Previous Month Sales}}$$

Sales Volatility:
$$\frac{\text{Maximum Monthly Sales} - \text{Minimum Monthly Sales}}{\text{Average Monthly Sales}}$$

207. What is the closest average number of $1\frac{1}{2}$ ton Window ACs sold by Torrent Enterprises during April 2014 - March 2015?

(a) 342

(b) 338

(c) 350

(d) 330

208. The absolute difference between average annual sales (in units) of which pair of WACs type is the highest

(a) 1 Ton and $\frac{1}{2}$ Ton

(b) 1 Ton and 2 Ton

(c) 2 Ton and $\frac{1}{2}$ Ton

(d) $1\frac{1}{2}$ Ton and $\frac{1}{2}$ Ton

209. Which type of WAC has performed the second best in Half Yearly Sales Performance? $\frac{1}{2}$

(a) Ton

(b) 1 Ton

(c) $1\frac{1}{2}$ Ton

(d) 2 Ton

210. In which of the months given below, the total WAC Monthly Sales Performance was the highest?

(a) May 2014

(b) June 2014

(c) October 2014

(d) February 2015

211. Which type of WAC has the least Sales Volatility?

(a) $\frac{1}{2}$ Ton

(b) 1 Ton

(c) $\frac{1}{2}$ Ton

(d) 2 Ton

Directions (Q. 212-215) : *Read the following information and graph, and answer the questions that follow.*

An International Organisation produces a Competitive Index of countries every two years based on eight factors (Institutions, Infrastructure, Macroeconomic Environment, Higher Education, Market Efficiency, Technological Readiness, Business Sophistication and Innovation). The last three indices were developed in 2010, 2012 and 2014. The scores for all eight factors of XYZ country are shown in the graph below:

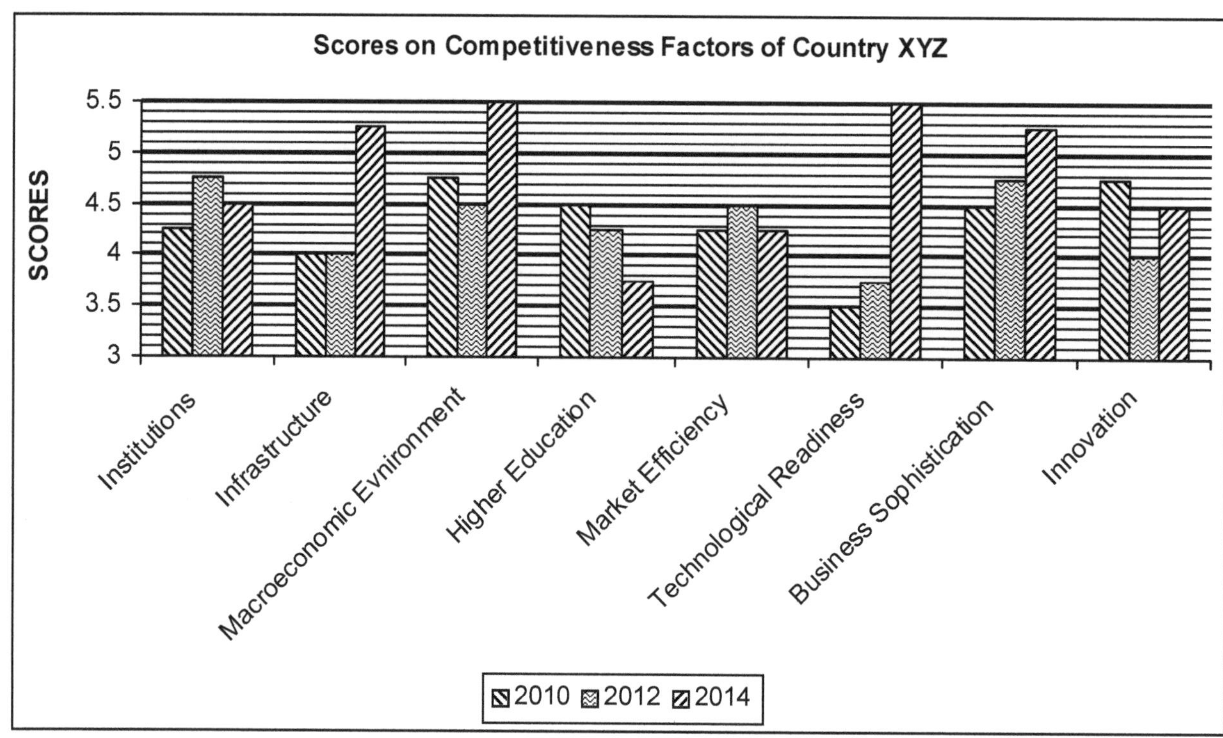

212. If Factor performance is measured as 0.30 × Factor Score in 2014 + 0.35 × Factor Score in 2012 + 0.35 × Factor Score in 2010, then which of the following has best Factor Performance?

(a) Innovation

(b) Business Sophistication

(c) Infrastructure

(d) Macroeconomic Environment

213. If Factor Performance is measured as

$$\left\{ \frac{\text{Factor Score 2014} - \text{Factor Score 2012}}{\text{Factor Score 2010}} \right\}$$

then which of the following has best Factor Performance?

(a) Innovation

(b) Business Sophistication

(c) Infrastructure

(d) Macroeconomic Environment

214. Which of the following factors has the highest average score across indices of 2010, 2012 and 2014?

(a) Infrastructure

(b) Institutions

(c) Technological Readiness

(d) Market Efficiency

215. Which among the following factors had the least growth rate in 2014 versus scores of 2010?

(a) Business Sophistication

(b) Institutions

(c) Technological Readiness

(d) Infrastructure

Directions (Q. 216-219) : *Read the following information and the accompanying graphs to answer the questions that follow.*

www.iav.com spent $ 5,57,000 during last 12 months for online display advertisements, also called impressions, on five websites (Website A, Website B, Website C, Website D and Website E). In this arrangement, www.jay.com is the Destination Site, and the five websites are referred to as the Ad Sites. The allocation of online display advertising expenditure is shown in Graph A. The online display advertisements helped www.jay.com to get visitors on its site. Online visitors, visiting the Ad Sites, are served display advertisements of www.jay.com and on clicking they land on the Destination Site (Graph B). Once on the Destination Site, some of the visitors complete the purchase process (Graph C).

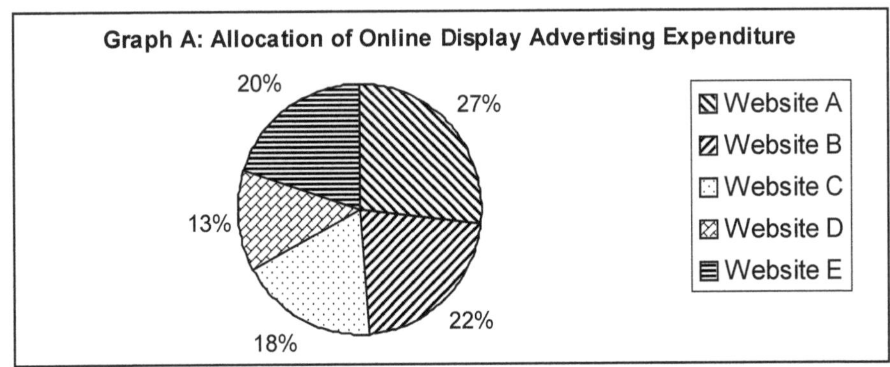

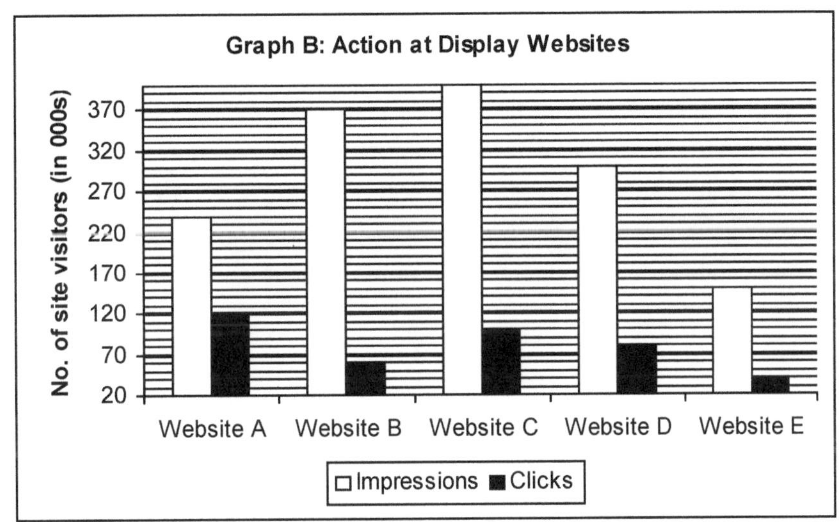

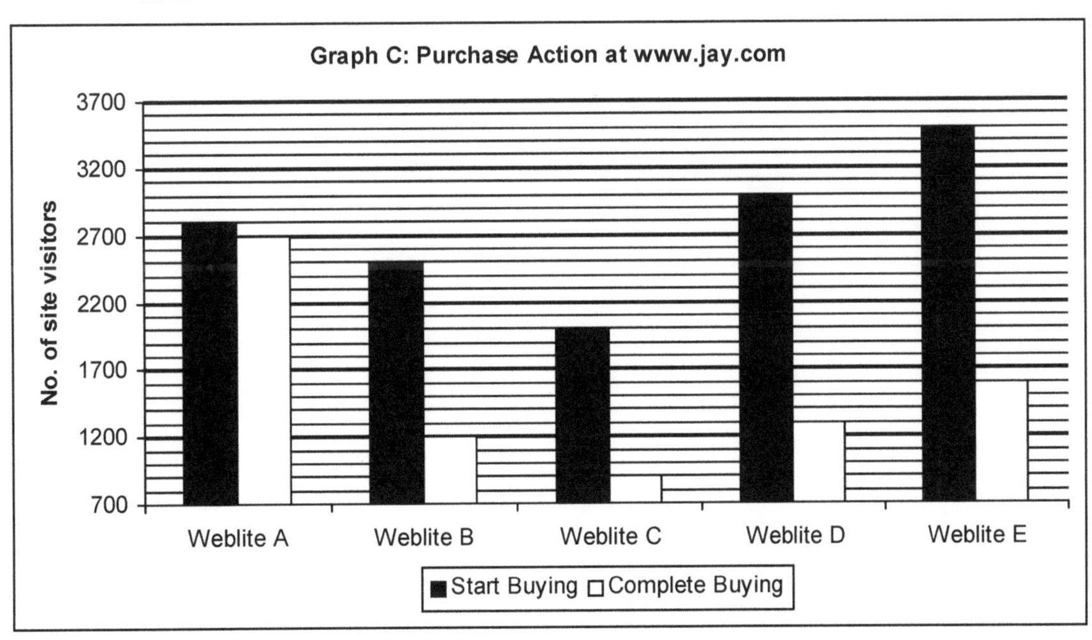

$$\text{Quality traffic} = \frac{\text{No. of site visitors who start purchase on destination site}}{\text{No. of visitors who click the online display advertisement}}$$

$$\text{Leakage in online buying} = 1 - \frac{\text{Complete buying on the destination website}}{\text{Start buying on the destination website}}$$

Efficiency of online display advertising expenditure on an Ad Site

$$= \frac{\text{No. of visitors from the Ad Site who complete the purchase process}}{\text{Amount spent on the Ad Site}}$$

216. Which of following Ad Sites provide facility of least cost per advertisement?

  (a) Website A   (b) Website B

  (c) Website D   (d) Website E

217. Which Ad Site has provided maximum quality traffic?

  (a) Website A   (b) Website B

  (c) Website D   (d) Website E

218. Which Ad Site sent traffic to www.jay.com with maximum leakage?

  (a) Website B   (b) Website C

  (c) Website D   (d) Website E

219. On which Ad Site is the advertising budget spent most efficiently?

  (a) Website A   (b) Website B

  (c) Website C   (d) Website E

2017-19

Directions (Q. 220-224) : *T-Nation, a T Shirt manufacturing company has unleashed 5-5-5 strategy, five brands (Ultimate, Supreme, Smash, Paramount, Astute), five sizes (S, M, L, XL, XXL), and five Stores (S1, S2, S3, S4, S5) to capture New Delhi market. Number of T-Shirts in each of the store is given in the stacked bar chart below.*

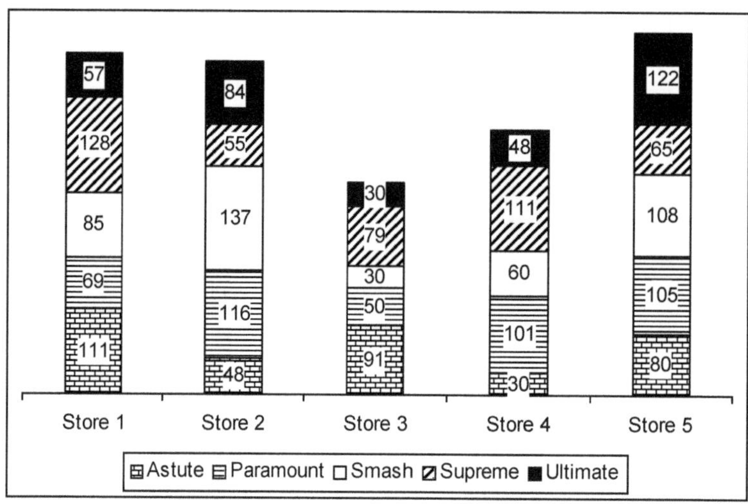

Note: Visibility of a brand in a store is given by number of T-shirts of the brand in the store by total number of T-Shirts in the store. Visibility across the stores is measured by sum of the scores of visibility of a brand in a store.

220. Which brand of T-shirt has more visibility across the stores?

  (a) Astute   (b) Supreme

  (c) Paramount   (d) Smash

221. Which brand has lowest visibility score in any of the stores?

  (a) Astute   (b) Smash

  (c) Paramount   (d) Ultimate

222. Suppose, size M constitutes 22% of all the T-shirts owned by T-nation. It is also given that 'size M T-shirts' in stores 1, 2 and 5 are 10% of the total T-shirts in these stores. Then, the total number of T-shirts of size M in store 4 cannot be less than

  (a) 23   (b) 28

  (c) 32   (d) 44

223. What is the approximate share of Supreme brand in all stores together?

  (a) 19   (b) 22

  (c) 18   (d) 20

224. Approximately, by what percentage are Smash T-shirts greater than Ultimate T-shirts in all the stores together?

  (a) 79   (b) 50

  (c) 35   (d) 23

Directions (Q. 225-229): *The following 2 bar charts represent revenues and expenses (in thousands) of A Ltd, B Ltd, and C Ltd over a period of five years.*

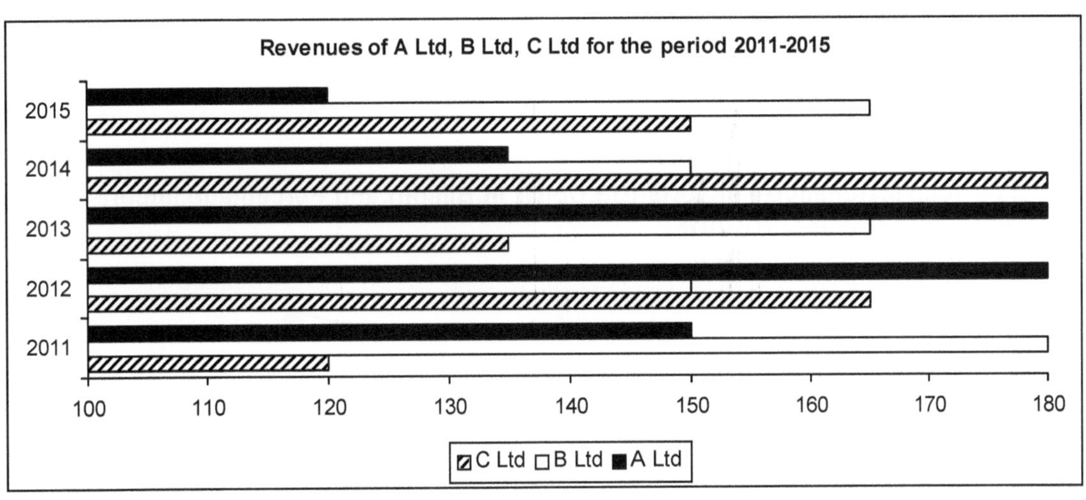

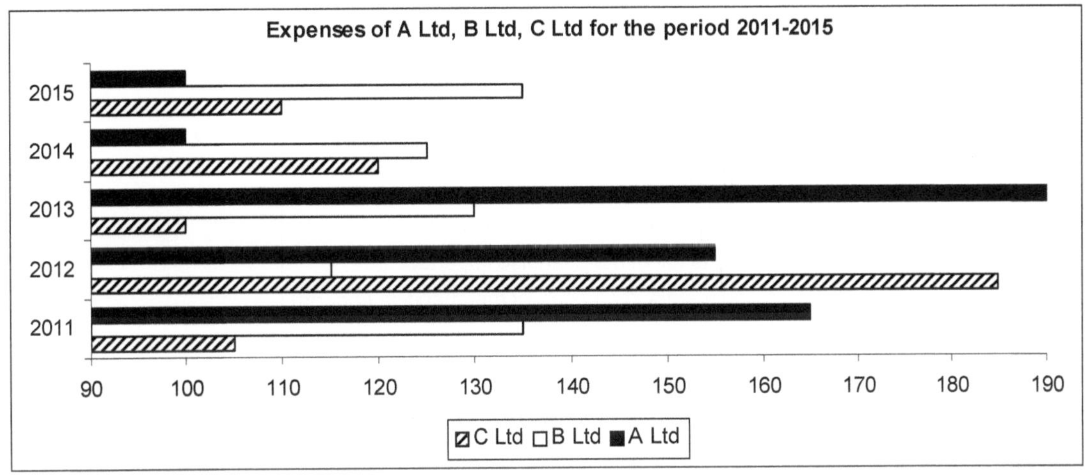

Profit = Revenues – Expenses

225. For which company, the average annual expenses were maximum in the given period?

  (a) A Ltd   (b) B Ltd

  (c) C Ltd   (d) Both A Ltd and B Ltd

226. For which year, the average annual revenue (considering all three companies) was the maximum?

  (a) 2011   (b) 2012

  (c) 2013   (d) 2014

227. What was the approximate percentage decline in the revenue of C Ltd in 2015 as compared to the revenue in 2012?

  (a) 16

  (b) 25

  (c) 33

  (d) 40

228. What was the approximate absolute difference between the average revenue of A Ltd in 2011,2012 and 2013 and the average revenue of B Ltd in 2013,2014 and 2015?

  (a) 20

  (b) 160

  (c) 20000

  (d) 26000

229. For which of the following years the percentage of rise/fall in profit from the previous year was the maximum for A Ltd?

  (a) 2012

  (b) 2013

  (c) 2014

  (d) 2015

2018-20

Directions for Questions 230-234: Exhibit 1 as under provides the data of India's Merchandize Imports (Billion US Dollar) on left axis and Percentage of Food, Fuel, Manufactures and Ores & Metals Imports of India's on the right axis. Similarly; Exhibit 2 provides data of India's Merchandize Exports (Billion US Dollar) on left axis and Percentage exports of Food, Fuel, Manufactures and Ores & Metals on the right axis. Attempt the questions in the context of information provided as under:

(a) Trade Balance = Import Minus Exports   (b) Trade Deficit = If Imports are more than Exports

(c) Trade Surplus = If Exports are more than Imports

Exhibit 1 : India's Total Merchandize Imports (US Dollar in Billion) and Percentage Imports of Food, Fuel, Manufactures and Ores & Metals (2012-2016)

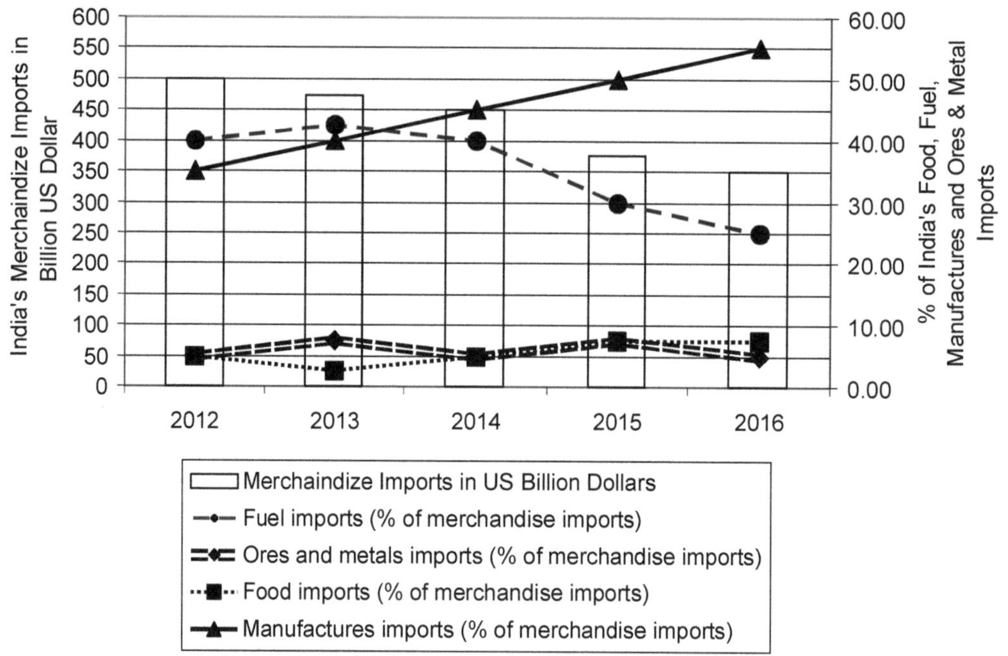

Exhibit 2: India's Total Merchandize Exports (US Dollar in Billion) and Percentage Exports of Food, Fuel, Manufactures and Ores & Metals (2012-2016)

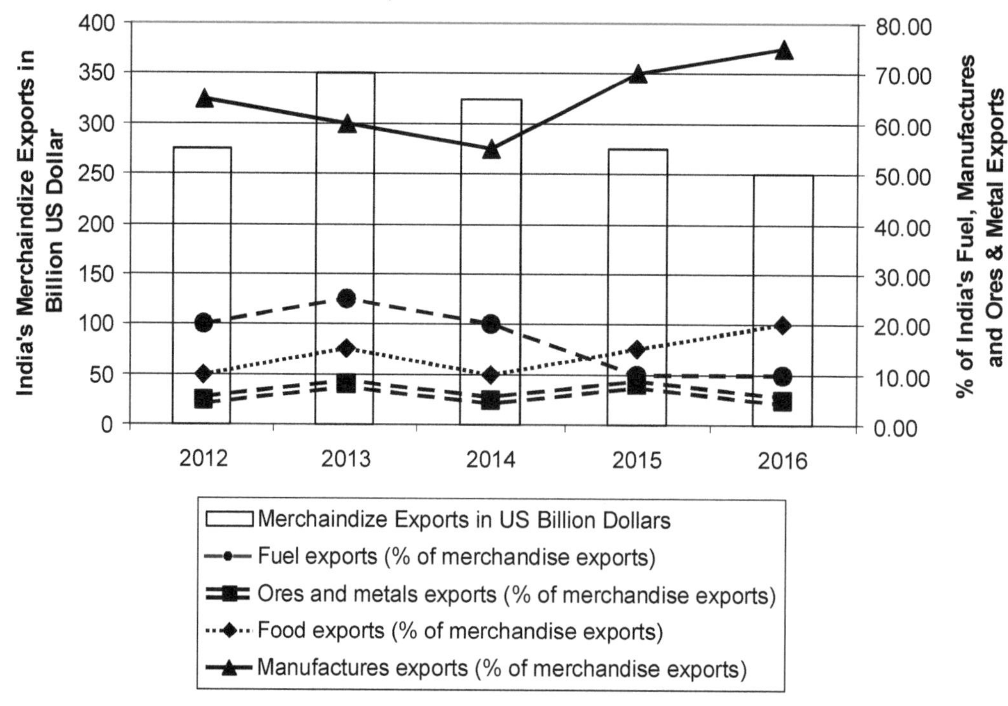

230. What shall be approximate Manufactures exports of India in the year 2016 based on average exports for the period 2012-2016?

(a) 221 Billion US Dollar

(b) 209 Billion US Dollar

(c) 239 Billion US Dollar

(d) 236 Billion US Dollar

231. What is the proportion of positive and negative Manufactures trade balance in the period 2012-2016?

(a) 3 : 2   (b) 2 : 3

(c) 1 : 4   (d) None of the above

232. In which year, trade deficit of fuel has been the second lowest?

(a) 2015   (b) 2014

(c) 2013   (d) 2016

233. Assuming India's imports and exports grow by 10% in 2017 and sectoral share of fuel in both imports and exports grow by 5 percentage basis, what shall be the approximate deficit of fuel trade in the year 2017?

(a) 88 Billion Fuel Trade Deficit

(b) 74 Billion Fuel Trade Deficit

(c) 85 Billion Fuel Trade Deficit

(d) 78 Billion Fuel Trade Deficit

234. Assuming India's absolute trade deficit grows by 54 Billion US Dollar and exports become 324 Billion US Dollar in the year 2017. What shall be India's absolute imports of food and fuel in 2017 if sectoral composition of food, fuel, manufactures, ores and metals remain same as that of 2016?

(a) 36 Billion US Dollar & 119.5 Billion US Dollar

(b) 38 Billion US Dollar & 117.5 Billion US Dollar

(c) 34 Billion US Dollar & 118.5 Billion US Dollar

(d) 38 Billion US Dollar & 116.5 Billion US Dollar

Directions for Question 235-236: *Table as under provides the monthly prices in US Dollars Per Tonne of Barley, Wheat, Maize and Sorghum for the period July 2016 to June 2017. Attempt the questions given as under in the context of information provided.*

Month	Barley Price	Wheat Price	Maize Price	Sorghum Price
16-Jul	140	134	162	174
16-Aug	128	128	150	141
16-Sep	125	123	148	141
16-Oct	128	123	153	139
16-Nov	132	123	151	139
16-Dec	128	123	153	139
17-Jan	132	137	160	140
17-Feb	136	147	163	141
17-Mar	137	146	159	142
17-Apr	139	138	156	143
17-May	142	146	159	144
17-Jun	141	157	158	167

235. In which of the following month, Wheat has the third highest percentage growth in monthly prices?

(a) June 2017   (b) February 2017

(c) January 2017   (d) None of these

236. How many times, the double digit growth in monthly prices occurs across the commodities in the given time period?

(a) 2   (b) 3

(c) 5   (d) None of the above

Directions for Questions 237-239*India has 13 major ports, out of which 6 ports are located in Eastern Coast and 6 ports are in Western Coast of India. 13th port is at Port Blair, located in Andaman & Nicobar Island, which has negligible cargo traffic. Table below provides the traffic data handled by 12 major ports (thousand tonnes) of India for the period 2011-12 to 2015-16. Based on the table, answer the questions:*

Table : Traffic Handled by Major Ports (Thousand Tonnes)					
Ports	2011-12	2012-13	2013-14	2014-15	2015-16
1. Kolkata	43248	39928	41386	46293	50195
2. Paradip	54254	56552	68003	71011	76386
3. Vizag	67420	59038	58504	58004	57033
4. Kamarajar	14956	17885	27337	30251	32206
5. Chennai	55707	53404	51105	52541	50058
6. Chidambaranar	28105	28260	28642	32414	36849
7. Cochin	20090	19845	20886	21595	22099
8. New Mangalore	32941	37036	39365	36566	35582
9. Mormugao	39049	17738	11739	14711	20776
10. Mumbai	56186	58038	59184	61660	61110
11. J.N.P.T.	65730	64488	62333	63801	64027
12. Kandla	82501	93619	87005	92497	100051

237. In which year, the average growth of all ports is the highest?

(a) 2014-15   (b) 2015-16

(c) 2013-14   (d) 2012-13

238. Which of the following port has registered the third highest growth in traffic (000) from year 2011-12 to 2015-16?

(a) Paradip   (c) Chidambaranar

(c) Kandla   (d) None of these

239. What shall be the total approximate traffic (000) of Kolkata, Vizag and Cochin Port in 2017-18 if traffic continues to grow at the annual growth rate of 10% per annum in each of these ports?

(a) 156500

(b) 142300

(c) 129500

(d) 161775

Instructions for Questions 240-244: *The table below relates to data on Wholesale Price of India (WPI) for the period 2001-02 to 2015-16. WPI-based inflation is defined as percentage Change in the value of the Index. Based on the table, answer the following questions:*

TABLE : WHOLESALE PRICE INDEX - ANNUAL AVERAGE						
Year	Index (Average of weeks)					
1	AC	PA	of which		F&P	MP
			FA	NF		
	2	3	4	5	6	7
					(Base: 1993-94 = 100)	
2001-02	161.3	168.4	176.1	152.9	226.7	144.3
2002-03	166.8	174	179.2	165.4	239.2	148.1
2003-04	175.9	181.5	181.5	186.3	254.5	156.5
2004-05	187.3	188.1	186.3	187.6	280.2	166.3
					(Base : 2004-05 = 100)	
2005-06	104.5	104.3	105.4	96.7	113.6	102.4
2006-07	111.4	114.3	115.5	102.3	120.9	108.2
2007-08	116.6	123.9	123.6	114.4	121	113.4
2008-09	126	137.5	134.8	129.2	135	120.4
2009-10	130.8	154.9	155.4	136.2	132.1	123.1
2010-11	143.3	182.4	179.6	166.6	148.3	130.1
2011-12	156.1	200.3	192.7	182.7	169	139.5
2012-13	167.6	220	211.8	201.9	186.5	147.1
2013-14	177.6	241.6	238.9	213.2	205.4	151.5
2014-15	181.2	248.8	253.4	212.1	203.5	155.1
2015-16	176.7	249.6	262.1	219.5	179.8	153.4
AC: All commodities						
PA: Primary articles.						
FA: Food articles.						
NF: Non-food articles.						
F&P: Fuel & Power.						
MP: Manufactured products.						
FA and NF are part of PA.						

240. What is the approximate percentage change in the WPI of F&P between 2001-02 and 2015-16?

(a) 115.5   (b) 122.2

(c) 130.7   (d) 136.4

241. Between 2001-02 and 2015-16, which of the following components - PA, AC, F&P and MP - have shown the second highest percentage increase in WPI?

(a) PA   (b) AC

(a) F&P   (d) MP

242. Between 2001-02 and 2015-16 which year has recorded the smallest percentage increase in WPI on FA?

(a) 2003-04   (b) 2004-05

(c) 2015-16   (d) None of the above.

243. If PA has a 40 percent weightage in the WPI-based inflation calculation in 2005-06, find the corresponding approximate percentage weights assigned to F&P and MP in the WPI- based inflation calculation for the same year.

(a) 12 and 48   (b) 15 and 45

(c) 18 and 42   (d) 20 and 40

244. Which component) in WPI has registered a decline more than once between two consecutive years?

(a) PA

(b) AC

(c) F&P

(d) None of the above

Instructions for Questions 245-249: Refer to the Table below. It provides quarterly output data of a company for four years (1998-2001) and its trend calculated through 4-quarter Moving Average Method.

Quarter wise Value of Output and its Trend

Value of Output			
	Quarter 1	Quarter 2	Quarter 3	Quarter 4
1998	65	58	56	61
1999	68	63	63	67
2000	70	59	56	52
2001	60	55	51	58
4 Quarter Moving Average (Trend)			
1998			60.38	61.38
1999	62.88	64.5	65.5	65.25
2000	63.88	61.12	58	56.25
2001	55.12	55.25		

245. In which year and which quarter the output has second highest positive deviation from its trend?

(a) 1999, Quarter 2   (b) 1999, Quarter 1

(c) 2001, Quarter 4   (d) None of the above

246. In which quarter, on an average there is maximum negative deviation of the output from the average value of trend of that quarter?

(a) Quarter 3   (b) Quarter 1

(c) Quarter 4   (d) Quarter 2

247. In which year the quarterly compound average growth rate (CAGR) is the second lowest?

(a) 2001   (b) 1999

(c) 2000   (d) 1998

248. In which year the annual output growth has been the lowest and what is the value?

(a) 2001, 8.75%   (b) 1999, -6.23%

(c) 2000, -9.20%   (d) 2000, -5.49%

249. Plot the quarterly output and its trend values. Identify the number of times the trend curve intersects the output curve

(a) 5 times

(b) 6 times

(c) 3 times

(d) Cannot be determined, more information required

2019-21

Directions (Questions 250-253): Based on the information given below, answer the questions which follow.

The occupancy rate of a hotel is the share of available rooms that are occupied during a given time. Figure-1 presents quarter wise average hotel occupancy in four regions (Asia-Pacific, America, Europe and Middle East & Africa) for the year 2016. Figure-2, shows the revenue of select hotel chains worldwide in 2016.

Figure-1 Region Wise Average Hotel Occupancy Rates

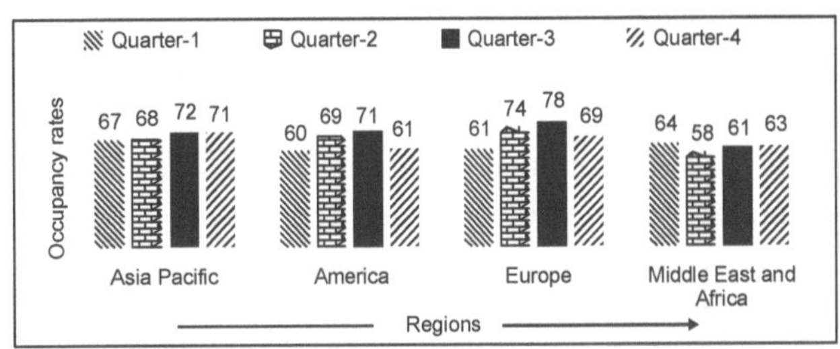

Figure-2 Revenue of Select Hotel Chains Worldwide

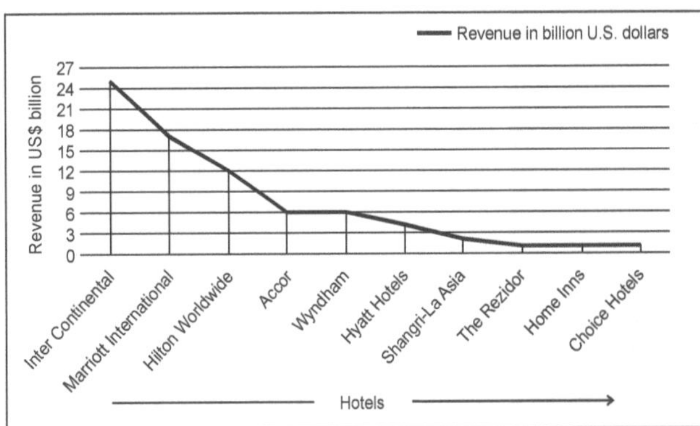

250. Considering the total revenue of the hotel industry in 2016 as 495.17 billion USD, what is the percentage contribution of revenue of select hotel chains to hotel industry revenue?

(a) 13   (b) 14

(c) 15   (d) 16

251. For Hilton Worldwide, considering 70% average occupancy rate for 365 days of operations and average room rent of 350 USD per day, the total number of rooms available (in 000's) in Hilton Worldwide per day approximately are:

(a) 150   (b) 130

(c) 160   (d) 170

252. If the number of available rooms in each of the four regions (Asia-Pacific, America, Europe and Middle East & Africa) are in the ratio 1 : 2 : 5 : 4, the average occupancy rate for Quarter-1 are:

(a) 62   (b) 66

(c) 58   (d) 60

253. Assuming that there is no change in the number of available rooms in a given year in all four regions, the correct arrangement in the increasing order of average annual occupancy rates is :

(a) Asia-Pacific, Europe, America and Middle East & Africa

(b) Middle East & Africa, America, Asia-Pacific and Europe

(c) Asia-Pacific, America, Middle East & Africa and Europe

(d) Middle East & Africa, America, Europe and Asia-Pacific

Directions (Questions 254-257): Based on the information answer the questions which follow.

IBM is one of the most valuable technology brand in the world. Visualizing the trends, IBM has added and dropped business segments across years. For example, *"Technology Services and Cloud Platforms (TSCP)"* which started in 2015 only, generated a revenue of approximately 34280 million U.S. Dollars in 2017. Table shows the Global Revenue generated by IBM in nine different segments of its business from 2010 to 2017 in millions USD.

IBM's Global Revenue from 2010 to 2017
(in millions U.S. Dollars)

Years	TSCP	CS	GBS	SYS	GF	Other	SOFT	GTS	S&T
2010			18,220		2,240	750	22,490	38,200	17,970
2011			19,280		2,100	720	24,940	40,880	18,990
2012			18,570		2,010	580	25,450	40,240	17,670
2013			18,400		2,020	490	25,930	38,550	14,370
2014			17,800		2,000	500	25,400	37,100	10,000
2015	35,140	17,840	17,160	9,550	1,840	210			
2016	35,340	18,190	16,700	7,710	1,690	290			
2017	34,280	18,450	16,350	8,190	1,700	170			

TSCP-Technology Services & Cloud Platforms, CS-Cognitive Solutions, GBS-Global Business Services, SYS-Systems, GF-Global Financing, Other, SOFT-Software, GTS-Global Technology Services and S&T-Systems and Technology

254. For the year 2017, if the revenue in different segments is represented on a pie-chart, what sector angle would be represented by 'Global Business Services (GBS)'?

(a) 75 Degree (b) 85 Degree
(c) 80 Degree (d) 70 Degree

255. Which segment has earned third highest cumulative revenue in the time period 2010-2017?

(a) Global Business Services
(b) Software
(c) Global Technology Services
(d) Systems and Technology

256. The profit booked by IBM in year 2012 is USD 49 billion. Considering equal percentage profit margins across all segments, then approximate profit made by 'Systems and Technology' in millions USD is

(a) 8200 (b) 8500
(c) 8700 (d) 8900

257. By how much is ratio of percentage of 'revenue from Global Business Services' to 'Total Revenue' lower than ratio of percentage of 'revenue from Cognitive Solutions' to 'Total Revenue' for the year 2016?

(a) 1
(b) 2
(c) 3
(d) 5

Directions (Questions 258-261): Based on the information answer the questions which follow.

The Logistics Performance Index (LPI) is an interactive benchmarking tool created by the World Bank to help countries identify the challenges and opportunities they face in their performance on trade logistics and what they can do to improve their performance. It is a measure of the country scores on six key indicators: Customs, Infrastructure, International Shipments, Logistics Competence, Tracking & Tracing and Timeliness. Table shows the LPI indicators (on the scale of 1 to 5) of select countries on these indicators. Figure below presents the perceived performance of these indicators (on the scale of 1 to 5) of India on these 6 indicators.

Table: LPI Indicators of Select Countries in 2018

Countries/ Indicators	Customs	Infrastructure	International Shipments	Logistics Competence	Tracking & Tracing	Timeliness
Austria	3.71	4.18	3.88	4.08	4.09	4.25
UK	3.77	4.03	3.67	4.05	4.11	4.33
USA	3.78	4.05	3.51	3.87	4.09	4.08
Switzerland	3.63	4.02	3.51	3.97	4.1	4.24
France	3.59	4.00	3.55	3.84	4.00	4.15

Figure: LPI Indicators for India

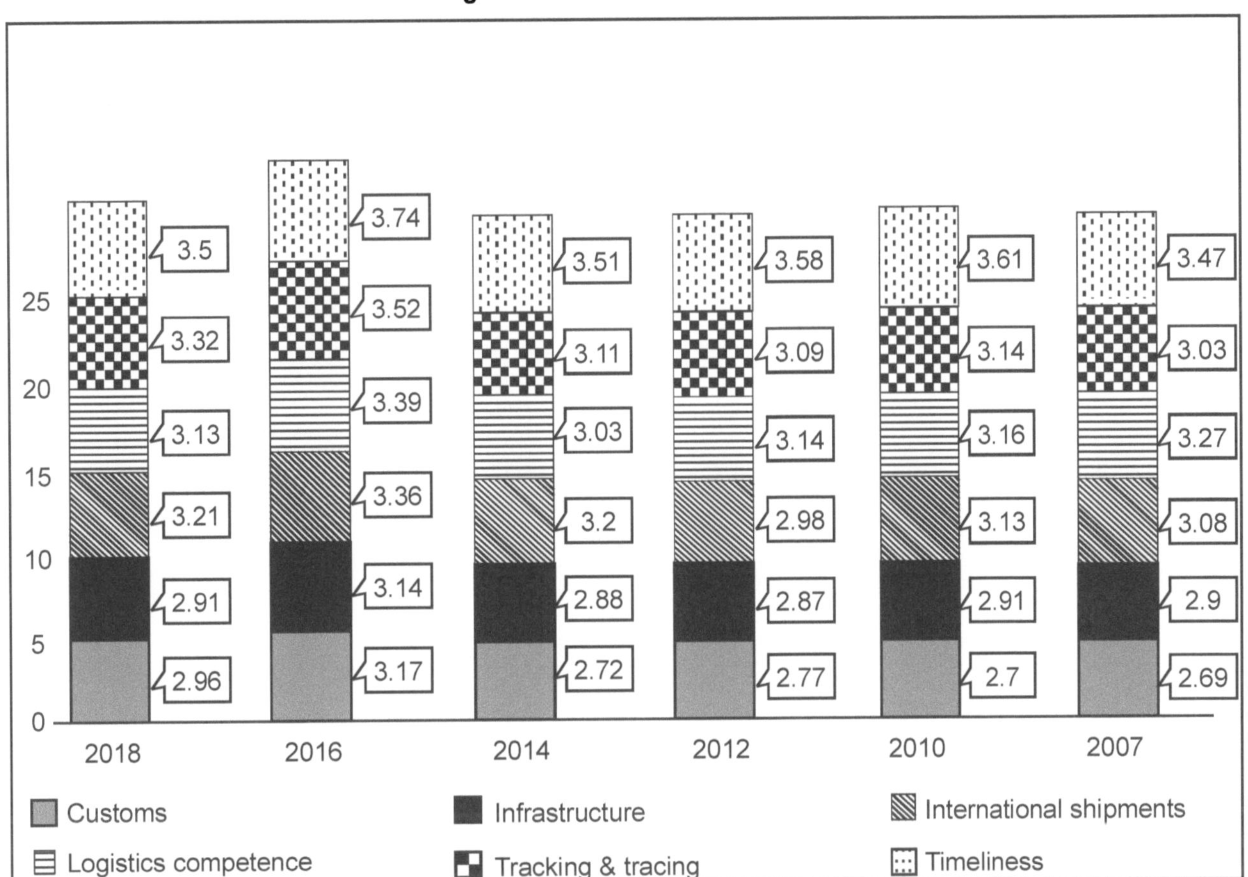

258. Considering Logistics Performance Index as the average of the scores obtained on the six parameters, the correct sequence of the countries in increasing order of LPI in the year 2018 is

(a) UK, Austria, USA, Switzerland and France

(b) Austria, UK, USA, Switzerland and France

(c) France, USA, Switzerland, UK and Austria

(d) UK, USA, Switzerland, Austria and France

259. Arrange the countries in ascending order on the basis of score obtained on (Timeliness) - (Logistics Competence)

(a) Austria, USA, Switzerland, UK and France

(b) Austria, USA, UK, Switzerland and France

(c) Austria, Switzerland, USA, UK and France

(d) Austria, USA, UK, France and Switzerland

260. In which year the difference between the score obtained on Timeliness between Germany and India is minimum considering the score obtained on Timeliness for Germany as 4.39, 4.45, 4.36, 4.32, 4.48 and 4.33 for 2018, 2016, 2014, 2012, 2010 and 2007 respectively?

(a) 2016   (b) 2014

(c) 2012   (d) 2018

261. The difference in performance of which indicator in 2018 as compared to that of 2007 is minimum for India?

(a) Customs

(b) International Shipments

(c) Timeliness

(d) Tracking & Tracing

Directions (Questions 262-265): Based on the information answer the questions which follow.

The data was collected for an industry in order to analyse the impact and importance of select parameters. The Figure represents performance of the industry on select parameters which are Fixed Capital, Materials, Value added and Number of Factories from the year 2008-09 to 2015-16. Total inputs = (Output – Value added). Table represents select performance indicators which are Output, Number of Workers and Emoluments from the year 2008-09 to 2015-16.

Figure: Industry Indicators from 2008-09 to 2015-16

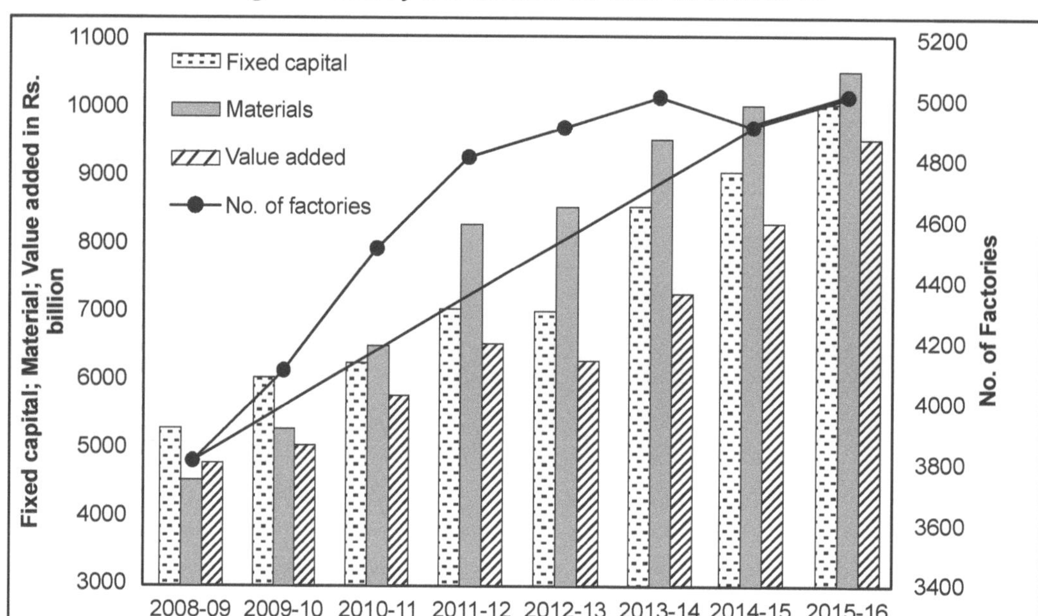

Table: Industry Indicators from 2008-09 to 2015-16

Year	Output in Rs. Billion	No. of workers	Emoluments in Rs. billion
2008-09	11442	2,39,966	65
2009-10	12241	2,50,009	81
2010-11	14993	2,89,965	102
2011-12	18250	3,25,000	135
2012-13	19249	3,30,000	147
2013-14	21493	3,80,000	177
2014-15	23251	3,69,996	202
2015-16	25506	3,99,988	245

262. In which of the following year annual growth rate in emoluments per worker is highest?

(a) 2009-10

(b) 2011-12

(c) 2014-15

(d) 2015-16

263. In which of the following year fixed capital per factory is lowest?

(a) 2008-09

(b) 2011-12

(c) 2013-14

(d) 2015-16

264. In which of the following year Material as a proportion of 'Total inputs' is highest?

(a) 2008-09

(b) 2009-10

(c) 2010-11

(d) 2011-12

265. For how many years annual percentage growth in fixed capital is greater than annual percentage growth in number of factories?

(a) 3

(b) 4

(c) 5

(d) 6

ANSWERS

1. (d)	**2.** (*)	**3.** (a)	**4.** (b)	**5.** (d)	**6.** (b)	**7.** (a)	**8.** (b)	**9.** (a)	**10.** (c)
11. (b)	**12.** (c)	**13.** (b)	**14.** (b)	**15.** (d)	**16.** (b)	**17.** (a)	**18.** (d)	**19.** (c)	**20.** (b)
21. (d)	**22.** (a)	**23.** (a)	**24.** (a)	**25.** (a)	**26.** (b)	**27.** (d)	**28.** (a)	**29.** (c)	**30.** (b)
31. (a,b,d)	**32.** (a,c)	**33.** (b,c,d)	**34.** (b,c)	**35.** (a,b,c,d)	**36.** (a,b)	**37.** (c,d)	**38.** (b,c)	**39.** (a,c)	**40.** (a,d)
41. (c,d)	**42.** (a,c)	**43.** (a,b,d)	**44.** (a)	**45.** (a,c)	**46.** (c)	**47.** (d)	**48.** (a)	**49.** (c)	**50.** (d)
51. (*c)	**52.** (*c)	**53.** (d)	**54.** (a)	**55.** (c)	**56.** (a)	**57.** (b)	**58.** (*d)	**59.** (b)	**60.** (a)
61. (c)	**62.** (a)	**63.** (a)	**64.** (b)	**65.** (a)	**66.** (*)	**67.** (c)	**68.** (c)	**69.** (a)	**70.** (b)
71. (c)	**72.** (a)	**73.** (d)	**74.** (b)	**75.** (c)	**76.** (c)	**77.** (a)	**78.** (c)	**79.** (b)	**80.** (b)
81. (d)	**82.** (c)	**83.** (b)	**84.** (c)	**85.** (c)	**86.** (a)	**87.** (c)	**88.** (c)	**89.** (c)	**90.** (d)
91. (c)	**92.** (b)	**93.** (d)	**94.** (b)	**95.** (b)	**96.** (b)	**97.** (c)	**98.** (c)	**99.** (b)	**100.** (d)
101. (c)	**102.** (a)	**103.** (d)	**104.** (b)	**105.** (b)	**106.** (a)	**107.** (d)	**108.** (b)	**109.** (c)	**110.** (b)
111. (a)	**112.** (c)	**113.** (a)	**114.** (b)	**115.** (a)	**116.** (d)	**117.** (b)	**118.** (d)	**119.** (*)	**120.** (*)
121. (*)	**122.** (*)	**123.** (d)	**124.** (b)	**125.** (d)	**126.** (c)	**127.** (*d)	**128.** (*c)	**129.** (b)	**130.** (a)
131. (d)	**132.** (a)	**133.** (a)	**134.** (d)	**135.** (c)	**136.** (b)	**137.** (c)	**138.** (*d)	**139.** (b)	**140.** (d)
141. (d)	**142.** (c)	**143.** (d)	**144.** (c)	**145.** (a)	**146.** (b)	**147.** (a)	**148.** (a)	**149.** (d)	**150.** (c)
151. (d)	**152.** (c)	**153.** (a)	**154.** (d)	**155.** (c)	**156.** (b)	**157.** (c)	**158.** (a)	**159.** (c)	**160.** (a)
161. (a)	**162.** (a)	**163.** (a)	**164.** (c)	**165.** (b)	**166.** (a)	**167.** (b)	**168.** (d)	**169.** (d)	**170.** (a)
171. (a)	**172.** (d)	**173.** (c)	**174.** (b)	**175.** (c)	**176.** (*a)	**177.** (b)	**178.** (c)	**179.** (b)	**180.** (d)
181. (b)	**182.** (a)	**183.** (d)	**184.** (c)	**185.** (a)	**186.** (c)	**187.** (d)	**188.** (b)	**189.** (a)	**190.** (c)
191. (b)	**192.** (d)	**193.** (c)	**194.** (a)	**195.** (d)	**196.** (c)	**197.** (b)	**198.** (d)	**199.** (d)	**200.** (d)
201. (c)	**202.** (c)	**203.** (b)	**204.** (b)	**205.** (d)	**206.** (b)	**207.** (b)	**208.** (a)	**209.** (c)	**210.** (d)
211. (d)	**212.** (d)	**213.** (c)	**214.** (b)	**215.** (b)	**216.** (c)	**217.** (d)	**218.** (c)	**219.** (a)	**220.** (b)
221. (a)	**222.** (a)	**223.** (b)	**224.** (d)	**225.** (c)	**226.** (b)	**227.** (c)	**228.** (c)	**229.** (b)	**230.** (a)
231. (a)	**232.** (a)	**233.** (b)	**234.** (a)	**235.** (b)	**236.** (d)	**237.** (a)	**238.** (d)	**239.** (a)	**240.** (b)
241. (c)	**242.** (a)	**243.** (a)	**244.** (c)	**245.** (b)	**246.** (b)	**247.** (d)	**248.** (c)	**249.** (b)	**250.** (c)
251. (b)	**252.** (a)	**253.** (b)	**254.** (a)	**255.** (b)	**256.** (a)	**257.** (b)	**258.** (c)	**259.** (a)	**260.** (a)
261. (c)	**262.** (a)	**263.** (a)	**264.** (b)	**265.** c)					

EXPLANATIONS

For questions 1 and 3:

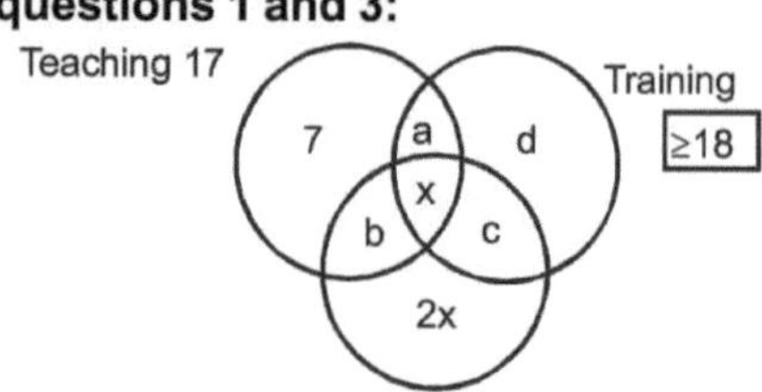

$$a + b + x = 10$$
$$x > 3.5$$
$$a + b + c + d + 3x = 30$$
$$\Rightarrow \quad c + d + 2x = 20$$

Case I: When $x = 4$

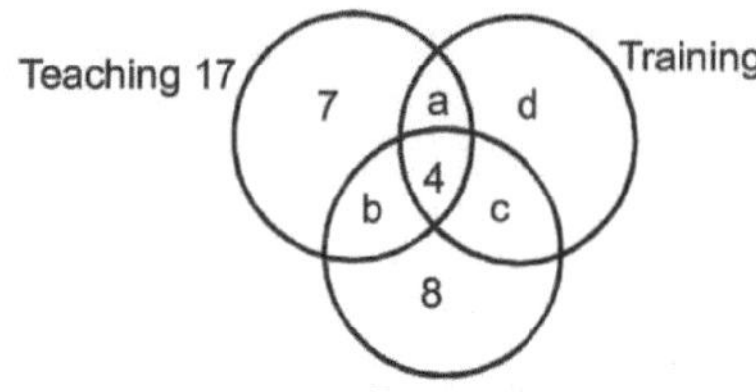

$$a + b = 6$$
$$c + d = 12$$
$$a + c + d + 4 \geq 18$$
$$\Rightarrow \quad a \geq 2$$

a	b	c	d
2	4	1	11
3	3	1	11
3	3	2	10
3	3	3	9
4	2	1	11
4	2	2	10
4	2	3	9
4	2	4	8
4	2	5	7
5	1	1	11
5	1	2	10
5	1	3	9
5	1	4	8
5	1	5	7
5	1	6	6
5	1	7	5
6	0	1	11
6	0	2	10
6	0	3	9
6	0	4	8
6	0	5	7
6	0	6	6
6	0	7	5
6	0	8	4
6	0	9	3

Case II: When $x = 5$

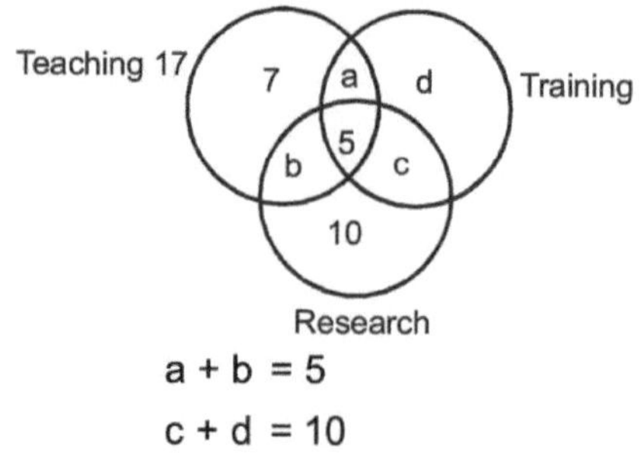

$$a + b = 5$$
$$c + d = 10$$
$$a + c + d + 5 \geq 18$$
$$\Rightarrow \quad a \geq 3$$

a	b	c	d
3	2	0	10
4	1	0	10
4	1	1	9
4	1	2	8
5	0	0	10
5	0	1	9
5	0	2	8
5	0	3	7
5	0	4	6

For any value of $x \geq 6$, training will not have maximum number of faculty members.

Following the table for variables a, b, c and d we can answer the two questions.

2. The minimum number of faculty members involved in both training and teaching, but not in research will be the minimum value of a, i.e., 2.

   ***None of the options match the correct answer**

3. Let 'x' be the number of kg of P1 variety and 'y' be the number of kg of P2 variety.

   Thus, $4x + 6y \leq 700$ and $6x + 10y \leq 1250$. Among the four given options, (c) and (d) do not satisfy the second inequality. The profit margin is $P = 20x + 30y$.

   Profit margin for option (a) = Rs.3900

   Profit margin for (b) = Rs.3800.

   Hence, option (a) is the correct choice.

4. For discrete random variables, the Expected Value - E is equivalent to the probability-weighted sum of all the possible values. There are 2 different possibilities in choice 3. These are:

   Possibility 1: M/s James will reach 75% of the customers. The probability of this possibility is 0.20. Under this possibility, M/s James is the distributor for each of the coming 5 years. The present value of the 5 years cumulative profit is: $5 \times (0.75) + 15 \times (0.75) =$ Rs.15 Crores.

Possibility 2: M/s James will continue to reach only 25% of the customers. The probability of this possibility is 0.80. Under this possibility, M/s James will be the distributor for the first year but M/s Jagan will be the distributor for the next 4 years. The present value of the 5 years cumulative profit is:

$$5 \times (0.25) + 15 \times (0.55) = \text{Rs.}9.5 \text{ Crores.}$$

The expected present value of the 5 years cumulative profit is:

$$E = 15 \times 0.20 + 9.5 \times 0.8 = \text{Rs.}10.6 \text{ Crores.}$$

5. In order to compare the 3 different choices, we need to compare the expected present values of the five years cumulative profit in each of the cases.

   Case 1: The expected present values of the five years cumulative profit under this case is: $(5 \times 0.55 + 15 \times 0.55) \times (1.00) = \text{Rs.}11 \text{ Crores.}$

   Case 2: The expected present values of the five years cumulative profit under this case is:

   $(5 \times 0.60 + 15 \times 0.60) \times (0.60) + (5 \times 0.40 + 15 \times 0.55) \times (0.40) = \text{Rs.}11.3 \text{ Crores.}$

   Case 3: As calculated in question above, the expected present values of the five years cumulative profit under this case is Rs.10.6 Crores.

   It is evident that the statements written in options (a), (b) and (c) are false.

6. The two possibilities for Case 3 are:

   Possibility 1: M/s James will reach 55% of the customers. The probability of this possibility is 0.70. The present value of the 5 years cumulative profit is:

   $$5 \times (0.55) + 15 \times (0.55) = \text{Rs.}11 \text{ Crores.}$$

   Possibility 2: M/s James will continue to reach only 25% of the customers. The probability of this possibility is 0.30. The present value of the 5 years cumulative profit is:

   $$5 \times (0.25) + 15 \times (0.55) = \text{Rs.}9.5 \text{ Crores.}$$

   The expected present value of the 5 years cumulative profit is:

   $$E = 11 \times 0.70 + 9.5 \times 0.30 = \text{Rs.}10.55 \text{ Crores.}$$

   The expected values for Case 1 and Case 2 will remain unaffected at Rs.11 Crores and Rs.11.3 Crores respectively.

7. Time taken in each of the given options case is shown below:

Places	Distance (in km)	Mode of Transportation	Speed	Time
Mumbai – Kanyakumari	950	Bus	40	950/40 = 23.75 hrs
Bhubaneswar – Chennai	950	Ship	30	950/30 = 730 hrs
Chennai – Kochi	901	Ship	30	901/30 = 30.03 hrs
Mumbai – Chennai	1000	Ship	30	1000/30 = 33.33 hrs

8. Costs of each route given in the options is as follows:

   Mumbai – Bhubaneswar (Bus) and Bhubaneswar – Kochi (Airplane)

   $$\text{Total fare} = 701 \times 2 + 798 \times 5$$
   $$= 1402 + 3990 = 5392$$

   Mumbai – Chennai (Ship) and Chennai – Kochi (ship)

   $$\text{Total fare} = 1000 \times 1.5 + 901 \times 1.5$$
   $$= 1500 + 1351.5 = 2851.5$$

   Mumbai – Kanyakumari (Bus) and Kanyakumari – Kochi (Train)

   $$\text{Total} = 950 \times 2 + 1100 \times 2.5$$
   $$= 1900 + 2750 = 4650$$

   Mumbai - Vizag (Airplane) and Vizag – Kochi (Airplane)

   $$\text{Total fare} = 500 \times 5 + 600 \times 5 = 5500$$

9. The cost will be minimum through the given route.

   Chennai $\xrightarrow{\text{Ship}}$ Bhubaneswar $\xrightarrow{\text{Train}}$

   Kanyakumari $\xrightarrow{\text{Ship}}$ Vizag $\xrightarrow{\text{Train}}$ Chennai

   Hence, the required cost (in Rs.)

   $$= (950 + 250) \times 1.5 + (700 + 300) \times 2.5 = 4300.$$

10. Time to reach each of the cities is shown below.

    Bhubaneswar – Chennai (by Ship)

    $$= 950 / 30 = 31.67 \text{ hrs}$$

    Bhubaneswar – Kanyakumari (by Train)

    $$= 700 / 25 = 28 \text{ hrs}$$

    Bhubaneswar – Mumbai (by Bus)

    $$= 701 / 40 = 17.525 \text{ hrs}$$

    Bhubaneswar – Vizag (by Train)

    $$= 1002/25 = 40.08 \text{ hrs}$$

11. The costs for each of the given route is shown below.

    Kochi – Vizag $= 600 \times 5$
    $$= \text{Rs. } 3000.$$

    Kochi – Chennai – Vizag $= 901 \times 1.5 + 300 \times 2.5$
    $$= \text{Rs. } 2051.$$

    Kochi – Kanyakumari – Vizag $= 1100 \times 2.5 + 250 \times 1.5$
    $$= \text{Rs. } 3125.$$

    Kochi – Mumbai – Vizag $= 300 \times 2.5 + 500 \times 5$
    $$= \text{Rs. } 3250.$$

For questions 12 to 16 :

Average Sales of Product A – Average Sales of Product B

$$= 214.29$$

$\Rightarrow$ Total Sales of Product A – Total Sales of Product B

$$= 214.29 \times 7$$
$$= ₹ 1500 \text{ Crores}$$

Let the Sale of Product A in the year 2013 be 'x'.

$\Rightarrow$ (1200 + 500 + 800 + 1200 + x + 1800 + 1300)

$\quad$ − (300 + 600 + 600 + 1000 + 1000 + 700 + 1600)

$\quad$ = 1500

$\Rightarrow$ x = 500

Let the Sales of Product C in 2010 be 'y'.

Total Sales of Product A − Total Sales of Product C

$$= -128.57 \times 7 = -900$$

$\Rightarrow$ 7300 − (1500 + y + 1400 + 1500 + 800 + 1200 + 1000)

$$= -900$$

$\Rightarrow \qquad y = ₹\,800$ Crores

Let the Sales of Product D in 2012 be 'z'.

Total Sales of Product A − Total Sales of Product D

$$= 142.86 \times 7$$

$$= 1000$$

$\Rightarrow$ 7300 − (600 + 1200 + 1100 + z + 100 + 900 + 1800)

$$= 1000$$

$\Rightarrow \qquad z = ₹\,600$ Crores

Average of All the Product Sales in 2009

$$= \frac{1500 + 1300 + 1200 + 600 + 300}{5} = 980$$

Similarly, in the year 2010, average $= \dfrac{4700}{5} = 940$

In 2011; average $= \dfrac{4200}{5} = 840$

In 2012, average $= \dfrac{4500}{5} = 900$

In 2013, average $= \dfrac{4400}{5} = 880$

In 2014, average $= \dfrac{5900}{5} = 1180$

In 2015, average $= \dfrac{6000}{5} = 1200$

13. Annual Sales average of all products is the least in 2011.

14. Product B has the least average Sales for the period 2009–15.

15. The difference between average Sales of Products for the Period 2009–15 is the least for the products A and E. But, It is not available in any option.

    So, As per given options the difference is the least for the Products D and E.

16. The YoY growth of Combined sales of all products has suffered maximum decline in year 2011.

    i.e. $\dfrac{4700 - 4200}{4700} = \dfrac{5}{47}$.

17. Overall pass percentage for Anga

$$= \frac{\text{Total Pass (all years)}}{\text{Total Appeared (all years)}} \times 100$$

$$= \frac{850 + 770 + 1200 + 750 + 1190}{5000 + 5500 + 6000 + 5000 + 7000} \times 100$$

$$= \frac{4760}{28500} \times 100 = 16.7\%$$

18. The total number of candidates passed in the given years is calculated as:

Year	Number of Candidates
2012	3503
2013	3570
2014	4226
2015	3360

Hence, total number of candidates passed from all the kingdoms is the lowest for the year 2015.

19. The pass percentage of Banga kingdom for the given

years $=$In 2012 $= \dfrac{640}{4000} \times 100 = 16\%$

In 2013 $= \dfrac{810}{4500} \times 100 = 18\%$

In 2014 $= \dfrac{1235}{6500} \times 100 = 19\%$

In 2016 $= \dfrac{660}{6000} \times 100 = 11\%$

Hence, it is the highest for 2014

20. Overall pass percentage for 2013 of all kingdoms

$$= \frac{770 + 810 + 275 + 1120 + 595}{5500 + 4500 + 2500 + 8000 + 3500} \times 100$$

$$= \frac{3570}{24000} \times 14.88\%.$$

21. The total number of candidates passed in the given kingdoms can be calculated as:

$$\text{Anga} = 4760, \text{Gandhar} = 3890$$
$$\text{Banga} = 4225, \text{Dwarka} = 4880$$

Hence, it is the highest for Dwarka.

22. The total investment in Energy sector in all the years

$$= 800 + 1200 + 500 + 1400 + 700 + 2500 + 600$$
$$+ 1000 + 1100 + 500$$
$$= 10300$$

The total investment in Financial sector in all the years

$$= 1800 + 500 + 400 + 2000 + 1200 + 1600$$
$$+ 1000 + 1500 + 700 + 1400 = 12100$$

Hence, the required ratio = 103 : 121 or 1 : 1.2.

23.

Sectors	Difference
Basic Materials	4800
Communications	1300
Consumer Cyclical	3900
Consumer Defensive	1800
Energy	2900
Financial Services	1900
Health care	6600
Real Estate	3400
Technology	8100

Hence, answer is option (a)

24.

Year	Total DI
2009	12400
2010	8100
2011	14500
2013	16000

Since total is maximum for 2013

So, average will also be highest for 2013.

25.

Sectors	Total DI
Basic Materials	10000
Communications	6300
Consumer cyclical	4700
Consumer Defensive	7300
Energy	3700
Financial services	5100
Health care	7500
Real estate	13500
Technology	8200

Hence, consumer cyclical sector has received the second lowest investment from DI for the total period.

26.   Total DI = 66300

Total FI = 78400

Hence, required ratio = 2 : 2.36.

27. Estonia $\Rightarrow \dfrac{1.3}{45} = 0.028$

Kyrgyz Republic $\Rightarrow \dfrac{6.5}{20} = 0.032$

Lao PDR $\Rightarrow \dfrac{7}{237} = 0.029$

Latvia $\Rightarrow \dfrac{2}{65} = 0.0307$

Therefore correct order is Estonia < Lao PDR < Latvia < Kyrgyz Republic

28. GNI per capita of word = total GNI/Total for population

$$= \frac{78000}{127498} = 0.611$$

GNI per capita of East Asia & Pacific

$$= \frac{23538}{42085} = 0.559$$

GNI per capita of Europe and Central Asia

$$= \frac{20738}{29793} = 0.697$$

GNI per capita of Latin America and Caribbean

$$= \frac{5282}{9838} = 0.536$$

GNI per capita of Middle East & North Africa

$$= \frac{3220}{8890} = 0.362$$

GNI per capita of North America $= \dfrac{20561}{21291} = 0.965$

GNI per capita of South Asia $= \dfrac{3118}{11697} = 0.266$

GNI per capita Sub-Sahara $= \dfrac{1543}{3908} = 0.394$

East Asia & Pacific is closest.

29. Total World's GNI = 78,000

GNI of India & USA = 2430 + 18980 = 21410

Percentage of India & USA to world

$$= \frac{21410}{78000} = 27.44\%$$

30. In this question, we need to check the difference of GNI per capita and PPP per capita. The following table provides data.

	GNI	PPP	Difference per capita
East Asia	23538	42085	8.0151
Europe	20738	29793	9.8907
Latin America	5282	9838	7.074
Middle East	3220	8890	12.7702
North America	20561	21291	2.011
South Asia	3118	11693	4.7958
Sub-Sahara	1543	3908	2.229

South Asia has the third lowest difference.

For questions 31 to 35:

31. Statement A: Correct

	2001	2002	2003
Wipro	0.1164	0.1189	0.1348
Tata Steel	0.156	0.1489	0.1495

Statement B: Correct

	2001	2003
Indo Rama	0.0111	0.0076
Arvind Mills	0.0316	0.0236
Raymond	0.0372	0.0389
Century Enka	0.00744	0.00811
Steel Authority	0.58412	0.5846
Tata Steel	0.1717	0.1909
Rashtriya Ispat	0.076	0.0636
Ispat Industries	0.0083	0.0086

Statement C: Incorrect

	2001	2002	2003
R & D expenditure of Tata Steel as a percentage of sales	0.117	0.096	0.152
Percentage of R & D expenditure to sales as iron and steel sector as a whole	0.134	0.115	0.105

Statement D: Correct as 5 companies show decline.

	2002	2003
Ranbaxy	0.4646	0.225
Dr.Reddy Lab	0.727	-0.004
Cipla Ltd.	0.3167	0.1206
Glaxosmithkline	0.0472	0.0375
Wipro	0.1115	0.1608
Infosys	0.3698	0.3913
Videocon	0.5332	-0.275
Bharat Electronics	0.1257	0.291

32. Statement A: Correct

Sectors	Required Percentage
Textiles	8.31%
Pharmaceuticals	7.77405%
Electronics	7.7704%
Iron and Steel	9.64%

Statement B: Incorrect (Ispat Industries will be ranked lowest.)

Companies	Required Percentage
Indo Rama	1.4%
Arvind Mills	6.57216%
Raymond Ltd.	16.23188%
Century Enka Ltd.	3.69979%
Ranbaxy	6.0099%
Dr. Reddy's	8.03519%
Cipla	4.64081%
Glaxo Smithkline	11.19163%
Wipro	15.85%
Infosys	46.31%
Videocon	1.4714%
Bharat electronics	14.62058%
Steel Authority	18.04016%
Tata Steel	11.58125%
Rashtriya Ispat Nigam	7.83028%
Ispat Industries limited	1.18076%

Statement C: Correct

Companies	Required Percentage
Indo Rama	0
Arvind Mills	0
Raymond Ltd.	0
Century Enka Ltd.	0
Ranbaxy	5.54753%
Dr. Reddy's	5.95794%
Cipla	3.35%
GlaxoSmithkline	0.33417%
Wipro	0.43017%
Infosys	0.57604%
Videocon	0
Bharat electronics	4.6225%
Steel Authority	0.30077%
Tata Steel	0.09665%
Rashtriya Ispat Nigam	0.0714286%
Ispat Industries limited	0

Statement D: Incorrect

Wipro did not make the highest profit as Indo Rama Synthetic Ltd. has made a higher growth than Wipro in the year 2001-2003.

33. Statement A: Correct

By observation.

Statement B: (Incorrect as the percentage is minimum for Electronics sector.)

Sectors	Required Percentage
Textiles	8.31%
Pharmaceuticals	7.77405%
Electronics	7.7704%
Iron and Steel	9.64%

Statement C: Incorrect

It is incorrect as for no company, the required percentage is greater than 20%.

Statement D: Incorrect

In the year 2002, the ratio of total profits to total sales is −0.02880 and in the year 2001, the given ratio is −0.0260.

34. Statement A: Incorrect

Because in the year 2002-2003, Cipla Ltd. had a 100% decline in the R & D expenditure.

Statement B: Correct

Company	Ratio
Ranbaxy	0.0541
Dr. Reddy's	0.0696
GlaxoSmithKline	0.0033501
Infosys	0.00565
Bharat Electrical	0.04655
Steel Authority of India Limited	0.0028
Tata Steel	0.00124

The ratio was highest for Dr. Reddy's.

Statement C: Correct

During the year 2001-2003, in terms of sales growth, the best performer in the Pharmaceutical sector was Ranbaxy which had a 79.55% growth and no company had a growth rate greater than any company in the Iron and Steel sector.

Statement D: Incorrect

Arvind Mills in the year 2001-2002 and Indo Rama Synthetic Ltd. in the year 2002-2003 have greater percentage decline than Videocon in any of the given years.

35.

Statement	2001	2002	2003
A	0.02779	0.01976	0.0196
B	0.156096	0.14891	0.1495
C	0.12161	0.11612	0.1119
D	0.2247	0.0883	0.0869

The values in the statements A, B, C and D for the given three years when plotted closely resemble in the figure.

For questions 36 to 39:

36. **Statement A: Correct**

From graphs, we can conclude that the vote share of Democrats and Labour party in 1998 is greater than their combined vote share in 2002.

Statement B: Correct

Number of seats lost by Democrats in 2002 elections

$$= (33.53 \times 5.01 - 25.48 \times 6.20)$$

$$= 168 - 158 = 10$$

Number of seats gained by the Republicans in 2002

$$= (7.9 \times 6.2 - 6 \times 5.01)$$

$$= 49 - 30 = 19.$$

Statement C: Incorrect

Independents gained the most in terms of vote share but in terms of the number of seats, labour gained the most over the 2000 election as they increased their seats from 105 in 2000 election to 165 in 2002 election.

Statement D: Incorrect.

In the year 2002 as well as in the year 1996, 70% of Independants and Labour are eligible to form the government as their share in the seats won is greater than 50% in each of the years.

37. **Statement A: Correct**

The percent increase in seats obtained by the Liberals and Labour together in 2002 over the year 1998 is 11.39% and the percentage increase in the vote share obtained by these parties during the same period is 1.34%.

Statement B: Correct

By observation, Labour party showed the greatest percentage increase in the vote share obtained in the year 2000 over the year 1998 across all the parties.

Statement C: Incorrect

Because in 2000 elections, three parties namely Independents, Democrats and Liberal faced a decline in the vote share, whereas in 1998 four parties (excluding democrats) faced decline.

Statement D: Incorrect

Highest jump in the percentage of seats obtained by any party (Independents in 2000 over the year 1998)

$$= (38.72 - 32.98) = 5.74\%$$

Highest jump in the percentage of vote share obtained by any party (Democrats in 1998 over the year 1996)

$$= (25.69 - 20.29) = 5.4\%$$

38. **Statement A: Incorrect**

Vote share of Labour and Liberal party taken together in the year 1996

$$= 28.8 + 1.97 = 30.77$$

Vote share of Labour and Liberal party taken together in the year 1998

$$= 25.82 + 1.75 = 27.57$$

$\therefore$ Loss of vote share = 3.2%

Number of seats won by Labour and Liberal in the year 1996 = 143

Number of seats won by Labour and Liberal in the year 1998 = 158

$\therefore$ Gain is 15 seats.

Statement B: Correct

Democrats, Republicans and 35% of the Independents could have formed the government in two elections 1998 and 2000.

Statement C: Correct

By observation, we find that no party increased its vote share in every succeeding elections.

Statement D: Incorrect

In 1996, vote share of the Republicans and Democrats

$$= (20.29 + 6.12) = 26.41\%$$

In 2000, vote share of the Republicans and Democrats

$$= (23.75 + 5.4) = 29.15\%$$

In 1996, percentage of seats of the Republicans and Democrats = (29.61 + 5.88) = 35.49%

In 2000, percentage of seats of the Republicans and Democrats = (33.53 + 6.00) = 39.53%.

Difference in the vote share = 2.74%

Difference in the percentage of the seats = 4.04%

39. Statement A: Incorrect

Percentage of seats obtained by Democrats and Labour together in years 1996, 1998, 2000 and in 2002 were 55.49%, 59.29%, 54.45% and 52.09% respectively. In 2002, they lost only 2.36% but in 2000 elections, they lost 4.84%. Hence, (a) is incorrect.

Statement B: Correct

Vote share of the Liberals and Republicans together in the year 1998 = 6.91%.

Vote share of the Liberals and Republicans together in the year 2000 = 6.88%.

Number of seats obtained by the Liberals and Republicans together in the year 1998 = 44.

Number of seats obtained by the Liberals and Republicans together in the year 2000 = 34.

Statement C: Incorrect

Difference in the number of seats won by Independents in 2000 and 1998 = +6

Difference in the number of seats won by Labour in 2000 and 1998 = −43

Difference in the number of seats won by Republican in 2000 and 1998 = −4

Difference in the number of seats won by Liberals in 2000 and 1998 = −6

Difference in the number of seats won by Democrats in 2000 and 1998 = −22

Statement D: Correct

Number of seats won by Labour party in the year 1996 = 132

Number of seats won by Labour party in the year 1998 = 148

Number of seats won by Labour party in the year 2000 = 105

Number of seats won by Labour party in the year 2002 = 165

For questions 40 and 41:

40. Statement A: Correct

	Gap	Rank
North America	-7.3	6
Latin America	9.9	3
Central and Eastern Europe	11.6	2
Western Europe	-1.4	5
Africa	14.4	1
Asia	2.6	4

Rank of Central and Eastern Europe is second.

Statement B: Incorrect (The highest percentage change in exports was highest in the year 2000.)

Year	Average Annual Percentage Change
1997	5.03333333
1998	- 3.85
1999	4.716
2000	18
2001	-3.61666
2002	3.5666
2003	16.5

Statement C: Incorrect (Rank of Asia is third)

	Gap	Rank
North America	0.2	5
Latin America	-1.5	4
Central and Eastern Europe	-5.9	2
Western Europe	2.5	6
Africa	-10.6	1
Asia	-1.7	3

Statement D: Correct

The lowest change (whether increase or decrease) is observed in year 1998 at −0.45.

Year	Average Annual Percentage Change
1997	6.98333
1998	-0.45
1999	0.51666
2000	13.1
2001	-3.4
2002	-2.9333
2003	16.1833

41. Statement A: Incorrect

North American regions average annual percentage change in exports is 2.25 is less than the average annual percentage change in exports of Latin America which is 6.3.

Statement B: Incorrect

Regions	Average Annual Percentage Change
North America	10.9
Latin America	9.375
Central and Eastern Europe	1.7
Western Europe	3.45
Africa	1
Asia	4.15

Africa region experienced the lowest average annual percentage change in imports as compared to other regions.

Statement C: Correct

In the year 1999-2000 Central and Eastern European region experienced a jump of 26.1 which is the highest across all companies in any of the given years.

Statement D: Correct

In the year, 2000-2001 Asian region suffered the maximum slump which is 30.1 and it is the highest across all companies in any of the given years.

For questions 42 to 45:

42. (a) Correct

Growth rate of female population during 2005-2010
$$= (3360 - 3189) / 3189 \times 100$$
$$= 5.4\%$$

Growth rate of male population during 2010-2015
$$= (3569 - 3403) / 3403 \times 100$$
$$= 4.88\%$$

(b) Incorrect

Growth rate of population of high income countries during 2005-2010
$$= 17 / 980 \times 100 = 1.73\%.$$

Growth rate of male population in East Asia and Pacific during 2010-2015
$$= 36 / 1001 \times 100 = 3.59\%.$$

(c) Correct

Growth rate of male population in low income countries during 2005-2010
$$= (1438 - 1330) / 1330 \times 100$$
$$= 8.12\%$$

Growth rate of female population in low income countries during 2005-2010
$$= (1400 - 1294) / 1294 \times 100$$
$$= 8.19\%$$

(d) Incorrect

Growth rate of world population during 2005-2010
$$= (6764 - 6418) / 6418 \times 100$$
$$= 5.39\%$$

Growth rate of world population during 2010-2015
$$= (7096 - 6764) / 6764 \times 100$$
$$= 4.90\%$$

43. (a) Incorrect

Share of high income countries in total world population in 2005
$$= 980 / 6418 \times 100 = 15.27\%$$

Share of high income countries in total female population in 2005
$$= 497 / 3189 \times 100 = 15.58\%$$

(b) Incorrect

Share of Europe and Central Asia in total male population in 2005
$$= 229 / 3230 \times 100 = 7.09\%$$

Share of Europe and Central Asia in total male population in 2010
$$= 229 / 3403 \times 100 = 6.73\%$$

Share of Europe and Central Asia in total male population in 2015
$$= 230 / 3569 \times 100 = 6.44\%$$

(c) Correct

Share of middle income countries in total female population in 2015
$$= 1512 / 3528 \times 100 = 42.86\%$$

Share of low income countries in total world population in 2010
$$= 2838 / 6764 \times 100 = 41.96\%$$

(d) Incorrect

Share of South Asia in total female population in 2015
$$= 821 / 3528 \times 100 = 23.27\%$$

Share of South Asia in total world population in 2010
$$= 1581 / 6764 \times 100 = 23.37\%$$

44. (a) Correct

Share of high income countries in total female population in 2005
$$= 497 / 3189 \times 100 = 15.58\%$$

Share of high income countries in total female population in 2010
$$= 505 / 3360 \times 100 = 15.03\%$$

Share of high income countries in total female population in 2015
$$= 511 / 3528 \times 100 = 14.48\%$$

Share of high income countries in total male population in 2005
$$= 483 / 3230 \times 100 = 14.95\%$$

Share of high income countries in total male population in 2010
$$= 491 / 3403 \times 100 = 14.43\%$$

Share of high income countries in total male population in 2015
$$= 497 / 3569 \times 100 = 13.92\%$$

(b) Incorrect

Growth rate of population of high income countries during 2010-2015
$$= (1008 - 997) / 997 \times 100 = 1.10\%$$

Growth rate of world population during 2010-2015
$$= (7096 - 6764) / 6764 \times 100$$
$$= 4.91\%$$

(c) Incorrect

Share of South Asia's females in total world population in 2005

$$= 715 / 6418 \times 100 = 11.14\%$$

Share of South Asia's females in total world population in 2015

$$= 821 / 7096 \times 100 = 11.56\%$$

Share of South Asia's females in total female population in 2005

$$= 715 / 3189 \times 100 = 22.42\%$$

Share of South Asia's females in total female population in 2015

$$= 821 / 3528 \times 100 = 23.27\%$$

Growth rate of Share of South Asia's female in total world population during 2005-2015

$$= (11.56-11.14)/11.14 \times 100$$
$$= 3.77\%$$

Growth rate of Share of South Asia's female in total female population during 2005-2015

$$= (23.27-22.42)/22.42 \times 100$$
$$= 3.79\%$$

(d) Incorrect

Growth rate in population of middle income countries during 2010-2015

$$= (3040 - 2928) / 2928 \times 100$$
$$= 3.82\%$$

Growth rate in population of middle income countries during 2005-2010

$$= (2928 - 2814) /2814 \times 100$$
$$= 4.05\%$$

Growth rate in population of high income countries during 2005-2010

$$= (997 - 980) / 980 \times 100$$
$$= 1.73\%$$

Growth rate in population of high income countries during 2010-2015

$$= (1008 - 997)/997 \times 100 = 1.10\%$$

45. (a) Incorrect

Share of South Asia in total world population in 2005

$$= 1470/6418 \times 100 = 22.90\%$$

Share of South Asia in total world population in 2015

$$= 1684/7096 \times 100 = 23.73\%$$

Share of low income countries in total world population in 2005

$$= 2624/6418 \times 100 = 40.88\%$$

Share of low income countries in total world population in 2015

$$= 3048/7096 \times 100 = 42.95\%$$

$$(23.73-22.90) < (42.95 - 40.88)$$

(b) Correct

Share of high income countries in total female population in 2010

$$= 505/3360 \times 100 = 15.02\%$$

Share of high income countries in total female population in 2015

$$= 511/3528 \times 100 = 14.48\%$$

Share of high income countries in total world population in 2010

$$= 997/6764 \times 100 = 14.73\%$$

Share of high income countries in total world population in 2015

$$= 1008/7096 \times 100 = 14.20\%$$

(c) Incorrect

Growth rate of female population in East Asia and Pacific region during 2010–2015

$$= (1001-963)/963 \times 100 = 3.94\%$$

Average annual growth rate = 3.94/5 = 0.79%

Growth rate of female population in South Asia region during 2010-2015

$$= (821-769)/769 \times 100 = 6.76\%$$

Average annual Growth rate = 1.35%

(d) Correct

Growth rate of female population in Europe and Central Asia during 2005-2015

$$= 1/248 \times 100 = 0.40\%$$

Growth rate of male population in Europe and Central Asia during 2005–2015

$$= 1/229 \times 100 = 0.43\%.$$

For questions 46 and 47: The average age of the different groups is in the range of 43 - 55. So whenever

(1) A 25 year old joins the group, the average age of the group dips by around 5 to 6 years.

(2) A 60 years old is retired, the average age of the group dips lesser than that in statement (1) above.

Logical Reasoning	Total Age
2004	49.33 × 3 = 148
2005	44 × 4 = 176,
	(Here, one faculty member joined whose age is 25 years)
2006	45 × 4 = 180
2007	46 × 4 = 184

Data Interpretation	Total Age
2004	$50.5 \times 4 = 202$
2005	$51.5 \times 4 = 206$
2006	$52.5 \times 4 = 210$
2007	$47.8 \times 5 = 239$ (One faculty member joined aged 25.)

English	Total Age
2004	$50.2 \times 5 = 251$
2005	$49 \times 4 = 196$ year (One faculty member retired aged 60.)
2006	$45 \times 5 = 225$ (One faculty member joined aged 25.)
2007	$46 \times 5 = 230$

Quant	Total Age
2004	$45 \times 6 = 270$
2005	$43 \times 7 = 301$ (One faculty member joined aged 25.)
2006	$44 \times 7 = 308$
2007	$45 \times 7 = 315$

46. Read the notes in the beginning of the solution. The average age dips twice first from 2004 to 2005 and then from 2005 to 2006. The dip is more when a 25 years old joins & lesser when somebody retires.

47. Let the person be X. From the data for 2004, as on April 1, 2004:

(Age of Sharma) + (Age of Verma) + (Age of X)

$$= 49.33 \times 3 = 148 \text{ years.}$$

Now the sum of ages of Sharma and Verma, as on 1 April 2004 is:

$$\begin{array}{r} 52y + 4m + 10d \\ +49y + 4m + 10d \\ \hline (101y + 8m + 20d) \end{array}$$

$\Rightarrow$ the age of X on 1 April 2004 is $47y + 3m + 10d$

$\Rightarrow$ X's age on 1 April 2009 is $\equiv 52y + 3m + 10d$

Hence, (d) is the correct option.

For questions 48 to 52:

Calculating the growth rates (in %) of the countries:

Country	2000	2001	2002	2003	2004	2005	Rate per year
Cambodia	23.03	7.99	28.2	10.14	32.1	10.79	18.71
China	27.84	6.78	22.36	34.59	35.39	28.37	25.89
India	18.82	2.32	13.58	15.91	32.37	25.85	18.14
Japan	14.76	-15.81	3.27	13.22	19.89	5.17	6.75
South Korea	19.89	-12.67	7.99	19.29	30.97	12.04	12.4
Myanmar	44.89	44.65	27.93	-18.48	-4.15	22.9	19.62
Singapore	20.16	-11.65	2.81	27.74	24.22	15.61	13.15
Thailand	18.17	-5.92	4.83	17.94	19.82	14.4	11.54
Vietnam	25.21	4.01	9.99	22.06	27.01	23.41	18.62

48. From the table given above, it is clear that Cambodia experienced the third highest average annual export growth rate over the period 1999 – 2005.

49. Option (a): During 1999-2000, Myanmar registered the highest annual export growth rate, i.e., 44.89%. Hence, (a) is true.

Option (b): During 2003-2004, India registered the second highest annual export growth rate, i.e., 32.37% after China. Hence, (b) is true.

Option (c): During 2001-2002, Cambodia registered the highest annual export growth rate, i.e., 28.2%. Hence, (c) is not true.

Option (d): The change in Thailand's export growth rate from 2000-2001 to 2001-2002 is $4.83 - (-5.92) = 10.75\%$. Hence, (d) is true.

50. Option (a): During 2000 – 2001, South Korea registered the second lowest export growth rate just above Japan. Hence, (a) is false.

Option (b): Sum of export growth rates of India and Vietnam during $2001 - 2002 = 13.58 + 9.99 = 23.57$, which is not lower than the growth rate of China (i.e. 22.36%) in that particular period. Hence, (b) is false.

Option (c): Cambodia, China, India and Vietnam witnessed maximum number of years of positive export growth rate during the entire period. Hence, (c) is false.

Option (d): During 2004 – 2005, difference between the growth rates of China and Japan $= 28.37 - 5.17 = 23.2\%$, which is lower than the export growth rate of Vietnam (23.41%) in the same period. Hence, (d) is not false.

51. *The language is slightly ambiguous. A likely solution is given below:

Difference between the highest and the lowest average annual export growth rates by the countries for the periods 1999-00 and 2004 – 05:

Cambodia $10.79 - 23.03 = -12.24\%$

China: 0.53%; India: 7.03%; Japan: –9.59%; South Korea: –7.85%; Myanmar: –21.99%; Singapore: –4.55%; Thailand: –3.77%; Vietnam: –1.8%

Clearly, China has the second highest difference.

52. *The language is slightly ambiguous. A likely solution is as below:

Difference between the highest and the lowest average annual export growth rates by the countries yearwise for the period:

$1999 - 00 : 44.89 - 14.76 = 30.13\%$

$2001 - 02 : 28.2 - 2.81 = 25.39\%$

$2004 - 05 : 28.37 - 5.17 = 23.2\%$

$2003 - 04 : 35.39 - (-4.15) = 39.54\%$

Hence, minimum is in the period 2004 – 05, i.e. option (c) is the correct answer.

53. The average annual level of SO_2 emission for Yamuna Nagar during 1997 – 2003 is 23.94 and not 23.74 μ^9/m^3. Hence, option (d) is false.

54. The highest average annual level of SO_2 emission on different years is as follows

$$1997 \rightarrow 112.3$$
$$1998 \rightarrow 114.9$$
$$1999 \rightarrow 93.3$$
$$2000 \rightarrow 64.6$$
$$2001 \rightarrow 46.5$$
$$2002 \rightarrow 40.9$$
$$2003 \rightarrow 39.3$$

So the different is maximum for the years 1998 & 2003.

55. In Faridabad, the emission level of SO_2 in the years 2001, 2002 and 2003 is less than in any years from 1997-2000. So definitely, the average level of SO_2 emission during 1997-2000 for Faridabad is higher than the average annual level for the city for the period from 1997-2003.

56. By options:

(a) Cochin & Pondichery during 1999 – 2000

Cochin $\rightarrow$ + 31.1

Pondichery $\rightarrow$ – 55.7

(b) Calcutta & Nagda during 1998 – 1999

Calcutta $\rightarrow$ + 26.7

Nagda $\rightarrow$ – 28.3

(c) Madras & Anpara during 2001 – 2002

Madras $\rightarrow$ + 14.8

Anpara $\rightarrow$ – 22.9

(d) Nagda & Pondichery during 1997 – 1998

Nagda $\rightarrow$ – 26.6

Pondichery $\rightarrow$ + 2.6

The difference is maximum in option (a) (Both cases when absolute difference is required or not) i.e. 86.8.

57. The annual emissile level decline for different years are as follows

1997 – 1998	8
1998 – 1999	4
1999 – 2000	5
2000 – 2001	7
2001 – 2002	6
2002 – 2003	10

It is maximum during 2002 – 2003.

Hence, the correct option is (b).

58. The average number of workers per factory for factory C decreased between 2003-04 by 7 so automatically by 6. All other statements are completely false.

***Note: The statement (D) must have been the average number of workers per factory for factory C decreased between 2003-2004 and 2004-2005 by 7.**

59.

	2003-04					2004-05				
	A	B	C	D	E	A	B	C	D	E
Invested Capital per worker	10.56	6.21	17.35	11.72	7.48	13.31	13.5	10.6	33.3	42.4

Hence, D is ranked second both between 2003-04 and 2004-05.

60.

	2004-05				
	A	B	C	D	E
Working Capital / Invested Capital	0.2	0.2	0.2	0.192	0.197

Hence, E has the second highest ratio.

61. Increase in gross fixed capital formation between 2003–04 and 2004–05 for D = 1010963 – 12369 = 9,98,594.

Corresponding increase for C and E = 739375 – 27821 = 7,11,554.

62.

	2003-04					2004-05				
	A	B	C	D	E	A	B	C	D	E
Average Profit per factory	121	61	–64	147	29	27	118	44	778	534

Hence, A has the second highest and the lowest average profit per factory for 2003-04 and 2004-05 respectively.

For questions 63 to 66:

63. Rank 1 → Europe to North America Iron and Steel export [81 − (− 9) = 90]

    Rank 2 → Intra-North America Iron and Steel export [41 − 4 = 37]

64. Rank 1 → Europe to North America Iron and Steel export (81 − 21 = 60)

    Rank 2 → Intra-Europe Iron and Steel export (45 − 10 = 35)

65. The difference between the highest and the lowest average export growth rate during 2005 among all three industries and regions is-

    39 {Europe to Asia Iron and Steel export} − (−1){Europe to Asia automotive parts export} = 40.

66. Option (b) should have been for the year 2003-05 to make all four statements consistent. Still **the answer is not available in any of the four options,** which is actually Europe to North America Iron and Steel export

    $$= \frac{81 + 21 - 9}{3} = 31.$$

67. The highest growth rate in FDI outflow projects was registered by Japan $\left(\frac{1025 - 878}{878} \times 100 = 16.74\%\right)$ amongst the developed nations and by Singapore $\left(\frac{103 - 90}{90} \times 100 = 14.44\%\right)$ amongst the developing nations.

68. China registered a decline of 22.68% which was the second highest decline after Japan 23.8% in 2004-05. Hence (c) is the correct option.

69. The highest growth rate in number of FDI projects inflow for Singapore was 42.59%

    $$\left(\frac{174 - 154}{154} \times 100 = 42.59\%\right)$$

    The highest growth rate in number of FDI projects outflow for UK was 61.87%

    $$\left(\frac{709 - 438}{438} \times 100 = 61.87\%\right)$$

    The difference is 19.28%.

    Hence, (a) is the correct option.

70. Average of FDI projects inflow growth rate in Germany

    $$= 46\left(= \frac{107.6 - 15.53}{2}\right)$$

    And average of FDI project out flow growth rate in Germany

    $$= 41.3\left(= \frac{76.10 + 6.61}{2}\right)$$

    Hence, (b) is the correct option.

71. The average growth rate figures for the inflow and the outflow are 39.2 % and 49.8% respectively. Hence option (c) is false.

72. FDI project outflow growth rate from India in 2002-03

    $$= \frac{179 - 117}{117} \times 100 = 96.63\%$$

    FDI project outflow growth rate from India in 2004-05

    $$= \frac{182 - 199}{199} \times 100 = -8.54\%$$

    ∴ Average growth rate of FDI outflow

    $$= \frac{96.63 - 8.54}{2} = 44.04\%$$

    Similarly, the average growth rate for FDI inflow in the same period for India = 31.75%.

    Hence, statement in (a) is true.

73. FDI outflow from India as a percentage of total FDI outflow from the developed countries in 2004

    $$= \frac{199}{1294} \times 100 = 15.378\%$$

    FDI inflow from US as a percentage of total FDI inflow from the developed countries in 2003

    $$= \frac{589}{3867} \times 100 = 15.231\%$$

    Hence, statement in (d) is false.

74. **Option (a):**

Year	Required %
1993	46.7
1994	44.4
1995	41.9
1996	40.6
1997	39.2
1998	38.7
1999	38.1
2000	36.7
2001	34.1
2002	33.3
2003	31.9

Hence, option (a) is not true.

Option (b): The special type wagons expressed as a percentage of total wagons is 17.531% and is maximum.

Hence, option (b) is true.

Option (c): The open high sided wagons expressed as a percentage of total wagons increased during 1994 to 2001 and also from 2001 to 2002.

75. Option (a): Required percentage in 1995 and 2001 is 16.45% and 17.5% respectively.

    Option (b): Required percentage in 1998 and 2004 is 16.61% and 17.3% respectively.

Option (c): Required percentage in 2000 and 2002 is 17.2% and 17.2% respectively.

Option (d): Required percentage in 1993 and 1994 is 14.89% and 15.75% respectively.

76. Required percentage in 2002, 2005, 2004 and 2003 is 4.4% 4.93%, 5% and 4.99% respectively.

77. Option (a): Required growth rate is – 4.18%

Option (b): Required growth rate is – 4.14%

Option (c): Required growth rate is – 4.13%

Option (d): Required growth rate is – 4.11%

Hence, the lowest of all the growth rate is – 4.18%.

78. The statement given in option (c) is false as the annual percentage growth rate of average wagon capacity is maximum in the year 2001.

79. Option (a): Required growth rate is – 6.73%

Option (b): Required growth rate is – 5.03%

Option (c): Required growth rate is – 8.25%

Option (d): Required growth rate is – 7.33%

For questions 80 to 84

	P	Q	R	S	Total
1990	45	99	75	115	334
1991	25	41	93	158	317
1992	40	108	107	166	421
1993	38	60	63	139	300
1994	76	41	132	88	337
1995	56	70	120	97	343
Total	280	419	590	763	2052

80. It can be easily concluded from the data given in the above table that the annual growth rate of total production is highest in 1992.

81. The stability of production during 1990 to 1995 for product P, Q, R and S is 0.92, 1.04, 1.43 and 1.63 respectively.

Hence, product S is the most stable one.

For questions 82 to 84:

	P (Rs.9)	Q (Rs.4)	R (Rs.13)	S (Rs.3)	Total
1990	405	396	975	345	2121
1991	225	164	1209	474	2072
1992	360	432	1391	498	2681
1993	342	240	819	417	1818
1994	684	164	1716	264	2828
1995	504	280	1560	291	2635
Total	2520	1676	7670	2289	

82. The total revenue of all the products is lowest in the year 1993.

83. The product Q fetches the lowest revenue.

84. It can be concluded from the data calculated in the table given above that the statement given in option (c) is true.

For questions 85 to 89:

85. Option (a): Required growth rate is 179.25%

Option (b): Required growth rate is 184.29%

Option (c): Required growth rate is 188.60%

Option (d): Required growth rate is 178.63%

86. Option (a): Required growth rate is – 68.52%

Option (b): Required growth rate is – 63.18%

Option (c): Required growth rate is – 67.78%

Option (d): Required growth rate is – 67.83%

87. Option (a): The annual FDI growth rate for Gujarat in 2001 is – 23.28 and the corresponding figure for Karnataka in 2005 is – 22.51%.

Option (b): The annual FDI growth rate for Kerala in 2001 is 42.29% and the corresponding figure for Uttar Pradesh in 2004 is 43.99%.

Option (c): The annual FDI growth rate for Kerala in 2005 is 45.73% and the corresponding figure for Punjab in 2007 is 45.55%.

88. Option (a): The absolute annual increase in FDI inflow in Bihar in 2001 is 4927 and the corresponding figure for Rajasthan in 2007 is 4957.

Option (b): The annual FDI growth rate for West Bengal in 2006 is – 14.05% and the corresponding figure for Uttar Pradesh in 2003 is – 16.56%.

Option (c): The absolute annual increase in FDI inflow in Madhya Pradesh in 2004 is 3870 and the corresponding figure for Maharashtra in 2005 is 3766.

89. Option (a): The absolute annual increase in FDI inflow in Haryana in 2006 is 2892 and the corresponding figure for Punjab in 2007 is 2888.

Option (b): Among all the States, in 2003 the absolute annual increase in FDI inflow was maximum for Maharashtra.

Option (c): The absolute annual increase in FDI inflow in Bihar in 2003 is 294 and the corresponding figure for Karnataka in 2001 is 254.

Option (d): The FDI inflow in Kerala over 2002 to 2007 was not the lowest across all the states. For, example in 2002, the FDI inflow was lowest in Bihar.

For questions 90 to 94:

90. Option (a): Export from Canada expressed as a proportion of export from North America in 2000 is 0.22583.

Option (b): Export from Germany expressed as a proportion of export from Europe in 2004 is 0.22461.

Option (c): Export from China expressed as a proportion of export from Asia in 2004 is 0.22363.

Option (d): Export from Japan expressed as a proportion of export from Asia in 2003 is 0.22065.

91. Option (a): The annual export growth rate of Argentina in 2003 was 15.27% and the corresponding figure for US in 2006 is 14.6%.

Option (b): The annual export growth rate of Africa in 2004 was 30.33% and the corresponding figure for Latin America in 2004 is 29.94%.

Option (c): The annual export growth rate of US in 2004 was 12.93% and the corresponding figure for Canada in 2005 is 13.54%.

92. Option (a): Required growth rate is 13.70%.

Option (b): Required growth rate is 13.87%.

Option (c): Required growth rate is 13.58%.

Option (d): Required growth rate is 13.22%.

93. Option (a): Export from Argentina expressed as a proportion of export from Latin America in 2001 is 0.14074 and export from Nigeria expressed as a proportion of export from Africa in 2004 is 0.13548.

Option (b): Export from UK expressed as a proportion of export from Europe in 2000 is 0.10837 and export from Argentina expressed as a proportion of export from Latin America in 2005 is 0.11366.

Option (c): The annual export growth rate in Argentina in 2004 is 0.16945 and the corresponding figure for Asia in 2005 is 0.15299.

Option (d): Export from South Africa expressed as a proportion of export from Africa in 2001 is 0.21294 and export from China expressed as a proportion of export from Asia in 2003 is 0.20494.

94. Option (a): The absolute annual increase in exports from Asia in 2003 is 330500 and the corresponding figure in 2006 is 518700.

Option (b): The absolute annual increase in exports from Germany in 2001 is 19827 and the corresponding figure for US in 2003 is 31668.

Option (c): The absolute annual increase in exports from Brazil in 2005 is 21833 and the corresponding figure for Japan in 2002 is 13230.

For questions 95 to 96:

Year	2000	2001	2002	2003	2004	2005	2006	2007	2008	2009	2010	Average
Revenue	700	1400	1200	900	1100	400	200	700	600	800	900	809.09
Profit	0	100	300	150	0	150	100	200	0	400	300	154.55
Selling Price per Unit	10	14	12	12	11	8	10	14	10	10	15	11.45
Number of Units	70	100	100	75	100	50	20	50	60	80	60	69.55
Cost Price	700	1300	900	750	1100	250	100	500	600	400	600	654.55
Cost price per Unit	10	13	9	10	11	5	5	10	10	5	10	8.91

95. From the data given in the above table, it can be easily concluded that the year in which per unit cost is HIGHEST is 2001.

Hence, option (b) is the correct choice.

96. Average quantity sold during the period 2000 – 2010 is close to 70 units.

97.

	Volatility
Price per Unit	0.61
Cost per Unit	0.9
Total Profit	2.59
Revenue	1.48

From the data calculated in the table given above, we can conclude that total profit has the highest volatility.

Hence, option (c) is the correct choice.

For questions 88 and 99:

Year	2000	2001	2002	2003	2004	2005	2006	2007	2008	2009	2010
Selling Price per Unit	8	11.2	9.6	9.6	8.8	8	10	14	10	10	15
Revenue	560	1120	960	720	880	400	200	700	600	800	900
Cost price per Unit	10	13	9	10	11	6	6	12	12	6	12
Cost Price	700	1300	900	750	1100	300	120	600	720	480	720
Profit	-140	-180	60	-30	-220	100	80	100	-120	320	180

98. From the data calculated in the table given above, we can see that in 5 years there is a loss.

99. Previous cumulative profit = Rs.1700 and after the change the cumulative profit is Rs.150.

Required difference = Rs.1700 – Rs.150 = Rs.1550.

100. The automobile production in 2004, 2005, 2006, 2007 and 2008 are 1775, 1700, 2175, 2325 and 2200 respectively.

The production shows decrease only in the year 2005 and 2008

The percentage decrease in 2005 $= \dfrac{1775 - 1700}{1775} = 4.22\%$

Percentage decrease in 2008 $= \dfrac{2325 - 2200}{2325} = 5.37\%$

Hence, 2008 exhibited highest percentage decrease.

101. In year 2004, exports of automobiles

$$= \text{Production} - \text{sales}$$
$$= 1775 - 1450 = 325$$

In year 2005, export of automobiles

$$= 1700 - 1525 = 175$$

In year 2006, export of automobiles

$$= 2175 - 1925 = 250$$

In year 2007, export of automobiles

$$= 2325 - 2025 = 300$$

In year 2008, export of automobiles

$$= 2200 - 1875$$
$$= 325$$

So highest growth in export is in year 2006

i.e, $\dfrac{250 - 175}{175} \times 100 = 42.85\%$.

102. Let 5x, 3x and 2x be the prices of a commercial vehicle, passenger vehicle and 3 wheeler respectively.

In the period 2004-08, earnings from domestic sales of :

Commercial vehicle = 2725 × 5x = 13625x

Passenger vehicle = 4300 × 3x = 12900x

3 wheeler = 1775 × 2x = 3550x

∴   Total sales = 30075x

∴   Required percentage $= \dfrac{13625x}{30075x} \times 100 = 43.3\%$

103. Average domestic sales = 1760

Closest year with sales is 2008 i.e., 1875

104. The percentage increase in:

$2005 = \dfrac{1525 - 1450}{1450} \times 100 = 5.17\%$

$2006 = \dfrac{1925 - 1525}{1525} \times 100 = 26.22\%$

$2007 = \dfrac{2025 - 1925}{1925} \times 100 = 5.19\%$

105. Domestic sales have increased in 2005, 2006, 2007 only and average production has increased in 2006 and 2007 only. Hence, we can find the required ratio for 2006 and 2007 only.

Ratio for 2006 = 400 : 475 ≈ 0.84

Ratio for 2007 = 100 : 150 ≈ 0.66

For questions 106 to 108:

	Absolute Return		
	Alpha	Beta	Gama
Auto	0.0745	0.299	-
Chemicals	0.3612	0.2412	0.6
Communication	–0.3505	–0.25	–0.2
Construction	0.2265	-	0.9015
Diversified	0.8228	0.7689	1.045
Energy	2.0979	3.675	4.305
Engineering	0.7208	0.8792	1.24
Financial	1.5588	1.44	1.0206
FMCG	3.625	0.5	0.5
Health Care	1.0764	-	0.54
Metals	-	–0.8792	–0.7984
Services	0.45	0.704	0.4
Technology	–0.1102	–0.15	–0.07
Textiles	0.6851	-	-
Total	11.2383	7.2281	8.8537

106. Refer to the above table.

107. Refer to the above table.

108. At the end of 1st year, 100 + 8.85 = 108.85%.

So investment of 10 lakhs in fund Gama will become

$10,00,000 \times 1.088 \approx 10.9$ lakhs.

109. Jowar yield for 2007 $= \dfrac{368}{673} = 0.546$

Soyabean yield for 2008 $= \dfrac{799}{650} = 1.229$

⇒ Required ratio = 0.546 : 1.229.

So the closest ratio is 0.89 : 2.09.

110. The top 3 crops by yield in 2006 are:

Sunflower = 1.864

Groundnut = 1.5488

Rice = 1.4299

111. The bottom 3 crops by yield in 2008 are:

Moth = 0.208

Seasmum = 0.25

Millets = 0.266

112. Statement I is wrong as productivity of pulses has increased in 2007.

Statement II is correct as the productivity of Maize over the years are 1.097, 1.094 and 1.073 respectively.

113. Statement I is correct as the productivity of Cereals over the years is 0.536, 0.757 and 0.756 respectively.

Statement III is also correct as the productivity over the years are 0.25, 0.297 and 0.3431 respectively.

For questions 114 to 118:

As per the data given in the question, following table can be derived.

	Total Oil used	Total Oil produced
1996	2608	3258
1997	2914	3646
1998	2870	3704
1999	2834	3936
2000	2920	3622
2001	3262	3754
2002	3658	4044
2003	3500	3944
2004	3822	4328
2005	3618	4650
2006	3826	4968
2007	4030	5484
2008	4152	5580

114. Oilused for Household:

In 1998 $= \dfrac{22}{2870} \times 100 = 0.76655$

In 1999 $= \dfrac{22}{2834} \times 100 = 0.776$

In 2000 $= \dfrac{20}{2920} \times 100 = 0.684$

In 2001 $= \dfrac{22}{3262} \times 100 = 0.6744$.

115. Loss as a proportion of Total production:

in 2002 $= \dfrac{386}{4044} = 0.095$

in 2003 $= \dfrac{444}{3944} = 0.1125$

in 2004 $= \dfrac{506}{4328} = 0.1169$

in 2006 $= \dfrac{1142}{4968} = 0.2298$

116. 'Suburban' as a Proportion of 'Total Oil used' in 2005

$$= \dfrac{230}{3618} = 0.063$$

In 2006 $= \dfrac{210}{3826} = 0.054$

In 2007 $= \dfrac{254}{4030} = 0.063$

In 2008 $= \dfrac{266}{4152} = 0.064$

117. A total of 4 years are there for which the growth rate in 'Production of Oil' is more than the growth rate in 'Total oil used' viz., 1997, 2004, 2006 and 2007.

118. As evident from the table, statement in option (d) is correct.

123. Percentage decline in cost per square feet for

Westside in 2005 $= \dfrac{687}{2411} \times 100 = 28.49\%$

Percentage decline in cost per square feet for

Pantaloon 2008 $= \dfrac{388}{2044} \times 100 = 18.98\%$

Percentage decline in cost per square feet for S.Stop

$= \dfrac{222}{2419} \times 100 = 9.17\%$

Percentage decline in cost per square feet for Vishal

2010 $= \dfrac{595}{1659} 100 = 35.86\%$

Hence, Vishal in 2010 shows sharpest decline.

124. Increase in cost per square feet for S Stop in 2006

$$= 2135 - 1889 = 246$$

Increase in cost per square feet for S Stop 2007

$$= 2464 - 2135 = 329$$

Increase in cost per square feet for Pantaloon 2006

$$= 1996 - 1729 = 267$$

Increase in cost per square feet for Vishal 2006

$$= 1802 - 1832 = -30$$

Hence, S Stop in 2007 shows maximum increase in cost per square feet.

125. Average of rate of cost per square feet in 2007

$$= \dfrac{2044 + 2464 + 1751 + 1525}{4} = \dfrac{7784}{4} = 1946$$

Average of rate of cost per square feet in 2010

$$= \dfrac{1396 + 2230 + 1064 + 1051}{4} = \dfrac{5741}{4} = 1435.25$$

Percentage change $= \dfrac{-510.75}{1946} \times 100 = -26.24\%$

$\therefore$ Required rate of change $= \dfrac{-26.24\%}{3} = 8.75\%$.

126. Rate of change for U.P.(E) $= \dfrac{5.85}{39.68} \times 100 = 14.74\%$

Rate of change for Bihar $= \dfrac{5.19}{33.17} \times 100 = 15.65\%$

Rate of change for Orissa $= \dfrac{2.32}{13.57} \times 100 = 17.09\%$

Rate of change for Haryana $= \dfrac{1.37}{13.59} \times 100 = 10.08\%$

Hence, Orissa shows the maximum rate of change.

127. ***There is a slight ambiguity in the question regarding the distribution of states across the eastern and southern telecom circle.** So avoid finding the exact figures in the region. A simple observation is that the subscribers of Idea and Airtel in south bears the ration 48 : 52 = 0.92. Going by options, only option (d) exactly matches this ratio.

Note: Though not advisable in exams, the figures can be calculated exactly if we consider Bihar, West Bengal, Orissa, Kolkata and Assam in the eastern circle and Tamil Nadu, Karnataka, Andhra Pradesh and Kerala in southern circle.

128. ***There is again ambiguity regarding the distribution of states in the eastern circle.** Moreover, no instruction has been given to use the data from previous question, without which the question is not likely to be answerable.

Considering the data from the above question holds true, we get the following solution:

R-com subscribers in the eastern circle was 28% of the total subscribers whereas it is the same 28% in UP and Madhya Pradesh.

∴ R-com subscribers in new eastern circle = 28%.

There was no Idea subscriber in eastern region whereas 32% in UP and Madhya Pradesh

∴ Idea subscribers in new eastern region

$$= 32\% \text{ of (UP + Madhya Pradesh)}$$

$$= \frac{32}{100} \times 111.05 = 35.536 \text{ million}$$

Total subscribers in new eastern circle

$$= 30.03 + 77.22 + 111.05$$

$$= 218.3 \text{ million}$$

∴ Percentage of Idea subscribers

$$= \frac{35.536}{218.3} \times 100 = 16.27\%.$$

∴ Remaining subscribers in new eastern circle using Vodafone

$$= 100\% - 28\% - 16.27\%$$

$$= 55.73\%.$$

129. Number of subscribers in December 2009

$$= 562.18 \text{ million}$$

Number of subscribers in March 2010

$$= 621.3 \text{ million}$$

Percentage change $= \dfrac{621.3 - 562.18}{562.18} \times 100$

$$= \frac{59.12}{562.18} \times 100 = 10.51\%$$

130. Brand Building score for Maheshwari & Co

$$= 10 + 20 + 2.5 + 5 + 0$$

$$= 37.50$$

Points scored for the sales

$$= 15 + 0.25 \times 6241$$

$$= 15 + 1560.25$$

$$= 1575.25$$

Therefore, total points = 1612.75

Hence, Maheswari & Co can redeem 2 Tupperware sets.

131. Brand Building score for Bhowmik brothers

$$= -20 + 2.5 + 2.5 + 10$$

$$= -5$$

Points scored for the sales = 12

$$\text{Total points } = -5 + 12 = 7$$

Hence, 33 more points are required to be eligible for minimum redemption.

132. Brand Building points of Saha H/W = 85

Points scored for sales in this quarter

$$= 512 \times 0.25 = 128 + 15$$

Brand building points of Saha H/W in next quarter = 85

Total points till now = 313

Points required to redeem the Kanjivaram Saree = 4000

Hence points required from sale in next quarter = 3687

Points for achieving 100% sale in next quarter = 15

Points required from extra units of sale = 3672

Hence, extra units required to be sold

$$= 4 \times 3672 = 14688$$

133. Points scored for sales by Malling Enterprise

$$= 15 + 250 = 265$$

Points required to redeem three Nike Caps and an Umbrella = 300 + 40 = 340

Hence, its brand building points = 340 − 265 = 75

134. Brand building score of Srikrishna Trader = 80

Points scored for sales by Srikrishna Trader

$$= 0.25 \times 2000$$

$$= 500 + 15 = 515$$

Hence, total points scored by Srikrishna Trader

$$= 80 + 515$$

$$= 595$$

Hence, it can redeem only first 3 items.

So from given options it can redeem only Nike Cap and T-Shirt.

135. CO_2 emission to per capita income ratio for US after

two years $= \dfrac{1200 \times 0.875 \times 0.875}{300 \times 1.02 \times 1.02} = 2.9$

CO_2 emission to per capita income ratio for China

after two years $= \dfrac{1180 \times 0.875 \times 0.875}{270 \times 1.04 \times 1.04} = 3.1$

CO_2 emission to per capita income ratio for Japan

after two years $= \dfrac{1125 \times 0.875 \times 0.875}{240 \times 1.03 \times 1.03} = 3.4$

136. Standard benchmark ratio = 0.75

So CO_2 emission for USA must be 225

Hence, it has to buy 975 × 2.5

$\qquad\qquad$ = 2437.5 carbon credit units.

Similarly CO_2 emission for China must be 202.5

Hence, it has to buy 977.5 × 2.5

$\qquad\qquad$ = 2443.75 carbon credit units

In one year a country can buy 15 + 20 + 30

$\qquad\qquad$ = 65 carbon credit units

Time taken by USA to achieve standard benchmark

$\qquad = \dfrac{2437.5}{65} = 37.5$ years

Time taken by China to achieve standard benchmark

$\qquad = \dfrac{2443.75}{65} = 37.59$ years

Hence, required number of years is 38 .

137. The combined per capita income of all five countries in 2010 is 845.

So, per capita income in 2011 = 861.9

$\qquad\qquad$ 2012 = 883.44

$\qquad\qquad$ 2013 = 914.37

The ratio of CO_2 emission to per capita income in 2010

$\qquad = \dfrac{2050}{845} = 2.426$

The ratio for next three years = 0.5 × 2.426 = 1.213

$\Rightarrow$ CO_2 emission of 2011 = 861.9 × 1.213 = 1045.48

$\Rightarrow$ CO_2 emission of 2012 = 883.44 × 1.213 = 1071.61

$\Rightarrow$ CO_2 emission of 2013 = 914.37 × 1.213 = 1109.13

The benchmark emission of CO_2 = 350 × 5 = 1750 million tonne

Savings for 2011 = 704.52

Savings for 2012 = 678.39

Savings for 2013 = 640.87

Hence, total carbon credits earned

$\qquad = \dfrac{(704.52 + 678.39 + 640.87)}{0.5} \times 1.25$

$\qquad$ = 5059.45 = 5060 (approx.)

138. If the countries are arranged according to the condition given in option (a), the order is as follows:

	Country	CO_2 emission / per capita income
1	AUSTRALIA	1.627906977
2	POLAND	1.632653061
3	UKRAINE	1.70212766
4	SPAIN	1.818181818
5	INDIA	2
6	FRANCE	2.142857143
7	ITALY	2.272727273
8	SOUTH AFRICA	2.368421053
9	CANADA	2.5
10	GERMANY	2.903225806
11	US	3.428571429
12	RUSSIA	3.451612903
13	UNITED KINGDOM	3.47826087
14	CHINA	3.6875
15	JAPAN	3.879310345

Therefore, option (a) is correct.

If the countries are arranged according to the condition given in option (b), the order is as follows:

	Country	CO_2 emission / per capita income
1	POLAND	2.051282051
2	AUSTRALIA	2.121212121
3	UKRAINE	2.162162162
4	SPAIN	2.222222222
5	INDIA	2.5
6	FRANCE	2.8125
7	ITALY	2.941176471
8	CANADA	3.157894737
9	SOUTH AFRICA	3.214285714
10	GERMANY	3.461538462
11	US	4
12	RUSSIA	4.115384615
13	CHINA	4.37037037
14	UNITED KINGDOM	4.444444444
15	JAPAN	4.6875

Therefore, option (b) is correct.

If the countries are arranged according to the condition given in option (c), the order is as follows:

	Country	CO_2 emission / per capita income
1	AUSTRALIA	0.909090909
2	POLAND	1.025641026
3	UKRAINE	1.081081081
4	SPAIN	1.333333333
5	INDIA	1.5
6	FRANCE	1.5625
7	ITALY	1.764705882
8	SOUTH AFRICA	1.785714286
9	CANADA	2.105263158
10	GERMANY	2.692307692
11	US	3.333333333
12	UNITED KINGDOM	3.333333333
13	RUSSIA	3.346153846
14	CHINA	3.62962963
15	JAPAN	3.854166667

Therefore, option (c) is correct.

If the countries are arranged according to the condition given in option (d), the order is as follows:

	Country	CO_2 emission / per capita income
1	AUSTRALIA	0.697674419
2	POLAND	0.816326531
3	UKRAINE	0.85106383
4	SPAIN	1.090909091
5	FRANCE	1.19047619
6	INDIA	1.2
7	SOUTH AFRICA	1.315789474
8	ITALY	1.363636364
9	CANADA	1.666666667
10	GERMANY	2.258064516
11	UNITED KINGDOM	2.608695652
12	RUSSIA	2.806451613
13	US	2.857142857
14	CHINA	3.0625
15	JAPAN	3.189655172

Therefore, option (d) is incorrect.

*** NOTE: It is advisable not to attempt this question.**

139. Units produced in Bihar exceed the number of units produced in Madhya Pradesh by

$$\frac{45 - 32.4}{360} \times 72000 = 12.6 \times 200 = 2520 \text{ units}$$

140. Number of females in 1995 = 300 million

Number of females in 1996 = 330 million

Percentage increase in number of females

$$= \frac{30}{300} \times 100 = 10\%$$

Number of females in 1998 = 320 million

Number of females in 1999 = 350 million

Percentage increase in number of females

$$= \frac{30}{320} \times 100 = 9.375\%$$

Number of females in 2003 = 350 million

Number of females in 2004 = 370 million

Percentage increase in number of females

$$= \frac{20}{350} \times 100 = 5.71\%$$

Number of females in 2004 = 370 million

Number of females in 2005 = 420 million

Percentage increase in number of females

$$= \frac{50}{370} \times 100 = 13.51\%$$

141. Number of educated people in 2002 = 545 million

Number of educated female in 2002

$$= \frac{4}{9} \times 545 \text{ million} = 242.22 \text{ million}$$

Number of uneducated female in 2002 = 107.78 million

Number of educated male in 2002

$$= \frac{5}{9} \times 545 \text{ million} = 302.78 \text{ million}$$

Number of educated male in 2003 = 378.475 million

Number of educated female in 2003 = 181.525 million

Number of uneducated female in 2003 = 168.475 million

Hence, required percentage change

$$= \frac{60.695}{107.78} \times 100 = 56.313 = +56\%$$

142. Population living in urban area in 2005

$$= 0.68 \times 600 = 408 \text{ million}$$

Population living in rural area in 2005 = 492 million

Rural population in 2010 $= \frac{12}{55} \times 1100 = 240$ million

Hence, required ratio $= \frac{492}{240} = 2.05$.

For questions 143 to 147:

143. Compound Average Growth Rate

$$= \left[\left(\frac{\text{Final Value}}{\text{Initial Value}} \right)^{\frac{1}{n}} - 1 \right] \times 100$$

$$= \left[\left(\frac{3701}{3075} \right)^{\frac{1}{4}} - 1 \right] \times 100$$

$$\approx 4.74\%$$

144. Country XX's Outward investment to Singapore dropped in March and April only.

Percentage growth in March $= \frac{741 - 1211}{1211} \times 100 \approx -38.8\%$

Percentage growth in April $= \frac{378 - 741}{741} \times 100 \approx -48.98\%$

145. Required percentage $= \frac{116 + 117}{3221} \times 100 \approx 7.23\%$.

146. Share of outwards investment to Singapore and UAE together in:

January $= \frac{273 + 86}{3075} \times 100 \approx 11.67\%$

February $= \frac{1211 + 227}{3221} \times 100 \approx 44.64\%$

March $= \frac{741 + 70}{2358} \times 100 \approx 34.4\%$

April $= \frac{378 + 157}{1390} \times 100 \approx 38.49\%$

May $= \frac{615 + 142}{3701} \times 100 \approx 20.45\%$

Therefore, it is highest in February.

147. Except USA, all the countries showed decline from February to April.

Percentage decline for:

$$\text{UK} = \frac{117 - 44}{117} \times 100 \approx 62.4\%$$

$$\text{Singapore} = \frac{1211 - 378}{1211} \times 100 \approx 68.8\%$$

$$\text{UAE} = \frac{227 - 157}{227} \times 100 \approx 30.84\%$$

$$\text{Others} = \frac{1551 - 686}{1551} \times 100 \approx 55.8\%$$

Therefore, it is highest for Singapore.

For questions 148 to 152:

148. Value (in Rs. crore) of tertiary sector in 2004-05

$$= 2971464 - (650454 + 744755)$$

$$= 1576255$$

Share of tertiary sector in 2004-05

$$= \frac{1576256}{2971464} \times 100 \approx 53.05\%$$

Value (in Rs. crore) of tertiary sector in 2009-10

$$= 6133230 - (1243566 + 1499601)$$

$$= 3390063$$

Share of tertiary sector in 2009-10

$$= \frac{3390063}{6133230} \times 100 \approx 55.27\%$$

149. Growth rate in GNP series between:

2005-06 and 2006-07

$$= \frac{3919007 - 3363505}{3363505} \times 100 \approx 16.52\%$$

2006-07 and 2007-08

$$= \frac{4560910 - 3919007}{3919007} \times 100 \approx 16.38\%$$

2007-08 and 2008-09

$$= \frac{5249163 - 4560910}{4560910} \times 100 \approx 15.09\%$$

2008-09 and 2009-10

$$= \frac{6095230 - 5249163}{5249163} \times 100 \approx 16.11\%$$

Therefore, it is highest between 2005-06 and 2006-07.

150. Value (in Rs. crore) of GDS in 2009-10

$$= 1.3 \times 1798347 = 2337851$$

$$\text{Required percentage} = \frac{2337851}{6550271} \times 100 \approx 35.69\%.$$

151. Percentage change in Gross Domestic Capital Formation between 2008-09 and 2009-10 is the highest and is equal to

$$\frac{2344197 - 1973535}{1973535} \times 100 \approx 18.78\%.$$

152. Gross Domestic Capital Formation as percentage of GDP (at Market Prices) in:

$$2004\text{-}05 = \frac{1052232}{3242209} \times 100 \approx 32.45\%$$

$$2005\text{-}06 = \frac{1266245}{3692485} \times 100 \approx 34.29\%$$

$$2006\text{-}07 = \frac{1540749}{4293672} \times 100 \approx 35.88\%$$

$$2007\text{-}08 = \frac{1896563}{4986426} \times 100 \approx 38.03\%$$

Therefore, option (c) is correct.

For questions 153 to 158:

153. Increase in Malaysia's Global Chemical Products export

$$= 0.7 - 0.4$$

$$= 0.3$$

Increase in India's global Office and Telecom Equipment export

$$= 0.3 - 0.1$$

$$= 0.2$$

Increase in Mexico's global Chemicals Products export

$$= 0.3 - 0.2$$

$$- 0.1$$

Increase in Thailand's global integrated circuits and Electronics export

$$= 2.1 - 1.9$$

$$= 0.2$$

154. Option (d): The increase in global import shares of India from 2000 to 2009 is highest for Chemicals products and is equal to $1.8 - 0.8$ i.e. 1.

155. Option (c): South Korea's global export share for Integrated circuits and Electronics Components from 2000 to 2009 decreased by $\frac{0.4}{8} \times 100$ i.e. 5%.

156. After 600% increase, India's market share in 2009 would be 0.7.

As seven countries are above India in exports Market share, therefore rank of India would be eighth.

157. Percentage change in Market share of China's Integrated Circuits and Electronics Components export is the highest and is equal to

$$\frac{11.4 - 1.7}{1.7} \times 100 \text{ i.e. } 570.58\%.$$

158. USA, Mexico and Canada come under North America and rest of the countries come under Asia.

For each of Chemical Products and Automotive Products, EU's rank is first and that of Asia's rank is second. Only option (a) satisfies this.

159. Total exports = 112.5 + 150 + 150 + 200 + 175
$$+ 200 + 275 + 200 + 262.5 + 250$$
$$= 1975$$

Total imports = 275 + 250 + 225 + 225 + 270 + 200
$$+ 175 + 175 + 200 + 175$$
$$= 2170$$

The percentage by which exports are smaller than imports

$$= \frac{2170 - 1975}{2170} \times 100 \approx 9\%.$$

160. The absolute difference between imports and exports for the given year are :-

2002	162.5
2003	100
2004	75
2005	25
2006	95
2007	0
2008	100
2009	25
2010	62.5
2011	75

Hence, the 4th rank while arranged in ascending order is in 2010.

161. The percentage increase in exports for the given years are:-

2003	33.33%
2004	0%
2005	33.33%
2006	−12.5%
2007	14.28%
2008	37.50%
2009	−27.27%
2010	31.25%
2011	4.76%

Hence, fifth largest increase is in the year 2007.

162. The imports increased only in 2006 and 2010 in the entire period.

The percentage increase in 2006

$$= \frac{270 - 225}{225} \times 100 = 20\%$$

The percentage increase in 2010

$$= \frac{200 - 175}{175} \times 100 = 14.28\%$$

Hence, the second largest increase was in the year 2010.

163. The maximum percentage increase in exports is in 2008 i.e. 37.5%.

The minimum percentage decrease in imports is in 2003 i.e.

$$= \frac{275 - 250}{275} \times 100 = 9.09\%$$

Hence, the required answer = 37.5 − 9.09 ≈ 28%.

164. Growth Rate $= \dfrac{\text{Final Value} - \text{Initial Value}}{\text{Initial Value}} \times 100$

Iron Ore $= \dfrac{163 - 100}{100} \times 100 = 63\%$

Aluminium $= \dfrac{105 - 69}{69} \times 100 = \dfrac{36}{69} \times 100 \approx 52\%$

Gold $= \dfrac{25 - 15}{15} \times 100 = \dfrac{10}{15} \times 100 = 66.67\%$

Copper $= \dfrac{103 - 71}{71} \times 100 = \dfrac{32}{71} \times 100 \approx 45\%$

Hence, Gold witnessed highest growth rate in production from 2005 to 2011.

165. The given information can be tabulated as:

Year	Total Production (in million tonnes)	Absolute increase (in million tonnes)
2005	346	
2006	376	30
2007	380	4
2008	449	69
2009	462	13
2010	486	24
2011	518	32

Hence, the highest absolute increase in total production was witnessed in the year 2008.

166. Iron Ore in 2008 $= \dfrac{131 - 102}{102} \times 100 = \dfrac{29}{102} \times 100 \approx 28\%$

Gold in 2011 $= \dfrac{25 - 20}{20} \times 100 = \dfrac{5}{20} \times 100 = 25\%$

Aluminium in 2008 $= \dfrac{98 - 81}{81} \times 100 = \dfrac{17}{81} \times 100 \approx 21\%$

Gold in 2006 $= \dfrac{18 - 15}{15} \times 100 = \dfrac{3}{15} \times 100 = 20\%$

Hence, Iron Ore in 2008 has the highest annual growth rate in production.

167. Annual average growth rate during 2006 to 2011 for

Aluminium $= \dfrac{1}{5} \times \dfrac{105 - 75}{75} \times 100 = 8\%$

Let the production of Aluminium in 2015 be 'A' million tonnes.

Annual average growth rate during 2011 to 2015 for

Aluminium $= \dfrac{1}{4} \times \dfrac{A - 105}{105} \times 100 = 8\%$

$$\Rightarrow A = 105 + \frac{8 \times 4 \times 105}{100} = 138.6 \text{ million tonnes}$$

Hence, the correct option is (b).

168. Percentage of Copper production in total minerals for

$$2010 = \frac{97}{486} \times 100 \approx 20\%$$

$$2008 = \frac{88}{449} \times 100 \approx 19.6\%$$

$$2009 = \frac{92}{462} \times 100 \approx 19.9\%$$

$$2007 = \frac{79}{380} \times 100 \approx 20.8\%$$

169. Growth rates in production from 2006 – 2010 for

$$\text{Aluminium} = \frac{99 - 75}{75} \times 100 = \frac{24}{75} \times 100 \approx 32\%$$

$$\text{Coal} = \frac{116 - 88}{88} \times 100 = \frac{28}{88} \times 100 \approx 31.8\%$$

$$\text{Copper} = \frac{97 - 75}{75} \times 100 = \frac{22}{75} \times 100 \approx 30\%$$

$$\text{Gold} = \frac{20 - 18}{18} \times 100 = \frac{2}{18} \times 100 = 11.11\%$$

Hence, Gold witnessed the minimum growth rate in production from 2006 to 2010.

170.

Region	2007	2010	Ratio (2010/2007)
Eastern Europe	152764	227650	1.49
Central & South America	42319	54728	1.29
West Asia	171661	235317	1.37
South East Asia	303475	409043	1.35

$$\text{Final Value} = \text{Initial Value}\left[1 + \frac{R}{100}\right]^3$$

where $R \rightarrow$ CAGR.

The region for which $\frac{\text{Final}}{\text{Initial}}$ ratio is highest will have the highest CAGR.

Hence, Eastern Europe has highest CAGR.

171. Ratio of final to initial will be calculated and if it is more than $(1.1)^3 = 1.331$ for any region, it will be considered.

Eastern Europe, West Asia and South East Asia qualify for this.

Hence, there are three such regions.

172. Highest annual growth rate is for East-Asia from 2009 to 2010 i.e. $\frac{411947 - 322797}{322797} \times 100 \approx 27.62\%$.

173. In 2006, the external trade for LCD = 875 – 400 = 475; for LED = 500 – 425 = 75 , Plasma = 850 – 825 = 25.

So total external trade = 475 + 75 + 25 = 575 units

In 2007, the external trade for LCD = 450 , LED = 25,

Plasma = 0

So total external trade = 450 + 25 = 475 units

In 2008, the external trade for LCD = 400, LED = 350, Plasma = 25

So total external trade = 400 + 350 + 25 = 775 units

In 2010, the external trade for LCD = 250, LED = 200, Plasma = 75

So total external trade = 250 + 200 + 75 = 525 units

Hence, the highest external trade in total number of TV units is registered in the year 2008.

174. In 2006, the export for LCD = 875 – 400 = 475 ; for LED = 425 – 500 = –75 , Plasma = 850 – 825 = 25.

Net exports = 475 – 75 + 25 = 425 units

Similarly, in 2007, net exports = 450 + 20 + 0 = 470 units

in 2009, net exports = 275 – 75 – 75 = 125 units

and in 2010, net exports = 250 – 200 + 75 = 125 units

Hence, the highest net exports is in the year 2007.

175. Statement I: For every year, the production of LCD TVs is more than its domestic sales, i.e. net exports (exports - imports) is positive. Hence, statement I is true.

Statement II: The net exports for the years are:

Year	2006	2007	2008	2009	2010	2011
Net exports (in units)	425	470	50	125	125	25

The net exports is equal to 1220 units. Hence, statement II is not true.

Statement III: From the two bar graphs, we can conclude that only in the year 2009 has the production of Plasma TVs fell short of sales. Hence, statement III is true.

For solution 176 and 177:

176. Sales of Figo in $2010 = 80{,}000 \times \frac{9}{100} = 7{,}200$

Sales of Figo in $2011 = 80{,}000 \times \frac{125}{100} \times \frac{44}{360} = 12{,}222$

$\therefore$ Approx. increase = 12,222 – 7,200

$$= 5{,}022.$$

The closest option is option (a).

177. Average growth rate for all the models is given as 25%. Hence, if the percentage share of a model remains constant next year, then the sales would have grown by 25%. Similarly if the percentage share would have increased or decreased, the total sales would have increased by more than 25% or less than 25% respectively.

The percentage share of all models in 2011 are:

$$\text{Alto} = \frac{111}{360} \times 100 = 30.83\%, \quad \text{Swift} = 67 \times \frac{100}{360} = 18.61\%$$

$$\text{i10} = 82 \times \frac{100}{360} = 22.78\%, \quad \text{Honda City} = 56 \times \frac{100}{360} = 15.56\%$$

$$\text{Figo} = 44 \times \frac{100}{360} = 12.22\%$$

Hence the percentage share increased for 3 models i.e. Figo, i10 and Honda City.

178. Out of the given sectors, the increase in FDI inflows from 2007 to 2012 was the highest for Automobile Industry and it was equal to (4.9 − 1.9) = 3.0.

179. The simple average of share of FDI inflows has been the lowest for Drug and Pharmaceuticals i.e. 2.61 and was the second lowest for the Automobile industry was i.e. 3.95

180. During 2007 to 2010, the percentage shares of FDI inflow in Chemicals (other than Fertilizers) sector were 1.3, 1.9, 1.7 and 2.1. Hence FDI inflow in Chemical (other than Fertilisers) did not witness continuous increase.

181. In 2011, the construction development sector was ranked fifth in terms of percentage share of FDI inflow in the country. Also in 2009, the Computer Software and Hardware sector was ranked sixth in terms of percentage share of FDI in flow in the country. Thus, A and B are true.

The rankings of Drugs and pharmaceuticals in terms of percentage share of FDI inflow in 2012 is the third lowest. Hence, only statement III is false.

182. Increase in FDI inflow percentage share for Telecommunications sector between 2007 and 2008 was the maximum among the given four options and it was (8.3 − 5.5) i.e. 2.8, which was the second highest among the given options.

183. The highest year to year decline in absolute terms for North African region was the highest from 2009-10 to 2010-11 and the decline witnessed was

$$\left| 1.59 - 1.75 \right| = 0.16.$$

184. For North American region the export shares declined the maximum number of times in a year and it was equal to 7.

185. The annual growth rate in India's export share in percentage was the lowest for North Africa and has been

$$\frac{1.59 - 1.75}{1.75} \times 100 = 9.14\%.$$

186. India's simple average expert share to Latin America during 2002-03 and 2004-05 was the highest and it was

$$\frac{2.06 + 2.15}{2} = 2.105$$

187. The annual growth rate in India's (percentage) export share between 2002 -03 and 2003-04 has been highest for South Asia and not for West Asia. Hence, D is false.

188. The average managerial wage was the highest for Industry 6 and it was equal to

$$\frac{6084 - 3117}{4271 - 3333} = \frac{2967}{938} = 3.163 \text{ lakh.}$$

189. Profit expressed as ratio of net value added is the highest for Industry 6 and it was

$$\frac{31219}{42434} = 0.7357.$$

190. The required difference is the maximum for option (c) and it was equal to

$$= \left(\frac{71739 + 25674}{7508} \right) - \left(\frac{2284 + 149}{877} \right) = 10.20.$$

191. Expenses on fuel as a percentage of input cost was the highest for Industry 7 and it was

$$\frac{32178}{171246} \times 100 = 18.79\%.$$

192. Only option (d) is true as the Emoluments expressed as percentage of net value added for industry 5 was

the lowest and it was $\dfrac{9284}{71739} \times 100 = 12.94\%$.

193. If the countries are ranked according to the number of days required to start a business, the top three countries would be Paraguay, United Kingdom and Chile. Among these three, the country with the least cost to per capita income ratio is Paraguay.

194. Ratio of the number of days required for export to

import is the least for U.K and it is $\dfrac{13}{17} = 0.764$.

195. In Georgia, the number of days required for exporting is 22 and the number of days required for importing is 23, so the days required for exporting is lower than required for importing. Hence, option (d) is the true statement.

196. The number of days required for importing in Georgia is less than the number of days required for exporting in Niger. Hence, option (c) is false.

197. Total number of mergers for the entire period = 1499

Total number of mergers and acquisitions = 5646

Thus, number of acquisitions = 5646 − 1499 = 4147

Percentage of mergers to acquisitions

$$= (1499/4147) \times 100 = 36.15\%.$$

198. The following table can be formed from the given information:

Sectors	Total 'Mergers & Acquisitions'	Total 'Acquisitions'	Percentage of 'mergers' to 'mergers & acquisitions'
Food & Beverage	465	97	>20%
Textile	371	77	>20%
Chemicals	584	116	<20%
Drugs &Pharma	350	74	>20%
Cement	48	6	<20%
IT & Telecom	643	96	<20%
Diversified	52	2	<20%
Financial Service	1041	452	>20%
Others Services	1709	512	>20%
Miscellaneous Manufacturing	192	34	<20%
Non Metallic Mineral Products	191	33	<20%

From the above table, it can be seen the required number is 5.

199. It can be observed that 5 sectors namely (1) Food & Beverage, (2) IT & Telecom, (3) Diversified, (4) Financial Services and (5) Other Services have more (> ½) merger activity in the first 3 years as compared to the last 3 years.

200. Turbulence = Sum of differences (in absolute terms) in number of mergers & acquisitions on a year-on-year basis. Going by the answer

Sectors	Financial Services	IT & Telecom	Food & Beverage	Other Services
2001-02	103 – 91= 12	134 – 19 = 115	96 – 17 = 79	207 – 90 = 117
2002-03	107 – 94 = 13	95 – 19 = 76	54 – 23 = 31	188 – 92 = 96
2003-04	87 – 73 = 14	71– 13 = 58	67 – 10 = 57	182 – 105 = 77
2004-05	75 – 41 = 34	64 – 16 = 48	55 – 19 = 36	200 – 81 = 119
2005-06	118 – 75 = 43	92 – 17 = 75	43 – 20 = 23	210 – 61 = 149
2006-07	126 – 51 = 75	91– 12 = 79	53 – 8 = 45	210 – 83 = 127
Total	191	451	271	685

It can be observed from the above table that 'Other Services' is the most turbulent for the given period.

201. The following table gives the number of acquisitions for all the sectors over the given period:

Sectors	2002-03	2003-04	2004-05	2005-06	2006-07
Food & Beverage	54	67	55	43	53
Textile	52	51	53	56	32
Chemicals	83	100	76	55	47
Drugs &Pharma	43	30	40	45	60
Cement	5	7	19	0	0
IT & Telecom	95	71	64	92	91
Diversified	8	12	4	7	5
Financial	94	73	75	118	126
Others Services	188	182	200	210	210
Miscellaneous Manufacturing	23	31	31	24	21
Non Metallic Mineral Products	19	26	22	39	23
Higher number of acquisitions	-	6	5	7	3

As we can see from the above table, maximum 7 sectors in the year 2005-06 had higher number of acquisitions compared to the previous year

202. In 2009, the consumption of:

Coal = 540 MTOE, Crude Oil = 290 MTOE,

Natural Gas = 80 MTOE

Nuclear energy = 20 MTOE

Hydro electricity = 50 MTOE

Others = 20 MTOE

Total consumption in 2010 of:

Coal = 540 × 1.15 = 621 MTOE

Crude Oil = 290 × 1.1 = 319 MTOE

Natural gas = 80 × 1.05 = 84 MTOE

Hydro Electricity = 50 × 1.1 = 55 MTOE

Others = 20 × 1.5 = 23 MTOE

Import in Coal = 25% of 621 = 155.25 MTOE

Import in Crude = 50% of 319 = 159.5 MTOE

Import in Natural Gas = 50% of 84 = 42 MTOE

Import in Hydro Electricity = 5% of 55 = 2.75 MTOE

Total Import = 155.25 + 159.5 + 42 + 2.75 = 359.5 MTOE

203. In 2010, the import of natural gas was 42 MTOE.

Consumption of natural gas in 2012

$$= 84 \times 1.1 \times 1.05 = 97 \text{ MTOE}$$

The import of natural gas in 2012

$$= 30\% \text{ of } 97 = 29.1 \text{ MTOE}$$

So, there was a decrease of 13 MTOE.

204. Consumption of Crude Oil in 2011

$$= 290 \times 1.1 \times 1.1 = 351 \text{ MTOE}$$

The import of Crude oil in 2011 is 45%. So, the production will be 55% of 351 = 193 MTOE.

205.

Year	Crude Oil	Natural gas	Coal	Nuclear energy	Hydro elecricity	Other
2009	290	80	540	20	50	20
2010	319	84	621	24	55	23
2011	350.9	92.4	683.1	27.6	57.75	26.45
2012	403.53	97	785.5	30.36	63.52	29.1

As it can be observed from the above table that the total domestic consumption of energy

= 403.53 + 97 + 785.5 + 30.36 + 63.52 + 29.1

= 1409

Thus, proportion of coal in 2012

= (785.5/1409) × 100 = 56%.

206. The following table gives consumption of nuclear and hydro electricity from 2009 to 2011:

Year	Nuclear energy	Hydro-electricity
2009	20	50
2010	24	55
2011	27.6	57.75

Thus, domestic production of nuclear energy in 2011

$$= 27.6 \times 1 = 27.6 \text{ MTOE}$$

Domestic production of hydro-electricity in 2011

$$= 57.75 \times 0.95 = 54.9 \text{ MTOE}$$

Thus, approximate sum of nuclear energy and hydro-electricity (domestic production) in 2011

$$= 27.6 + 54.9 = 82.5 \text{ MTOE}.$$

For questions 207 to 211:

Months	Two ton	One & half ton	One ton	Half ton
April-14	253.20	240.54	177.24	595.02
May-14	253.60	240.92	177.52	595.96
June-14	318.00	419.76	152.64	381.60
July-14	323.00	426.36	155.04	387.60
Aug-14	401.76	246.24	440.64	207.36
Sep-14	259.20	246.24	181.44	609.12
Oct-14	324.50	428.34	337.48	207.68
Nov-14	325.00	429.00	338.00	208.00
Dec-14	325.00	429.00	156.00	390.00
Jan-15	332.50	438.90	345.80	212.80
Feb-15	415.40	254.60	455.60	214.40
Mar-15	418.50	256.50	459.00	216.00
Total	3,949.66	4,056.40	3,376.40	4,225.54

207. Required average $= \dfrac{4056.4}{12} \approx 338.$

208. For the absolute difference between average annual sales to be the highest, the absolute difference between total sales should be the highest.

From the above table, It is clear that the difference between total Sales is maximum for 1 ton and $\frac{1}{2}$ ton WACs.

209.

Time period	2 ton	1½ ton	1 ton	½ ton
Apr'14 to Sep'14	1808.76	1820.06	1284.52	2776.66
Oct'14 to Mar'15	2140.9	2236.34	2091.88	1448.88
Half yearly sales	0.18363	0.22872	0.62853	-0.47819

Half yearly Sales Performance for 2 Ton WACs

$$= \frac{2140.9 - 1808.76}{1808.76} = 0.184$$

Half yearly Sales Performance for $1\frac{1}{2}$ Ton WACs

$$= \frac{2236.34 - 1820.06}{1820} = 0.229$$

Half yearly Sales Performance for 1 Ton WACs

$$= \frac{2091.88 - 1284.52}{1284.52} = 0.629$$

Half yearly Sales Performance for $\frac{1}{2}$ Ton WACs

$$= -0.478$$

Hence, $1\frac{1}{2}$ Ton WACs has performed the Second best in Half yearly Sales Performance.

For questions 212 to 216:

212. Factor performance for Innovation

$$= 0.30(4.5) + 0.35(4 + 4.75)$$

Factor performance for Bussiness Sophistication

$$= 0.30(5.25) + 0.35(4.75 + 4.5)$$

Factor performance for Infrastructure

$$= 0.30(5.25) + 0.35(4 + 4)$$

Factor performance for Macroeconomic Environment

$$= 0.30(5.5) + 0.35(4.75 + 4.5)$$

From above, it is clear that Macroeconomic Environment has the best Factor Performance.

213. Factor performance for Innovation

$$= \frac{4.5 - 4}{4.75} = 0.105$$

Factor performance for Bussiness Sophistication

$$= \frac{5.25 - 4.75}{4.5} = .111$$

Factor performamce for infastructure

$$= \frac{5.25 - 4}{4} = .3125$$

Factor performance for macroeconomic Environment

$$= \frac{5.5 - 4.5}{4.75} = .211$$

From above, It is clear that Infrastructure has best factor performance.

214. Average Score for Infrastructure

$$= \frac{4 + 4 + 5.25}{3} = \frac{13.25}{3}$$

Average Score for Institutions

$$= \frac{4.25 + 4.75 + 4.5}{3} = 13.5$$

Average Score for Technological Readiness

$$= \frac{3.5 + 3.75 + 5.5}{3} = \frac{12.75}{3}$$

Average Score for Market Efficiency

$$= \frac{4.25 + 4.5 + 4.25}{3} = \frac{13}{3}$$

So, we can Say that Institutions has the highest average Score among the given options.

215. It is clear from the graph that among the given options, Institutions has the least growth rate in 2014 versus Scores of 2010.

216. Cost per Advertisement for Website

$$A = \frac{557000 \times \frac{27}{100}}{(230+120)}$$

Cost per Advertisement for Website

$$B = \frac{557000 \times \frac{22}{100}}{(370+60)}$$

Cost per Advertisement for Website

$$D = \frac{557000 \times \frac{18}{100}}{(300+80)}$$

Cost per Advertisement for Website

$$E = \frac{557000 \times \frac{20}{100}}{(150+40)}$$

From above, It is clear that cost per Advertisement for Website D is the least.

217. Quality traffic on Website

$$A = \frac{2800}{120}$$

Quality traffic on Website

$$B = \frac{2500}{60}$$

Quality traffic on Website

$$D = \frac{3000}{80}$$

Quality traffic on Website

$$E = \frac{3500}{40}$$

From above, It is clear that Website E has provided maximum quality traffic.

218. Leakage in website

$$B = 1 - \frac{1200}{2500} = 0.52$$

Leakage in website

$$C = 1 - \frac{900}{2000} = 0.55$$

Leakage in website

$$D = 1 - \frac{1300}{3000} = 0.57$$

Leakage in website

$$E = 1 - \frac{1600}{3500} = 0.54$$

Hence, website D sent traffic to www.jay.com with maximum leakage.

219. From the given Pie-chart and graph C, It is clear that on website A advertising budget was spent most efficiently. i.e. the ratio of the Advertising expenditure and the number of visitors who completed buying is minimum.

For questions 220 to 224:

Checking the visibility of given brands across the stores:

1. Astute : $\dfrac{111}{450} + \dfrac{48}{440} + \dfrac{91}{280} + \dfrac{30}{350} + \dfrac{80}{480}$

    = 0.94 (approx.)

2. Supreme : $\dfrac{128}{450} + \dfrac{55}{440} + \dfrac{79}{280} + \dfrac{111}{350} + \dfrac{65}{480}$

    = 1.13 (approx.)

3. Paramount : $\dfrac{69}{450} + \dfrac{116}{440} + \dfrac{50}{280} + \dfrac{101}{350} + \dfrac{105}{480}$

    = 1.1 (approx.)

4. Smash : $\dfrac{85}{450} + \dfrac{137}{440} + \dfrac{30}{280} + \dfrac{60}{350} + \dfrac{108}{480}$

    = 1.06 (approx.)

5. Ultimate : $\dfrac{57}{450} + \dfrac{84}{440} + \dfrac{30}{280} + \dfrac{48}{350} + \dfrac{122}{480}$

    = 0.82 (approx.)

221. Astute has the lowest visibility in any store (i.e. in store 4).

222. Total T-shirts given = 2000.

So, T-shirts of size M = $\dfrac{22}{100} \times 200 = 440$.

Total T-shirts of size M in stores 1, 2 & 5 = 10% of 1370 = 137. Hence, the remaining T-shirts of size M = 440 − 137 = 303.

Now, since we want to minimize size M in store 4, so we maximize size M in store 3 which can be 280 only.

Hence remaining will be in store 4 = 303 − 280 = 23.

223. Share of Supreme brand in all the stores

128 + 55 + 79 + 111 + 65 = 438

Percentage share = $\dfrac{438}{2000} \times 100 = 21.9\%$

224. Smash T-shirts = 420

Ultimate T-shirts = 341

Difference = 79.

The Required percentage = $\dfrac{79}{341} \times 100 = 23.16\%$

225. Company A:

$$\frac{105+185+100+120+110}{5} = \frac{620}{5} = 124$$

Company B:

$$\frac{135+115+130+125+135}{5} = \frac{640}{5} = 128$$

Company C:

$$\frac{165+155+190+100+100}{5} = \frac{710}{5} = 142$$

So company C has maximum average annual expenses.

226. For 2011: $\dfrac{120+180+150}{3} = \dfrac{450}{3} = 150$

For 2012: $\dfrac{165+150+180}{3} = \dfrac{495}{3} = 165$

For 2013: $\dfrac{135+165+180}{3} = \dfrac{480}{3} = 160$

For 2014: $\dfrac{180+150+135}{3} = \dfrac{465}{3} = 155$

So maximum average annual revenue is in the year 2012.

227. Revenue of C in 2015 = 120

Revenue of C in 2012 = 180

The required percentage decrease

$$= \frac{180-120}{180} \times 100 = 33\%.$$

228. Average revenue of A in 2011, 2012, 2013

$$= \frac{120+165+135}{3} = \frac{420}{3} = 140$$

Average revenue of B in 2013, 2014, 2015

$$= \frac{165+150+165}{3} = \frac{480}{3} = 160$$

Difference = 20 × 1000 = 20000.

229. Profit in 2011 = 120 − 105 = 15

Profit in 2012 = 165 − 185 = − 20 (loss)

Profit in 2013 = 135 − 100 = 35

Profit in 2014 = 180 − 120 = 60

Profit in 2015 = 150 − 110 = 40

So by observation, % increase in 2013

$$= \frac{35-(-20)}{20} \times 100 = \frac{55}{20} \times 100 = 275\%$$

Hence it is maximum, so answer is (b) option.

230. Average exports of years from 2012–2016

$$= \frac{1475}{5} = 295.$$

Manufacture's exports is given to be 75%.

Value of manufacture exports

$$= 295 \times \frac{75}{100}$$

= 221 billion US dollar

231. In this question, we will have to calculate Exports & Imports of Manufacturing for all the five years.

Years	Exports	Imports	Surplus Deficiency
2012	182	175	Surplus
2013	210	188	Surplus
2014	181.5	202.5	Deficiency
2015	196	185	Surplus
2016	187.5	192.5	Deficiency

3 times there is surplus, 2 times Deficiency

∴ Option (a)

232. We will have to calculate

Export & imports of fuel for all years:

Years	Exports	Imports	Deficiency
2012	56	200	144
2013	87.5	199.75	112
2014	65	180	115
2015	28	112.5	84.5 (second lowest)
2016	25	87.5	62 (lowest)

∴ Year 2015

Option (a) is correct

233. According to this question.

Exports of fuel in 2017 ⇒ 275 x 15% = 41.25

Imports of fuel in 2017 ⇒ 385 x 30% = 115.5

∴ Deficit = 74

234. Now exports in 2017 = 324

Previous trade deficit = 100

∴ New trade deficit = 100 + 54 = 154

∴ Imports in 2017 = exports + Trade deficit

$$= 324 + 154$$

$$= 478$$

Now that we have calculated imports, we can calculate the imports of food and fuel taking same sectoral composition

∴ option (a) is correct

235. The highest percentage growth is for Jan 2017 (123 − 137), 2nd highest percentage growth is for June 17 (146 − 157) and third highest percentage growth is for Feb 2017 (137 − 147). Hence answer is option (b).

236. Now, if we check across all the commodities, double digit growth is taking place 4 times, which are 123 to 137, 137 to 147, 146 to 157 and 144 to 167. Therefore (d) option is correct answer.

237. Total traffic handled by major ports: 2011-12 = 560187, 2012-13 = 545831, 2013-14 = 555489, 2014-15 = 581344, 2015-16 = 606372. So average growth is highest for the year 2014-15, which is equal to

$$\frac{581344 - 555489}{555489} \times 100 = 4.6\%.$$

238. Highest growth in traffic from 2011-12 to 2015-16 is for Paradip, next is Kandla, and the third highest growth is for Kamarajar.

239. Required value = $(50195 \times 1.1 \times 1.1) + (57033 \times 1.1 \times 1.1) + (22099 \times 1.1 \times 1.1) = 156485$. So closest is 156500. Hence answer is option (a).

240. In 2001-2002, WPI of F & P was 226.7. In 2015-16, by unitary method, $\dfrac{280.2 \times 179.8}{100} = 503.8$. From 226.7 to 503.8, there is 122.2% increase. Option (b) is correct.

241. By using same method in previous question we need to calculate for all the commodities

	2001 - 02	2015 - 16	
PA	168.4	$\dfrac{188.1 \times 249.6}{100} = 469$	(Highest growth)
AC	161	$\dfrac{187.3 \times 176.7}{100} = 330$	
F & P	226.7	$\dfrac{280.2 \times 179.8}{100} = 504$	(Second Highest growth)
MP	144	$\dfrac{166.3 \times 153.4}{100} = 254$	

∴ F & P is correct answer.

242. By observing all the values, we can see that smallest percent increase in WPI on FA is from 179.2 to 181.5. Hence 2003-04. So answer is option (a).

243. Given that PA has 40% weightage. Total WPI for all commodities is 104.5. Going by options, if we assign percentage weight 12 to F & P, and assign percentage weight 48 to MP, then total weightage would be $(104.3 \times 0.4) + (113.6 \times 0.12) + (102.4 \times 0.48) = 41.72 + 13.63 + 49.15 = 104.5$ which is matching the given value. Hence answer is option (a).

244. This question is to be done by observation. PA & AC do not decline more than once. However, F & P declines twice.

2008-2009 to 2009-2010 & 2013-2014 to 2014-2015. Therefore, option (c) is correct.

247. For 1998, it would be $61 = 56\left(\dfrac{1 + R}{100}\right)$.

Therefore, R = 9%

For 1999, it would be $67 = 63\left(\dfrac{1 + R}{100}\right)$.

Therefore R = 6%.

There was no growth in case of any quarters for 2000.

For 2001, it was $58 = 51\left(\dfrac{1 + R}{100}\right)$

Therefore R = 14%.

248. Annual output for 1998 = 240, Annual output for 1999 = 261, Annual output for 2000 = 237, Annual output for 2001 = 224.

So annual output growth is lowest for the year 2000 which is equal to $\dfrac{261 - 237}{261} \times 100 = 9.20\%$ decrease.

250. Contribution

$$= \frac{(25 + 17 + 12 + 6 + 6 + 4 + 2 + 1 + 1)}{495.17} \times 100 = 15010$$

251. Let rooms available per day = x

According to questions

$$0.7x \times 365 \times 350 = 12000000000$$
$$x = 130 \text{ (approx.)}.$$

252. Average occupancy rate

$$= \frac{67 \times 1 + 60 \times 2 + 61 \times 5 + 64 \times 4}{12} = 62 \text{(approx)}$$

253. Average occupancy rate of Asia pacific = 69.5

Average occupancy rate of America = 65.25

Average occupancy rate of Europe = 70.5

Average occupancy rate of Middle east = 61.5

So answer is option (b).

254. Total revenue in 2017

$$34280 + 18450 + 16350 + 8190 + 1700 + 170$$
$$= 79,140$$
$$\text{GBS share} = 16,350$$

$$\text{GBS share in pie chart} = \frac{16350 \times 360}{79140} = 75°$$

255. Total revenue for GBS = 14,2580

Total revenue for software = 12,4210

Total revenue for GTS = 194970

Total revenue for CS = 54480

Total revenue for TSCP = 104760

Total revenue for SYS = 25450

Total revenue for S&T = 70,000

Total revenue for other = 3690

Total revenue for GF = 15,600

Therefore, software is the third height

256. As profit is divided equally in 6 countries

$$\therefore \text{ profit earned by S\&T} = \frac{1}{6} \times 49 \times 10^9 = 8200 \times 10^6$$

257. Percentage revenue from GBS

$$= \frac{18190}{79920} \times 100 = 22.7\%$$

Percentage revenue from cognitive

$$= \frac{16700}{79920} \times 100 = 20.8\%$$

$$\text{Difference} = 22.7 - 20.18 = {\sim}1.9 = 2\%$$

258. Average score of Austria = 4.031

Average score of UK = 399.33

Average score of USA = 389.66

Average score of Switzerland = 391.16

Average score of France = 385.5

So answer is option (c)

259. Difference of Austria = 0.17

Difference of UK = 0.28

Difference of USA = 0.25

Difference of Switzerland = 0.27

Difference of France = 0.31

So answer is option (a)

260. Difference is minimum in 2016 (4.45 − 3.74 = .71)

261. The difference in performance is minimum in timeliness (3.5 − 3.47 = .03)

262. $2009 - 10 \Rightarrow \dfrac{323988 - 270871}{270871} \times 100$

$$\frac{53117}{270871} \times 100 = 19.6\%$$

$2011 - 12 \Rightarrow \dfrac{415384 - 351766}{351766} \times 100$

$$\frac{63616}{351766} \times 100 = 18.1\%$$

$2014 - 15 \Rightarrow \dfrac{545952 - 465789}{465789} \times 100$

$$= \frac{80163}{465789} \times 100 = 17.2\%$$

$2015 - 16 \Rightarrow \dfrac{612518 - 545252}{545252} \times 100$

$$= \frac{66566}{545952} \times 100 = 12.2\%$$

263. $2008 - 09 \Rightarrow \dfrac{280}{3800} \Rightarrow 1.38\,/\,\text{factor}$

$2011 - 12 \Rightarrow \dfrac{6000}{4175} \Rightarrow 1.43\,/\,\text{factor}$

$2013 - 14 \Rightarrow \dfrac{8500}{5000} \Rightarrow 1.7\,/\,\text{factor}$

$2015 - 16 \Rightarrow \dfrac{10000}{5000} \Rightarrow 2\,/\,\text{factor}$

264. $2008 - 09 \Rightarrow \dfrac{4500}{1142 - 4750} = \dfrac{4500}{6692} = .672$

$2009 - 10 \Rightarrow \dfrac{5200}{12240 - 5000} = \dfrac{5200}{7241} = .7181$

$2010 - 11 \Rightarrow \dfrac{6500}{14993 - 5500} = \dfrac{6500}{9493} = .68$

$2011 - 12 \Rightarrow \dfrac{8200}{18250 - 6500} = \dfrac{8200}{11750} = .69$

265.

Fixed Cap		No. of factors	
5200	15.3	3800	7.30%
6000	3.3	4100	9.70%
6200	12.9	4500	6.60%
7000	0	4800	2.00%
7000	21.4	4900	2.00%
8500	5.85	5000	−2%
9000		4900	
10000	11.11	5000	2%

Hence we can see these all 5 years

General Knowledge & Current Affairs

General Knowledge & Current Affairs

Science

2007-09

Directions for Questions 1 to 7: Mark <u>all</u> the correct statements

1. (a) The full form of AIDS is Abnormal Immune Deficiency Syndrome.

   (b) Petrology refers to the study of the economy in relation to petroleum products.

   (c) A diverging lens can be used as magnifying glass.

   (d) Laparoscopy is concerned with gynaecological operations.

2. (a) In an eye donation, it is the lens that is donated.

   (b) Dialysis of kidneys involves the process of reverse osmosis.

   (c) IC chips used in computers are usually made of chromium.

   (d) The age of the tree can be found by counting the annual growth rings in a section of its stem.

3. (a) All metals are solids at ordinary temperatures.

   (b) Nitric acid is, when pure, a colourful liquid, possessing great oxidising power, turning yellow the skin and other organic bodies.

   (c) Ammonia gas may be synthetically prepared from its elements by passing the silent electric discharge through a mixture of nitrogen and hydrogen.

   (d) The composition of the air by weight maybe shown by passing a given volume of pure dry air over a weighed quantity of heated metallic copper, the increase in weight showing the weight of oxygen present in the volume of air, the nitrogen also being collected and the weight ascertained.

4. (a) Four scientists shared the Nobel Prize in Physics in the year 2005.

   (b) International Atomic Energy Agency was the co-recipient of Nobel Peace Prize in the year 2005.

   (c) The flow of heat by conduction occurs via collisions between atoms and molecules in the substance and the subsequent transfer of potential energy.

   (d) Madam Curie, pioneer in the early field of radiology, was born in France.

5. (a) The two planets - Mercury and Mars - that move within the Earth's orbit are known as inferior planets.

   (b) All planets can be seen at night.

   (c) An ion is an atom or molecule that has become electrically charged by the loss or gain of one or more electrons.

   (d) Human eyelids open and close about 20 times a minute.

6. (a) Chlorine may be collected by downward displacement of air, as it is two and a-half times heavier than air, or it may be collected over warm water.

   (b) Chlorine is a greenish yellow gas, easily condensed to a liquid; it does not burn in air, but many substances burn in it, forming chlorides, just as bodies burning in oxygen form oxides.

   (c) Because of combining with free hydrogen, chlorine is not able to separate hydrogen from some of its compounds and to combine with it.

   (d) Chlorine bleaches mineral colouring matters.

7. (a) Doppler effect refers to the phenomenon whereby the pitch of a sound appears to change as the object moves away.

   (b) The equation $V = d \times d$, where V is the volume and d is the diameter of the sphere is dimensionally correct.

   (c) Bernoulli's principle states that the pressure of a fluid is inversely proportional to its volume.

   (d) Northern lights are caused by energetic particles released from the sun reacting in earth's atmosphere.

2009-11

8. The antibiotic penicillin is obtained from:

   (a) a bacterium (b) fungus

   (c) synthetic means (d) virus-infected cells

9. Select the correct Inventions/Discoveries – Inventors/ Discoverers match:

Inventions/Discoveries	Inventors/Discoverer
i. Cassette (Audio)	a. Philips Co.
ii. Super Computer	b. J. H. Van Tassel
iii. Cloning (Mammal)	c. Wilmut, et al
iv. HIV	d. Mortagnier

   (a) i-a, ii-b, iii-c, iv-d (b) i-b, ii-a, iii-d, iv-c

   (c) i-c, ii-a, iii-b, iv-d (d) i-a, ii-b, iii-d, iv-c

10. Select the correct Diseases – Plants affected match:

Diseases	Plants affected
i. Black heart	a. Peas
ii. Red Rot	b. Wheat
iii. Karnal Bunt	c. Sugarcane
iv. Powdery Mildew	d. Patatos

    (a) i-a, ii-b, iii-d, iv-c   (b) i-d, ii-c, iii-b, iv-a

    (c) i-b, ii-c, iii-a, iv-d   (d) i-a, ii-b, iii-c, iv-d

11. In April 2008 ISRO launched the following satellite form Sriharikota:

    (a) KITSAT-3   (b) CARTOSAT-2A

    (c) HAMSAT   (d) INSAT-4CR

2011-13

12. Match the following measuring instruments to the formal test methods which define the use of the Instrument.

Instruments	Use of instrument
a. Squid	i. Heating of power radiation
b. Actinometer	ii. Viscosity of a fluid
c. Dilatometer	iii. Boiling Temperature of a liquid
d. Ebulliscope	iv. Coefficient of thermal expansion
e. Rheometer	v. Magnetic Field

    (a) a-v, b-i, c-iv, d-iii, e-ii

    (b) a-ii, b-i, c-v, d-iii, e-iv

    (c) a-v, b-iv, c-i, d-ii, e-iii

    (d) a-iii, b-iv, c-v, d-i, e-ii

2012-14

13. Which of the following is a space mission by ISRO?

    (a) SROSS-C2   (b) QuickScat

    (c) SAMPEX   (d) Stardust

2013-15

14. In ecology, what name is given to the measure of diversity that is often used to quantify the biodiversity of a habitat, by taking into account the number of species present, as well as the abundance of each species?

    (a) Simpson Index

    (b) Herfindahl-Hirschman Index

    (c) Flintstone Index

    (d) Bio-volatility Index

15. The 'God Particle' is the name given to

    (a) The Meson particle

    (b) The Higgs Boson Particle

    (c) The Proton Particle

    (d) None of the above

2014-16

16. Which is the most abundant element in the universe?

    (a) Hydrogen   (b) Helium

    (c) Oxygen   (d) Carbon

2016-18

17. A person with 'AB' blood group is also called a universal recipient because of the

    (a) Lack of antigens in the bipod

    (b) Lack of antibodies in the blood

    (c) Lack of both antigens and antibodies in the blood

    (d) Presence of both antigens and antibodies in the blood

18. Who discovered 'Pluto' in the year 1930?

    (a) Clyde Tombaugh   (b) Albert Einstein

    (c) Carl Sagan   (d) Jacques Cousteau

19. Mark the wrong combination

    (a) James Watt: Steam Engine

    (b) (a)G. Bell: Telephone

    (c) J.L. Baird: Television

    (d) J. Perkins: Penicillin

20. The British Cosmologist Stephen Hawking and the Russian entrepreneur Yuri Milner have launched a project to search for the extra terrestrial life. This project is called:

    (a) The Breakthrough Listen Project

    (b) The Cosmic Breakthrough Project

    (c) The Extra Terrestrial Project

    (d) The Edge of the Universe Project

2017-19

21. Which of the following best represents baking soda?

    (a) Potassium Carbonate

    (b) Sodium Chloride

    (c) Potassium Hydroxide

    (d) Sodium Bicarbonate

2019-21

22. Correctly match the following terms?

    1. Isobront : a. Joins points with the same light intensity

    2. Isocheim : b. Joins points with the same wind direction

    3. Isogon   : c. Joins points with the same mean temperature in winter

    4. Isophote : d. Joins points of a given phase of a thunderstorm activity

    (a) 1-d, 2-c, 3-b, 4-a   (b) 1-a, 2-b, 3-c, 4-d

    (c) 1-d, 2-a, 3-b, 4-c   (d) 1-a, 2-c, 3-d, 4-b

23. Which of the following company has designed the humanoid 'Sophia'?
    (a) Hansen Robotics Ltd.
    (b) Hanson Robotics Ltd.
    (c) Hansan Robotics Ltd.
    (d) Hemsen Robotics Ltd.

Polity

2007-09

Directions for Question 24 : Mark <u>all</u> the correct statements

24. (a) The parliamentary term 'crossing the floor' may be best described as leaving a house by a minister in between a session to attend the other house.
    (b) It is necessary to be a member of either house of parliament to be appointed as governor of a state.
    (c) A cognizable offence is one where arrests can be made without warrants.
    (d) The Chief Minister of a State in India is not eligible to vote in the Presidential elections if he is a member of the Upper House of the State Legislature.

2009-11

25. Select the WRONG Country – Name of Parliament match:

	Country	Name of Parliament
A	Iran	Majlis
B	Norway	Riksdag
C	Tansania	Bunge
D	Israel	Knesset

26. Which of the following is not part of the Central Police Forces under the Union Government of Indian?
    (a) Sashashatra Seema Ball
    (b) Assam Rifles
    (c) National Security Guard
    (d) Anti-Naxalite Force

2011-13

27. The Constitution of which country has influenced the inclusion of the "Emergency Provision" in the Indian Constitution.
    (a) Germany   (b) Canada
    (c) USA   (d) Britain

28. Which one of the following Indian Union Territory is having the legislative assembly as of 2010.
    (a) Dadra and Nagar Haveli
    (b) Lakshadeep
    (c) Puducherry
    (d) Andaman and Nicobar Islands

2013-15

29. What was the picture shown on the first stamp of independent India?
    (a) The new Indian flag
    (b) Ashoka Lion Capital
    (c) A portrait of Mahatma Gandhi
    (d) A Douglas DC-4 aircraft

30. Who, among the following, has not been a Vice President of India before becoming the President of India?
    (a) S. Radhakrishnan
    (b) R. Venkatraman
    (c) Shankar Dayal Sharma
    (d) Giani Zail Singh

2015-17

31. Shri Pranab Mukherjee is the __________ President of the Republic of India.
    (a) 11th (b) 12th
    (c) 13th (d) 14th

2017-19

32. General elections were held in Myanmar on 8th November 2015. This has been the first openly-contested election held in the country since 1990. Which political party received the highest number of seats?
    (a) National League for Democracy
    (b) United Socialist Party
    (c) Union Solidarity and Development Party
    (d) National Peoples Party

33. Which of the following is not an elected post in India?
    (a) President
    (b) Prime Minister
    (c) Governor
    (d) Chief Minister

2019-21

34. IIFT has been entrusted with the responsibility of setting up of India-Africa Institute of Foreign Trade as a Centre of Excellence in the area of International Business and Trade with Pan-Africa reach. This effort of Government of India will come under which of the following types of Diplomacy?
    (a) Track-III Diplomacy
    (b) Track-II Diplomacy
    (c) Track-V Diplomacy
    (d) Track-VII Diplomacy

Geography

2007-09

Directions for Questions 35 to 36: Mark <u>all</u> the correct statements

35. (a) Sand dunes occur only in arid desert regions.

(b) Central Africa is home to the second largest rainforest.

(c) The heat buildup inside the earth reached a high early in the earth's history.

(d) The troposphere is a layer of the earth's atmosphere near its surface which is cooler higher up and warmer farther down.

36. (a) The Aravalli is the oldest mountain range in India, running from northeast to southwest across Rajasthan in western India.

(b) The Satpura Range is a range of hills in central India. It begins in eastern Gujarat near the Arabian Sea coast, then runs east through Maharashtra, Madhya Pradesh and ends in the state of Bihar.

(c) The Himalayas extend from the state of Jammu and Kashmir in the west to the state of Assam in the east.

(d) The Cardamom Hills located in Kerala, are named after the cardamom grown in the hill's cool regions.

2008-10

37. Which of the following state-river match is correct?

	River	State
A.	Koodor	Maharastra
B.	Girnar	Kerala
C.	Mahi	Goa
D.	Tunga	Karnataka

38. State wise largest producers of following crops (in quantity) are given in descending order. Mark which is not correct combination?

S. No.	Crops	States
A	Saugarcene	Uttar Pardesh, Maharashtra, Tamil Nadu
B	Coffee	Karnataka, Kerala, Tamilnadu
C	Wheat	Punjab, Uttar Pradesh, Haryana
D	Soybeans	Madhya Pradesh, Maharshtra, Rajasthan

2009-11

39. In descending order, which of the following group of countries is correct about the length of India's land borders with its neighbors?

(a) Bangladesh, Pakistan, China, Myanmar, Nepal

(b) China, Pakistan, Bangladesh, Myanmar, Nepal

(c) China, Bangladesh, Pakistan, Nepal, Myanmar

(d) Bangladesh, China, Pakistan, Nepal, Myanmar

40. Which of the following mountain peak is not located in India?

(a) Daulagiri

(b) Mt. Kamet

(c) Saltoro Kangri

(d) Nanga Parbat (Diamir)

41. In descending order, which one of the following is the correct sex ratio of states in India?

(a) Kerala, Chhatisgargh, Tamil Nadu, Andhra Pradesh, Orissa

(b) Kerala, Chhatisgargh, Orissa, Tamil Nadu, Andhra Pradesh

(c) Kerala, Tamil Nadu, Orissa, Andhra Pradesh, Tamil Nadu

(d) Kerala, Tamil Nadu, Chhatisgargh, Orissa, Andhra Pradesh

42. Select the correct Sobriquets – Primary Names match:

Sobriquets	Primary Names
i. Emerald Island	a. Bahrain
ii. Island of pearls	b. Ireland
iii. Holy land	c. Bhutan
iv. Land of thunderbolt	d. Palestine

(a) i – b, ii – d, iii – c, iv - a

(b) i – c, ii – d, iii – a, iv – b

(c) I – b, ii – a, iii – d, iv – c

(d) i – c, ii – a, iii – d, iv – b

43. Select the correct Railway Zone – Head Quarter match:

Railway Zone	Head Quarter
i. South-East Central	a. Jablpur
ii. North-East Frontier	b. Maligaon
iii. North Eastern	c. Bilaspur
iv. West Central	d. Gorakhpur

(a) i-c, ii-b, iii-d, iv-a

(b) i-a, ii-d, iii-b, iv-c

(c) i-a, ii-b, iii-c, iv-d

(d) i-c, ii-a, iii-d, iv-b

2011-13

44. Name the Indian state having maximum number of Major Seaports.

(a) West Bengal

(b) Goa

(c) Gujarat

(d) Tamil Nadu

45. Match the National Highway route number to States that it covers?

National Highway Route Number	Name of the Indian States which the NH covers
a. National Highway Number 6	1. Punjab, Rajasthan, Gujarat
b. National Highway Number 7	2. Delhi, Haryana, Rajasthan, Gujarat, Maharashtra
c. National Highway Number 8	3. Orissa, Jharkhan, West Bengal, Gujarat
d. National Highway Number 15	4.Uttar Pradesh, Madhya Pradesh, Maharashtra, Andhra Pradesh, Karnataka, Tamil Nadu

(a) a-4, b-2, c-1, d-3   (b) a-2, b-3, c-4, d-1   (c) a-3, b-4, c-2, d-1   (d) a-4, b-1, c-2, d-3

46. Match the old name to the new name of the countries.

Old Name	New Name
a. South West Africa	1. Ethiopia
b. Rhodesia	2. Zambia
c. Northern Rhodesia	3. Namibia
d. Abyssinia	4. Zimbabwe

(a) a-2, b-4, c-3, d-1   (b) a-3, b-4, c-2, d-1
(c) a-4, b-3, c-2, d-1   (d) a-1, b-4, c-2, d-3

47. Match the Country, City and River.

Country	City	River
a. Germany	i. Lisbon	1. Vistula
b. Poland	ii. Chittagaon	2. Karnafuli
c. Portugal	iii. Dreden	3. Tagus
d. Bangladesh	iv. Warsaw	4. Elbe

(a) a-i-3, b-iv-1, c-iii-2, d-ii-4

(b) a-iii-1, b-iv-3, c-i-4, d-ii-2

(c) a-iv-4, b-iii-1, c-i-2, d-ii-3

(d) a-iii-4, b-iv-1, c-i-3, d-ii-2

48. Match the Geographical Epithet to Country/ City.

Epithet	Country / City
a. Quaker city	1. Budapest
b. Twin city	2. Chicago
c. White city	3. Philadelphia
d. Windy city	4. Belgrade

(a) a-1, b-4, c-3, d-2

(b) a-4, b-3, c-2, d-1

(c) a-3, b-1, c-4, d-2

(d) a-1, b-2, c-4, d-3

49. Which one of the following national park established by government of India is the relatively the latest one?

(a) Madhav National Park, Madhya Pradesh

(b) Khangchendzonga National Park, Sikkim

(c) Corbett National Park, Uttaranchal

(d) Tadoba National Park, Maharashtra

2012-14

50. Which of the following rivers do *not* flow across Uttarakhand?

(a) Bhagirathi and Ganga

(b) Ramaganga and Yamuna

(c) Gandak and Gomti

(d) Tons and Kali

51. Match the *correct* Country with its Capital City and Currency:

	Country		Capital City		Currency
a.	Argentina	i.	Ashgabat	1	Birr
b.	Ethiopia	ii.	Buenos Aires	2	Rial
c.	Turkmenistan	iii.	Addis Ababa	3	Peso
d.	Yemen	iv.	Sana	4	Manat

(a) a-iv-2; b-i-3; c-iii-4; d-ii-1

(b) a-ii-2; b-iii-1; c-iv-4; d-i-3

(c) a-ii-3; b-iii-1; c-i-4; d-iv-2

(d) a-ii-2; b-iii-3; c-i-1; d-iv-4

2013-15

52. What is a good estimate for the length of the coastline of mainland India?

(a) 6000 kms   (b) 7500 kms

(c) 9000 kms   (d) 11,000 kms

53. When it is 11:15 hours as per Greenwich Mean Time, what will be the time in Delhi?

(a) 04:45 hours   (b) 05:45 hours

(c) 17:45 hours   (d) 16:45 hours

54. Mullaperiyar Dam is a matter of controversy between which of the following states?

(a) Karnataka - Tamil Nadu

(b) Kerala - Tamil Nadu

(c) Kerala - Karnataka

(d) Karnataka - Andhra Padesh

55. Arrange the following Indian rivers from North to South

1. Narmada   2. Kaveri

3. Jhelum   4. Godavari

(a) 3-1-2-4   (b) 1-4-3-2

(c) 1-3-4-2   (d) 3-1-4-2

2014-16

56. Mt. Everest is the highest mountain summit of the world. Rank the following summits in descending order of their heights?

i.   Makalu;
ii. Kanchenjunga;
iii. Godwin Austen;
iv. Lhotse

(a) iv-i-iii-ii
(b) ii-iii-i-iv
(c) iii-ii-iv-i
(d) i-iv-ii-iii

57. Which country has the longest coastline?

(a) USA
(b) Australia
(c) India
(d) Canada

58. Arrange the following Indian port cities beginning from East to West.

i.   Jamnagar
ii. Kochi
iii. Chennai
iv. Visakhapatnam

(a) i-ii-iii-iv
(b) iv-iii-ii-i
(c) ii-iv-i-iii
(d) iii-i-iv-ii

59. Which of the following cities is at the junction of the highways known as North-South and East-West Corridors?

(a) Delhi
(b) Nagpur
(c) Jhansi
(d) Hyderabad

60. Which countries are separated by the McMahon line?

(a) India and Pakistan
(b) India and Bangladesh
(c) China and India
(d) China and Tibet

2015-17

61. The Ebola virus disease is named after the Ebola River. The River is located at.

(a) The Federal Republic of Nigeria
(b) The Democratic Republic of the Congo
(c) The Republic of Senegal
(d) The Commonwealth of Virginia, US

62. A cording to the Primary Census Abstract 2011, which of the following states in India has the highest population density?

(a) Gujarat
(b) Bihar
(c) Kerala
(d) Goa

2016-18

63. Match the name of the city with the river on whose banks it is located

City	River
I. Budapest	a. Tigris
II. Baghdad	b. Tiber
III. Rome	c. Han
IV. Seoul	d. Danube

(a) I-d; II-a; III-b; IV-c
(b) L-b; II-c; III-d; IV-a
(c) I-c; II-d; III-a; IV-b
(d) I-a; II-b; III-c; IV-d

2017-19

64. Which of the following Indian states share border with multiple countries?

(a) Manipur
(b) Mizoram
(c) Tripura
(d) Bihar
(e) Sikkim
(f) West Bengal
(g) Assam

(a) (f), (e), (a) and (g)
(b) (b), (f), (g) and (e)
(c) (a), (f), (b) and (c)
(d) (f), (c), (e) and (a)

65. The Panama Canal expansion project is also referred to

(a) Dead Locks
(b) Third Set of Locks
(c) New Horizon
(d) Cut Across the Sea

2019-21

66. Which of the following is the most exported agricultural commodity from India in terms of value?

(a) Tea
(b) Rice
(c) Rubber
(d) Cotton

67. Which of the following is a correct sequence of Sea Ports of India from "South to North"?

(a) Cochin $\to$ Vizhinjam $\to$ Kozhikode $\to$ Mangalore
(b) Kozhikode $\to$ Vizhinjam $\to$ Cochin $\to$ Mangalore
(c) Vizhinjam $\to$ Cochin $\to$ Kozhikode $\to$ Mangalore
(d) Vizhinjam $\to$ Kozhikode $\to$ Mangalore $\to$ Cochin

History

2007-09

Directions for Questions 68 to 70: Mark <u>all</u> the correct statements

68. (a) The only Veda to have been rendered musically is the Sama Veda.

(b) Port Blair is situated in North Andaman.

(c) The outermost layer of the Sun is called photosphere.

(d) Nhava Sheva, a major Indian port, is in the state of Gujarat.

69. (a) Chandragupta, who ruled from 324 to 301 (b)(c), was the architect of the first Indian imperial power -- the Mauryan Empire (324 - 184 (b)(c)).

(b) The period from 1707 AD - the year when Aurangzeb died, 1857, the year of the Indian Uprising, saw the gradual increase of the European influence in the India.

(c) Between 1746 - 48, the French and English finally came to blows in the first Carnatic War.

(d) Tilak, who was one of the first nationalist leaders with a following and deep understanding of the grassroots of India, voiced the thought of Home Rule in 1825.

70. (a) The Montagu-Chelmsford Reforms were introduced by the British Government in India towards women's participation in active politics.

(b) The first Governor-General of India - Warren Hastings, remained in India until 1874 and was succeeded by Cornwallis, who initiated the Permanent Settlement.

(c) Lord Dalhousie's notorious Doctrine of Lapse, whereby a native state became part of British India if there was no male heir at the death of the ruler, was one of the principal means by which native states were annexed by the British.

(d) In the third Carnatic war, the British East India Company defeated the French forces at the battle of Wandiwash ending almost a century of conflict over supremacy of India.

2008-10

71. Match the correct combination in the following:

Age	Period	Composer
(i) Madieval	(a) 476-1400 AD	(A) Hohann Christian Bach
(ii) Renaissance	(b) 1400-1600 AD	(B) Gioachino Rossini
(iii) Baroque	(c) 1600-1760 AD	(C) Thomas Campion
(iv) Classical	(d) 1730-1820 AD	(D) Dante Alighieri
(v) Romantic	(e) 1850-1910 AD	(E) William Byrd

(a) I-A-e, II-B-c, III-C-D, IV-D-a, V-E-b

(b) I-A-d, II-B-a, III-c-B, iv-d-C, v-e-E

(c) i-a-A, ii-b-C, iii-c-E, iv-d-d, v-e-B

(d) i-a-D, ii-b-E, iii-c-C, iv-d-A, v-E-B

2009-11

72. Which of the treaty was signed amongst the European nations for entering into the monetary union?

(a) Treaty of Nice (b) Treaty of Versailles

(c) Maastricht Treaty (d) Treaty of Paris

2011-13

73. The State Bank of India was know as Imperial Bank of India in 1921, which was an amalgamation of three banks namely.

(a) Bank of Bengal, Bank of Bombay and Bank of Madras

(b) Bank of Bengal, Bank of Punjab and Bank of Mysore

(c) Bank of Bombay, Syndicate Bank of Union Bank

(d) Bank of Madras, Mercantile Bank, Bank of Travancore

2012-14

74. Who did declare, "The only hope for India is from the masses. The upper classes are physically and morally dead"?

(a) Gopalkrishna Gokhale

(b) Bal Gangadhar Tilak

(c) Mahatma Gandhi

(d) Swami Vivekananda

75. Which of the following facts is *not true* about Mahatma Gandhi?

(a) He was chosen for the Nobel Peace Prize in 1948, but because of his unfortunate assassination, the Peace Prize was not awarded that year.

(b) Time magazine named him the "Man of the Year" in 1930.

(c) In 1999, he was declared the "Person of the Century" by the Time magazine, and the runner-up was Albert Einstein.

(d) He was shoved out a train in 1893 in Pietermaritzburg in KwaZulu Natal province of South Africa, because he refused to move to a third class coach while holding a first class ticket.

2013-15

76. Which year is known as the year of the great divide in the demographic history of India?

(a) 1857 (b) 1947

(c) 1921 (d) 1951

2014-16

77. Under an agreement with which of the following countries did Subhas Chandra Bose organise the Indian soldiers into Azad Hind Fauj?

(a) Germany (b) Japan

(c) Italy (d) Russia

78. Which religion was propounded by Mughal Emperor Akbar in 1582 (a)(d), with the intention of merging the best elements of different religions?

(a) Akbarnama (b) Ain-i-Akbari

(c) Zij-i Ilkhani (d) Din-e-Ilahi

2016-18

79. The remains of which ancient civilization can be seen at the site of Machu Pichu in Peru?

(a) Incas (b) Aztecs

(c) Mayans (d) Indians

80. Who is acknowledged as the creator of Chandigarh's Rock Gardens?

(a) E. Sridharan (b) Nek Chand Saini

(c) Charles Correa (d) Geoffrey Bawa

2017-19

81. "Satyameva Jayate" inscribed on one side of all Indian currency, has been derived from which of the following ancient Indian scripture?

(a) Mundaka Upanishad (b) Rigveda

(c) Ramayana (d) None of the above

Art and Culture

2008-10

82. Match the right combination of the numbered boxes from the positions below:

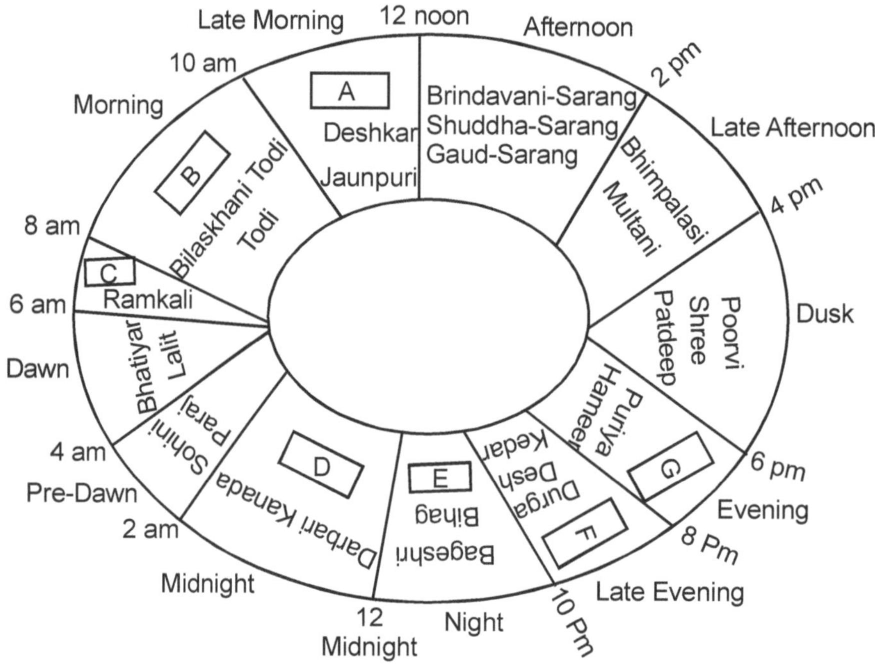

(a) A-Bhairavi, B-Ahir Bhairav, C-Bhairavi, D-Yaman, E-Jayjaiwanti, F-Chandrakauns, G-Malkauns

(b) A-Bhairavi, B-Ahir Bhairav, C-Bhairav, D-Malkauns, E-Chandrakauns, F-Jayjaiwanti, F-Chandrakauns

(c) A-Bhairavi, B-Ahir BAhirav, C-Chairavi, D-Malkauns, E-Yaman, F-?Jayjaiwanti, G-Chandrakauns

(d) A-Ahir Bhairav, B-Bahiravi, C-Bhairav, D-Malkauns, E-Chandrakaus, F-Jayjaiwanti, G-Yaman

83. Match the following:

State	Festival	Fair
(i) Bihar	(a) Chhath	(A) Madia Fair
(ii) Andhra Pradesh	(b) Gugga Naumi	(B) Yellaramma Jatara
(iii) Harayana	(c) Margazh	(C) Sonepur Cattle Fair
(iv) Madhya Pradesh	(d) Koqsar	(D) Bsdod Fain

(a) i-a-D, ii-b-B, iii-c-C, iv-d-A

(b) i-d-C, ii-c-B, iii-a-A, iv-b-D

(c) i-a-C, ii-c-B, iii-b-D, iv-d-A

(d) i-b-A, ii-a-C, iii-d-D, iv-c-B

2009-11

84. Select the correct Artists – Instruments match:

Artists	Instruments
i. N. Rajam	a. Santoor
ii. Satish Vyas	b. Violin
iii. Vilayat Khan	c. Rudra Vina
iv. Asad Ali Khan	d. Sitar

(a) i-c, ii-b, iii-d, iv-a

(b) i-b, ii-a, iii-d, iv-c

(c) i-d, ii-a, iii-b, iv-c

(d) i-c, ii-d, iii-b, iv-a

2012-14

85. Identify the *correct* match of the Folk Dances and States given below:

	Folk Dances		States
a.	Dhalo	i.	Goa
b.	Ghoomra	ii.	Kerala
c.	Gidda	iii.	Orissa
d.	Thullal	iv.	Punjab

(a) a-i; b-ii; c-iv; d-iii

(b) a-i; b-iii; c-iv; d-ii

(c) a-iii; b-i; c-iv; d-ii

(d) a-iii; b-ii; c-iv; d-i

2013-15

86. In a painting, what is the vanishing point?

(a) The point beyond which things are too small to be seen

(b) The point where the sky meets the ground

(c) The point on the horizon where parallel lines appear to meet

(d) The point where an object disappears behind another

Economy

2008-10

87. From which country did India receive the highest FDI inflow during 2006-2007?

(a) United States of America

(b) United Kingdom

(c) Netherlands

(d) Mauritius

88. Match the following:

State	Location	Type of Special Economic Zone
(i) Andhra Pradesh	(a) Hassan	(A) Auromobile and Automobile Component
(ii) Maharashtra	(b) Ranipat	(B) Leather
(iii) Karnataka	(c) Hydrabad	(C) Textile
(iv) Tamil Nadu	(d) Waluj	Gems and Jewellery

(a) i-b-D, ii-d-A, iii-a-C, iv-c-B

(b) i-b-B, ii-a-A, iii-d-C, iv-c-D

(c) i-c-B, ii-d-A, iii-a-C, iv-b-D

(d) i-c-D, ii-d-A, iii-a-C, iv-b-B

89. With which of the following country, India currently <u>does not</u> have a Preferential Trade Agreement?

(a) Sri Lanka   (b) Thailand

(c) Chile   (d) Peru

2009-11

90. Select the correct Organization – Purpose match:

	Organization		Purpose
1	NABARD	i	Financial assistance for warehousing
2	NCDC	ii	Refinancing agricultural credit
3	SCARDB	iii	Inter-state sale of agricultural products
4	NAFED	iv	Land development

(a) 1 – ii, 2 – i, 3 – iv, 4 – iii

(b) 1 – iii, 2 – i, 3 – iv, 4 – ii

(c) 1 – ii, 2 – iii, 3 – iv, 4 – i

(d) 1 – iii, 2 – iv, 3 – ii, 4 – i

2010-12

91. Which is the correct Legal Act and Jurisdiction Match?

Act	Jurisdiction
a. Companies Act 1956	i. Facilitating external trade and payments
b. Competition Act 2002	ii. Formation and regulation of companies
c. SEBI Act 1952	iii. Prohibition of anti-competitive agreements
d. FEMA Act 1999	iv. Investors' protection

(a) a-ii, b-iii, c-iv, d-i   (b) a-iv, b-ii, c-iii, d-i

(c) a-iv, b-i, c-ii, d-iii   (d) a-iv, b-ii, c-iii, d-i

92. The abbreviations given in the first column are explained in the second column. Select the option which has all wrong explanations of the abbreviations.

a. UNCTAD:	I. United Nations Conference on Trade and Development
b. UNCED:	ii. UN Conference on Education and Development
c. TAFTA:	iii. Trans-Atlantic Financial Trade Agreement
d. FEMA	iv. Foreign Exchange Management Act
e. PFRDA:	v. Pension Fund Reporting and Development Authority
f. NASSCOM:	vi. National Association of Software and Service Companies
g. MODVAT:	vii. Modified Value Added Tax
h. FCNRA:	viii. Foreign Currency Non-Resident Accounts
i. ASSOCHEM	ix. Association chamber of Commerce Trade and Industry

(a) b-ii, c-iii, e-v, i-ix   (b) a-i, f-vi, h-viii

(c) b-ii, d-iv, g-viii   (d) e-v, i-ix, h-viii

93. CDS which has been in news recently stands for?

(a) Collateral Default swap

(b) Credit Demand Swap

(c) Credit Default Swap

(d) Collateral Demand Swap

94. In the financial year 2008-09, the top three investing countries in terms of FDI inflows were:

(a) USA, UK, Mauritius

(b) Mauritius, Singapore, USA

(c) UK, Japan, Mauritius

(d) Mauritius, USA, Japan

95. Negative inflation is also called:

(a) Disinflation

(b) Deflation

(c) Both

(d) None of the above

96. Which of the following statements does not relate to the concept of carbon credits?

(a) For one tonne of carbon dioxide emission reduction a company receives a carbon emission certificate which can be traded like any other commodity.

(b) The carbon emission certificates are sold to companies in developed economies like power utilities.

(c) Carbon credit certificates are traded under UN-mandated international convention on climate change.

(d) Developing economies are allowed to offset some of their emissions from cars, factories and homes by funding clean energy projects in developed ones.

2011-13

97. Which one of the following state is having maximum number of special economic zone (SEZ), notifies under the SEZ Act, 2005.

(a) Andhra Pradesh

(b) Maharashtra

(c) Tamil Nadu

(d) Karnataka

98. Select the country that has maximum share in FDI equity inflow in India as on June 2010.

(a) Germany

(b) UAE

(c) France

(d) Netherland

99. Which sector attracted minimum FDI equity Inflow in India in the year 2009-2010?

(a) Construction activities

(b) Housing and real estate

(c) Telecommunications

(d) Power

2012-14

100. Indian Rupee received a unique symbol ₹ which blends the scripts of ____________.

(a) Devanagari and Palli

(b) Sanskrit and Roman

(c) Devanagari and Roman

(d) None of the above

101. Mark the *correct* match of Public Programmes with the Ministry:

	Public Programmes		Ministry of
a.	MNREGS	i.	Rural Development
b.	JNNURM	ii.	Panchayati Raj
c.	RHM	iii.	Urban Development
d.	IAY	iv.	Health & Family Welfare

(a) a-i; b-ii; c-iii; d-iv

(b) a-ii; b-iv; c-i; d-iii

(c) a-i; b-iv; c-iii; d-ii

(d) a-ii; b-iii; c-iv; d-i

102. Which of the following is *not* an eligibility condition placed in the 'Draft Guidelines for Licensing of New Banks in the Private Sector' issued by the Reserve Bank of India on 29th August 2011?

(a) New banks must have a minimum capital of Rs. 500 crores from the beginning.

(b) Only credible groups with 10 years track record will be eligible to set up banks.

(c) Foreign shareholding in the new bank shall not exceed 5% for the first 5 years.

(d) Groups having 10% or more income or assets or both from real estate construction or broking business or both in last 3 years will not be eligible.

2014-16

103. From the year 2014 onwards, the London Interbank Offered Rate (LIBOR)will be administered by

(a) NYSE Euronext

(b) Thomson Reuters

(c) British Bankers' Association

(d) UK's Financial Services Authority

104. Dr. Raghuram Rajan has not served in which of the following positions

(a) Governor, RBI

(b) Economic Counsellor, IMF

(c) Chief Economist, World Bank

(d) Chief Economic Advisor, GO I

105. If India exports more than it imports, which of the following is likely to happen?

(a) INR is likely to appreciate against other currencies

(b) The supply of INR is likely to exceed the demand in the foreign exchange market, ceteris paribus.

(c) INR would be under pressure to depreciate against other currencies.

(d) Both B and C are correct

106. According to the "Doing Business Report (2013)" of the World Bank, which BRIC nation holds the best ranking?

(a) Russian Federation   (b) Brazil

(c) India   (d) China

2015-17

107. According to the Economic Survey for 2013 – 14, India had the second fastest growing services sector over the 11 – year period from 2001 to 2012. Which country had the fastest growing service sector, in the corresponding period?

(a) China   (b) Russia

(c) Thailand   (d) Philippines

108. According to the Human Development report published by UNDP in July 2014, which among the following South Asian countries have the highest and the least rank. in Human Development Index (2013)? In each option first name is indicated for highest rank and second name for the least rank.

(a) India, Afghanistan

(b) Maldives, Nepal

(c) Srilanka, Afghanistan

(d) India, Bangladesh

109. In the Union Budget for 2014 - 15, the Government proposed to keep a side Rs. 500 crores for "Deen Dayal Upadhyaya Gram Jyoti Yojna" for:

(a) augmenting power supply to rural areas

(b) encouraging rural youth to take up local entrepreneurship program

(c) providing impetus to watershed development in the country

(d) the welfare of the tribal

110. The Prime Minister of India has laid the foundation of which of the following port-based Special Economic Zone (SEZ) in August 2014?

(a) JNPT   (b) Chennai port

(c) Cochin Port   (d) Mundra Port

2016-18

111. Which multilateral development bank has been set up by BRICS as an alternative to the World Bank and the International Monetary Fund?

(a) The New Development Bank

(b) The Asian Development Bank

(c) The Bank for Emerging Nations

(d) The Economic Cooperation Bank

112. Given below are some popular stock indices of the world. Match the stock index with the country and stock market it represents

Stock Index	Stock Market
I. DAX	a. Japan
II. Nikkei	b. Brazil
III. KOSPI	c. Germany
IV. Bovespa	d. South Korea

(a) I-d; II-b; III-a; IV-c   (b) I-b; II-d; III-c; IV-a

(c) I-a; II-c; III-b; IV-d   (d) I-c; II-a; III-d; IV-b

113. Who launched a 'crowd funding' campaign to raise funds for bailing out Greece?

(a) Thomas Feeney   (b) Thomas Friedman

(c) Thomson Reuters   (d) Thomas Edison

114. As per the monetary policy agreement between RBI and the Finance Ministry, the RBI is required to maintain inflation in the range of:

(a) 2% to 6%   (b) 4% to 10%

(c) 3% to 9%   (d) 5% to 8%

115. According to the World Investment Report 2015 published by UNCTAD, which of the following countries was the largest recipient of FDI inflows in 2014?

(a) China   (b) India

(c) USA   (d) Singapore

116. Euro dollars are

(a) A currency issued by European Union

(b) Special currency issued by the Federal Government of USA for Europe

(c) US dollars held in Europe

(d) European currencies exchanged for the US dollar in US

2017-19

117. The Trans Pacific Partnership (TPP)or Trans Pacific Partnership Agreement (TPPA)is a trade agreement among twelve Pacific Rim countries, signed on 4 February 2016 in Auckland, New Zealand. Which of the following countries is not a member of TPP?

(a) Mexico

(b) United States

(c) Vietnam

(d) Indonesia

118. Sustainable Development Goals have replaced

(a) Millennium Environment Goals

(b) Sustainable Environment Goals

(c) Millennium Development Goals

(d) Sustainable Triple Bottom Line Goals

119. Match the Organisation with the location of its Headquarter

Organisations	Headquarters
(a) World Bank	(i) Brussels
(b) North Atlantic Treaty Organisation	(ii) Washington
(c) Anmesty International	(iii) Frankfurt
(d) Food and Agricultural Organisation	(iv) London
(e) European Central Bank	(v) Rome
(f) Organization for Economic Cooperation and Development	(vi) Paris

(a) (a)-(ii), (b)-(i), (c)-(v), (d)-(iv), (e)^(iii), (f)-(vi)

(b) (a)-(vi), (b)-(iii), (c)-(iv), (d)-(v), (e)-(i), (f)-(ii)

(c) (a)-(i), (b)-(iii), (c)-(v), (d)-(iv), (e)-(vi), (f)-(ii)

(d) (a)-(ii), (b)-(i), (c)-(iv), (d)-(v), (e)-(iii), (f)-(vi)

120. Which global credit information company is associated with Credit Information Bureau (India) Limited (CIBIL)?

(a) Moody

(b) Standard and Poor

(c) American Express

(d) TransUnion

121. Bitcoin is

(a) A type of new coin introduced by the USA

(b) A type of digital currency that uses cryptography

(c) A type of currency used by Paytm

(d) A type of commemorative coin issued by Mints

2018-20

122. Method to safeguard against losses due to currency fluctuations is popularly known as:

(*a*) Risk Premium

(*b*) Hedging

(*c*) Round Tripping

(*d*) Bond Indexation

123. Which of the following is not correct about Regional Comprehensive Economic Partnership (RCEP)?

(a) It is a Free Trade Agreement of 16 countries of Asia Pacific Region including India.

(b) Member states account for a population of 3.4 billion people with a total Gross Domestic Product (GDP)of $49.5 trillion (at PPP).

(c) RCEP potentially includes more than 3 billion people or 45% of the world's population.

(d) Combined GDP of negotiating member states is about $21.3 trillion, accounting for about 40 percent of world trade.

124. The 'Ease of Doing Business Index' is an index created by the World Bank Group. Which of the following is not correct about 'Ease of Doing Business Index'?

(a) Economies are ranked on their ease of doing business, from 1-190.

(b) A high Ease of Doing Business ranking means the regulatory environment is more conducive to the starting and operation of a local firm.

(c) Regulations covering financial markets, levels of employment and intellectual property are an important parameter in determining the country rankings.

(d) The rankings are determined by sorting the aggregate distance to frontier scores on 10 topics, each consisting of several indicators, giving equal weight to each topic.

125. Which of the following stock market index is not correctly matched with the country?

(a) Japan-Nikkei

(b) South Korea- KOSPI

(c) France-CAC

(d) United Kingdom-MTSE

2019-21

126. Which of the following is **NOT** an activity generally carried out by using a shell company?

(a) Production and Manufacturing

(b) Transfer Pricing

(c) Tax Evasion

(d) Raising funds for starting business

127. Which of the following agreement is NOT related to the World Trade Organization (WTO)?

(a) Agreement on Trade Related Intellectual Property Rights

(b) General Agreement on Trade in Services

(c) Multilateral Agreement on Transport and Logistics

(d) Agreement on Agriculture

128. Why are the Indirect Taxes termed as "Regressive Taxing Mechanisms"?

(a) Indirect taxes are charged uniformly to all income groups.

(b) Indirect tax with different tax rates are charged differentially to different people.

(c) Indirect taxes have progressive tax schedule, meaning high income group may pay more taxes.

(d) None of the above

129. Which of the following industry is the not covered in the 'Index of Eight Core Industries' in India?

(a) Electricity

(b) Crude Oil

(c) Natural Gas

(d) Pharmaceutical

Current Affairs

2007-09

Directions for Questions 130 to 138: Mark all the options (a)..d of List 1 that have corresponding matches <u>anywhere</u> (not necessarily in the same row) in <u>each</u> of the other lists (List II, List III and List IV)

130.

List I	List II	List III	List IV
A. Kumar Mamglam Birla	Steel	Sahitya Parishad Award	SUN TV
B. I. G Patel	Voice and radio products	Ernst & Young Enterpreneur Award 2005	Bajaj Auto
C. Pawan Munjal	Aluminium & Copper	NDTV Automobiles Man of theYear 2005	RBI
D. Kalanithi Maran	Policy Formulation	CNBC Business Excellence Award 2005	Grasim

131.

List I	List II	List III	List IV
A. Padmasree Warrior	Integrated Communications Solutions	Sahitya Parishad Award	Maruti
B. Rana Kapoor	IGNIS	Chennai	Motoraola
C. Jagdish Khattar	Integrated Business Solutions	Farady Medal	Wipro
D. Azim Premji	Rabobank	Start – Up Enterpreneur Award 2005	YES Bank

132.

List I	List II	List III	List IV
A. Namibia	Textiles	Copenhagen	Dollar
B. Norway	Diamonds	Abuja	Dinar
C. New Zeland	Oil	Windhoek	Naira
D. Nigeria	Dairy Products	Melbourne	Kroner

133.

List I	List II	List III	List IV
A. Sir Walter Scott	Rip Wan Winkle	The life of Napolean Bonaparte	Russia
B. Cervantes	Ivanhoe	Noveleas Ejmplares	Scotland
C. Washington Irving	Dr Zhivago	My sister – life	New York
D. Boris Pasternak	Don Quixote	Stratford – on – Avon	Spain

134.

List I	List II	List III	List IV
A. L. N. Mittal	Berkshire Hathway Inc	Slovakia	Steel – Industry
B. Warren Buffet	Microsoft	Paris	Bill & Melindia Gates Foundation
C. Bill Gates	ISPAT International	Omaha	Har var d University
D. JRD Tata	Air India	Gopalur SEZ	Severstal

135.

List I	List II	List III	List IV
A. Infosys	Hyderabad	Computer software	Nandan Nilekani
B. Tata Steel	Kolkata	Finished Steel	Sanjay. S. Lalbhai
C. Escorts Steel	Faridabad	Tractors	Rajan Nanda
D. Arvind Mills	Pune	Textiles	B. Muthuraman

136.

List I	List II	List III	List IV
A. Dr. Reddy's	Pfizer	Generic drugs	Italy
B. Tata	Eight O'Clock	Razor	Germany
C. Holcim	L & T	Textiles	US
D. Johnson & Johnson	Betapharm	Cement	Indian

137.

List I	List II
a. B. V. Rao	i. Automobiles Manufacture
b. C. K. Prahalad	ii. Fisheries Economy
c. John Kurien	iii. Information Technology and Software
d. Kiran Karnik	iv. Poultry Farming
	v. Managment Science

(a) a i, b v, c ii   (b) b v, c ii, d iii   (c) a iv, c ii, d iii   (d) a i, c iv, d ii

138.

List I	List II
a. My Presidential Years	i. S. Radhakrishnan
b. The Hindu Way of Life	ii. V. V. Giri
c. Voice of Conscience	iii. N. Sanjiva Reddy
d. Without Fear or Favour	iv. R. Venkatraman
	v. K. R. Narayanan

(a) a iv, c ii, d iii   (b) b v, c iv, d ii   (c) b i, c ii, d iv   (d) b i, c ii, d iii

Directions for Questions 139 to 142 : Mark <u>all</u> the correct statements

139. (a) Hanumantha Rao replaced Verghese J. Kurien as the chairman of the National Dairy Development Board.

(b) Dabur is the best known institution of Unani medicine worldwide which ploughs back nearly 90% of its 1200 odd unani products into social welfare.

(c) Pascal Lamy is current the Director General of the World Trade Organization.

(d) Jawahar Lal Nehru had said that it was his ultimate aim to wipe every tear from every eye.

140. (a) 198 nations attempted to qualify for the 2006 FIFA World Cup.

(b) South Africa will host the FIFA World Cup 2010.

(c) Special Olympics 2005 took place during 2-9 August 2005 at Glasgow.

(d) New Zealand was the Champion in Sultan Azlan Shah Hockey tournament in 2005.

141. (a) Mukhya Mantri Gram Sadak Yojana is one of the major rural development initiatives in India.

(b) Dogri and Gojri are two festivals celebrated in Jammu & Kashmir.

(c) The Surajkund Craft Mela of international fame is held every year in the month of December.

(d) Prasar Bharati is the public service broadcaster in India with All India Radio and Doordarshan as its two constituents.

142. (a) Six Indians have been awarded Nobel Prize till date.

(b) No Indian has ever received Nobel Prize for Medicine.

(c) Two Indians have received Nobel Prize for Literature.

(d) S. Chandrashekar was awarded the Nobel Prize for physics.

2008-10

143. Which of the following teams secured the runner-up position in India's National Football League 2006-2007?

(a) East Bengal Club   (b) Mahindra United

(c) JCT, Phagwara   (d) Dempo SC

144. Which one of the following is the correct combination?

	i	ii	iii	iv
	Year	Author	Creation	Award
1	1997	Arundhati Roy	The Inheritance of Loss	Booker
2	2006	Salman Rushdie	Interpreter of Maladies	Booker
3	2000	V.S. Naipaul	The God of Small Things	Pulitzer
4	1981	Kiran Desai	Midnight's Children	Booker
5	1971	Jhumpa Lahiri	In a Free State	Booker

(a) 1-ii, 3-i, 3-iii, 5-iv   (b) 5-i, 2-iv, 3-ii, 5-iii   (c) 3-i, 5-ii, 2-iii, 4-iv   (d) 2-i, 4-ii, 5-iii, 1-iv

145. Which of the following combination for Sahitya Academy Awards given in English literature and the Awardees is correct?

	i	ii	iii	iv
	Year	Author	Creation	Type
1	1978	Ruskin Bond	The Sahdow Lines	Noval
2	1989	Anita Desai	Rajaji: A Life	Short Stories
3	1992	Upamanyu Chatterjee	Our Trees Still Grow in Dehra	Noval
4	2001	Amitav Ghosh	Fire On the Mountain	Biography
5	2004	Rajmohan Gandhi	Mammaries fo the Welfare State	Noval

(a) 1-i, 2-ii, 1-iii, 5-iv   (b) 2-i, 1-ii, 3-iii, 2-iv   (c) 4-i, 5-ii, 2-iii, 4-iv   (d) 5-i, 3-ii, 4-iii, 1-iv

146. Which of the following film personality had received the Dadasaheb Phalke Award for lifetime contribution to Indian Cinema in the year 2005?

(a) Shyam Benegal   (b) Mrinal Sen   (c) Yash Chopra   (d) Adoor Gopalakrishan

147. which of the combination of the Arjuna award winners are correct?

	i	ii	iii
	Year	Name	Field
1	2002	Deepak Thakur	Badminton
2	2004	Anju Bobby George	Hockey
3	2003	Pullela Gopichand	Shooting
4	1999	I. M. Vijayan	Athletics
5	2002	Mahesh Bhpati	Football
6	1995	Rajyavardhan Singh Rathore	Lawn Tennis

(a) 5-i, 1-ii, 2-iii   (b) 4-i, 3-ii, 1-iii   (c) 2-i, 6-ii, 3-iii   (d) 3-i, 4-ii, 5-iii

148. Which of the following chess player became India's second Grandmaster in world chess after Viswanathan Anand?

(a) Krishan Sasikiran

(b) Pravin Thipsay

(c) Dibyendu Barua

(d) Abhijit Kunte

149. In the recent WTA Bank of the West Classic tennis tournament in Stanford, USA Sania Mirza won the Women's Doubles Title pairing up with __________.

(a) Vania King

(b) Shahar Peer

(c) Lezel Huber

(d) Bethanie Mattek

150. Match the following:

Name	Hobby/Profession
(i) Numismatists	(a) Linguist who focuses on the origin of words
(ii) Epigraphist	(b) Person expert in the art of the fine handwritting
(iii) Calligraphist	(c) Scientist who study insects
(iv) Etymologist	(d) Collectors of Coin
(v) Entomologists	(e) Study fo inscriptions engraved into stone or other durable material Scientists who styudy insects

(a) i-a, ii-b, iii-d, iv-e, v-c   (b) i-d, ii-e, iii-b, iv-a, v-c

(c) i-d, ii-a, iii-c, iv-b, v-e   (d) i-b, ii-c, iii-e, iv-d, v-a

151. Which of following combination is correct?

(a) Andaman Express: Chennai to Jammu Tawi

(b) Gitanjali Express: Mumbai to Jammu Tawi

(c) Hirakud Express: Puri to Amritsar

(d) Navyug Express: Mangalore to Howrah

152. Which of the fallowing is not correct about Palagummi Sainath?

(a) Development journalist

(b) Expert on famine and hunger

(c) Was a student of Delhi University

(d) Grand son of former president V. V. Giri

153. Which of the following countries with their capital and currency is not correct?

	Country	Capital	Currency
A.	Botswana	Gaborone	Peso
B.	Bulgaria	Sofia	Lev
C.	Combodia	Phnom Penh	Riel
D.	Macedonia	Skopje	Denar

154. What is common to Steve Martin and Peter Sellers?

(a) Both of them have feature in the title role of Inspector Blake

(b) Both of them have featured in the title role of Inspector Lynley

(c) Both of them have featured in the title role of Inspector Jacques Clouseau

(d) Both of them have Featured in the title role of Inspector Migraet

155. The CEO of Arcelor at the time of its acquisition by the Ispat group was ___________.

(a) John M. Cassaday   (b) David Lev

(c) Guy Dolle   (d) Antonio Murta

156. Match the following:

Name of the Retailer	Country of origin
Wal-Mart (a)	France (i)
Carrefour (b)	USA (ii)
TESCO (c)	Australia (iii)
Woolworth (d)	UK (iv)

(a) a-iii, b-i, c-iv, d-ii   (b) a-ii, -iv, c-iii, d-i

(c) a-ii, b-i, c-iv, d-iii   (d) a-iv, b-ii, c-iii, d-i

157. Match the following:

Country	President
(i) Ghana	(a) Umaru yar' Adua
(ii) Tanzania	(b) Yoweri Museveni
(iii) Nigeria	(c) John Agekum Kufuor
(iv) Uganda	(d) Jkaya Mrisho Kikwete

(a) i-a, ii-b, iii-c, iv-b   (b) i-c, ii-d, iii-a, iv-b

(c) i-b, ii-a, iii-c, iv-d   (d) i-a, ii-b, iii-d, iv-c

158. Match the correct combination in the following:

Cartoon Characters	Creators
(i) Asterix	(a) Bill Watterson
(ii) Dilbert	(b) Jim Davis
(iii) Calvin and Hobbes	(c) Charles Shulz
(iv) Peanuts	(d) Albert Uderzo& Rane Coscinny
(v) Garfield	(e) Scott Adams

(a) i-a, ii-c, iii-b, iv-e, v-d   (b) i-d, ii-e, iii-a, iv-c, v-b   (c) i-d, ii-d, iii-a, iv-e, v-c   (d) i-c, ii-a, iii-b, iv-d, v-e

159. Match the correct combination in the following:

Actresses	Featured in a James Bond Movie
(i) Izabella Scorupco	(a) The world is not enough
(ii) Teri Hatcher	(b) Die Anotehr Day
(iii) Sophie Merceau	(c) Golden Eye
(iv) Roasmund Pike	(d) Tommorrow Never Dies

(a) i-c, ii-d, iii-a, iv-b   (b) i-a, ii-c, iii-d, iv-b   (c) i-c, ii-d, iii-b, iv-a   (d) i-a, ii-b, iii-c, iv-b

160. Match the following:

Painter	Title of Creation
(i) Leonardo Da Vinci	(a) The Last Supper
(ii) Jonannes Vermeer	(b) The descent from the cross
(iii) Vincent Van Gogh	(c) Starry Night
(iv) Rembrandt Harmensz Van Rijn	(d) Christ in the house of Martha and Mary
(v) Salvador Dali	(e) the distintegration of the persistence of memory

(a) i-a, ii-d, iii-c, iv-b, v-e   (b) i-a, ii-b, iii-c, iv-d, v-e   (c) i-c, ii-d, iii-e, iv-b, v-a   (d) i-e, ii-b, iii-d, iv-c, v-a

161. Who were the founders of the company Hewlett Packard (HP)?

(a) Dave Hewlett and Bill Packard

(b) Bill Hewlett and Dave Packard

(c) Jack Hewlett and Edwards Packard

(d) Edwards Hewlett and Jack Packard

162. Who won the 'Asia Business Leader of the Year' award at the CNBC Asia Business Leaders Awards in 2006?

(a) ahul Bajaj

(b) Ratan Tata

(c) Anand Mahindra

(d) Vijay Mallya

163. Which of the following Indian ports is a private port?

(a) Bedi Bunder

(b) Navlakhi

(c) Ratnagiri

(d) Pipavav

2009-11

164. Which of the following country is not a member of Nuclear Suppliers Group?

(a) Belarus

(b) Malta

(c) Turkey

(d) Albania

165. Select the correct Bharat Ratna recipient – Year match:

	Bharat Ratna recipients		Year
1	Pandit Ravi Shankar	I	1992
2	Ustad Bismillah Khan	Ii	1999
3	M S Subbulakshmi	Iii	2001
4	Satyajit Ray	Iv	1998

(a) 1 - ii, 2 – iii, 3 – iv, 4 - i

(b) 1 – iii, 2 – i, 3 – iv, 4 – ii

(c) 1 – iv, 2 – ii, 3 – i, 4 – iii

(d) 1 – iii, 2 – iv, 3 – ii, 4 – I

166. Select the WRONG Country-River-Currency match:

	Country	River	Currency
A.	Nigeria	Benue	Naira
B.	South Korea	Nakdong	Won
C.	Colombia	Magdalena	Peso
D.	Malaysia	Siouguluan	Ringgit

167. Select the WRONG International Organization – Location of Headquarter – Country match:

	International Organization	Location of Headquarter	Country
A.	International Atomic Energy Agency	Vienna	Austria
B.	World Health Organization	Geneva	Switzerland
C.	International Monetary Fund	New York	USA
D.	International Court of Justice	The Hague	Netherlands

168. Select the WRONG Venue of Hockey World Cup – Year – Winner match:

	Venue of Hockey World Cup	Year	Winner
A.	Kuala Lumpur	1975	India
B.	London	1986	Australia
C.	Sydney	1994	Netherlands
D.	Monchengladbach	2006	Germany

169. Which of the following country is not a member of G8 group of countries?

(a) United Kingdom

(b) China

(c) Germany

(d) Canada

170. Which prominent intergovernmental organization launched the movement, 'Education For All' (EFA):

(a) UNCTAD

(b) UNIDO

(c) UNDP

(d) UNESCO

171. Which of the following country is a member of OECD group?

(a) Venezuela

(b) Brazil

(c) Mexico

(d) South Africa

172. Select the correct Year – Olympic host cities match:

	Year		Olympic host cities
1	1976	i	London
2	1992	ii	Tokyo
3	1964	iii	Montreal
4	2012	iv	Barcelona

(a) 1 – ii, 2 – iii, 3 – iv, 4 - i

(b) 1 – iii, 2 – I, 3 – iv, 4 – ii

(c) 1 – iv, 2 – ii, 3 – i, 4 – iii

(d) 1 – iii, 2 – iv, 3 – ii, 4 – i

173. Select the correct IPL Franchise – Owner match:

	IPL Franchise		Owner
1	Mumbai Indians	i	UB Group
2	Royal Challengers	ii	GMR Holdings
3	Chennai Super Kings	iii	Reliance Industries
4	Delhi Daredevils	iv	India Cements

(a) 1- ii, 2 – iii, 3 – iv, 4 - i

(b) 1 – iii, 2 – i, 3 – iv, 4 - ii

(c) 1 – iv, 2 – ii, 3 – i, 4 – iii

(d) 1 – iii, 2 – iv, 3 – ii, 4 – I

174. Select the WRONG Book – Author match:

	Book	Author (s)
A.	The Google Story	David A. Vise and Mark Malseed
B.	Accidental Empires: How the Boys of Silicon Valley Make Their Millions, "Battle Foreign Competition, and Still Can't Get a Date	Robert X. Kennedy
C.	The Monk Who Sold His Ferrari	Robin S Sharma

	Book	Author (s)
D.	Freakonomics: A Rogue Economist Explores the Hidden Side of Everything	1998

175. Which one of the following books has been authored by P. Chidambaram?

(a) View from the outside: Why good economics works for everyone

(b) Propelling India from Socialist Stagnation to Global Power

(c) Interpreting the Indian Economy

(d) Strategic consequences of India's economic performance

176. Which of the following Indian automobile major has a tie – up with a German insurer?

(a) Hindustan Motors   (b) Maruti

(c) Bajaj   (d) Ashok Leyland

177. Which Indian company has acquired General Chemical Industrial Products Inc. of USA in 2008?

(a) Tata Chemicals

(b) Mody Chemical Industries

(c) Gujarat Heavy Chemicals Ltd

(d) Hindustan Chemicals.

178. Chronologically which one of the following is correct?

(a) (1) India's first nuclear test,

    (2) Comprehensive Test Ban Treaty comes to force,

    (3) "France and China sign Non Proliferation Treaty

(b) (1) India conducts its second nuclear test – 1998,

    (2) N. Korea conducts test of nuclear weapon,

    (3) Chernobyl nuclear power station accident in Ukraine

(c) (1) International Atomic Energy Agency set up,

    (2) France conducts first nuclear test,

    (3) China conducts its first nuclear test

(d) (1) France and China sign Non Proliferation Treaty,

    (2) India conducts its second nuclear test,

    (3) France conducts first nuclear test

179. Which of the following is an incorrect Award – Person match?

(a) Indra Nooyi – Padma Shri

(b) M Sukumaran – Sahitya Academy Award

(c) Dr. Jagannath Prasad Das – Saraswati Samman

(d) Rahman Rahi – Jnanpith Award

2010-12

180. Arcelor, acquired by Mittal steel, was formed by merger of which of the following three steel companies?

(a) Arcel, Arecalia and Usinor

(b) Arcel, Acer and Lucinor

(c) Arbed, Aceralia and Usinor

(d) None of the above

181. Select the correct author – book match.

Author	Book
a. Narayan Murthy	i. Imagining India
b. Nandan Nilekani	ii. Remaking India
c. Ratan Tata	iii. A Better India A Better World
d. APJ Abdul Kalam	iv. A Vision For The New Millennium

(a) a-iii, b-i, c-ii, d-iv   (b) a-i, b-iii, c-iv, d-ii

(c) a-I, b-ii, c-iii, d-iv   (d) a-ii, b-i, c-iii, d-iv

182. The company Fem Care Pharma Limited, the manufacturer of Feb Bleach, was acquired by?

(a) Hindustan Unilever Limited

(b) Godrej Industries Limited.

(c) Dr. Reddy's Laboratories

(d) Dabur India Limited

183. Which is the correct Stock Index- Country Match?

STOCK INDEX	COUNTRY
a. HANG SENG	i. United States
b. NASDAQ	ii. South Korea
c. FTSE	iii. Hong Kong
d. KOSPI	iv. United Kingdom

(a) a-i, b-ii, c-iii, d-iv   (b) a-iii, b-i, c-iv, d-ii

(c) a-iv, b-i, c-iii, d-iii   (d) a-iv, b-ii, c-i, d-iii

184. Match the President, Country and Currency.

President	Country	Currency
a. Nicolas Sarkozy	i. Russia	1. Rouble
b. Dmitry Medvedev	ii. Uganda	2. Euro
c. Yoweri Museveni	iii. Germany	3. Shilling
d. Horst Kohler	iv. France	4. Dollar

(a) a-i-1, b-ii-2, c-iii-3, d-iv-4

(b) a-iii-2, b-i-1, c-ii-3, d-iv-4

(c) a-iv-2, b-i -1, c-ii-3, d-iii-2

(d) a-ii-2, b-i-1, c-iii-4, d-iv-4

185. Who amongst the following was not nominated by the Government of India on the board of Satyam Computer Services?

(a) T.N. Manoharan

(b) Ketan Parekh

(c) Suryakant Balakrishnan Mainak

(d) Kiran Karnik

186. The table given below matches the company with its auto brand. Choose the correct match.

Company	Brand
a. Mahindra	i. Land Rover
b. Tata	ii. Jetta
c. Toyota	iii. Lexus
d. Volkswagen	iv. Xylo

(a) a-i, b-ii, c-iii, d-iv

(b) a-iv, b-i, c-ii, d-iii

(c) a-iv, b-i, c-iii, d-ii

(d) a-iv, b-ii, c-iii, d-iv

187. The slogans in the table given below have been matched with the company they relate to. Choose the correct match.

Slogan	Company
a. Let's make things better	i. HP
b. Technology you can trust	ii. Phillips
c. Sponsors of tomorrow	iii. Microsoft
d. Your potential our passion	iv. Intel

(a) a-ii, b-i, c-iii, d-iv

(b) a-iii, b-ii, c-I, d-iv

(c) a-ii, b-i, c-iv, d-iii

(d) a-ii, b-iv, c-I, d-iii

188. The co-founders of Google are:

(a) Sergey Brin & Eric Schmidt

(b) Larry Page & Eric Schmidt

(c) Sergey Brin & Larry Page

(d) Shirley M tilghman & Ric Schmidt

189. Which of the following Public Sector Units does not fall in the category of 'Navratna' PSUs:

(a) Steel authority of India (SAIL)

(b) Indian oil corporation (IOC)

(c) National Thermal Power corporation (NTPC)

(d) National Hydroelectric Power Corporation limited(NHPC)

190. India signed the Kyoto Protocol in the year

(a) 2000   (b) 1998

(c) 2002   (d) 1995

191. Match column A with Column (b)

Column A	Column B
a. C K Prahlad	i. Capability & Equality
b. Paul Krugman	ii. Climate Change & Global Warming
c. Al Gore	iii. International Trade and Geography
d. Amartya Sen	iv. Core Competence Of the Corporation

(a) a-i, b-ii, c-iii, d-iv

(b) a-iv, b-iii, c-ii, d-i

(c) a-ii, b-iii, c-I, d-iv

(d) a-iii, b-ii, c-I, d-iv

192. Match the women CEOs with the company

Column A	Column B
a. Ms Shikha Sharma	i. HSBC
b. Ms Naina Lal Kidwai	ii. Axis Bank
c. Ms Indira Nooyi	iii. Biocon India
d. Ms Kiran Mjaumdar Shaw	iv. Pepsico

(a) a-iii, b-I, c-ii, d-iv

(b) a-I, b-ii, c-iv, d-iii

(c) a-ii, b-I, c-iv, d-iii

(d) a-I, b-iii, c-iv, d-ii

193. Match the company and the place where it originates from

Column A	Column B
a. Toyota	i. Finland
b. Nokia	ii. Japan
c. Volvo	iii. South Korea
d. LG Electronics	iv. Sweden

(a) a-ii, b-i, c-iv, d-iii

(b) a-ii, b-I, c-iii, d-iv

(c) a-iii, b-ii, c-I, d-iv

(d) a-iii, b-iv, c-I, d-ii

2011-13

194. Name the South Korean President who attended the Indian Republic Day Parade in 2010 as a chief guest.

(a) Kim Yoon - Ok   (b) Ban Ki - Moon

(c) Lee Myung - Bak   (d) Chung Mong Koo

195. The Indian government auctioned the 3G spectrum in 22 telecom circles in 2010. Which three companies won the maximum number of circles in the auction?

a. R - Com   b. Airtel

c. Vodafone   d. Aircel

(a) a, b & c   (b) b, c & d

(c) a, c & d   (d) a, b & d

196. Which one of the following group of banks formed a joint venture in Life Insurance Sector?

(a) Canara Bank, HSBC, Oriental Bank of Commerce Limited

(b) Canara Bank, HDFC, Syndicate Bank

(c) HDFC, HSBC, Oriental Bank of Commerce Limited

(d) Canara Bank, Axis Bank, HDFC

197. Match the International Organization - Location - Country

International Organization	Location	Country
a. North Atlantic Treaty Organization (NATO)	i. Lyons	1. Austria
b. World Wild Life fund (WWF)	ii. Vienna	2. Switzerland
c. Organization of Petroleum Exporting Countries (OPEC)	iii. Gland	3. France
d. International Police (INTERPOLE)	iv. Brussels	4. Belgium

(a) a-iii-2, b-iv-4, c-i-3, d-ii-1   (b) a-iv-4, b-iii-2, c-ii-1, d-i-3

(c) a-ii-4, b-iv-3, c-iii-1, d-i-2   (d) a-i-4, b-iii-1, c-iii-3, d-iv-2

198. Match the Women CEOs in 2010 and their respective Company and its Location.

Name of CEOs	Name of the Company	Location
a. Carol A Bartz	i. Dupont	1. Colorado
b. Ellen J Kullman	ii. Western Union	2. California
c. Ursula Burns	iii. Yahoo Inc	3. Connecticut
d. Christina A Gold	iv. Xerox Corporation	4. Deleware

(a) a-ii-4, b-iii-3, c-iv-1, d-i-2   (b) a-iii-3, b-iv-4, c-i-1, d-ii-2

(c) a-iii-2, b-i-4, c-iv-3, d-ii-1   (d) a-ii-1, b-iii-2, c-i-4, d-iv-3

199. Match the Acquiring Company with its Target Company.

Acquiring Company	Target Company
a. United Breweries Group	1. Schoneweiss
b. Mahindra & Mahindra	2. RSM Ambit
c. Price Water Cooper	3. Ambuja Cement
d. Holcim	4. Shaw Wallace

(a) a-4, b-3, c-1, d-2

(b) a-1, b-4, c-2, d-3

(c) a-2, b-1, c-3, d-4

(d) a-4, b-1, c-2, d-3

200. Match the Company and its Tagline

Company	Tagline
a. Toyota	1. Express Yourself
b. BSNL	2. The easy way to stay in touch
c. Airtel	3. Connecting India
d. Trump (MTNL)	4. Touch the perfection

(a) a-2, b-4, c-1, d-3

(b) a-4, b-1, c-3, d-2

(c) a-4, b-3, c-1, d-2

(d) a-2, b-4, c-3, d-1

201. Match the name of the Indian Banks with their Brand Ambassadors for the year 2010.

Name of the Banks	Name of the Brand Ambassador
a. Canara Bank	1. Rahul Dravid
b. Dena Bank	2. Hema Malini
c. Bank of Rajasthan	3. Venkatesh Prasad
d. Bank of Baroda	4. Juhi Chawala

(a) a-4, b-3, c-1, d-2

(b) a-3, b-1, c-4, d-2

(c) a-2, b-3, c-1, d-4

(d) a-3, b-4, c-2, d-1

202. Who among the following is a recipient of the prestigious Dara Shikoh award by Indo-Iran Society for contributing towards nurturing the value of peace, harmony and brotherhood in 2010.

(a) Sheikh Hasina

(b) Sonia Gandhi

(c) Shiela Dixit

(d) Fatima Bhutto

203. Match the Lt Governors - India Union Territories - and the Capital.

Lt. Governors	Union Territories	Capital
a. J.K. Dadoo	i. Dadra and Nagar Haveli	1. Kavaratti
b. Satya Gopal	ii. Puducherry	2. Port Blair
c. Iqbal Singh	iii. Andaman and Nicobar Island	3. Silvassa
d. Lt. Gen. (Retd). Bhopinder Singh	iv. Lakshadweep	4. Puducherry

(a) a-iii-2, b-i-3, c-iv-1, d-ii-4
(b) a-ii-4, b-iii-2, c-iv-3, d-i-1
(c) a-i-3, b-iv-1, c-ii-4, d-iii-2
(d) a-iv-1, b-i-3, c-ii-4, d-iii-2

204. Which one of the following structure has been included in UNESCO in 2010 as world cultural heritage list?

(a) Chhatrapati Shivaji Terminus
(b) Jantar Mantar
(c) Mahabodhi Temple Complex at Bodh Gaya
(d) Red Fort Complex

205. Match the following Head of the Staff to the Concerned Defense forces.

Head of the Staff	Defense Force
a. Pradeep Vasant Naik	1. Chief of Integrated Defense Staff
b. Vijay Kumar Singh	2. Chief of Naval Staff
c. Nirmal Verma	3. Chief of Army Staff
d. Suresh Chand Mukul	4. Chief of Air Staff

(a) a-3, b-4, c-1, d-2   (b) a-4, b-3, c-2, d-1   (c) a-3, b-2, c-1, d-4   (d) a-1, b-2, c-4, d-3

206. Match the following Brand to the Company.

Brand	Company
a. Santoor	1. Hindustan Unilever Limited
b. Margo	2. Wipro
c. Camay	3. Henkel
d. Hamam	4. Proctor and Gamble

(a) a-4, b-1, c-2, d-3   (b) a-2, b-3, c-4, d-1   (c) a-3, b-1, c-4, d-2   (d) a-2, b-4, c-1, d-3

207. Match the Countries- Name of the parliament - Currency

Country	Name of the Parliament	Currency
a. Sweden	i. Diet	1. Yen
b. Japan	ii. Riksdag	2. Zloty
c. Poland	iii. Knessat	3. Krona
d. Israel	iv. Sejm	4. New Shekkel

(a) a-iii-2, b-iv-1, c-i-4, d-ii-3
(b) a-ii-3, b-i-1, c-iv-2, d-iii-4
(c) a-iv-2, b-iii-1, c-ii-4, d-i-3
(d) a-ii-3, b-i-1, c-iii-4, d-iv-2

208. Name the sports personality who is not an ambassador for the Common Wealth Games 2010?

(a) Samaranth Jung   (b) Sushil Kumar   (c) MC Mary Kom   (d) Tejeswini Sawant

209. Match the Central Public Sector Enterprises in India and their Position.

CPSE	Position
a. Steel Authority of India Limited	1. Mini Ratna Category – I
b. Gas Authority of India Limited	2. Maharatna
c. Bharat Sanchar Nigam Limited	3. Mini Ratna Category – II
d. Hindustan Machines and Tools.	4. Navratna

(a) a-3, b-2, c-4, d-1   (b) a-2, b-4, c-1, d-3   (c) a-2, b-4, c-3, d-1   (d) a-4, b-2, c-1, d-3

210. Match the Indian TV Channel to its Owners/ Parent Company

TV Channel	Owner/ Parent Company
a. CNBC	1. Bennett, Coleman and Co Ltd
b. Times Now	2. Raghav Bahal
c. Star News	3. India Today Group
d. Aaj Tak	4. Anand Bazar Publication

(a) a-2, b-4, c-3, d-1   (b) a-2, b-1, c-4, d-3

(c) a-2, b-3, c-4, d-1   (d) a-3, b-1, c-4, d-2

2012-14

211. Who won the 2011 FIFA Women's World Cup Final?

(a) Sweden   (b) Japan

(c) USA   (d) France

212. Match the correct Celebrity Endorser with the Brand of Vests:

	Celebrity Endorser		Brand of Vests
a.	Hrithik Roshan	i.	Amul Macho
b.	Saif Ali Khan	ii.	Dollar Club
c.	Neil Nitin Mukesh	iii.	MacroMan
d.	Akshay Kumar	iv.	GenX

(a) a-ii; b-i; c-iii; d-iv   (b) a-iii: b-i; c-iv; d-ii

(c) a-iv; b-iii; c-ii; d-i   (d) a-iii; b-iv; c-i; d-ii

213. Elzie Crisler Segar is best known as the creator of the cartoon character of ___________.

(a) Garfield   (b) Popeye

(c) Scooby Doo   (d) Blondie

214. Identify the *correct* match for the Personality with what he/she is known for:

	Personality		Known for
a.	Bhagwan Dass	i.	Bharat Ratna
b.	Annie Besant	ii.	Theosophical Society
c.	Bharat Muni	iii.	Natya Shastra
d.	Bhavabhuti	iv.	Malatimadhava

(a) a-i; b-ii; c-iii; d-iv

(b) a-ii; b-i; c-iv; d-iii

(c) a-ii; b-i; c-iii; d-iv

(d) a-i; b-ii; c-iv; d-iii

215. Which book among the following is not written by Dr. A.P. J. Abdul Kalam?

(a) Wings of Fire

(b) India in the New Millennium

(c) India My Dream

(d) Envisioning an Empowered Nation

216. In the table below, match the *correct* Trade Name of medicine with its Generic Name and the name of the pharmaceutical company that manufactures it:

	Trade Name		Generic Name		Manu-facturer
a.	Viagra	i.	Acetaminophen	1	Roche
b.	Tylenol	ii.	Ibuprofen	2	Pfizer
c.	Tamiflu	iii.	Sildenafil Citrate	3	Johnson & Johnson
d.	Brufen	iv.	Oseltamivir	4	Abbott Laboratorie

(a) a-i-4; b-ii-3; c-iii-2; d-iv-1

(b) a-iii-2; b-i-3; c-iv-1; d-ii-4

(c) a-iii-1; b-i-2; c-iv-3; d-ii-4

(d) a-i-4; b-iv-3; c-iii-2; d-ii-1

217. By what name were the Commonwealth Games known when they were first held in 1930 in Ontario, Canada?

(a) British Commonwealth Games

(b) British Empire and Commonwealth Games

(c) British Empire Games

(d) Queen's Empire games

218. Which of the following group of countries is *not* member of the United Nations?

(a) Taiwan, Yemen, Tunisia

(b) Tunisia, Vatican City, Turkish Cyprus

(c) Tunisia, Turkish Cyprus, Vatican City

(d) Vatican City, Turkish Cyprus, Taiwan

219. Given below are names of select personalities who have been recently rated among the most powerful women of the world by Forbes. Identify the option that ranks them in the right order (from 1 to 4) as they are ranked in the Forbes list of the world's 100 most powerful women in 2011:

Angela Merkel; Hillary Clinton; Michelle Obama; Oprah Winfrey; Indira Nooyi; Irene Rosenfeld; Dilma Rousseff

(a) (1) Hillary Clinton   (2) Angela Merkel   (3) Michelle Obama   (4) Oprah Winfrey

(b) (1) Michelle Obama   (2) Irene Rosenfeld   (3) Oprah Winfrey   (4) Indira Nooyi

(c) (1) Angela Merkel   (2) Michelle Obama   (3) Hillary Clinton   (4) Dilma Rousseff

(d) (1) Angela Merkel   (2) Hillary Clinton   (3) Dilma Rousseff   (4) Indira Nooyi

220. Match the *correct* name of the Regulator / Association with the name of its Chairman (as on 31st August 2011):

	Regulator / Association		Chairman's Name
a.	Securities and Exchange Board of India	i.	J. Hari Narayan
b.	Forward Markets Commission	ii.	Ramesh Abhishek
c.	Insurance and Regulatory Development Authority	iii.	Milind Barve
d.	Association of Mutual Funds of India	iv.	U.K. Sinha

(a) a-iv; b-iii; c-ii; d-i   (b) a-iii; b-i; c-iv; d-ii

(c) a-iii; b-iv; c-i; d-ii   (d) a-iv; b-ii; c-i; d-iii

221. Which of the following group of companies have agreed to merge their Liquid-Crystal-Display businesses as at August 2011?

(a) Sony Corp., Samsung Electronics, Chimei Innolux Corp.

(b) Sony Corp., Toshiba Corp., Hitachi Ltd.

(c) Samsung Electronics Co., LG Electronics Co., Hitachi Ltd.

(d) Samsung Electronics Co., Toshiba Corp., Chimei Innolux Corp.

222. Match the *correct* name of the Film with its Lead Actor and Director:

	Film		Lead Actor		Director
a.	The Aviator	i.	Russell Crowe	1	Richard Attenborough
b.	A Beautiful Mind	ii.	Colin Firth	2	Martin Scorsese
c.	Gandhi	iii.	Leonardo Di Caprio	3	Ron Howard
d.	The King's Speech	iv.	Ben Kingsley	4	Tom Hooper

(a) a-iii-2; b-i-3; c-iv-1; d-ii-4

(b) a-ii-4; b-i-3; c-iv-1; d-iii-2

(c) a-i-2; b-ii-1; c-iv-3; d-iii-4

(d) a-iii-4; b-iv-2; c-ii-1; d-i-3

2013-15

223. Which of the following venues has hosted the Summer Olympic Games the maximum number of times?

(a) Athens

(b) Paris

(c) London

(d) Los Angeles

224. Which treaty led to the creation of the single European Currency "Euro"?

(a) Maastricht Treaty

(b) Vienna Monetary Treaty

(c) Plaza Accord

(d) Bretton Woods Agreement

225. Match the Memoir/Autobiography in Column 1 with the person on whom it is based in Column 2:

Column 1	Column 2
1. Open	i. Hillary Rodham Clinton
2. Living History	ii. Lance Armstrong
3. The Elephant to Hollywood	iii. Andre Agassi
4. Every Second Counts	iv. Michael Caine

(a) 1-iv; 2-i; 3-iii; 4-ii   (b) 1-i; 2-iv; 3-ii; 4-iii

(c) 1-iii; 2-i; 3-iv; 4-ii   (d) 1-iii; 2-ii; 3-iv; 4-i

226. Which of the following is NOT TRUE about the Millennium Development Goals (MDGs) of the United Nations (UN)?

1. There are 8 MDGs that 193 UN Member states have agreed to achieve

2. The year set for achieving the MDGs is 2020

3. Ensuring environmental sustainability is not one of the MDGs

4. Eradication of extreme poverty and hunger is one of the prime MDGs

(a) 1 & 2   (b) 2 & 3

(c) Only 3   (d) Only 4

227. Match the Country in Column 1 with its Capital city in Column 2 and its Currency in Column 3:

Column 1	Column 2	Column 3
1. Hungry	a. Tehran	i. Dirham
2. Iran	b. Rabat	ii. Rial
3. Morocco	c. Bucharest	iii. Leu
4. Romania	d. Budapest	iv. Forint

(a) 1-d-iv; 2-a-i; 3-b-ii; 4-c-iii

(b) 1-d-iv; 2-a-ii; 3-b-i; 4-c-iii

(c) 1-b-i; 2-a-iv; 3-d-ii; 4-c-iii

(d) 1-b-i; 2-a-ii; 3-d-iii; 4-c-iv

228. Who is the Indian to be named as one of the six winners of the prestigious Magsaysay award for 2012?

(a) Medha Patkar

(b) Jeet Thayil

(c) Kulandei Francis

(d) Arvind Kejriwal

229. Match the name of the automobile company in Column 1 with the brand of cars owned by them in Column 2:

Column 1	Column 2
1. BMW	i. Bentley
2. Fiat	ii. Cadillac
3. General Motors	iii. Chrysler
4. Volkswagen	iv. Mini

  (a) 1-iv; 2-iii; 3-ii; 4-i   (b) 1-iii; 2-iv; 3-i; 4-ii
  (c) 1-i; 2-ii; 3-iii; 4-iv   (d) 1-ii; 2-i; 3-iv; 4-iii

230. GAAR has been in news recently. What does GAAR stand for?

  (a) Global Accounting Alliance Regime

  (b) General Anti-Avoidance Rules

  (c) Government Affairs Assessment Rules

  (d) Generally Accepted Accounting Rules

231. Match the description given Column 1 with the name of the film in Column 2 :

Column 1	Column 2
1. First Hindi Film	a. Mother India
2. First Hindi Colour Film	b. Alam Ara
3. First Hindi film nominated for Oscars	c. Kisan Kanya
4. First Hindi film with sound	d. Raja Harishchandra

  (a) 1-d; 2-c; 3-a; 4-b   (b) 1-b; 2-a; 3-d; 4-c
  (c) 1-b; 2-d; 3-a; 4-c   (d) 1-d; 2-a; 3-c; 4-b

232. Match the position in Column 1 with the person who holds it (as on 31st August 2012) in Column 2:

Column 1	Column 2
1. Chief Information Commissioner of India	i. V.S.Sampath
2. Central Vigilance Commissioner of India	ii. S.H. Kapadia
3. Chief Election Commissioner of India	iii. Satyananda Mishra
4. Chief Justice of India	iv. Pradeep Kumar

  (a) 1-ii; 2-iii; 3-i; 4-iv   (b) 1-iii; 2-i; 3-ii; 4-iv
  (c) 1-iii; 2-iv; 3-i; 4-ii   (d) 1-i; 2-iii; 3-iv; 4-ii

233. Which among the following cities hosted the 4th BRICS Summit in 2012?

  (a) Brasilina, Brazil

  (b) Sanya, China

  (c) New Delhi, India

  (d) None of the above

234. Match the celebration day in Column 1 with the date in Column 2:

Column 1	Column 2
1. World AIDS Day	i. April 22
2. UN Day	ii. October 24
3. Earth Day	iii. March 8
4. International Women's Day	iv. December 1

  (a) 1-ii; 2-iv; 3-iii; 4-i   (b) 1-iii; 2-ii; 3-iv; 4-i
  (c) 1-i; 2-iii; 3-iv; 4-ii   (d) 1-iv; 2-ii; 3-i; 4-iii

235. Which country has won the Gold Medal for Men's Football in the 2012 Olympic Games?

  (a) Brazil   (b) Spain

  (c) Germany   (d) Mexico

236. What is the name given to the civil reformist movement for eradication of ragging in India?

  (a) Aman   (b) Mitra

  (c) Sahyog   (d) Aadhar

237. Which of the following teams have been in at least one of the ten final matches of the ICC Cricket World Cup played from 1975 through 2011, but have never been a winner?

  (a) England   (b) South Africa

  (c) New Zealand   (d) Zimbabwe

238. Match the Leader's name in Column 1 to the Party headed by them in Column 2:

Column 1	Column 2
1. Hosni Mubarak	i. National League for Democracy
2. Aung San Suu Kyi	ii. Socialist Party
3. Francois Hollande	iii. National Democratic Party

  (a) 1-iii; 2-ii; 3-i   (b) 1-ii; 2-iii; 3-i
  (c) 1-iii; 2-i; 3-ii   (d) 1-ii; 2-i; 3-iii

239. According to Greek Mythology, what is the name of the beautiful youth who was loved by Echo; and in punishment for not returning her love, was made to fall in love with his image reflected in a pool; and finally unable to possess the image, is believe to have pined away and turned into a flower?

  (a) Midas   (b) Narcissus

  (c) Hercules   (d) Adonis

240. Of which of the following trade groupings is Myanmar a member?

  (a) SAARC

  (b) ASEAN

  (c) NAFTA

  (d) MERCOSUR

2014-16

241. In Column 1 are the names of some great Indians, whose birthdays are celebrated as special days, which are given in Column 2. Match the birthday with the day of celebration

Column 1: Birthday of	Column 2: Celebrated in India as
i. Swami Vivekananda	a. Harmony Day
ii. M. Visvesvaraya	b. Doctors Day
iii. Rajiv Gandhi	c. National Youth Day
iv. B.C. Roy	d. Engineers Day

(a) i-a; ii-b; iii-c; iv-d
(b) i-c; ii-b; iii-d; iv-a
(c) i-c; ii-d; iii-a; iv-b
(d) i-d; ii-c; iii-b; iv-a

242. Which of the following fictional characters was created by Agatha Christie?

(a) Hercule Poirot
(b) Father Brown
(c) Perry Mason
(d) Sherlock Holmes

243. Bashar al-Assad is/was a leader of which of the following countries?

(a) Oman
(b) Jordan
(c) Tunisia
(d) Syria

244. Which of the following countries is not a member of SAARC?

(a) Nepal
(b) Myanmar
(c) Pakistan
(d) Afghanistan

245. Given in Column 1 are some Latin phrases commonly used in English. Their meanings are given in Column 2. Match the phrase in Column 1 with its correct meaning in Column 2:

Column 1	Column 2
i. Caveat Emptor	a. That is to say
ii. Quid Pro Quo	b. In the same place
iii. Videlicet	c. Let the buyer beware
iv. Ibidem	d. One thing for another

(a) i-c; ii-d; iii-a; iv-b
(b) i-b; ii-a; iii-c; iv-d
(c) i-d; ii-c; iii-b; iv-a
(d) i-a; ii-b; iii-d; iv-c

246. What is the name of the novel that was published in April 2013 and authored under the pseudonym Robert Galbraith?

(a) Ghana Must Go
(b) Savage Continent
(c) The Cuckoo's Calling
(d) Who says Elephants Can't Dance?

247. Which of the following persons purchased the Washington Post in 2013?

(a) Warren Buffet
(b) Jeff Bezos
(c) Carlos Slim
(d) Steven-Spielberg

248. For which franchise did Parupalli Kashyap play in IBL 2013?

(a) Pune Pistons
(b) Banga Beats
(c) Mumbai Masters
(d) Hyderabad Hotshots

249. Who amongst the following is not associated with Egypt?

(a) Mohammed al-Magariaf
(b) Adly Mansour
(c) Mohammed.Morsi
(d) Hosni Mubarak

250. Which of the following is Narayan Murthy not associated with?

(a) Padma Vibhushan
(b) Patni Computers
(c) Unique Identification Authority of India
(d) Both A and C

251. Pick the odd one out.

(a) Ban Ki- Moon
(b) Boutros Boutros- Ghali
(c) Pascal Lamy
(d) Kofi Annan

252. Pick the odd one out

(a) Abhinav Bindra
(b) Sushil Kumar
(c) Gagan Narang
(d) Vijay Kumar

253. In the Tapi gas pipeline, the word "Tapi" refers to which of the following?

(a) Turkey, Afghanistan, Pakistan, India
(b) Tajikistan, Azerbaijan, Pakistan, Iran
(c) Tajikistan, Afghanistan, Pakistan, Iran
(d) Turkmenistan, Afghanistan, Pakistan, India

254. Match the names in column 1 with their organization in column 2:

Column 1	Column 2
i. Christine Lagarde	a. UNFCCC
ii. Roberto Azevedo	b. IMF
iii. Christiana Figueres	c. World Bank
iv. Jim Yong Kim	d. WTO

(a) i-b; ii-a; iii-c; iv-d
(b) i-b; ii-d; iii-a; iv-c
(c) i-b; ii-a; iii-d; iv-c
(d) i-a; ii-c; iii-b; iv-d

255. Match the Countries with Trade Agreements/Regional Blocs:

Country	Trade Agreement/ Regional Blocs
i. Brazil	a. ASEAN
ii. Indonesia	b. APTA
iii. Bangladesh	c. MERCOSUR
iv. Mexico	d. NAFTA

(a) i-b; ii-c; iii-a; iv-d
(b) i-b; ii-a; iii-c: iv-d
(c) i-c; ii-b; iii-a; iv-d
(d) i-c; ii-a; iii-b; iv-d

256. The nomenclature of which of the following schemes is incorrect?

(a) Rajiv Gram Samridhi Yojana

(b) Jawahar Rozgar Yojana

(c) Rajiv Awas Yojana

(d) Pradhan Mantri Gram Sadak Yojana

2015-17

257. Match the Indian Gold Medal Winners at the 2014 Commonwealth Games held at Glasgow with the sports type in which the medal was awarded:

Name of the Player	Sports Type
a. Joshana Chinappa	1. Weightlifting
b. Vinesh Phogat	2. Squash
c. Vikas Gowda	3. Discuss Throw
d. Satish Sivalingam	4. Wrestling

(a) a - 3, b - 2, c - 4, d - 1

(b) a - 2, b - 3, c - 1, d - 4

(c) a - 2, b - 4, c - 3, d - 1

(d) a - 4, b - 2, c - 1, d - 3

258. Which of the following countries did not qualify for the 2014 FIFA World Cup semi-final?

(a) Brazil   (b) Germany

(c) Belgium   (d) Argentina

259. Lifebuoy is a brand of soap marketed by which of the following companies?

(a) ITC   (b) Procter & Gamble

(c) Godrej   (d) Unilever

260. Which of the following Indian-origin academician became the Dean of the Harvard College with effect from July 2014?

(a) Nitin Nohria   (b) Rakesh Khurana

(c) G Anandalingam   (d) Ajit Rangnekar

261. In the Pro-Kabaddi league played in India in 2014, the Future Group is the owner of which team?

(a) Bengaluru Bulls

(b) Bengal Warriors

(c) Dabang Delhi

(d) Jaipur Pink Panthers

262. Which of the following is headquartered in USA?

(a) Goldman Sachs Group

(b) Barclays

(c) HSBC Holdings

(d) Standard Chartered PLC

263. Match the following:

Financial Institution	Tagline
a. ICICI Bank	1. India's International Bank
b. Bank of Baroda	2. Jiyo sar utha ke
c. HDFC Std Life	3. Zindagi ke sath bhi Zindagi ke baad bhi
d. LIC	4. Khayal Aap Ka

(a) a - 3, b - 2, c - 4, d - 1

(b) a - 4, b - 3, c - 1, d - 2

(c) a - 4, b - 1, c - 2, d - 3

(d) a - 4, b - 2, c - 1, d - 3

264. Who among the following legends has been the latest recipient of the preestigious Dadasaheb Phalke Award?

(a) Shyam Benegal   (b) Manna Dey

(c) Gulzar   (d) Adoor Gopalkrishnan

265. Who is the Brand Ambassador of Telangana State?

(a) Sania Mirza   (b) Saina Nehawal

(c) V. V. S. Laxman   (d) P. V. Sindhu

266. Which country has become the latest number of the World Trade Organisation?

(a) Yemen   (b) Republic of Moldova

(c) Vietnam   (d) None of the above

267. Which among the following options is the oldest surviving brand of Tata Group?

(a) Tate Steel   (b) Tata Motors

(c) Tate Tetley   (d) Taj Hotels

268. Who among the following is the first woman to become MD / Chairman of a Bank in Inda?

(a) Ms. Ranjana Kumar

(b) Ms. Chanda Kochhar

(c) Ms. Arundhati Bhattacharya

(d) Ms. Shubhalakshmi Panse

269. Who amongst the following has not won the Man Booker Prize?

(a) Chitra Banerjee Divakaruni

(b) Arundhati Roy

(c) Khan Desai

(d) Arvind Adiga

270. Match the Country with the Leader:

Country	Leader
a. Japan	i. Kim Jong-un
b. China	ii. Benigno Aquino
c. HDFC Std Life	iii. Shinzo Abe
d. Philippines	iv. Xi Jinping

(a) a - i, b - ii, c - iii, d - iv

(b) a - iii, b - i, c - ii, d - iv

(c) a - iv, b - iii, c - i, d - ii

(d) a - iii, b - iv, c - i, d - ii

271. Which of the following is not headquartered in China?

    (a) Weibo　　　　　　(b) We-Chat

    (c) Alibaba　　　　　(d) Jabong

272. Who is the first CEO of AirAsia India?

    (a) Mukund Rajan　　(b) Srinivas Kini

    (c) Y. P. Teik　　　　(d) Mittu Chandilya

273. Who among the following has been appointed as the Chief Justice of India in September 2014?

    (a) Justice Markandey Katju

    (b) Justice R M Lodha

    (c) Justice H L Dattu

    (d) None of the Above

274. The winner of the Wimbledon Men's singles Final 2014 has been:

    (a) Roger Federer　　(b) Rafael Nadal

    (c) Andy Murray　　　(d) Novak Djokovic

275. Pradhan Mantri Jan Dhan Yojana has been launched in which year?

    (a) 2011　　　　　　(b) 2012

    (c) 2013　　　　　　(d) 2014

2016-18

276. Which is the first Eurozone nation to exit its bailout package?

    (a) Portugal　　　　(b) Italy

    (c) Ireland　　　　　(d) Spain

277. What is the motto of the 2016 Summer Olympics to be held in Rio de Janeiro?

    (a) Live Your Passion

    (b) One World, One Dream

    (c) Friends Forever

    (d) Harmony and Progress

278. Which film won the 2015 Oscar Award for the "Best Animated Feature Film"?

    (a) Song of the Sea

    (b) How to train your Dragon 2

    (c) Big Hero 6

    (d) The Boxtrolls

279. Who among the following has won the maximum all time Grand Slam Women's Singles title?

    (a) Serena Williams

    (b) Margaret Court

    (c) Steffi Graf

    (d) Martina Navratilova

280. Match the name of the Multinational Firm with whom the following Indians are/have been associated as CEO

Indian CEO	Multinational Firm
I. Anshu Jain	a. MasterCard
II. Shantanu Narayen	b. Reckitt & Colman
III. Ajaypal Singh Banga	c. Deutsche Bank
IV. Rakesh Kapoor	d. Adobe

    (a) I-c; II-d; III-a; IV-b

    (b) I-b; II-a; III-c; IV-d

    (c) I-d; II-c; III-b; IV-a

    (d) I-a; II-b; III-d; IV-c

281. Who is the Vice Chairman of the NITI Aayog?

    (a) Arvind Panagariya

    (b) Arun Maira

    (c) Raghuram Rajan

    (d) Arvind Subramaniam

282. The first Export Processing Zone of Asia was set up in

    (a) Singapore　　　　(b) Kandla

    (c) Shanghai　　　　(d) Dubai

283. Match the name of the book with its author.

Book	Author
I. To Kill a Mockingbird	a. E.M. Forster
II. A Passage to India	b. Joseph E. Stiglitz
III. Globalization and its Discontents	c. Thomas L. Friedman
IV. The World is Flat	d. Harper Lee

    (a) I-a; II-b; III-d; IV-c

    (b) I-d; II-a; III-b; IV-c

    (c) I-d; II-c; III-a; IV-b

    (d) I-a; II-d; III-c; IV-b

284. The U.S. recently announced that its redesigned ten-dollar bill, to be issued in 2020, will include the

    (a) Face of a Lion

    (b) Face of an Elephant

    (c) Face of a Woman

    (d) Face of a Dragon

285. The new Centre-State tax sharing model promised a 10% increase in the State's share. This 10% increase will result from increasing the share from

    (a) 32% to 42%

    (b) 22% to 32%

    (c) 42% to 52%

    (d) None of the above

286. Which of the following countries is not a member of European Union?

(a) Sweden   (b) Finland

(c) Norway   (d) Denmark

287. Match the Prime Ministers and Presidents of India who have been contemporaries in Office

Prime Minister	President
I. Indira Gandhi	a. Shankar Dayal Sharma
II. Rajiv Gandhi	b. V.V.Giri
III. I.K.Gujral	c. A.P.J. Abdul Kalam
IV. Manmohan Singh	d. Giani Zail Singh

(a) I-a; II-b; III-c; IV-d

(b) I-b; II-a; III-d; IV-c

(c) I-a; II-c; III-b; IV-d

(d) I-b; II-d; III-a; IV-c

288. Mother Teresa was born in

(a) Switzerland

(b) India

(c) Germany

(d) Macedonia

289. In 1985-86, an official policy introduced by Gorbachev in Soviet Union that stressed on honest discussion about the country's social issues and concerns was called

(a) Glasnost

(b) Gosplans

(c) Irredentism

(d) Oligarchs

290. Match the name of the organization with the name of the city in which it is headquartered

Organization		Headquarters
I.	International Monetary Fund	a. Lausanne
II.	International Olympic Committee	b. Geneva
III.	International Labour Organisation	c. Washington
IV.	International Chamber of Commerce	d. Paris

(a) I-d; II-c; III-a; IV-b

(b) I-a; II-b; III-d; IV-c

(c) I-c; II-a; III-b; IV-d

(d) I-b; II-d; III-c; IV-a

291. Match each Brand with the most appropriate Industry Type it represents:

Brands	Industry Types
(a)Facebook	(i) Financial Services
(b) Louis Vuitton	(ii) Business Services
(c) Visa	(iii) Technology
(d)UPS	(iv) Luxury
(e) Accenture	(v) Transport

(a) (a) - (iii),.(b) - (v), (c)- (i), (d) - (iv), (e) - (ii)

(b) (a) - (iii), (b) - (V), (c)- (ii), (d) - (iv), (e) - (i)

(c) (a) - (iii), (b) - (iv), (c)- (i), (d) - (v), (e) - (ii)

(d) (a) - (ii), (b) - (iv), (c)- (v), (d) - (iii), (e) - (i)

292. Which of the following country was not there in the UEFA Euro 2016 (Soccer Tournament)quarter-final?

France, Belgium, Wales, Germany, Italy, England, Poland, Portugal, Iceland

(a) Iceland   (b) Poland

(c) England   (d) Italy

293. Alvin Toffler (October, 1928 - June, 2016) was an American writer and futurist, known for his works discussing modem technologies, including the digital revolution and the communication revolution, with emphasis on their effects on cultures worldwide. Toffler was an associate editor of Fortune magazine. Identify the book authored by Alvin Toffler from the following list

(a) Previews and Premises

(b) The Fourth Protocol

(c) The End of Eternity

(d) The Time Machine

294. What was the theme of the 2016 National Youth Festival of India?

(a) Youth For Better India

(b) Celebrating Diversity in Unity

(c) India Youth for Skill, Development and Harmony

(d) Youth For Drugs Free World

295. Which Indian player has created junior world record in "Javelin throw" in July 2016?

(a) Neeraj Chopra

(b) Annu Rani

(c) Rajesh Bind

(d) Devendra Jhajharia

296. Match the famous personality in Column II from the information given in Column I.

Column I	Column II
a. He was born in 1966 in New York. He won his first title of the World Boxing Council (WBC), heavyweight championship in 1986. He virtually remained at the top of the world for next few years. However, his professional career was in chaos in early 1990s and he was sentenced to jail for a grave crime in 1992. Later, he was diagnosed with bipolar disorder. Who is this famous person?	i. Rocky Marciano ii. Shraddha Kapoor iii. Sonakshi Sinha iv. George Foreman v. Alia Bhatt vi. Dilip Doshi vii. Bishan Singh Bedi viii. Kareena Kapoor ix. Srinivas Venkataraghavan x. Mike Tyson xi. Muhammad Ali
b. He was India's spin bowler. He had test debut in 1979 and total wicket taken was 136 (Test + One day). He had immaculate control on flight and has been one of India's finest left arm spinner. Who is this cricketer?	
c. She was born in 1989 in Mumbai and daughter of a famous Bollywood actor. She had her first presence in Hindi film in 2010. Who is she?	

(a) a-x, b-ix, c-iii   (b) a-xi, b-vi, c-ii   (c) a-x, b-vi, c-ii   (d) a-x, b-vii, c-ii

297. What is the Currency of Bulgaria?

(a) Lev   (b) Lira

(c) Lek   (d) Loto

298. Bharat Heavy Electricals Ltd. (BHEL) commissioned 2 units each of 14 Megawatts at the Salma Hydro Electric Project in 2016. Identify the country where this project is located.

(a) Nigeria   (b) Iran

(c) Turkmenistan   (d) Afghanistan

299. Which country inaugurated the first electric road in the world for hybrid heavy transports?

(a) Sweden   (b) Poland

(c) Iceland   (d) France

300. Which of the following Company has acquired Jabong in July 2016?

(a) Shopclues

(b) Snapdeal

(c) Amazon

(d) Myntra

301. Match the movie with the personality on whose life it is based

Movies	Personalities
a. The Social Network	i. Aung San Suu Kyi
b. The Special Relationship	ii. Mark Zuckerberg
c. The Lady	iii. Stephen Hawking
d. The Theory of Everything	iv. Tony Blair

(a) a-iii, b-iv, c-i, d-ii

(b) a-ii, b-iv, c-i, d-iii

(c) a-ii, b-i, c-iv, d-iii

(d) a-iv, b-iii, c-i, d-ii

302. The 2016 Joint Military Exercise "Maitree" has been conducted between India and which of the following countries?

(a) Indonesia

(b) Maldives

(c) Malaysia

(d) Thailand

303. What is Director Identification Number (DIN)?

(a) An identification number which the individual company allots to the intending director

(b) A number which the Central Government allots to any individual intending to be appointed as director or to any existing director of a company

(c) A number which the SEBI allots to any individual intending to be appointed as director or to any existing director of a company

(d) A number which the Central Government allots to retired directors so as to build data base

304. Match the Bollywood Actors with their debut Hindi Film

Actors	Films
a. Shahnikh Khan	i. Aur Pyaar Ho Gaya
b. Sushmita Sen	ii. Dastak
c. Aishwarya Rai Bachchan	iii. Refugee
d. Rani Mukheijee	iv. Deewana
e. Kareena Kapoor	v. Raja ki Aayegi Barat

(a) a.-ii, b.-iv, c.-i, d.-v, e.-iii

(b) a.-ii, b.-iv, c.-iii, d.-v, e.-i

(c) a.-iv, b.-v, c.-iii, d.-ii, e.-i

(d) a.-iv, b.-ii, c.-i, d.-v, e.-iii

2018-20

Directions for questions 305-306: Read the paragraphs carefully and identify the factual mistakes.

305. News Item dated 22 Jan 2017: Saina Nehwal's Triumph at Malaysia Masters Final

Days after recovering from knee injury during Rio Olympics, Saina Nehwal is back with a bang as this Indian badminton ace thrashes Pornpawee Chochuwong of Thailand by 22-20 and 22-20, thereby claiming the Malaysia Masters Grand title.

Quashing the air about her ability to win titles, the world No 10 Nehwal clinched her first Masters within five months since knee injury. Nehwal had to undergo surgery after an early exit from the Rio Olympics where her fellow citizen PV Sindhu created history by claiming the first silver medal for Indian badminton.

Silencing the critiques, Saina returned to action within a quarter of her surgery setback. Once the absolute queen of Indian badminton, she faced early exits and missed the qualification mark for Sharjah World Super Series Finals. Also, she lost to Sindhu in the Premier Badminton League. However, Malaysia Masters Grand title has been her winning start to 2017.

(a) Saina received a knee injury during Rio Olympics

(b) Pornpawee Chochuwong is from Thailand

(c) Saina missed her qualification mark for Sharjah World Super Series Finals

(d) None of the above

306. News Item dated, April 2017: West Bengal Won the Santosh Trophy

West Bengal won the Santosh Trophy for the 32nd time after a 1-0 win over Goa, extending their domination in the premier domestic football tournament. Playing in front of a vociferous home crowd, five-time winners Goa tried their best and controlled the match, but ran out of steam in the extra time. The hosts had their chances to score but the rival keeper pulled off some great saves. West Bengal, thus, ended a six-year wait having last won the title in 2011. Goa last won it in 2010. Goa, who had hosted the tournament thrice, lost to West Bengal in the semi-final in 1972 and the final in 1996, while winning against Kerala in 1990.

(a) West Bengal won the Santosh Trophy for the 32nd time after a 1-0 win over Goa

(b) Goa tried their best and controlled the match, but ran-out of steam in the extra time.

(c) West Bengal, thus, ended a six-year wait having last won the title in 2011

(d) Goa last won it in 2010

307. 'Soulmate" is a famous Indian music band. Identify the genre of music for which they are famous. Also, name the place from where the music band comes from.

(a) Blues Rock, Shillong

(b) Hard Rock, Goa

(c) Punk Rock, Puducherry

(d) Psychedelic, Mumbai

308. XYZ is an Indian English-language broadsheet daily Newspaper founded in 1875 and published simultaneously in various cities of India. It is a direct descendant of two newspapers, The Englishman (1821)and The Friend of India (1818) which later merged with XYZ. It was managed by a British corporate group until it transferred ownership to the Tata Group, with J.R.(d)Tata as Chairman in the mid-1960s. It is currently owned by Nachiketa Publications, Kolkata. Identify XYZ out of the following:

(*a*) Times of India   (*b*) Business Standard

(*c*) The Statesman   (*d*) Tribune

309. Which London-based Group founded in mid-1910, started out as a moneylender before expanding the business to include imports of dried fruit, jute, textiles and tea. The business grew steadily under the late Shah of Iran as they were having large presence in Iran and continued to flourish even after Islamic Revolution forced it to move to Europe. It is now a multibillion-dollar energy, transport, media and agriculture conglomerate. The company had been in a bidding war to acquire the Express Newspapers group, and was one of several bidders for Go Fly, British Airways' low-cost airline. This famous conglomerate has a large presence in India also. Identify the Group.

(*a*) Ruia Group   (*b*) Mittal Group

(*c*) Oswal Group   (*d*) Hinduja Group

310. Match the companies with their CEOs of Indian origin (either in the past or present).

(a) Adobe	(i) Geoge Kurian
(b) Cognizant	(ii) Sanjay Mehrotra
(c) Micron	(iii) Rajeev Suri
(d) NetApp	(iv) Francisco D'souza
(e) Nokia	(v) Sanjay Kumar Jha
(f) Global Foundries	(vi) Shantanu Narayen

(*a*) a-iii, b-i, c-ii, d-vi, e-iv, f-v

(*b*) a-i, b-iv, c-v, d-ii, e-vi, f-iii

(*c*) a-vi, b-iv, c-ii, d-i, e-iii, f-v

(*d*) a-vi, b-iii, c-iv, d-v, e-i, f-ii

311. Choose the odd match from the following Fortune 500 Companies with their respective sector / industry and headquarters:

Name of the Company	Sector / Industry	Headquarter
(a) Berkshire Hathaway	(i) Financial	1. New York, NY
(b) Walgreens Boots Alliance	(ii) Wholesalers: Health Care	2. Deerfield, IL
(c) Verizon	(iii) Telecommunications	3. New York, NY
(d) Amazon.com	(iv) Technology	4. Seattle, WA

    (a) a - i - 1   (b) b - ii - 2

    (c) c - iii - 3   (d) d - iv - 4

312. Match the name of the famous conglomerate/company with its particular tagline:

Tagline	Name of Conglomerate / Company
(a) Growth is Life	(i) General Electric
(b) Imagination at Work	(ii) Reliance Industries Limited
(c) High Performance. Delivered	(iii) Accenture
(d) Because You're Worth It	(iv) L'Oreal

    (a) (a) - (i), (b) - (iii), (c)- (iv), (d) - (ii)

    (b) (a) - (i), (b) - (ii), (c)- (iii), (d) - (iv)

    (c) (a) - (i), (b) - (ii), (c)- (iv), (d) - (iii)

    (d) (a) - (ii), (b) - (i), (c)- (iii), (d) - (iv)

313. Which of the following is not correct for Government of India's initiative "Make in India"?

    (a) It is launched by Prime Minster of India in 2014

    (b) It aims to attract Foreign Investment for faster industrial development of India.

    (c) It aims to substitute the imports of India

    (d) It focuses on the twenty-five sectors of the economy for faster economic growth, export promotion and employment generation

314. Given as under, are part logo of different Organizations. Match the part logo of each with their type of Organization:

Type of Organization	Part Logo
i. Multilateral Organization	a.
ii. International Airlines	b.
iii. Sports Goods Manufactures	c.
iv. Media Production House	d.
v. Japanese Conglomerate	e.

    (a) i-a, ii-e, iii-b, iv-d, v-c

    (b) i-d, ii-c, iii-a, iv-b, v-e

    (c) i-d, ii-c, iii-b, iv-e, v-a

    (d) i-e, ii-a, iii-c, iv-b, v-d

315. Who among the following cricketers has highest individual score in Women's One Day International Cricket?

    (a) Belinda Clark

    (b) Harmanpreet Kaur

    (c) Chamari Atapattu

    (d) Charlotte Edwards

316. India is building which of the following port in Iran in order to improve the trade connectivity with Iran, Afghanistan and Central Asian countries.

    (a) Chabahar Port

    (b) Bandar Khomeini

    (c) Bandar Abbas

    (d) Bandar Mahshahr

317. Which of the following pair of country – present currency is not correctly matched?

    (a) Tunisia- Dinar

    (b) Israel-Israeli Lira

    (c) Syria- Syrian Pound

    (d) Qatar- Riyal

318. Megastar Amitabh Bachchan is one of the most popular actors of Bollywood. It is said that the advertisers line up to rope him in as their brand ambassador. Which of the following brands has not been endorsed by Amitabh Bachchan till date?

    (a) Everest Masala

    (b) TATA SKY

    (c) ICICI Bank

    (d) Rasna '

2019-21

319. Match the Trophies and Cup associated with each Sport:

    1. Badminton   a. Durand Cup

    2. Hockey   b. Bama Belleck Cup

    3. Table Tennis   c. Rangaswamy Cup

    4. Football   d. BWF World Championships

    (a) 1-d, 2-c, 3-b, 4-a

    (b) 1 -c, 2-b. 3-d, 4-a

    (c) 1-d, 2-b, 3-c, 4-a

    (d) 1-b. 2-c, 3-d, 4-a

320. Match the Biographies/Autobiographies of India's sport players:

1. The World Beneath His Feat	a. Milkha Singh
2. Imperfect	b. Mary Kom
3. The Race of My Life	c. Sanjay Manjrekar
4. Unbreakable	d. Pullela Gopichand

(a) 1 -d, 2-c, 3-a, 4-b

(b) 1-a, 2-b, 3-d, 4-c

(c) 1-c, 2-a, 3-d, 4-b

(d) 1-b, 2-a. 3-d, 4-c

321. Which of the following Telecom Operator has launched the app based internet calling service "WINGS" in India?

(a) BSNL

(b) JIO

(c) Airtel

(d) Vodafone

322. Which of the following country is not a member of BIMSTEC?

(a) China

(b) Bhutan

(c) Nepal

(d) Myanmar

323. Given below are the logos of various global firms. On the basis of their logo, select the correct functional area they operate in.

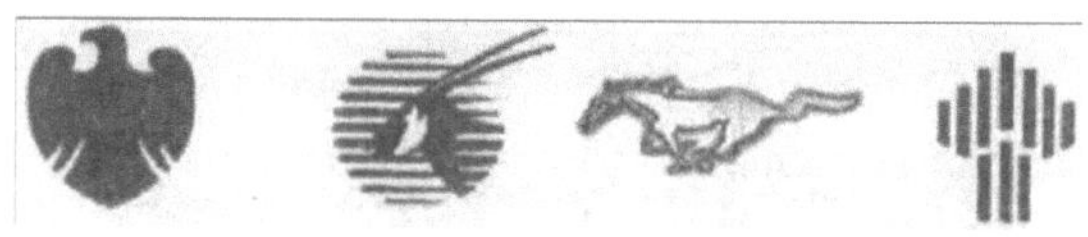

(a) Airlines, Automobiles, Banking, Petroleum

(b) Banking, Airlines, Automobiles, Petroleum

(c) Airlines, Petroleum, Automobiles, Banking

(d) Banking, Airlines, Petroleum, Automobiles

324. To strengthen its maritime network and enhance trade & economic ties, Government of India has decided to invest in a port in Indonesia. The name of this port is

(a) Sabang

(b) Samarinda

(c) Sibolga

(d) Sorong

325. Which of the following statement about American Businessman Elon Musk is not correct?

(a) His full name is Elon Reeve Musk

(b) He is Argentina-born American entrepreneur and businessman

(c) He founded www.X.com in 1999 (which later became PayPal), SpaceX in 2002 and Tesla Motors in 2003

(d) He is instrumental in leading the design and manufacture of electric Sedan and SUV cars

326. Rand is the currency of which of the following country?

(a) Tanzania

(b) Somalia

(c) Sudan

(d) South Africa

327. Bharat Desai and Neerja Sethi, the Indian-American couple has made USD 2 Billion jackpot by selling their company to French IT major, ATOS. Name the company they sold.

(a) Syntel

(b) Symtel

(c) Syotel

(d) Simtel

ANSWERS

1. (d)	2. (b,d)	3. (b,c,d)	4. (b)	5. (c,d)	6. (a,b,d)	7. (d)	8. (b)	9. (a)	10. (b)
11. (b)	12. (a)	13. (a)	14. (a)	15. (b)	16. (a)	17. (b)	18. (a)	19. (d)	20. (a)
21. (d)	22. (a)	23. (b)	24. (c)	25. (b)	26. (d)	27. (a)	28. (c)	29. (a)	30. (d)
31. (c)	32. (a)	33. (c)	34. (a)	35. (b,c,d)	36. (a,d)	37. (d)	38. (c)	39. (d)	40. (a)
41. (a)	42. (c)	43. (a)	44. (d)	45. (c)	46. (b)	47. (d)	48. (c)	49. (b)	50. (c)
51. (c)	52. (a)	53. (d)	54. (b)	55. (d)	56. (c)	57. (d)	58. (b)	59. (c)	60. (c)
61. (b)	62. (b)	63. (a)	64. (b)	65. (b)	66. (b)	67. (c)	68. (a)	69. (b,c)	70. (c,d)
71. (d)	72. (c)	73. (a)	74. (d)	75. (c)	76. (c)	77. (b)	78. (d)	79. (a)	80. (b)
81. (a)	82. (b)	83. (c)	84. (b)	85. (b)	86. (c)	87. (d)	88. (d)	89. (d)	90. (a)
91. (a)	92. (a)	93. (c)	94. (b)	95. (b)	96. (d)	97. (a)	98. (d)	99. (c)	100. (c)
101. (d)	102. (c)	103. (a)	104. (c)	105. (a)	106. (a)	107. (a)	108. (c)	109. (a)	110. (a)
111. (a)	112. (d)	113. (a)	114. (a)	115. (a)	116. (c)	117. (d)	118. (c)	119. (d)	120. (d)
121. (b)	122. (b)	123. (a)	124. (c)	125. (d)	126. (a)	127. (c)	128. (a)	129. (d)	130. (a,d)
131. (b,c,d)	132. (a,d)	133. (a,b,d)	134. (a,b)	135. (c)	136. (a)	137. (b,c)	138. (a,d)	139. (c,d)	140. (a,b)
141. (a,d)	142. (d)	143. (c)	144. (b)	145. (c)	146. (a)	147. (a)	148. (c)	149. (b)	150. (b)
151. (a)	152. (c)	153. (a)	154. (c)	155. (c)	156. (c)	157. (b)	158. (b)	159. (a)	160. (a)
161. (b)	162. (c)	163. (d)	164. (d)	165. (a)	166. (d)	167. (c)	168. (c)	169. (b)	170. (d)
171. (c)	172. (d)	173. (b)	174. (b)	175. (a)	176. (c)	177. (a)	178. (c)	179. (a)	180. (c)
181. (a)	182. (d)	183. (b)	184. (c)	185. (b)	186. (c)	187. (c)	188. (c)	189. (d)	190. (c)
191. (b)	192. (c)	193. (a)	194. (c)	195. (d)	196. (a)	197. (b)	198. (c)	199. (d)	200. (c)
201. (d)	202. (c)	203. (d)	204. (b)	205. (b)	206. (b)	207. (b)	208. (d)	209. (b)	210. (b)
211. (b)	212. (b)	213. (b)	214. (a)	215. (b)	216. (b)	217. (c)	218. (d)	219. (d)	220. (d)
221. (b)	222. (a)	223. (c)	224. (a)	225. (c)	226. (b)	227. (b)	228. (c)	229. (a)	230. (b)
231. (a)	232. (c)	233. (c)	234. (d)	235. (d)	236. (a)	237. (a)	238. (c)	239. (b)	240. (b)
241. (c)	242. (a)	243. (d)	244. (b)	245. (a)	246. (c)	247. (b)	248. (b)	249. (a)	250. (d)
251. (c)	252. (b)	253. (d)	254. (b)	255. (d)	256. (a)	257. (c)	258. (c)	259. (d)	260. (a)
261. (b)	262. (a)	263. (c)	264. (c)	265. (a)	266. (a)	267. (d)	268. (a)	269. (a)	270. (d)
271. (d)	272. (d)	273. (c)	274. (d)	275. (d)	276. (c)	277. (a)	278. (c)	279. (b)	280. (a)
281. (a)	282. (b)	283. (b)	284. (c)	285. (a)	286. (c)	287. (d)	288. (d)	289. (a)	290. (c)
291. (c)	292. (c)	293. (a)	294. (c)	295. (a)	296. (c)	297. (a)	298. (d)	299. (a)	300. (d)
301. (b)	302. (d)	303. (b)	304. (d)	305. (c)	306. (d)	307. (a)	308. (c)	309. (d)	310. (c)
311. (a)	312. (d)	313. (c)	314. (c)	315. (a)	316. (a)	317. (b)	318. (d)	319. (a)	320. (a)
321. (a)	322. (a)	323. (b)	324. (a)	325. (b)	326. (d)	327. (a)			

EXPLANATIONS

1. (a) Acquired Immune Deficiency Syndrome (AIDS or Aids)

   (b) Petrology is a field of geology, which focuses on the study of rocks and the conditions by which they form.

   (c) A diverging (concave lens) always form virtual image. Convex lens is used for magnifying glass.

2. (a) Only the transparent section of the eyes called cornea is taken out and not the full eye ball.

   (c) IC chips are usually made of silicon, not chromium.

3. Mercury, Gallium, Francium are metals and are liquid at room temperature

4. (a) Three scientists shared the Nobel Prize in physics in the year 2005.

   (c) The flow of heat by conduction occurs via collisions between atoms and molecules in the substances and the subsequent transfer of kinetic energy not potential energy.

   (d) Madam Curie was born in Poland not in France.

5. (a) Only mercury and venus are inferior planets.

   (b) All planets cannot be seen at night.

6. Only (c) is the false statement.

7. Statements (a), (b) and (c) are incorrect, only (d) is correct.

24. (a) Crossing the Floor- In politics, crossing the floor is to vote against party lines, especially where this is considered unusual or controversial.

Statement (b) and (d) are incorrect.

35. Sand dunes occur throughout the world, from coastal and lakeshore plains to arid desert regions.

36. (b) The Satpura Range is a range of hills in central India. The range rises in eastern Gujarat state near the Arabian Sea coast, running east through Maharashtra and Madhya Pradesh to Chhattisgarh.

(c) The Himalaya range runs for about 2,400 km, from Nanga Parbat (Pakistan) in the west to Namche Barwa (Tibet) in the east.

68. (b) Port Blair is the largest town and a municipal council in Andaman's district in the Andaman Islands and the capital of the Andaman and Nicobar Islands union territory of India. It lies on the east coast of South Andaman Island and is the main entry point to the islands.

(c) The photosphere is the zone from which the sunlight we see is emitted. The outermost layer of the sun is the corona. Only visible during eclipses, it is a low-density cloud of plasma with higher transparency than the inner layers.

69. (c) Chandraupta ruled from 322 BC-298 BC not 324 to 301 B.C.

(d) On April 28, 1916, the Home Rule League was set up with its headquarters at Pune. Tilak went on a whirlwind tour of the country, appealing to everybody to unite under the banner of Home Rule League.

70. (a) The Montagu-Chelmsford Reforms were reforms introduced by the British Government in India to introduce self-governing institutions gradually to India.

(b) Warren Hastings (December 6, 1732 - August 22, 1818) was the first governor-general of British India, from 1773 to 1786. He was famously impeached in 1787 for corruption, and acquitted in 1795. He remained in India untill 1874 is the wrong statement rest part of the statement is correct.

130. Correct Matches are:

(a) Kumar Mangalam Birla-Aluminium & Copper-Ernst & young Entrepreneur Award 2005-Grasim.

(d) Kalanithi Maran-Voice and radio products-CNBC Business Excellence Award 2005-Sun TV.

131. Correct Matches are:

(b) Rana Kapoor-Rabobank-Start-up Entrepreneur Award 2005-Yes Bank.

(c) Jagdish Khattar-IGNIS-Gurgaon-Maruti

(d) Azim Premji-Integrated Business Solution-Faraday Medal-Wipro

132. Correct Matches are:

(a) Namibia-Diamonds-Windhoek-Dollar

(d) Nigeria-Oil-Abuja-Naira

133. Correct Matches are:

(a) Sir Walter Scott-Ivnhoe-The Life of Napolean Bonaparte-Scotland

(b) Cervantes-Don Quixote-Novelas Ejemplares-Spain

(d) Dr. Zhivago-My sister life-Russia

134. Correct Matches are:

(a) L.N. Mittal-ISPAT International-Gopalpur SEZ-Steel Industry

(b) Warren Buffet-Berkshire Hathaway Inc-Omaha-Bill & Melinda Gates Foundation

135. Correct Match is:

(c) EscortsLtd-Faridabad-Tractors-Rajan Nanda

136. Correct Matches are:

(a) Dr Reddy's-Betapharm-Generic drugs-Germany.

137. Correct Matches are:

(a) B.V. Rao-Poultry Farming

(b) C.K Prahalad-Management Science

(c) John kurien-Fishries Economy

(d) Kiran karnik-Information Technology & Software

138. Correct Matches are:

(a) My Presidential Years - R Venkatraman

(b) The Hindu way of life - S Radhakrishnan

(c) Voice of Conscience - V. V. Giri

(d) Without Fear or Favour - N Sanjiva Reddy.

139. (a) It was founded by Dr. Verghese Kurien and Dr. Amrita Patel is the current Chairman of the National Dairy Development Board, Anand.

(b) Dabur is well known for Ayurvedic medicine, Hamdard is world largest producer of unani medicine.

140. (c) Special Olympics 2005 took place during 2-9 July 2005 at Glasgow

(d) Australia was the champion in the Sultan Azlan Shah Hockey tournament in 2005

141. (b) Dogri and Gojri are two languages of Jammu & Kashmir.

(c) Surajkund mela, from 1st to 15th February rural India basks in the warmth of admiration at Surajkund mela village that lies some 8 km from South Delhi.

142. (a) Statement is not clear, till now Eight persons of Indian origin have been honoured, Nobel Prize.

(b) Hargobind Khorana (born 1922), a person of Indian origin, shared the 1968 Nobel Prize in Physiology or Medicine for his work on genes.

(c) Three person of indian origin won Nobel Prize for Literature. These are Rudyard Kipling, Literature, 1907. Rabindranath Tagore, Literature, 1913 and Sir Vidiadhar Surajprasad Naipaul, Literature, 2002.

Printed by Libri Plureos GmbH in Hamburg,
Germany